INTERNATIONAL RELATIONS

INTERNATIONAL RELATIONS

FOURTH EDITION

PEU GHOSH

Assistant Professor
Department of Political Science
Lady Brabourne College
Kolkata

PHI Learning Private Limited

Delhi-110092
2017

₹ 395.00

INTERNATIONAL RELATIONS, Fourth Edition
Peu Ghosh

ISBN-978-81-203-5240-7

The export rights of this book are vested solely with the publisher.

Twelfth Printing (Fourth Edition)   ···   ···   **May, 2017**

Published by Asoke K. Ghosh, PHI Learning Private Limited, Rimjhim House, 111, Patparganj Industrial Estate, Delhi-110092 and Printed by Rajkamal Electric Press, Plot No. 2, Phase IV, HSIDC, Kundli-131028, Sonepat, Haryana.

Contents

v

Preface

This edition has been revamped and rewritten after getting the tremendous response from the academicians, students, young scholars and teaching faculties all over India since the book was published in 2009. Current international scenario has compelled us to look afresh at the events happening all around the globe. The global recession that set in 2008 send shock waves and international political economy witnessed a massive depression. This depression touched the Eurozone too and the Euro debt crisis is known to all. Moreover, turbulence in Syria, Iraq and Afghanistan and the rise of new terror axis has complicated the situation in these countries. The deteriorating political conditions in these countries called for international action, including air strikes that have forced thousands to leave their countries and voyage into other countries, especially, Europe. The massive influx of 'boat people' has given rise to an unprecedented humanitarian crisis in Europe. Another development in international political economy is the falling crude price. The world is grappling in coming to terms with these crises amongst many. The book cannot disregard such developments. Therefore, a new chapter (Chapter 21) on **Current Concerns in International Relations: India and the World** has been also added to this new edition.

Chapters 1–5 deal with the theoretical aspects of International Relations. These chapters primarily focus on the evolution, nature and scope of International Relations, different approaches to the study of International Relations, detailed discussion on international system and states and non-state actors, national power, national interest, balance of power and foreign policy and its determinants and various techniques. Chapters 6–9 deal with the major world events and patterns of international relations that emerged in the post-Second World War era. Chapter 10 deals with regionalism in international relations and major regional organizations of the world and their role in world politics. Chapter 11 carries an in-depth analysis of the United Nations. Chapters 12–16 contain an analysis of the newer concerns of International Relations. They deal with the various attempts at disarmament, challenges posed by globalization, question of development and sustainable development, issue of human rights and the menace of terrorism. Chapter 14 which deals with different perspectives on development has now an added section on gender and development in IR. Chapter 17 brings about the importance of international law, international morality and world public opinion in world politics. Chapter 18 deals with the Indian foreign policy as it has evolved from the days of Pandit Jawahar Lal Nehru to the present. The bilateral relations of India with the major powers and her neighbours have been discussed at length in this chapter. Chapter 19 deals with international relations and its connection with the environment. This chapter has been updated against the backdrop of Climate Conference in Paris, 2015. Keeping in mind the working of the international political economy, Chapter 20 focuses on the prominent emerging economic groupings/initiatives, as well as the existing international and regional arrangements and institutions.

This book is not only a useful guide for students and teachers of International Relations, Political Science, History but also for those aspiring for various competitive examinations such as NET, SLET and other Central and State Services.

I am thankful to all my Professors of Department of International Relations, Jadavpur University for infusing me with the knowledge of International Relations and providing me with the encouragement that have helped me to traverse the dynamic terrain of International Relations in this book. I am thankful to my colleagues of Lady Brabourne College for being so cooperative.

It is pertinent on my part to take the opportunity to thank the editorial and production team of my publishers, PHI Learning, for their careful processing of the manuscript and continuous cooperation. My most sincere regards go to my parents, Mr. Subhas Kumar Ghosh and Mrs. Krishnasree Ghosh for their love and affection. It was only because of their inspiration and enthusiasm that this book could take the final shape.

Peu Ghosh

1

The Discipline of International Relations—Meaning, Evolution, Nature and Scope

INTRODUCTION

The world that we live in is in a flux. The change, whether in technologies, telecommunications or travel, affects our daily lives. Our everyday choices get influenced by such changes. In this fast moving globalized world, from the time we vote in an election or work on a political platform or simply purchase commodities or even trade services in the world market, we become part of the international community. Whether it is the rules of world trading system or war or catastrophes or increased people-to-people contact, our perspectives about world are shaped by the contemporary world events. The discipline of International Relations makes an endeavour to encapsulate such international politics and processes.

International Relations (IR) represents the study of foreign affairs and global issues among states including the roles of states, inter-governmental organizations (IGOs), non-governmental organizations (NGOs), and multinational corporations (MNCs). It is both an academic and public policy field, and can be

1

either positive or normative as it seeks both to analyze as well as formulate the foreign policy of particular states. It is often considered a branch of political science.

Apart from political science, IR draws upon such diverse fields as economics, history, law, philosophy, geography, sociology, anthropology, psychology, and cultural studies. It involves diverse range of issues including but not limited to: globalization, state sovereignty, ecological sustainability, nuclear proliferation, nationalism, economic development, global finance, terrorism, organized crime, human security, foreign interventionism, and human rights.

Since global developments touch upon the lives of every individual, the domain of International Relations cannot be the sole right of the Presidents, Prime Ministers or Diplomats. It becomes relevant for every single person living under the Sun. The evolution of this discipline which began after the First World War is still in a developing stage and its scope is expanding everyday. It becomes a challenge for academicians and students to master the discipline in this fast changing world.

MEANING OF INTERNATIONAL RELATIONS

It is not an easy task to give the precise meaning of international relations which when capitalized and reduced to the acronym 'IR', specifies a field of study taught in universities and colleges as a 'subject' or a 'discipline'. The difficulty increases manifold because of the tendency to use the terms 'international relations' and 'international politics' interchangeably. Often it is taken for granted that IR is the study of international politics only. Morgenthau[1] and others viewed the core of international relations to be international politics and the subject matter of international politics to be struggle for power among sovereign nations. Padelford and Lincoln[2] also opine that, when people speak of 'international relations', they are usually thinking of the relationships between states. They further contend that such relationships between states constitute 'international politics' which is the interaction of state policies within the changing patterns of power relationship.

But international relations means more and, as Palmer and Perkins[3] point out, international relations is related to not just politics of international community centring on diplomacy and relations among states and other political units, it means 'the totality of the relations among peoples and groups in the world society'. Therefore, the term 'international relations' is not only broad but means more than the official political relations between governments on behalf of their states. As Hoffman[4] suggested, the discipline of IR "is concerned with the factors and activities which affect the external policies and the power of the basic units into which the world is divided".

Palmer and Perkins[5] observe that IR "encompasses much more than the relations among nation-states and international organizations and groups. It includes a great variety of transitional relationships, at various levels, above and below the level of the nation-state, still the main actor in the international community".

Wright[6] contended that international relations include "relations between many entities of uncertain sovereignties" and that "it is not only the nations which international relations seek to relate. Varied types of groups—nations, states, governments, peoples, regions, alliances, confederations, international organizations, even industrial organizations, cultural organizations, religious organizations—must be dealt with in the study of international relations, if the treatment is to be realistic".

A more convincing definition has been provided by Frankel[7]: "This new discipline is more than a combination of the studies of the foreign affairs of the various countries and of international history—it includes also the study of international society as a whole and of its institutions and processes. It is increasingly concerned not only with the states and their interactions but also with the web of trans-national politics".

Mathiesen[8] gives a much broader definition of international relations and suggests that "International Relations embraces all kinds of relations traversing state boundaries, no matter whether they are of an economic, legal, political, or any other character, whether they be private or official", and "all human behaviour originating on one side of state boundary and affecting human behaviour on the other side of the boundary".

Goldstein[9] opines that the field of IR primarily "concerns the relationship among the world's governments". But defining IR in such a way, he argues, may seem simplistic, and therefore, to understand IR holistically, the relationship among states is to be understood in relation to the activities of other actors (international organizations, MNCs, individuals), in connection with other social structures (including economic, cultural and domestic politics), and considering historical and geographical influences.

Jackson and Sorenson[10] observe that "the main reason why we should study IR is the fact that the entire populations of the world are divided into separate territorial communities, or independent states, which profoundly affect the way people live". This definition points to the centrality of states and state system in the study of IR but there are other issues as well in contemporary IR. Jackson and Sorenson thus reflect that "at one extreme the scholarly focus is exclusively on states and inter-state relations; but at another extreme IR includes almost everything that has to do with human relations across the world. Therefore, IR seeks to understand how people are provided or not provided, with the basic values of security, freedom, order, justice and welfare".

According to Lawson[11] "in the simplest and narrowest senses, IR is taken to denote the study of relations between states". She contends that, in a broader sense, "IR denotes interactions between state-based actors across state boundaries" meaning thereby that, besides the intimate concern with the state system as a whole, there is an equal concern with the activities of a variety of non-state actors.

A somewhat standard definition of international relations has been provided by Frederick S. Dunn 1948. He is of the view that international relations may "be looked upon as the actual relations that take place across national boundaries, or as the body of knowledge which we have of those relations at any given time"[12]. It is considered to be a comprehensive definition because it does not limit the subject to official relations between states and governments.

Thus, it may be observed that there has been a tremendous effort on the part of the IR scholars to come out of a state-centric thinking and embark on a perspective, recognizing the presence of other actors as well. Therefore, summing up the above viewpoints, it may be ascertained that IR is a vast field encompassing the relationships among states in all their dimensions, including interactions with various other political and non-political groups along with the study of international history, international law, international society and international political economy.

EVOLUTION OF THE STUDY OF IR

The First World War resulted in unparalleled destruction and devastation of almost every country involved, with millions of lives lost—perhaps a proper estimate can never be done. Total economic collapse, widespread famine, and rampant disease continued to add to the death toll, many years after the fighting had ended, even for the winning side, the victorious nations. It is from this awesome and traumatic experience of the First World War that the inspiration to study IR, as a separate academic discipline, grew.

The origin of IR can be traced to the writings of political philosophers such as, Thucydides, an ancient Greek historian who wrote the *History of the Peloponnesian War* and is also cited as an intellectual forerunner of *realpolitik*, Chanakya's *Arthashastra*, and Niccolò Machiavelli's *Il Principe* (*The Prince*). However, IR as an academic discipline in its own right only came to be studied after the horrifying experiences of the First World War. Before that, IR had always existed as a branch of history, law, philosophy, political science and other related subjects. But World War I, resulting in a loss of 20 million lives, proved the bankruptcy and limitations of traditional European diplomacy as a method of maintaining world order, and there grew an urge for alternatives.

This gave birth to the liberal approaches to IR which is often collectively referred to as *idealism* or sometimes as *utopianism*. Their focus was on the ills of international system, and, "what ought to be done" to avoid major disasters in the future and to save the future generations from the scourge of wars. There were many strands of liberal thinking, but the basic assumption, running throughout the many liberal writings, was that human beings were rational and, when they apply reason to international relations, they can set up organizations for the benefit of all. Therefore, emphasis was laid on outlawing war, disarmament, international law and international organizations during this phase of evolution of liberal thinking. The chief advocates of post-World War I (WWI) idealism were Alfred Zimmern (1879–1957), Norman Angell (1872–1967), James T. Shotwell (1874–1965), and Woodrow Wilson (1856–1924). In particular,

Wilson's "14 Points" speech, delivered before the US Congress in 1918 is an expression of the sentiments of the idealist exposition. He made a pledge to the world community for:

- Making the world safe for democracy.
- Creation of international organization for promotion of peaceful cooperation among nation-states.

In fact, Wilson's points were adopted in the post-War peace settlement. The birth of the League of Nations and the Covenant, which was finally drawn in 1919, were the final expressions of Wilsonian principles. The main line of thinking was that *realpolitik* is like a "jungle, where dangerous beasts roam and the strong and cunning rule, whereas under the League of Nations the beasts are put into cages reinforced by the restraints of international organization, i.e., into a kind of zoo".[13]

International Relations, which emerged against such a backdrop, soon made its way into the American universities. The first University Chair that formally established the discipline was the Woodrow Wilson Chair of International Politics at the University College of Wales, Aberystwyth in 1919. It was endowed by philanthropist David Davies. Sir Alfred Zimmern was the first holder of the prestigious chair. Simultaneously, Montague Burton also endowed chairs of international relations in Jerusalem (1929), Oxford University (1930), the London School of Economics (1936) and the University of Edinburgh (1948). Their firm belief was that by promoting the study of international relations it would be possible to bring about peace, that is, the systematic study of international relations would lead to increased support for international law and the League of Nations. Despite several shortcomings of the liberal thought, it is acknowledged that Zimmern, Wilson and Davies laid the foundation of the study of IR as an academic discipline.[14]

As the leading academicians were still reeling under the shock and awe of the First World War, they adopted a legalistic–moralistic approach and were highly descriptive and prescriptive, unable to satisfy the need to understand the complex nature of international relations as they tried to establish ideals to be achieved while ignoring the harsh realities of international relations. The optimism and ideals of the liberal thinkers therefore, got a rude shock with the outbreak of the Second World War (WWII) in 1939. The idealists' failure to answer the questions regarding the failure of the League of Nations to prevent the war and also the behaviour of certain states with respect to some others, which aggravated conflict-like situations in the inter-War period ultimately culminating in the Second World War led to severe criticisms.

Contrary to Wilson's hope to spread democracy, Fascism and Nazism grew in Italy and Germany and coupled with this was the rise of authoritarianism in Central and Eastern Europe. The League of Nations proved to be too weak an international organization to control aggressive states. Russia and Germany always had strained relationship with the League. Germany joined the League in

1926 and left in the early 1930s. Following its invasion of Manchuria, Japan left the League. Russia joined the League in 1934 but was expelled in 1940, following its attack on Finland. Britain and France never had regards for the principles of the League. USA, though a forerunner in the creation of the League, could not join it because of the Senate's refusal to ratify the Covenant of the League as well as their intention to pursue their age-old policy of isolationism. Severe economic crisis of the 1930s again forced the states to follow zealously the policy of protectionism rather than interdependence. As some scholars put forth, the situation was like each country for itself, each country trying as best it could to look after its own interests, if necessary, to the detriment of others—the 'jungle' rather than the 'zoo'.[15] Therefore, the stage was ready for a more critical and in-depth understanding of IR.

When the Second World War (1939–1945) finally broke out, the idealists were blamed for their utopian thinking and their legalistic–moralistic assumptions were alleged to be far from the realities of power politics. IR soon came to be occupied with a critique of liberal idealism and out of this emerged a new paradigm—Realism, sometimes also known as *Realpolitik*—an anti-thesis of Idealism. The principal advocates of this worldview were E.H. Carr (1939), George F. Kennan (1954, 1956), Hans J. Morgenthau (1948), Reinhold Niebuhr (1947), Kenneth W. Thompson (1958, 1960) and others. This was the emergence of the first 'Great Debate' in IR in the post-World War II period.

The realist paradigm puts singular importance to states as the principal actors and their activities, guided by their interests to be the only reality. To the realists, conflict of interest is inevitable, which results in an anarchical international system and it is this situation of world politics that shapes the choices of the states where each state defines its interest in terms of power. Interest, defined in terms of power devoid of any moral consideration, according to the realist, gives meaning to international politics. Realism with its forceful exposition soon became the dominant paradigm of understanding IR. Nevertheless, dissatisfaction also arose about the shortcomings of the realist paradigm around 1960s and 1970s.

The discontent was more with the language and the method of studying IR. This was largely because of the behavioural revolution in the whole gamut of social sciences. The main emphasis was on application of scientific methods of study. Thus, emerged the second Great Debate in IR. But this 'new' Great Debate was different from the first in the sense that the first Great Debate was related to the subject matter or the content of IR, whereas the second was purely a methodological movement focusing on the mode of analysis in IR. As Kegley and Wittkopf[16] point out that the central focus was on "theorizing about theory" rather than "theorizing about international relations". They tried to replace subjective belief with verifiable knowledge and wanted to supplant impressionism and intuition with testable evidence along with an endeavour to substitute data and reproducible information for mere opinion. The major works which tried to incorporate scientific methods were Quincy Wright's *A Study of*

*War****, Morton A. Kaplan's *Systems and Processes in International Politics******* and Charles McClelland's† *Theory of the International System.*

The methodologies of theorists like Morton Kaplan and Karl Deutsch‡ repudiated the moralism and legalism of the traditional approaches. Kaplan conceived the international system as an "analytical entity" for explaining the behaviour of international actors and the "regulative", "integrative" or disintegrative" consequences of their policies. Deutsch understood international system as "clusters of settlement, modes of transport, centers of culture, areas of language, decisions of caste and class barriers between markets, sharp regional differences in wealth and interdependence". Said[17] states that "what has been the ideological commitment of the traditional theorists became a devalued hypothesis to analyse causation in the real political world" for these theorists in IR.

The second Great Debate was neither won by the behaviouralists nor by the traditionalists and, gradually the controversies receded but left a long-lasting impact on the IR scholars, especially those from USA. Ultimately, this led to the reformulation of both realism and liberalism, both of which were highly influenced by the behaviouralist methodologies. The new avatars of realism and liberalism in the form of neo-realism and neo-liberalism again fermented the renewal of the first major debate in the 1970s. Side by side there sparked off another major debate between the neo-liberalism and neo-realism on one hand and neo-Marxism on the other. This 'neo–neo' debate came to constitute the third Great Debate of IR.

The neo-liberals renewed the old liberal ideas about the possibility of progress and change, but they discarded idealism. They tried to formulate theories and apply new methods that were scientific. Among several strands of neo-liberalism, the most prominent, which tried to face the realist challenge, was generally known as *pluralism,* and associated with it was the *Interdependence Model* of international relations. The chief proponents of the neo-liberal approach were E. Haas (Influential American Political Scientist), Robert Keohane§ and Joseph Nye§§.

---

*Quincy Wright, *A Study of War,* University of Chicago, Chicago, 1942.

**Morton A. Kaplan, *Systems and Processes in International Politics,* Wiley and Sons, New York, 1957.

†Charles McClelland's, *Theory of the International System,* The Macmillan Company, New York, 1967.

‡Karl Deutsch, *The Analysis of International Relations,* Prentice Hall, Englewood Cliffs, New Jersey, 1968.

§Robert Keohane is an American academic and a neo-liberal institutionalism theorist in international relations. He is the Professor of International Affairs at the Princeton University.

§§Joseph Nye Voted as one of the ten most influential scholars of international relations in the US. Along with Robert Keohane, he developed the neo-liberal theory of international relations.

The main line of thinking of this neo-liberal school was the plurality or multiplicity of actors. The neo-liberalists rejected the singular simplicities of the realist approach which considered states to be the only significant actors in international relations. This new school of liberal thought put a much greater emphasis on the plurality of actors and their activities in international relations. They acknowledged that side by side the UN and other regional organizations like the European Union (EU), Association of South East Asian Nations (ASEAN), the African Union (AU) which remained state-based, there was an increasing importance of non-state actors such as the multinational corporations (MNCs), International Monetary Fund (IMF), the World Bank, several international non-governmental organizations such as the Red Cross, Red Crescent, Médecins sans Frontiers, Amnesty International, and a host of other non-state actors. These actors operate between the domestic and the international spheres, thereby transcending states and making the boundaries irrelevant to some extent.

The other idea which the neo-liberals put forward is the concept of *complex interdependence*, which is dramatically different from that of the realists. They argue that, besides the political relations of governments, there are other forms of connections between societies including transnational links between the business corporations. Here, military force is not given much importance. Hence, an "absence of hierarchy among issues" is found and military power is no longer useful as an instrument of foreign policy as the other actors; besides, the states do not have violent conflict on their international agenda. Therefore, it can be said that the neo-liberals put forward non-military paradigms of international relations and continuously argued for peaceful and cooperative international relations.[18]

The pluralists' arguments soon caught the attention of the realists and it was Kenneth Waltz[*] who renewed realism in its new form—Neo-Realism—and revived the debate between the realists and the liberals. This stream of neo-realism tried to build upon the principles of classical realism, especially those of Hans J. Morgenthau and tried to draw from classical realism those elements of a theory adequate to the world of the late twentieth century as well as link conceptually to other theoretical efforts. Waltz's pathbreaking work *Theory of International Politics*[**] (1979) laid the essential basis of the neo-realists' debate. He focused on the 'structure' of the international system and the consequences of that structure in the international system. For the neo-realists, international politics became more than the summation of the foreign policies of the states and the external balance of other actors. Waltz, therefore, emphasized patterned relationships among actors in a system that is anarchical. For him, states were power-seeking and security-conscious, not because of human nature viewed as

---

[*]Kenneth Waltz is one of the most prominent scholars of international relations.

[**]Kenneth Waltz, *Theory of International Politics*, McGraw Hill, New York, 1979.

'plain bad' by classical realists, but because the structure of the international system compels them to do so. Therefore, neo-realists did not overlook the prospects of cooperation among states. But the point of contention was that states, while cooperating with each other, tried to maximize their relative power and preserve their autonomy. Therefore, the neo-realists were successful in putting the neo-liberals on the defensive in the 1980s.[19]

However, during this period, efforts were embarked on by scholars to bring the two schools of thought closer. The efforts of Robert Keohane and Bary Buzan[20] were noteworthy. Bary Buzan along with Charles Jones and Richard Little tried to synthesize neo-realist and neo-liberal institutionalist positions and they introduced the concept of *deep structure*, which meant that political structure encompasses anarchy as well as hierarchy and it includes not only power and institutions but also rules and norms. They believed that anarchic society produced states that are sovereign but that in no way meant that anarchy is incompatible with cooperation. Buzan, Jones and Little were of the opinion that units of the international system have differing structures, extending from empires to republics and including state and non-state actors, in their international action, exhibit cooperative and competitive behaviours. This resulted in alliances, coalitions, regimes, norms and institutions for international cooperation. Change and continuity were brought about by the interaction between the international system and its units. On the whole, Buzan, Jones and Little retained the core elements of Waltz's structural realism but broadened it by looking into the international system as being based on anarchy but still including patterns of cooperation.

Another challenge, which came up during this time and straightaway confronted the neo-realists and neo-liberalists, was the Marxists viewpoint. The main contributions came from neo-Marxists such as Andre Gunder Frank (1967), Immanuel Wallerstein (1974) and others who formed the School of International Political Economy (IPE). Their fundamental contributions were in providing powerful insights into the origin and development of the international system which is roughly divided into the dominant North and the dependent South. Their effort was to locate the causes of most developing countries' persistent underdevelopment in the patterns of dominance and dependence. Two strands of structural theorists need attention: the World System Theory and the Dependency Theory. A core-periphery bifurcation of the world was developed by the dependency theorists who took their cue from Lenin's work *Imperialism: The Highest Stage of Capitalism*. In the 1970s, Immanuel Wallerstein[*] added another category of semi-periphery to the dual structure model while developing the Modern World System Theory. The line of thinking that reflected in the works of these structural Marxists is that the striking feature of the world system is the transfer of wealth and resources from the peripheral countries to the core countries. The result is that the rich get richer and the poor get poorer. The core

---

[*]Immanuel Wallerstein is an American Sociologist.

periphery bifurcation symbolizes the "relative economic strength of rich countries (i.e. those in North America and Europe as well as Japan), which forms the core of the world economy, and the poorer ones on the periphery, with the Soviet Union occupying the semi-periphery".[21]

The 1970s and 1980s were thoroughly preoccupied with the neo-liberalism and neo-realism debate. But after the end of the Cold War from the 1990s onwards, there was a change in the way IR was seen. The preponderance of the American scholars lessened, and this made way for assertion by IR scholars of Europe and other places of the globe. The school of thought that emerged around this time in the United Kingdom came to be referred to as "the English School", with its emphasis on *society of states* or *international society*[22]. Though the school had come to be associated with the English, but its major figure Hedley Bull was an Australian. The other chief proponents of this school were E.H. Carr, C.A.W. Manning, F.S. Northedge, Martin Wight, Adam Watson, R.J. Vincent, James Mayall, Robert Jackson, and newer scholars like Timothy Dunne and Nicholas Wheeler.[23] The International Society theorists made an attempt to provide an alternative set of premises which are neither Hobbesian nor utopian. In fact, they tried to arrive at non-Hobbesian conclusions from Hobbesian premises. They did not reject the realists' emphasis on power and national interest and they did acknowledge that world politics is an "anarchical society" but, at the same time, they do contend that under conditions of anarchy, states act within a system of norms which, most of the time, is constraining. Therefore, the core element in their thought is that there is a presence of a world of sovereign states where both power and law are present. Power and national interest do matter, but norms and institutions also have great significance.[24]

However, with the end of Cold War and the dismemberment of the Soviet Union, the dominant paradigms in IR seemed unable to explain the prevailing situations. Therefore, new reflective critical ideas started gaining ground, which were a departure from the mainstream liberal, realist and orthodox Marxist thinking in IR. New debates have, therefore, arisen in IR addressing methodological as well as substantial issues. Currently a fourth debate is on its way, which challenges the established traditions in IR by alternative approaches. The new voices in IR are identified as *post-Positivist approaches* and the era that it has heralded has been identified by Yosef Lapid* as *a post-Positivist era*.

Steve Smith[25] while considering the present theoretical perspectives of IR, puts IR theories into two broad categories:

- Explanatory theories that see the world as something external to our theories. Realists, pluralists and structural neo-Marxist theories tend to be explanatory theories, with their task being to report on a world that is external to theories. In this endeavour, they attempt to find regularities in

*Yosef Lapid, 'The Third Debate: On the Prospects of International Theory in a Post-Positivist Era', *International Studies Quarterly*, 33(3), 1989.

human behaviour and thereby explain the social world in the way a natural scientist would do.

- Constitutive theories are those that help construct the world. Most of the recent approaches, ranging from critical theories to post-modernist theories, tend to be constitutive in the sense that these theories are not external to the things they are trying to explain and they just attempt to construct how one thinks about the world.

Smith contends that present theoretical perspectives as based on:

- Foundational theoretical position which states that all truth claims can be judged true or false. Neo–neo debate, historical sociology and critical theory seem to be foundational.
- Anti-foundational theoretical position which contends that truth claims cannot be so judged since there are never neutral grounds for doing so. Post-modernism, some feminist theories, normative theories tend to be anti-foundational.

Smith further characterizes the theories into two categories:

- Rationalist, constituting the neo-liberal and neo-realist theoretical positions.
- Reflectivist, constituting the non-positivistic theories.

Smith argues that present day IR is, therefore, characterized by three principal trends: [Figure 1.1]

- Continuing dominance of the three theories—Realism, Liberalism and Modern World System theory—constituting the rationalist position and epitomized by the 'neo–neo' debate.
- Emergence of non-positivistic theories marking the reflectivist position.
- Development of an approach that seeks a rapprochement between the rationalist and reflectivist positions and is epitomized by the social constructivist position.[25]

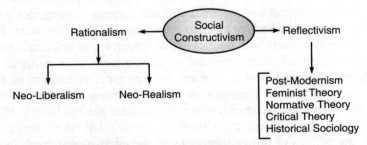

Figure 1.1   Classification of international relations theory in the late 1990s.
[Source: Adapted from Steve Smith][25].

NATURE OF INTERNATIONAL RELATIONS

From the birth of IR, it has been facing uncertainty regarding its boundaries. Before its academic study as a separate discipline began in the aftermath of the First World War, IR was treated as a part of history, law and political theory. Even after the intellectual development started and the discipline was successful in establishing its foothold, some still considered it as a subdivision of the greater field of Political Science and emphasized the need to study political phenomena at the global level. Still, some universities today offer separate degrees and have separate departments for IR (especially at the PG level) while others teach IR along with Political Science. Some others view that the subject matter of IR can only be studied by interdisciplinary research teams drawing on the expertise of many disciplines including Political Science, Economics, Sociology, Psychology, Anthropology, Medicine, Cybernetics and Communications and other related fields of study and not separately. Zimmern[26] (a British academician and the Wilson Professor of International Politics, the first Professor of International Politics, also known as International Relations in the World) commented that "the study of international relations extends from the natural sciences at one end to moral philosophy ... at the other". He defined the field not as a single subject or discipline but as a "bundle of subjects...viewed from a common angle".

POLITICAL SCIENCE AND INTERNATIONAL RELATIONS

Even though IR has to be treated as a 'bundle of subject' yet, more often controversy unfolds between the discipline of Political Science and IR. One treats the other as an offshoot or rather part of its own discipline, while the other claims to be an autonomous discipline. It is truly very difficult to compartmentalize both Political Science and IR, as both are inextricably related to one another, and such controversies must be avoided. For a more matured and holistic study, both have to work hand-in-hand. What can be done is to look at the emphasis of both and levels of entry of one another into the discipline of each other. Political Science, if it is treated as a science of politics and working towards studying formal and informal political patterns existing in a particular state, IR is more concerned with trans-territorial affairs of the state. Political Science involves concern with politics within the territorial unit that is called the State. The legislative, executive and judicial actions of a political system affecting the political life of a state are the core areas of concern of Political Science. Very little is the emphasis on foreign relations of the state concerned and comes into discussion when it affects the national policies mainly. IR, on the other hand, is more concerned with the external relations of the states and studying the politics of power bargaining at the international level. Individual foreign policies of states, bilateral and multilateral engagements, interactions with trans-national non-state actors, conflict and cooperation, questions of international peace and security become the main concern of IR. However, it is not possible to draw an iron curtain between these two disciplines. It is not possible to study domestic politics totally disregarding the international politics, as international agreements and even international organizations might affect the national economic and political policies of State. Similarly, IR is also touched by domestic politics. The ruling government or regime, the bureaucrats, the political parties and public opinion come to have an impact on the external relations of the State. For example, the IMF, World Bank and WTO known as the Triad in international political economy, with their policies of Structural Adjustment Programmes (SAPs) affect the economic and financial policies of the countries, which take loans from them. On the other hand, to analyze the foreign policy trend of any state, one has to study the internal functioning of the political system, including the study of political institutions, political parties and interest groups and public opinion. What can be said is that domestic politics and international politics cannot be studied in isolation. IR, therefore has to make an entry into the domain of Political Science for a proper understanding by developing methodologies and theories to understand international politics.

The Approaches to the Study of IR: Theories and Methodologies

In reality, the complexities in IR makes it impossible to study with a limited knowledge. What is needed is a systematic analysis of the subject matter of IR. For this, as Goldstein[27] observes that both descriptive and theoretical knowledge are required as he contends that "It would do little good only to describe events without being able to generalize or draw lessons from them. Nor would it do much good to formulate purely abstract theories without being able to apply them to the finely detailed and complex real world in which we live". Equally important is the use of methods in developing and testing various theories. Whether one builds theories from facts or predict facts from theories, one can utilize them to the learning of IR in myriad ways. But given the complexities and unpredictability of IR, it can be said that even the best theories provide only a rough guide to understand the international processes and interactions and eventually make decisions.

Nevertheless, overtime different paradigms in IR which sparked grand debates have ultimately led to the gradual evolution of the discipline as already discussed. The main debates in IR are between:

1. Utopian Liberalism/Idealism and Realism
2. Traditional Approaches and Behaviouralism
3. Neo-liberalism/neo-Realism and neo-Marxism
4. Positivism and post-Positivist Alternatives.

Most IR scholars do agree that a single set of theories or even a single set of concepts would not be in a position to explain IR. Still three paradigms are found to dominate the study of IR.

1. Realism and neo-realism
2. Liberalism, pluralism and neo-liberalism
3. International political economy—structuralism and neo-Marxism.

Scholars like Abdul A. Said[17] observed that five categories of theories have emerged to examine the unexplored terrain of international relations:

1. *Theory of theory:* how 'scientific' the discipline of IR can become.
2. *Systems analysis:* This refers to the development of hypotheses about the international system. The two primary foci are the state as a responding unit within the international system and the configuration of the international system on the whole.
3. *Action theories:* the analysis of the ways states and their decision makers conduct foreign policy including decision-making capabilities, institutions and the interaction of the political system and national society.
4. *Interaction theory:* which attempts to generalize about the 'patterns' of interactions and the internal behaviour of the interacting units like the theory of balance of power, world equilibrium, gaming, "challenge and response", international processes involving competition, cooperation, bargaining and conflict.
5. *Newer research techniques:* borrowed from other disciplines; content analysis borrowed from the study of communications, psychometrics useful in measuring such attitudes as 'friendship' or 'hostility' among states, game theory and the like.[28]

Several alternative approaches have also developed into the study of contemporary IR.

1. Post-modernist theories propounded by Richard Ashley (1988), R.B.J. Walker (1993), James Derian (1989) and others.
2. Critical theories advocated by Andrew Linklater (1990), Robert Cox (1996) and others.
3. Historical sociology propounded by Michael Mann (1986 and 1983), Charles Tilly (1990), Theda Skocpol.
4. Feminist theories advocated by J. Ann Tickner (1988), Cynthis Enloe (1988, 1990, 1993 and 1999) and Christine Sylvester (1998).[29]

Despite such breakthroughs in theory building and paradigm development and improvisations, IR is difficult to study by utilizing such theories. At best, a mixture of combination of theories is required to obtain acceptable results. The aim is to provide the IR scholars and students with a choice of IR theories that will help to comprehend the multi-layered and cultural complex world as well as recognize the processes and difficulties involved in coming to understand them.

SCOPE AND SUBJECT MATTER OF IR

International Relation is a dynamic discipline. With the world fast changing in the face of globalization, along with the threats of fundamentalism, ethnicity and terrorism, ebbing state system, crisis in sovereignty of states, human rights, newer international regimes, the discipline has been forced to move beyond its traditional themes and incorporarte a 'new agenda' in its study.

Initially, the discipline devoted itself to the study of diplomatic history, foreign policies of states, international law, international organizations. Since the outbreak of the Second World War and in the years following it, the world was not only engulfed in a Cold War between the United States and the Soviet Union but it also witnessed the birth of many new states due to rapid decolonization, which led to an expansion of the scope of IR. As a result, new theories, and newer methodologies to study IR emerged. As in the 1960s and 1970s, when behaviouralism made a pathway into the study of IR, motives and behaviours of states as well as political leaders came to be studied. It is quite an extensive discipline embracing diplomatic history, international politics, international organization, international law, area studies, behaviour of states and their mutual relations, international trade and foreign policy. Its scope is still expanding and will expand in future too. As Frederick S. Dunn contends that the word 'scope' is ambiguous because it implies fixed boundary lines readily identifiable as a surveyor's mark. Therefore, he suggested that the "subject matter of international relations consists of whatever knowledge, from any sources, may be of assistance in meeting new international problems or understanding old ones".[30] IR scholars have never agreed on where the boundaries of their field lie.

Goldstein projects IR as a field of study focussing on:

1. Issue areas—diplomacy, war, trade relations, alliances, cultural exchanges, participation in international organizations, etc.
2. Conflict and cooperation in relationship among states concerning issue areas.
3. International security—questions of war and peace.
4. International political economy—between 1970 and 1980—increasing concern with economic issues made international political economy (IPE) inextricably woven into IR, especially with regard to security issues.[31]

Palmer and Perkins[32] include such topics within the domain of IR such as state system, national power, diplomacy, propaganda, war, imperialism, balance of power, collective security, international organizations, international law, regional conflicts, national interests, nuclear weapon and changing international system.

According to Frankel,[33] the contents of IR must take care of the changes in the international system, i.e., the rise in the number of states, MNCs and terrorist groups; the shift of the major danger spots geographically, from Europe to

Middle East and Africa, from the strategic to the economic field; the growing recognition of the need for some form of global or regional regimes, overriding sovereign states. Therefore, the study should include the making of foreign policies, the mutual interactions among states, conflicts, competitions and cooperations among them, national power, diplomacy, propaganda, international system and international organization.

Coloumbis and Wolfe[34] emphasize that the study of IR should involve the approaches to the study of IR, theories of IR, nation-states and nationalism, national power, national interest, foreign policies of nation-states and nationalism, national power, decision making, diplomacy, war, balance of power, international law, international economy, international organizations, functionalism and regional integration, gap between the rich and poor nation-states, new actors in international system, threats facing humankind.

Kal Holsti[35] points out that during the heydays of the Cold War, the field was characterized by three distinct sets of normative concerns or discourses which tried to answer the question 'what to study?' They are:

- Security, conflict and war
- Cooperation and the conditions for peace
- Equity, justices and the sources of international inequality

According to Jackson and Sorenson[36], traditional IR was concerned solely with the development and change of sovereign statehood in the context of the larger system or society of states which might help in explaining the questions of war and peace. However, they assert that contemporary IR is concerned not only with political relations between states but also with a host of other subjects such as economic interdependence, human rights, transnational corporations, international organizations, the environment, gender inequalities, development, terrorism, and so forth.

Baylis and Smith[37] in their effort to include upcoming agenda in IR tried to incorporate several new themes. They looked not only into the historical context of international society and world history till the end of Cold War and discussed the main theories in IR, including the new approaches to IR theory in the post-Cold War era, but also focussed chiefly on international security in the post-Cold War era, international political economy in the age of globalization, international regimes, diplomacy, the UN and international organizations, transnational actors, environmental issues, nuclear proliferation, nationalism, cultural conflicts in IR, humanitarian intervention in world politics, regionalism and integration, global trade and finance, poverty, development and hunger, human rights, and gender issues.

A more wider content has been provided by Kegley and Wittkopf[38]. By using macropolitical perspective, they draw our attention to:

- Charateristics, capabilities and interests of the principal actors in world politics (nation-states and various non-state participants in international affairs).

- The principal welfare and global issues that populate global agenda.
- The patterns of cooperation and contention that influence the interactions between and among actors and issues.

Further, they state that the scope of contemporary IR has to expand to accommodate such questions as:

- Are states obsolete?
- Is interdependence a cure or a curse?
- Is technological innovation a blessing or a burden?
- Will geo-economics supersede geo-politics?
- What constitutes human well-being in an ecologically fragile planet?

Lawson[39] points out that, although the traditional concern for war and inter-state warfare in particular is still the focus of IR, but IR's "new agenda" embraces a "vast range of policy issues". They include global environment concerns, the epidemiology of AIDS, legal and illegal migration, including refugee movements, the North–South gap, human rights, reform of the UN and its agencies, extension of international law, and the prosecution of crimes against humanity, whether involving terrorism, religious fundamentalism or international organized criminal activities that range from drug production and trafficking to money laundering, smuggling goods of all kinds including weapons, diamonds, endangered species and people and 'new wars' arising from 'identity politics' linked with religious, ethnic or cultural factors. Lawson highlights that the "notion of 'human security' rather than 'state security' is now very much in ascendance."

The vast topics which have now come to dominate the study of IR may again not be sufficient with the changing needs of time. Prospects of change remain as world conditions change.

EXERCISES

1. Elucidate on how scholars, over time, have tried to define international relations. Also try to trace the evolution of international relations.

2. Discuss the nature and scope of international relations.

3. Disucss how after the end of First World War, since 1919, the study of international relations has evolved to its present form.

4. Discuss the different stages of evolution of international relations as an academic discipline with special emphasis on the *Great Debates*.

REFERENCES

[1] Morgenthau, Hans J., *Politics Among Nations: The Struggle for Power and Peace*, Kalyani Publishers, New Delhi, 1985, p. 31.

[2] Padelford, Norman J. and George A. Lincoln, *International Politics: Foundations of International Relations,* New York, 1954, pp. 4, 6.

[3] Palmer, Norman D. and Howard C. Perkins, *International Relations—The World Community in Transition,* A.I.T.B.S. Publishers, New Delhi, 1997, p. xiv.

[4] Hoffman, Stanley (Ed.), *Contemporary Theory of International Relations,* Prentice Hall, Englewood Cliffs, New Jersey, 1960, p. 6.

[5] Palmer and Perkins, *op. cit.*, n. 3, p. xi.

[6] Wright, Quincy, *The Study of International Relations,* Appleton-Century Crofts, New York, 1955, p. 5.

[7] Frankel, Joseph, *International Relations in a Changing World,* Oxford University Press, London, 1979, p. 6.

[8] Quoted in Palmer and Perkins, *op. cit.*, n. 3, p. xiv.

[9] Goldstein, Joshua S., *International Relations*, Pearson Education, New Delhi, 2006, p. 29.

[10] Jackson, Robert and George Sorensen, *Introduction to International Relations—Theories and Approaches*, Oxford University Press, London, 1999, pp. 2–3.

[11] Lawson, Stephanie, *International Relations,* Polity Press, UK, 2004, p. 4.

[12] Dougherty, James E. and Robert L. Pfaltzgraff, Jr, *Contending Theories of International Relations—A Comprehensive Survey,* Longman, New York, 1997, p. 18.

[13] Jackson and Sorensen, *op. cit.*, n. 10, p. 38.

[14] Lawson, Stephanie, *op. cit.*, n. 11, pp. 41, 44.

[15] Jackson and Sorensen, *op. cit.*, n. 10, pp. 40, 41.

[16] Kegley, Charles W., Jr. and Eugene R. Wittkopf, *World Politics—Trends and Transformation,* St. Martin's Press, New York, 1997, pp. 26–27.

[17] Said, Abdul A., *Theory of International Relations—The Crisis of Relevance,* Prentice-Hall of India, New Delhi, 1969, p. 18.

[18] Lawson, Stephanie, *op. cit.*, n. 11, pp. 49–50.

[19] Dougherty and Pfaltzgraff, *op. cit.*, n. 12, pp. 80–82.

[20] Buzan, Bary, Charles Jones and Richard Little, *The Logic of Anarchy: Neo-realism to Structural Realism*, Columbia University Press, New York, 1993, p. 36.

[21] Lawson, Stephanie, *op. cit.*, n. 11, pp. 53–54.

[22] Jackson and Sorensen, *op. cit.*, n. 10, p. 53.

[23] Brown, Chris, *Understanding International Relations,* Macmillan Press, London, 1997, pp. 52–53.

[24] Jackson and Sorensen, *op. cit.*, n. 10, pp. 53–55.

[25] Smith, Steve, "New Approaches to International Theory," *in* John Baylis and Steve Smith, *The Globalization of World Politics,* Oxford University Press, London, 1997, pp. 166–173.

[26] Dougherty and Pfaltzgraff, *op. cit.*, n. 12, p. 17.

[27] Goldstein, Joshua S., *op. cit.*, n. 9, pp. 32–35.

[28] Jackson and Sorensen, *op. cit.*, n. 10, p. 35.

[29] Baylis, John and Steve Smith, *op. cit.*, n. 25, pp. 172–186.

[30] Dougherty and Pfaltzgraff, *op. cit.*, n. 12, p. 18.

[31] Goldstein, Joshua S., *op. cit.*, n. 9, pp. 30–31.

[32] Palmer and Perkins, *op. cit.*, n. 3, p. xv.

[33] Frankel, Joseph, *op. cit.*, n. 7.

[34] Couloumbis, Theodre A. and James H. Wolfe, *Introduction to International Relations—Power and Justice,* Prentice-Hall of India, New Delhi, 1986.

[35] Holsti, Kal J., "The Study of International Politics during the Cold War," *in* Tim Dunne, Michael Cox and Ken Booth (Eds.), *The Eighty Years' Crisis—International Relations—1919–1999,* Cambridge University Press, London, 1998, p. 26.

[36] Jackson and Sorensen, *op. cit.*, n. 10, p. 34.

[37] Baylis, John and Steve Smith, *op. cit.*, n. 25, pp. xiii–xviii.

[38] Kegley and Wittkopf, *op. cit.*, n. 16, pp. 10–15.

[39] Lawson, Stephanie, *op. cit.*, n. 11, p. 6.

2

Theories and Approaches to the Study of International Relations

CONTENTS

The Liberal Approach
Political Realism
E.H. Carr and Realism
Morgenthau and Realism
Neo-Realism
Pluralism
Marxist Approach and the Modern World System Theory
World System Theory
The Indian Approach: North over South
Systems Theory
Communications Approach
Decision-Making Theory
Post-Structuralism in International Relations
Constructivism
Feminism in International Relations

INTRODUCTION

Theory is considered to be a systematic reflection of phenomena, designed to explain them and to show how they are related to each other in a meaningful, intelligent pattern, instead of being merely random items of an incoherent universe. Theory is essential for every discipline to help in research and provide the basis for explanation and prediction. However, even the grand theories in social sciences, particularly in IR, have no21t provided with generalizations, principles or hypotheses with that force or vigour that they might be considered as the foundations for universally accepted comprehensive theories of IR. As we have seen in Chapter 1, the effort towards comprehensive theory-building in IR began with the first Grand Debate between the Idealists and the Realists. Subsequently in the 1940s, development towards theory-building was given a boost by growing interests in newer methodologies and techniques for research, analysis and teaching in IR. Further, the 1960s behavioural revolution opened up new avenues for research and methodological usage. Inputs were taken from biological, psychological, anthropological, sociological, economic and other behavioural sciences to explain international political behaviour. Contemporary IR is also witnessing a steady growth of several new approaches of the post-Positivist tradition. Despite such initiatives of theory building, Dougherty and Pfaltzgraff (Jr.)[1] point out that like all other social science disciplines, theory is more diffused and less precise in IR than found in the physical sciences. Till date, the mainstream IR discourse, however, is under the influence of three main theoretical perspectives on world politics—liberalism, political realism and world system theory. Of these again, political realism seems to have preponderance over the others.

THE LIBERAL APPROACH

The tradition of liberal political thought as propounded by liberal thinkers like Immanuel Kant, Thomas Jefferson, James Madison, John Stuart Mill, John Locke, David Hume, Jean–Jacques Rousseau and Adam Smith was revived, adopted and transformed to give birth to the liberal approach to IR. The chief proponents of post-World War I liberalism were Alfred Zimmern, Norman Angell, James T. Shotwell and Woodrow Wilson. They are sometimes referred to as *liberal idealists* or simply *idealists*. E.H. Carr (1939), however, ascribed them as *utopians*.

At the heart of the liberal worldview lie certain basic assumptions about the human rationality and morality, belief in reforming institutions as solutions to problems and most importantly idea about human progress. In the words of David Sidorsky[2] liberalism consists of "In simplest terms, first a conception of man as desiring freedom and capable of exercising rational free choice. Second, it is a perspective on social institutions as open to rational reconstruction in the light of individual needs. It is third, a view of history as progressively perfectible through the continuous application of human reason to social institutions".

Based on their optimism, the liberalists conceptualize the individual as the possessor of rationality and a seat of moral values and virtues and also capable of controlling their basic impulses. They try to justify the irrational and immoral behaviour of the individuals as not the manifestations of flawed human nature but the result of ignorance and misunderstanding, which is possible to overcome through education and reforming of social and political institutions.

Alongside such positive picturization of human beings, the liberals tend to be less emphatic about social and individual conflicts as inevitable. They believe that it is possible to bring about the greatest good for the greatest number that would reap benefits for all and create an order that would maximize individual freedom and material and economic prosperity. The logical corollary of this is the concept of "**harmony of interests**".

Contrary to the realist position that focuses on the possibility of conflict of interests and clashes, the liberals lay emphasis on the common interests. The belief is that people and nations share common interests and the prospects of cooperative activities among them will satisfy these interests. Liberals are critical about the realist perspective of international conflict and war and consider them as a distortion of reality. On the other hand, they believe that on the whole the majority of interactions among nations are cooperative and non-conflictual. Wars do take place but they contend that the majority of nations live in peace and the fact that they are at peace is not because of any balance of power.

Most importantly, the liberal contention for human progress is worth mentioning. At the core of this thinking is also the implicit trust (or liberal faith) that human beings by nature are rational creatures. The liberals reject the realist position that the basic dynamics and fundamental realities of international relations remain unchanged. They contend that as people are rational, they would learn that certain things such as war is irrational and undesirable and, as they learn more about how the world they live in works they will gain knowledge which ultimately will help them to solve problems. As Robert Gilpin (*War and Change in World Politics*, 1981) noted that, just as realism "is founded on a pessimism regarding moral progress and human possibilities", so too liberalism is founded on an optimism regarding moral progress and human possibilities.

Kegley and Wittkopf[3] present the underlying beliefs of the liberalist worldview and uphold that the basic assumptions of liberalism are:

1. Human nature is essentially "good" or altruistic and people are, therefore, capable of mutual aid and collaboration.

2. The fundamental human concern for others' welfare makes progress possible.

3. Bad human behaviour, such as violence, is the product not of flawed people but of evil institutions which encourage people to act selfishly and to harm others.

4. War is not inevitable and its frequency can be reduced by eradicating the institutional arrangements that encourage it.

5. War is an international problem requiring collective or multilateral, rather than national, efforts to control it.

6. The international society must reorganize itself in order to eliminate the institutions that make war likely and nations must reform their political

systems so that self-determination and democratic governance within states can help pacify relations among states.[3]

However, there were several manifestations of idealisms before and after the inter-War period. It can be said that there were "contending liberalisms" at work in world politics during that time and later. They can be classified as:

Liberal Internationalism: This strand of liberal thinking puts faith in human reason and believes that this reason could deliver freedom and justice in international relations. Their emphasis was on transformation of individual consciousness, abolishing war, setting up of a world government, promoting free trade and maintaining peace. Liberal internationalists talked about the 'harmony of interests' in international relations, which was vehemently criticized by E.H. Carr in his famous work *The Twenty Years' Crisis* (1939). Jeremy Bentham (1748–1832) and Immanuel Kant (1724–1804) were the leading exponents of liberal internationalism.[4]

Idealism: Unlike the liberal internationalists, the idealists believed that peace and prosperity is not a natural condition but is one which must be constructed and for which the requirement is of "consciously devised machinery". In other words, they talked about the establishment of an international institution to secure peace and, with this objective, they supported the moves for the establishment of the United Nations after the failure of the League of Nations. They were also the proponents of collective security, human rights, "New International Economic Order" peace and disarmament.

Liberal Institutionalism: David Mitrany (1966) and Ernst Haas (1968) were the earlier liberal institutionalists who believed that integration through international and regional institutions would help to solve common problems. Their work provided impetus for increased cooperation between the European states. The later liberal institutionalists such as Keohane and Nye emphasized the centrality of actors other than the states and focused on transnationalism and interdependence.

The core content of these contending liberalisms was, however, akin to the emphasis on economic freedom, support for national self-determination, international system organized and regulated on the basis of norms and rules, doctrine of non-intervention, opposition to authoritarian rule, outlawing war and disarmament.

Neo-Liberal Internationalism: This strand of neo-liberal thinking is dominated by the supporters of democratic peace thesis whose core thinking is based on the assumption that liberal states do not go to war with other liberal states. To this end Francis Fukuyama (1989) in his article entitled "The End of History" in *The National Interest*, championed the victory of liberalism over all ideologies and contended that liberal states were internally more stable and more peaceful in international relations. He believes that liberal states have established pacific union within which war becomes unthinkable.

Neo-Idealism: Advocates of neo-idealism like David Held[*], Norberto Bobbio[**] and Danielle Archibugi[†] believe that global politics must be democratized. David Held even prescribes a "cosmopolitan model of democracy" in place of Westphalian and UN models, and creation of regional parliaments, extension of the authority of regional bodies such as the European Union, as well as democratization of international organizations like the UN. He also recommends the realization of human rights through national parliaments and monitoring by a new International Court of Human Rights.

Neo-Liberal Institutionalism: Proponents of neo-liberal institutionalism like Axelrod, Keohane and Nye put forward their ideas in response to Kenneth Waltz's theory of neo-realism in his famous work *Theory of International Politics* (1979). This strand of neo-liberal institutionalism shares with the realists the assumption that states are the most significant actors and the international environment is anarchic. But the neo-liberal institutionalists try to focus on the task of initiating and maintaining cooperation among states under conditions of anarchy.

Criticisms

Most of the assumptions of the idealist have been criticized on a number of grounds. They have been considered as impracticable, utopian and most of the liberal principles are charged of being culture-specific and ethnocentric. They portray Western values and try to impose those on the non-Western values. Free trade, interdependence, democracy are concepts wedded to Western liberal tradition and looked at with much contentions by the developing world. For, it is the big and powerful states which control the functioning of international politics. The liberals attempt for peace, effective international organization and disarmament efforts have met with little success. Further, idealism has been criticized vehemently by the realists for not taking into account the realities of human nature and, hence, politics. Pursuit of self-interest becomes the sole guiding principle in case of individual actions and state activities. Morality has least importance in the arena of politics. As Couloumbis and Wolfe[5], observed, "The Realists argue that the adoption of legalistic, moralistic and even ideological behaviour in politics tends to run contrary to the forces of nature and it results either in pacifism and defeatism on the one hand and a fierce exclusivist, and crusading spirit on the other". Kegley and Wittkopf also pointed out that "Much of the idealist programme for reform was never tried, and even less of it was ever achieved".

---

[*]David Held a British political scientist and a prominent scholar in the field of international relations.

[**]Norberto Bobbio was an italian political scientist.

[†]Danielle Archibugi is an italian social scientist.

This does not mean that idealism is without any value. A scholar at this point of time can ask the question whether realism and idealism can be synthesized to get a comprehensive approach in the study of international relations. Reinhold Niebuhr[6] (*The Children of Light and the Children of. Darkness* 1944) opines that it is possible to combine the wisdom of the Realists with the optimism of the idealists or one can discard the pessimism of the realists and the foolishness of the idealists. The essence of this line of thinking is to retain the reality of power struggle among the states as well as directing the efforts of the states towards building up of international peace and security and peaceful coexistence. Reinhold Niebuhr spoke of **children of light** and **children of darkness.** The former, children of light, regard subordination of self-interest to universal laws so that they are at harmony with universal good and the latter, children of darkness, regard self-interest as the prime guiding principle. On the basis of this criterion, Niebuhr regards the children of darkness as evil and wicked and the children of light as virtuous. But again, he realizes that the children of darkness are wise and the children of light are foolish for they fail to understand the power of self-interest and underestimate anarchy. Niebuhr, therefore, suggests that the children of darkness should learn something from the children of light and the children of light should borrow something from the children of darkness. It is the only possible way to evolve a comprehensive approach to understand international relations.

POLITICAL REALISM

Realism has been the most dominant school of thought in the post-World War II international relations and still continues to have relevance in the present international relations scenario. The principal line of thinking of the realist school is in terms of power and its exercise by states. In other words, it is chiefly concerned with *realpolitik.*

The basic assumptions of realism are:

1. The international system is anarchic.
2. Sovereign states are the principal actors in the international system.
3. States are rational unitary actors each acting under the consideration of its own national interest.
4. National security and survival are the primary 'national interest' of each state.
5. In pursuit of national security, states strive to increase national power.
6. National power and capabilities determine the relations among states.
7. National interest, defined in terms of national power, guides the actions of the states in international relations.

The seeds of realism, however, could be traced to the writings of political philosophers like Thucydides, an ancient Greek historian who wrote the *History of the Peloponnesian War* and is also cited as an intellectual forerunner of realpolitik; Chanakya's *Arthashastra;* Machiavelli's, *Il Principe (The Prince)*; Thomas Hobbes' *Leviathan*; Otto von Bismarck, a Prussian statesman who coined the term *balance of power* and Carl von Clausewitz a nineteenth century General Prussian and military theorist who wrote *On War (Von Kriege)* in which he propounded his greatest dictum that *war is nothing but a continuation of politics by other means*.

Their understanding of *realpolitik* deeply influenced the political realists' perspective of looking at world politics especially from the viewpoint of human nature which they relocated in the sphere of reified states. This will lead us to a discussion on the propositions put forward by some of the political philosophers and how they helped in the "construction of state", "construction of masculinity" and "construction of warrior mentality" in the discipline of IR.

Machiavelli's[7] classic work *The Prince* is an embodiment of what a prince should actually be and the ways he should wield his power in order to gain and maintain his sway over his state. To do this, he could resort to unprincipled means not sanctioned by religious or ethical standards and still be virtuous. The prince should combine in him the qualities of the man and the beast. He should be able to assume the potentialities of the fox and the lion at the same time. Machiavelli's contention is that new princedoms are either acquired or are held through a man's own armies and his virtú, and not through fortune. Here, he gives a masculine character to the statecraft as he describes fortune as a female who is always to be trusted and is always attracted by the 'vir', the man of true manliness, a friend of the brave and those who are "less cautious and more spirited".[8] If a virtuous and prudent ruler wishes to master fortune, then Machiavelli's advice is to "strike and beat her and you will see that she allows herself to be more easily vanquished by the rash and the violent than by those who proceed more slowly and coldly".

Chanakya's[9] *Arthashastra,* written in Sanskrit, discusses the principles of statecraft at length. The title, *Arthashastra*, which means "the Science of Material Gain" or "Science of Polity", does not leave any doubt about its ends. Kautilya suggested that the ruler should use any means to attain his goal and his actions require no moral sanction. The problems discussed are of the most practical kind faced by the kings, and the solutions suggested are still relevant and practicable in the modern administrative world. Espionage and the liberal use of provocative agents are recommended on a large scale in Chapter XI of Book I on *The Institution of Spies*. Murder and false accusations were to be used by a king's secret agents without any thoughts to morals or ethics. There are chapters for kings to help them keep in check the premature ambitions of their sons, and likewise chapters intended to help princes to thwart their fathers' domineering authority too [Book I on *Concerning Discipline*].

Hobbes[10] in his *Leviathan* portrays a state of nature, which is horrific and undoubtedly anarchic. The root cause of this anarchy lies at the basic characteristics of human nature, which persuades every man to be enemy of every man for three principal causes—competition, diffidence and glory. Therefore, in such a condition there are "no arts; no letters; no society; and which is worst of all, continual fear, and danger of violent death; and the life of man, solitary, poor, nasty, brutish, and short". Force and fraud are the two cardinal virtues. To come out of this situation, man entered into a contract—'a covenant of every man with every man' and thus the multitude united in one person—the Commonwealth, in Latin, *civitas*. Therefore, the Leviathan,—the immortal God, was born and with it came into existence the sovereign, the civil society and the political authority.

Political realists, deriving their basic assumptions from these philosophic expositions, believe that mankind is not inherently benevolent but rather self-centred and competitive. From this, they propagate that states are also inherently aggressive (offensive realism) and/or obsessed with security (defensive realism); and that territorial expansion is only constrained by opposing power(s). This aggressive build-up, however, leads to a security dilemma where increasing one's own security can bring along greater instability as the opponent(s) builds up its own arms. Thus, security is a zero-sum game where only *relative gains* can be made. The chief proponents of political realism were E.H. Carr (1939), N.J. Spykman (1942), Reinhold Niebuhr (1947), George F. Kennan (1954 and 1966), Hans J. Morgenthau (1948) and Keneneth W. Thompson (1958 and 1960).

E.H. CARR AND REALISM

The efforts of the liberals to establish a peaceful world order through international organizations, disarmament, open diplomacy, self-determination and other lofty ideals were vehemently criticized by Carr[11] (1939) in his polemical work *Twenty Years' Crisis: 1919–1939*. He was of the opinion that "The teleological aspect of the science of international politics has been conspicuous from the outset. It arose from a great disastrous war; the overwhelming purpose which dominated and inspired the pioneers of the new science was to obviate a recurrence of this disease of the international body politic". Therefore, it was the passionate desire to prevent war that determined the direction of the study. The obvious outcome was that international politics came to be marked by utopianism. The liberal doctrine of harmony of interest seems to be untenable because in reality whatever common interests are present, are "nothing more than an expression of the satisfied powers with a vested interest in the preservation of the status quo". Actually, the doctrine of harmony of interests, according to Carr, serves as an ingenious moral device invoked in perfect sincerity by privileged groups in order to justify and maintain their position. The crux of the matter is that what seems to be absolute universal principles are nothing but the unconscious reflections of national policy based on a particular interpretation of national interest at a particular time. They are nothing but transparent disguises of selfish vested interests. He opines that "The inner meaning of the modern international crisis is the collapse of the whole structure of utopianism based on the concept of harmony of interest". The bankruptcy of utopianism resides, according to Carr, not in its failure to live up to its principles but in the exposure of its inability to provide any absolute and disinterested standard for the conduct of international affairs. Therefore, the importance of power politics has to be acknowledged in international relations. But Carr suggested that to get sound political theories, both elements of utopianism and realism, namely, power and moral values are required.

MORGENTHAU AND REALISM

Political realism in IR reached its zenith and assumed a grotesque stature in the hands of Hans J. Morgenthau in his seminal work *Politics Among Nations: The Struggle for Power and Peace* (1948). His six principles or signposts are:

1. Politics, like society in general, is governed by objective laws that have their roots in human nature which is unchanging. Therefore, it is possible to develop a rational theory that reflects these objective laws.

2. The main signpost of political realism is the concept of interest defined in terms of power which infuses rational order into the subject matter of politics, and thus makes the theoretical understanding of politics possible. Morgenthau views international politics as a process in which national interests are accommodated or resolved on the basis of diplomacy of war. He upheld that "The concept of national interest presupposes neither a naturally harmonious, peaceful world nor the inevitability of war as a consequence of the pursuit by all nations of their national interests. Quite to the contrary, it assumes continuous conflict and threat of war to be minimized through the continuous adjustment of conflicting interest by diplomatic action".

3. Realism assumes that interest defined as power is an objective category which is universally valid but not with a meaning that is fixed once and for all. In a world in which sovereign states compete for power, survival constitutes the minimum goal of foreign policy and the core national interest. The protection of "their physical and cultural identity against encroachments by other nations" constitutes the vital interest which is common to all states. Therefore, the basic minimum national interest identifiable is national survival and other interests are determined by the requirements of time, place, culture, socio-economic and political condition of the states.

To support his argument, Morgenthau gives classic examples from history. One such is the policy of Great Britain in 1939–40 towards Finland which, he says, was not based on legalistic–moralistic foundations but backed by massive military aid on the face of Soviet aggression that might have backfired on Britain's survival only. It would have faced destruction in the hands of Nazi Germany and would not have been able to restore the independence of Finland thus endangering its vital national interest, i.e., national survival. Morgenthau remarks asking: When the national interest related to national survival has been safeguarded, can nations pursue lesser interests?

4. Universal moral principles cannot be applied to state action. They must be filtered through concrete circumstances of time and place. To confuse individual morality with state morality is to court disaster, as states in pursuit of their national interest are governed by a morality that is different from the morality of individuals in their personal relationships.

5. Political realism refuses to identify the moral aspirations of a particular nation with the moral laws that govern the universe. It is the concept of interest defined in terms of power that saves us from the moral excess and political folly.

6. The political realist maintains the autonomy of the political sphere in the same way as the economist, the lawyer and the moralist do.[12] A political realist thinks in terms of interest defined in terms of power as the economist thinks in terms of interest defined as wealth, the lawyer in terms of the conformity of action with legal rules, and the moralist, who thinks in terms of the conformity of action with moral principles. Thus intellectually, political realist maintains the autonomy of the political sphere but never-the-less the political realist disregard the existence and importance of standards of thought other than political ones. It implies that each standard of thought should be assigned its proper sphere and function. The development of standards of thoughts in the field of politics, as in case of economics and other disciplines, is the main purpose of political realism.

Therefore, this Hobbesian, Machiavellian and Kautilyan understanding of human nature, as selfish and conflictual unless given appropriate conditions, has been succesfully adopted, internalized and transformed into a modern theory of international relations. During the Cold War it became the most widely accepted perspective of world politics. As Rothenstein[*][13] pointed out, realism became the "doctrine which provided the intellectual frame of reference for the (US) foreign policy establishment for something like twenty years... it did determine the categories by which they assessed the external world and the state of mind with which they approached prevailing problems". Realism prevailed as the dominant paradigm with its emphasis on the autonomy of political action and the "billiard ball" model in IR till it was challenged by the behavioural revolution. But it again re-emerged in the form of neo-realism in the 1970s.

---

[*]R. Rothenstein, "on the Costs of Realism", *Political Science Quarterly*, Vol. 87, No. 3, 1972, p. 38.

NEO-REALISM

The realist tradition suffered a setback due to the emergence of the neo-liberal thought, especially the challenge posed by 'pluralism'. State-centrism of the traditional realists received a serious jolt as pluralists emphasized the fact that the state may be a significant actor in international relations but it is not the sole actor. In other words, they acknowledged a plurality of actors in international relations as will be discussed just now. The pluralist's challenge to realism was soon met by a new brand of realists, and the forerunner among them was Kenneth Waltz. Waltz in his famous works, *Man, the State and War* (1959) and *Theory of International Politics* (1979), came up with his idea of world politics which is popularly known as **neo-realism**. Waltz argues that the key difference between international and domestic politics lies not in the regularity of war and conflict but in the **structure** of international system. In the absence of higher authority in the international system, there is no other way to secure oneself other than **self-help** which will ultimately lead to **security dilemma** because security build-up of one would lead to insecurity of others. The resultant anarchy for the neo-realists is, therefore, due to the presence of a system characterized by the absence of a higher power over the sovereign states. It is this structure of international system which decisively shapes up the behaviour of states in international relations and their struggle for power. Thus, the sources of conflict or causes of war, unlike what the traditional or classical realists argue, do not rest on the human nature but within the basic framework of the anarchic structure of international relations. Waltz uses game theory (an economic concept which is widely used in many fields today) in addressing the balance of power and self-help in this environment. He says that balance of power results in this kind of a system irrespective of the intentions of a particular state. But in international politics, in the absence of authority to effectively prohibit the use of force, the balance of power among states becomes most often a balance of capabilities, including physical force, which states choose to use in pursuing their goals. Thus, in a self-help system, the logic of self-interest provides a basis of understanding the problem of coordinating the interests of individual versus the interests of the common good and the pay-off between short-term interests and long-term interests.[14] Neo-realists did not overlook the prospects of cooperation among states also. But the point of contention was that, states, while cooperating with each other, tried to maximize their relative power and preserve their autonomy.

Criticisms

The first major criticism which can be levelled against realism is that like idealism, realism is also lopsided and stresses solely on power and power struggle, i.e., 'power monism'. The traditional realists formulated their views in reaction to the liberal utopians of the 1920s and 1930s. Consequently, they put greater emphasis on 'power politics', state sovereignty, balance of power and war. For the realists, states were the only important actors in international relations. Besides, scholars point out that Morgenthau's realism was based on *a priori* assumptions about human nature, such as the rational pursuit of self-interest, utility maximization and the like, which are hardly verifiable and tested. Benno Wasserman, Robert Tucker, Stanley Hoffman and others have criticized traditional realism on the ground, that it is neither realistic nor consistent with itself. According to Stanley Hoffman[15], this theory is full of anomalies and ambiguities and ignores the discussion of ends. Quincy Wright observed that the realist theory has ignored the impact of values on national policy. Robert Tucker criticized the theory because he thought it was inconsistent both with itself and with reality. Vasquez (1979) contends that a statistical analysis of international relations would reveal that though there was overwhelming dominance of realist paradigm in the 1950s and 1960s, but it failed to adequately explain international politics. According to the findings, over 90 per cent of the 7000 realist hypotheses were falsified. Linklater (1990) opined that there is a need to go beyond the structural realists' emphasis on constraints and the liberal realists' predilection for order, in order to develop an emancipatory form of theory which seeks to deepen the sense of solidarity and widen the bonds of community in global politics. Neo-realism is also not without flaws as Linklater has pointed out that a major problem with Waltz's unit-structure relationship is that it leaves little or no room for systemic change induced by the units themselves.[16] He further argues that by emphasizing recurrence and repetition in the international system, neo-realism cannot envisage a form of statecraft which transcends the calculus of power and control. Cox (1986) places the neo-realist theory in the category of 'problem-solving approach' to international relations when this may be little more than a cover for and rationalization of immoral and unethical behaviour. By deconstructing realism, neo-realism and neo-liberalism, post-modern critical theory observes that the concept of inter-state anarchy is in reality an artificial construction of the dominant discourse and the state practices associated with it. It is contrived and generated by the dominant international relations discourse.[17]

There has also been a feminist critique of realist theory from the point of exclusion of the women throughout the whole discourse. The most common motif in feminist analyses of peace and war depicts masculinity as a transcendentally aggressive force in society and history. Women are bystanders or victims of men's wars. Most feminist commentary, through the 1980s, followed this framework. In particular, the extraordinary outburst of concern over the nuclear threat in the 1970s and early 1980s resulted in a spate of feminist writings explicitly or implicitly founded on a critique of masculinist militarism. In her appraisal of Hans J. Morgenthau, for instance, Tickner (1988) criticizes realism as only "a partial description of international politics", owing to its deeply embedded masculinist bias. But partial descriptions are partial descriptions; they are not dead wrong. Tickner attacks Morgenthau's paradigm on several grounds. But her main concern is to offer a *feminist reformulation* of certain realist principles. In a similar vein, the central problem may not be with objectivity as such, but with objectivity "as it is culturally defined ... [and] associated with masculinity". The idea of the "national interest" likewise needs to be rendered more "multidimensional and contextually contingent", but not necessarily abandoned. Tickner stresses: "I am not denying the validity of Morgenthau's work" but only asking for a negotiation with the 'contentious others'.[18]

PLURALISM

The intellectual roots of pluralism can be found in the concepts, arguments and perspectives of liberal thinking that have directly or indirectly influenced the pluralist image of international politics, especially the liberal institutionalism.

The state-centricism of the realist paradigm, its sole concern with security and military issues and national interest came under scrutiny in the late 1960s and the early 1970s. The changing patterns of international system as well as the emergence of new issues posed a challenge to the 'realist' image of the world order, and the challenge came from the pluralist thinkers. The 'transnationalist' image or the pluralist perspective takes into account the existence of such non-state actors like the MNCs, international organizations such as the Amnesty International, the Catholic Church, OPEC, cartels, and other organizations like terrorist outfits and hijackers. Their main point of argument is that the presence of states as actors cannot be perceived in the absence of **non-state actors**.

They also looked into the existence of **intra-state actors** playing an important role and often influencing foreign policy decisions. For instance, Richard C. Snyder (1954) with his associates had tried to show the foreign policy behaviour of a particular state in terms of both the subjective perceptions of the individuals involved in foreign policy decision-making and the intra-state 'setting' in which they operate, including domestic politics, public opinion, and non-governmental actors.

Some other pluralists such as Alexander George and Ole Holsti[17] have emphasized the role of individuals, their belief patterns and their psycho-pathological traits in the making of foreign policy. Others like Robert Jervis draws attention to the role of cognitive factors in decision-making foreign policy. Scholars such as Irving L. Janis have emphasized the importance of what they call "group think" in the making of foreign policy. Taking the instances of the Bay of Pigs invasion by the USA in 1961, the US unpreparedness regarding the Japanese Pearl Harbour incident in 1941, and the US decision to escalate the Korean and Vietnam wars, as case studies, he argues that the small groups which make foreign policy decisions tend to act more under the compulsion of group norms rather than rational thinking. Other pluralists have tried to make an in-depth study and looked into the specific role of the bureaucracy, its inner conflicts, contradictions and relationship with the political executive as a major determinant of foreign policy of a state. Graham

T. Allison has argued on the basis of an empirical study, the role of the US bureaucracy during the Cuban Missile Crisis of 1962. He comments that the rational actor model of foreign policy, which assumes the state to be a monolithic and rational maker of foreign policy, is an unreal abstraction and, in reality, foreign policy is the composite resultant of intense bureaucratic 'imperialism' and rivalry in the form of non-cooperative games, and is often irrational on that account.

Keohane and Nye (1972 and 1977) took this pluralist image a major step forward by contending that the state may not be able to confine these bureaucratic actors. Organizations, whether private or governmental, may transcend the boundaries of states forming coalitions with their foreign counterparts. Such **transnational actors** may well act at cross-purposes with the governmental leaders in their home states who possess the formal authority of decision-making in international relations. The best example can be that the British Defence Ministry and the US Defence Department may have a common view but this is in fact contrary to the stands taken by both the British Foreign Office and the US State Department which again may be in unison on a particular issue. Further, certain non-governmental interest groups in both countries may form coalitions supportive of one or the another trans-governmental coalition.[19]

The pluralists, therefore, try their best to differentiate themselves from the realists, old and new, by asserting the presence of non-state, intra-state and transnational actors in international relations. They recognize the multivariate character of the processes of international relations, thereby devaluing the dimension of political power of international relations and emphasizing the 'complex-interdependence' of nations as against a state-centric and conflict-ridden perspective of international system of the realists.

This transnationalism and model of complex interdependence came to be reflected in the celebrated work *Transnational Relations and World Politics* edited by Robert Keohane and Joseph Nye[*]. In another of their major works, *Power and Interdependence: World Politics in Transition* (1977), they proposed the complex interdependence as a new account of IR to run alongside realism. Keohane and Nye elucidate the key characteristics of complex interdependence juxtaposing them against the basic assumption of the realist approach to international relations. They identify three main characteristics of complex interdependence:

1. *Societies connected by multiple channels of communication*: The inter-state, trans-governmental and transnational communications, which the realist framework tends to overlook.

2. *An absence of hierarchy among issues*: The agenda of inter-state relations consists of multiple issues that may not be arranged

---

[*]Robert Keohane and Joseph S. Nye, *Power and Inter dependence: World Politics in Transition*, Little Brown, Boston, 1977.

hierarchically. This means that the realist assumption that military security tops the agenda is not acceptable.

3. *Lesser importance of military force*: Against the realist assumption that military force is dominant, Keohane and Nye contend that military force is expensive and in some cases may be irrelevant to a wide range of issues.[20]

From this complex interdependence, there emerges a political process which is quite distinct from the conventional one where there is no fixed goals and distinction of power. Under the traditional analysis of international system, one is expected to anticipate similar processes on a variety of issues. Under the conventional system, militarily and economically strong states tend to dominate a variety of organizations and a variety of issues, by linking their own policies on some issues to other states' policies on other issues. This will result in the stronger states prevailing on even weak issues by using their dominance and ultimately bringing about congruence between the overall structure of military and economic powers and the pattern of outcome on any one issue. World politics, thus, becomes a seamless web. Under the complex interdependence model, however, lack of congruence between various issues increases the difficulties of states to construct linkage strategies. As military force is devalued, militarily strong states find it difficult to dominate outcomes on issues in which they are weak. Similarly, unequal distribution of power resources in trade shipping or oil result in variations in patterns of outcomes of political bargaining, creating political processes which differ from one set of issues to another.[21]

Management of interdependent relations may involve construction of rules and associated institutions and international organizations to govern the interactions in the issue areas. These definitely would give rise to international regimes and the scope of activity of the international organizations will increase in this interdependent world. In the absence of superordinate central authority, these rules are voluntarily established by states to provide some degree of order in international relations. Voluntarism, thus, becomes central to this mode of thought.[22]

Overall, increased transnational and trans-governmental relations blur the distinction between national and international politics and create political processes in which results cannot be predicted by assuming the dominance of the states.

The basic assumptions of the pluralist models are:

1. Acknowledgement of the presence of non-state actors.
2. Non-military and non-security issues such as population, pollution, distribution of food, depletion of natural resources, dependency and outer space are the priority areas.

3. An increase of interdependence—trade, technology transfer, investment, travel migration, student exchanges and other interactions have risen manifold.

4. War is no longer a major option for foreign policy decision-makers, and the more powerful a nation is, the less viable the war becomes. As one pointed out: "We are moving to an era dominated by economic power—an era in which war between major states may virtually disappear".[21]

Criticisms

The first and foremost shortcoming of the pluralist theory is that islands of theory are constructed rather than building such general theory as propounded by realists. Some concentrate on the perception of decision-making processes, some on regional integration, others on impact of domestic and bureaucratic politics on foreign policy or the roles played by transnational actors in world politics. To attempt to combine islands of theory does not necessarily result in a general theory.

Further, the pluralists downplay the role of anarchy and security dilemma in analysing international relations, which has been criticized by the realists as an incomplete analysis. For, no analysis of world politics is complete unless the anarchical structure of the system is not taken into account. The realists allege that such kinds of thinking tend to be utopian.

The pluralists have also been criticized by many for viewing the world through the lenses of American political system. This has been refuted by the pluralists who acknowledge cultural, societal and other differences. They argue that bureaucracies, interest groups and transnational actors are important for a better understanding of international relations and deny that this image is purely American ethnocentrism imposed on the globe. Yet, critics do find the pluralist vision of the world suffering from American ethnocentrism.[22]

MARXIST APPROACH AND THE MODERN WORLD SYSTEM THEORY

The Marxists theory has not been able to secure a formidable place within the discipline of international relations. Mostly, Marxist discussion is confined to the question of 'imperialism' and one-sided interpretation of the phenomena. Marxism's emphasis on economic factors at the international level also has not been very successful in explaining the political, ideological and security issues falling within the domain of international relations. Therefore, Marxism has faced great difficulties in carving a niche for itself in the realm of IR theories.

Karl Marx did not provide a theory of international relations, but in his works with Engels, for example, *Manifesto of the Communist Party* (1848), or his legendary work *Capital: A Critique of Political Economy (Das Capital,* originally published in 1867), there is reference to wars, proletarian internationalism, world revolution, expansion of capitalism on a world scale leading to a revolutionary socio-economic transformation and the like. Later, Lenin, Stalin, Mao, and a host of other communist scholars tried to elaborate Marx's views according to the changing needs of time and world scenario with an ardent effort to explain the events of international relations with the help of the principles propounded by him.

Basic Assumptions of Marxian Approach

1. Economic or materialistic determination provides a clue to understand international relations.
2. Historical determination provides a guideline to understand international relations.
3. The centrality of the concept of class and class struggle is evident in international relations.
4. The capitalist states seek economic exploitation and political subjugation of the weaker states.
5. A scramble for colonies follows.
6. Wars erupt as a result of the clash between capitalist nations themselves in their bid to establish colonies. The First World War (1914–1918) is a glaring example in this context.
7. Proletariats or working classes would unite globally and proletarian internationalism would lead to world revolution.
8. Lasting peace can only be established after the world revolution, as it would signify the collapse of imperialism and ushering in of a classless and stateless society.

Professor Arun Bose[23] provides insights into Marxist view of international politics. According to him, the basic framework of international politics includes four basic tenets. These are now briefly discussed.

Proletarian Internationalism: The essence of proletarian internationalism is contained in the Communist Manifesto, which ends with the call: "workers of the world unite". The ideal of proletarian revolution includes:

1. The word proletariat has a common interest, independent of all nationality.
2. Working men have no country since the proletariat of each country must first acquire political supremacy and constitute itself as a nation; it is itself national.

3. United action by the proletariat is one of the first conditions for the emancipation of the proletariat.

4. In proportion, as the exploitation of one individual by another is put to an end, similarly, the exploitation of one nation by another will also be put to an end ..., and thus, hostility of one nation by another will come to an end.

Anti-Imperialism: The main line of thinking is contained in Lenin's seminal work *Imperialism—The Highest Stage of Capitalism*. As capitalism has its inherent contradiction, so has imperialism. According to Lenin imperialism is capitalism in transition as represented by moribund capitalism. Lenin depicted imperialism as the "monopoly stage of capitalism". He also forewarned certain features of imperialism.

1. Concentration of production and capital leads to the creation of national and multinational monopolies—not as in liberal economics, but as *de facto* power over their markets—while "free competition" remains the domain of local and niche markets.

2. The fusion of banking capital with industrial capital and the creation, on the basis of this financial capital, of a financial oligarchy.

3. Finance capital exportation replaces the exportation of goods (though they continue in production).

4. The economic division of the world, by multinational enterprises via international cartels.

5. The political division of the world by the great powers, wherein exporting finance capital to their colonies allows their exploitation for resources and continued investment.[24]

The central themes of anti-imperialism are:

1. Capital has become international and monopolistic.

2. Uneven political and economic development is an absolute law of capitalism.

3. Proletarian socialist revolution is possible not only in several countries of Europe, but also in one capitalist country, taken singly, which, would form the nucleus, the base, the hegemony, of world socialist revolution, attracting to its cause the oppressed classes of other countries.

Self-Determination: The goal of national self-determination was to be realized through "proletarian self-determination" as the class which attains political supremacy, comes to constitute the nation. The crux of this line of thought was that all nations of the world must be free to determine their political destiny and colonial system must be abolished. The main ideas include:

1. Lenin makes no distinction between the oppressor and the oppressed nations of the world.

2. Oppressed nations are identified as the victims of imperialism as national revolutionary reserve or allies of the proletariat in the world socialist revolution.
3. Recognition of the right of the oppressed nation to self-determination is now interpreted to mean not only the right of oppressed nations to secede freely, but the desirability of secession to remove 'distrust' and 'prejudices' among the oppressed nations.

Peaceful Coexistence: This line of thinking upheld that all nation-states of the world must live peacefully without criticizing or undermining other's social, economic and political systems. It includes:

1. Proletarian socialist revolution could be victorious first in several countries, or even in one country.
2. It has to survive capitalist encirclement by relying on anti-imperialistic contradictions.
3. The best way to achieve this is to try to work at the relations of peaceful coexistence between socialist states and, at least some, if not all the capitalist states.

Therefore, the essence of all these four basic tenets of Marxist approach to international relations includes the end of capitalism and imperialism, unity of the proletariat as one national, and internationalism in its true form. There was a revival of interest in Marxian, approach to international relations in the 1970s, which led to major contributions by scholars like Immanuel Wallerstein (1974), Frank (1967), Galtung (1971) and others. Their perspective came to be identified as *Dependencia Model or the World System Theory.*

WORLD SYSTEM THEORY

The roots of the World System Theory can be traced to the writings of Lenin. In his monumental work, *Imperialism—The Highest Stage of Capitalism,* Lenin contended that imperialism created a two-tier structure within the capitalist world economy. He identified the dominant structure as the 'core' and the less-developed structure as the 'periphery'. It is the location of the states within this capitalist world economy, which determines the patterns of interaction and relation of domination and dependence between them. Galtung (1971) and Wallerstein (1974) further developed this theory and provided powerful insights into the working of the world capitalist economy. Among other proponents of this theory, the noteworthy were Andre Gunder Frank (*Capitalism and Underdevelopment in Latin America,* 1967), Raúl Prebisch[*] (1963), the first Executive Director of the United Nations Economic

---

[*]Raúl Prebisch, *Towards a Dynamic Development Policy for Latin America,* United Nations, New York, 1963.

Commission for Latin America, John Gallagher and Ronald Robinson[**] (1953), and Gunnar Myrdal[†] (1957), the author of *Asian Drama*.

The main line of argument of the World System theorists is that the dependency situation of the developing countries is the direct result of the economic exploitation by the advanced countries. They define the situation of dependency, as a "situation in which a certain number of countries have their economy conditioned by the development and expansion of another…, placing the dependent countries in a backward position exploited by the dominant countries".

Dependency theorists not only reflect upon the external factors like foreign states, MNCs, international banks, multilateral lending institutions, foreign control of technology and an international bourgeoisie as causes of dependency but also highlight the internal constraints on development such as patterns of land tenure, social structures, class alliances, and the role of the state. These internal factors strengthen and reinforce the instruments of foreign domination. As a result of the interplay between these internal and external factors, the nature of development or underdevelopment of society will vary.

With this line of thinking in mind, some of the World System theorists use Marxist terminology and Leninist insights to explain this situation of dependency. Here the structural theories of dependency of the two chief proponents will be discussed.

Immanuel Wallerstein and His World System Theory

Wallerstein represents the most powerful exposition of the modern World System theory in his seminal work *Modern World System: Capitalist Agriculture and the Origins of the European World-Economy in the Sixteenth Century* (1974). Tracing the emergence of capitalism in the sixteenth century Europe, he examines its evolution into a world capitalist system that contains a **core,** a **periphery** and a **semi-periphery** (see Figure 2.1). The 'core' has come to constitute historically the most advanced economic areas, which are engaged

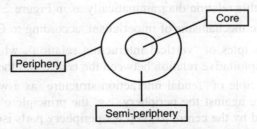

Figure 2.1 Configuration of the modern world system.

[**]John Gallagher and Ronald Robinson, 'The Imperialism of Free trade,' *Economic History Review,* Vol. 6, No. 1, 1953.

[†]Gunnar Myrdal, *Economic Theory and Underdeveloped Regions,* Gerald Duckworth, London, 1957.

in activities like banking, manufacturing, technologically advanced agriculture, ship building and others. The 'periphery' has been providing raw materials such as minerals and timber to support the core's economic expansion. Unskilled labour is repressed and the peripheral countries are denied advanced technology from the core countries in those sectors where they may give the core countries a tough competition. The semi-periphery is involved in a mix of production activities, some associated with core areas and others with peripheral areas. It also serves as an outlet for investment when wages in core economies become too high. Over the time, particular regions of the world may gravitate between core, peripheral and semi-peripheral status. Class structure in each zone varies depending on how the dominant class relates to the world economy.

Johan Galtung and His Structural Theory of Imperialism

Galtung[25] presents his version of imperialism as a relation between a Centre and a Periphery. The relationship is unequal and his theory tried to illuminate on the structure of this unequal relationship, which resists any change in the *status quo*. It is this inequality that results in the formation of a centre and a periphery and he contends that those in power in the centre have a community of interest with those in power in the periphery. The consequence that follows is a kind of relationship that operates at the expense of the majority of the people in the peripheral countries, but this primarily serves the interest of the majority of the people in the centre countries.

The basic assumptions of Galtung are:

1. Harmony of interest between the centre in the Centre nation and the centre in the Periphery nation.
2. Disharmony of interest within the Periphery nation than within the Centre nations.
3. Disharmony of interest between the periphery in the Centre nation and the periphery of the Periphery nation.

He depicted this relation diagrammatically as in Figure 2.2.

The two basic mechanisms of imperialism, according to Galtung, are:

1. The principles of 'vertical interaction relation', which involves the actual exploitative relation between the centre and the periphery.
2. The principle of 'feudal interaction structure' as a way of protecting the centre against the periphery, e.g. the principle of divide and rule employed by the centre to keep the periphery parts isolated from each other.

The first mechanism is the major factor behind the inequality, and the second helps to sustain and reinforce the inequality. The consequence is a continuous dependency of the periphery on the centre.

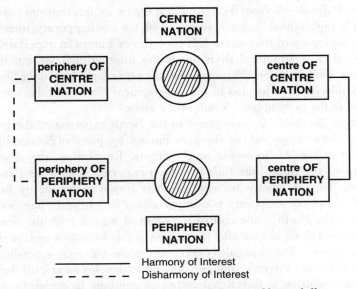

Figure 2.2   Galtung's structural theory of imperialism.

[**Source:**   Adapted from Johan Galtung, "A Structural Theory of Imperialism"]

He further enumerates four rules defining the interaction structure between the centre and the periphery:

1. Interaction between the Centre and Periphery is 'vertical'
2. Interaction between the Periphery and Periphery is 'missing'
3. Multilateral interaction involving all three is 'missing'
4. Interaction with the outside world is 'monopolized' by the centre with two implications:
   - Periphery interaction with other Centre nations is 'missing'
   - Centre as well as Periphery interaction with periphery nations belonging to other centre nations is missing.

The operation of the two mechanisms just mentioned creates "subtle grid of protection" measures against any potential threats to the system, i.e., trouble in the periphery in the Periphery. The more finer and sophisticated mechanisms of imperialism are introduced within and between nations; there will be lesser needs to resort to oppression or violence and warfare. Galtung asserts: "Only imperfect, amateurish imperialism needs weapons; professional imperialism is based on structural rather than direct violence".

THE INDIAN APPROACH: NORTH OVER SOUTH

Almost the same theme was provided by a renowned Indian scholar of international relations, Prof. Jayantanuja Bandyopadhyaya in his famous work

North Over South—A Non-Western Perspective of International Relations (1984). He highlighted that the structure of the contemporary international system is the legacy of four-and-a-half centuries of European imperialism. This has resulted in a structural division of the international system into two subsystems. One small but dominant, and the other large but subordinate. The dominant subsystem is located in the geographical North and the subordinate subsystem in the geographical South of the globe.[26]

Whereas the dominant subsystem in the North experienced the industrial revolution centuries ago and has also gone through the phase of Second Industrial Revolution or the Technotronic or Cybernetic Revolution, the subordinate subsystem of the South has failed to even experience their first industrial revolution. This is mostly because of their impoverishment by historical imperialism and contemporary neo-imperialism, which again has caused the affluence of the North at the cost of the drain of wealth from the South. The situation has not changed even after the process of decolonization and the so-called "transfer of power". The imperialist gain continues through more sophisticated and finer mechanisms. Poverty, hunger and underdevelopment still haunt the developing countries as developed countries continue to enrich themselves. Therefore, the North–South contradiction is the central or primary contradiction within the international system.

Criticisms

Professor Jayantanuja Bandyopadhyaya has shown that the World System Theory has given us deep insights into the working of international system which tends to be oligarchic and hegemonistic. He says, however, that this reductionist determinism of the theory detracts from its ability to explain the impact of domestic structures on the foreign policies of state in detail or in a methodologically and logically acceptable manner. There is no reference to the role of any structural elements other than class in the analysis. Political parties, armed forces, ethnic and religious groups, bureaucracy and other factors have been totally ignored. Professor Bandyopadhyaya observes that the dependency on the World System theories are too simplistic and fail to provide satisfactory explanation on the relationship between the domestic structure of a state and the magnitude and direction of its foreign policy. They are preoccupied with the centre–periphery relationship and pay insufficient attention to all these factors. There is also the question of causality involved. Some critics question whether dependency creates economic and social backwardness, as World System theorists claim, or it is economic and social backwardness which create a situation for dependency. There is no agreement on causality, whether dependency is the cause of backwardness or it is the effect of this condition.

Despite such criticisms, World System Theory is not without value. It has made some positive contribution in revealing the real structure of international system which, according to Prof. Bandyopadhyaya, is divided roughly between the dominant North and the dependent South. It also has given a clue to understanding the causes and mechanisms of creation and continuation of this dependency, subordination and marginalization of the poor and developing countries by the oligarchic and hegemonic powers of the international system.

SYSTEMS THEORY

The systems theory originated primarily due to the behavioural revolution in social science. The desire of the new genre of social scientists, to evolve a general body of knowledge by integrating the various disciplines of social sciences, finally led to the emergence of a host of theoretical approaches inspired by natural science methods. The chief among them was the systems analysis, and prominent contributions in the field of international politics were made by Easton (1965), Kaplan (1957), McClelland (1966), Rosenau (1961), and Boulding (1956), among others.

Morton Kaplan[27] has been the chief exponent of systems theory in international relations. He conceives international system as an analytical entity for explaining the behaviour of international actors and the regulative, integrative and disintegrative consequences of their policies. The positive element in Kaplan's thinking is the consideration of the possibility of 'change'. Thus he studied the behaviour of a system under changing conditions. He stated that there is some coherence, regularity and order in international relations and it is constituted of two things: "international system" and "nation-state system". The international system is composed of subsystems and a set of actors, both international and supranational, and is characterized by interactions among them. Nation-states are the primary actors and their role changes with the change in the international system. Kaplan describes six models of international system. They are:

1. The Balance of Power System
2. The Loose Bipolar System
3. The Tight Bipolar System
4. The Universal System
5. The Hierarchical System
6. The Unit Veto System.

The Balance of Power System: According to Kaplan, the period between 1815 and 1914 experienced a golden age of Balance of Power (BOP). Since the beginning of the twentieth century, the system started faltering as rules started to be flouted by major international actors. Finally, the whole BOP system collapsed with the outbreak of the First World War in 1914. Kaplan also suggested certain basic rules for the functioning of the balance of power system. These rules meant that one takes the following steps:

1. Act to increase capabilities but negotiate rather than fight.
2. Fight rather than pass up an opportunity to increase capabilities.
3. Stop fighting rather than eliminate an essential national actor.
4. Act to oppose any coalition or single actor which tends to assume a position to predominance with respect to the rest of the system.
5. Act to constrain actors who subscribe to supranational organizing principles.
6. Permit defeated or constrained essential national actors to re-enter the system as acceptable role partners or act to bring some previously inessential actor within the essential actor classification.
7. Treat all essential actors as acceptable role partners.

In Kaplan's view, these features would help keep intact the *balance* in relations. Failure would mean an end to balance and, ultimately, the system.

The Loose Bipolar System: The loose bipolar system, often recognized as the 'Cold War' model, envisages an international system that comes into operation when there is only two superpowers leading their respective competitive blocs and there is also a simultaneous presence of non-member bloc-actors and universal actors. Thus, this system would comprise two major bloc actors: the non-aligned states and international organizations like the United Nations. Both blocs try to increase their capabilities and are willing to run at least some risks to eliminate rival bloc. Both blocs also attempt to subordinate the objectives of the universal actors to their own objectives. Non-aligned states, on the other hand, try to support the universal actor to check the power of the two blocs and reduce the danger of war between them. Both blocs strive to increase their membership but at the same time tolerate the status of the non-aligned states.

The Tight Bipolar System: The loose bipolar system may get transformed into a tight bipolar system where two major powers lead their respective blocs and it virtually becomes different forms of interactions between the two blocs. In this system, therefore, the role of non-aligned states or non-member states either disappears or become less significant. Even universal actors such as international organizations become too weak to mediate.

The Universal System: This system emerges when the world gets transformed into a federal world state based on the principle of mutual tolerance and universal rule of law. The system almost resembles a world federation. It, therefore, works through a universal actor such as an international organization like the United Nations or such other agencies, which would have the necessary capacity to maintain peace and security and prevent war, once the bipolar system ceases. It would be performing judicial, economic, political and administrative work although the states would enjoy sufficient autonomy.

The Hierarchical System: Such system will come into existence when a single universal actor absorbs all the other states either through conquest or treaty. The system will be directive if found on the basis of world conquest. It would be non-directive when power would be distributed among units according to hierarchy under the domination of a single national actor. The states as territorial units are, thus, transformed into functional units. The non-directive system is based on will, and the directive system on force.

The Unit Veto System: This is a kind of system when all the states would possess equal potentialities to destroy each other. The mere possession of deadly weapons and nukes would deter the attacks on a particular state. Therefore, this system reaches stability when a state can resist and retaliate threats from every other state.

Criticisms

Major criticisms have been launched against the systems approach. The general criticisms against the system analysts are that they have not evolved any theories but only frameworks, which cannot make significant contributions to international relations. The theory is also difficult to operationalize as empirical testing is difficult. There is a gap between theory and research. It is, therefore, limited in scope.

Kaplan's models of international system has been subjected to rigorous criticisms. It is argued that the system not only offers limited possibilities but its merit is also limited. The first two models roughly correspond to real situations in the backdrop of particular historical trajectories. The other four models are totally hypothetical, impracticable and arbitrary. It was almost like an intellectual exercise on Kaplan's part without any reference to reality. Kaplan's model also neglected the role of geo-strategic factors as well as national and sub-national factors. However, the criticisms do not mean that the systems approach is absolutely without merit. It has made significant contribution in the scientific study of behaviour in international relations. It can be used along with other approaches to the study of international relations.

COMMUNICATIONS APPROACH

Another noteworthy theory in the field of international relations is the communications approach. The term 'communication' has been borrowed from the concept of 'cybernetics', which means 'steering'. Norbert Weiner (1948) developed the concept of cybernetics in his famous work *Cybernetics,* to signify the control of communications in political systems. Cybernetics is "a body of theory and technique for the study of probabilities in different but analogous universes such as certain types of machines, animals, individual human beings, societies and nation-states—and the ways in which message transactions function to control such universes".[28] Communication is treated as the cement that makes organizations. It alone enables a group to think together, to see together and to act together. All social sciences require the understanding of communication.

This approach in international relations was developed by Deutsch[29] in his celebrated work *The Nerves of Government: Model of Political Communication and Control* (1963). In this book, Deutsch applies the concept of the theory of information, communication and control to problems of political and social science borrowing from Weiner's concepts of 'feedback', 'channel capacity', and 'memory'. From these, Deutsch developed his concepts of "consciousness," "will" and "social learning". Since 1960s, the communications approach became popular in social sciences, and terms like 'feedback', 'steering' and 'learning capacity' have become a common usage while analysing political systems.

For Deutsch, communications, in the true sense of the word, are the nerves of government. A government is analogous to steering of a ship and it is a form of administration of communication channels. Control of steering is central to the problem of steering. A government, which can lessen the uncertainty of the international environment, has an advantage and can steer clear in the troubled waters of international relations. For this, the main component is information which is vital to the state's decision-making, both present and future, vis-à-vis other states as well as non-state actors about their present and future courses of actions. Very important in this respect is the *feedback*. This means the government is able to assess the impact of its decisions on other actors through the feedback mechanism. This helps the government, especially those charged with the decision-making to carefully steer through the troubled waters of international relations. Therefore, the main focus of communications approach is communication and information flows and not unitary emphasis on power.

Criticisms

According to the critics of the communications approach, there is enormous difficulty in either applying a model or making use of it for a purposeful study of IR, which has been directly influenced by natural sciences. The terminology borrowed from electrical or mechanical engineering also makes it more complex in its application, and there are chances that the model can be misapplied. The most vehement criticism has been launched by scholars from the developing world who contend that the communication flow and feedback is not among equals but among unequal subsystems characterized by domination and subordination. The controls of information flow is vital as this determines who dominates the rest. Obviously, it is the dominant North which controls the communication facilities and thus the flow of information and consequentially the feedback form the weaker subsystem, the subordinate South. The proponents of communications approach have not addressed this phenomenon of dependence and dominance of North over South. Therefore, the complete landscape of international relations cannot be understood by this approach alone.

DECISION-MAKING THEORY

Another approach to the study of international relations is the decision-making approach. It is quite common that decisions are made at various levels and in various ways in all political and international systems. The decision-making approach tries to comprehend the complete process of decision making at national, international or comparative levels and its relation to policy formulation. This approach became more popular in the United States as there was a growing urge among the scholars to focus on decision making and governmental process. The names which came to be associated with this approach were of Richard C. Snyder, H.W. Bruck and Burton Sapin, in their monumental work *Decision-Making as an Approach to the Study of International Relations*[30] (1954) tried to provide the theoretical framework for analysis of the behaviour of actors in international relations.

They began with the assumption that the key to political action lies in the way in which decision-makers as actors define their situations and that determines the course of actions of the actors, for action taken by states in reality are the actions of those acting in the name of the state. To understand why a particular state acts in a particular manner, one has to take into consideration the manner in which the decision-makers as actors define their situation which is again built on the projected course of action as well as the reasons behind such actions. Therefore, decision-making is a "process which results in the selection from a socially defined, limited number of problematical, alternative project to bring about the particular future state of affairs envisaged by the decision-makers". There are external and internal factors which also influence the process of decision-making. The internal factors include the role of public opinion, socio-economic conditions of the people, geographical and demographic factors and others. Among the external factors the important ones are the actions reactions and counteractions of other states as a result of the decisions taken by the men in authority there. The actions of the decision-makers are also determined by three basic determinants: (i) spheres of competence, (ii) communication and information and (iii) motivation. However, there are also certain limitations to decision-making and decision outcome. The limitations can arise from outside the decisional system and limitations arising from the nature and functioning of the decisional system.

Criticisms

Though the decision-making approach became a handy tool to study foreign policy processes, it has been criticized on several grounds. Scholars, though they acknowledge the positive contribution of this approach, at the same time contend that this approach is partial. Decision-making approach is impressive and is an innovation over the traditional power-centric approaches but it has failed to provide a comprehensive study of international relations. Again, it itself suffers from state-centrism by putting more emphasis on states as actors. It neglects objective realities. It also focusses more on the motives and actions of the decision-makers and completely ignores the impact of other factors on international politics. It helps understand the foreign policy processes and importance of the decision-makers in that respect but, in doing so, it focusses more on images and perceptions rather than on ground realities. This approach also disregards the importance of norms and values in national and international politics. Further, there are no uniform methods or techniques of analyzing the decision-making process. Nevertheless, this theory is an improvement upon the institutional approaches as it tried to provide an explanation of the behavioural pattern of the states under different circumstances.

POST-STRUCTURALISM IN INTERNATIONAL RELATIONS

From the discussions in the preceding sections especially the sections on Liberalism, and Realism and Neo-Realism one thing can be understood clearly that what we take to be real, timeless and universal in the field of IR is the result of imposition of a form of order. The dominant interpretations of the 'world' which have been established traditionally talks of states and their policy-makers pursuing their national interests. Therefore, the way the discipline of IR perceives the world makes it evident that the discipline is characterized by different paradigms competing in 'great debates'.

Post-structuralism engages itself with these issues of representation, the relationship of power and knowledge and the politics of identity to the production and understanding of global politics. One should not perceive Post-structuralism as a new set of paradigm in IR. Rather it is critical attitude, approach, or ethos that calls attention to the importance of representation, the relationship of power and knowledge and the politics of identity in an understanding of global affairs.

The critical attitude of Post-structuralism can be traced in the writings of Michael Foucault*. Post-structuralism as an approach emerged in the field of IR in the 1980s. The prominent scholars who introduced Post-structuralism are Richard Ashley, James Der Derian, Michael and Shapiro, David Campbell and R.B.J. Walker to name a few. Post-structuralism mainly focusses on the following points which may be summarized as:

1. Articulate the meta-theoretical** critique of the dominant paradigms like the realist theories of IR.

---

* Michel Foucault (1926–1984): He was a French historian and philosopher, associated with the structuralist and post-structuralist movements, and often labeled as a post-modernist too. Foucault's work is inter-disciplinary in nature, ranging across the concerns of the disciplines of history, sociology, psychology, and philosophy.

** Meta-theoretical: A meta theory is a broad perspective that overarches two, or more, theories like positivism, post-positivism, hermeneutics, and so on – of importance in sociology and other social sciences.

2. Connects IR to its inter-disciplinary context by introducing new sources of theory.
3. Concerned about how the relations of inside and outside were mutually constructed.
4. Focusses on identity, subjectivism and powers.
5. Shiftes analysis from assumptions about pre-given subjects to the problematic of subjectivity and its political enactment.
6. Employs a methodological precepts of interpretation, representation and politics instead of narrativizing historiography.

Richard K. Ashley's famous article, "The Poverty of Neo-Realism", led to the development of critical approach to IR. He pointed out that neo-realism, which tried to replace subjectivism of realism by a 'scientific' approach, tried to identify the 'objective' structures of social power behind or constitutive of states and their interests. Critical scholars were dissatisfied with the way realism and neo-realism remained dominant even in the face of global transformation. Post-structuralists, highlighted the neglect of realism of the importance of transnational actors, issues and relationships as well as voices of excluded people and perspectives.

Post-structural influence in IR opened newer dimensions in the study of IR. The newer research work included studies of the gendered character of state identity in the context of US intervention in the work of Weber (1994, 1999), studies of centrality of representation in North-South relations and immigration policies by Doty (1993, 1996), a deconstructive account of famine and humanitarian crises (Edkins, 2000), interpretative readings of diplomacy and European security (Dillon, 1996), a rethinking of finance and the field of international political economy (de Goede 2005, 2006) to mention a few.[31]

Evaluation

While assessing Post-structuralism it must be seen as an approach, attitude, or ethos that pursues critique with the purpose of inherently positive exercise that establishes the conditions of possibility for pursuing alternatives. It is in this context that post-structuralism makes other theories of IR one of its objects of analysis and approaches those paradigms with meta-theoretical questions designed to expose how they are structured. Post-structuralism reorients analysis away from the prior assumption of pre-given subjects to the problematic of subjectivity. This involves rethinking the question of power and identity such that identities are understood as effects of the operation of power and materialized through discourse. However, Post-structuralism often has been marginalized in the discipline of IR, and their over critical attitude have made them controversial being labelled as skeptical.

CONSTRUCTIVISM

To discuss constructivism, it will be easier if one follows Figure 1.1 (Chapter 1). Constructivism can be seen to be occupying a 'middle ground' between rationalism comprising the traditional theories of IR and reflectivism consisting of Post-structuralist approaches to IR. The timing of the rise of constructivism is quite striking. The sudden end of the Cold War, the collapse of the Soviet Union and certitude of possible changes that swept over Europe following the end of Cold War marked a need for a new theoretical orientation towards understanding of international events. The factor that spurred the constructivist critique is that the pre-dominant theories in IR failed to predict, and even recognize the possibility that such a dramatic change would happen in international politics. The other thing which became clear is that international relations is not static or fixed, and exists independently of human action and cognition. It can be said that international relations is a consequence of social construction. Constructivism thus became popular with scholars like Alexander Wendt, Nicholas Onuf, Peter Katzenstein and Friedrich Kratochwil giving their valuable insights while contending neo-realists debates forwarded by Kenneth Waltz in his famous work *Theory of International Politics* (1979).

Niclolas Onuf argues that constructivism is not a theory but a way of studying social relations. The core themes of constructivism can be summarized as:

1. International relations is a social construction. Social phenomena such as states or alliances or international institutions or any other phenomena such as states or alliances or international institutions or any other phenomena may build on the basic material of human nature, but they take specific historical, cultural and political forms that are a product of human interaction in a social world.

2. There is a 'social' dimension of international relations. There is an importance of norms, rules and languages in this context apart from exclusive emphasis of realist theory on material interest and power.

3. Far from an objective reality, international politics is 'a world of our making'. Interactions among actors bring historically, culturally and politically distinct 'realities' into being. This is because actors are not totally free to choose their circumstances and process of interactions make possible for them to determine their choices.

4. International relations is a social construction rather than existing independently of human meaning and action.

5. The idea of social construction suggests difference across context rather than a single objective reality. In place of regularities for the purpose of generalizations and theory construction constructivists have sought to explain or understood 'change' at the international level.

Alexander Wendt's book *Social Theory of International Politics*, (1999) builds a constructivist theory. In his article "Anarchy is What States make of It:

The Social Construction of Power Politics", (1992), published in *International Organizations*, while contending neo-realist assumption of anarchy in the absence of a global authority, Wendt, provides a framework for thinking about identity and interests as constructed, which is subject to process of transformation. He sets out to build a bridge between Rationalist and Reflectivist traditions by developing a Constructivist argument drawn from structural and symbolic interactional sociology.[32]

Evaluation

Constructivism can be said to be epistemologically about the social construction of knowledge and ontologically about the construction of social reality. The basic aim therefore, what seems of constructivism is increasing the reflexivity in both theoretical and empirical studies in IR on the basis the fact that analysis of the social world is very much a part of the real world and might affect it also. A constructivist looks at international relations with an eye open to social construction of actors, institutions and events. However, it does not mean that constructivism sets aside the ideas that material power is important or that actors make instrumental calculations of their interests; nor does it necessarily assume the *apriori* existence of sovereign states, epistemological positivism, or the anarchy problematique. Rather, it means that what goes on in these categories and concepts is constructed by social processes and interactions, and that their relevance for international relations is a function of the social construction of meaning. For example, the realist assumptions for competitions among states may be for status, prestige, hegemony but they will only make sense in terms of either legitimized power or shared understandings or are constructed. Therefore, a constructivists analysis opens a space for greater reflexivity in the analysis of any situation or event in international relations where the actors can for a moment think how their own actions may contribute to the very problems they seek to address. The glaring example in the recent international politics is the US War on Terror. What started as a largely militarized response to the 9/11 attack in the US, but later has assumed politicization of the US actions, and later the mission of remaking countries of Middle-east into liberal democracies involving human rights violations, disregard of international law and thus War on Terror becoming a war of infinite duration. A Constructivist approach to this War on Terror would rather emphasize on how identities and human sufferings are constructed through a process of interaction and move away from the emphasis on states.

FEMINISM IN INTERNATIONAL RELATIONS

International Relations (IR), being a discipline studying the politics among nations within a changing pattern of power relations among them, has been the last of the body of knowledge to be influenced by the feminist perspective.

Women have always remained 'hidden' in International Relations, which has been predominantly treated as a masculine discipline. In international politics, men are always in the forefront and women as heads of states or diplomats are hard to find. If one looks at international summits like the G-8 or the UN conferences or conferences and summits of several regional organizations like the European Union or SAARC, the number of men is always greater than the number of women. So, where do we find women in international relations? For long, women have been located as wives of diplomats, wives of politicians or as 'comfort women' for military personnel. But women have always been the victim of decisions taken by men in international politics regarding war and peace. During war or ethnic clashes or separatist movements, they are the worst victims and in the aftermath too, especially if they are forced to leave their country as refugees, their conditions become deplorable. In peace time, women become victims of trafficking, trading in women workers or easy recruits in sex tourist industry flourishing globally. Thus, it is not justified to keep women out of the purview of any sort of discussion in the discourse of International Relations. From the late 1980s and 1990s, attempts were made for re-evaluation of traditional IR theory from the feminist perspectives, which opened up a space for gendering International Relations.

Several conferences and published literature marked a new outlook for examining world events. Jean Bethke Elshtain's *Women and War* (1987), Cynthia Enloe's *Bananas, Beaches and Bases: Making Feminist Sense of International Politics* (1989), J. Ann Tickner's *Gender in International Relations: Feminist Perspectives on Achieving Global Security* (1992), V. Spike Peterson and Anne Sisson Runyan's *Global Gender Issues* (1993), and Christine Sylvester's *Feminist Theory and International Relations in a Postmodern Era* (1994) made their mark in the early 1990s.

Several international conferences also paved the way for highlighting women's issues. The important among them were Mexico Women's Conference (1975), Copenhagen Women's Conference (1980), Nairobi Women's Conference (1985), Vienna Human Rights' Conference (1993), Beijing Women's Conference (1995), and the like. The year 1975 was declared as the International Women's Year and 1976–1985 was declared as the UN Decade for Women. These were milestones in bringing women issues to the forefront. The adoption of UN Convention on the elimination of All Forms of Discrimination Against Women (CEDAW) (1979) and the UN General Assembly Declaration on the Elimination of Violence Against Women (1993) symbolized the victory of Women's political campaigns held globally. Three conferences also boosted the launch of feminist thought into the IR study. They were the *Millennium: Journal of International Studies* Conference at the London School of Economics (1988), the Conference at the University of Southern California (1989), and the Conference at Wellesley (1990).

In 1997, in a debate led by J. Ann Tickner in the International Studies Association's *International Studies Quarterly*, she suggested three types of misunderstandings that were to be blamed for the lack of insight of IR scholars regarding woman's issues. They are: (i) misunderstandings about the meanings of gender; (ii) different ontologies; and (iii) epistemological divides. Tickner in her *Hans Morgenthau's Principles of Political Realism: A Feminist Reformulation* (1988) presented a reformulation of Morgenthau's six principles of Political Realism, which is the dominant perspective in International Relations and very much masculine in nature, focusing only on power politics.

Therefore, Tickner criticizes realism as only "a partial description of international politics," owing to its deeply embedded masculinist bias. Her main concern is to offer a *"feminist reformulation"* of certain realist principles. They were:

- Objectivity is culturally defined – and is associated with masculinity – so objectivity is always partial.
- National interest is multi-dimensional – so not one set of interests can (or should) define it.
- Power as domination and control privileges masculinity
- All political action has moral significance – cannot or should not separate them.
- Perhaps look for common moral elements.
- Feminists deny the autonomy of the political realm – building boundaries around a narrowly defined political realm defines political in a way that excluded the concerns and contributions of women.

However, contemporary world affairs have forced the feminist to face challenges and consequently respond to, analyze, and confront forces of globalization and fragmentation. Globalization with its market forces has severe impact on women. It affects and often devastates women's lives, family and livelihood, and drastically reduces political space for making claims against the state. Further, the political identity movements producing 'new wars,' mostly in non-western states, have women as victims in such movements. Therefore, these new developments need a feminist understanding of nationalism, militarization, war and peace, identity conflicts, religious fundamentalism, functioning of the global political economy and impact of forces of globalization. Unfortunately, despite sincere efforts of the feminists, IR still remains a male-dominated field. International Relations scholars have worked out their own exclusions and inclusions and it is very hard for them to think beyond the issues of power and national interest when it comes to the question of politics among nations.

Criticism

Two of the most well-known scholars to raise criticism against feminist IR have been Robert Keohane and Francis Fukuyama. For Keohane, feminist IR needs to develop scientific, testifiable theories. Fukuyama questions the feminist IR scholars' view that if women ran the world, we would live in a much more peaceful world which, to him, is doubtful. In the face of such criticism, the feminist IR scholars need to develop a much more nuanced and sophisticated argument in order to meet the overwhelming challenge posed by Political Realists.

However, the impact of feminist engagement on politics and on public policies across the world cannot be denied. That several conventions recognize women's rights itself is a positive development. Untiring efforts of the feminist have raised consciousness about gender issues. Feminists and international lawyers have been successful in getting rape classified, for the first time, as a war crime, and categorized by the international tribunals on former Yugoslavia and Rwanda as a form of torture. Sexual discrimination and maltreatment has been accepted by some countries like Canada and Spain as grounds for political asylum. International non-governmental organizations and also aid agencies involved in providing assistance to the developing countries have specified in their development policy in general gender concerns as the centre of their donation policies. Even participation of women in political decision-making has been made possible through reservation of seats for women, as in India, in the case of local self-governmental institutions (a national bill is still pending). In practice, however, a lot has to be done to increase the level of gender sensitivity in IR.

EXERCISES

1. What are the basic assumptions of liberal approach to the study of international relations? Examine critically the liberal approach to politics.
2. Discuss the liberal approach to the study of international relations.
3. Analyse the basic principles of liberal approach to international relations. How was it revived in the 1970s?
4. Discuss liberal and neo-liberal approach to the study of international relations.
5. Analyse the basic principles of political realism in the study of international relations. In this connection elucidate E.H. Carr's and Morgenthau's views on political realism.
6. Examine the realist approach to international relations. In this context also discuss the emergence of neo-realism and its basic tenets.
7. Discuss the six main principles of Morgenthau's theory of political realism.
8. Critically examine the pluralist approach and point out its difference with political realist approach.
9. Discuss the Marxist approach to the study of international relations.
10. Analyse the basic principles and significance of the modern world system theory of international relations.

11. Elucidate Johan Galtung's structural theory of imperialism.

12. Discuss Morton Kaplan's six models of international system.

13. Examine how far the communications approach is applicable to the study of international relations.

14. Briefly discuss the decision-making theory to the study of international relations.

15. Examine the post-structuralist approach to international relations.

16. Analyze constructivism as an approach to the studys of international relations.

17. Discuss the feminist approach to international relations.

REFERENCES

[1] Dougherty, James E. and Robert L. Pfaltzgraff, Jr., *Contending Theories of International Relations: A Comprehensive Study*, Longman, USA, 1997, pp. 14–22.

[2] Sidorsky, David (Ed.), *The Liberal Tradition in European Thoughts*, Capricorn Books, New York, 1970, p. 2, cited in Keith L. Shimko, *International Relations—Perspectives and Controversies*, Houghton Mifflin Company, New York, 2005, pp. 51–52.

[3] Kegley, Charles W., Jr. and Eugene R. Wittkopf, *World Politics—Trends and Transformation*, St. Martin's Press, New York, 1997, p. 20.

[4] Dunne, Timothy, "Liberalism", *in* John Baylis and Steve Smith (Eds.), *The Globalization of World Politics*, Oxford University Press, London, 1997, pp. 150–151.

[5] Couloumbis, Theodore A. and James H. Wolfe, *Introduction to International Relations: Power and Justice*, Prentice-Hall of India, New Delhi, 1981, p. 7.

[6] Cited in Mahendra Kumar, *Theoretical Aspects of International Relations*, Shiva Lal Agarwal & Co. Educational Publishers, Agra, 1995, pp. 58–59.

[7] Machiavelli, *The Prince*, Wordsworth Classics of World Literature, Hertfordshire, 1997.

[8] Skinner Quentin, *Machiavelli*, Oxford University Press, London, 1981, pp. 25–29.

[9] Arthashastra, http://www.mssu.edu/projectsouthasia/history primary-docs/Arthashastra/index.htm, see also http://www.wsu.edu:8080/~wld-civ/world_civ_reader/world_civ_reader_1/arthashastra.html.

[10] Hobbes, Thomas, *Leviathan*, http://oregonstate.edu/instruct/phl302/texts/hobbes/leviathan-contents.html.

[11] Carr, E.H., *The Twenty Years' Crisis: 1919–1939*, Macmillan Press, Bangalore, 1981, p. 80.

[12] Morgenthau, Hans. J, *Politics Among Nations: The Struggle for Power and Peace*, Kalyani Publishers, New Delhi, 1985, pp. 4–14.

[13] Cited in Radharaman Chakrabarti and Gautam Kumar Basu (Eds.), *Theories of International Relations: Search for Alternatives*, Sterling Publishers, New Delhi, 1992, p. 91.

[14] Dunne, Timothy, "Realism", *in* John Baylis and Steve Smith (Eds.), *The Globalization of World Politics*, Oxford University Press, London, 1997, pp. 117–119.

[15] Hoffman, Stanley (Ed.), *Contemporary Theory in International Relations*, Prentice Hall, Englewood Cliffs, New Jersey, 1960, p. 34.

[16] Burchill, Scott, "Realism and Neo-Realism," *in* Scott Burchill, Richard Devetak, Andrew Linklater, Matthew Paterson, Christian Reus-Smit and Jacqui True (Eds.), *Theories of International Relations*, Palgrave, New York, 2001, p. 92.

[17] Bandyopadhyaya, Jayantanuja and Amitava Mukherjee, *International Relations Theory: From Anarchy to World Government*, Manuscript India, Kolkata, 2001, p. 44–46.

[18] Review of International Studies, Adam Jones, *Does Gender Make the World Go Round, Feminist Critiques of International Relations*, http://adamjones.freeservers.com/does.htm.

[19] Viotti, Paul R. and Mark K. Kauppi (Eds.), *International Relations Theory: Realism, Pluralism, Globalism and Beyond*, Allyn & Bacon, USA, 1998, p. 210.

[20] Keohane, R.O. and J.S., Nye, "Realism and Complex Interdependence," *in* William Marc (Ed.), *International Relations in the Twentieth Century: A reader*, Macmillan Education, London, 1989, pp. 243–254.

[21] Sullivan, Michael P., "Transnationalism, Power Politics, and the Realities of the Present System," *in* William Marc (Ed.), *International Relations in the Twentieth Century: A reader*, Macmillan Education, London, 1989, pp. 255–274.

[22] Viotti, Paul R. and Mark K. Kauppi (Eds.), *International Relations Theory: Realism, Pluralism, Globalism and Beyond*, Macmillan, London, 1990, p. 215.

[23] Bose, Arun, "The Marxian Theory of International Relations", *in* K.P. Misra and R.S. Beal (Eds.), *International Relations Theory: Western and Non-western Perspective*, Vikas Publishing, New Delhi, 1980, pp. 161–165.

[24] Lenin, V.I., *Imperialism: The Highest Stage of Capitalism*, Left Word, New Delhi, 2000, pp. 113–123.

[25] Galtung, Johan, "A Structural Theory of Imperialism", *Journal of Peace Research*, International Peace Research Association, Groningen, Vol. 13, no. 2, 1971, pp. 81–94.

[26] Bandyopadhyaya, Jayantanuja, *North Over South: A Non-Western Perspective,* South Asian Publishers, New Delhi, 1984, pp. 1–2.

[27] Kaplan, Morton A., *System and Process in International Politics*, Wiley and Sons., New York, 1957, pp. 21–53.

[28] Weiner, Norbert, *The Human Use of Human Beings,* Boston, Houghton, Mifflin, 1950.

[29] Deutsch, Karl W., *The Nerves of Government: Model of Political Communication and Control,* The Free Press of Glencoe III, 1963.

[30] Snyder, Richard C., H.W. Bruck and Burton Sapin, *Decision-Making as an Approach to the Study of International Relations,* Princeton University Press, Princeton, 1954.

[31] Tim Dunne, Milja Kurki and Steve Smith, *International Relations Theories: Discipline and Diversity,* Oxford University Press, New Delhi, 2013.

[32] *ibid.*

3

International System and the Role of Actors and Non-State Actors

INTRODUCTION

The present international system comprises 192 states who are members of the United Nations, and 6 others such as Kosovo, Palestine, Sahrawi Arab Democratic Republic(Western Sahara), Turkish Cyprus, Taiwan and the Vatican City, who are non-members of the United Nations. Alongside, there has been a parallel increase of other kinds of actors besides the states, who are also challenging the might of the state. It is because of the increase in interdependence among all these actors that the international system has now become more extensive and is not just limited to states and their activities. To comprehend the complexities and functioning of this international system, it is important to identify the major actors and their crucial roles in international politics. Therefore, there has been an increase in interest among the scholars to assess the changing patterns of international system along with its component units.

THE INTERNATIONAL SYSTEM

The structure of the present day international system is quite complex and is increasingly becoming more complex. This is more so because of the changes in the nature of the component units of the system. Traditionally, it was only the states which were considered to be the vital parts of the international system or the primary actors, but now there has been an increasing recognition of the existence of other agents, or as they are now called *non-state actors* in international relations. Therefore, international system can be thought of as one combining several kinds of actors of varying degrees of autonomy in their international behaviour, with the states among them retaining a leading but by no means an exclusive role.[1]

By international system, some scholars mean a more complex concept involving a set of states and other actors interacting with each other. Any system is defined by the combination of the attributes of its component units and the nature, pattern, and number of interactions among those units. If this idea is applied to the international system, then the factors, which become important are:

- The number of state actors
- The relative size of various actors
- The number and types of non-state actors
- Linkages or interactions among state actors
- Interdependence among the units of the system.[2]

However, as Frankel points out, international system lacks two prerequisites of domestic political systems, namely, the social basis of a community and the political structure of a government. International system does not possess any unconditional agreement on cooperation, on the precedence of some basic common good over sub-group or individual interests. It is built only on some limited and conditional cooperation, which sometimes degenerates into anarchy. In the absence of a hierarchically arranged government, there is no authority to determine the jurisdiction of all the social sub-groups and enforce norms and laws. What exists is only a loose structure and weak sets of norms to regulate the behaviour of the states. Nevertheless, the international system has been characterized by the presence of sovereign states and ensuing anarchy, security dilemma, balance of power, hegemony, alliances, regional alignments, international regimes, collective security, conflict and conflict resolution from time to time. At present, in the contemporary international system, there is an increasing crisis of the territorial states vis-à-vis the challenges posed by the non-state actors.

ACTORS IN INTERNATIONAL SYSTEM

Actors in the theatrical sense, mean the lead roles in any play or movie. Different actors play different roles on stage or a film. If this concept is transferred to the realm of international system, then the whole international system becomes an arena of dramatic politics where lead roles are played by several actors who may be individuals, groups or organizations. Here, actors are on the one-hand states personified and on the other several non-state actors. Therefore, as Frankel says that conceiving international society as a system and its major components, the states as well as non-state actors, as subsystems, it is possible to conceptualize the reality of world politics in a sensible way. The reality is about influencing and getting influenced. The question here arises who influences and who gets influenced? The answer obviously can be found out by analysing the behavioural patterns of the actors of the international system. The dominant actors always are in an advantageous position and do possess the capabilities to influence and manipulate the behaviour of not so powerful actors. Bargaining and leveraging are the core processes through which the actors try to extend their influence on each other in the international system, although force does retain its importance even in the present time.

STATES AS ACTORS

Despite several arguments forwarded by a number of scholars regarding the crisis of territorial state, in the age of increased global interdependence and the proliferation of the nuclear and space technologies, the state remains the primary actor in the international system. Most scholars date the birth of the state system from 1648 and the Treaty of Westphalia (1648), although some contend that the state as it existed in the seventeenth century, was nothing but the culmination of the processes that had been happening for over 500 years before the Westphalia Treaty. However, a sojourn into history would testify that the period of 200 years from about 1450 to 1650 marked the evolution of the territorial state system. The Treaty of Westphalia brought an end to the thirty years war in Europe and, by virtue of this Treaty, the rulers of Europe shook themselves off from the authority of the Church and the Roman Empire. The apparently simple but central principle of this Treaty was "the ruler of the territory would determine the religion of that territory" which had major consequences. The pretense of religious and political unity in Europe was broken and authority was dispersed among various kings and princes, and the base for the sovereign nation-states was established. From this time onwards the important elements of statehood was conceived—a people, a territory where they lived and a government with the authority to rule over the people and the territory. The government was seen as an agent of the state, which was now considered as a legal entity enjoying sovereignty.[3]

In the course of time, the state system has undergone further development and changes due to increase in the number of states, interdependence among them in all spheres, especially in the economic sector, technological development, rise of democratic institutions, growth of international law, international regimes, regional alliances, development of military warfare and weaponries. Whatever may be the situation, it can be said with certainty that states still remain as dominant actors in the international system. As Palmer and Perkins[4] assert, the state-system "may be in its sunset period, but there seems to have been little change in its basic design, which is the coexistence of a large number of states, including some pre-eminent military powers, all subject to the drive of their special interests and emotions, all subscribing to the theory of sovereignty, and all impelled to develop national power as the instrument of their national policies".

Elements of Statehood

Elements of statehood can be discerned from the definition of state given by L. Oppenheim (*International Law*, 1905), a British authority on international law. He said that a state "is in existence when a people is settled in a country under its own sovereign government".[5] This definition focuses on the four distinct elements of statehood. They are a people, a territory, a government and the attribute of sovereignty. A careful analysis of all these four elements is necessary.

The People

Most often definition of a state refers to "any body of people occupying a definite territory and politically organized under one government". Therefore, the first vital requirement to qualify as a state, population is important. It is impossible to conceive of a state until and unless people live together in an associated life. This is because state is a form of social organization and people must be its essential component. The number of people who live in a state is a matter of great importance. There is, however, no fixed idea about the exact number of population. Most scholars are of the opinion that what counts is the quality and character of the population. These involve obvious concerns about age, sex distribution, trends in birth rates, standards of living, health, literacy, productive capacity and skills, customs and beliefs, moral standards and morale and national character.

Territory

The second most vital element of statehood is, territory. There can be no state without a fixed territory. Nomadic tribes wandering from one place to another cannot be considered as a state. The modern state unquestioningly requires a definite portion of the earth as its territory over which it has undisputed authority. Again, like the population, it is difficult to fix the limit of the territory. There may be states such as the Soviet Union with huge territory or small states such as Tuvalu, Nauru, Vatican City, Monaco, Maldives or Malta with territory as small as it can be. What matters is the geographic location of the states. Otherwise, it would not have been possible for a small foggy island in the Atlantic, Great Britain to hold its sway over the world for centuries. In fact, the United States also enjoyed a strategic location so unique that it was possible for it to follow the policy of isolationism in the past. The United States is also less vulnerable from land or naval attacks because of the huge water body (Atlantic Ocean) surrounding it. An approaching enemy can be intercepted in the mid-seas by the powerful US navy. Therefore, size does not really matter. What matters is how far a state is vulnerable or not, which again depends on a lot of geo-strategic calculations and political, economic and military factors, especially in this nuclear and space age.

Government

The third important element is the government, which is the political organization of the state. The government is like the eyes and ears of the state, and the state wills and acts through the government. Whatever may be the form of government, it is absolutely necessary to have a government. It is through the government that the sovereign will of the state is expressed. What should be the nature of the government is no doubt important as far as foreign policy orientation is considered, but it is tough to state what should be the 'model' government for a state. From Aristotle till the present day this is a puzzle to which there is no clear-cut answer. Therefore, there are democratic forms of government to authoritarian regimes in the world. What counts is that whether or not the government of a particular state is recognized by the governments of other countries. Once it receives this recognition, it becomes the legal representative of the country, for instance the case with Peoples Republic of China, which did not receive the recognition of the United States after its birth in 1949 and was only recognized by the USA and admitted to the permanent seat in the United Nations Security Council in 1971 and replaced Nationalist China (Taiwan).

Sovereignty

The most important element of statehood is, sovereignty. The term 'state' was derived from the Latin 'status' which means the 'position' or 'standing' of a ruler. The position of the state is supreme. Sovereignty is the supremacy of the state. The state is supreme in internal as well as external matters. As Hedley Bull (The Anarchical Society, 1977) observes, sovereignty includes "internal sovereignty, which means supremacy over all other authorities within that territory and population" and "external sovereignty, by which is meant not supremacy but independence of outside authorities".[6] This implies then that the state has supreme power to govern its land and resources and population within its territory as well as in external relation it has no restrictions on its authority, except those, which it has on its own accepted.

In international relations, sovereignty is accepted as a fact and government as representatives of their states, no matter where the jurists or political scientists locate the seat of the ultimate sovereign power. Sovereignty should be seen as a special theoretical relationship between each state and all other states. Though all states on the face of this Earth is considered sovereign and equal, this equality is *legal* and *not factual*. There is a simultaneous presence of states of varied dimensions. Some are considered as major powers, others as middle range powers, yet some others as small and weak. Here, the interplay between sovereignty becomes crucial. As each state tries to pursue its national interests, each of them has to accommodate, make compromises and adjustments, which limits their absolute sovereignty. International law and international regimes also impose restrictions on the behaviour of the state. Clyde Eagleton (1945) took a realistic view of the problem of inter-relationship between international law and sovereignty of states. He said, "sovereignty cannot be an absolute term. It is just as foolish to say that sovereignty must be surrendered or eliminated as to say that it must be absolute and unrestrained...."[7] There are scholars who point out to the fact that the states often agree to limit their sovereignty through the conclusion of international agreements and through their memberships of international institutions. Therefore, the principle of 'consent' becomes important as, in reality, states can and indeed bind themselves to observe certain rules and contract certain obligations.[8] There are few supporters to the idea that states, by participating in various kinds of international agreements or gaining membership to various international organizations like the United Nations or the Commonwealth of Nations, lose their status as sovereign states. There may be contentions about limited sovereignty in the present day globalized world yet it is not possible to deny that so long as the nation-state system remains the basis of the prevailing pattern of international society, the substance of sovereignty will remain even if the word "sovereignty" disappears.

The fact is that all the states on the face of this earth are considered equal and enjoy political independence. The United Nations Charter under Article II acknowledges that it "is based on the principle of sovereign equality of all its Members". This may be legally true but factually incorrect. There can be many reasons. No state is equivalent to other in terms of size, resources and economic development, and hence power. It is true that some states may be more equal than others, but reality shows that differences between states are numerous which affect their capabilities in international relations to manoeuvre and exert its power and influence on others. As Palmer and Perkins talked about the conventional classification of the states in power-political terms as "great powers" or "major powers" and "small powers" or "lesser powers," and also a category like "middle powers." Undoubtedly, there is another category of states that is weak and not so powerful in the international arena. Therefore, it is obvious that "great powers" would have leverage in bargaining and also manipulating the techniques of using rewards and punishments vis-à-vis "small powers" and weak states. Therefore, what constitutes power, obviously, brings us to the discussion about national power.

NATIONAL POWER

What makes the United States of America the most powerful state in the world? Should India follow a favourable policy towards USA? What should be the equation between USA and Russia in their relationships? How does USA figure in the Indo-Pak relations? Thousands of such questions can be raised, but the answer is that the disposition of a particular state in the international arena is based on its national power.

Power is seen "as the ability to get another actor to do what it would not otherwise have done (or not to do what it would have done).[9] Power, therefore, is a relationship. If thought in terms of international relations, then the state's attempt to influence others, to a great extent, is determined by its own capabilities, goals, policies and actions which is similarly affected by the behaviour of those with which it interacts.

Power, in the context of world politics, can be seen as:

- A set of attributes or capabilities
- An influence process
- Ability to control resources, behaviour of other states, events, outcomes of interaction (cooperative or conflictual).

Couloumbis and Wolfe produced an umbrella concept of power that denotes anything that establishes and maintains control of one actor over the other. They conceive power as having three elements—force, influence and authority (see Figure 3.1). Force, can be defined as the explicit threat or the use of military, economic and other instruments of coercion by one actor against another in pursuit of its political objectives. Influence, is seen as the use of instruments of persuasion, short of force, in order to maintain or alter the behaviour of one actor in the way as preferred by the other actor. Authority, means the compliance by one actor to the directives issued by another actor nurtured by its own perception of respect, solidarity, affection, affinity, leadership, knowledge and expertise regarding that actor.[10]

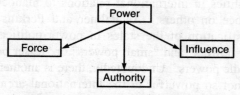

Figure 3.1   Illustration of power.

[**Source:** Adapted from Theodore A. Couloumbis and James H. Wolfe][10]

From the realist's perspective, international politics becomes nothing but an incessant struggle for power. As its chief proponent, Hans J. Morgenthau[11] pointed out in his classic text, *Politics Among Nations*, in the section entitled "International Politics as a Struggle for Power": "International politics like all politics is a struggle for power. Whatever the ultimate aims of international politics, power is the immediate aim". To him power "may comprise anything that establishes and maintains control of man over man [and it] covers all social relationships which serve that end, from physical violence to the most subtle psychological ties by which one mind controls another".

According to Organski[12], power is "part of a relationship between individuals or groups of individuals" and cannot therefore be "disentangled from the rest of the relationship but it is influenced by it and changes with it. For, power is that part of relationship in which each party is able to influence the behaviour of the other, and almost any tie between two nations may be utilized in this fashion". Power is, thus, the ability to influence the behaviour of others in accordance with one's ends. Unless a nation can do this, even if it is large, wealthy, or even great, it cannot become powerful.

Padelford and Lincoln[13] define national power "as the sum total of the strength and capabilities of a state harnessed and applied to the advancement of its national interests and the attainment of its national objectives".

As Ebenstein (1948) puts national power more than the sum total of certain quantitative factors, it is "The alliance potential of a nation, its civic devotion, the flexibility of its institutions, its technical know-how, its capacity to endure privations". These may be referred to as a few qualitative elements that determine the strength of a nation.[14]

Whatever may be the varying notions about national power, if we try to define it from a broad perspective, it means the ability to prevail in conflict and overcome obstacles, and this is more so because relations among states involve some form of incompatibility. Therefore, power helps in getting one's way. Influence is one of the methods by which states, like people, try to get their way in international relations. Influence can range from compellance, switching sides in international fora, leaving one alliance and joining another and economic embargo, to deterrence. Deterrence as a policy became very popular during the Cold War when both the superpowers, USA and USSR mutually deterred each other by using the threat of nuclear missiles rather than actually using it to maintain their foothold in world politics and maintaining their spheres of influence. Holsti lists six different tactics in the influence ladder:

1. Use of force
2. Infliction of non-violent punishment
3. Threat of punishment (the *stick*)
4. Granting rewards (the *carrot*)
5. Offer of rewards
6. Persuasion.[15]

States often use a combination of all the above tactics to gain leverage in a particular bargain, either tacit or explicit. Therefore, power becomes an important factor in international relations and to know how it contributes to a states' prowess involves an effort to estimate power. The Chinese strategist *Sun Tzu* advised the rulers to accurately estimate their own power—ranging from money to territory to popular domestic support—and that of their potential enemies. He wrote that it is essential to "Know the enemy and know yourself", and when it comes to the question of estimating national power, it is necessary to know about the elements of national power, since measurement of national power is impossible. As Ebenstein noted that "In the field of international relations, the central problem of the strength of a nation is essentially a problem of qualitative judgement and measurement, as national power is more than the sum total of population, raw materials and qualitative factors". Seen in the present context of global interdependence, power can be seen as having an impact on the sensitivity and vulnerability of other actors. Therefore, it is rational to discuss the elements of national power, which would help us to comprehend the pattern of interaction in international arena.

Elements of National Power

Geography: Geo-politicians such as Sir Halford Mackinder (1869–1947), Admiral Alfred Thayer Mahan (1840–1914), Karl Haushofer (1869–1946) and Nicholas J. Spykman (1893–1943) attached great importance to geography. Mackinder forwarded the "Heartland Theory". He expounded, "Who rules East Europe commands Heartland; Who rules Heartland commands World Island; and Who rules World Island commands the World". Haushofer distorted the thesis to support German imperialist ambitions. He propounded the idea that to have a healthy life a state must be nourished by acquiring new lands or what he called *Lebensraum*. Spykman revised the Heartland theory and forwarded what came to be popularly known as the *Rimland Theory*. He propounded, "Who controls the Rimland rules Eurasia; Who rules Eurasia controls the destinies of the World". Mahan in his book *The Influence of Sea Power* looked at the rise and exploits of British naval power by virtue of its control of seas. His writings had a great influence on the national policy of the United States to develop a huge and powerful navy. Geography, therefore, may be regarded as the most stable determinant national power. This includes the size of the territory, topography, location relative to sea, and landmasses relative to other nations and control of strategic places.

Size: It means the total land mass that a state controls or exercises its sovereign authority. The size of states varies from one state to another, but the most important factors, which contribute to its national power, are the state's internal organization, its capacity for forging political unity and its ability to defend itself. A large area contributes only to a state's power if it is capable of providing it with the capacity of containing a large population and a large varied supply of natural resources. Nevertheless, size does have an influence on a state's decision-making capacity as two of the greatest powers in the world, the United States and the Soviet Union have huge land masses under their control.

Location: More important than size is the geo-strategic location of the state in the sense that, position of a state in relationship to other land bodies and to other states which profoundly affects the culture, economy and both its military and economic power. Location tends to make a state, a land power or a sea power. It is also intimately related with the power of foreign policy decision-making. The insularity of Great Britain and the isolated position of the United States have greatly affected the foreign policy decisions of these states.

Climate: It is another geographical feature that plays a crucial role in determining the national power. Climate affects the health, temperament and energy level of the population. It is also closely related to productivity. Extremes of climate may make functioning and development of a modern industrial society difficult. Climate does affect national power of states through its direct impact on agriculture, which is required to support its population. Uncertain rainfall and drought might limit the power of a state while too much dependence on food import might be obstructed from adopting an independent foreign policy posture.

Topography :   It is another important geographical feature affecting foreign policy decisions. It, not only determines the density of population, which a region can support, but also the climate of the land. Wind, rainfall, temperature and consequently soil conditions are influenced by the position of the land, sea and mountains. The strategic position of mountain, valleys, rivers and plains and deserts not only helps in communication but also in matters of security; for example, the Himalayas and the Alps are like natural barriers. Topography sets limit to natural expansion of states. The Himalayas serving as a natural barrier between India and China has checked Chinese expansionism. The Pyrenees serve as a fortress of Spain, and the English Channel gives a natural insularity to Great Britain.

Natural Resources and Availability of Raw Materials: All these improve the bargaining capacity of a state internationally. Natural resources are available naturally to the states in the form of soil and its products, water and its products and minerals. These in turn helps the states to develop industrially, economically and also militarily. However, huge possession of resources does not add up to one's strength, but the utilization of the particular product is important. The possession of oil, uranium and atomic energy has been utilized by various states to their advantage, which have contributed to the strengthening of their position in international arena. Thus, huge quantities of oil have helped the West Asian and Gulf countries to embark on the policy of oil diplomacy. The most noteworthy incident shaking the international economy, was the oil embargo by the OPEC countries in 1973. Self-sufficiency in food, mineral and energy resources has also helped the United States and Russian foreign policy choices.

Economic Development: The economic performance of a state in terms of GNP per capita provides the key to understand the state's ability to utilize its natural and human resources which adds up to its national power and determines its policy choices and menu. The United States, by far the largest economy recording a highest Gross National Product (GNP), is always able to secure its objectives vis-à-vis underdeveloped and developing states and also to some extent in relation to certain developed states too such as Britain and France. The levels of high economic development provide leverage to the countries to flex their muscles in relation to economically weak countries. However, the United Nations Development Programme (UNDP) has forwarded a different view of development. The GNP is not always an indicator of the well-being of the masses. Therefore, UNDP has introduced the Human Development Index (HDI) to calculate economic development of a state. This includes three basic components of human development—longevity, knowledge and standard of living. But it had also been revealed that those countries ranking high in HDI group have also high GNP per capita. Therefore, whether it is HDI or GNP measure of economic development, it is the developed countries who are in an advantageous position and are able to call the shots in international relations. Therefore, economic development is a crucial factor as far as national power is concerned. The level of economic development also determines the state's ability to gear up its military preparedness and improvise its military capabilities, which in turn determines its foreign policy objectives.

Military Preparedness: Military capability is the most determining factor as far as national power and prestige is concerned. Russia, the United States and China have huge army under their command as compared to Iceland, Costa Rica, Maldives, Mauritius and other small countries. Manpower backed by sophisticated technology and upgradation through continuous research and development is what makes a state militarily strong and powerful. The US high-tech war during the 1991 Gulf War brought about revolutionary changes and introduced new thinking in the history of warfare. It symbolized radical changes from strategy, to research and development to procurement, so much so, that other states had to rethink about the efficacy of their military establishment. Therefore possession of conventional forces as well as nuclear arsenal gives certain leverage to states in negotiation with others. Exhibition of sheer military might projects the prowess and prestige of a state.

National Character and National Morale: Though many scholars disregard the importance of national character as an important input of foreign policy because of its metaphysical overtones yet national character finds expression in international relations through the perceptions, reactions and behavioural patterns of decision-makers. As Prof. Jayantanuja Bandyopadhyaya suggests that, if worship of wealth and power are regarded as chief attributes of American national character, the foreign policy becomes logically one, which is consistent with these attributes. In India, the culture and belief system has moulded the outlook and foreign policy perspective of the decision-makers.

National Morale: It is also an elusive category and consists of a state of mind, which sometimes can be called **patriotism or love of country.** Morgenthau opined, "National Morale is the degree of determination with which a nation supports the home and foreign policies of its government in times of peace or war. It permeates all activities of a nation, its agricultural and industrial production as well as its military establishment and diplomatic service". Willingness to stand up and sacrifice for one's country is not only an ingredient of national morale of troops fighting but also of the civilian population's.

Political Structure and Leadership: The political structure of a state and the nature of the ruling elite determines to a great extent the direction and realization of national policies and also influences the formulation of foreign policy of a state. In other words, a mature and responsible government and decision-makers contribute to the national power of a state. A democratic state, with a high degree of political accountability, is both responsive and responsible than totalitarian and authoritarian states. But it is the quality of leadership which determines the extent to which the state is able to secure its national interest. The democratically elected government of Pakistan, since 2008, has failed either to secure the safety of its individual citizens or of the foreign nationals visiting that country. The Sri Lankan team, to the shock and awe of the world became a target of terror during their tour in Pakistan on March 03, 2009. It is alleged that Pakistan's soil is being used by international terrorist outfits to carry out their plans. Unfortunately, the ruling elites are unable to tackle the rising problem, which is further weakening Pakistan and in reality disturbing the peace and security of South Asia. Therefore, the quality of rule is also an important factor in considering the effectiveness of national power.

Ideology: Ideology is also an important element of national power. Padelford and Lincoln[16] defined ideology "as a body of ideas concerning economic, social and political values and goals which pose action programme for attaining these goals". An ideology accepted within a state, whether it is democracy, socialism or communism or some other, serves certain interests of the state. Ideological principles may be used by state, or group of states to advance their national interests through justifying or disguising their policies and deeds in the struggle for power. The world has experienced dangerous ideologies such as Fascism and Nazism which run counter to internationalism. Again, the Soviet Union has used Marxist–Leninist ideologies to promote Soviet expansionism. Clash of Capitalism with communism was a source of Cold War between the United States and the Soviet Union. However, ideology alone cannot contribute to national power. One has to have the propaganda machinery, publicity facilities and media coverage at one's disposal to effectively use and propagate ideology to further one's national interest.

Population: Population is another factor which contributes to national power. As Morgenthau[17] pointed out, "since size of population is one of the factors upon which national power rests and since the power of one nation is always relative to the power of others, the relative size of the population of countries competing for power and especially the relative rate of growth desire careful attention". But it is difficult to ascertain whether size of the population adds up to national power. Large population may be a source of strength or weakness in the modern world. The test is whether a state can utilize its human resources effectively, support them at tolerable standard of living, and provide constructive outlets for their talents and energies. In developed countries, large numbers are usually a source of their strength, but in underdeveloped and developing countries, large numbers usually become their burden.

NATIONAL INTEREST

Power defined in terms of national interest gives meaning to international politics. This realist proposition, propounded by Morgenthau, as the second and most important signpost of *realpolitik* may seem to be a little exaggerated but, nevertheless, it is true to some extent. It is the position of a particular state in the international arena by virtue of its national power that determines how it is going to exercise its will over others. When the question of will of a state comes into consideration, undoubtedly, the concept of national interest figures in one's own idea. But to pinpoint at certain basic national interests of any particular state it becomes very difficult. For, as Frankel[18] wrote 'National interest' is a singularly vague concept. It assumes a variety of meanings in the various contexts in which it is used and, despite its fundamental importance, these meanings cannot be reconciled. Hence, no agreement can be reached about its ultimate meaning.

However, certain attempts have been made to provide a bare meaning of the concept. This has been tried from subjective and an objective angle. The former interprets national interest as "a constantly changing pluralistic set of objective preferences", the latter assumes that national interest can be objectively defined, or at least, can be examined with the help of some objectively definable criteria.

Rosenau[*] had proposed a distinction between the use of the concept for the purpose of political analysis and that of political action. He was of the opinion that as an analytical tool, it can be employed to explain or evaluate the sources of adequacy of a nation's foreign policy, and as an instrument of political action, it can serve as a means for justifying, denouncing or proposing policies.

Frankel proposed a classification of the uses of the term 'national interest' into 'aspirational', 'operational', 'explanatory' and 'polemical'. On the aspirational level, national interest refers to some ideal set of goals, which the state would like to realize, if possible. At the operational level, national interest is the sum total of interests and policies actually pursued. On the 'explanatory' and 'polemical' level, in political argument, the concept of national interest is used to explain, evaluate, rationalize or criticize foreign policy.[19]

However, a powerful objective exposition of national interest was given by Morgenthau. Though highly criticized, yet not without value and relevance, he contended that statesmen think and act according to interest defined in terms of power. The content of national interest is determined by the political traditions

---

[*]James N. Rosenau, "National Interest", *International Encyclopaedia of Social Sciences*, 1968.

and the total cultural context within which a nation operates. Inherent in the meaning of national interest is the minimum requirement of states to protect their physical, political and cultural identity against aggressions by other states. Therefore, the residual meaning inherent in national interest is 'survival'. 'Survival' involves preservation of physical identity, i.e., maintenance of territorial integrity, preservation of political identity, i.e., preservation of existing politico-economic regimes, preservation of cultural identity, i.e., conservation of ethnic, religious, linguistic and historical norms found in a state. From these general objectives, Morgenthau, argues that the statesmen derive their specific policies which may range from cooperative to conflictive policies like competitive armaments, balance of power, foreign-aid, alliances, subversion and economic and propaganda 'warfare'. [20]

On the whole, as Clinton[21] points out 'the national interest' refers to a general regulative principle of diplomacy, which represents the common good of the society, in its relations with other national units, as the end of diplomatic action. But the usage of the term 'the national interests' refers to myriad narrower goals which serve the broader end of 'the national interest' by maintaining or increasing the power of the state. National interests may range from vital or primary interests to secondary interests and again from permanent to variable interests. There can also be general interests and specific interests. Simultaneously, there can be in the international arena a play between identical interests, complementary interests and conflicting interests. The main purpose of the whole idea of national interest is in giving direction to long-term objectives of the foreign policy of a state and giving meaning to its actions in a short-term context.

CRISIS OF TERRITORIAL STATE

International system has been defined by some scholars as "any collection of independent political entities—tribes, city-state, nations, or empires—that interact with considerable frequency and according to regularized process". However, this does not present the whole picture of the international structure. This structure is conceived as being composed of several primary actors, the states and other equally important international actors, the non-state actors. The presence of these non-state actors has a great deal of influence in developing and promoting the menu of constraints and possibilities of state actions. The international and regional inter-governmnetal organizations such as the United Nations, NATO, ASEAN, SAARC, OAU, IMF, WHO and others have come to affect the menu for choice of the states. These supranational actors have the power to act separately and make and implement decisions that are binding on members, and to some extent, non-members too. Some non-governmental organizations (NGOs) such as the Amnesty International, International Red Cross Society, several human rights bodies and environmental groups have significant influence on the policy decisions of states. With the growing interdependence of the world system individual acts also produce impact on state actions. Steady growth of world public opinion has, in many instances, influenced state policies pertaining to human rights, environment, and matters relating to war and peace.

Globalization and agents of globalization are also now restricting the sovereignty of states to such an extent that questions are being raised about the erosion of state authority. Multinational corporations, flow of capital and information technology, opening up of markets, convertibility of currencies, free trade, global stock and bond trading, and mass media are delimiting the authority of the state more and more. The present state is quite incapable of controlling phenomena such as global satellite sensing, global social and ecological problems, which might spearhead global social and ecological movements, as well as internet hacking all having great consequences on the international system.

Pathbreaking technological revolution in military technologies has changed the whole perception of security for the state. States are no longer invincible. They have become vulnerable preys to the latest technological discoveries of long-range cruise missiles, inter-continental ballistic missiles (ICBMs), short-range ballistic missiles (SRBMs), Multiple Independently Targetable Reentry Vehicles (MIRVs) and a host of other improved newer weapons of mass destruction. Added to this are the dangers of biological and chemical weapons. As John Herz (*International Policies in the Nuclear Age*, 1959) suggested that, given the nature of available weaponry, the traditional state system and security have become obsolete. States are no longer capable of protecting the lives of their citizens in the traditional sense. The Gulf War of 1991, and the US War on terror in Iraq and Afghanistan bear testimony of how helpless states have become in the face of brazen use of modern weapons of tremendous precision.

Further, today we find that there is a sharp decline in the ability of many governments to govern. This often results from the domestic challenges being faced by the states, which have international implications. Ethnic and religious forces are resulting in divided loyalty between these ethno-national and religious movements and states. These have resulted in disintegration of states in some cases, and in some such fissiparous forces have made the task of governance difficult. The ethnic strife in former Yugoslavia and Czechoslovakia led to the dismemberment of the states. Rwanda, Burundi and Somalia are experiencing clashes along ethnic lines that are horrific and often spill over into warfare. Therefore, observers contend that ethno-national multiculturalism is a potential long-term threat to the state's survival because the aspirations of ethno-national groups to a separate statehood becomes possible only through the fragmentation of the territorial integrity of the existing states. Partha Chatterjee (*The Nation and its Fragments*, 1993) points out that states are inherently fragile because all are weak coalitions of multiple nationalities that can splinter. The forces of religious fundamentalism, sometimes assuming international manifestation in the form of terrorist assaults, are now shaking the pillars of state authority.

However, to argue that the state, as the most primary unit in international relations is fading away, is ignoring the reality. It is true that the overwhelming control of the state over the lives and activities of its citizens or its external as well as internal concerns has loosened, but this has in no way affected its position as the premier form of political organization—a unit that provides myriad services to its people. It is clear that the state remains the only organization that can provide the two essential services that allow the society to survive—security and welfare broadly conceived. Forces of ethnicity, religious fundamentalism, terrorism, the 9/11 attacks on the World Trade Center, the London blasts, Jaipur blasts, serial blasts in Ahmedabad (July 2008), Bangalore (July 2008), and the recent Mumbai siege (26/11) 2008 are no doubt challenging the states' might, yet, states continue to be the dominant units in international relations and the decisions and actions of their governments and their interrelations still remain the focus of inquiry.

If one considers the case of state vis-à-vis the non-state actors, one is sure to conclude that non-state actors work towards realization of their specific interests, few of which may be directly resulting in war or peace. But, even then, the governments remain the primary arbiters in these matters. As Holsti[22] contends, states remain critical actors in international politics because:

1. They command the allegiance of people occupying a definite territory.

2. They are the ones who possess the capabilities to employ the ultimate threat (war).

3. They, unlike the transnational organizations, are concerned with allround development, welfare and security of their population.

4. Only states enjoy sovereignty.

Frankel also explains that "by the end of the seventies, when the scattered residual remains of colonial empires were still achieving statehood and adding new, ostensibly even less 'viable' new members to the family of nations, no cases of disintegration or disappearance of a legitimate state had been recorded". The disintegration of Yugoslavia, Czechoslovakia and the Soviet Union in the late eighties and nineties had added to the number of states, but the world community did not experience any demise of territorial state as such. Frankel[23] points out six reasons for the survival of territorial states despite several crises challenging them. They are:

1. States generally retain their legitimacy, both domestically and internationally.

2. They remain the largest-scale meaningful communities and command supreme loyalty of the vast majority of their citizens, particularly as political representatives of nations and as guardians of national cultures.

3. They retain the monopoly of territory and the near monopoly of large-scale legitimate force.

4. They remain the only truly comprehensive large-scale multifunctional organizations with great built-in powers of inertia due to the built-in bureaucratic and other sectional interests, which have a stake in their survival.

5. Negatively, they have not been generally faced with really serious rivals.

6. Perhaps most importantly, as the discontinuation of any state could undermine the stability of the international system as a whole and threaten others with a possibility of a major war, disastrous to all, everybody has now a substantial stake in the continuation of the status quo.

Therefore, while acknowledging the growing importance of non-state actors, it has to be admitted also that sovereign states would continue to be the basic unit of international system. No viable alternative institution is thinkable in the distant future. It is true that interdependence and interpenetration of domestic and international politics, the movement of capital and information, forces of globalization, technological innovations, newer weaponry, the increasing influence of transnational social movements and organizations pose challenges to the state's supremacy, yet, these do not mean the end of the state as the primary unit in international relations. The state system is now facing new challenges, internationally and also on the domestic front, to which it has to adjust, and its survival remains linked to such adjustments.

NON-STATE ACTORS IN INTERNATIONAL RELATIONS

John Burton (*The Study of World Society: A London Perspective* (1974), a famous theorist of international relations, opined that for ages there have been several images, models of abstractions to focus on the different aspects of world society. One such image is that of the realist perception of the world. This conventional image projects a vision of the world composed of nation-states, which are of different size and power. This image became popularized as the 'billiard ball' model. These models upheld the presence of sovereign, independent states represented by their governments as units and the interactions or contacts among them are like those of different sized billiard balls, only the hard exteriors touch and heavier or faster moving ones push others out of the way. In other words, the points of contact are government to government. Therefore, this image only focussed on diplomatic relations, on governments as the main actors in world affairs, on their relative power and on the personal characteristics of their leaders. But a sea-change has occurred since the formulation of this image especially since the Second World War. Thus, there was the need to revise this world image.[24] Burton and his colleagues highlighted that with the growth in technology, communication, transportation and weaponry, the classical European model of balance of power model has become inadequate. Further, they neglected the internal processes and components within the states and interactions among various non-state actors such as political parties, ethnic groups and multinational corporations, which have greatly influenced and sometimes manoeuvred governmental decisions.

Therefore, Burton suggested a contrast to the realist model, which he termed as the cobweb model—a pluralist image of the world society. He argues that a cobweb or series of superimposed and intermeshing cobwebs would be in a better position to give an almost accurate image of the world society than a set of billiard balls. Though it would be difficult to theorize but nevertheless it would reflect, with less distortion, the actual political and economic processes that crisscross the globe. The cobweb model, he suggested, would not only take into account the activities of multinational corporations like Unilever or General Motors (before the economic meltdown of 2008 after which they have filed for bankruptcy) but also account for the activities of separatist ethnic organizations such as the Irish Republican Army (IRA) in Ulster, Palestinian Liberation Organization (PLO) and others and would also include the activities of individuals and non-governmental organizations having a powerful transnational impact such as the Green Peace, Amnesty International, the Roman Catholic Church and others. This, obviously, in no way undermines the importance of the states and their governments as they are still treated as extremely important international actors but are no longer the only actors.[25] The increasing presence of non-state actors must be admitted.

Holsti refers to three kinds of non-state actors:

- Territorial non-state actors
- Non-territorial non-state actors
- Inter-governmental actors.

Frankel also recognizes the existence of mainly three categories of non-state actors:

- Inter-state governmental organizations
- Inter-state non-governmental actors
- Intranational actors.

Following Frankel we will now discuss about these three non-state actors.

Inter-State Governmental Organizations (IGOs)

IGOs are important non-state actors in world politics. They are formed when several states come together in some common interest. These organizations most often develop a common external policy that might at times contravene the interests of any single member state.

IGOs can be classified according to the scope of their memberships and their purpose. On the one hand, there are universal political organizations such as the erstwhile League of Nations and the present day United Nations and its specialized agencies which endeavour to include international membership as far as possible. On the other hand, there can be several regional groupings of states or even groupings based on some specific or general purposes and, therefore, the membership is also regional and sometimes specific. They might be performing political, economic, developmental, military, socio-cultural or other functions for their member states. The most prominent of these kinds of IGOs are the North

Atlantic treaty Organization (NATO), the Organization of American States (OAS), the Organization of African Unity (OAU), the South Asian Association for Regional Cooperation (SAARC), Association of Southeast Asian Nations (ASEAN), the Arab League, Organization of Petroleum Exporting Countries (OPEC) and, the most notable one the European Union. To mention a few others, IGOs which are concerned with social or developmental matters, are the World Health Organization (WHO), the International Monetary Fund (IMF), the International Labour Organization (ILO) and the World Bank.

The number of IGOs increased between the period of 1945–1985 with a post-World War II high of 378 but, by 1990, the number has declined to around 300 IGOs. Nevertheless, IGOs are considered as crucial actors in international relations because their policy and behaviour have definite impact on the foreign policy of their members and also on the non-members. Most often, sending representatives to the IGOs or funding the IGOs or interacting with other states through the IGOs leads the statesmen to believe that IGOs are behaving like international actors and must be given importance in their foreign policy considerations.[26]

Inter-State Non-Governmental Actors

Inter-state non-governmental or non-territorial transnational organizations have also found prominence in international relations because of the kind of impact they have on the political, economic and socio-cultural life of states. They can be categorized into two types—religious and economic.

According to Holsti[27] they are characterized by:

- Organized activities occurring simultaneously in a number of countries.
- Objectives that do not relate to interests within any given territory.
- Çomponent parts that are essentially non-political.

As far as religious non-state actors are concerned, no actor has been so powerful as the Roman Catholic Church, with the Pope as its universal head who is also the head of state of Vatican or the Holy See. Frankel points out that traditionally, the Vatican has been treated as a sovereign state and it maintains diplomatic relations with a number of states, which may also include non-Christian states Vatican or the Pope the supreme head of over one billion acts as Catholics all over the world. The Pope has made pronouncements on a variety of international issues including economic development, abortion, arms control, and the nature of political regimes. However, the non-Catholic Christian churches, organized around 1954 into the World Council of Churches do not play such a massive role nor does any other religion as such.

The other most important transnational actors are those who are economic in character but have a tremendous impact on all aspects of lives of states. They are the multinational corporations (MNCs). MNCs have been defined in different ways. Some see them as a "cluster of corporations of diverse nationality joined together by ties of common management strategy". Others view them as "companies that control production facilities in two or more countries".[28] Whatever way an MNC is defined, it has a presence in the present-day context unperceived of previously by the state-centric thinkers. To name a few of the prominent MNCs: GE, the Daimler–Chrysler, General Motors Corporation (before they filed for bankruptcy after the global recession of 2008), Ford Motor Company, Exxon Corporation, Procter & Gamble, Unilever, Microsoft, IBM, Toyota, Sony, LG, Mitsubishi, Coca Cola, Pepsi Co., and others.

MNCs reflect the increasing globalization of world economy. By their sheer size in physical and financial assets, they have a tremendous impact on the global economic system. Allocation of factors of production and control of investment flows give them a leverage vis-à-vis international political units, such as the states. It is said that through payment of royalties and taxes, establishment of new plants, or closure of old ones, decisions on location of plants and advertising through MNCs can affect developing countries' economic structure, tax revenues, level of employment and consumption patterns which might sometimes lead to social strains.

The MNCs might also be politically involved as evident from the oft cited cases of the "banana republics" and the involvement of the United Fruit Company which tried to keep in power that government which would allow them to operate uninterruptedly. When a hostile regime under general Arbenz came to power, the company's vital interest stood threatened. In 1952, the Arbenz government introduced land reforms aiming to expropriate uncultivated portions of large plantations. As the United Fruit Company had the largest land holding with most of it being uncultivated, it became apprehensive of Arbenz's reform programme. The company, therefore, assisted the American government's efforts to overthrow the hostile regime by supporting the exiles in Honduras and Nicaragua. The coupd'état ultimately toppled the Arbenz government and he had to flee. Another most cited case is that of the International Telephone and Telegraph Company, which promoted a scheme to topple the Allende government in Chile where the US government officials already had undertaken programmes to topple the Allende government.[29] There have been cases where the interest of the home government and that of the MNC had coincided, leading to the intervention of the host country by the home government ultimately serving the interest of the MNC. Some of the most cited cases of MNCs and host government nexus are the American government's involvement in the overthrow of Mossadegh regime in Iran in 1953, resulting in new operating privileges for American oil companies and European oil companies, strong support of the French–British–Israeli invasion of the Suez Canal in 1956, and the American government's abortive Bay of Pigs invasion of 1961 to oust Castro and to do something to preserve the interests of American oil companies.

MNCs also have their own sphere of influence through the division of world markets. They are often found to be engaged in diplomacy and espionage, traditional tools of state interaction. The huge economic resources at their disposal make them more powerful than several newer and smaller states as well as old states. In 1993, General Motors was listed first in the Fortune Global 500 (though today it is thinking of filing for bankruptcy) and it had gross sales larger than the GNP of Finland or Denmark. The number and importance of MNCs, therefore, have grown in the present day. Frankel observed that in 1972 "The Year Book of International Organizations" listed as many as 2,190 MNCs, compared to 1,000 in 1958. By 1990s, it is noted by most observers, that there were at least 10,000 firms with business activities spreading all over the globe to several countries and controlling over 90,000 subsidiaries. The United States was home to, 159 such MNCs, Japan to 135, and Britain to 41.[30]

MNC-optimists view the multinationals as "the most powerful agent for the internationalization of human society". To them MNCs are "as huge economic combines that have the capacity, know-how, and wisdom to treat the world as a single unit and to combine the factors of production (labour, land, capital and management) for maximum efficiency and productivity, in accordance with the rules of the resuscitated law of comparative advantage". Further, the MNCs can also act as powerful agents of modernization, especially among less-developed countries by creating new jobs, introducing advanced technologies, training local citizens and thereby, contributing to the development of the state. The managers and employees of the MNCs become globally oriented and world minded as opposed to anachronistic nationalism and war, thereby paving the way for the development of world peace. They will be humanity's best hope for producing and distributing the resources of the earth.

Quite contrary to these views, the MNC-pessimists place their own objections while critically looking at the functioning of the MNCs. Barnet and Muller* in their "*Global Reach*" placed a very powerful argument that the MNCs are "the most powerful human organization yet devised for...colonizing...the future" and they offer little hope for solving the problems of mass starvation, mass unemployment and gross inequality. They even neglect the socially vital issues like nutrition, clean air and public health and also the environmental factors. They argue that the MNCs are colonizing the poor and less-developed countries and increasingly weakening them to maintain their strong hold and flow of profit and at the same time destabilize the rich countries. They predict that the rich countries simultaneously would also be hit by increasing unemployment and inflation which is true to some extent in the present context. The Third World and even the industrialized West are not in a position to stop the process of concentration of wealth in the hands of the big MNCs.

Intra-National Actors

These sort of non-state actors refer to political movements, national liberation movements, activities of ethnic, racial, religious or some ideological minority

---

*Richard J. Barnet and Ronald E. Muller, "*Global Reach*", Simon and Sehuster, New York, 1974.

groups. Their activities have a great impact on the actions of the states of their origin when these groups are able to gain support from external sources, either from the members of own national groups, or from governments hostile to their own government. This tends to complicate the relations among states and also have significant consequences on the international system.

During the Cold War, both the superpowers were engaged or gave tacit support to violent groups taking their sides in the ideological battle between the two. National liberation struggles like the Palestine Liberation Organization (PLO), or the African National Congress (ANC), and the South West African National People's Organization (SWAPO), known for its struggle against Apartheid regime, are noteworthy examples of such non-state actors. Even the Jews in the United States act as a powerful lobby, called the **Zionist lobby,** a pressure group aiming at making the foreign policy of America more favourable to the state of Israel.

INCREASING ROLE OF NON-STATE ACTORS

Undoubtedly, the non-state actors have come to occupy a place of significance in the international scenario whether they are IGOs, or transnational organizations or intranational actors. The role of many IGOs has become institutionalized in that the comity of nations expect them to act in a particular pattern, as in the case of the United Nations. The UN is expected to make efforts to resolve international conflicts or situations, which might give rise to conflict and perturb peace. The UN's role in international peacekeeping and peacemaking is well acknowledged. The specialized agencies of the UN are also expected to deliver their respective service as per their mandate. The World Bank and the IMF have roles to play with respect to the developmental aspects of the developing states. MNCs have now come to occupy important place in international relations and, quite significantly, are playing a more decisive role in the internal as well as external policies of states.

Keohane and Nye[31] contend that the transnational relations increase the sensitivity of societies to one another and, thereby, alter relationships between governments. They have pointed out five major effects of transnational interactions and organizations, all with direct or indirect consequences for mutual sensitivity and, thereby for inter-state politics. Four of these, they point out, may result from transnational interactions even without the presence of transnational organizations, although transnational organizations may produce them as well. The fifth effect necessarily depends on the presence of transnational organizations as autonomous or quasi-autonomous actors.

The five effects are summed up as follows:

1. *Attitudinal Changes:* These may be brought about by face-to-face interactions between citizens of different states that may alter the opinions and perceptions of reality of elites and non-elites within national societies, which may have possible consequences for state politics. New attitudes can also be fostered by transnational organizations as they create new myths, symbols and norms to provide legitimacy for their activities. It is argued that advertising by these multinational enterprises affects popular attitudes in less developed societies to the detriment of their autonomy and economic development.

2. *International Pluralism:* This means the linking of national interest groups in transnational structures, usually involving transnational organizations for purposes of coordination. There has been a rapid growth of international transnational organizations which link national organizations having common interests. The creation of such organizational linkages may in turn affect attempts by national groups to influence government policy and even contribute to internationalization of domestic politics.

3. *Dependence and Interdependence:* This is often associated with international transportation and finance movements. Integration into a world monetary system may make it impossible for a state to follow an autonomous monetary policy without drastic changes in economy, and dependence on foreign companies for technologies, capital and managerial skills may deter less-developed countries from following highly nationalistic and socialistic eco-policies. Further, where transnational organizations become important within a host society, they may alter the patterns of domestic economic policies too.

4. *Increases in Ability of Certain Governments to Influence Others:* Some governments have often attempted to manipulate transnational interactions to achieve results that are explicitly political. The use of tourists as spies or the cultivation of sympathetic ethnic or religious groups in other states are examples of such "informal penetrations". Powerful governments would always try to direct the flow of international trade or produce changes in international monetary arrangements by unilateral actions. Transnational organizations are particularly serviceable as instruments of government's foreign policy, whether through control or willing alliance. USA sought to retard the development of French nuclear capability by simply forbidding IBM-France to sell certain types of computers to the French government.

5. *Growth of Autonomous Actors:* The emergence of autonomous actors with private foreign policies many a times deliberately oppose or impinge upon state policies. Such organizations include revolutionary movements, trade unions, multinational companies and the Roman Catholic Church among others. Thus, it would not be possible to understand British–Iranian relations during 1951–1953 or American–Cuban relations between 1959–1961 without taking into account the role of certain oil companies in both the cases.[31]

Holsti[32] identifies certain roles played by non-state actors. These roles imply that these non-state actors:

1. Introduce an issue into international diplomatic agenda.
2. Publicize and raise citizen consciousness regarding certain global or regional problems.

3. Lobby national governments and international organizations to make decisions favourable to their cause.

4. Seek outcome through direct action, sometimes (though relatively rare) involving the threat or use of force.

Therefore, it can be said with certainty that any organized unit that commands the identification of interests, and loyalty of individuals, which affects inter-state relations becomes a major competitor of states as actors. If the international processes are analyzed it can be seen without doubt that there may be tussle not only between the states but also between the states and non-state actors. Examples include the United Nations and Iraq, between OPEC and the industrialized West, between PLO and Israel, between an MNC and a state in the case of toxic gas accident at Union Carbide's plant resulting in the Bhopal Gas tragedy in India. Nevertheless, it can also be said that there may be several competitors to the power and authority of the states as actors, yet the states continue to enjoy predominance over any other international non-state actor.

EXERCISES

1. What do you mean by actors in international system? Do you think that the state is the only actor in the international system? Justify your answer.

2. Discuss the crisis of territorial state in the face of globalization.

3. What do you mean by non-state actors? Examine the role of non-state actors in international relations.

4. What do you mean by national power? Discuss the elements of national power.

5. What are the main components of national power? Elucidate.

6. Bring out the significance of national interest in international politics.

REFERENCES

[1] Frankel, Joseph, *International Relations in a Changing World*, Oxford University Press, London, 1979, p. 8.

[2] Russet, Bruce and Harvey Starr, *World Politics : The Menu for Choice*, W.H. Freeman & Company, New York, 1996, pp. 74–75.

[3] *ibid.*, pp. 50–54.

[4] Palmer, Norman D. and Howard C. Perkins, *International Relations—The World Community in Transition*, A.I.T.B.S. Publishers, New Delhi, 1997, p. 10.

[5] Frankel, Joseph, *op. cit.*, n. 1, pp. 16–17.

[6] Russet and Starr, *op. cit.*, n. 2, p. 54.

[7] Palmer and Perkins, *op. cit.*, n. 4, p. 13.

[8] Frankel, *op. cit.*, n. 1, p. 20.

[9] Quoted in Vinay Kumar Malhotra, *International Relations,* Anmol Publications, New Delhi, 2006, p. 48.

[10] Couloumbis, Theodore A. and James H. Wolfe, *Introduction to International Relations: Power and Justice,* Prentice-Hall of India, New Delhi, 1981, pp. 86–87.

[11] Morgenthau, Hans J., *Politics among Nations: The Struggle for Power and Peace,* Kalyani Publishers, New Delhi, 1985, p. 31.

[12] Organski, A.F.K., *World Politics,* Alfred A. Knopf, New York, 1960, pp. 96 and 98.

[13] Padelford, Norman J. and George A. Lincoln, *International Politics: Foundations of International Relations,* The Macmillan and Co., New York, 1954, p. 193.

[14] Palmer and Perkins, *op. cit.,* n. 4, p. 35.

[15] Russet and Starr, *op. cit.,* n. 2, pp. 116–120.

[16] Padelford and Lincoln, *op. cit.,* n. 13, p. 136.

[17] Morgenthau, *op. cit.,* n. 11, p. 144.

[18] Frankel, Joseph, *National Interest,* Macmillan, London, 1970, p. 15.

[19] *ibid.,* p. 17.

[20] Couloumbis and Wolfe, *op. cit.,* n. 10, p. 113.

[21] Clinton, W. David, "The National Interest: Normative Foundation," *in* Richard Little and Michael Smith (Eds.), *Perspectives on World Politics,* Routledge, London, 1991, p. 50.

[22] Holsti, K.J., *International Politics: A Framework for Analysis,* Prentice-Hall of India, New Delhi, 1995, p. 65.

[23] Frankel, Joseph, *op. cit.,* n. 1, p. 55.

[24] Viotti, Paul R. and Mark K. Kauppi (Eds.), *International Relations Theory: Realism, Pluralism Globalism and Beyond,* Macmillan, London, 1990.

[25] Couloumbis and Wolfe, *op. cit.,* n. 10, pp. 369–370.

[26] Russet and Starr, *op. cit.,* n. 2, pp. 65–67.

[27] Holsti, *op. cit.,* n. 22, p. 61.

[28] Couloumbis and Wolfe, *op. cit.,* n. 10, pp. 370–371.

[29] Holsti, *op. cit.,* n. 22, pp. 62–63.

[30] Russet and Starr, *op. cit.,* n. 2, p. 69.

[31] Keohane, Robert O. and Joseph S. Nye, Jr. *Transnational Relations and World Politics,* Harvard University Press, Cambridge, Massachusetts, 1973, pp. xii–xxii.

[32] Holsti, *op. cit.,* n. 22, p. 64.

4

Balance of Power

CONTENTS

INTRODUCTION

The presence of states with varying degrees of power makes it necessary to study the pattern of relationship among them. If one goes by the realist assumption, the international system is unrestrained and unprotected by any international government, where states have to look after their own national interests and, obviously, national security, thereby inducing insecurity in others. Therefore, the picture that emerges is one in which "each is against the other". Though international relations may seem anarchic in the absence of any world government, yet it is not so in the sense of lawlessness and disorder.[1] The key to the puzzle, as the realists suggest, is the principle of balance of power which is "a basic principle of international relations and a fundamental law of politics as it is possible to find". The political relations of independent nations, especially the great powers, traditionally have been explained by the theory of the balance of power.[2]

83

BALANCE OF POWER

European history has experienced long periods when actual large-scale conflict did not take place. The chief reason behind this was the absence of one single sovereign authority and presence of many sovereign states, each zealously guarding its autonomy. Power was distributed in such a way that each state was able to balance the others. In theory, if any state tried to increase its power, thereby posing a threat, all the others would unite to prevent it. This was what came to be known as the *balance of power* (see Figure 4.1).

The basic assumption is that, as long as power is not abolished, it must be met by countervailing power. To rely on the goodwill of powerful neighbours would be naive and only matching power can provide adequate protection under all circumstances. *Mutual deterrence* becomes the buzzword. Any potential aggression is deterred by the potential combined powers of all the other states. Therefore, in such a case, balancing power, either by one single nation or by a group of nations, will prevent any one particular nation from imposing its will upon others. If state A increases its power, state B must try to equalize it. If B alone cannot match A's might, it can join other states and together they can offset the power of A.

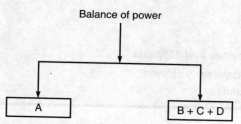

Figure 4.1   Illustration of balance of power.

The balance of power that existed in Europe during the eighteenth and nineteenth centuries are classic examples of balance of power systems. The focus was not on matching a rival's power by building up one's army but by forming a coalition of one or more other states threatened by the growing power of the rival. Thus, deterrence was achieved by alliances and not by arms races. Historically, under this kind of balance of power systems, there was no increase in the power of a single state or even in the system as a whole. Only power was re-arranged to counter aggression. States pursued independent policies and was not bound to each other by permanent alliances. Only when one state threatened the independence of another, did a group begin to coalesce to oppose the belligerent power.

There are instances when such balance of power principles became operative in Europe between 1740 and 1763. There were many alliances between France, Prussia, Saxony, Bavaria on the one hand and Austria, England and Hanover on the other in 1740–1743. In 1744–1745, the line-up was like France, Prussia and Bavaria on the one hand, and Austria, England, Hanover and Saxony on the other. In 1756–1763, the line-up was Prussia and Hanover on one side, and Austria, Russia, France and Saxony on the other. These arrangements were not fool proof and did not prevent war, but what mattered was that there was no ideological crusades as seen in the twentieth century. There was no call for "deFredericking" Prussia as the US "de-Nazified" Germany after the Second World War. Further, those wars were mainly fought over Silesia and did not result in large-scale civilian casualties although a large number of soldiers were killed.[3]

MEANING

The balance of power is one notion which is central to the study of international relations. The term is in no way an innovation of the present times and can be traced to the sixteenth century, only to be theorized in the eighteenth century and after. It appeared in treaties like the Treaty of Utrecht of 1713, in the memoirs of statesman, and in the writings of diplomats historians and lawyers. The diplomats of *Ancien Régime* (refers to the political system established in France from fourteenth century to eighteenth century under the Valois and Bourbon dynasties) considered it as the underlying principle that created stability. In the twentieth century it has been invoked many a times but the problem is that there is a lack of unanimity on the exact meaning of the term.[4] Inis L. Claude (1962) observed that "the trouble with the balance of power is not that it has no meaning but that it has too many meanings".

Professor A.F. Pollard (1923) stated that there are several thousand meanings of the phrase, but "The essential idea is simple enough: it is 'equilibrium' of the type represented by a pair of scales. When the weights in the scales are equal, balance results".

George Schwarzenberger (1951) viewed balance of power as 'an equilibrium' or "a certain amount of stability in international relations".

G. Lowes Dickinson(1926) clarified the two uses of the term 'balance'. He said that "it means, on the one hand, an equality, as of the two sides when an account is balanced, and on the other hand, an inequality, as when one has a 'balance' to one's credit at the bank". He also added "the balance of power theory professes the former, but pursues the latter".

According to Professor Sidney B. Fay (1937), balance of power is such a "just equilibrium in power among the members of the family of nations as will prevent any one of them from becoming sufficiently strong to enforce its will upon others".

Kaplan[5] in his *System and Process in International Politics,* distinguished between the balance of power system and other international systems. To him balance of power system is an international social system without a political subsystem. The actors within the system are international actors who fall within the sub-class, "national actor". 'Essential' being used as an undefined term, the number of essential actors must be at least five and preferably more.

Morgenthau in his *Politics Among Nations: The Struggle for Power and Peace* has given four meanings of the term:

1. A policy aimed at a certain state of affairs
2. An actual state of affairs
3. An approximately equal distribution of power
4. Any distribution of power.

Haas[6] has given eight mutually exclusive versions of the concept of balance of power:

1. Equilibrium resulting from equal distribution of power among nation-states.
2. Equilibrium resulting from unequal distribution of power among nation-states.
3. Equilibrium resulting from the dominance of one nation-state (the balancer).
4. A system providing for relative stability and peace.
5. A system characterized by instability and war.
6. Another way of saying power politics.
7. A universal law of history.
8. A guide for policy makers.

Kenneth Waltz[*][7] in his *Theory of International Politics* (1979) does not assume that states are self-aggrandizing and aggressive bodies but he does assume that they have a necessity to preserve themselves. Thus, they are obliged to be concerned with their security and take into considerations the existence of other states, posing to be potential threats. This induces the states to continually adjust their stance in international relations according to their reading of power of other states and their own power. The result of these movements is the emergence of the balance of power.

Hedley Bull[**][8] in his *The Anarchical Society* (1977) considers the balance of power as a kind of artefact, something that states, or a significant proportion of states, are willing to see as a desirable end and are committed to the idea and must 'want' it to work.

Despite several meanings and implications, balance of power remains, as Morgenthau pointed out, "a manifestation of a general social principle" in international relations.

---

[*]Kenneth Waltz, *Theory of International Politics,* McGraw Hill, New York, 1979 [given details in Chap 1 (p. 8)].

[**]Hedley Bull, *The Anarchical Society: A Study of Order in Politics,* Columbia University Press, New York, 1977.

The Prerequisites for Balance of Power

1. A multiplicity of states.
2. Absence of a centralized legitimate and strong authority over these sovereign actors.
3. Relatively unequal distribution of national power.
4. Requirement of a balancing power.
5. Perpetuation of existing power distribution which benefits the balancer nations mutually, i.e., status quo.[9]

From these assumptions arise a set of informal widely understood principles or rules:

1. Be suspicious of an increase in power by another country—any country. Be concerned with the capabilities, not intentions.
2. Always ally with the weaker side. Ignore considerations such as friendship or morality.
3. Support a state or group of states only until, it is out of danger. Remember that no alliance is permanent.
4. Show moderation towards the aggressor after it is defeated because no alliance is permanent; today's enemy may be tomorrow's ally.
5. Settle non-essential quarrels in peripheral areas in a way that does not disturb the central balance.[10]

Kaplan[11] also suggests certain basic rules for the functioning of the balance of power system:

1. Act to increase capabilities but negotiate rather than fight.
2. Fight rather than give up an opportunity to increase capabilities.
3. Stop fighting rather than eliminate an essential national actor.
4. Act to oppose any coalition or single actor which assumes a predominant position with respect to the rest of the system.
5. Act to constrain actors who subscribe to supranational organizing principles.
6. Permit defeated or constrained essential national actors to re-enter the system as acceptable role partners or act to bring some previously inessential actor within the essential actor classification.
7. Treat all essential actors as acceptable role partners.

Characteristics of Balance of Power System

Professor Palmer and Perkins have enumerated certain basic characteristics of balance of power system:

- The term 'balance of power' itself suggests equilibrium but it is subjected to constant changes, i.e., from equilibrium to disequilibrium.
- Nicholas J. Spykman (1942) remarked that balance of power is not "a gift of the gods" and it must be achieved by "the active intervention of man". States cannot wait until it 'happens' if they are willing to survive, and as Spykman says, that "they must be willing to go to war to preserve a balance against the growing hegemonic power of the period.
- Balance of power tends to be in favour of status quo; but to be effective, a balance of power policy must be changing and should be a dynamic one.
- A real balance of power rarely exists and its real test, presumably, is war. When war actually breaks, the whole system gets upset.
- It offers both subjective approach of a statesman and an objective approach of a historian. As was observed by Martin Wight (1946) who suggested that the difference in the perspectives of a historian and a statesman is that "The historian will say that there is a balance when the opposing groups seem to him to be equal in power. The statesman will say that there is a balance when he thinks that his side is stronger than the other. And he will say that his country *holds* the balance, when it has freedom to join one side or the other according to its own interests". Hence, states, which play the game of balance, actually indulge in imbalance—in their favour.
- The balance of power game is a game for the great states although small and weaker states are vitally concerned with the outcome; they become mere spectators, or more often victims, rather than players.
- To maintain the balance there is a need for a balancer.

Hartman[12] looking back into history, identified four types of balance of power process since 1815.

1. "The balancer form in which the balancer promotes flexibility to a simple, two-bloc form restraining either bloc".
2. "The Bismarckian form in which the potential troublemaker is restrained by isolating her through a complex and flexible alliance system built on the utilization of the counter balancing interests of other powers".
3. "The Munich Era form in which the flexibility stems from the lack of coordination of interests upon the part of the likely victims of attack".
4. "The simple two bloc form such as existed in 1907–1914 and again from 1949–1963 or so, in which each bloc is the direct sole deterrent or restraining influence upon the other".

TECHNIQUES/DEVICES AND METHODS

There are different techniques of maintaining the balance of power system. These are now briefly discussed.

1. *Alliances and Counter-Alliances:*   These are the most commonly used devices for maintaining the balance of power. If one state increases its strength, its adversaries have no other option but to balance it by forming coalitions against it. This has happened quite often in Europe, where, whenever one particular state threatened the balance in Europe, other states formed coalitions against it. Coalitions of one group of states may be met by counter-coalitions formed by another group of states. Twentieth century Europe saw two such alliances and counter-alliances, one of them being the Triple Entente formed by France, England and Russia in 1907 as a response to the Triple Alliance of Imperial Germany, Austria–Hungary and Italy. Another was the Axis formed in 1936 to counter the alliance between France and European nations. Again, the Allied powers formed a coalition against the Axis power during the Second World War.

Alliances can be both offensive and defensive, and even a world balance or a regional balance. It is not too much to say that balance of power considerations, whether regional, hemispheric or worldwide, are a controlling factor in virtually every alliance formed by states. This has proved to be true during the Cold War days when the United States formed several military regional arrangements such as NATO, SEATO, CENTO and others, with West European States, Central Asian states and Pakistan, which were countered by Soviet led coalitions like the WARSAW Pact.

2. *Compensations:*   Morgenthau points out that "the bargaining of diplomatic negotiations issuing in political compromise is but the principle of compensation in the most general form, and as such it is originally connected with the balance of power". Compensation usually involves annexation or division of territory. Territorial compensations have been frequently used by powerful states at the expense of the smaller and weaker ones and by victorious powers at the end of a war. Between 1870 and 1914, this principle was applied on a large-scale, resulting in distribution of colonial territories and the delineation of spheres of influence in China and elsewhere, among the European powers. Partition or division of territories has also been used in the maintenance of balance of power. A Plethora of examples are available in this regard, like the division of the Spanish possessions in Europe and outside among the Hapsburg and the Bourbons under the Treaty of Utrecht, the partition of Poland and later its division among Russia, Prussia and Austria, partition of Germany by the Treaty of Versailles and again after the Second World War among Britain, France, Russia and the United States, and division of Korea and Vietnam after the Second World War.

3. *Buffer States:*   Geo-strategically, some states may be placed in between some powerful states in such a way that they tend to keep rival powers out of direct contact with each other. They come to constitute a buffer between the two. Palmer and Perkins point out that buffer states are of great importance because of their cushioning effect between the great powers. They may be neutral or neutralized states, satellite states or dependent territories, or even may be actively associated with one of two or more aggregations of power in a relatively honourable way.

One of the important buffer regions of the world has been the one separating the Soviet Union from the non-Communist powers, an area comprising weak states, vast distances, geographical barriers, conflicting interests of superpowers during the post-War period and rising nationalisms. This may roughly correspond to the idea of a large part of the *Inner Crescent* of Mackinder and the *Rimland* of Spykman. Afghanistan long served as a buffer state between Russia and pre-independent India. Similarly, Tibet was also a buffer between China and India during the British India and even during the initial years of independence of India. But in both the cases, the Soviet intervention in Afghanistan in 1979 disturbed its buffer status, and recent Chinese occupation of Tibet has destroyed its buffer character. Nepal and Bhutan also serve as a buffer between China and India. Thus both India and China follow a cautious foreign policy towards Nepal and Bhutan. Several lines, such as the 17th Parallel in Vietnam and the 38th Parallel in Korea, also serve similar purposes, as that of the buffer states.

4. Armaments and Disarmaments: Military power is vital for the survival of a state and is directly linked to the maintenance of the security of that particular state. Therefore, states put great emphasis on their military preparedness, either in terms of their conventional forces or nuclear arsenal. The fact is that military preparedness of one state makes it a necessity for another state to follow the suit. This leads to a perilous and unending arms race and intensified rivalries among the major powers, as it had happened in the post-War era between the United States and the Soviet Union, and as it happens in every part of the globe. India and Pakistan are again contenders in the South Asian region and arms race between them tends to disturb the balance in the region. India, vis-à-vis its neighbour to match the Chinese prowess, pursues a policy of improvising and adding to its military arsenal, conventional and nuclear armaments, which again is most likely to send shocks to her South Asian neighbours, especially Pakistan, and escalate an arms race in the region.

But constant arms race increases the fear of destruction. Therefore, in theory, a more stable balance of power can be attained by ending the armament race and proportionately reducing the armaments. The first effort towards disarmament was the Treaty of Versailles of 1919 and then the Washington Naval Treaty of 1922. Following the reduction of tension between the two superpowers, both have attempted to reduce their armament efforts and have signed many accord in this regard like the Partial Test Ban Treaty (PTBT) of 1963, Strategic Arms Limitation Treaty (SALT-I) of 1972 and SALT-II of 1979, Intermediate Range Nuclear Force (INF) Treaty of 1987 and the Strategic Arms Reduction Treaty (START) of 1991. Globally, several disarmament efforts have also been taken up by the United Nations, such as the Non Proliferation Treaty (NPT), Comprehensive Test Ban Treaty (CTBT), the

Chemical Weapons Treaty and others. But the problem with disarmament is that the state, which disarms first, runs a serious risk. Therefore, disarmament is often discussed and its practice involves difficulties until there are assurances that all will disarm together in such a way that it will not disturb the current distribution of power. As this assurance is lacking in most cases, disarmament measures are looked upon with suspicion and this is the primary reason why most states having the potential to develop nuclear power refrained from signing the NPT and the CTBT. They feared a nuclear hegemony of the nuclear haves and their calculative measures to prevent the have-nots from joining the nuclear club.

5. *Intervention and Non-Intervention:* Intervention is a weapon used by a powerful state, usually the balancer to intervene, in the internal affairs of another state to extract certain concessions necessary to preserve the status quo in the existing balance of power. There have been several instances where such interventions have taken place. Germany intervened in the Spanish Civil War in favour of General Franco, Britain in Greece, the United States in Cuba, Lebanon, Laos, Guatemala, and others and the Soviet Union in North Korea, Hungary, Czechoslovakia, Afghanistan and elsewhere. In the post-Cold War world, there have been cases of intervention by the United States in the Middle-East in Iraq, Kuwait and Afghanistan.

Again, non-intervention is a kind of policy usually followed by the powerful states as well as the small states, which satisfies the political order and follows peaceful methods to preserve the balance. Unlike Germany, France and Britain followed the policy of non-intervention in the Spanish Civil War.

6. *Divide and Rule:* This had been a policy pursued for long to preserve the balance of power by making the competitors divide among themselves. It had been used by the Romans to maintain their control over the scattered people. The French had prominently used this policy towards Germany ever since the seventeenth century. The British had historically pursued this policy towards the Continent. In the post-War period, when the world politics was ripped apart by the tensions between the two superpowers, generally known as Cold War, this policy again came to feature in the foreign policy orientations of the superpowers. Both the superpowers aimed at keeping the rival camps, i.e., Western and Eastern Europe disintegrated and divided in order to retain a balance as well as preserve their spheres of influence.[13]

Criticism

The balance of power theory was an attempt on the part of some of the international relations scholars to devise a law for international politics like other sciences. But the greatest difficulty one faces in the field of international relations is in the application of the theories derived from other disciplines. Therefore, it becomes difficult to accept the idea of balance of power just because it is old and a respectable theory.

Most scholars have come up with their suggestions that the principles of the theory are correct but the altered conditions prevent the balance of power system from operating correctly. As Morgenthau pointed out "...the balance of power in international affairs is only a particular manifestation of a general social principle to which all societies composed of a number of autonomous units owe their autonomy; that the balance of power and policies aiming at its preservation are not inevitable but are an essential stabilizing factor in a society of sovereign nations; and that the instability of the international balance of power is due not to the faultiness of the principle but to the particular conditions under which the principle must operate in a society of sovereign states".[14]

Organski points out several drawbacks of the concept. To him, the concept is based on erroneous assumptions that nations are fundamentally static units whose power is not changed from within and also the assumption that nations have no permanent ties with each other but move freely, motivated primarily by consideration of power. He says that nations are not static units that increase their power only through military aggressions, territorial aggrandizements and alliances. Given the modern changes in the pattern of international relations, nations can change by mobilizing national sentiments, improving the efficiency of social organizations, and by industrialization. Such increase and shifts in power cannot be counteracted through traditional mechanisms of the balance of power because a variety of economic, technological and socio-cultural changes may lead to the breakdown of one actor and the emergence of another. A theory which assumes that the major road to national power lies in waging wars and forming alliances has missed the most important developments of modern times.

He further contends that nations are not free to make and break alliances at will for power considerations alone. Even the 'balancer' is often not in a position to change sides whenever the distribution of power changes. The truth is that a nation selects its friends and foes depending upon its national interest, which may range from purely military-strategic to political, economic, cultural, and even psychological. It supports a nation as long as its national interest is best served from the preservation of the present international order and opposes those, who tend to disturb or seek a change in status quo.

Organski also points out that there is no such thing as a 'balancer' and never has been so. England, which was long thought to be playing a role of a balancer, actually was motivated by its self-interest and acted in world politics in such a way to uphold her preponderance of power, and not a balance at all.[15]

The other truth lies in the fact that balance of power does not ensure peace. On the contrary, almost all greatest wars recorded in modern history have occurred at times when one of the challengers balanced the preponderant power or when, through miscalculation, a challenger thought that its power was as great as that of its rivals.

Morgenthau[16] has forwarded a threefold criticism of the concept of balance of power. He has pointed out the uncertainty, unreality and inadequacy of the balance of power concept.

1. Uncertainty: Morgenthau points out that if balance of power is conceived mechanically, it would require an easily recognizable quantitative criterion by which the relative power of a number of nations can be measured and compared. It is only by means of such a criterion it can be ascertained that a particular nation tends to be more powerful than another or they tend to maintain a balance of power among themselves. But in reality, it is difficult to make quantitative measurement of power, and national power is composed of so many elements that the quality of these components is also subjected to constant change. Thus, rational calculation of the relative strength of several nations becomes a series of guesses, the correctness of which is doubtful. The uncertainty of power calculation is inherent in the nature of national power itself. This uncertainty is, however, magnified when the weights in one or the other or in both scales are composed not only of single units but also of several nations forming alliances.

2. Unreality: The uncertainty of power calculations incapacitates the balance of power system from operating and also leads to its very negation in practice. Since nations are incapable of calculating the distribution of national power, they will at least attempt to make sure that whatever error they might commit in calculation, these will not land them in serious disadvantage in the competition of power and that they have a margin of safety.

Thus, in the struggle for power, nations actually aim not at a balance, which is equality of power, but a superiority of power in their favour. The limitless aspiration for power is always present in the mindset of nations and this transforms into an armament race which ultimately may cause war. Preventive war, however, abhorred in diplomatic language and abhorrent to democratic public opinion is, in fact, a natural outgrowth of the balance of power. The First World War is a pointer in that direction. The use of balance of power as an ideology aggravates difficulties and dangers inherent in the mechanics of the balance of power.

3. Inadequacy: Morgenthau observed that the actual contribution made by the balance of power system in the seventeenth, eighteenth and nineteenth centuries had helped in the establishment of stability of the modern state system and the preservation of the independence of its members. But it was not the balance of power system alone that helped in achieving these things; there were other factors such as the restraining influence of moral consensus present in Europe. Morgenthau also observed that the balance of power thus assumes a reality and function that it actually does not have and therefore, tends to disguise, rationalize and justify international politics as it actually is.

RELEVANCE OF BALANCE OF POWER

Based on the criticisms and shortcomings, Organski has asked the scholars of international relations to reject the balance of power theory because its concepts are fuzzy, it is logically unsound, full of contradictions, inconsistent with the events that have occurred, and fails to explain such events.

Richard Cobden[17] (1867) commented, "The balance of power is a chimera! It is not a fallacy, a mistake, an imposture—it is an undescribed, indescribable, incomprehensible nothing; mere words, conveying to the mind not ideas, but sounds".

Even the rules or the basic principles propounded by the balance of power theorists are not applicable in the ever-changing scenario of international relations. For example, the principles propounded by Morton Kaplan in 1957 hardly hold today. He had prescribed how the statesmen should or ought to behave rather than how they actually behave. Further, his rule 6, "treat all major powers as acceptable partners" is hardly tenable because, in the present context, given the importance of public opinion and a simultaneous increase in nationalism, it is not possible for a state to ally with another disregarding these restraining factors. Further, during the Cold War it was witnessed that ideological differences delayed the rapprochement between the United States and China for long.

Neither of the rules seems to be valid in contemporary international relations. A total all-out war now might lead to extremes and any unsuccessful venture might lead to loss of popular support as happened in the case of US during the Vietnam War. Moreover, if public opinion swings between interventionism and isolationism, it becomes difficult for a state to oppose a dangerously growing opponent. There can also be a system change without a great war as it had occurred in the Soviet Union.

Moreover, the spread of weapons of mass destruction, for example, the nuclear weapons, has created situations which are quite different from the pre-nuclear international scenario. The possession of nuclear weapons may work as a deterrent and induce the leaders to use the force with restraint and prevent escalation of small wars to big ones. Nevertheless, this situation, commonly known as **mutually assured destruction,** also creates a kind of balance of power where the nuclear might of a state matches with that of its adversaries. This is, however, a balance of terror, and not of power, as it was evidenced during the Cold War days between the United States and the Soviet Union, which reached a climax during the Cuban Missile Crisis in 1962. However, even during the climax, both powers restrained from using nuclear power though usage would have given a lead to one over the other. Therefore, even if major wars are less frequent in a nuclear world than in a conventional system, the high intensity of such wars probably cancels out the gains from the wars. This situation is sometimes referred to as *Pax Atomica*.

Prof. Palmer and Perkins pointed out the difficulties that balance of power faced in a bipolarized world:

1. The confusing bipolar–multipolar pattern of power and the disappearance of a balancer

2. The sudden increase in the power of the offensive over the defensive and the character and the frightening implications of total war

3. Ideological considerations and other less tangible elements of power

4. The increasing disparities in the power of the states, with the superpowers becoming more powerful and the lesser states becoming weaker, at least in relative terms.[18]

Presently, with the dissolution of one of the superpowers, the post-Cold War situation drastically changed the power equation between the two poles. There was no such power transition as suggested by Organski when he said that "if great change occurs within a single lifetime, both challenger and dominant nation may find it difficult to estimate their relative power correctly, and may stumble into a war that would never have been fought if both sides had foreseen where the victory would lie". Systemic changes took place without a general war. The changes in relative strength came from the differing economic growth rate and from the loss of allies of the Soviet Union. This left the United States as the unchallenged dominant actor in world politics. But again, another question seems to be coming up whether a united Western Europe will be an ally or become a competitor of the United States. Although the United States at present seems to be the unchallenged power, there are also several power centres and the international system tends to become multipolar. Therefore, the functioning of the balance of power system in such a multipolar world cannot be ruled out completely. As US Secretary of State, Lawrence Eagleburger proclaimed in 1989 that "We are now moving into... a world in which power and influence [are] diffused among a multiplicity of states – [a] multipolar world". Scholars suggest that such multipolar system is more likely to consist of the United States, China, Germany, Japan, Russia and a consolidated European Union. They envisage that such multipolarity will result in an enlarged global chessboard of multiple bilateral geo-strategic relationships.[19]

COLLECTIVE SECURITY

Balance of power, as a method of crisis management, is a lesser used method, and a modern device of collective action by international community, has become a more viable option. **Collective security**, as it is popularly known, has become a device that seeks to confront the would-be aggressors or aggressors with concerted power of states, determined to keep peace. Collective security, though at a glance might seem simplistic and self-explanatory, is difficult to define.

As Quincy Wright (1942) observed: "The relations of the balance of power to collective security have...been at the same time complementary and antagonistic". It is not antithetic but supplementary and "International organization to promote collective security is ... only a planned development of the natural tendency of balance of power policies", and, again, the basic assumptions of the two are different. The substance of collective security is the creation of a world front against a possible aggressor and that of balance of power is to approximately equal the opposing fronts. But collective security involves a far greater degree of systematization than balance of power. As Inis Claude observed: "Balance of power is a system only by courtesy; while the accusation that it amounts to anarchy is too strong, it is assuredly a most unsystematic system ... Collective security, on the other hand, represents the urge for systematization, the institutionalization of international relations".[20]

Collective security is based on the principle that "Aggression against any one member of the international community is an aggression against international peace and security. As such it has to be met by collective efforts of all the nations". It stands for "One for All and All for One".

An effective collective security system should be strong enough and capable to meet any aggression from any power or combination of powers invoked as soon as aggression occurs. George Schwarzenberger[*] (an eminent scholar on power politics) observed collective security as a "machinery for joint action in order to prevent or counter any attack against an established international order". Organski[21] stated that collective security is not a scheme to keep some nations in check and not others. Rather, it is a plan by which any nation that uses force illegally is defeated. Organski underlined the five basic assumptions of collective security:

1. In any armed combat, all nations will agree on which combatant is the aggressor.

2. All nations are equally interested in restraining aggression from whatever source it comes.

3. All nations are equally free and able to join in action against the aggressor.

4. The combined power of the collectivity will be great enough to defeat the aggressor.

5. Knowing that overwhelming power stands ready to be used against it, an aggressor nation will either sheathe its sword or go down in defeat.

Morgenthau[22] highlights three basic conditions that must be fulfilled for the successful operation of collective security as a device to prevent war:

1. The collective security system must be able to gather, at all times, such overwhelming strength against any potential aggressor or coalition of aggressors that the latter would not dare to challenge the order defended by the collective system.

2. At least those nations whose combined strength would meet the requirements under the first principle must have the same conception of security which they are supposed to defend.

---

*George Schwarzenberger, *Power Politics*, 2nd rev. ed. (New York: Frederick A. Praeger, 1951), p. 8.

3. Those nations must be willing to subordinate their conflicting political interests to the common good defined in terms of the collective defence of all member states.

Under the League of Nations, the sanctions against Italy following the Italo–Ethiopia War in 1935–1936 and the United Nations intervention, in defence of the territorial integrity of South Korea, following an invasion from North Korea in 1950 and 1953, are examples of application of the principle of collective security.

The League of Nations failed drastically to implement the provisions of collective security as contained in Article 16 of the Covenant of the League. It was never implemented. The League was impaired from the beginning due to the abstention of the superpowers like the United States to join it and also due to mutual rivalries among the member states, each zealously guarding its national interest. The League failed to take effective measures either during the Manchurian crisis or against the acts of aggression by Nazi Germany, culminating in the attack of Poland. It was only during the Italo–Ethiopian crisis that the League, for once, made extensive effort to implement the collective security provisions. As Claude observed, "The league experience might be summarized as an abortive attempt to translate the collective security idea into a working system. The failure of collective security in this period was not so much the failure of the system to operate successfully as its failure to be established".[23]

The Charter of the United Nations contains provisions relating to collective security. Article I of the Charter stating the purposes and principles of the UN, aims at maintaining international peace and security as its top priority and, to that end declares to take effective collective measures for the prevention and removal of threats to peace. Chapter VII of the Charter with regard to *Action with respect to Threats to the Peace, Breaches of the Peace, and Acts of Aggression* contains provisions from Articles 39–51 relating to the collective security system. The Charter invests supreme power on the Security Council to initiate collective security action in cases of breach of international peace of security. The United Nations evoked the collective security measures during the Korean crisis of 1950. Another test of the collective security system came during the Congo crisis of 1960. The more current operation includes the one during Iraq's invasion of Kuwait in 1991. But it was more so on the insistence and preponderance of the United States that the collective actions were taken. The 2003 invasion of Iraq by the United States on the plea of eliminating weapons of mass destruction, and USA's War on Terror against Afghanistan, were unilateral decisions and the United Nations was bypassed in these cases of intervention. This has undermined the credibility of collective action measures under the auspices of the United Nations. Further, during the heydays of Cold War, the superpower relations affected the operation of Security Council and hence the implementation of collective security system. The international community has failed to evolve a workable system of collective security for the preservation of peace and security.

Since the end of the First World War, there were active initiatives among the states to develop the system of collective security. But the machinery of collective security has never been developed effectively. Hence, the success rate of operation of the principle is low. It is a vague principle underlying the obligation of states coming together to uphold some vague obligations and perform unspecified actions in response to hypothetical events brought out by some unidentifiable state.[24] Inis Claude observed that this concept of collective security has been much talked about, persistently advocated and attacked, defended and criticized, but efforts towards developing this as a working principle in managing international relations have often been thwarted.

A survey of historic experiences has revealed that the nature of international politics is such that conflicts of interest would continue and this would create obstruction in banding together of states. Furthermore, under the assumptions of collective security, any war anywhere in the world assumes the stature of the World War. Therefore, instead of localizing an actual or threatened conflict between two or more states, the collective security system has the potential to make war universal. It is a dangerous principle to operate, as Morgenthau points out, and it is bound to destroy peace among all states.

Therefore, collective security in essence has not been totally disbanded but, as operation of the principle becomes difficult, the United Nations has its own peacekeeping mechanisms which in essence contain the principle of collective action in order to ensure international peace and security.

EXERCISES

1. Explain the concept of balance of power pointing out its characteristic features. Discuss the different techniques of maintaining balance of power.

2. What do you mean by Balance of Power? What are the various techniques of balance of power? Discuss whether the concept is still relevant in the contemporary world.

3. Analyze the concept of collective security. Is it a substitute for balance of power system?

REFERENCES

[1] Brown, Chris, *Understanding International Relations*, Macmillan Press, London, 1997, p. 103.

[2] Organski, A.F.K., *World Politics*, Alfred A. Knopf, New York, 1960, p. 270.

[3] Ziegler, David W., *War, Peace and International Politics*, Little Brown & Company, Boston, 1987, pp. 165–173.

[4] Brown, Chris, *op. cit.*, n. 1, pp. 104–105.

[5] Kaplan, Morton A., *System and Process in International Politics*, Wiley&Sons, New York, 1957, pp. 22–23.

[6] Hass, Ernst, "The Balance of Power: Prescription, Concept, or Propaganda", *World Politics*, Vol. 5, July 1953, pp. 442–477 cited in Theodore A. Couloumbis and James H. Wolfe, *Introduction to International Relations: Power and justice*, Prentice-Hall of India, New Delhi, 1981, p. 43.

[7] Brown, Chris, *op. cit.*, n. 1, p. 47.

[8] *ibid.*, p. 109.

[9] Couloumbis and Wolfe, *op. cit.*, n. 6, p. 43.

[10] Ziegler, David W., *op. cit.*, n. 3.

[11] Padelford, Norman J. and George A.Lincoln, *International Politics: Foundations of International Relations,* The Macmillan & Co, New York, 1954, pp. 213–215.

[12] Hartman, F.H., *The Relations of Nations,* The Macmillan Company, New York, 1967, p. 368.

[13] Palmer and Perkins, *op. cit*, n. 12, p. 224–227.

[14] Morgenthau, Hans J., *Politics Among Nations: The Struggle for Power and Peace*, Kalyani Publishers, New Delhi, 1985, pp. 187.

[15] Organski, *op. cit.*, n. 2, pp. 287–297.

[16] Morgenthau, *op. cit.,* n. 16, pp. 223–233.

[17] Organski, *op. cit.*, n. 2, pp. 298.

[18] Palmer and Perkins, *op. cit.*, n. 12, p. 231.

[19] Kegley, Charles W., Jr. and Eugene R. Wittkopf, *World Politics—Trends and Transformation,* St. Martin's Press, New York, 1997, pp. 458–459.

[20] Palmer and Perkins, *op. cit.*, n. 12, p. 242.

[21] Organski, *op. cit.*, n. 2, p. 373.

[22] Morgenthau, *op. cit.*, n. 16, p. 452.

[23] Palmer and Perkins, *op. cit.*, n. 12, p. 246.

[24] *ibid.*, p. 241.

5

Foreign Policy—Concepts and Techniques

INTRODUCTION

States as units of international system cannot remain isolated from each other. Especially, in this age of growing interdependence, there are always reasons for interactions among them. Their interactions constitute what is known as the **international processes.** These interactions are best reflected by the policies pursued by the states towards other states. These policies are generally identified as the foreign policies which involve regulating and conducting external relations of the states, with respect to others in the international scenario.

DEFINITIONS OF FOREIGN POLICY

To put in simple terms, foreign policy is the output of the state into a global system. 'Policy' is generally considered as "a guide to an action or a set of actions intended to realize the goals of an organization that it has set for itself" which involves 'choice' or choosing actions (or making decisions) to achieve one's goal. 'Foreign' implies those territorially sovereign units that exist beyond the legal boundaries of a particular state. That is to say, anything beyond that legal territorial boundary, not under the legal authority of the state concerned, is foreign. Therefore, "foreign policy" is considered to be a set of guidelines to choices being made about people, places and things beyond the boundaries of the state concerned.[1]

Padelford and Lincoln[2] point out that foreign policy consists of courses of actions which a state generally undertakes to realize its national objectives beyond the limits of its own jurisdiction. They further contend that foreign policy of a state is "something more than a mere collection of several specific policies which it pursues with respect to individual countries". A state's foreign policy takes into account several factors such as an estimate of its own power and capabilities, the broad principles of conduct which the state holds and its government advocates with respect to international affairs, the specific objective of national interest which the state seeks for itself in foreign relations as well as for the course of world affairs generally. Foreign policy also involves the strategies and commitments and tactics which are undertaken for the realization of a state's objectives and interests.

There are others who have tried to give a definition of foreign policy. C.C. Rodee and others in *Introduction to Political Science* (1957) defines foreign policy as involving "the formulation and implementation of a group of principles which shape the behaviour of a state while negotiating with (contracting) other states to protect or further its vital interest". Professor Charles Burton Marshall (*The Exercise of Sovereignty*, 1965) defines foreign policy as "the course of action undertaken by authority of state and intended to affect situations beyond the span of its jurisdiction". According to Prof. F.S. Northedge (The Nature of Foreign Policy, in F.S. Northedge (Ed.) *The Foreign Policies of Powers*, 1968) foreign policy implies "the use of political influence in order to induce other states to exercise their law-making power in a manner desired by the state concerned: it is an interaction between forces originating outside the country's borders and those working within them". Frankel sees foreign policy as consisting of "decisions and actions which involve to some appreciable extent relations between one state and others" (all these definitions are cited in Sharma and Sharma).[3]

George Modelski[4] (*A Theory of Foreign Policy*, 1962) defined foreign policy as "the system of activities evolved by communities for changing the behaviour of other states and for adjusting their own activities to the international environment". But scholars like Mahendra Kumar (*Theoretical Aspects of International Politics*, 1995) have pointed out the limitations of such a definition. According to Mahendra Kumar the definition of foreign policy should "include within its range all activities of a state to regulate the behaviour of other states, either through change or status quo, in order to ensure the maximum service of its interest". To him foreign policy should be conceived of "as a thought-out course of action for achieving objectives in foreign relations as dictated by the ideology of national interest".

Whatever may be the definitions of foreign policy, the important point is that foreign policy involving the process of creating decisions, making decisions or implementing decisions is 'relational'. It is 'relational' in the sense that the intention of foreign policy is to influence the behaviour of other actors because nothing is equal in the international system. Every state requires resources, economic goods, military know-how, political and strategic support, and cooperation of others as well as coordination with all other actors. Foreign policy, as both process and output, is also a link between the activities taking place within a state and the world environment outside it. James Rosenau (*Domestic Sources of Foreign Policy*, 1967; *Linkage Politics*; *Essays on the Convergence of the National and International System*, 1969 and *The Scientific Study of Foreign Policy*, 1971) considers foreign policy as a "bridging discipline" that "takes as its focus of study the bridges that whole systems called nation-states build to link themselves and their subsystems to even more encompassing international systems of which they are a part".[5]

On the whole, it can be said that foreign policies are strategies devised by governments to guide their actions in the international arena. Therefore, they spell out the basic objectives that the state leaders have decided to pursue in a given relationship or situation as the general means by which they intend to realize their basic objectives. The arduous task before the decision-makers is to identify the political, economic and psychological needs of their country and also to recognize the limitations involved in their pursuit and to work out "a well-defined and well-ordered set of foreign policy objectives".[6]

OBJECTIVES OF FOREIGN POLICY

Professor Jayantanuja Bandyopadhyaya (*The Making of India's Foreign Policy*, 1970) perceives the making of foreign policy as a continuous exercise in the choice of ends and means on the part of the nation-state in an international setting. A broad end or goal is necessary to give a sense of direction to foreign policy.

Broadly speaking, by foreign policy objectives, one means those things that statesmen pursue in the course of their interactions with other states. Objectives evolve, and there is hardly any consensus on how those objectives are best pursued or what the foreign policy objectives should be. This brings us to a discussion on the relation between objectives and strategy or between ends and means. Few things thought of as objectives appear to be ends in themselves, but are rather means for the achievement of still more abstract or distant ends (happiness, security, success, prestige, etc.) and objectives, which originated as a means of attaining something sometimes become an end in itself. The commonly cited example is that of the United States, objective of winning the war in Korea and Vietnam. The real motive was to contain communism which in turn was ultimately linked to the US interest to maintain stability in the international system to protect American security. Again, the objective of winning the Vietnam War was containing communism but gradually it became an end in itself because the reputation of the policy-makers depends upon the victory in the war although it became evident that the outcome of the Vietnam War was surely going to weaken the US and place the communists in a favourable position.[7]

Therefore, according to Legg and Morrison[8], a rational policy-making process to a large extent is the process of organizing clear and reliable, (i.e., the means actually lead to the desired end) means–ends chain, controlling the tendency of means to become ends in themselves and seeing that the original and more fundamental objectives are kept in perspective.

Holsti[9] identifies objectives of the states, which he arranges according to the priorities depending upon a variety of external circumstances and domestic pressures as:

- Security
- Autonomy
- Welfare in the broadest sense
- Status and prestige.

Not all the states pursue similar kinds of priorities and there may be options between 'guns' and 'butter'. Foreign policy objectives can, therefore, be described as "the discovery of goals as much as it involves using decisions to achieve particular outcomes". The objectives, may include projecting "image of future state of affairs and future conditions that governments through individual policy makers aspire to bring about by wielding influence abroad and by changing or sustaining the behavior of other states". Objectives may be immediate, concrete or abstract, long-term or less concrete. Expansion of territory like China's aim in Tibet, or China's boundary tussles with India, and the wars fought and persisting animosity over the border issues, several wars in the Middle East like the Iran–Iraq war over the control of Shatt al-Arab, or Iraq's attack on Kurdistan may be seen as involving concrete objectives. Promotion of specific set of values like "making the world safe for democracy", creating a new world order, such as the demand for New International Economic Order, or "War on Terror" may be visualized as long-term and abstract objectives. Sometimes governments pursue incompatible objectives, either incompatible with the objectives of another state as was the case during the Cold War days between the United States and the Soviet Union, or incompatible with their domestic objectives. This was the case with the Nixon administration's wheat deal with the Soviet Union in 1971–1972 which on the one hand aimed to help in the betterment of relations with the Soviet Union, thereby facilitating American withdrawal from Vietnam and on the other hand tried to control inflation, prices of foods and ensuring the well-being of American society.

Undoubtedly, the ends that the states seek vary from one state to another depending on several factors such as geo-strategic location, needs, political culture, national interests and power factors. From the many aims of states, Padelford and Lincoln have identified four basic aims:

1. National security
2. Economic advancement
3. Safeguarding or augmenting national powering relation to other states
4. International prestige.

Generally speaking, a wide range of private and public objectives, some concrete, some abstract and some incompatible, are pursued by states. To the realists, these objectives appear to be solely concerned with military/security issues, and not involving economic ones. For the transnationalists, the objectives involve long-term economic and social welfare as well as security, issues, but not solely military objectives, like the realists.

DETERMINANTS OF FOREIGN POLICY

Various factors influence the making of foreign policy of a particular country. Even the basic determinants vary in importance according to circumstances. It is impossible to lay down any general rule regarding the relative importance of each of these factors or a scale of priorities which the decision-makers must permanently adhere to in making their policy decisions. Nevertheless, certain basic determinants can be identified which most of the states take into account while making their policy.

Among the **domestic determinants or internal determinants** the most significant ones are discussed now.

1. *Geography:* Perhaps this is the most stable determinant of foreign policy. This includes the size of the territory, topography, location relative to sea and landmasses relative to other nations and control of strategic places.

Size means the total landmass that a state controls or exercises its sovereign authority on. But a large area contributes only to a state's power if it is capable of providing it with the capacity of containing a large population and a large and varied supply of natural resources.

More important than size is the geo-strategic **location** of the state in the sense that the position of a state in relationship to other land bodies and to other states profoundly affects the culture, economy and both its military and economic powers. The insularity of Great Britain and the isolated position of the United States have greatly affected the foreign policy decisions of those states.

Climate is another geographical feature that plays a crucial role in determining a state's foreign policy. Extremes of climate make functioning and development of a modern industrial society difficult. Climate does affect national power of states and, therefore, its foreign policy through its direct impact on agriculture, which is required to support its population.

Topography is another important geographical feature affecting foreign policy decisions. It not only determines the density of population which a region can support, but also the climate of the land. Wind, rainfall, temperature and, consequently, soil conditions are influenced by the position of the land, sea and mountains. The strategic position of mountains, valleys, rivers and plains and deserts not only helps in communication but also in matters of security like the Himalayas, the Alps which are like natural barriers.

Natural resources of a state improve its bargaining capacity, internationally. Huge possession of resources does not add up to one's strength but the utilization of the particular product does. Thus, huge quantities of oil have helped the West Asian and Gulf countries to embark on the policy of oil diplomacy. The most noteworthy incident that shook the international economy was the oil embargo by the OPEC countries in 1973. Self-sufficiency in food, mineral and energy resources has also helped the United States and Russian foreign policy choices.

2. *History and Culture:* The political tradition of a state has its roots in its history and culture. The historical and cultural traditions provide the basic guidelines for formulating the basic foreign policy objectives. The bitter experiences of colonialism, imperialism and racialism have strengthened the resolve of many countries for developing anti-imperialist, anti-colonial and anti-racist stance. Gandhi's idea of *ahimsa* (non-violence) and India's policy of *peaceful coexistence*, as reflected in the **panchsheel**, also have roots in the history and culture of the country.

3. *Economic Development:* The economic performance of a state in terms of GNP provides the key to understanding the state's ability to utilize its natural and human resources which, in turn, influences its foreign policy choices and menu. The United States, by far the largest economy recording the highest GNP, is always able to secure its foreign policy objectives vis-à-vis underdeveloped and developing states, and to some extent in relation to certain developed states too, such as Britain and France. The levels of high economic development provide leverage to the countries to flex their muscles in their relations with economically weak countries. The developing world, to a great extent, is dependent on the developed world for capital, technology and military research and development and supply of armaments. This places them in a disadvantageous position and they have serious impediments in pursuing an independent foreign policy. The level of economic development also determines the state's ability to gear up its military preparedness and improvise its military capabilities, which in turn determines its foreign policy objectives. Economic power has worked as a positive leverage for USA, whereas economic decline has worked as a negative factor in the case of Russia as far as their foreign policy stances are concerned.

4. *National Interest:* To the realists, 'national interest' is the key factor in determining a state's behaviour with respect to other states. National interest, whether political, economic or military, changes with the changing needs of time and circumstances either in the domestic front or internationally. But undoubtedly, national interest while formulating the of foreign policy of a state, is of supreme importance.

5. *National Character and National Morale:* Though many scholars disregard the importance of **national character** as an important input of foreign policy because of its metaphysical overtones, yet national character finds expression in international relations through the perceptions, reactions and behaviour patterns of decision-makers. As Prof. Jayantanuja Bandyopadhyaya suggests if worship of wealth and power are regarded as chief attributes of America's national character, the foreign policy becomes logically one that is consistent with these attributes. In India the culture and belief system has moulded the outlook and foreign policy perspective of the decision-makers too.

National morale is also an elusive category and consists of a state of mind, which sometimes can be called **patriotism** or **love of country.** Willingness to stand up and even sacrifice one's life for one's country is not only an element of national morale of the troops that fight in the front but also of the civilian population.

6. *Political Structure:* The political structure of a state and the nature of the ruling elite to a great extent influence the formulation of foreign policy of a state. A democratic state, with a high degree of political accountability, is both responsive and responsible. Therefore, the foreign policy pursued by such a system would be different from the foreign policies pursued by totalitarian and authoritarian states.

Sudden changes in the government of a state are also a source of changes in the course of foreign policy. For example, changes of government in Pakistan, from military regime to democratically elected government for a brief period in the past and a new democratic governmental coalition after the general election of 2008, have led to some changes in their foreign policy outlook. Similarly, changes in governments in India also have influenced foreign policy choices from time to time. For instance, irrespective of the government in power whether it is a full-fledged Congress led government, or a BJP led NDA coalition, or a Janata Dal led government, or Congress–UPA government— there have been changes in foreign policy stances.

7. *Social Structure:* Foreign policy cannot be generated in a vacuum. Just as political inputs are important, social factors too are important. A strong cohesive society provides chances for a strong foreign policy, whereas, a society with tensions along ethnonational or religious factors or societies with unequal distribution of wealth have a strong possibility of pursuing a weak policy due to the lack of cohesion and cooperation among various groups. Thus, it is not possible to ignore the internal components of the external policy of a state.

8. *Ideology:* Ideology is defined as a cluster of interrelated, though not necessarily logically interdependent, ideas about government, economies, society and history. Ideology does often come to play an important role in the conduct of foreign policies of states. But most often, ideological principles are used by states or group of states, to advance national interests through justifying or disguising their policies and deeds in the struggle for power. The operation of ideology many a time is a source of international conflict. The rise of Fascism and Nazism had a profound impact in the international ideological arena. After the Second World War, the world witnessed strong ideological overtones in the foreign policy objectives of Soviet Russia and the United States. The struggle was between communism and efforts of Western democracies to 'contain' communism. However, one should not overestimate the importance of ideology as a determinant of foreign policy because, in its true sense, it is primarily used as a garb to hide the real intentions of the actors in international relations.

9. *Public Opinion:* In a democratic state it is impossible for the government to ignore the importance of public opinion in both domestic and foreign policies. This is true today more than ever before because of the revolution in information technology, mass media, telecommunications, internet and the like. People are now far more informed than was the case earlier. As such public opinion dose set the limit for the domestic as well as the foreign policies. In case of foreign policy, public opinion sets: (i) broad limits of constraint regarding the choice of policies—the 'mood' of the public; (ii) constraints in the policy execution. As in the case of the Vietnam War, the then American government had to succumb to the public opinion and was compelled to withdraw. In India, after the 1962 jolt given by China and the defeat of the Indian army, there was severe dent in Krishna Menon's image as a Defence Minister, and he had to face hostile public opinion which resulted first in his demotion to the Position of Minister of Defence Production ; ultimately he had to resign even though he had great personal equations with Prime Minister Nehru.

External Determinants

International Regimes and Organization: The foreign policies of the states have to operate taking into consideration the external environment also. The first and the most important factor that constrains or influences the making of the foreign policies is the presence of international laws, international treaties, pacts, trading blocs and various international and regional organizations. Several bilateral and multilateral treaties and agreements have to be taken into consideration when foreign policy choices are set. Activities of international organizations like the United Nations and its agencies, the IMF,

World Bank, WTO and regional organizations like ASEAN, SAARC, NAFTA, APEC and military pacts like NATO have an important bearing on the foreign policies of every state.

World Public Opinion: Domestic public opinion is an important determinant of foreign policy. Likewise, world public opinion has now come to play a crucial role in constraining foreign policy choices. In this present world of fast communication and information exchange, there has been an increased consciousness among the people at large, and there is also an extensive people-to-people contact, all of which have facilitated the generation of world public opinion on issues such as human rights, environment, war and peace and other related issues.

Foreign Policies of Other States: The external environment of a state consists of the presence of other states. Therefore, the formulation and the operation of foreign policy of a particular state has to take into consideration the behaviour of their states as well as their foreign policy choices. Foreign policy objectives of a state have to be state specific in the sense that it should manoeuvre its foreign policy choices according to its relations with states those that are friendly and those that are hostile. Ultimately, it is the reaction of the states that matter most. Therefore, foreign policy has to be engineered to get the desired result.

TECHNIQUES OF FOREIGN POLICY

DIPLOMACY

The coexistence of separate political units necessitates a certain degree of contact among them. There is a need for communication between governments, and the business of communicating between governments is technically termed as **diplomacy.** In the broadest sense, diplomacy is often used to mean both the making and execution of the foreign policy.

Diplomacy as an instrument of foreign policy is nothing new and can be traced to antiquity. Greece, Byzantium and Renaissance Italy made the most notable contributions to its evolution. But the origins of organized diplomacy dates back to the Congress of Vienna, 1815. The Congress of Vienna, The *Reglement* of 19 March 1815 and the subsequent regulations of Aix-la-Chappelle ultimately established the diplomatic services and representation of the powers on an agreed basis. Four categories of representatives were defined, namely: (a) ambassadors, papal legates and papal nuncios; (b) extraordinary envoys and plenipotentiary ministers; (c) ministers resident; (d) Chargè d'Affaires.[10] Finally, at the Vienna Conference on Diplomatic Intercourse and Immunities, attended by 81 states in 1961, a comprehensive agreement relating to almost all aspects of diplomatic practices was signed.

The Oxford Dictionary (Second edition, 1989) defines diplomacy as "the management of international relations by negotiation". Sir Ernest Satow (*Guide to Diplomatic Practice*, 1922) defined diplomacy as "the application of intelligence and tact to the conduct of official relations between governments of independent States". Another definition, which closely relates the method to the substance, is that diplomacy "represents the accumulative political, economic and military pressures upon each side formalized in the exchange of demands and concessions between negotiators".[11]

Nicolson[12] gives five different meanings of diplomacy. He says that in current language diplomacy is carelessly taken to denote several things. Diplomacy is taken as:

1. Synonym for foreign policy
2. Negotiation
3. The machinery by which such negotiation is carried out
4. A branch of the foreign service
5. "An abstract quality or gift, which, in its best sense, implies skill in the conduct of international negotiation; and, in its worst sense, implies the more guileful aspects of tact".

Ultimately he agrees to the definition given by the Oxford Dictionary.

Organski[13] considers diplomacy as "only one part of the process by which foreign policy is formulated and executed". Morgenthau referred to diplomacy as the brain of the state power.

Foreign Policy and Diplomacy

Although the terms diplomacy and foreign policy are used interchangeably, the distinction between the two must be kept in mind. In the interest of maintaining some precision of language in the description of international relations, diplomacy encompasses a "method or technique whereby states conduct their relationships with one another". Hence, diplomacy is not the substance of foreign policy nor does it represent the process whereby governments formulate foreign policy. It is but one of the ways in which policies are being implemented, day-to-day, throughout the world.

Palmer and Perkins also point out the distinction between diplomacy and foreign policy by quoting J.R. Childs (*American Foreign Service,* 1948) who suggested foreign policy as "the substance of foreign relations", and diplomacy as "the process by which policy is carried out". The purpose of diplomacy is to provide the machinery and personnel by which foreign policy is executed. More precise distinction has been provided by Sir Harold Nicolson in his study, *The Congress of Vienna* (November 1814–June 1815). He said that "foreign policy is based upon a general conception of national requirements... Diplomacy, on the other hand, is not an end but a means; not a purpose but a method... It is the agency through which foreign policy seeks to attain its purpose by agreement rather than by war". He further opines that diplomacy becomes inoperative with the outbreak of hostilities, as foreign policy, the final sanction of which is war, becomes inoperative too. But Palmer and Perkins have serious reservations on this and they contend that diplomacy does not cease to function, as Nicolson suggests, in times of war. Although its role may be different in wartime, the work of diplomats and ministers expands during wartime. They cite the examples of two World Wars as a convincing support for their argument. The crux of the whole debate is that diplomacy is the method and foreign policy is the substance, which is executed by the use of diplomatic technique. A British diplomat once remarked, "foreign policy is what you do; and diplomacy is how you do it".

FUNCTIONS OF DIPLOMACY

Morgenthau[15] provides four functions of diplomacy. These functions imply that one must:

1. determine the objectives of diplomacy in light of power actually and potentially available for the pursuit of these objectives;
2. assess the objectives of other nations and the power actually and potentially available for the pursuit of those objectives;
3. determine to what extent these different objectives are compatible with each other; and
4. employ the means suited to the pursuit of its objectives.

To him a diplomat fulfills three basic functions for his government: symbolic, legal and political.

Palmer and Perkins classify the functions of diplomats as:

1. Representation
2. Negotiation
3. Reporting
4. Protection of national interests and nationals abroad.

To this category another one, can be added, that is, the maintenance of international peace and promotion of international cooperation.

Poullada[16] points out that diplomacy performs five substantive functions:

1. Conflict management
2. Problem solving
3. Cross-cultural interaction on a wide range of issues
4. Negotiation and bargaining
5. Programme management of the foreign policy decisions of one country to another.

For the performance of these substantive functions, procedurally communicating the views of one's government and exchanging information, is involved. This is best done by the diplomats using certain procedural arts and crafts such as the refinements of protocol, diplomatic drafting, press relations and even gastronomy.

White[17] has pointed out five major functions of diplomacy:

1. Information gathering
2. Policy advice
3. Representation
4. Negotiation
5. Consular services

Some basic functions of diplomacy are discussed below:

Representation: The diplomat is the symbolic, legal and political representative of his country and government. His **symbolic** functions involve attending ceremonial and social occasions, address foreign groups and be present in all events with which his country has a connection. In their symbolic capacity, the diplomats have to deal with the totality of relations in all its facets between their government and their host country.

As the **legal and political** representative of the country, he conducts negotiations, signs treaties, represents his country in international conferences and organizations, and casts vote according to the directives of his government. He is also involved in the protection of interests of his country abroad and protects nationals abroad. He is also supposed to gather information and report to his government, which are like raw materials, which help the government to chalk out its foreign policies. Morgenthau points out, "As the foreign office is the nerve center of foreign policy, so are the diplomatic representatives its outlying fibres maintaining the two-way traffic between the center and the outside world".

Negotiation: This is by far the most important function of diplomacy. This involves a variety of activities ranging from simple consultation, exchange of views to full-fledged negotiation of specific issues. Negotiation can be conducted through persuasion, compromise, inducement and even pressure. It is said that the ability to persuade other governments is central to the art of diplomacy. If persuasion fails, then other measures are available, for example, imposing time limits on the negotiation, seeking to isolate the other state diplomatically or, in extreme situations, the threat of breaking off diplomatic relations. Overall, the negotiation has to take into account the mentalities, value system, and public opinion of both domestic and foreign political systems. Professional diplomats conduct negotiations or provide supportive roles if the political leaders or other envoys are involved in the negotiation.

Obtaining Information: This is the most delicate task of the diplomat as information and data are the raw materials of foreign policy. Data concerning military potential, personalities and economic trends or problems must be supplied to the policy makers in his country so that they can decide their course of action. The diplomat's chief function is providing information by using his skills and familiarity with the foreign society in order to interpret the data and make reliable assessments and forecasts of responses of the receiving government towards the policies of his own government.[18]

Reporting: The data and information collected from the receiving country must be reported to the diplomat's own government. These reports cover every conceivable subject, which may be important for his country. As a publication of the United States Department of State states the American Foreign Service expects its diplomats to "observe, analyze, and report on political, social and economic conditions and trends of significance in the country in which they are assignees".[19]

Protection of National Interests: Although a diplomat is expected to be *persona grata* to the government of the state, i.e., he must get along with the government of the country he is accredited to, yet protecting and furthering the national interest of his country is his prime duty. This is the bedrock of the practice of the diplomacy.

Protection of Nationals Abroad: This involves protecting the lives and promotion of interests of nationals residing or travelling abroad. This is a routine task but during catastrophes or civil disorders, the role of diplomats becomes crucial especially when the local government fails or does not provide the security of the lives and property of the foreign nationals.

   Though diplomacy has evolved from its traditional form to its modern form and considerable changes have taken place in foreign relations, the essential functions of diplomacy and those of the diplomats have remained unchanged. The chief functions of diplomacy: the transmission of information and viewpoints between governments, the representation of policy positions vis-à-vis others, the protection of the interest of one's nationals and perhaps, above all, the negotiation of existing differences of interests and policy aims through the process of finding the formulae to accommodate those differences still continues to be the same. As Morgenthau wrote in *The Art of Diplomatic Negotiation,*

> *that a nation which exists among other nations can deal with the outside world in one of three ways: it can deny the importance of the links between itself and other countries—which will lead to a policy of isolation and nonparticipation; it can deny the equality of other nations and try to impose its will on the others by coercion—which will lead to a policy of hegemony and imperialism; or it can attempt to pursue interests in contact with other countries on the assumption that there are possibilities of defining, redefining, adjusting and accommodating varying interests of countries to one another*

and the third course of action is the function which, in Morgenthau's judgement, diplomacy should serve.[20]

TRADITIONAL AND NEW DIPLOMACY

Till the end of eighteenth century, diplomacy was branded as old or traditional diplomacy. The nineteenth century diplomacy is referred to as *modern diplomacy* which involved newer methods and personnel because of change in the very nature of diplomacy.

An academic interpretation of old European kind of diplomacy has been provided by Kenneth W.Thompson (American academic and author in the field of international relations). He described the background of diplomacy in the following terms: "In theory at least, it sought to mitigate and reduce conflicts by means of persuasion, compromise and adjustment. It was a diplomacy rooted in the community of interests of a small group of leaders who spoke the same language, catered as often to one another as their own people, and played to one another's strengths and weaknesses. When warfare broke out, they drew a ring around combatants and sought to localize and neutralize the struggle. The old diplomacy... carried out its tasks in a world made up of states that were small, separated, limited in power and blessed ironically enough, by half-hearted political loyalties. Patience was a watchword; negotiations and talks would be initiated, broken off, resumed, discontinued temporarily and reopened again by professionals in whose lexicon there was no substitute for diplomacy".

There were certain factors which brought about changes in the theory and practice of diplomacy and ushered in a new era of diplomacy. Nicolson speaks of "Old Diplomacy" and its disreputable variant "Secret Diplomacy" which, he points out, saw a great white light in the year 1918 and gradually moved on to its new form of new diplomacy. Seventeenth or eighteenth century diplomacy now stood in sharp contrast with its modern form—the nineteenth century diplomacy. Nicolson[21] however, contends that no sudden conversion has taken place, neither sharp contrasts of principle or method could be recognized; only what has happened was that the art of negotiation has gradually adjusted itself to changes in the political conditions. Nicolson has called attention to these developments as:

- The "growing sense of the community of nations"
- The "increasing appreciation of the importance of public opinion
- The "rapid increase in communications"

Features of Traditional Diplomacy

The system of diplomacy, which is referred to as "traditional diplomacy", is also identified as "old diplomacy", "bilateral diplomacy", the 'French' or the

'Italian' system of diplomacy. Whatever may be the label, traditional diplomacy is characterized by some distinctive features with regard to its structure, process and agenda broadly relating to questions such as: Who is involved in diplomacy? How is diplomatic activity carried out? What is the substance of diplomacy?

Structure: The first and foremost feature of traditional diplomacy, which marked its difference from its predecessors in the ancient and medieval worlds, was that it constituted a communication process between recognizably modern states rather than any other forms of political organization such as the Catholic Church. Traditional diplomacy was also Europe-centric, and five big powers England, France, Prussia, Austria and Spain were the main actors? who could act in harmony to an unusual extent and, hence, the system was often referred to as the *Concert of Europe*. Most of Asia, Africa and Latin America were either isolated or became subjected to colonization. Therefore, diplomacy was virtually *European diplomacy*.

Traditional diplomacy also witnessed gradual institutionalization and by the seventeenth century, the diplomatic institutions became professionalized because diplomacy ceased to be an ad hoc activity and needed a permanent and dedicated workforce of diplomats.

Traditional diplomacy was the monopoly of the aristocratic class and of the professional diplomats who shared a rapport with each other.

Process: Traditionally, diplomacy was organized largely on a bilateral basis and was usually undertaken in secrecy characterized by distinctive rules and procedures. From fifteenth century onwards, diplomacy became a regularized process with the development of diplomatic protocol and a series of rights, privileges and immunities attached to both diplomats and diplomatic activities.

Agenda: The agenda of traditional diplomacy was parochial and narrow in comparison to the present era. As White points out, the agenda was not only set by the relatively underdeveloped state of bilateral relationships between states but, more importantly, "the preoccupations of diplomacy reflected the preoccupations of political leaders". Perhaps, the significant contribution of traditional diplomacy came to be known, in a classic piece of overstatement, as the "century of peace" in Europe between 1815–1914.

Features of New Diplomacy

The golden age of diplomacy together with the balance of power system, which was soon followed by the drastic changes in international politics since 1918, came to be replaced by the so-called popular or new diplomacy. At the heart of this transition lay the suspicion of the public about the whole system of balance of power which they identified as the main cause of the First World War. They were also suspicious about the role of diplomacy with its tradition of secrecy. President Woodrow Wilson in his "14-points" agenda expressed this new view of diplomacy when he said: "Open Covenants of peace, openly arrived at, after which there shall be no private international understandings of any kind, but diplomacy shall proceed always frankly and in public view".[22]

A number of other factors also led to the change in the nature of diplomacy. The first and foremost among them is the development in technology and communication which, to a great extent, has changed the role of a diplomat. Even an ambassador of the highest level can no longer conduct his office as an independent agent, far removed from the seat of his government, as he once could and was expected to do. He has to shuffle between his own office and his home office. Improved communications have reduced the authority of a professional diplomat to make decisions and generally to 'represent' his own country. The superfast communication system has reduced the importance of the diplomats, and to a large extent, diplomacy now overlaps with policy making. New means of mass communication have also opened up means of direct approach to the people of other countries through other means like propaganda.

Moreover, public opinion has now come to play an important role which, to a large extent, has intruded in the conduct of foreign policy. Diplomacy has ceased to be dynastic or a matter of a handful of people. It has assumed a democratic character where the statesmen have to take the public into confidence.

Further, the structure of international society has also undergone several changes. Europe is no longer the centre of international affairs. Post-Second World War, following massive decolonization of Asian and African countries, the number of independent countries has increased. Therefore, the influence of non-European powers—both Asian and African, has considerably increased; indeed, today they have a greater say in international affairs. Multilateral diplomacy, summit diplomacy or diplomacy by parliamentary procedure have gained importance alongside bilateral diplomacy, and "Open Covenants Openly Arrived" at these summits or conferences show a consuming interest of significant numbers of private citizens and groups. This has been regarded as the "democratization" of foreign policy which is a significant development in this regard. The United Nations has become an important international organization which represents this new genre of diplomacy.

Nicolson has criticized open diplomacy as he says that negotiations require "concessions and counter concessions" and once the news of concessions is divulged, the public might acquire a negative attitude and force the diplomats to abandon the negotiations. Nicolson has also raised serious shortcomings of diplomacy by conference. Such kinds of multilateral diplomacy suffer from several defects and cannot therefore function properly because political statesmen are not often competent to handle diplomatic negotiations. Further, as it involves many people, it fails to solve certain fundamental problems because the members tend to take rigid positions. Still, this new kind of diplomacy is popular and has some basic characteristics as we now discuss.

Structure: The structure of new diplomacy almost remained the same as that of the old diplomacy. States still remained the major actors in this diplomatic system and there was well-established permanent embassies abroad. The only difference was that the stage had to be shared by the state with other non-state actors like inter-governmental organizations and non-governmental organizations.

Process: The changing international scenario influencing the menu for choice of the states as actors, as also the increase in the number of non-state actors, have all led to the changes in the nature of new diplomacy and its process of negotiation. Diplomacy has become a more complicated activity involving states and non-state actors. Alongside bilateral negotiations on a state-to-state basis, groups of states negotiated multilaterally in inter-governmental organizations like the United Nations and with other non-governmental organizations.

Agenda: The agenda of new diplomacy contained a number of new issues like economic, social and welfare, commonly identified as *low politics,* as well as military issues, and issues of war and peace, identified as *high politics.*

TYPES OF NEW DIPLOMACY

Palmer and Perkins noted the most effective forms of diplomacy that could be perceived in the twentieth century till the present. The chief forms of diplomacy, among others, are democratic diplomacy, totalitarian democracy, summit diplomacy, personal diplomacy, diplomacy by conference, and parliamentary diplomacy.

Democratic Diplomacy: This had, particularly become the commonest form of diplomacy by the turn of twentieth century. The participation of the people in the politics of a state and the importance of public opinion led to a democratization of diplomacy where the governments were no longer the domain of aristocrats and diplomacy the sole affair of diplomats and ministers. But the experience of democratic diplomacy had not been satisfactory and a number of shortcomings had been pointed out by Nicolson. The most vehement criticism about democratic diplomacy is that it has come to be associated with the diplomacy of the market place. Further, Nicolson points out that the most potent source of danger is the "irresponsibility of the sovereign people" which means the failure of the common people to understand foreign policy intricacies which arise not from the absence of facts but from their ignorance and inability to apply their thoughts and intelligence to comprehend foreign affairs. Foreign affairs appear too foreign for them; as a result they create situations of embarrassment for diplomats and even strong public opinion may pull down a diplomatic negotiation or dog it with delay and imprecision.

Totalitarian Diplomacy: The rise of totalitarian states such as Germany, Italy, the Soviet Union after the First World War introduced a new but disturbing kind of diplomacy which was far different from its predecessors. These totalitarian states used modern techniques of military, political and psychological power to expand their spheres of influence, gain control over other states and subvert other regimes and further their aggressive policy of expansion. For this, they invoked doctrines of racial superiority, mysticism, materialism and militarism to further their national interests. Diplomacy came to be used as an instrument of national policy and, in doing so, the language and practice of diplomacy was thoroughly degraded. In dealing with these totalitarian states, the old techniques of diplomacy seemed quite inadequate as diplomats of these totalitarian regimes became agents of conquest, double-dealing and espionage. Lord Vansittart (The Decline of Diplomacy, "*Foreign Affairs*, XXVIII, January, 1950) remarked that the object of totalitarian diplomacy, quite contrary to the eighteenth or nineteenth century diplomacy, was to create and maintain 'bad' relations among states.

Summit Diplomacy: This involves the direct participation of foreign ministers, Heads of States and Heads of Governments in diplomatic negotiations. This is nothing new and, during the course of Second World War and even in the post-War years, a number of personal meetings were held between Churchill and Roosevelt. The meeting of 1941 resulting in the signing of Atlantic Charter, the Teheran meeting with Stalin, the Yalta (February, 1945) and the Potsdam Conferene (July–August, 1945) are the most noteworthy. Meetings of Asian and African Prime Ministers, either through exchange of visits on a bilateral basis or at major international conferences, have been quite frequent in the past and also in the present, such as the Asian–African Conference at Bandung in 1955, Conference of Non-Aligned states in Belgrade in 1961 and in Cairo in 1964, the meetings of OAU, SAARC and other international and regional organizations.

Personal Diplomacy: Personal diplomacy also takes other forms where the normal channels of diplomacy are used only to a limited degree. Heads of states have embarked on a practice of using their personal agents or representatives to handle delicate problems in international relations. They even sometimes grow a tendency to consult their personal favourites rather than the foreign ministers. This has been a practice for many decades as Henry Wriston[*] pointed out in his study of *Executive Agents in American Foreign Relations* that they have been

---

[*]Henry Wriston, *Executive Agents in American Foreign Relations,* The John Hopkins Press, Baltimore, 1929.

employed in American diplomatic relations from the colonial times. Wriston's reliance on Colonel House and Roosevelt's on Harry Hopkins are best known examples. Besides employing personal agents, another very common practice, among Heads of states is to directly approach his counterpart in the other country. Churchill and Roosevelt developed this practice to a fine art and later on was used by Kennedy and Khrushchev, during the détente days, through hotline.

Diplomacy by Conference: In the post-War period, international conferences have proliferated in the conduct of foreign policies and have assumed greater significance than normal channels of diplomacy through foreign offices and diplomatic and consular establishments. These, in most parts, involve periodic meetings of regional and international organizations attended by a number of representatives of the member states and sometimes the non-member states too. The stimulus to this form of diplomacy was provided by the League of Nations after the First World War. A number of conferences followed the post-First World War period, such as the Paris Peace Conference (1918), the Disarmament Conference at Geneva (1927), the London Conference (1930), and others. During the Second World War, a number of important conferences were held. The most noteworthy among them are: the Teheran Conference (1943), the Bretton Woods Conference (1944), The Yalta Conference (1945), and the San Francisco Conference (1945). Contemporary international relations have witnessed a number of conferences pertaining to disarmament, nuclear regimes, sustainable development and environmental issues.

Parliamentary Diplomacy: Kenneth W. Thompson has pointed out that there has been a "novel, revolutionary and worldwide institutionalizing of diplomacy". This has generally been the result of three developments, which are quite striking:

1.   Increasing incidence of public multilateral negotiations

2.   Expansion of diplomatic activity into the cultural and educational fields

3.   Multiplication of informal channels of contact among people and nations.

These factors have led to the growing importance of what has been called 'parliamentary diplomacy'. Dean Rusk (Parliamentary Diplomacy—Debate vs. Negotiation, *World Affairs Interpreter*, XXVI, Summer, 1955) suggested that this type of multilateral negotiation involves "a continuing organization", a "regular public debate exposed to the media of mass communication", "rules of procedure which govern the process of debate", and "formal conclusions, ordinarily expressed resolutions". The United Nations General Assembly and other UN bodies are examples of diplomacy through parliamentary procedures.[23]

Economic Diplomacy: Economic diplomacy as a concept is not new. In fact, trade diplomacy has a long history. But trade and aid have been widely in use since the Second World War to obtain a favourable outcome in negotiations. Hence, trade and aid are continuously being used as a part of 'carrot and stick' policy in the sense that either can be offered or withheld. During the Cold War, economic trade and aid were used as instruments to win over allies and to maintain respective spheres of influence by both the United States and the Soviet Union. The Truman Doctrine and the Marshall Plan are prominent examples of such aid to European countries aiming at containing the spread of communism. The Soviet response to Marshall Plan was the Molotov Plan which was a series of bilateral agreements with the East European countries to help them tide over their economic crises and, thereby, preserve communism. Post-Cold War trade and aid, along with transfer of technology, capital and information, are still used while conducting economic diplomacy. Mostly the third world countries are the targets, and the usage of these techniques by the rich countries gives leverage in bargaining situations to the developed countries. Therefore, while economic diplomacy between equal partners may bring out outcomes beneficial to both, such diplomacy between rich and poor states might result in inequitable returns from the negotiations. Even in economic diplomacy, the quality of rule and pattern of governance in a particular country might just take a back seat and national trading interest might just become supreme. As human rights violations in Myanmar surpassed all limits in September, 2007, ASEAN member states—India, China, Russia and Japan—did little more than issue bland statements calling for restraint after the September protests followed by severe repressions by the junta. This is primarily due to the economic interests, alongside strategic interests, that these states have in Myanmar.

Nuclear Diplomacy: Nuclear diplomacy takes different forms and meanings depending on whether the negotiating states are nuclear haves or nuclear have–nots. Under these circumstances there can be either deterrence or compellance or coercive diplomacy. Deterrence comes into being if the parties involved in the negotiation are all nuclear haves. Then possession of nuclear arsenal will deter them from using the nukes. On the other hand if the other party does not possess nukes then that party may be compelled into doing certain things which the nuclear-haves might desire. But there is an unprecedented risk attached to this type of nuclear diplomacy and a crisis situation might escalate and reach the threshold of nuclear war as manifested during the Cuban Missile Crisis.

Public Diplomacy: This form of diplomacy which became popular in the US in the 1960s signifies engagement with the foreign public in the context of realising foreign policy objective. This assumes the form of people-to-people contact which involves the inclusion of academicians, NGOs, cultural groups, tourism, films, theatres, internet and blogging. The chief aim is to increase people-to-people contact and improve the image of a country abroad alongside the traditional mechanisms of diplomacy. This public-private partnership has immensely increased due to the improvement in communications, information exchanges and media and internet revolution. The USA, aptly uses public diplomacy to improve public relations and its image in other countries through the Voice of America, organization of academic exchanges (students and teachers), seminars, film shows and host of other activities. These activities are conducted by USIS in several countries. Educational exchange programmes in India are conducted through USIEF (United States-India Educational Foundation). However, for long, public diplomacy was seen as a euphemism for propaganda. Nevertheless, scholars and practitioners of public diplomacy have tried to overcome this parochial interpretation of the term and have embarked on policies that aim at enhancing people-to-people contact.

DIPLOMACY AS A TECHNIQUE OF FOREIGN POLICY

As already noted, diplomacy entirely involves direct government-to-government interactions so that a particular state can persuade governments in their countries to act in the manner in which it wants them to do. Therefore, diplomacy is considered as the central technique of foreign policy implementations and effectively the only direct technique where the central feature is communication. Most of the rules of protocol, diplomatic immunities and non-interference have been established and codified to facilitate communication and reduce misunderstanding and distortion in inter-state communication.

From the perspective of world politics "diplomacy refers to a process of communication that is central to the working of the international system". If world politics is identified as being the interplay between conflict and cooperation, then, war and diplomacy can be said to represent the two defining institutions (see Figure 5.1). If conflict and cooperation are placed at the two ends

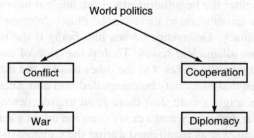

Figure 5.1   Illustration of world politics.

[**Source:** Adapted from Brian White][17]

of a spectrum, diplomacy will feature at the cooperation and war on the conflict end. This is because, the main focus of diplomacy is the resolution of conflict by negotiation and dialogue and an attempt to create some sort of order within the world politics to prevent a conflict spilling over into war.[24]

"Diplomacy offers one instrument that international actors might use to implement their foreign policy either as its own right or as a means of communicating the use or threatened use of other instruments to other parties concerned".[25] "Pure diplomacy" based on negotiation and persuasion is often linked with other instruments of conducting foreign relations. This gives rise to a 'mixed' kind of diplomacy. Here, diplomacy "becomes a communication channel through which the use or threatened use of other instruments is transmitted to other parties". Diplomacy is often linked with a policy of either 'carrot' or 'stick' to successfully mould the behaviour of other parties concerned. This is done by using either potential rewards or punishments.

The message to use or the threat to use military force to obtain leverage in a bargaining situation has long been used by the states. The combination of the duo, diplomacy and military force may be regarded as traditional instruments of foreign policy. The aim is to convey to others the knowledge of the military capabilities one possesses, in order to influence the menu of choice of the adversaries that is done by using diplomacy.

Another instrument which is short of force is the use of economic measures, sanctions and embargos. Trade and aid or the withdrawal or refusal have been used increasingly since World War II to influence the outcome of negotiations. This was amply illustrated in the case of Iraq (where UN approved economic sanctions were enforced for many years) and other countries for non-compliance of international norms and regulations. Here also diplomacy gets mixed up with the job of communicating either the offering or the suspension of trade and aid.

The third and recently used instrument is subversion. This instrument might not be linked to diplomatic process in a strict sense. It is not directed towards government but targeted towards specific groups within the other state through various techniques of propaganda, intelligence activities and giving assistance to rebel groups. All these are done with the ultimate aim of gaining leverage in the diplomatic bargaining with the threat of undermining or overthrowing the government of the opponent state.

However, the use of other instruments of conducting foreign policy depends upon a number of factors, among which two important considerations are the capability and availability of other instruments and the cost effectiveness of these instruments. Therefore, diplomacy continues to be the most favoured, advantageous and cost-effective method.

After the conclusion of the Cold War, diplomacy has become more global with the dilution of ideological differences and inclusion of more states into normal diplomatic intercourse with others. It has also made diplomacy more diverse and complex involving multiple actors, complex bilateral and multilateral processes at work, levels of interconnectedness or interdependence between societies and revolution in communications technology. Complex political and economic problems are being handled more by negotiations at an international level than at the domestic level. Therefore, process of negotiation, which was considered as an art in the past, still continues to be an art but an art of management, as practised in large bureaucracies, than the art of guile and concealment of any particular diplomat.

PROPAGANDA

Propaganda is the next effective weapon used by the states after diplomacy in conducting their foreign relations. It is completely different from the diplomacy in essence and style. Propaganda is more like a *psychological warfare* targeted at specific groups. It is usually an attempt to persuade or influence leaders as well as the general population of other countries. Since propaganda is generally directed at the enemy or those who are hostile, it involves the manipulation of facts and symbols to attain the desired effects on the minds of an audience. Therefore, some scholars consider the term 'propaganda' to be too narrow and only a part of *psychological methods* of conducting international relations. Scholars like W.P. Davison (1963) prefer to use the term 'political communication' in its place. Whatever one calls this method, it is undoubtedly true that this particular method was and is being continuously used by governments to realize their objectives.[26]

Holsti points out to the fact that due to the widespread involvement of average citizens or subjects in foreign affairs and increasing people-to-people contact between different nationalities, the psychological and public opinion factors have now come to play a decisive role in the conduct of foreign policy. The American involvement in the Vietnam War witnessing a massive loss of lives of American soldiers had a definite impact on the minds of the American people, which got reflected in the ensuing Presidential elections. The minds of people have evolved as an essential element in international relations. It is hard to ignore public opinion, either domestic or worldwide. Therefore, one of the unique aspects of modern international political relationships "is the deliberate attempt by governments, through diplomats and propagandists, to influence the attitudes and behaviour of foreign populations, or of specific ethnic, class, religious, economic, or language groups within those populations" with the aim that these foreign groups or the entire population will influence and mould the attitudes of their domestic government as desired by the propagandists. The aim is "to create a favourable image of their country abroad".[27]

Palmer and Perkins refer to propaganda as "any attempt to persuade persons to accept a certain point of view or to take a certain action" which has a specific aim and method of action.

Couloumbis and Wolfe[28] point out that propaganda has been effectively defined as a process involving a communicator whose attention is to change the attitudes, opinions and behaviour of a target population using spoken, written and behavioural symbols and employing media such as books, pamphlets, films, lectures and so on. They also project the disaggregation of the cooperative from the conflictual types of propaganda in terms of white, gray and black propaganda.

White Propaganda: It is referred to as those cooperative and straightforward campaigns designed to explain the policies of a state to audiences across its borders and over the seas. This generally involves activities in cultural and educational domains involving cultural and educational exchange programmes. Magazines, pamphlets, films and lectures are the usual methods of orchestrating the message for cultivation of mutually beneficial friendship and cooperation.

Gray Propaganda: It begins when the relationship between the communicator and the government of the target state begins to deteriorate. Therefore, exaggeration and falsehood creep into the communications and propaganda becomes combative and competitive in content and philosophy (of propaganda).

Black Propaganda: It usually refers to those techniques, that are used during the time of war when actual hostilities break out and diplomacy and formal negotiations fail. Verbal and audio-visual weapons are used in communication hiding the true identities of the communicators and producing forged and fabricated documentations aimed at creating confusion and chaos in the ranks of the enemy, for example, forecast for large-scale unemployment, food scarcity, labour, ethnic unrest, and famine.

According to Joseph Frankel, propaganda is generally understood as any systematic attempt to affect the minds, emotions, and actions of a given group for a specific purpose. Like diplomacy, it is also verbal, but it is different from diplomacy in two respects, though the dividing line is not fully clear.

- Propaganda is addressed to the people of other states and rarely to their governments.
- Propaganda is often guided by selfish motives, governed solely by national interests of the propagandist and is therefore, usually unacceptable to other states.

Selection of targets is essential in conducting propaganda. The important factor is the identification of the targets whose attitudes have to be changed. It is undeniable that despite increasing development in communication, media, computer technologies, internet, only a relatively small section of people in any given society has access to the newer technologies and means of communication. Therefore, this section of people becomes the likely targets of foreign-oriented information because, in many developing countries, most of the population is denied access to the means of communication and is confined to their small region or province. Propaganda again seems to be effective when directed towards people sharing wholly or partially, the attitudes of the communicator. The job becomes an easier one in strengthening the existing attitudes or crystallizing the predispositions than in concerting those that are already hostile. It is often seen that propaganda becomes effective when targeted towards the crowds. Holsti points out that there is some evidence that the arousal of any strong emotion may make the individual in the crowd more suggestible, even if that emotion is directed initially against the leader of the crowd.

To influence the target population or group is a difficult job and it becomes tougher when the targets are hostile to the communicator. Therefore, the propagandists use devices that tend to be spectacular, colourful, unusual, and in no way related to the substance of the message. The assumption is that the images of other states, which the foreign populations possess, are generally based on news reports, movies, cultural events, television programmes and information on the Internet, rather than direct experience. The effort, therefore, is to present spectacular news-making foreign policy actions, which will be noticed by a larger section of the foreign population whereas regular government information will reach only to a smaller audience. The objective of foreign information programmes is to sustain or alter the attitudes and behaviours of politically relevant groups within the society.

TECHNIQUES OF PROPAGANDA

Holsti lists several techniques of conducting propaganda with the ultimate aim to deliver the specific message to the targeted group. These techniques are now enumerated.

Name Calling: It is the attaching of an emotion-laden symbol to a person or country, for instance, calling the Soviet Union as the "evil empire" during the Cold War days, or the "axis of evil" (used by president George Bush) for Libya, Iraq and North Korea after the Cold War, or naming the communists as "Reds" or constitutional governments as "capitalist cliques".

Glittering Generality: It is similar to the previous one but aimed at describing a policy rather than an individual, for example, "free world" used by the Western propagandists, or "Socialist solidarity" used by the communists.

Transfer: It means identifying an idea, person, country or policy with some other in order to make the target approve or disapprove it, for instance, evoking hostility among religious people against communism is equating it with atheism.

Plain Folks: It is to do away with the image as foreigner propagandists appear to identify themselves as closely as possible with the values and lifestyle of the targets using local slang, accent and idiom.

Testimonial: It means using an esteemed person or institution to endorse or criticize an idea or a political entity.

Selection: It refers to the selection of facts, although seldom, specific in factual content. Propagandists tend to use those facts only which required to prove predetermined objectives.

Bandwagon: This technique plays on the audience's desire to belong to or be in accord with the crowd. Similar to the testimonial, but rather a mass of people and not a single esteemed person or institution, serves as the attraction. The messages of the communist propagandists used such phrases as "the whole world knows that…," "all peace-loving people recognize that…" and others.

Frustration Scapegoat: It means releasing frustration by creating a scapegoat and directing hostility and hatred towards it like the myth created by Hitler that Germany's internal and external problems were created by "the Jews", which led to the holocaust.

Fear: It means raising of consciousness resulting in changes of attitudes when the audiences are made aware of an impending or imminent threat to their lives and welfare, for example, fear of a nuclear war to promote arms control and disarmament issues.[29]

Palmer and Perkins refer to four major methods and techniques of propaganda:

1. Methods of presentation
2. Techniques of gaining attention
3. Devices for gaining response
4. Methods of gaining acceptance.

When propaganda is directed at foreign population, certain results or consequences are kept in mind. Propaganda can be both offensive and defensive. Where the policies of another government oppose the purposes of the government employing propaganda, the techniques might be used to create internal dissension and opposition, thereby weakening the domestic support which those policies might otherwise promote. A given government will leave no stone unturned to create a positive support base for its own policies and ward off negative impact emanating from the use of similar policies by other states, in the absence of counter propaganda. This might give rise to a counter-counter propaganda and at the end the original purpose may be lost in the never-ending battle of words.

EFFICACY OF PROPAGANDA IN CONDUCTING INTERNATIONAL RELATIONS

Political communication and the systemic use of psychological methods, of which propaganda is a prominent part, are nothing new in the history of international relations. It was the Roman Catholic Church which first used it and institutionalized it as the propagation of faith through a special Sacred Congregation (Congregation de Propaganda Fide, that is, the congregation of the Propagation of Faith), from the title of which the word 'propaganda' is derived. Though the British Government was the first to organize and systematize the use of propaganda at home and abroad during the First World War, it was the communists and then the Nazis who developed the mechanism of propaganda during the inter-war period. They built up such costly propaganda machineries that the Western democracies were forced to develop the same to match theirs. Post-Second World War and, even, in the present time, the states continue to use propaganda as a useful tool for statecraft.

In the United States, the agency incharge of propaganda activities is the United States Central Information Agency (CIA) and in the former Soviet Union it was the Agitation and Propaganda Section of the Central Committee of the Soviet Communist Party. British propaganda (officially referred to as *information services*), though it suffers from fund crunch, has been relatively successful in operating through decentralized organs, the Central Office of Information, the Overseas Services of the BBC, and also through the British Council.[30]

In the Soviet Union before World War II, after the Bolshevik revolution, they put into practice the process of 'indoctrination' on individual. For this, they used mechanisms of propaganda through party workers, the local Soviets of towns and villages, and the army. As Lenin wrote, as early as 1905: "Propaganda is of crucial importance for the triumph of the Party". Twelve years later he remarked that the revolution had succeeded "because it knew how to combine force with persuasion". The Soviets were masters in both developing propaganda devices and in adapting techniques to specific situations. The communist propaganda always had a vocabulary of its own and they used such terms as 'proletariat', 'communism', 'socialism', 'toiling masses', and 'revolution', which had a favourable meaning and 'capitalism', 'bourgeoisie', 'classes', 'imperialism', and 'parliamentarism' were treated as epithets that communists used while referring to their enemies. After 1918, the communists promoted the Third International (the Comintern), which was a useful medium for directing the communist parties throughout the world and exerting pressure on the foreign governments to follow favourable policies towards the Soviet Union. After 1935, on the face of an imminent Nazi attack, it was seen that the communist parties of Europe followed the Moscow directive for a "People's Front" which meant cooperation with liberal groups against the Nazi threat. Therefore, the former Soviet Union was highly successful in utilizing its propaganda machinery.[31]

Nazi Germany had also used propaganda to hype several 'big lies'. It was effectively used by Hitler who believed that a lie, provided that it is sufficiently big and is frequently repeated, will be at least partly believed by the masses because the conviction is that most of the people lack the imagination to conceive that repeated statements are not all true. Hitler established a National Ministry of Popular Enlightenment and Propaganda headed by the infamous Joseph Goebbles. Goebbles defined his job as the achievement of "one single opinion". A few ideas circulated among the people soon after the defeat of Germany and conclusion of the Treaty of Versailles (1919) were: (i) the Versailles Treaty had been unjustly imposed upon them; (ii) the leaders of the Weimar Republic had betrayed their country; (iii) 'Jew-Communists' were the cause of their grievances, and (iv) the 'Herrenvolk' "master race" needed

'Lebensraum' "living space". Hitler and his followers manipulated these ideas and made appeals to all the sections of society and got unemployed youths recruited in the Storm Troops—all by means of successfully using the propaganda machinery.

As far as Fascist Italy is concerned, Mussolini developed propaganda machinery earlier to the Nazis, and the Nazis copied some of his techniques. In his quest to consolidate power, Mussolini appealed to all groups present within the society, like the army, navy, monarchists, irredentists, clerics, discontented masses and others. He used the "plain folks" technique that highlighted his low background and distributed his pictures showing him toil on some humble job. His role as IL Duce "the leader" was glorified and heightened.[32]

The United States lacked proper machinery till 1939 either for foreign propaganda or general public information programme. The Office of War Information (OWI), incorporating the "Voice of America" was established during World War II which functioned to support the national policies in the war effort, both at home and abroad. The OWI was abolished later and its functions were transferred to the Department of State. To match the Soviet propaganda post-Second World War, the US Congress enacted foundations of a comprehensive programme of information and cultural relations in tune with the US foreign policy. The purpose of such programme was defined as "to promote mutual understanding between the people of the United States and other countries and also to try to correct the misunderstandings about America". In 1953, the then US President Eisenhower, by a reorganization plan, established the United States Information Agency (USIA) as a separate executive branch. Since its creation the USIA has played a major role in official propaganda abroad. The well-known branch of USIS, USIA is the "Voice of America".

During the Cold War days, both the superpowers utilized their propaganda machineries against each other in order to maintain their spheres of influence. USA often identified the Soviet Union as an "evil empire". Post-Cold War, after the dissolution of the Soviet Union, it identified as the "axis of evil" (a term used by president George Bush) Libya, Iraq, Iran and North Korea. Again, after the 9/11 terrorist attacks in its "War on Terror", it identified Saddam Hussain as an abettor of Osama bin Laden and Iraq as a potential threat to humanity being the possessor of weapons of mass destruction (WMDs). In all these cases, though the periods may be different, yet the Americans used their propaganda machinery consisting of press, media, television, Internet blogs, and websites to carry out massive propaganda campaigns against them. At the same time, it also utilized the same to project a favourable image of itself in the international arena.

From the foregoing discussion it is clear that propaganda has an effective role in the conduct of the foreign policy of states. Morgenthau[33] points out the importance of propaganda in his celebrated work Politics Among Nations as "an autonomous instrument of foreign policy" which "is a novelty". He says that all foreign policy aims at promoting one's interests by changing the mind of the opponent. To that end he remarks that "diplomacy uses persuasiveness of promises and threats in terms of the satisfaction or denial of interests; military force, the physical impact of actual violence upon the opponent's ability to pursue certain interests; propaganda, the use and creation of intellectual convictions, moral valuations, and emotional preferences in support of one's interests". He, therefore, concludes that "all foreign policy, then is a struggle for minds of men; but propaganda is so in the specific sense that it endeavors to mould the minds of men directly rather than through the intermediary of the manipulation of interests or physical violence". From the given discussion it becomes clear that propaganda as a technique of foreign policy can be effective depending upon the content of the propaganda, relations between propaganda and the life experiences of those whom one tries to reach, i.e., the target group, and the relations between propaganda and the foreign policy whose instrument propaganda serves and evaluates as to what extent psychological warfare is capable of supporting the policy.

However, as Holsti[34] points out, there are serious limitations to the use of propaganda as a technique of foreign policy. Information and communication are central to propaganda and almost its life-blood. But the point to be taken into consideration is the availability of information and means to disseminate such information to the target groups. In North, communication media and facilities such as newspapers, magazines, radios, televisions, video recorders, computer technologies and Internet connections are available along the length and breadth of the country. But this is not a global picture. The people in the poor, underdeveloped South do not have access to most of these facilities.

Further, there is also asymmetry in communication patterns. The governments of the major industrialized countries have an advantage of accessing the global media and, hence, control the flow of information. The messages of public and private communication move predominantly between industrial countries and towards South to the Third World countries, and never in the opposite direction. Films, news service, products and television programmes from the North flow to Third World countries with little reciprocity. The Third World countries are always at a disadvantageous position as far as the control of flow of information and availability of means of transmission are concerned. The developed countries of the North utilize the technique of propaganda to carry out their neo-imperialist designs and impose a kind of cultural imperialism through the control of the means of communications and flow of information.

MILITARY POWER AS A TECHNIQUE OF FOREIGN POLICY

According to Garnett[35] the term 'military power' refers to the capacity of a state to kill, maim, coerce and destroy. Though there may be contenders of states in matters of use of violence as a means to attain specific goals yet it is usually accepted, till date, that military power and its use is exercised by states and used primarily by governments to protect their countries from external aggression and internal subversion. Even the Charter of the United Nations under Article 51 acknowledges the use of force in self-defence. According to the Article nothing in the present Charter shall impair the inherent right of individual or collective self-defence if an armed attack occurs against a Member of the United Nations, until the Security Council has taken necessary measures to maintain international peace and security. Military power is therefore, "the legally sanctioned instrument of violence that governments use in their relations with each other, and, when necessary, in an internal security role".

From this definition, two assumptions can be derived. One is that military power is a purposive and second is that it is a functional thing. It is functional because it is one of the many instruments in the orchestra of power that states use at various times in pursuit of their national interests. It is purposive because use of military power, which results in war or acts of aggression, is not always used as an instrument of policy but as a purposive political act.

If the international system is thought to be like the Hobbesian 'state of nature', following the realists, then to survive in that ungoverned environment, military power has proved to be a powerful weapon. Therefore, the use of military power as a rational technique for pursuing foreign policy has been accepted under such situations of insecurity. Its frequent use determines not who is right, but who is going to prevail in the constant struggle for prosperity, prestige and security. Michael Howard suggested "the capacity of states to defend themselves, and their evident willingness to do so, provides the basic framework within which the business of international negotiations is carried on". Military power is an intrinsic part of the rather fragile international order associated with the international system.[36]

Traditionally, the utility of military power has been upheld by several strategic thinkers and political philosophers and its value is self-evident despite mounting criticisms against its usage. Karl Von Clausewitz, the Prussian strategic thinker, gave a dictum in which he said "war is the continuation of politics by other means".

His book 'Von Kriegg' (On War) contains ample examples from history to illustrate the various concepts propunded by him. Some of the prominent Clausewitzian principles are:

1. War must never be seen as a purpose to itself, but as a means of physically forcing one's will on an opponent.

2. The military objectives in war that support one's political objectives fall into two broad types: "war to achieve limited aims" and war to "disarm" the enemy: "to render [him] politically helpless or militarily impotent".

3. The course of war will tend to favour the party who has more resolve and resources.

Carr[37] in his *Twenty Years Crisis* upheld that the "supreme importance of the military instrument lies in the fact that the *ultima ratio* of power in international relations is war". Every act of a state from the aspect of its power is directed to war not as a desirable weapon but as a weapon which it may require as the last resort. He said that "war lurks in the background of international politics just as revolution lurks in the background of domestic politics". Therefore, potential war becomes a dominant factor in international politics and military strength becomes a recognized standard political value. Military power is not only an essential element in the life of the state but it sometimes becomes an end in itself. Carr contends that fewer wars are fought for trade or territorial expansion, and he points out that most serious wars had been fought to make one's country militarily strong or for preventing another country from becoming militarily stronger. He says that "the principal cause of war is war itself".

Quincy Wright[*] in his *Study of Wars* defines war as "a violent contact of distinct but similar entities" in a broadest sense, and in a narrow sense, as " the legal condition which equally permits two or more hostile groups to carry on a conflict by armed forces". He further suggested the possible causes of war in his *Causes of War and Conditions of Peace* (1935) as being in a sense the obverse of the conditions of peace which are related to the following aspects of the world situation:

- A state of opinion violently hostile to the existing state of affairs
- Inadequacy of international organization to deal with conflicts
- Inadequate system of law
- Unstable equilibrium of material forces.

Wright points out that there can also be politico-technological, juro-ideological, socio-religious, and psycho-economic causes of war.

However, the role of military power as an instrument of national policy is often considered in a political rather than in a purely military context. The validity of Clausewitz's strictures against a rigid compartmentalization of politics and military strategy turns out to be more true, especially in the present context when advances in military technologies have transformed war from a diversion of monarchs to a potential menace against humanity. In the nuclear age particularly military forces exist not solely for the purpose of inflicting damage on enemies but also as a threat to gain leverage in diplomatic bargaining or as a means of communicating one's intentions to potential adversaries.

Force and threat of use of force have existed in international relations and development of military technologies has an important impact on the structures and processes of political systems. Thermonuclear weapons and long-range ballistics missiles are qualitatively different from their predecessors or conventional forces. Long range missiles such as intercontinental ballistic missiles (ICBMs), and short-range ballistic missiles (SRBMs) have come to

---

[*]Quincy Wright, *A Study of War*, University of Chicago, Chicago, 1942.

constitute major strategic delivery vehicles which carry a warhead up along a trajectory and let it drop on the target. Military analysts consider the period starting from the 1991 Gulf War as a revolution in military affairs, especially in the US forces. The 1999 Kosovo campaign, and the 2001 US campaign in Afghanistan against the Talibans witnessed sea changes in war tactics. Integration of diverse forces, using information-rich battle management systems, forced the adversaries to succumb. The 2003 Iraq war was another incident where the chief aim was to 'shock and awe' the enemy. To this end, the US used cruise missiles to disarm the enemy. In 1993, President Bill Clinton attacked the Iraqi intelligence with dozens of cruise missiles which became the first all-cruise-missile attack in history.[38] Therefore, these newer generations of military technologies have changed the military power calculation and have a definite impact on the adversaries, which conventional forces might not have. States often want to be perceived as militarily strong and are willing to use their capabilities and thus do not want to be challenged or thwarted. Demonstration of prowess might be explicit through display of military capabilities or implicit, as may be the case with the possession of nuclear weapons. India's nuclear explosion of Pokhran I and Pokhran II was an attempt to attain the status and prestige among her neighbours which is, to a great extent, thwarted by the presence of her northern neighbour China.

Possession of nukes has shaped the nuclear strategy adopted by the nuclear powered states. Either it may be "first strike" as Pakistan has adopted or "second-strike" as India has adopted. There can also be a situation as was the case during the Cold War between USA and the Soviet Union, which came to be known as **mutually assured destruction** or **MAD** because both possessed second-strike capabilities. But the important point is that mere possession of nukes would deter an adversary from using its missile. During the Cold War days it was acknowledged by both the Soviet and American leaders that there are few, if any, goals that can be served by the actual 'use' of nuclear weapons and the 'threat' to use nuclear weapons plays a more decisive role. It is said, "A nuclear war cannot be won and never be fought". Therefore, deterrence can be considered as one of the means by which one state can prevent certain actions of political adversaries. Effective deterrence should be 'stable' as well as 'credible'. It should be both 'threatening' in the sense that it will be sufficiently credible that adversaries are not attempted to undertake prohibited actions and stable in the sense that it will be reassuring enough to reduce any incentives to launch a pre-emptive strike out of fear.[39] Deterrence or dissuasion is easier to achieve than compellance. In Vietnam the Americans faced not only the task of compelling a particular action but also of promoting an effective political order which was hard to achieve. The Cuban Missile Crisis was a test of nerves and undoubtedly it proved that possession of nuclear arsenal is not a decisive factor. From these arguments many scholars conclude that utility of military forces has been reduced in this nuclear age because:

- Nuclear might of one superpower balances that of the other. Therefore, their effective power is reduced to zero. The best and distinctive forces are least usable. As John Herz remarked, "Absolute power equals absolute impotence".

- The fear of escalation strongly inhibits even the use of conventional forces, especially by the USA or the Soviet Union. Nuclear powers must fear escalation more than other states, for, in any war that rises to the nuclear level, they will be primarily targeted. They may resort to conventioal forces, but the risks in doing so are higher than in the past. Besides, in the nuclear age, enormous military power no longer ensures effective control over even the most feeble opponents.

- The weak states of the world have tried to change world opinion by asking the powerful nations to exercise restraint on the use of force, either nuclear or conventional.[40]

The given arguments might give us the impression that advent of nuclear and thermonuclear weapons has imposed new restraints upon those who control them and has undermined the utility of military power. But in the true sense, as Garnett[41] puts it, states have developed strategies that emphasize the "political uses" of military power even in war itself. T.C.Schelling (1966) has defined war as a "bargaining process" or a sort of "tough negotiation" and as "the diplomacy of violence". All of these actually suggest that war has become a part of diplomacy. He uses the terms 'coercive warfare' and 'compellance' to describe the significance of military power for achieving goals that are not strictly military at all and the "object is to make the enemy behave". The core of this policy is to hurt, to cause pain and suffering. The classic example is that the two atom bombs dropped on Hiroshima and Nagasaki at the end of the Second World War which were not really aimed at these cities, but rather the target was the decision-makers in Tokyo. In Schelling's words: "The effect of the bombs and their purpose were not mainly the military destruction they accomplished but the pain and the shock and the promise of more". This was again illustrated during the 2003 US military campaign against Iraq post 9/11 terrorist attacks on USA. The whole strategy was to create "shock and awe" in the minds of the enemies in order to force it to behave in the way desired by the UN as well as the US.

Related to the military power there is the growing influence of a powerful "military–industrial complex". The whole concept of "military–industrial complex" includes both labour unions and politicians whose districts would benefit directly from military spending. Even if American economy as a whole could survive and prosper without military spending, some industries and geographic areas would suffer from any sort of reduction in military expenditure. Military–industrial complex tries hard to maintain their business and add new contracts and, in this endeavour, they are helped by government policies. Post-Cold War closures of domestic military bases and the end of the

Cold War itself have renewed the debate of the importance of military–industrial complex. There have been serious questions whether there will be a "peace dividend" of money formerly spent on arms race to meet the welfare needs of the civilian population. USA and many other countries are faced with a dilemma between its large military establishment and its liberal democratic prrinciples. President Eisenhower called the military–industrial complex as a very real symptom of this dilemma. There have been several attempts of disarmament and arms control, but without much effect, and military security and use of military power still remains central to the conduct of international relations.

EXERCISES

1. What do you understand by foreign policy? Discuss briefly the determinants of foreign policy.

2. What are the objectives of foreign policy?

3. What are the different techniques of foreign policy? In this connection, discuss the role of diplomacy as a technique of foreign policy.

4. What do you understand by diplomacy? What are the functions of diplomacy?

5. Discuss the various forms of diplomacy.

6. How do you think traditional diplomacy differs from new diplomacy? Elucidate.

7. Discuss the role of propaganda as a technique of foreign policy.

8. What do you mean by propaganda? What are the different techniques of propaganda?

9. How far can the use of military power be an effective technique of foreign policy?

10. In a nuclear world do you think military prowess can serve as a powerful technique of foreign policy? Argue.

REFERENCES

[1] Russett, Bruce and Harvey Starr, *World Politics: The Menu for* Choice, W.H. Freeman and Company, New York, 1996, pp. 162–163.

[2] Padelford, Norman J. and George A. Lincoln, *International Politics*, The Macmillan Company, New York, 1954, p. 306.

[3] Sharma, Urmila and S.K. Sharma, *International Relations: Theory and History*, Vol-I, Atlantic Publishers, New Delhi, 2000, pp. 112–113.

[4] *ibid.*

[5] Russet and Starr, *op. cit.*, n. 1, p. 164.

[6] Legg, Keith R. and James F. Morrison, "The Formulation of Foreign Policy Objectives", *in* Richard Little and Michael Smith (Eds.), *Perspectives on World Politics*, Routledge, London, 1991, p. 59.

[7] *ibid.*, p. 60.

[8] *ibid.*, p. 61.

[9] Holsti, K.J., *International* Politics: *A Framework for Analysis*, Prentice-Hall of India, New Delhi, 1967, p. 126.

[10] Nicolson, Sir Harold, *Diplomacy,* Oxford Universty Press, London, 1969, p. 14.

[11] Mclellan, David S., William C. Olson, Fred A. Sondermann, *The Theory and Practice of International Relations*, Prentice-Hall, Englewood Cliffs, New Jersey, 1974, p. 189.

[12] Nicolson, *op. cit.*, n. 10, pp. 3–4.

[13] Organski, A.F.K., *World Politics*, Alfred A. Knopf, New York, 1960, p. 341.

[14] Russet and Starr, *op. cit.*, n. 1, p. 138.

[15] Morgenthau, Hans. J., *Politics among Nations:* Kalyani Publishers, New Delhi, 1985, pp. 563–564.

[16] Poullada, Leon B., "Diplomacy: The Missing Link in the Study of International Politics", *in* David S. Mclellan, William C. Olson, Fred A. Sondermann (Eds.), *The Theory and Practice of International Relations*, Prentice-Hall, New Jersey, 1974, p. 194.

[17] White, Brian, "Diplomacy" *in* John Baylis and Steve Smith (Eds.), *The Globalization of World Politics,* Oxford University Press, London, 1997, p. 259.

[18] Holsti, K.J., *International Politics: A Framework for Analysis*, Prentice-Hall of India, New Delhi, 1995, p. 138.

[19] Palmer, Norman D. and Howard C. Perkins, *International Relations: The World Community in Transition,* A.I.T.B.S. Publishers, New Delhi, 1967, p. 87.

[20] Mclellan, *op. cit.*, n. 11, pp. 189–193.

[21] Nicolson, *op. cit.*, n. 10, pp. 36–39.

[22] Frankel, Joseph, *International Relations in a Changing World,* Oxford University Press, London, 1979, p. 125.

[23] Palmer and Perkins, *op. cit.*, n. 19, p. 106.

[24] White, Brian, *op. cit.*, n. 17, p. 250.

[25] *ibid.,* 251.

[26] Mclellan, *op. cit.*, n. 11, p. 207.

[27] Holsti, *op. cit.*, n. 18, pp. 152–153.

[28] Couloumbis, Theodore A. and James H. Wolfe, *Introduction to International Relations: Power and Justice*, Prentice-Hall of India, New Delhi, 1981, pp. 182–183.

[29] Holsti, *op. cit.*, n. 18, pp. 158–159.

[30] Frankel, Joseph, *op. cit.*, n. 22, pp. 131–132.

[31] Palmer and Perkins, *op. cit.*, n. 19, p. 116.

[32] *ibid.,* 115–117.

[33] Morgenthau, *op. cit.*, n. 15, p. 353.

[34] Holsti, *op. cit.*, n. 18, p. 163.

[35] Garnett, John, "The Role of Military Power", *in* Richard Little and Michael Smith (Eds.), *Perspectives on World Politics*, Routledge, London, p. 69.

[36] *ibid.*

[37] Carr, E.H., *The Twenty Years' Crisis:1919–1939,* The Macmillan Press, London, 1981, pp. 109–111.

[38] Goldstein, Joshua S., *International Relations*, Pearson Education, New Delhi, 2006, pp. 261–263.

[39] Holsti, *op. cit.*, n. 18, pp. 214–224.

[40] Waltz, Kenneth N., "International Structure, National Force and the Balance of Power", *in* David S. Mclellan, William C. Olson, Fred A. Sondermann (Eds.), *The Theory and Practice of International Relations*, Prentice-Hall, Englewood Cliffs, New Jersey, 1974, pp. 297–303.

[41] Garnett, John, *op. cit.*, n. 35, p. 80.

6

Cold War and Evolution of Post-Cold War World

CONTENTS

INTRODUCTION

Soon after the conclusion of the Second World War, the world was engulfed in a different sort of a struggle for global leadership between the two former allies, the United States and the erstwhile Soviet Union. Both emerged as superpowers immediately after the Second World War. Great Britain was exhausted and no longer was able to hold on to the position of a global power. Germany being partitioned and Japan being devastated by atomic bombs, failed to emerge as great powers. This left only the United States and the Soviet Union to play a decisive role in the international scenario. However, the relation between the two became strained for a number of reasons and assumed the form of **Cold War**, which was short of hot war. This resulted in the bifurcation of the world into two rival blocs and creation of a number of military alliances and counter alliances. Though there was a temporary thaw in their relations, regarded as détente, but that too was short-lived and soon degenerated into another round of tensions and strained relations, often called **New Cold War.** Ultimately, the Cold War ended in 1990, with the dismemberment of the former Soviet Union.

MEANING

The term **Cold War** was popularized by the columnist, Walter Lippmann and it came into common use by 1947. It came to acquire a special meaning, signifying that the relations between the East and the West, though bad and war like, and strained but had not reached the point of hot war. It symbolized intense competition in political economic fronts and even on ideological grounds but never assumed the stature of hot war or actual armed conflict between the two blocs. Calvocoressi[1] observes that Cold War was not an episode like other wars, which had beginnings and ends, winners and losers. It signified a state of affairs.

ORIGIN OF COLD WAR

It is an arduous task to trace the origin and development of Cold War. Young and Kent[2] point out that there had been innumerable debates regarding the nature and origin of the early Cold War which had a definite impact on the ways the historians and social scientists had interpreted the nature of international system, till 1989. The origin of Cold War still remains a matter of long-standing historical dispute.

The orthodox theories assume that the alleged Soviet aggression or Soviet expansionism resulted in American counter reactions. They opine that in essence the Cold War became a battle for global influence because Stalin and the Soviet system made cooperation impossible. For them, Stalin and Soviet Communism had to be confronted and contained by the Western capitalist states for the sake of international peace and security and the survival of the liberal democratic values. To be more specific, an allegedly expansionist Soviet Union threatened the 'national security' of the United States and the Western Europe which required an economic and military response. This can be viewed more or less as the realist or neo-realist perception of the superpower rivalry. In this perception, power and security as well as functioning of the capitalist and communist states and their respective external requirements figure more importantly rather than ideology or internal structure.

The orthodox view was challenged in the 1960s by the revisionist historians who focussed less on the international state system and the struggle to gain greater power and influence and more on the alleged requirements of international capitalism, especially of the United States in the 1940s. Revisionist interpretation laid emphasis on the foreign policy requirements of the United States, which they viewed was designed to meet the expansionist requirements of capitalism. The Soviets, therefore, sought security in the form of resisting expansion of capitalism into areas that would threaten the existence of Soviet

Communism. Thus, for the revisionists, the blame for the Cold War lies with the aggressive US policies to which the Soviets had to respond. According to this perception, therefore, rather than Soviet expansionism creating insecurity for the United States, the US commitment to the expansion of capitalism created a sort of Soviet insecurity.

The post-revisionist writers have sought to focus more on factors such as geo-politics, cultural traits and elite perceptions on psychology, bureaucratic politics, security requirements, misunderstandings and misperceptions, none of which is mutually exclusive. Geo-politically, the pre-1917 development of two land-based empires in Eurasia and the Western Hemisphere inevitably meant that these two exploitative land-based systems would come into conflict.[2]

Whatever may be the different perspectives on the origin of Cold War, it can be said that the Cold War broke out because of ideological confrontation, post-Second World War complications and irreconcilability of vital interests of USA and the Soviet Union.

Causes of Cold War

The first and the foremost reason for antagonism between the two superpowers was the opening of the Second Front to divide the German army. The Soviet Union was pressurizing the opening of the Second Front from June 1941 but finally, the Supreme Commander, General Dwight Eisenhower (who later became the US president) opened the Second Front in June 1944. The delay in opening the Second Front created suspicion in the minds of the Soviets resulting in antagonism between the two.

Soon after the conclusion of the Second World War, the two wartime allies stood divided on the Polish and German questions. In the case of Poland, though at the Potsdam Conference of July 1945, the Oder–Neisse line was considered the *de facto* line between Poland and Germany whose ultimate fate would be finalized through a peace treaty with Germany, yet the future democracy or governance of Poland remained undecided. The Soviets, considering that Eastern Europe lay within their sphere of influence, installed a Polish government dominated by the communists. The US president Harry S. Truman, after assuming office, with the support of British Prime Minister Churchill demanded that the composition of the Polish government should be equally divided between the communists and the so-called London Pols or the London-government-in-exile backed by the British. Lend-lease aid to the Soviet Union was suspended by Washington but Stalin refused to give in and the emergent Polish government remained firmly oriented towards the Soviet Union.

German question proved to be another stumbling block in the superpower relations, which unfolded at the Potsdam Conference of July 1945. The question of post-war reparations from Germany led to sharp arguments. Soviet Union insisted that goods and assets worth 20 billion dollars should be ceased from Germany, of which 50 per cent should be given to the Soviet Union and the rest to be shared between the USA and the UK as war indemnity. But an element of suspicion was harboured by the USA and the UK. The Western powers insisted their right to fix the level of reparations in their own zones of occupation and, by spring 1946, they suspended further reparation payments to the Soviet Union from their zones of occupation in West Germany.[3]

Post-Second World War, Soviet activities in Iran, Turkey and Greece gave birth to suspicions in the West. Initially these factors embittered the relations between the two superpowers, once the allies and gradually assumed the shape of the Cold War. As years passed by the Cold War between the two intensified because of different misconceptions, misperceptions, threats to each other's sphere of influence, increased arms race, and alleged threats to each other's vital interests. Hence, the theatre of Cold War shifted from one part of the world to the other and had unfurled itself in different phases, virtually dividing the world into two antagonistic blocs. The antagonism between the two became evident from the 'long telegram' assessing the sources of Soviet conduct sent by George F.Kennan, the then Diplomat in the American embassy in Moscow. Kennan concluded "In summary, we have here a political force committed fanatically to the belief that with [the] US there can be no permanent *modus operandi*, that, it is desirable and necessary that the internal harmony of our society be disrupted, our traditional way of life be destroyed, the international authority of our state be broken, if Soviet power is to be secured". Thus, what Kennan contended was that "In these circumstances it is clear that the main element of any United States policy toward the Soviet Union must be that of a long-term, patient but firm and vigilant *containment* of Russian expansive tendencies". His ideas became very popular soon after its publication in an article in the *Foreign Affairs* under the pseudonym 'X'. This came to be known as the famous "X article".[4]

Soon, situations in Greece and Turkey took such a turn that President Truman made Kennan's assessment the keystone of the US foreign policy in the post-War years. The violence in Greece and Turkey was viewed by the Americans as inspired and instigated by the communists and, thus, Truman declared in March 1947, "I believe that it must be the policy of the United States to support the free peoples who are resisting attempted subjugation by armed minorities or by outside pressures". This ultimately came to be identified as the **Truman Doctrine**. Thus, was born **the policy of containment** which aimed at preventing the expansion of the Soviet influence by encircling the Soviet Union and intimidating it with the threat of a military attack. Therefore, by late 1940s, the world witnessed the beginning of the formation of the two opposing blocs and it was reinforced by the **Marshall Plan** of 5 June 1947. Earlier on 5 March 1946, Churchill's Fulton speech had signalled the beginning of the Cold War as he described in his speech that an Iron Curtain across Europe from Stettin in the Baltic to Trieste in the Adriatic had been drawn.[5] Only the Truman Doctrine and the Marshall Plan reaffirmed his contention and set an emerging new paradigm in the US foreign policy.

PHASES OF COLD WAR
1946–1949

The first phase of the Cold War was triggered off with the gradual consolidation of the Soviet influence in Eastern Europe and its inroads into the geo-strategic sphere of influence of the Western powers in Iran, Turkey and Greece. The situations in Greece, Turkey and Iran incited the United States to adopt an **interventionist foreign policy** against its erstwhile policy of isolationism.[6]

The crisis in Iran started, especially when the Russian troops failed to withdraw as per an allied agreement of 1942. Further, it was alleged that in the Soviet-occupied Iran, the Soviets encouraged local independence movements and even instigated a rebellion in Northern Iran and forced it to sign a Treaty which would give Russian access to Iranian oil. To ward-off the Soviet threat of expansion, the United States mounted pressure in the United Nations Security Council. With the United Nations intervention the Soviets finally withdrew, but the damage was already done. Determined US support for Iran was based on the belief that further Soviet expansion must be contained at any cost.

In Turkey, the Soviets demanded the internationalization of the Bosporus Strait, which had been under the Turkish control since 1936. During the Second World War, Churchill backed the Soviet claim but, when the divisions between the superpowers became evident, he fundamentally changed his position. Following the Soviet activities in Iran, the Allies apprehended a possible effort on the part of Soviet Union to expand its sphere of influence, and therefore, adopted gestures to resist the Soviet expansion.

In Greece, the Civil War, resulting from the guerilla warfare, led by the communists that launched attacks on the Greek government posed a threat to the Western powers. Britain, the traditional arbiter of the region, however failed to control the situation. Therefore, USA was called upon to counter the growing threat of the communist guerilla attacks. President Truman responded by approving legislation passed in the US Congress that permitted the President to send aid and military advisers to Greece. Subsequently, Truman dispatched military forces to tackle the situation. It was in this context that the **Truman Doctrine** was born which constituted a call to resist outside forces which clearly was directed against international communism and, by implication, it pointed at the Soviet Union.

This was soon followed by the Marshall Plan of 5 June 1947. The conditions in Greece and Turkey made it inevitable to preserve Western Europe from the Soviet influence. Around this time, the communists were able to garner support in Europe, especially in countries like Belgium, Greece, Italy and Hungary. In Belgium, Denmark, Norway, the Netherlands and Sweden, the communists were able to mobilize an average of 10 per cent of the vote. Further, the dwindling European national economies led to the instability of these countries. Therefore, to thwart communist subversion and restore stability of European countries by revamping the national economies, the Marshall Plan was announced. The

Marshall Plan envisaged the transfer of significant amount of funds to Europe on the assumption that only a massive monetary infusion would allow Europe to resurrect from the ravages of war and stabilize its material condition and political atmosphere. The main line of thinking was that a stable Europe would be able to resist the indigenous and exogenous communists.

The Soviet response to the Marshall Plan was the Molotov Plan of July 1947 which included a series of bilateral agreements linking the Soviet Union with the East European countries. This was the economic response to the Marshall Plan. The political response was the establishment of the Communist Information Bureau (COMINFORM) (September 1947) to provide Moscow with the institutional means to control foreign communist parties.

A year after the execution of the Marshall plan and the creation of COMINFORM, the Soviets had been successful in repressing all undesirable non-communists elements in Hungary, Romania, Bulgaria and Poland. In Czechoslovakia there was a Prague Coup in the end of February, 1948 and installation of a communist government under Clement Gottwald. The fall of Czechoslovakia raised apprehensions in the West European minds of a possible military threat from the Soviet Union. Hurriedly, the Europeans concluded the Pact of Brussels on 17 March 1948. It was a mutual defence treaty, which directed the signatories to extend military support to any member state in case of an attack by Germany or any third party in Europe. Undoubtedly, it implied the threat coming from the Soviet Union.

In protest to this Brussels Pact, in March 1948 the Soviet representatives withdrew from the Allied Control Council, which was the governing body of occupied Germany. But now the Cold War tensions started over Germany. This, coupled with the creation of West Germany in early June 1948 and the introduction of a separate currency, the Deutsche mark, in the French, US and British zones resulted in a strong Soviet response in the form of the **Berlin Blockade** in the same year. The United States to beat the Soviet blockade, which continued for 324 days had to airlift 13,000 tonnes of supplies of food per day.[7] Finally, the blockade was lifted but it increased rivalries and suspicions among the two superpowers. The Berlin Blockade also led to the militarization of Europe resulting in the formation of a military alliance—North Atlantic Treaty Organization (NATO), 4 April, 1949—to counter Soviet expansionist designs.

1949–1953

In the late 1940s, the theatre of Cold War shifted to Asia. Around this time China became an important factor in the superpower relations. The Korean War also dragged the superpowers to this region.

The formation of the Peoples Republic of China by the Chinese communists under the leadership of Mao-Tse-Tung and the defeat of the Chinese Nationalists (Kuomintang) under General Chiang Kai-shek were seen with great apprehension by the Western powers. They perceived the rise of China as a part of an 'ascendant monolithic communist bloc'. Therefore, the vision of global expansion of communism deeply influenced the US foreign policy.

The Korean War of 1950 further brought the two superpowers into confrontation, if not directly, and embittered the relationship between the two. North Korea under Kim II Sung, the leader of North Korean Communist Party, wanted to unite the peninsula which South Korea proceeded to proclaim as the Korean Republic. Therefore, the stage was set for a major confrontation. Along the 38 parallel, skirmishes broke out and on that pretext North Korea invaded South Korea on 25 June 1950. South Korea was battered badly by North Korean forces and its Capital Seoul was conquered by the latter. On the other side of the 38 parallel, substantial Soviet support to North Korea further fuelled US fears of another communist bid to expand further into Asia. So, USA came to the relief of South Korea and it launched a counter-attack from Japan. Matters became worse when Chinese intervention took place in the Korean War.

Simultaneously, USA was successful in moving a resolution in the United Nations Security Council and declared North Korea as an aggressor, and launched a full-fledged offensive against North Korea with the help of UN troops. USA took advantage of the long absence of the Soviet representation in the Security Council, bypassed the Security Council, and passed the Uniting for Peace Resolution (UPR), in 1950. By virtue of UPR, it could take actions even in the absence of Soviet representation. However, with an armistice signed in July 1953, after the death of Stalin there was a cessation of hostility but much damage was done to the relations between the two superpowers.

Further, the detonation of the first Soviet nuclear device in August 1949, also ended the US nuclear monopoly and created a sort of fear in the minds of the Western European states. They now lacked confidence in the United States and also in the Western military strength, and harboured a fear of nuclear attack from Soviet Union.

1953–1959

After the Korean crisis, the Indo-China became the theatre of Cold War tensions between the superpowers. The riding tensions between the French colonial administration and the communist national liberation movement, the Viet Minh was looked at with suspicion by USA. By January 1950, the Soviets and the new regime of China had given diplomatic recognition to the Viet Minh. By 1954, the Viet Minh controlled large tracts of North Vietnam and made its presence felt in the southern part of the country too. Further, to much shock and awe of the Western powers, the communist influence spread from Vietnam to the adjacent areas of Laos and Cambodia .

The United States tried to support the French economically and militarily and President Eisenhower elaborated his apprehensions regarding the situation in Vietnam in his famous **Domino theory**. He said, "You have a row of dominoes set, you knock over the first one, and what will happen to the last one is the certainty that it will go over very quickly. So you have a beginning of a disintegration that would have the most profound influences".[8] This Domino theory or, in other words, "knocking over" one South-east Asian State after another, led the United States into the Indo-China War, known as the **Vietnam War** in the United States and the greatest debacle faced by the United States in this war is known worldwide.

Finally, in the Indo-China Conference convened in Geneva in 1954, Vietnam was divided along the 17 parallel and there was also the recognition of Laotian and Cambodian independence.

Another flash point of Cold War rivalry was the Peoples Republic of China and its tensed relation with the island of Formosa, better known as Taiwan, which was taken over by the Nationalists under Chiang Kai-shek with active support of USA. But in 1954, Beijing declared that it is going to liberate Taiwan. Despite US warning, that any action against Taiwan would prompt a determined response on the part of the US, the People's Liberation Army commenced shelling of Quemoy and the proximate Tachen islands. The US Congress passed the Formosa Resolution under which it pledged to defend Formosa. After much nerve-wracking situations the Chinese expressed their willingness for negotiation and accommodation with the Nationalists. The First Taiwan Crisis came to an end, only to begin soon after, with the re-equipping at a massive scale by the US of the Nationalist army of Taiwan, raising suspicion in the Chinese mind about a mounting threat. Followed by this was Khrushchev's visit to Beijing to assure the Chinese communists of the reliability of Soviet nuclear deterrent in the face of an American nuclear attack. This visit caused much unease and antagonisms in the United States. Coupled with this was the increasing hostile relations between Mao and Chiang Kai-shek which ultimately led to shelling of Quemoy and Matsu, by the Chinese communist troops in August 1958. Ultimately, Eisenhower dispatched the Seventh Fleet in the Taiwan Strait and reinforced US troops, stationed in Taiwan, and realizing his determined stance China called off the attack in October. But this incident ruptured the Sino-Soviet bonhomie on the one hand as the Chinese communists realized the unreliability of Soviet support and on the other escalated the tension between the superpowers.

The Middle East became a hot bed of tension in the mid 1950s. The Suez crisis set the stage for another bout of hostility between the superpowers in the Middle East. Following the nationalization of the Anglo-French Suez Canal Company on 26 July 1956, Great Britain, France and Israel decided to initiate a concerted attack against Egypt as their trade and security interests were suddenly jeopardized. Israel especially was vociferous against Egypt because of the understanding between the Soviet Union and Egypt, followed by mass influx of Soviet arms in the region. The Western powers also apprehended a Soviet–Egyptian alliance. The French and the British motive was to overthrow the Arab Nationalist Government of Nasser because his **pan-Arabism** gave much trouble in the respective overseas colonies of French and British in this region and the

Suez crisis gave them a pretext to save them from the dissolution of their colonial empire.

President Eisenhower, in the face of a nuclear threat against Britain and France by Moscow and decision to send Soviet volunteers to support Egypt, proclaimed the so-called **Eisenhower Doctrine** in January 1957. In a message to the Congress, he maintained that the US troops would be used to protect the nations in the region from the countries that were "controlled by international communism". The Eisenhower Doctrine had the same objective in regard to Middle East as Truman Doctrine had towards Greece and Turkey, i.e., **containment of communism**[9], which automatically added to the superpower rivalry.

The Soviet intervention in Hungarian Revolt of 1956 also embittered the relations between the superpowers. Following the decision of the Hungarian Prime Minister, Imre Nagy, to withdraw from the WARSAW Pact and establish the country's neutrality, on 4 Nov 1956, the Red Army intervened in a bid to prevent Hungary from joining the Western bloc and weakening the Eastern bloc. Secretary of State, John Foster Dulles adopted the aggressive rhetoric of roll back, i.e., "rolling back" communism and used all means like Radio Free Europe to encourage a Hungarian rebellion against Soviet intervention. But his rhetoric rang hollow as thousands of Hungarians lost their lives.

Side by side, the Berlin crisis again resurfaced following Khrushchev's Berlin ultimatum. He demanded the West to agree on a peace Treaty along the lines of the Potsdam Accord for the constitution of a confederated German state and exclude the two Germanies from the two blocs and granting privileges of a free city to Berlin. Therefore, there ensued serious tensions among the superpowers. Ultimately, the Camp David of 1959 eased the tensions.

Added to these developments was the US bid to consolidate its sphere of influence, after the Korean War. The US entered into treaties and made commitments in a number of different regions. Before the Korean War, the US was only bound by the military treaty, outside the Western hemisphere, the NATO. After the Korean War the US concluded The Security Treaty between Australia, New Zealand (ANZUS) on 1 September 1951, The Japanese Peace Treaty on 8 September 1951, the South East Asian Treaty Organization (SEATO) on 8 September 1954 and the Middle East Defence Organisation on 24 February 1955. In 1955 the Baghdad Pact was signed with the United Kingdom, Turkey, Pakistan, Iran and Iraq as members. In 1953, the US also entered into a defence agreement with South Korea guaranteeing the security of South Korea. With Taiwan also, after the island of Quemoy was bombed, the Eisenhower administration entered into a Mutual Defence Treaty to ensure the security of Taiwan in the event of Chinese communist aggression. As Secretary of State, Dulles declared in the report on the first 90 days of the administration that "the Far East has received a high priority. Furthermore, it has been made clear that we think our friends in the Far East, from Japan, Korea and Formosa to Indo-China and Malaya face a united enemy front, which has to be met by a common attitude and greater cooperation among the separate links of freedom".[10] The Soviet Union was not far behind and it also organized its sphere of influence in the form of a military alliance, the WARSAW Pact which was concluded on 14 May 1955. Pacts and counter pacts, therefore, added to the Cold War tensions.

1959–1962

After the Camp David, it was decided to convene a four-power summit meeting in Paris in May 1960. But the U-2 incident, where the Soviets downed an American U-2 'spy plane' loaded with photographic equipment for gathering of intelligence data, came as a setback to this effort. The diplomatic battle that started after the incident made it inevitable that the Soviets would again raise the Berlin problem. Undoubtedly, the Berlin problem again came to the fore in 1961 and matters became worse with the erection of a 25-mile long Berlin wall on 13 August 1961, which cordoned off the East from the West and with the construction of the Berlin Wall, the 'Iron Curtain' became a reality.

In Cuba, the failed Bay of Pigs, a counter-revolution against Fidel Castro, signified the survival of a communist base from where the Soviets could threaten the United States and also cause security threats to other Western nations. Added to this apprehension, in the fall of 1962, a U-2 reconnaissance plane photographed missile-launching sites under construction by the Soviets in Cuba. The two superpowers looked eyeball-to-eyeball and the world was on the verge of witnessing a massive nuclear war. Ultimately, sanity prevailed and the conventional superiority, especially naval superiority of the United States, in the Caribbean, forced Khrushchev to retract. In the words of the Secretary of State, Dean Rusk, "We were eyeball to eyeball, and the other fellow just blinked". The period following the Cuban Missile Crisis was a period of restraint and both the superpowers took interest in easing of tensions between them. This period is regarded in the history of Cold War as **Détente**.

TOWARDS TEMPORARY THAW—DÉTENTE

Détente—Meaning

The Cuban Missile Crisis was an eye-opener for both the superpowers and also a *catalytic* learning experience for them. This experience made them aware of the impending threat of mutual destruction with the growing parity of American and Soviet military capabilities that made co-existence or non-existence appear to be the only alternative. Therefore, easing of tensions between the two superpowers became necessary. At the American University, in 1963, President John F. Kennedy explained the necessity of reduction of tensions and lessening the risk of war.

"Today, should total war ever break out again—no matter how—our two countries would become the primary targets. It is an ironical but accurate fact that the two strongest powers are the two in the most danger of devastation. We are both caught up in a vicious and dangerous cycle in which suspicion on one side breeds suspicion on the other and new weapons beget counter weapons.

In short, both the United States and its allies, and the Soviet Union and its allies, have a mutually deep interest in a just and genuine peace and in halting the arms race....

So let us not be blind to our differences, but let us also direct attention to our common interests and to the means by which those differences can be resolved. And if we cannot end now our differences, at least we can help make the world safe for diversity".[11]

Though Kennedy's exposition signalled a shift in the American policy towards Soviet Union, but the chief architect of détente was Richard Nixon and his National Security Adviser, Henry Kissinger. In the words of Kissinger, détente sought to create "a vested interest in cooperation and restraint", "an environment in which competitors can regulate and restrain their differences and ultimately move from competition to cooperation".

Later, President Jimmy Carter defined détente as the easing of tension between two nations and the evolution of new means by which the two nations could live together in peace. The Soviets looked at détente as a peaceful coexistence between different political and social systems, as a need to prevent nuclear war and resolve disputes by peaceful means and mutually advantageous cooperation.

It is very difficult to give an exact meaning to such ambiguous concepts like détente. Nevertheless, the initiatives and serious developments that took place during the period of détente "were a far cry from sustained cooperation between the ideological antagonists, but they did signal a departure from the posture of confrontation that had previously typified Soviet–American relations. Cooperative behaviour was evident, however, intermittent and fleeting, amidst a pattern of continued competition for advantage and influence".[12]

Causes of Détente

Détente, as it came to occupy the centre stage of US–Soviet relations, naturally raised the question as to why both the superpowers suddenly sought détente or temporary relaxation of tensions. The point to be noted here of course is that before the Cuban Missile Crisis also there were attempts to ease tensions. After the Potsdam Summit, the two superpowers met in Geneva in 1955. Though there was no such pathbreaking achievements, yet the meeting was an expression of the altered climate between the East and the West, the 'spirit of Geneva' as it came to be known. President Eisenhower and Bulganin exchanged assurances that nuclear warfare had no rational purpose and both the powers were not interested in beginning such a war. Following the Geneva Summit, Moscow joined the Olympic Winter Games in 1956, negotiations on arms control also proceeded, though no final agreement was reached. The death of Stalin in March 1953 also brought about changes in the Soviet policy. Yet the spirit could not be carried forward due to the suppression of Hungarian revolution by the Soviets, the Suez Crisis and the German problem. But given the intensity of the Cuban Missile Crisis of 1962, which almost turned the Cold War into a hot war, the two superpowers gave a rethinking to their strategies towards each other.

The causes for Détente can be seen as many. Some of the major factors leading to détente are:

Attainment of Strategic Parity by the Superpowers: The shift in the balance of power signalled a shift in the policies of both the superpowers towards the path of détente. The USA so long used its Strategic Air Command (SAC), later supplemented by the navy's nuclear submarines, to deter the Red Army. The US bombers and missiles deterred the Soviets with their implied threat of destroying their cities. But this strategic superiority, that was enjoyed by the United States was soon challenged by the Soviets. The American–Soviet balance had been asymmetric so far: the USA enjoyed strategic superiority and an intercontinental reach, and the Soviet Union enjoyed conventional superiority and a regional reach. But the Soviets gained its inter-continental capability and capacity of destroying USA as well as Western Europe from its massive build-up that began after 1964. The number of Soviet intercontinental missiles had surpassed the number of American land-based missiles. As Northedge and Grieve[13] observed, "The fear of thermonuclear war, which could annihilate both sides, and determination to avoid the kind of confrontations between two superpowers from which thermonuclear war could spring".

American Compulsions: The first and the foremost factor, which compelled the United States to walk in the path of détente, was the rising public opinion which was very much critical about America's role as a "global policeman". The mood within the United States reflected its weariness resulting from its foreign policy burdens. For Nixon and Ford, détente was necessary until the nation could "recover its nerve" and once more play the leading role. Therefore, détente was required to protect the US interests against Soviet expansion. The Vietnam debacle had placed the United States in a difficult position. Due to heavy involvement in the Vietnam War huge amount of US resources had to be committed. The more the Americans fought, the higher was the morale of the North Vietnam and the Viet Cong. Even extensive bombing by the United States could not prevent escalation of the war on the part of North Vietnam. But the US involvement in the warfare and massive bombing raised criticisms from many quarters, including the Americans themselves. The truth was that the massive effort did not result in any visible success, especially after the Tet offensive of North Vietnam and the Viet Cong in 1968. Therefore, the United States wanted to end the Vietnam War in an honourable way and thought that Soviet help was necessary as the Soviets were also actively involved in the war and provided economic and military assistance to North Vietnam. Disengagement from Vietnam became the prime motivation for Nixon and Kissinger to seek détente.

Soviet Compulsions: The change in the attitude of the policy makers in Kremlin also became a factor for Moscow to seek détente. Malenkov, who became the Russian Prime Minister after Stalin's death, had started his drive towards détente but it became more evident in Khrushchev and later in Brezhnev–Kosygin period. They embarked upon a policy of peaceful coexistence. Besides, there were also economic compulsions on the part of the Soviet Union. The lopsided development created shortage of wage-goods and other consumer durables as a result unemployment was on the rise. As Northedge and Grieve observed, "Again the rising living standards in the Soviet Union probably gave that country a strong interest, like Americans'; in reducing the massive scale of arms expenditure in the cold war by arms control agreements, in increasing its lagging technology by agreements with the Western powers to make their skills and equipment available to Russian industry and perhaps above all, in keeping *status quo* stable in eastern Europe, when it was threatened by liberalization programme of Dubchek of Czechoslovakia".[14]

The China Factor: The emergence of China as another major power led not only to easing of tensions between the two superpowers but also ushered in the Sino–American rapproachement. The rise of Communist China posed a direct challenge to the Soviet Union as China became the alternative source of aid and encouragement to the liberation movements in South-East Asia and even communist states in Eastern Europe, such as Albania and Rumania. Further, in 1964 China detonated its first atomic bomb. What became evident was the growing Sino–Soviet rift, which erupted into open clash in 1969 over the border dispute regarding the number of islands located in the Ussuri River.

The bipolar world of the Cold War was becoming tripolar. The worsening of relation of China with the Soviet Union led the United States to take leverage of the Sino–Soviet split. Nixon and Kissinger played the China card well. USA took the initiative to recognize Mao's regime as the rightful government of China in early 1971. USA also sent a US table-tennis team to China, dubbed as a ping-pong diplomacy, which was well-acknowledged by the Chinese. In July 1971, Kissinger's secret visit to China, followed by Nixon's tour, only six months later surely showed the US intentions of playing China against the Soviet Union. Therefore, the US fostered good relations with both the communists giants, and more precisely, towards the Soviet Union using the policy of 'carrot' and 'stick'.

Brandt's Ostpolitik: The German Chancellor, Willy Brandt's *Ostpolitik* was largely responsible for easing of tensions between the two superpowers. Bonn initially tried to extend relations with the countries of Eastern Europe but that got a jolt with the Soviet invasion on Czechoslovakia in 1968. Bonn realized that without Moscow's support this could not be achieved. Therefore, improvement of relations with Moscow became a priority. On 12 August 1970, Soviet Union entered into a non-aggression treaty with West Germany. This agreement with the Soviet Union laid the foundation for similar agreements with Poland and East Germany. Even Brandt acceded to the Oder–Neisse line as Polish frontier and this was designed to propagate the spirit of *Ostpolitik*. This normalized relations not only between West Germany and Soviet Union but also between the Eastern and the Western blocs. Thus, Summits between the East and the West became common.

Linkage Theory: The chief architects of détente, Richard Nixon and Henry Kissinger, envisaged the easing of tensions on the basis of **linkage strategy**. This aimed at binding the two rivals in a common fate by making peaceful superpower relations dependent on the continuation of mutually rewarding exchanges (such as trade concessions), thereby lessening the incentives for conflict and war.

Implications of Détente

The crux of the matter is that shifts in the policy produced results as relations between the Soviets and Americans 'normalized'. Détente was marked by several major visits, cultural exchanges, trade agreements, joint technological ventures and, obviously arms reduction endeavours, in place of threats, warnings and confrontations.

Détente witnessed several developments such as the following:

1. Immediately after the Cuban Missile Crisis, a "hotline" was installed in 1963 linking the White House and the Kremlin.

2. The Partial Test Ban Treaty was signed in 1963, the Outer Space Treaty was signed in 1967, and the Nuclear Non-Proliferation Treaty (NPT) was signed in 1968. The Sea-Bed Pact banned the testing of nuclear devices on the bottom of the world's oceans in 1971, and a year later, the Biological Warfare Treaty aimed at curbing the use of biological agents for the purpose of war.

3. Nixon's visit to Moscow in 1972 culminated in the signing of the Strategic Arms Limitation Talks (SALT). The talks produced two agreements: The first in 1972, known as the SALT I, and the second in 1979, called SALT II. However, the SALT II Agreement was never ratified by the United States due to strong congressional opposition.

4. A number of agreements pertaining to trade, agriculture, oceanography, economic and culture followed. In 1973,Brezhnev paid a visit to Washington. The newly elected US President, Gerald Ford also visited Russia and in Vladivostok there was a US–Soviet Agreement on guidelines for arms control and reduction.

5. In Europe, détente culminated symbolically with the Conference on Security and Cooperation in Europe (CSCE) in Helsinki in

August 1975. It was attended by 34 countries of Europe and North America and formulated certain agreed principles regarding the relationship between the states of the two blocs. Though nothing concrete was achieved, yet it contributed to the easing of tensions.

6. The spirit of détente was carried forward with the United States and Soviet Union's Apollo–Soyuz joint mission in July 1975.

7. Détente also gave an opportunity to the United States to mend its relationship with China.

Certain Uncertainties and End of Détente

Despite careful nurturing of détente, its spirit did not live long and several irritants cropped up. Czechoslovakia experienced **Prague Spring** or socialism with a human face, under the reformist leader, Alexander Dubèhèk in 1967 who also decided to withdraw from the WARSAW Pact. Brezhnev apprehended that Dubèhèk's reforms had been intended to foment a nationalist counter-revolution within the Soviet sphere of influence and Dubèhek's move signalled its defection towards the West. Soon, Brezhnev proclaimed what came to be known as the **Brezhnev Doctrine** which stipulated in no uncertain terms that a communist state was within its rights when it intervenes in the internal affairs of an East European state if such action would prevent the re-introduction of a capitalist social system. Working along the lines of this doctrine Brezhnev took steps to crush the **Prague Spring.** This became an irritant in the East–West relations.[15]

The Indo–Pak War of 1965–66 and the War of liberation of Bangladesh in 1971 fuelled the superpower rivalry. Then there was the Middle East crisis which also dampened the mood of the détente in 1973. After the six-day-war, Israel occupied the Sharm El-Sheikh, Sinai and drove the Jordanian troops from Jerusalem and savaged the Syrian army in the Golan Heights. The defeat was a great humiliation to the pan-Arab national pride. The Arab nations continued their refusal to recognize Israel resulting in intermittent raids and skirmishes. But matters came to a head again when Anwar Sadat, who succeeded Nasser, with a combined Egyptian–Syrian force, launched a surprise attack on 6 October 1973—the Jewish Day of Atonement (*Yom Kippur*)—against Israel. After the initial shock, the Israelis were capable of stopping the advance of the combined forces. At this stage the Arab nations imposed an oil embargo on any country aiding Israel. The United States was the largest supplier of arms to Israel and the oil embargo placed the US and its allies in inconvenience. Added to this was the Israeli non-compliance to the US–Soviet plan presented before the United Nations, that earned the Soviet wrath. Brezhnev threatened to take necessary steps to force Israeli compliance with the truce. The superpower competition in the region raised the intensity of Israeli–Arab wars. Though the Yom Kippur war ended with the Israeli victory and ultimately an Israeli–Arab rapproachement reached at Camp David in 1978, the spirit of détente was hard hit.[16]

The final blow to détente came with the Soviet invasion of Afghanistan in 1979 and symbolized the beginning of the **New Cold War**.

END OF DÉTENTE BEGINNING OF NEW COLD WAR

Causes of New Cold War

Soviet invasion of Afghanistan was perceived by the then US President, Jimmy Carter as "Soviet Aggression in Afghanistan—unless checked—confronts all the world with the most serious strategic challenge since the Cold War began". He retaliated by proclaiming the famous **Carter Doctrine**, which declared America's willingness to use military force to protect its interests in the Persian Gulf. He proclaimed that "any attempt by any outside force to gain control of the Persian Gulf region will be regarded as an assault on the vital interests of the United States. It will be repelled by the use of any means necessary, including military force".[17] The overthrow of the Shah of Iran, in 1979, gave impetus to the American Plan for Rapid Deployment Force under consideration. The United States tried to secure bases in Kenya, Somalia and Oman in order to protect the American interests in the Indian Ocean and Persian Gulf regions. Along with this, he tried to organize a worldwide boycott of the 1980 Moscow Olympics and suspended the US grain exports to the Soviet Union.

Further the non-ratification of the SALT II by the American Senate also increased tensions between the superpowers. The Soviets were bitter regarding the US involvement in Nicaragua, Grenada and El Salvador. The Americans, on the other hand, were critical about the Soviet activities in Angola and the Middle East.

At this critical juncture the ascendancy of Ronald Reagan to the Presidency of the United States led to the beginning of a **New Cold War.** Brezhnev, in October 1982, admitted "Russia declares détente with the USA as dead".

President Ronald Reagan and his Russian counterparts, first Andropov and then Chernenko, soon got embroiled in a barrage of confrontational rhetoric. Reagan declared that Soviet Union "underlies all the unrest that is going on" and considered the Soviet Union as the "focus of evil in the modern world". American statements regarding the use of nukes and military intervention in Grenada and Libya and US activities in Central America, especially support for the *contras* in Nicaragua, increased the tensions between the superpowers. Arms race resumed and arms control talks were ruptured. The Soviets boycotted the 1984 Olympic Games in Los Angeles. Under such 'hot' circumstances, Reagan proclaimed his famous doctrine, generally known as the **Reagan Doctrine.** He pledged US support to anticommunists insurgents to overthrow Soviet-supported governments in Afghanistan, Angola and Nicaragua.

President Reagan vowed to take the wars to the space. His **Strategic Defence Initiative (SDI),** dubbed **Star Wars**, had grave consequences on the superpower relations. The SDI was a research programme designed to explore opportunities of space-based defences against ballistic missiles. This was not welcomed by the Soviets and they took the threats seriously and it dampened the relations. Ultimately, the SDI did not materialize and later on was abandoned by Reagan's successors. Nevertheless, the situations became explosive and more complex because of the moves and countermoves of the superpowers.

Though the situation became alarming it did not explode primarily with the ascendancy of Mikhail Gorbachev as the President of Soviet Union in 1985. His *new thinking* in foreign policy and his domestic reforms (*glasnost* and *perestroika*) marked a new beginning in the East–West relations. Therefore, there was again easing of tensions between the two superpowers, which was followed by what is known as **New Détente** and ultimately the **end of Cold War.**

END OF COLD WAR: THE NEW DÉTENTE

The ascendancy of Gorbachev as the President of the Soviet Union marked a new beginning in the East–West relations. His ascendancy to the Presidency paved the way for agreements on nuclear and conventional forces. The Geneva Summit of 19–21 November 1985 was the first Soviet–American summit held after the outbreak of the Afghanistan crisis. Here, both USA and the Soviet Union focussed on the need for preventing any sort of war—nuclear or conventional—between them. The Reykjavik Summit of 11–12 October 1986 was the Second Summit where President Reagan and President Gorbachev met to discuss various major problems of international politics and other issues of mutual interest. This was followed by the pathbreaking Washington Summit of 7–10 December 1987. In 1987, Gorbachev travelled to the United States and signed the Intermediate Range Nuclear Forces (INF) Treaty banning intermediate range nuclear missiles including Cruise and Pershing II missiles. Gorbachev and Reagan met at the Moscow Summit of May 1988, and the Malta Summit of 1989 marked a new beginning in the US and USSR relations as well as in international politics. A host of summits followed between Gorbachev and the new American President George Bush (Sr.) symbolizing several agreements on arms control, trade and also the question of German reunification. There was also the Helsinki Summit regarding the Gulf Crisis of 1990, but the most important breakthrough came in the Moscow Summit of 1991 and signing of Strategic Arms Reduction Treaty (START). In July 1991, President Bush and President Gorbachev signed the START for deep cuts in their strategic arsenals.[18] The Conventional Forces in Europe (CFE) Treaty also reduced the Soviet presence in Europe. The Soviet Union also agreed to withdraw their aid and support to Cuba, Afghanistan and Eastern Europe. All these developments signalled the beginning of the end of Cold War.

In 1991 and early 1992, President Bush declared massive unilateral nuclear arms cut and this was matched by Russia by substantial reduction in the former Soviet nuclear arsenal. He had proclaimed the end of Cold War in the early nineties but, on 1 February 1992, President Bush and the visiting Russian

Federation President, Boris Yeltsin made a formal declaration of the end of the Cold War and to beginning of a new era of relationship between the United States and the Russian Federation. After intense talks at Camp David in February 1992, the two leaders signed a declaration, which sought to highlight the new relationship based on trust and commitment to economic and political freedom. In June 1992, Yeltsin and Bush signed the "Washington Charter" and six other documents relating to economic, scientific and military cooperation between the two.[19] Therefore, decades of hostility, antagonism and suspicion ended and paved way for post-Cold War development in the relation between the US and the Russian Federation and changes in the international system in the post-Cold War era.

End of Cold War

Gorbachev's *new thinking* reflected in his **glasnost** (openness) and **perestroika** (political and economic restructuring) unleashed such forces which ultimately became the reason of destruction of the Soviet Union. Internally, there were several reasons which led to the collapse of communism. Richard Crockatt pointed out some long- and short-term causes which included structural weaknesses in the economy, inflexible planning system, inability to modernize; economic stagnation; poor harvest and ironically, Gorbachev's glasnost and perestroika also contributed to the disintegration of the Soviet Union. The last one heavily damaged the existence of the Soviet Union as it undermined the role of the Communist party and also loosened the control over media which made the public opinion out of control of Gorbachev. Following the elections of 1989, a number of communist candidates were defeated and there took place "a whirlwind of free debate that scattered every known communist taboo".[20] This was coupled with the demand for independence and secessionist movements which finally led to the crumbling of the Soviet Union. In reality, Gorbachev underestimated the task of changing the Soviet Union overnight. This led to policy errors and contributed to the failure of his programme of resurrecting socialism built on the foundation of successful implementation of **perestroika** and **demokratzatsiya.**[21]

Externally, as soon as Gorbachev became reluctant to enforce the Brezhnev Doctrine marking non-intervention in the internal affairs of its East European allies, the political changes in Poland, Hungary, Czechoslovakia and East Germany gathered momentum. The Bulgarian and Romanian Communist governments collapsed by the end of 1989. The climax was reached in November 1989 when thousands of ordinary citizens broke the Berlin Wall and the security guards stood there as mere spectators. The collapse of the Berlin Wall marked the effective end of the Cold War. Ultimately, on December 1991 the Union of Soviet Socialist Republics (USSR) ceased to exist and the Commonwealth of Independent States (CIS) emerged. Once the Soviet Union ceased to exist, there was much jubilation in the capitalist camps and scholars such as Francis Fukuyama came up with *The End of History and the Last Man,* a thesis where he celebrated the victory of liberalism over all other ideologies and the globalization of liberal capitalism. The other thesis which became very popular was Samuel Huntington's *Clash of Civilization.* Here, he upheld the implications of a post-Cold War World which would come to witness an escalation of deadly conflicts around the issues of 'identity' politics including culture, ethnicity and religion. This changed scenario would induce the world community to set a new agenda for international relations.

INTERNATIONAL SYSTEM IN THE POST-COLD WAR ERA

The Cold War was an important episode in the world history but, by early 1990s, it was accepted that 'Cold War' is over. General Colin Powell, former Chairman of Joint Chiefs of Staff commented, "We have seen our implacable enemy of 40 years vaporize before our eyes". But the fact of the matter is that the end of Cold War may have signalled a victory for the US as is evident from President Bush's (Sr.) much known hype that "We have won" but, at the same time, the World witnessed a fundamental shift in the structure and patterns of international relations.

The end of Cold War witnessed the dismantling of the Soviet bloc in Eastern Europe, the collapse of communism in Eastern Europe, the disintegration of the Soviet Union with the simultaneous unification of Germany, all of which redrew the map of Europe.

With the end of the Cold War and the dismemberment of the Soviet Union, the WARSAW pact also met its doom. The alliance and counter-alliances of the Cold War days presently have assumed a peculiar characteristic with the ones formed by the United States still continuing, for example, the NATO and its activities pertaining to the politics of Europe. A reminder in this direction is the NATO bombing of Kosovo. The gearing up of NATO activities during the mini-war between Georgia and Russia in 2008 also suggests the same.

Post-Cold War scenario has come to be characterized by the return of multipolarity where there is a presence of great powers and small powers. Some scholars also uphold the view that the world has become unipolar with the presence of the sole surviving superpower, the United States. On the other hand, there are other scholars who profess multipolarity and project the emergence of a five-way balance of power system rotating around the United States, Europe, Japan, China, and the present Soviet Union.[22]

Military power, though not a salient feature of world politics in the post-Cold War scenario, still continues to be the most reliable technique serving the interest of the big and powerful states. This became evident soon after the end of the Cold War on the wake of Iraq's invasion of Kuwait and action taken by the US led coalition powers under the auspices of the UN. The War on Terror, being carried out by the US initially against Afghanistan and thereafter against Iraq, post 9/11, show that the use of military power is still important and its use by the reigning superpower and its allies to the protection of their own interest is the rule of the day. The United Nations is just side-tracked by these powers and, in these current cases, unilateral actions are taken on the basis of the principle of pre-emptive self defence by the states on their own.

The UN has been hijacked by the sole superpower, the United States and it is used by the United States and the West to serve their own interest and solidify their domination over the small and weak states. It is a long way to establish the New International Economic Order or an international system based on the rule of law and greater sharing between the North and the South.

The condition of the Third World has remained unchanged in the post-Cold War scenario. Although the superpower relationships were formulated in the context of the Cold War, with the collapse of the Soviet Union, the United States and the industrialized North continue their old policy of intervention and domination. Only they have modified it to make it more relevant in the current post-Cold War scenario.

The Third World, especially the Middle East, still continues to be the vital interest zone for the West, especially the United States. The first post-Cold War National Security strategy report sent to the US Congress in March 1990, recognized that military power must target the Third World, primarily the Middle East, where the "threats to our interests" that have required force "could not be laid at the Kremlin's door".[23] Therefore, the prime concern continued to be the control of the countries of the South.

The domination of South is now ensured not through the use of force but by the use of economic weapons. The international financial regimes such as the IMF, the World Bank and WTO (the Triad), with their policies of structural adjustments, are spreading their tentacles of domination all over the developing South. The other mechanism includes multinational corporations (MNCs) through which the developed West tries to reduce the functions of the Third World governments merely to police functions while the MNCs and TNCs gain free access to their resources, control their decision-making, pattern of development, new technology and global investment. All in all, the entire dependency syndrome and neo-colonialism would continue even in the post-Cold War scenario.

In the post-Cold War context, the relevance of Non-Aligned Movement (NAM) is questioned. NAM originated against the backdrop of the superpower rivalry but once that is over, scholars question the relevance of NAM. Nevertheless, NAM countries, in the post-Cold War scenario, are continuing to use this forum to achieve a set of agenda relevant in the post-Cold War world. It includes, among others, independence in foreign relations, sustainable development, protection of environment, international cooperation in political, economic and cultural fields, equity in trade relations, democratization of the United Nations and NAM's long-standing goals of international peace and security, disarmament and arms control, and protection of human rights.

The post-Cold War world is witnessing an increased regional integration and growth of regional arrangements such as the European Union, SAARC, ASEAN, OPEC, NAFTA, APEC, OAS, AU and a host of others.

Post-Cold War, international relations has become more complex with ethnic and identity movements in former Yugoslavia, Czechoslovakia, Angola, Cyprus, Somalia, Ethiopia, Rwanda, Burundi, Russia, Georgia, and elsewhere, rise of fundamentalist forces gradually spreading over the world and often assuming the character of international terrorism jeopardizing international peace and security.

Last but not the least, the post-Cold War scenario did not witness a cessation of arms build-up and all around the globe there has been a proliferation of nuclear weapons and weapons of mass destructions (WMDs). The dangers increase manifold as there are chances of the terrorists outfits of getting access to the nukes, especially in the "failed states" where there is a lack of quality governance and government is weak to control the polity as well as the nuclear establishments.

EXERCISES

1. Examine the causes of the origin of the Cold War in international politics.
2. Discuss the phases of Cold War till its end in the 1990s.
3. What do you understand by détente? What were the causes of détente between the United States and the Soviet Union?
4. Bring out the significance of détente with special reference to the various developments in the relationship between the two superpowers.
5. What were the causes of the demise of détente and the emergence of the New Cold War?
6. Examine how the Cold War came to an end.
7. Discuss the features of international system in a post-Cold War era.

REFERENCES

[1] Calvocoressi, Peter, *World Politics: 1945–2000,* Pearson Education, New Delhi, 2005, p. 3.

[2] Young, John W. and John Kent, *International Relations Since 1945: A Global History,* Oxford University Press, London, 2004, pp. 19–27.

[3] Heller, Henry, *The Cold War and the New Imperialism: A Global History, 1945–2005,* Cornerstone Publications, Kharagpur, India, 2006, pp. 29–30.

[4] Kegley, Charles W., Jr. and Eugene R. Wittkopf, *World Politics—Trends and Transformation,* St. Martin's Press, New York, 1997, pp. 85–86.

[5] Young and Kent, *op. cit.,* n. 2, p. 49.

[6] Wenger, Andreas and Dorn Zimmermann, *International Relations: From Cold War to the Globalized World*, Viva Books, New Delhi, 2006, p. 20.

[7] Young and Kent, *op. cit.*, n. 2, pp. 92–93.

[8] *ibid.*, p. 46.

[9] Lundestad, Geir, *East, West, North South: Major Developments in International Politics since 1945*, Oxford University Press, London, 1999, p. 71.

[10] *ibid.*, p. 61.

[11] Kegley and Wittkopf, *op. cit.*, n. 4, pp. 88–89.

[12] *ibid.*

[13] Northedge, F.S. and M.J. Grieve, *A Hundred Years of International Relations,* Gerald Duckworth and Co., London, 1971, p. 268

[14] *ibid.*, pp. 269–270.

[15] Zimmermann, *op. cit.*, n. 6, p. 119.

[16] *ibid.*, pp. 148–150.

[17] Lundestad, Geir, *op. cit.*, n. 9, p. 124.

[18] Scott, Leon, "International History: 1945–1990", *in* John Baylis and Steve Smith (Eds.), *The Globalization of World Politics,* Oxford University Press, London, 1997, pp. 83–84.

[19] Malhotra, Vinay Kumar, International Relations, Anmol Publications, New Delhi, 2004, pp. 253–256.

[20] Crockatt, Richard, *in* John Baylis and Steve Smith (Eds.), *The Globalization of World Politics,* Oxford University Press, London, 1997, pp. 93–94.

[21] Garthoff, Raymond L., "Why did the Cold War Arise, and Why did it End?" *in* Michael J. Hogan (Ed.), *The End of the Cold War : Its Meaning and Implications,* Cambridge University Press, Cambridge, 1992, p. 131.

[22] Alperovitz, Gar and Kai Bird, "The Fading of the Cold War–and the Demystification of Twentieth Century Issues," *in* Michael J. Hogan (Ed.), *The End of the Cold War: Its Meaning and Implications,* Cambridge University Press, Cambridge, 1992, pp. 207–208.

[23] Chomsky, Noam, "A View from Below", *in* Michael J. Hogan (Ed.), *The End of the Cold War: Its Meaning and Implications,* Cambridge University Press, Cambridge, 1992, pp. 137–138.

7

The Third World

INTRODUCTION

Post-Second World War, international relations not only did witness the bifurcation of the globe into two rival camps, each headed by two former allies, the Soviet Union and the United States but also the emergence of a new group of states, the Third World countries. They were mostly the countries belonging to the 'South', Asia, Africa and Latin America. More on the economic criteria of growth and development these countries were regarded as the Third World or developing, rather than their ideological orientation. These Third World countries shared a common history of exploitation by the formal colonial powers and struggle for liberation from the yoke of the colonial powers and post-Independence share the common problem of economic underdevelopment. Each one of them, thus, strives for economic growth and development. In this arduous task, they seek to retain their economic independence and therefore, try to keep themselves out of the power bloc rivalry and forge their solidarity through forums like Non-Alignment Movement or United Nations General Assembly and even fight for a just and equitable international political and economic order.

DECOLONIZATION AND EMERGENCE OF THE THIRD WORLD

The end of Second World War witnessed a complete change in the international scenario. Not only did the globe witness a tussle between the capitalist world, led by the United States and communist bloc led by the Soviet Union, but also there were major upheavals in the Third World. There was a continuous struggle for liberation from the colonial masters to seek political as well as economic independence from the European imperialist powers.

By the end of the eighteenth century, the Third World struggle for independence became manifest in many countries. History provides numerous examples of such movements, for instance, the Tupac Amaru revolt in Bolivia and Peru, the Pontiac rebellion in North America, and the Great Slave Revolt in Haiti against the Spanish, British and French colonial powers. Among other examples, the Indian Sepoy Mutiny, the Save the Emperor Movement in Vietnam, the Boxer Rebellion in China and others show the growing resistance to the growing European incursions in the early nineteenth and twentieth centuries. Nationalist movements further matured between 1914 and 1945 as traditionalist leaders like chiefs or royal princes were replaced by nationalist leaders who were equipped with western education and ideology. Thus, the colonies once the prized possession of the colonial masters now became the real burden of White men.

Such struggles for independence in the Third World, in principle however, received support from both the Soviet Union and the United States. The Soviet perspective considered such struggle for national independence as progressive and constricted the field of operation of imperialism and monopoly capitalism. Thus, there was a growing support for national liberation movements in the Third World by the Soviet Union. The United States, in principle, opposed colonialism in the name of democracy and the right to self-determination. But the real intention was market driven. The colonies were part of the trading blocs, which hampered the progress of US trade and investment. Therefore, post-1945, the US position was tempered by strategies of tackling the ongoing weakness of their European allies, containment of communism and threats to the US interests.

Post-war decolonization began in Asia and the Middle East and then spread to other parts of the world. The late 1940s saw a number of countries emerging. These included the Phillipines (1946), India and Pakistan (1947), North and South Korea (1948), Myanmar (1948), Ceylon (1948), Indonesia (1949). Indo-China (Vietnam, Laos and Cambodia) became independent from the French colonizers in the 1950s. Middle East experienced struggle for independence with the expulsion of the French from Syria in 1946. North Africa, in the 1950s, witnessed a wave of political independence like Libya (1951), Sudan (1956) and the French colonies of Morocco and Tunisia (1956). Egypt remained a British protectorate until the overthrow of monarchy in 1952 and proclamation of a Republic in 1953. Iraq could also free itself from the British masters only with the ouster of King Faisal II in a nationalist revolution of 1958. In sub-

Saharan Africa, Ghana got its independence in 1957 and Guinea in 1958. By late 1960s, almost all the colonies of Africa were successful in establishing their political independence.[1]

Causes for Decolonization

1. *Bankruptcy of the Imperial Powers*: The First World War had already exhausted the imperial powers and the Second World War, fought in quick succession, left them bankrupt. Huge losses incurred in terms of military, human and material resources exhausted them economically and politically. Further, the growing resistance to their domination in the colonies also made them fatigued and it became almost impossible for them to retain the colonies in Asia, Africa and Latin America. They had to concentrate on their socio-economic reconstruction back home, which implied that they had to withdraw from the colonies.

2. *United States and Decolonization*: USA, as already pointed out, in principle, supported decolonization efforts in order to contain the spread of Communism in these colonies. It championed the principles of self-determination and efforts to establish democratic governments that gave further impetus to the struggle against colonial powers.

3. *Rise of Communism*: The Communist movement spearheaded by the Soviet Union gave an undeniable support to the people struggling for liberation in the colonies. The success of the Russian Revolution of 1917 resulting in the overthrow of the Tsarist autocracy and the rise of the USSR as a strong socialist state gave inspiration to the anti-colonial movements in Asia and Africa. The belief that ran high was that the imperialists were the exploiters and, therefore, should be ousted. This boosted the spirit of the nationalists, to fight against colonialism, with renewed vigour.

4. *Rise of Nationalism and Nationalist Struggle and the Principle of Self-Determination*: While the roots of European nationalism can be found in the European Renaissance, the emergence of Third World nationalism can be traced to the struggle of the Third World people against colonial powers. Imbued with the principle of self-determination, various nationalist struggles launched massive assault on their colonial masters. The struggle reached its peak in the aftermath of the Second World War, finally culminating in the withdrawal of the colonial powers and their subsequent independence.

5. *Role of the United Nations*: The Declaration regarding Non-Self-Governing Territories in the UN Charter imposed an obligation on the members regarding the administration of territories, whose people had not yet reached a full measure of self-government. The Declaration, contained in Article 73 of the Charter states, "Members of the United Nations which have to assume responsibilities for the administration of territories whose peoples have not yet attained a full measure of self-government recognize the principle that the interests of the inhabitants of these territories are paramount, and accept, as a sacred trust the obligation to promote to the utmost, within the system of international peace and security established by the present Charter, administration of territories whose people had not yet reached a full measure of self-Government".

Article 74 states that "Members of the United Nations also agree that their policy in respect of the territories to which this Chapter applies, no less than in respect of their metropolitan areas, must be based on the general principle of good-neighbourliness, due account being taken of the interests and well-being of the rest of the world, in social, economic, and commercial matters".[2] This would be done to:

(a) Ensure, with due respect for the culture of the peoples concerned, their political, economic, social, and educational advancement, their just treatment and their protection against abuses.

(b) Develop self-government, to take due account of the political aspirations of the people, and to assist them in the progressive development of their free political institutions, according to the particular circumstances of each territory and its people and their varying stages of advancement.

(c) Further international peace and security.

(d) Promote constructive measures of development, to encourage research, and to cooperate with one another and, when and where appropriate, with specialized international bodies with a view to the practical achievement of the social, economic and scientific purposes set forth in this Article.

(e) Transmit regularly to the Secretary-General for information purposes, subject to such limitation as security and constitutional considerations may require, statistical and other information of a technical nature relating to economic, social and educational conditions in the territories for which they are respectively responsible other than those territroies to which Chapters XII and XIII apply.

These provisions in the United Nations Charter gave an impetus to the movement for decolonization. There were long debates and tensions between the colonial and non-colonial powers regarding the granting of status of self-governing territory and, most often, the colonial powers deliberately kept the question of independence outside the United Nations as was done by France in the case of Indo-China, Morocco and Algeria. But still it is undeniable that the United Nations did play an important role in ending the colonial rule in certain African trust territories, such as Libya, Eritrea and Somaliland.

6. *Role of Third World Countries:* Outside the United Nations, the Non-Aligned Movement (NAM), launched by the Third World countries also played an important role in providing support to the people fighting for liberation, and was vociferous against colonial designs. By 1960, the number of decolonized countries also grew and these countries now came to enjoy numerical superiority in the General Assembly so much so that they tried their best to utilize the General Assembly and speed up the process of decolonization and ensure emancipation of those territories still under the colonial domination. To this end, on 14 December 1960, with a majority vote of 90–0 and nine abstentions by the colonial powers, a resolution was passed, which was in the form of a declaration. It came to be known as the Declaration on the Granting of Independence to Colonial Countries and Peoples. The Declaration proclaimed the necessity of bringing speedy and unconditional end to colonialism in all its forms and manifestations and to that end it declared that:

(a) The subjection of peoples to alien subjugation, domination and exploitation constitutes a denial of fundamental human rights, is contrary to the Charter of the United Nations and is an impediment to the promotion of world peace and cooperation.

(b) All peoples have the right to self-determination; by virtue of that right they can freely determine their political status and pursue their economic, social and cultural development.

(c) Inadequacy of political, economic, social or educational preparedness should never serve as a pretext for delaying independence.

(d) All armed actions or repressive measures of all kinds, directed against dependent peoples shall cease in order to enable them to exercise peacefully and freely their right to complete independence, and the integrity of their national territory shall be respected.

(e) Immediate steps shall be taken, in Trust and Non-Self-Governing Territories or all other territories which have not yet attained independence, to transfer all powers to the peoples of those territories, without any conditions or reservations, in accordance with their freely expressed will and desire, without any distinction as to race, creed or colour, in order to enable them to enjoy complete independence and freedom.

(f) Any attempt aimed at the partial or total disruption of the national unity and the territorial integrity of a country is incompatible with the purposes and principles of the Charter of the United Nations.

(g) All states shall observe faithfully and strictly the provisions of the Charter of the United Nations, the Universal Declaration of Human Rights, and the present Declaration on the basis of equality, non-interference in the internal affairs of all states, and respect for the sovereign rights of all peoples and their territorial integrity.[3]

All these factors increased the momentum of decolonization in the Third World. The rise in the number of newly independent countries changed the architecture of international relations. Once independent, these countries began to support the struggle against colonialism and racial discrimination of the other fellow Third World countries. They became a powerful force and opposed any sort of military alliances or alignment with any of the power blocs of the Cold War days and established a strong position in the form of NAM. They, by their sheer numerical majority, soon emerged as a powerful voice in the United Nations and there arose a strong demand from the Third World countries to change the unequal pattern of economic relations and usher in a New International Economic Order (NIEO) and also a New World Information and Communication Order (NWICO).

CONCEPT OF THE THIRD WORLD

The nomenclature, "*Third World*", definitely calls for a review, particularly the usage of the term in common parlance. Though there is no precise agreement on the meaning of the term yet what constitutes the Third World or why certain countries are categorized as the Third World is a matter of concern for academicians and scholars of IR. It is true that the rapid decolonization of Asia, Africa and Latin America had led to an immense increase in the number of independent states but, at the same time, they were placed in a lower tier of the international hierarchy. Generally, the countries belonging to the Southern hemisphere were classified as belonging to the Third World characterized by underdevelopment and poverty. A wide array of terms have been used over the years to categorize the countries falling under the Third World, and most of the time, the vocabulary used is not neutral. Eric Toussaint[4] draws attention to the variety of terms used to designate the countries belonging to the Third World. In most cases the index of classification is economic. 'Underdeveloped' is the oldest term used and now it has become obsolete as it appeared to be derogatory and carried a reference to the developed countries. Developing countries, developed countries, poor countries, countries of the South, peripheral countries, emerging countries or countries in transition are some of the popular terms used to refer to the Third World countries, presently. Frantz Fanon*, the Algerian writer and author of *The Wretched of the Earth* used the word "third world" at a time when the former colonies of Africa, Asia and Latin America were emerging as newly independent states. To Fanon, these former colonies, struggling for independence, fighting against exploitation of the imperialist powers and neo-colonialism constituted the Third World which lay between the Capitalist and Socialist worlds.

If one tries to look into the origin of the term Third World, it would be found that it was the French scholar, Alfred Sauvy who invented the term and it became very popular during the Cold War. It was used to refer to those countries adopting a position of non-alignment with either of the bloc. Sauvy said, "We readily speak of two opposing worlds, of their possible war, of their

---

*Frantz Fanon, *The Wretched of the Earth,* translation, Constance Farrington, (1963 translation of the 1961 book), Grove Weidenfeld, New York, 1963.

coexistence, etc., all too often forgetting that there exists a third one, the most important, and in fact the first one in chronological terms. This is the body of those that we call, in United Nations fashion, the underdeveloped countries. (…) The underdeveloped countries, the 3rd world, have entered into a new phase (…). Because at last this ignores, exploited Third World, looked down on as the Third State, also wants to be something else".

The term soon figured in the Bandung Conference of 1955, the first forum of the Third World countries which laid the foundation of the non-aligned movement. During the heydays of Cold War, the term designated the countries neither aligned with the western powers (the first world), nor the communist bloc (the second world). From this perspective, the Third World more or less represented a kind of 'Third Force'.

As Calvocoressi[5] pointed out, "It was a Third World because it rejected the notion of a world divided into two worlds in which only the United States and the USSR counted and everybody else had to declare for the one or the other. It feared the power of the superpowers, exemplified and magnified by nuclear weapons. It distrusted their intentions, envied their superior wealth and rejected their insistence that, in one case in democratic capitalism and in the other in communism, they had discovered a way of life which others need do no more than copy". Therefore, these countries were neither in favour of Moscow's rigid communism nor Washington's hatred for communism and believed in non-alignment with any of the power blocs.

The Chinese concept forwarded by Mao looked at the Third World from a different perspective. For Mao, "The United States and the Soviet Union form the First World. Japan, Europe and Canada the middle section, which belong to the Second World. We are the Third World. The Third World has a huge population. With the exception of Japan, Asia belongs to the Third World. The Whole of Africa belongs to the Third World and Latin America". It is believed by the scholars that the Chinese stratification was based on power and there was a hidden objective of propounding this theory of Third World. China wanted to declare itself as the leader of the Third World.

Yet, more often the term 'Third World' has been used to refer to underdeveloped, less developed and the developing countries and, obviously, the reference point is the developed countries. The goal of the Third World countries is "catching up" with the developed countries. Economically speaking, the First World was defined as the countries with industrialized and free market economies. The Second World countries were those with socialist and centrally planned economies. The Third World countries form the largest group consisting of countries of the three continents of Africa, Asia and Latin America.

Irving Horowitz[*] also defined the Third World in terms of development in his *Three Worlds of Development*. The First World, made up of Western

---

[*]Irving Horowitz, *Three Worlds of Development,* Oxford University Press, New York, 1966.

Europe, USA and Japan was characterized by competitive capitalism. The Second World, that of Soviet bloc, was characterized by socialism of both Soviet and Chinese models. The Third World was made up of those newly independent countries that faced the problems of development belonging to the three continents of Africa, Asia and Latin America.[6]

According to Kegley and Wittkopf[7], "The Third World comprises the poorer, economically less developed countries of the world. So numerous are they that it is easier to say than to say who is not. The underdeveloped countries include all of Asia and Oceania except Japan, Australia and New Zealand, all of Africa except South Africa, and all of the Western Hemisphere except Canada and the United States. Some formulations also include a few European nations in the class of developing economies" like Portugal, Spain, Greece, Turkey, (erstwhile) Yugoslavia and Rumania.

In whatever way one tries to look at the Third World, it would seem to reveal that the Third World is a geo-political concept based on inclusion in a geographical area comprising the Southern hemisphere sharing the common colonial past and put under similar circumstances of underdevelopment. The dismemberment of the Soviet Union and the fast dilution of the socialist model and the socialist bloc has resulted in the gradual disappearance of the Second World and there is a growing tendency of the Second World getting merged with the First. Therefore, more than the term *Third World* what is in vogue nowadays are the terms like *developing world* or *developing countries*.

FEATURES OF THE THIRD WORLD

Colonial Past: The Third World countries share a common history of being subjugated under European colonialism. The European powers imposed their domination on the peoples of Africa, Asia and Latin America as they carved out colonies for themselves. They virtually converted these colonies into 'raw material appendage' in order to feed their economies. The prosperity of the European countries was at the cost of the underdevelopment and exploitation of these colonies. Frustrations and discontent against the colonial rule gave rise to nationalist struggles in all these colonies, which ultimately forced the European colonial powers to grant them independence. This colonial legacy prompted the Third World countries to zealously guard their independence and gear up their resources and energy towards development.

Poverty and Underdevelopment: Poverty and underdevelopment linger in the South. The onus is not only on the North but also on the internal structure of the South. If the South's uncommitted leadership, misallocation of its limited resources, huge population growth and sluggish economic growth contribute to poverty, the North's tactics of trade and aid, WTO and IMF's structural adjustment programmes, world price fluctuations, financial instability in the global stock markets, global financial crisis (2008), protectionist regime of the

North, and the role of MNCs have also increased the underdevelopment of the Third World countries. The World Bank has produced a list of 140 'failed states' that are either developing countries or former socialist countries, but with huge natural resources. This has again given the North another opportunity to intervene in these developing countries, and justify their activities as efforts to save the failed states and spread democracy so that they do not become the breeding grounds of international terrorists.

Debt Crisis: In the 1980s there was a huge Third World debt crisis from which the developing countries found it difficult to re-emerge. The developing countries were encouraged to borrow more until the trap finally closed on them. 1979 was the turning point, as we will discuss in Chapter 14, when the theoretical *virtuous circle* of taking out external loans to promote development and well-being, which would result in self-perpetuating growth, turned into a *vicious circle* of permanent debt for the Third World countries with enormous capital flow to the creditors.

Dependence and Neo-Colonialism: The collapse of colonial empire had put an end to the colonial domination of the European powers after the Second World War. This, however, did ensure political independence but not economic independence. The underdevelopment of the former colonial countries made them dependent again on their former colonial masters for finance, aid, technology transfer, and research and development. The former colonial masters, therefore, devised means of utilizing this dependence to serve their own purposes. The colonies being important source of raw materials and markets for their products, the colonial powers sought newer methods to establish their domination over them. The new form of colonial domination is referred to as *neo-colonialism*. This concept, at present, covers the relationship of the Third World with the United States, which was not a formal colonizer, and the North–South relations.

A United Force: Resistance to Inequitable International Order: The common problems of the Third World countries inspired them to form a united front to fight for a just and equitable international political and economic order. They had changed the architecture of international relations since the 1960s. They had bargained collectively since the 1970s for a New International Economic Order in the United Nations. Along with NIEO, they have also demanded a New International Information and Communication Order (NIICO). They had also evolved the Non-Aligned Movement (NAM) to not only safeguard their political independence but also to insulate themselves from the superpower rivalry since the Cold War days. The NAM also gave them a platform where they could fight for the NIEO and crusade against neo-colonialism and initiate a North–South dialogue. They have also forged a common front with the creation of Group of 77. The Third World played a commendable role in mobilizing world opinion and exploring the possibilities of an alternative to the existing international order.

EXERCISES

1. Discuss the concept of the Third World. Briefly analyze the features of the Third World.

2. Examine the causes of decolonization and the emergence of the Third World.

REFERENCES

[1] Heller, Henry, *The Cold War and the New Imperialism: A Global History, 1945–2005,* Cornerstone Publications, Kharagpur, India, 2006, pp. 75–79.

[2] The United Nations Charter.

[3] Declaration on the Granting of Independence to Colonial Countries and Peoples.

[4] Toussaint, Eric, *The World Bank: A Never Ending Coup d'état,* The Hidden Agenda of Washington Consensus, Vikas Adyayan Kendra, Mumbai, 2007, p. xxvii.

[5] Calvocoressi, Peter, *World Politics: 1945–2000,* Pearson Education, New Delhi, 2005, p. 184.

[6] Melkote, Rama S. and A. Narasimha Rao, *International Relations,* Sterling Publishers, New Delhi, 1983, p. 130.

[7] Kegley, Charles W., Jr. and Eugene R. Wittkopf, *World Politics—Trends and Transformation,* St. Martin's Press, New York, 1997, p. 101.

8

Non-Aligned Movement

INTRODUCTION

The Non-Aligned Movement (NAM) belongs to the developing world and is a coalition of small and middle-sized states of the developing world, mostly former colonies. Taking its roots from the Belgrade Conference in 1961 with the participation of 25 countries, NAM has grown over the years through several conferences and now more than 100 countries are its members. The non-aligned countries devised a flexible organizational structure and they meet from time to time in different regions of the world to garner support for some specific issues and also to promote their objectives. The NAM has been a major movement in international relations, primarily aiming at changing the existing global structure and creating a more just, equal and peaceful world order. In essence, it is an anti-imperialist movement.[1]

NAM: GENESIS

The rapid decolonization process that followed after the Second World War brought into existence numerous states in Africa, Asia and the Caribbean which were mostly small or middle-sized and were underdeveloped and politically weak. They faced twin tasks of nation-building as well as tackling the internal dissenting forces within their societies. Alongside they had a Herculean task of coping up with underdevelopment and working towards development. It is these nations whose governments came together under the umbrella of the NAM.

Post-Second World War also witnessed the outbreak of Cold War resulting in the hostilities of the two major powers, the United States and the Soviet Union. The Cold War was further fuelled when the USA adopted a policy of containment of Communism throughout the world, as the USSR was doing the same by giving support to the national liberation movements. The ultimate result was military pacts and counter pacts, an increase in arms race, gradual polarization of the world into different blocs, and the threat of nuclear war, which could result in the total annihilation of mankind. The newly independent states that wanted to tide over their own problems of development and shared a similar kind of exploitative colonial past, wanted to belong to neither of the camps and envisioned a position of neutrality—non-alignment. The NAM originated under the leadership of Jawaharlal Nehru (India), Marshal Tito (Yugoslavia), Kusno Sukarno (Indonesia), Kwame Nkrumah (Ghana) and Gamal Abdel Nasser (Egypt). They forged a strong coalition of states from Asia, Africa, Europe, The Arab World and Latin America and the Caribbean.

The rationale behind the adoption of the policy of non-alignment by the developing countries reflects numerous objectives, each differing from one state to the other. For instance, in the case of India, her foreign policy objectives rested on the pillars of peace, freedom from colonialism, racial equality and non-alignment, which were very much grounded in her experiences of colonial rule and her freedom struggle against British colonialism. The Cold War that emerged immediately after the conclusion of the Second World War and the strategies of superpowers to maintain their spheres of influence resulted in the formation of military pacts like the Australia, New Zealand, United States Security Treaty (ANZUS, 1 Sept, 1951), Central Treaty Organization, also known as Baghdad Pact, 1955, (CENTO, 1958–1979, dissolved in 1979) and Southeast Asia Treaty Organization, or the Manila Pact (SEATO, 8 Sept, 1954, dissolved in 1977), to which India's neighbour Pakistan was being drawn into, prompted India to embark upon the policy of non-alignment. Nehru made it clear that India would belong to one camp—the camp of peace, goodwill and cooperation. An essential aspect of the policy of non-alignment is, in the words of Nehru, "the enlargement of freedom and replacement of colonization by free and independent countries and a large degree of cooperation among nations".[2]

The Arab leaders' choice of the policy of non-alignment primarily arose from their desire to ward off a conflict in their area between the great powers, or at any rate not to provide them a pretext for intervention. The Suez Crisis was an eye-opener and the Arabs realized the possibilities of other infamous self-serving intrusions in their region. To this end, they pursued a non-aligned course and also harped on Arab solidarity and enhanced military strength to deter potential aggression from the Zionist [incubus] in the heart of the Arab world.[3]

The African states imbibed the spirit of non-alignment in an effort to retain the sovereignty of the newly independent states. They further worked towards a common purpose to keep off the foreign powers out of Africa, to solve *inter se* (their own) problems themselves, to aid African National Liberation Movements and to fight against white racism. The decision of the African states to join the non-aligned group en bloc can be considered as essentially an anti-imperialist gesture.

Cuba's decision to join the non-aligned movement was one of its pragmatic considerations. The US military base at Guantanamo was one of the reasons that prompted Cuba to join a movement that was opposed to the foreign military bases. Further, being isolated in Latin America in the 1960s, Cuba felt a compelling need to belong somewhere and non-alignment seemed to be a good choice which would presumably secure a political insurance against the erosion of its sovereign independence, which is otherwise impossible to retain through proximity to one or the other of the major powers.[4]

However, non-alignment as a concept has often created confusion as well as earned criticisms from different quarters. It is wrongly perceived to be somewhat similar to neutrality which enjoys legal recognition for several centuries as a position of non-belligerency defined by some specific treaty obligations and rights. Nehru attempted to dispel the confusion between the two concepts by observing that "neutrality as a policy had little meaning except in time of war", whereas India preferred "to keep away from the power politics of groups aligned against one another which had led in the past to two world wars, and which might again lead to disasters on an even vaster scale".[5]

In practice, non-alignment has come to mean more than not joining the military alliances or maintaining neutrality during cold or hot war. Its main aim has been to reduce the risks of conflict between the hostile blocs by keeping out of them and to broaden the area of peace in the world. But like neutrality, which has sometimes destroyed neutral nations and most of the time stood violated once war broke out, non-alignment also ran the risk of a similar kind of fate. Therefore, the non-aligned states embarked on the policy of "peace, commerce and honest friendship with all nations and entangling alliances with none".

Nevertheless, the negative connotation in non-alignment has been a constant source of irritation to those who believed in the rightness of formation of military blocs for preserving security. John Foster Dulles once declared non-alignment as "immoral", and Stalin too doubted its motive. Stalin doubted India as "a running dog of British imperialism" and ironically Dulles thought that Soviet Communism exercised a strong influence in India.

Nehru at the first NAM Summit at Belgrade in 1961 said "We call ourselves non-aligned countries. The word 'Non-Aligned' may be differently interpreted, but basically it was coined and used with the meaning of being Non-Aligned with the great power blocs of the world...Non-aligned has a negative meaning. But if we give it a positive connotation, it means nations which object to lining up for war purposes, to military blocs, to military alliances and the like. We keep away from such an approach and want to throw our weight in favour of peace".[6] Krishna Menon, once replying to a reporter's insistent questioning said, "Yes, in a sense non-alignment is an ugly word; it is a negative word but when you use it in the way we do, it becomes positive". Professor J. Bandyopadhyaya contends that the negative nomenclature bears the imprint of India's cultural heritage, which expresses many positive values in the negative terminology.

Nehru, the architect of non-alignment, once said, "I have not originated non-alignment; it is a policy inherent in the circumstances of India for freedom, and inherent in the very circumstances of the world today".[7] He also confessed to the Indian National Assembly that "the natural result of our non-alignment has been that neither of the big blocs looks upon us with favour. They think that we are undependable, because we cannot be made to vote this way or that way". Krishna Menon, too, had observed that "Non-alignment is more or less a residue of historical circumstances,...we cannot align with the west with its colonialism, and there is no question of course of joining the Soviet bloc".[8]

The Bandung Conference of 18–24 April 1955 in Indonesia was an Afro-Asian Conference, and it marked the beginning of the non-alignment movement although it was formally initiated at the Belgrade Conference in 1961. As Prof. V.P. Dutt observed that non-aligned countries "despite their inner contradictions, their oft-differing needs, their lack of military muscle and power, and their economic backwardness, have become some kind of a force to reckon with and at least one significant factor in international affairs".[9]

MAJOR OBJECTIVES OF NAM

The leaders of 25 non-aligned countries met at the Belgrade Conference in 1961 to create an independent path in world politics that would shield them from becoming pawns in the struggle between the major powers. Their common concerns became the fundamental principles upon which the non-aligned countries based their decisions and activities. They are a commitment to:

- Peace and disarmament, especially the reduction of tensions between the major powers.
- Independence, including the right of self-determination of all colonial peoples and the right of equality between all races.
- Economic equality, with an emphasis on restructuring the existing international economic order, particularly with respect to the growing and persistent inequality between the rich and the poor nations.

- Cultural equality, with an emphasis on restructuring the world information and communication order, and opposing cultural imperialism and the Western monopoly of information systems.
- Universalism and multilateralism through strong support for the United Nations system.[10]

These principles have been the underlying guidelines of the Movement from its beginning, and no attempt was formally made to enunciate them until the Sixth Summit in Havana in 1979. It should be noted at this point that though the non-aligned countries share a commitment to these basic principles, there are ideological differences within the Movement as the Movement is a complex grouping of states representing different histories, languages, religions and cultures and a variety of political, social and economic systems. These differences sometimes have come to influence the course of the Movement, but it can be said that despite such tendencies the Movement continues to reflect one single primary concern—to engage in policies that reduce structural inequality in the global system.

GROWTH OF THE MOVEMENT—FROM BANDUNG TO TEHRAN

The growth of NAM can be traced through various major meetings from one Summit conference to another within the context of global events. The various Summit conferences of NAM which have been held till date are as follows:

Place	Year
Bandung (Indonesia)	1955
Belgrade (Yugoslavia)	1961
Cairo (Egypt)	1964
Lusaka (Zambia)	1970
Algiers (Algeria)	1973
Colombo (Sri Lanka)	1976
Havana (Cuba)	1979
New Delhi (India)	1983
Harare (Zimbabwe)	1986
Belgrade (Yugoslavia)	1989
Jakarta (Indonesia)	1992
Cartagena (Colombia)	1995
Durban (South Africa)	1998
Kuala Lumpur (Malaysia)	2003
Havana (Cuba)	2006
Sharm el-Sheikh (Egypt)	2009
Tehran (Iran)	2012

Prelude: The Bandung Conference (1955)

The Bandung Conference of 18–24 April 1955 was a landmark in the process of giving a concrete shape to the collective thought on non-alignment. It was an Afro-Asian Conference being attended by leaders of 29 states which were mostly former colonies. Many Arab states too joined the Conference to discuss the common concerns with an objective to formulate joint policies in international relations. Messages of goodwill were sent by the Soviet Union and the presidiums of five Soviet Central Asian Republics, but the US government was sceptical and secretly tried to control the outcome of the meeting. Nehru, Sukarno and Nasser played pioneering roles, along with the other Third World leaders, sharing their common problems of resisting the pressures of major powers, maintaining their independence, and opposing colonialism and neo-colonialism as well as western domination. The Conference issued a final communiqué on Economic and Cultural Cooperation, Human Rights and Self-determination following the United Nations Charter which highlighted:

(i)   problems of dependent peoples and colonialism,

(ii) ways to promote a new world order based on the principles of respect for fundamental human rights,

(iii) sovereignty and territorial integrity of all nations,

(iv) recognition of the equality of all races and equality of all nations, large and small,

(v)   abstention from interference in the internal matters of other countries,

(vi) refraining from acts or threats of aggression or the use of force, and

(vii) promotion of mutual interests and cooperation.

The conference instilled in the participants what came to be recognized as 'the spirit of Bandung'—the recognition of the similarity of purpose and unity of action among oppressed people—to address their common problems and take an active role in changing the existing world order. The final recommendation was that another conference should be held.

First NAM Summit, Belgrade (Yugoslavia), 1–6 September 1961

The spirit of Bandung was carried forward to the Belgrade Summit Conference of 1961. If Bandung was the prelude, the Belgrade Conference marked the official beginning of NAM in the history of international relations. It was attended by 25 participant states and three observer states, all from Latin America, observers from 19 liberation movements, all from Africa, representatives of 11 labour and socialist parties from Europe, Asia and Latin America, and a host of other organizations.

The timing of the Belgrade Summit was very crucial as it was marked by nuclear testing in France (1960–1961) by *Gerboise Bleue*, increased East West tensions over Berlin, Laos, Cuba and the Congo. In the Belgrade Declaration, the NAM countries expressed their confidence in humanity to establish a peaceful world. They strongly opposed the existence of military blocs, which "necessarily provoke periodical aggravations of international relations" and sought peaceful coexistence to avoid the possibility of a nuclear disaster. They upheld the idea that peaceful coexistence was based on the rights of the people to self-determination, independence and the form of development of their own choice. NAM supported the UN Declaration on the Granting of Independence to Colonial Countries and Peoples and demanded an immediate stop to armed action and other repressions against liberation movements. The Conference condemned apartheid in South Africa, foreign intervention in Tunisia and the Congo, demanded restoration of all the rights of the Arab people of Palestine in accordance with the UN Charter and resolutions, and respect for Cuba's right to choose its own path of development. In sum, The Belgrade Declaration listed 27 separate items, 14 dealing with anti-colonialism, self-determination and non-interference, six relating to disarmament and three on economic development.

Apart from the Belgrade Declaration, on Nehru's suggestion, a separate Statement on the Danger of War and Appeal for Peace was approved. This was directed towards sending messages to the United States and the USSR to suspend their preparations for war in a nuclear age which might result in a total annihilation and start negotiations on disarmament.

Second NAM Summit, Cairo (Egypt), 5–10 October 1964

The second NAM Summit was attended by 47 states as compared to 25 in Belgrade. Of the 22 new members, 20 were African states. The number of observer states had increased from three to ten with the majority coming from Latin America and the Caribbean. The Movement stood strengthened by its increased membership and wider international representation.

The international scenario at this point of time was marked by the thaw in the Cold War and increase in the national liberation struggles. Also, between 23 March and 15 June 1964, the First UN Conference on Trade and Development (UNCTAD) met in Geneva and the Group of 77 was born, composed of countries primarily from the non-aligned movement.

The Cairo Declaration was anti-colonialist and anti-imperialist. It also welcomed the improvement in the East–West relations. The question of disarmament also received equal attention and the Partial Test Ban Treaty was commended, and there was a plea for a total ban on nuclear weapons. There was also recommendation for setting up of denuclearized zones, wherever feasible. The Conference also opposed racial discrimination and the Declaration strongly condemned the policy of apartheid in South Africa and called for sanctions against the Republic of South Africa. It also recognized nationalist movements as being the 'authentic representatives' of colonial peoples and affirmed that those under the colonial rule, foreign occupation or racist regime, might legitimately resort to arms to secure their full independence. The Conference called upon the member States to provide necessary material support—financial and military—to the peoples engaged in freedom struggle. The NAM countries asserted that political independence and self-determination were primary conditions for peace and drew attention to the tensions being caused by external interference in the Congo, Cyprus, Cuba and Indo-China where people were trying to grapple with the problems of development. Therefore, the Conference claimed that world peace could only be established with the abolition of imperialism, colonialism and neo-colonialism. On economic matters, the NAM countries stated that "Persistence of poverty poses a threat to world peace and prosperity". They opined that peoples and nations should have the right to control their national wealth and resources for their own economic development and concluded that "a new and just economic order" must be established to foster development in the Third World countries. The Declaration also called for cultural, scientific and educational cooperation at international and regional levels. A number of recommendations made in Cairo, especially those with regard to national liberation struggles, were later adopted at the UN, largely through the untiring efforts of the NAM countries.

Third NAM Summit, Lusaka (Zambia), 8–10 September 1970

The Third NAM Summit was held after a lapse of six years, mostly at the insistence of Marshal Tito. Certain world events during the intervening period had been very interesting. Explosion of China's first nuclear bomb in October 1964, shortly after the Cairo Summit, removal of Khrushchev from his office, India's war with Pakistan in 1965, followed by normalization of relations between the two neighbours, primarily due to the mediatory role played by the Soviet Union and not the NAM countries, end of specific policies of non-alignment pursued by Indonesia, Ghana and Algiers due to coups against Sukarno, Nkrumah and Ben Bella, Middle-East and Vietnam were the major events influencing the course of NAM. However, there was easing of tensions between the major powers following the détente between them. But the Soviet intervention in Czechoslovakia in 1968 revived the threat perception of Yugoslavia and Tito was galvanized into convening a consultative meeting in Belgrade in July 1969. At this meeting the non-aligned countries decided to take a more active approach internationally and within the United Nations. This was followed by a preparatory meeting at Dar-es-Salaam from 13 to 17 April 1970. In this meeting it was agreed to have a Third Summit Conference of NAM, prior to the 25th Session of the United Nations, at Lusaka.

Thus, the Third Summit was held at Lusaka, 8–10 September 1970. Fifty-three member countries, ten observer countries and two guest countries, Austria and Finland, attended the Third Conference of Heads of State or Government. Representatives from the United Nations and the Organization of African Unity (OAU) were also present as observers. The Lusaka Conference called upon the members to rededicate themselves to the fundamental goals and objectives of the Movement. Given the lack of progress during the first UN Decade of Development, the major concerns of this Conference were peace, decolonization, non-interference, and support for the UN as well as economic development. The Summit, therefore, recognized the need for more action and elaborate programmes to create a *new world order*.

The Final Declaration consisted of two separate declarations, one political and the other economic, along with a number of other resolutions. The Political Declaration on "Peace, Independence, Development, Co-operation and Democratization of International Relations" was not only a reaffirmation of the raison d'être of the Movement but also reiterated the opposition of the Movement to intervention in the internal affairs of the states, especially regarding the wars being waged in the Middle-East and Indo-China, the continued oppression of the African peoples in South Africa, and the arms race to racism, apartheid, colonialism and imperialism. The Movement also demanded democratization of international relations, cooperation between developing countries, and lessening of the gap between the developed and developing countries.

In their Declaration on "Non-Alignment and Economic Progress", the NAM countries, for the first time, concluded that a "structural weakness in the present world economic order" was responsible for poverty and economic dependence, and pledged themselves to a "spirit of self-reliance", national socio-economic progress and mutual cooperation. They expressed their determination to strengthen the UN system to support the restructuring of the global economic system.

At Lusaka, the NAM countries started a practice of adopting resolutions on concerns that they deemed critical and in need of support. Therefore, there were separate resolutions condemning foreign intervention, occupation and wars in Indo-China, the Middle-East, Cyprus, Zimbabwe, Namibia, and the Portuguese colonies of Angola, Mozambique and Guinea-Bissau. In their Resolution on Disarmament, the non-aligned countries sought their earlier demand for world disarmament and welcomed the United Nations' designation of the 1970s as the "Disarmament Decade".

With the deaths of Nehru and Nasser and advanced age of Tito, the Lusaka Conference recognized the need for developing new leadership. It also decided to continue with the Standing Committee established at Lusaka and designated President Kenneth Kaunda of Zambia as the Chairman, with specific responsibilities till the next Summit.

Fourth NAM Summit, Algiers (Algeria), 5–9 September 1973

The Algiers Conference was a historic moment for NAM for it was the largest international gathering at that time outside the United Nations. Seventy-five non-aligned countries attended, which was an increase of 22 over the previous Summit, which equalled to nearly two-thirds of the UN membership and over

90 per cent of the newly independent countries post-Second World War. There were eight observer states, all from Latin America and the Caribbean, and three guest states, all from Europe. In addition, 15 national liberation movements and political parties attended the Summit as observers and made presentations. But the remarkable event was the address by the Secretary-General of the UN, Kurt Waldheim, which indicated the growing importance of the Movement.

Current international situation influenced the proceedings of the Summit. The shift from confrontation to détente between the major powers was welcomed by the NAM countries, but concerns were expressed at the tensed situations in the Middle-East, continued apartheid in South Africa, Sino–Soviet split and Chinese accusations of Soviet 'imperialism', the situation in Indo-China, Liberation struggles of Latin America being crushed by the United States, its opposition to the Allende government in Chile, and continued surveillance by USA to ensure Cuba's political and economic isolation in Latin America.

The Political Declaration reflected the outlook of the non-aligned leaders to link the political and economic dimensions of global security. Genuine independence was defined broadly and made exhaustive by including cultural and social aspects as well as economic and political concerns. Alongside, anti-imperialist and anti-colonialist tenor of the Movement continued. Concerns were expressed over the massive assault on the national liberation struggles and the Movement reaffirmed its historic support for these struggles and adopted a separate Declaration on the Struggle for National Liberation. The Algiers Summit was noteworthy in the sense that the NAM members adopted an Economic Declaration and Action Programme, a radical statement demanding the establishment of a New International Economic Order (NIEO).

For institutionalization of the Movement, a significant step was taken towards maintaining the Standing Committee in the form of a 15-member Co-ordinating Bureau which was to prepare for the Fifth Summit Conference and other non-aligned gatherings and also to coordinate the non-aligned activities, particularly at the UN and the G-77, and to assist in the implementation of the Action Programme for Economic Cooperation.

The oil embargo of the Arab countries against the Western supporters of Israel had increased the price of oil by the OPEC and placed many non-aligned countries in serious hardship and sort of created a discontent against the Arab countries which took a long time to heal.

Fifth NAM Summit, Colombo (Sri Lanka), 16–19 August 1976

One of the first Summits to be held in Asia was in Colombo, Sri Lanka. The new Head of the Movement was Mrs. Bandarnaike, Prime Minister of Sri Lanka. It was attended by 86 states—increase of 11 states from the last Summit—which was attended by 75 states. A number of observer states and guest states were present as well. The number of heads of liberation movements attending the Summit got significantly reduced from 15 at Algiers to five at Colombo due to the success of the national liberation movements in gaining independence. The Portuguese empire had crumbled and five new African states joined the movement.

The Conference identified specific problems relating to Middle-East, Cyprus, Southern Africa and Korea. Other concerns were the militarization of Diego Garcia and unabated arms race, despite the atmosphere of détente between the two major powers. But Southern Africa was really an important region of concern for it was the one region which still remained under colonial domination. Particularly, independence for Zimbabwe and Namibia and majority rule for South Africa were the disturbing factors, and the NAM countries condemned the Western power's collaboration with South Africa. The NAM states, thus, reaffirmed their faith and support for national sovereignty and the right of self-determination, especially for the struggles in southern Africa. The NAM countries were extremely critical about the use of veto by the five permanent members in the Security Council of the UN which would be tantamount to abuse of power.

The Political Declaration was the reaffirmation of non-aligned principles of peace, disarmament, international cooperation, faith in the UN, adoption of an 'integrated approach' linking both political and economic aspects to solve problems of peace, development, and disarmament and condemnation of increased interference in the internal matters. The Colombo Summit reiterated NAM's rejection of a global system based on the power blocs, balance of power, and spheres of influence in favour of mutual interdependence and the democratization of international relations.

The economic concerns over the disparity between the rich and the poor states were seen as the cause of tensions and conflicts. The only possible solution was the establishment of the New International Economic Order, which could be realized through a programme of action, by UNCTAD. The Economic Declaration and the Action Programme were reflections of the vision of the NAM countries.

The Colombo Summit witnessed the beginning of the institutionalization of NAM with a major resolution being adopted on the composition and mandate of the Coordinating Bureau. Another important milestone was the setting up of the Press Agencies Pool of Non-Aligned Countries and the formation of its one-member Coordination Committee with a view to foster cooperation in the field of information and mass media.

However, internal strains among the Movement also became visible during this Summit. The ASEAN countries were uncomfortable with the Economic and Political Declarations that were adopted and the support being given to the liberation movements in South-East Asia, and they expressed their concerns about the role of US lobby in the Movement, especially of Singapore and Malaysia. Egypt's rapprochement with the West also raised concerns among the Arab countries.

Sixth NAM Summit, Havana (Cuba), 3–9 September 1979

The Havana Summit of 1979 was held after much speculation about the venue of the Sixth Summit. The Summit was attended by all except two of the 95-member states of NAM. The new governments of Grenada and Nicaragua also attended the Summit for the first time as full-fledged members of the Movement. There was an overwhelming presence of Latin American countries. Though it has been a long-standing policy of the United States to isolate Cuba from the rest of Latin America and the Caribbean, yet 22 delegations from the region came to the Havana Summit.

As far as the issues were concerned, they were similar to the previous Summits. They were the struggles against neo-colonialism and the right of the peoples to choose their own path of social, economic and political development, including their choice of external relations, without interference from the major powers in the region.

However, there were several irritants in this summit. Disputes over the position of non-aligned states erupted between Marshal Tito, the sole surviving founding father of non-alignment and representative of the 'old guard' of the theory of equidistance, and Castro, the 'young Turk' who floated the theory of Socialist bloc as a 'natural ally'. The question of Kampuchean representation regarding the representation at the Movement by the Pol Pot Government or the Heng Samrin Government, and attempts to expel Egypt for the Camp David Agreements, and the Egyptian–Israeli Separate Peace Treaty seen as betrayal of the Arab cause—all seemed to create split within the movement inevitable.

Yet, the final Political Declaration made no specific mention of the natural ally thesis, sought by Cuba but cited the Western countries for their violation of non-aligned principles and aggression against a number of non-aligned states. Otherwise, peace and disarmament support for national liberation, opposition to racism and strengthening of the United Nations remained the chief concerns.

Seventh NAM Summit, New Delhi (India), 7–12 March 1983

The New Delhi Summit was attended by 99 member states. Twenty countries were invited as observers and 19 countries and organizations as guests. The Summit adopted political, economic and other declarations in which it reiterated the need for collective self-reliance among the non-aligned countries and other developing countries by enforcing South–South cooperation.

The Political Declaration contained a call for immediate prohibition of the use of the nuclear weapons and a comprehensive treaty, nuclear disarmament under effective international control, nuclear-free regions in different parts of the world, reduction of military presence by the big powers in the Indian Ocean, and the return of Diego Garcia to Mauritius. There was a call for withdrawal of foreign troops from Afghanistan and Kampuchea as well as support for the people of Palestine, Namibia and South Africa.

The Economic Declaration reaffirmed the position of the non-aligned countries to usher in a New International Economic Order, early establishment of a food security system for NAM member countries and other developing countries, and also condemned the use of food as an instrument of political pressure. Further, it reiterated the old demand for elimination of restrictive, conditional, selective and discriminatory measures with a view to promote world trade.

Eighth NAM Summit, Harare (Zimbabwe), 1–7 September 1986

The Eighth NAM Summit was held at Harare, the capital of Zimbabwe and was attended by 101 states including Pakistan. Among other issues, the punitive measures against the racist Pretoria government were noteworthy. The Summit unanimously adopted several punitive measures to be applied against the white government in South Africa. These included prohibition of transfer of technology to South Africa, cessation of export, sale or transport of oil, snapping of air links, and termination of free entry privileges to South Africa. The other issues discussed were the Iran–Iraq War, the Afghan crisis, the Kampuchea crisis, the Palestine problem, the US aggression in Libya, disarmament, debt burden of developing countries, and strengthening of South–South cooperation.

Ninth NAM Summit, Belgrade (Yugoslavia), 4–7 September 1989

102 member states attended the Summit. The Summit, upholding the principles of the Movement, called for a complete disarmament, especially pertaining to weapons of mass destruction (WMDs). It also called for an increasing pressure and tightening of sanctions against South Africa with a view to isolating the regime. The Summit also urged for a speedy solution of problems pertaining to Afghanistan, Kampuchea, democratization of Latin America, restoration of rights of the people of Palestine, and establishment of independence of Namibia. In the economic front, the Summit highlighted the growing disparity between the wealthy North and the poor South, the growing debt burden of the South, and called for a collective self-reliance of the countries of the South.

Tenth NAM Summit, Jakarta (Indonesia), 1–7 September 1992

This summit was held in the backdrop of the dissolution of Cold War and dismemberment of the Soviet Union. This was attended by 108 member states. Alhough discussions were held on crucial issues on South Africa, Somalia, Palestine and the Middle East, the ethnic problem of Yugoslavia occupied the centre stage of debates. Despite differences over the Yugoslav issue, there was a consensus over the policy of ethnic cleansing perpetuated by the local Serbs and deployment of UN peacekeeping forces in Bosnia–Herzegovina in place of external troops. Alongside, there was a discussion on NAM's agenda, for example, democratization of the United Nations, North–South dialogue, and the forging of a South–South cooperation. The Summit also demanded the convening of a special UN General Assembly Session to finalize the independence of Namibia.

Eleventh NAM Summit, Cartagena (Colombia), 18–20 October 1995

The member countries, reiterating their faith in the spirit of NAM, called for a unified effort to promote the restructuring, revitalization and democratization of the United Nations based on the principles contained in its Charter, as well as the restructuring of the international financial system, including the Bretton Woods institutions, all on the basis of the principle of sovereign equality of states. They also took a pledge for achieving general and complete disarmament, including the nuclear disarmament and the elimination of type of weapons.

The Heads of state or government also emphasized that the high social cost of the structural adjustment had hit the developing countries hard. It is the developed countries that derived the greatest benefits from the existing structure of the world economy. Therefore, they found it unacceptable that the rich and the powerful nations should continue to establish unilateral conditionalities on open trade to gain advantages from the countries constituting the Movement. While pressing for opening up of the economies of the developing countries, developed countries imposed restrictions and tariff obstructions on the products of the developing countries in their own country. Thus, the Movement expressed grave concern over the new protectionism of the developed countries.

Twelfth NAM Summit, Durban (South Africa), 2–3 September 1998

The NAM countries met at Durban, South Africa from 2 to 3 September 1998, to address crucial global issues affecting their people with a view to agreeing to a set of actions in the promotion of peace, security and development, conducive to a new system of international relations based on the principles of justice, equality and democracy.

There was a wide array of issues discussed in this summit. While reviewing the international situation and the role of NAM, the member countries discussed matters relating to agenda for peace, strengthening and democratization of the United Nations, disarmament, terrorism, and a host of other issues. They expressed their concern at the slow pace of progress towards nuclear disarmament, which constitutes their primary disarmament objective. They further stressed the significance of universal adherence to the CTBT, including adherence by all nuclear weapon states, and commencement of negotiations in the Conference on disarmament of fissile materials, which, interalia, should accelerate the process of nuclear disarmament. They also reiterated their positions against unilateral, coercive or discriminatory measures, which have been applied against the non-aligned countries. They stressed the need for bilateral dialogue to secure peaceful solutions on all outstanding issues and the promotion of confidence and security-building measures and mutual trust.

Thirteenth NAM Summit, Kuala Lumpur (Malaysia), 20–25 February 2003

This was attended by 116 members and observers, guest countries and guest organizations. There was a pledge to make the NAM more relevant and effective. Along with this there was a general consensus on international issues such as terrorism and disarmament.

Fourteenth Ministerial Conference of NAM, Durban (South Africa) (Mid-Term Review), 17–19 August 2004

Along with the member countries of the Movement, the Summit was attended by observers from the African Union, Afro-Asian Peoples Solidarity Organization (AAPSO), the League of Arab States, United Nations Assistant Secretary-General, China, Costa Rica, Croatia, Kazakhstan, Mexico, Ukraine, Paraguay, Serbia and Montenegro. There were also 19 guest countries and 13 guest organizations.

The ministers reaffirmed the positions as expressed in the Final Document of the Thirteenth Kuala Lumpur Summit on the review of the international situation, and reiterated the determination of their leaders to make every effort to further strengthen the Movement's capacity for action and to develop concrete modalities to enhance the influence and impact of its decisions on world affairs. They also reaffirmed their determination to preserve the noble ideals and principles of the Movement as articulated at the Bandung Conference in 1955, as well as the principles set forth in the United Nations Charter, in order to consolidate the Movement's role as a leading force in the twenty-first century. The ministers reaffirmed and reiterated the long-standing principled positions of the Movement on disarmament and international security, including the decisions taken at the Twelfth Summit in Durban, the Thirteenth Summit in Kuala Lumpur and the Fourteenth Ministerial Conference in Cartagena. They also upheld the adoption of the concept of Disarmament, Demobilization, Reintegration and Rehabilitation (DDRR). This was to be implemented during the United Nations peacekeeping operations, along with the post-conflict peacebuilding (PCPB) activities, which will boost the post-conflict reconstruction, upon request and with the consent of the state concerned.

Fourteenth NAM Summit, Havana (Cuba), 15–16 September 2006

This was the second NAM Summit held in Havana (Cuba) after the Sixth NAM Summit in 1979. Once again, in this Summit, Cuba tried to give an anti-US outlook, but this was controlled and discussions merely focused on the unilateral and hegemonistic approach of some states. Terrorism became the focal point of discussion. Concerns were expressed over issues such as cross-border terrorism as experienced by India, functioning of terrorist groups including former Talibans who were again regrouping in certain parts of Afghanistan, providing support, protection and shelter to the terrorists by some states. Condemnation of terrorism was followed by a call for fighting terrorism by the international community. Other issues discussed were: the inalienable rights of developing countries to engage in research, production and development of nuclear energy for peaceful purposes without any discrimination and North–South dialogue and better cooperation among developing countries in the WTO negotiations with a view to project and protect interests of the developing countries.

Fifteenth NAM Summit, Sharm el-Sheikh (Egypt), 11–16 July 2009

This Summit has been held at a time when the world is passing through a phase of global meltdown which started around mid 2008. Alongside, the world is also experiencing increasing terrorist onslaughts and threats to international peace and security. Therefore, the focus of the Fifteenth NAM Summit has been, on one hand, on creating a "new world order" to save the globe from further economic recessions and on the other hand, addressing the ways and means of combating terrorism. The NAM members expressed their willingness to work for fundamental reform of the international economic and financial systems, to address the flaws that have come to the fore in the wake of global meltdown. Further, the 118 members of NAM took a pledge to bolster NAM Solidarity in combating terrorism in accordance with the principles of the UN Charter, international law and relevant conventions. The members also upheld their commitment to enhance the voice and participation of developing countries in international decision making and norm setting including international financial institutions. They also showed an urge for "expeditious" reform and expansion of the United Nations Security Council. The spirit of the Fifteenth NAM Summit got expression in the Sharm el-Sheikh Summit Declaration.

Sixteenth NAM Summit, Tehran (Iran), 26–31 August 2012

The Sixteenth NAM Summit was held in Tehran, Iran from 26–31 August 2012. The theme for the Sixteenth NAM Summit was *Lasting Peace Through Joint Global Governance*. The Egyptian President, Mohammad Morsi, officially handed over the Presidency of the Non-Aligned Movement (NAM) to Iranian President Mahmoud Ahmadinejad, during the inaugural ceremony of Leaders' Meeting. Iran will hold the NAM Presidency for three years until the Seventeenth Summit in Venezuela, in 2015. The *Tehran Declaration* was adopted which undertook a review of international situation and reaffirmed faith in the NAM principles articulated in Bandung (1955) and Belgrade (1961). In the Declaration, the NAM members declared to build a fair, inclusive, transparent and effective system of joint global governance, based on justice and equitable participation of all countries and to address present challenges and risks stemming from global security threats, environmental hazards, climate change, migration, contagious diseases and extreme poverty. The Sixteenth NAM Summit also adopted the *Tehran Plan of Action* (2012–2015) which focused on global issues, reaffirmation of faith on UN Charter and international law, promotion of multilateralism through the UN and multilateral processes, peaceful settlement of disputes and non-use or use of threat of force, culture of Peace, dialogue among civilizations, religions and cultures, and cultural diversity, right to self-determination and decolonization, reform of the UN, and terrorism. NAM also adopted a *Declaration on Palestine Political Prisoners* in which NAM members expressed grave concerns regarding the deteriorating situation of Palestinian political prisoners in the Occupied Palestinian Territory, including East Jerusalem. *A Solidarity Declaration on Palestine* was also adopted in which they regretted that Israel's obstructive policies have made it impossible for the NAM Committee on Palestine to convene the Extraordinary Ministerial Meeting in Ramallah, Palestine, on 5 August 2012. The *Final Document* contains detailed report of the discussions on global issues, regional and sub-regional political issues involving Occupied Syria Golan, African countries like Libya, Somalia, Sudan and others, certain countries of Asia like Afghanistan, Iraq and Kuwait and others, Latin American and Caribbean countries. The *Final Document* also contains reports on development, social and human rights issues.

Structure and Organization

The founders of NAM and their successors recognized the possible difficulties the Movement could face if formal structures like a constitution or an internal secretariat were established. They also realized that the Movement, being a multicultural transnational organization made up of states with differing ideologies and purposes, it would be difficult to create, a rational administrative structure and even if created, be accepted by all. As a social movement, it calls upon its members to respond to specific issues relevant at that particular time. Therefore, to best suit its purpose, the NAM members have created a unique form of administrative style. The NAM administration is non-hierarchical, rotational and inclusive, providing all member-states, regardless of size and importance, with an opportunity to participate in global decision-making and world politics. The structure of NAM is depicted in Figure 8.1.

The NAM countries meet from time to time in various regions and hold discussions, share concerns, formulate policies and plan of actions. The Summit conferences are of utmost importance because at these conferences Heads of states or governments of non-aligned countries meet to analyze the current

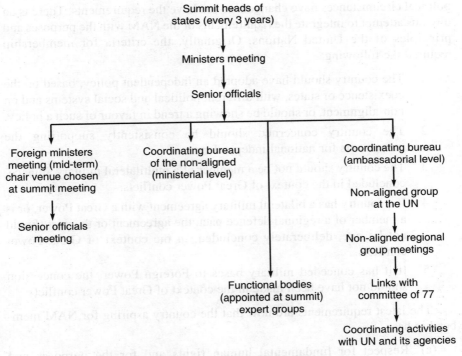

Figure 8.1   Structure of NAM.

[**Source:** Adapted from A.W. Singham and Shirley Hune, *Non-alignment in an Age of Alignments.*]

international scenario. During these summits, the Movement formally rotates its chairmanship, and this happens generally in every three years. The Chair is the head of the state of the host country of the Summit and holds office between the Summits, who is also delegated some responsibilities for promoting the principles and activities of the Movement. The creation of the rotating chair was envisaged with the objective of delegating the administrative responsibilities, with appropriate administrative structure, to the country assuming the Chair. Therefore, when a country assumes the Chair, it creates or designates an entire section of foreign ministry to deal particularly with the NAM issues and concerns. At each Summit, the venue for the next NAM Summit is also selected. The NAM uses the method of consensus to arrive at decision-making. Though there have been at times difficulties in reaching a consensus, the NAM has achieved consensus on many difficult problems in world politics over the years. It can be said that the consensus has been achieved, in part, by a shared commitment to certain basic principles and also by the use of many levels of discussion before a decision is reached.[11]

The criteria for membership in the organization have changed from the original requirements as well. As the organization has matured and international political circumstances have changed, so too have the requirements. There is an obvious attempt to integrate the requirements of the NAM with the purposes and principles of the United Nations. Originally, the criteria for membership required the following:

1. The country should have adopted an independent policy, based on the coexistence of states, with different political and social systems and on non-alignment, or should be showing a trend in favour of such a policy.
2. The country concerned should be consistently supporting the movements for national independence.
3. The country should not be a member of a multilateral military alliance, concluded in the context of Great Power conflicts.
4. If a country has a bilateral military agreement with a Great Power, or is a member of a regional defence pact, the agreement or the pact should not be one, deliberately concluded, in the context of Great Power conflicts.
5. If it has conceded military bases to Foreign Power, the concession should not have been made in the context of Great Power conflicts.

The latest requirements are now that the country aspiring for NAM membership has:

(a) Respect for fundamental human rights and for the purposes and principles of the Charter of the United Nations.
(b) Respect for the sovereignty and territorial integrity of all nations.
(c) Recognitzed the equality of all races and of the equality of all nations, large and small.
(d) Abstained from intervention or interference in the internal affairs of another country.
(e) Respect for the right of each nation to defend itself singly or collectively, in conformity with the Charter of the United Nations.
(f) Refrained from acts or threats of aggression or the use of force against the territorial integrity or political independence of any country.
(g) Settled all international disputes by peaceful means, in conformity with the Charter of the United Nations.
(h) Promoted mutual interests and cooperation.
(i) Respect for justice and international obligations.

CONTRIBUTION OF NAM

The NAM, which was born in the backdrop of the Cold War tensions between the two superpowers, worked for peace, security, disarmament, independence, development and cooperation among nations. In short, it can be said that

NAM's contribution can be best assessed in terms of six Ds—Decolonization, Détente, Disarmament, Development, Democratization and Dissemination.

From its inception, the Movement primarily focused on peace and disarmament and the need for peaceful coexistence among states. There was also a strong support for freedom struggle against the colonial rule in Algeria, Angola, Tunisia, South Africa and Cuba. The process of decolonization also received support and attention in Mozambique and other Portuguese colonies, French Somaliland, Southern Rhodesia, Aden and Oman. The Movement vehemently criticized the apartheid in South Africa and even went to the extent of breaking off diplomatic ties with South Africa.

In the economic front, the NAM drew attention to the rising neo-colonialism, and in the Lusaka Summit it was stated that "classical colonialism is trying to perpetuate itself in the garb of neo-colonialism—a less obvious, but in no way a less dangerous means of economic and political domination over the developing countries". Therefore, the NAM demanded a revision of the unequal global economic structure with a New International Economic Order based on equity and justice.

As far as the institutionalization of NAM was concerned, a major resolution was adopted in the Colombo Summit with the composition and mandate of the Coordinating Bureau. Another important step was the setting up of the Press Agencies Pool of non-aligned countries with a view to foster cooperation in the field of information and mass media and set up a New World Information and Communication Order (NWICO) also known as New International Information Order. The NAM also highlighted the need for collective self-reliance among the developing countries, which would augment their development and help in the establishment of New International Economic Order (NIEO). In other words, it sought a South–South cooperation.

Despite differences among the member countries on several international and regional issues such as the Iran–Iraq war, and problems in Kampuchea, Afghanistan, Lebanon, Central America, South Africa, Namibia and others, the achievements of the Movement in the field of Decolonization, Detente, Development, Dissemination and Democratization of international relations cannot be denied. The incoming Chairperson of NAM, Mrs. Indira Gandhi, the Indian Prime Minister in her closing address to the Seventh Summit (7–12 March 1983) stated, "the resolution to the two dominating issues of our day, disarmament and development, cannot be dramatic". "We have only established the base camp and have a long climb to the attainment of our goals and ideals".[12]

The Tenth NAM Summit at Jakarta in 1992, the Eleventh at Cartagena in 1995 all called for an introspection into the formulation of new, elaborated platform of the non-aligned states through a comprehensive world-view on the contemporary global issues, given the post-Cold War scenario and the newer challenges of socio-economic and political fronts. The Twelfth Summit at Durban conceded that the non-aligned countries were standing on a threshold of a new era—"an era that offers great opportunity yet poses special danger for the developing world". The Movement, to make positive contribution in contemporary international relations, should emerge as the power of the new millennium, the voice of the peoples living in the South and work towards the noble principles for which the Movement was established—international peace and security. As Dr. G.N. Srivastava observed, "it has to be realized that the world is interdependent as never before. The South–South Co-operation is important to achieve North–South Co-operation. And North–South Co-operation is essential to ensure a world based on tolerance and genuine coexistence as aspired by NAM".[13] To usher in the New World Order, the NAM has a definite role to play and the need of the hour is that the NAM-member countries should act in unison and revive the Movement's assertive role and forge a stronger solidarity between South and South, ultimately leading to North–South cooperation.

RELEVANCE OF NAM IN CONTEMPORARY INTERNATIONAL RELATIONS

The question which is raised under the given circumstances, when the rivalry between the two ideologically driven power blocs led by the United States and the erstwhile Soviet Union have ceased around 1990 followed by the dismemberment of the Soviet Union with the world becoming unipolar, is the need and relevance of non-alignment. Milos Minic, a Foreign Minister of Yugoslavia has expressed his observation for such situation as one cropping out of the end of the Cold War followed by the cessation of hostilities between the superpower blocs and being replaced, in many instances, by dialogue, negotiation and accommodation. The emergence of this kind of new situation in international relations calls for solution of international problems through negotiations and understanding on a greater plane and more successfully by revitalizing the United Nations. Under such changed circumstances the NAM cannot historically and practically play the same role.[14]

The end of the Cold War has replaced the "nuclear bomb" with "social bomb", with poverty, underdevelopment, violence and terrorism topping the priority list and getting intertwined with the security problem of the South to which there can be no military solution. The richest—20 per cent of the world population—hold almost 83 per cent of the wealth and the poorest—20 per cent—hold only 1.4 per cent.[15] Such adverse economic global structure continues to negatively affect the developing countries, and NAM has a definite role in working towards a New World Order to help its member countries to alleviate the sufferings of its population.

India's assertion at the Colombia Summit highlights that the culture and logic of NAM are not passé, but "The cold war had been so compulsive that many forgot the rationale of the origins of the Non-Aligned Movement and understood it as only an exercise in acrobatics between the overwhelming blocs.

The permanent principles of peace, struggle against dominations, cooperation between nations, and the establishment of a world order more or less took a back seat".[16] But the culture of peace, cooperation, striving for a new and just world order will continue as long as the world is based upon an inequitable international system.

I.K. Gujral, the Indian Prime Minister put forward certain proposals for rejuvenation of NAM before the Twelfth meeting of the NAM Foreign Ministers while highlighting the re-emergence of the new imperialism of the West. NAM, he asserted, should assume its supreme responsibility to deplore the fundamentalism of globalization and the market alongside addressing the burning issues of terrorism, civil wars, ethnicity, human rights, respect for democratic ideals, poverty, underdevelopment and democratization of the United Nations. He reaffirmed that NAM should strive for a more equitable World Order, and has to play a crucial role of projecting the views of the developing countries in the international fora. But to one's dismay, NAM has not made any remarkable breakthrough in either promoting the South–South cooperation or adopting a positive plan of action regarding the problems of human rights and social justice, environmental degradation, trafficking of drugs and weapons, international terrorism other than expressing concerns about them. Therefore, NAM should tide over such identity crisis and establish its relevance and efficacy, once again, for it is an international platform which provides opportunity to small, poor and underdeveloped countries to have their voices heard.[17]

The need of the hour is an effort by all the member states to strengthen the bargaining capacity of NAM, which can partly be done by reaffirming faith in the Movement and by building a strong bond among its member states once again, and partly by organizing some form of institutional machinery for collective bargaining with the developed countries. The latter was proposed by the Chairman of the South Commission, late Julius Nyerere, the former President of Tanzania. In a report published in 1990, he reaffirmed that the Third World countries are in extremely weak bargaining position in their dealings with the well-organized groupings of the developed countries or with the transnational corporations, and that the Third World countries are often ill-prepared for discussions with the North which often decides the agenda of the meeting. The report recommended, *inter alia*, "the Commission is firmly of the view that the developing countries should establish a well-staffed Secretariat for the South that would provide continuing institutional support for analysis, interaction, negotiation and follow-up action—the technical foundation for their collective function". [18] The NAM should work towards this end and establish a Secretariat to serve, coordinate and follow-up the implementation of its decisions. A rejuvenated NAM is the need of the hour. The NAM countries should come forward with a vision to:

- Reform and strengthen the United Nations
- Encourage the South–South cooperation

- Strive for an equitable world order
- Consolidate the movement through necessary reforms
- Adhere to the principles and objectives of the movement by its members and build a common bargaining platform.

EXERCISES

1. Trace the origin and evolution of the non-aligned movement. What are its objectives?

2. Discuss the growth of the non-aligned movement. Has the non-aligned movement lost its relevance?

3. Write a note on the growth, significance and contribution of the non-aligned movement. Is it relevant in the contemporary world?

REFERENCES

[1] Singham, A.W. and Shirley Hune, *Non-alignment in an Age of Alignments*, Lawrence Hill and Co., Westport, USA and Zed Books Ltd., London, 1986, p. 1.

[2] Jaipal, Rikhi, *Non-alignment: Origins, Growth and Potential for Worlds Peace,* Allied Publishers, New Delhi, 1983, p. 10.

[3] *ibid.*, p. 52.

[4] *ibid.*, pp. 55–56.

[5] *ibid.*, pp. 1–2.

[6] Jain, Narendra P., "A New Approach to International Relation", *in* D.R. Goyal (Ed.), *Non-Alignment: Concept and Concerns*, Ajanta Publications, New Delhi, 1986, pp. 3–4.

[7] Jaipal, Rikhi, *op. cit.*, n. 3, p. 10.

[8] *ibid.*

[9] Jain, N.P., *op. cit.*, n. 6, p. 5.

[10] Singham and Hune, *op. cit.*, n. 1, pp. 14–15.

[11] *ibid.*, pp. 33–42.

[12] Misra, K.P., "Non-Alignment: Concept and Concerns", *in* D.R. Goyal (Ed.), *Non-Alignment: Concept and concerns*, Ajanta Publications, New Delhi, 1986, p. 36.

[13] Josh, Harcharan Singh, "NAM and the New World Order", *in* Pramila Srivastava (Ed.), *Non-Aligned Movement: Extending frontiers*, Kanishka Publishers, New Delhi, 2001, pp. 82–83.

[14] Misra, K.P., "Aspects of Non-Alignment", *in* Pramila Srivastava (Ed.), *Non-Aligned Movement: Extending Frontiers*, Kanishka Publishers, New Delhi, 2001, pp. 17–18.

[15] Vidyasekera, E.A., "Non-Aligned Movement and the Challenge of Sustainable Development, *in* Pramila Srivastava (Ed.), *Non-Aligned Movement: Extending Frontiers*, Kanishka Publishers, New Delhi, 2001, p. 56.

[16] Misra, K.P., *op. cit.,* n. 14, p. 19.

[17] Singh, K. Natwar, "The Importance and Relevance of Non-Alignment," *in* Pramila Srivastava (Ed.), *Non-Aligned Movement: Extending Frontiers*, Kanishka Publishers, New Delhi, 2001, p. 29.

[18] Amate, C.O.C., "The Non-Aligned Movement Today", *in* Pramila Srivastava (Ed.), *Non-Aligned Movement: Extending Frontiers*, Kanishka Publishers, New Delhi, 2001, p. 47.

9

Neo-Colonialism

CONTENTS

Imperialism: An Overview
Neo-Colonialism: Concept
Mechanisms of Neo-Colonialism
Demand for NIEO
Fate of NIEO Proposal

INTRODUCTION

Post-Second World War, international system experienced a kind of subjugation of the weak, underdeveloped and newly independent states of the world by those powers who held their sway over these states as parts of their colony. Though traditional or classical colonialism did fade away with the former colonies asserting their independence and establishing themselves as sovereign states yet, in essence, their economic backwardness had made them heavily dependent on their former colonial masters. This is a situation when the former colonial powers exploit the resources of these newly independent states and impose their domination over them by using political, economic, social, military and technological forces—a situation, which has come to be identified as neo-colonialism or neo-imperialism. But before going into details about neo-colonialism it would be most effective to have an overview on imperialism.

IMPERIALISM: AN OVERVIEW

The subjugation of large parts of the world constitutes an important episode in the history of international relations. Realpolitik involves the urge of states to acquire jurisdiction and exercise domination over the territories and peoples of other states. The ultimate aim is expansion and enhancement of national prestige and asserting their power. This has led to the acquisition of colonies, setting up of economic dependencies and satellites. When such practices become a part and parcel of a foreign policy objective of a state, it is often said that the state is engaging in imperialism.

Though imperialism and colonialism have long been employed as instruments of national policy, there is no agreed definition about imperialism. Some scholars try to define imperialism as "a policy which aims at creating, organizing, and maintaining an empire; that is, a state of vast size composed of various more or less distinct national units and subject to a single centralized will". According to Charles A. Beard[*] "Imperialism is ... employment of the engines of government and diplomacy to acquire territories, protectorates, and/ or spheres of influences occupied usually by other races or peoples, and to promote industrial, trade, and investment opportunities". Parker T. Moon[**] defines imperialism as "domination of non-European native races by totally dissimilar European nations".

Joseph Schumpeter[†], a distinguished Austrian economist, regarded imperialism as an "atavistic force, ancient in inception, decadent and self-conscious in an age of rationalism, yet still powerful enough to lord it over its rival, the upstart capitalism".

Charles Hodges[††] offered a much more convincing definition of imperialism as "a projection externally, directly or indirectly, of alien political, economic, or cultural power of one nation into the internal life of another people. ... it involves the imposition of control—open or covert, direct or indirect —of one people by another" and it "is to affect the destinies of the backward people in the interest of more advanced from the stand point of world power".[1]

The terms 'colonialism' and 'imperialism' are used interchangeably although they mean two different things. Usually, 'colony' is a people detached from a larger entity and settled in a distant place. 'Imperium' is the exercise of command or domination of one people by a stronger people. Therefore, 'imperialism' implies pacification and domination.[2]

---

[*]Charles A. Beard, *American Foreign Policy in the Making, 1932–1940: A Study in Responsibilities*, Yale University Press, New Haven, 1946.

[**]Parker T. Moon, *Imperialism and World Politics*, The Macmillan Company, New York, 1926.

[†]Joseph A. Schumpeter, "Imperialism and Social Classes", 1951 (essay).

[††]Charles Hodges, *The Background of International Relations*, Wiley and Sons, New York, 1932.

Palmer and Perkins[3] point out that some scholars like Hobson, in his famous work, *Imperialism: A Study,* gave the essence of colonialism as "a natural overflow of nationality wherein groups of colonists are sent out to a foreign, and ordinarily more backward, land or go of their own volition to settle and take up the land", followed by the transplantation of their civilization and political institutions and retaining the territory of the home country. Imperialism, on the other hand, is regarded as "something more organized, more military, more self-consciously aggressive". The distinction can be understood in teleological terms and in terms of purposes and ends sought. When rule over foreign territories is sought primarily for the economic, political or military benefit of the central homeland, the action assumes the characteristics of imperialism, though it may not always be regarded as such. Where rule is undertaken within a colonial area, primarily for retaining the control over the territory, it is said to be identified with colonialism.

Whatever may be the distinction between the two, both imperialism and colonialism pertain to a relationship of domination and subordination of one area and its people by another area and its government. The most significant thing about colonialism and imperialism is not that they can be precisely defined or that they cannot always be distinguished from each other, but both express a kind of relationship and thus used interchangeably and the distinction is often not preserved.[4] In the modern times, colonialism acquired more or less the same connotation as imperialism with the rise of the British, French, Dutch, Portuguese and Spanish Empires.

Over the past 400 years or more, European nations had subjugated two-thirds of the non-European world. Spain and Portugal were the early colonizers but their supremacy was challenged since 1600 AD by Holland, England and France who joined the race for scramble for colonies. The peak of colonization was reached in 1775 when the entire American, Asian and African continents became subjugated to European domination. A second peak was reached in about 1900 AD when about half the earth's surface and a third of its population were colonial possessions. By that time England had the highest colonial possessions; second was France, and Germany held the third position.

This experience of colonialism was not an uncommon feature in history, because colonialism goes back to the ancient world. Great colonial empires were created by Phoenicians, the Greeks, the Romans and the Carthaginians. The Indians and the Chinese, the Arabs and the Turks all had colonies. But the facts which distinguished modern colonialism from the earlier forms of colonialism are:

- Modern colonialism was basically a European phenomena.
- The colonies have all been far from homeland.
- The colonies were inhabited by populations different from their conquerors in both culture and race.

Modern colonialism got a spurt of life in the nineteenth century due to the industrial revolution in Europe that induced the European states to search for new markets for their products. The best opportunities were held out by the Third World countries. Therefore, subjugation of the Third World countries became the primary aim of the European states and these often led to inter-imperialistic wars like Anglo–French rivalry in India, France–Germany conflict over Morocco, Anglo–French rivalry over Sudan, France–Germany conflict over Congo, and so on. Nevertheless, a pattern of colonial relationships, one that was of domination and subjugation, was created when the European nations established and maintained their sway over geographically external political units inhabited by different people.

Primary motives behind imperialistic policies arise from a state's political motives, which may be aimed at increasing national power. Spain, Britain and France setup colonies because it added to their power and prestige. Imperialistic policy may also be pursued for national defence as is reflected in the United States' acquisitions of bases in the Caribbean, the purchase of the Virgin Islands and the exercise of influence in Central America from time to time which has been determined by United States vital interest of protection of Panama Canal and the American continent. In most cases, however, imperialist policies have been motivated by economic interests. Sometimes altruism has been emphasized as a motivating factor and in most cases English colonialism was justified by some as "shouldering the white man's burden". France also justified its colonizing moves as a sort of civilizing mission. Sometimes missionary zeal worked as a factor for colonialism. Religious missionaries were active in Africa, India and China. In England, Protestant missionary societies were a vocal impetus to British imperialism. Although strong economic forces have worked behind much of the growth of modern imperialism, it would be illogical if other factors are ignored. "No simple explanation, no dogmatic theory, will suffice"[5] as Imperialism is, in all its manifestations, the result of the interplay of complex forces that may have psychological, sociological, religious, political, military, intellectual, and personal-rule roots.

Professor Joseph Schumpeter suggested that imperialism is "the objectless disposition on the part of a state to unlimited forcible expansion". He further stated, "It would never have been evolved by the 'inner logic' of capitalism itself", but must be regarded "not only historically, but also sociologically, as a heritage of the autocratic state".[6]

A systematic economic explanation of the urge of the states to expand was given by Marx. When "Capital grows in one place to a huge mass in a single hand because it has in another place been lost by many" a stage of monopoly capitalism is reached. Each capitalist tries to increase profits by reducing the production costs, especially by saving the wages, and competes to win larger sales of product, which results in search for raw materials and new markets, and hence outward expansion. Hobson attributed this expansion as the "economic taproot of imperialism". Lenin[7] in his seminal work *Imperialism: The Highest*

Stage of Capitalism, viewed imperialism as a stage of capitalist development and not merely as one possible set of foreign policy options among many. To him, monopolist capitalist stage exhibits five basic features. They are:

1. Concentration of production and capital leads to the creation of national and multinational monopolies—not as in liberal economics, but as *de facto* power over their markets—while "free competition" remains the domain of local and niche markets:

> Free competition is the basic feature of capitalism, and of commodity production generally; monopoly is the exact opposite of free competition, but we have seen the latter being transformed into monopoly before our eyes, creating large-scale industry and forcing out small industry, replacing large-scale by still larger-scale industry, and carrying concentration of production and capital to the point where out of it has grown and is growing monopoly: cartels, syndicates and trusts, and merging with them, the capital of a dozen or so banks, which manipulate thousands of millions. At the same time the monopolies, which have grown out of free competition, do not eliminate the latter, but exist above it and alongside it, and thereby give rise to a number of very acute, intense antagonisms, frictions and conflicts. Monopoly is the transition from capitalism to a higher system. (Ch. VII)

2. The fusion of banking capital with industrial capital and the creation, on the basis of this financial capital, of a financial oligarchy.

3. Finance capital exportation replaces the exportation of goods (though they continue in production).

4. The economic division of the world, by multinational enterprises via international cartels.

5. The political division of the world by the great powers, wherein exporting finance capital to their colonies allows their exploitation for resources and continued investment.

Though Lenin did not provide a foolproof theory of imperialism nevertheless, he had set the tenor for analysing the causes of inequalities in the world which have been later developed by full names, Marxists like Andre Gunder Frank, Johan Galtung Immanuel Wallerstein (discussed in Chapter 2) and others who, in their own version utilizing the Marxian vocabulary, have tried to understand the pattern of relationship between the developing and developed parts of the world.

By the end of the nineteenth century, almost the entire globe was under the colonial rule. Scholars have pointed out that the age of discovery (fifteenth and sixteenth centuries), stimulated by ship-building and navigation, the politico-economic theory of mercantilism which held that national strength and security in a world of competing states were dependent on a favourable balance of trade and the accumulation of gold in the treasury, the rise of monopoly capitalism, all brought the Third World countries under imperialistic exploitation. As history moved on, colonialism and imperialism created their own contradictions in the forms of national liberation and urge for democracy. By the end of World War II, a process of decolonization had started and almost all states under colonial domination were able to shake off the yoke of this domination. This, formally put an end to colonialism but the former colonies continued and still continue to be dominated and exploited by the former colonial powers. Thus, political economy of dependence and exploitation continues. As Organski[8] remarks that classical colonialism might have met a natural death but new forms of colonialism are arising in its place. Nations, those who have won nominal political independence, are not necessarily free and those states which have never been colonies before also cannot escape the new forces of colonialism commonly known as **neo-colonialism.**

NEO-COLONIALISM: CONCEPT

The term 'neo-colonialism' was popularized in the wake of decolonialization, largely through the activities of scholars and leaders from the newly independent states of Africa and the Pan-African Movement. Many of these leaders came together with those of other post-colonial states at the Bandung Conference of 1955, leading to the formation of the Non-Aligned Movement. The All-African Peoples' Conference (AAPC) meetings of the late 1950s and early 1960s spread the critique of neo-colonialism. The Tunis conference of 1960 and Cairo Conference of 1961 specified their opposition to what they labelled as neo-colonialism. Their four-page *Resolution on Neocolonialism* is cited as a landmark for having presented a collectively arrived at definition of neo-colonialism and a description of its main features. Throughout the Cold War, NAM as well as organizations like the Organization of Solidarity with the People of Asia, Africa and Latin America defined neo-colonialism as a primary collective enemy of these independent states.

Neo-colonialism is best described as "The survival of the colonial system in spite of formal recognition of political independence in emerging countries which became the victims of indirect and subtle form of domination by political, economic, social, military and technical forces".[9]

The mechanisms of neo-colonialism are designed to serve the interest of continuation of economic dependence of former colonies by the former colonial powers. This is ensured by the integration of the dependent countries into colonial economic blocs through capital investments, loans, aid, unequal exchange and finances directly controlled by the colonial powers.

Difference between Colonialism and Neo-Colonialism

Kwame Nkrumah, who in 1957 became the leader of the newly independent Ghana, expounded his idea in his book *Neo-Colonialism: The Last Stage of*

Imperialism, in 1965. He stated, "The essence of neo-colonialism is that the State which is subject to it is, in theory, independent and has all the outward trappings of international sovereignty. In reality, its economic system and thus its political policy is directed from outside. Neo-colonialism is also the worst form of imperialism. For those who practice it, it means power without responsibility and for those who suffer from it, it means exploitation without redress".[10]

Therefore, to Kwame Nkrumah, the neo-colonialism of today represented imperialism in its final and perhaps its most dangerous stage. In the past, it was possible to convert a country into a colonial territory. Today, this process is no longer feasible due to the presence of international laws and world public opinion. Once a territory has become nominally independent, it is no longer possible, as it was in the last century, to reverse the process. Existing colonies lingered on for quite some time but no new colonies were created. Therefore, in place of colonialism as the main instrument of imperialism what exists today is neo-colonialism.

Denunciations of neo-colonialism also became popular with some national independence movements while they were still waging anti-colonial armed struggle and, after they gained independence, they rejected both traditional colonialism and neo-colonialism. The NAM countries were pioneer's in their struggle against colonialism and neo-colonialism and wanted the establishment of a New International Economic Order.

In the late twentieth century, the Western nations, especially the United States, were often charged for the perpetration of neo-colonialism. They were charged with involvement in the affairs of the developing nations. Proxy wars, many in former colonized nations, were funded throughout this period. Cuba, the Soviet bloc, Egypt under Nasser, as well as some governments of newly independent African states, charged the United States with supporting regimes which they felt did not represent the will of their peoples, and by both covert and overt means, toppled governments which rejected the United States.

The Third African People's Conference held in Cairo in 1961 made a comprehensive summary of manifestations of neo-colonialism. The Conference considered neo-colonialism to be the survival of the colonial system in spite of formal recognition of political independence in emerging countries, which became victims of an indirect and subtle form of domination by political, economic, social, military or technical [forces].

The manifestations of neo-colonialism, as highlighted and denounced by the Cairo Conference, are:

1. Puppet governments represented by stooges and based on some chiefs, reactionary elements, antipopular politicians, big bourgeois-compradors or corrupted civil or military functionaries.
2. Re-grouping of state, before or after independence, by an imperial power in federation or communities linked to that imperial power.

3. Balkanization as a deliberate political fragmentation of states by creation of artificial entities, as in the case of Katanga, Mauritiana, Buganda and others.
4. The economic entrenchment of the colonial powers before independence, and the continuity of economic dependence after formal recognition of national sovereignty.
5. Integration into colonial economic blocs which maintain the underdeveloped character of African economy.
6. Economic infiltration by a foreign power after independence through capital investments, loans and monetary aids or technical experts of unequal concessions, particularly those extending for long periods.
7. Direct monetary dependence as in those emergent independent states whose finances remain in the hands of and are directly controlled by the colonial powers.
8. Military bases sometimes introduced as scientific research stations or training schools, introduced either before independence or as a condition for independence.[11]

The neo-colonialism of the present time substitutes older form of controls over the former colonies and uses newer and subtle methods to perpetuate it. The mechanisms of neo-colonialism may be political devices, economic instruments, treaties and agreements, arms trade, technology transfer, military mechanisms and cultural mechanisms.

MECHANISMS OF NEO-COLONIALISM

Political Devices

Formal or informal modes of political control of the old form of colonialism are replaced by establishing the political control in varied forms. They may range from nurturing the old economic and political ties, wherever possible, like relationships formed within the Bristish Commonwealth and the French Community, closed currency, preferential trading systems, military alliances and political–military pacts. Other forms of political control include economic, political and cultural missions, labour union delegations, joint military training programmes, military grants and bribes to local ruling classes in the form of economic 'aid'. When these fail, the older policies of force are brought back, for example, the United States instigated counter-revolution in Guatemala in 1954 against the Arbenz Government and the accomplishments following it. The United States extracted an agreement for the return of property expropriated by the 'Arbenz Guzman*' government (of Guatemala) for the United Fruit

---

*Jacobo Arbenz Guzman was the centre-left President of Guatemala from 1951 to 1954 when he was ousted in a coup d'état by CIA and was replaced by a military junta headed by colonel Carlos Castillo Armas.

Company subsidiary there. Post-1954, the Castillo Armas regime was maintained in office via contracts with the United Fruit, Bond and Share and other monopolies. Therefore, puppet governments serve as important mechanisms of reinforcing neo-colonialism with vigour.[12]

Foreign Aid

Foreign aid is the assistance given to the developing countries to help them speed up their development or meet their basic humanitarian needs. The foreign assistance given take different forms and all serve different purposes. Some are humanitarian, some are political, and yet others try to create advantages for the donors. Most often, aid is used more as a weapon of foreign policy of the donor states or international agencies and always released with certain strings or conditions attached to it. But the truth is that the Third World countries are reeling under the onus of debt-burden which is making them more and more dependent on the developed states. They are suffering from the problem of debt servicing which is a constant drain of whatever surplus is produced by them. They may default on debt repayment or attempt debt re-negotiation. Either way, the Third World countries are losers and, as a result of heavy debt-burden in the 1980s, a Third World debt crisis emerged, particularly in Latin America. Africa today pays more money every year as debt service payments to the IMF and World Bank than it receives in loans from them, thereby often depriving the inhabitants of those countries from actual necessities.

The conditions attached to the debt or aid given reveal the true intention of the donor countries. The American PL 480 or "Food for Peace" given to the Third World countries, including India, was nothing but a US plan to dump their agricultural surpluses in the name of aid. It also opened up opportunities for future commercial markets for the US agriculture. Food aid also intended to discourage local production thereby hindering self-sufficiency and ultimately leading to continuous dependence of food supply from the foreign countries.

Aid through international agencies such as the IMF and the World Bank is also not less motivated. Generally an agreement to loan IMF funds is based on the condition that certain government policies are adopted, is worked out which is referred to as *IMF conditionality agreement*. This means implementation of these conditions agreed upon by the recipient country as a part of the "structural adjustment programme". Adjustments largely consisting of privatization programmes, which they say, result in deteriorating health, education, inability to develop infrastructure, and in general, lower living standards. Undoubtedly, implementation of these conditionality leads to the hardships of the average citizens and fails to deliver any good, and sometimes may even result in political disturbances within the country resulting in the toppling of the government. As in the case of Ghana, the local poultry industry collapsed, impoverishing 400,000 small farmers because the market was flooded with cheap subsidized frozen chickens from the EU and the United States. Ghana's attempt to raise the tariffs to prevent this dumping was blocked by the IMF and the WTO because the conditionality of structural adjustments had to be continued. The sub-Saharan countries are suffering from the IMF and the WTO conditionality of structural adjustments because they have been forced to open up their economies to import from the industrialized North.[13]

Though aid from these agencies helps in fostering development of the Third World countries, nevertheless, as the major contribution to these International financial agencies comes from the United States and Western countries, they have a greater say in the decision-making of these agencies. They decide the amount of aid to be given and conditions to be attached as a result of which, to a great extent, the rate of economic development and the economic policies of the poor countries get determined by the rich North. It is said that "The benefits of such international aid have been marginal in the long run; and had only perpetuated the dependence of third world countries on such aid".[14]

Multinational Corporations (MNCs)

Multinational Corporations are becoming crucial and powerful non-state actors in international relations. Some of the industrial MNCs have annual sales of tens of billions of dollars each and international firms such as the IBM, Unilever, Coca Cola and others have become more powerful than the sovereign states. Whether MNCs serve as agents of national governments or national governments serve as agents of MNCs, the truth is that both guard each other's interests and state interventions whether military or economic result when their interests in the Third World countries are jeopardized. For instance, nationalization of the Suez Canal Company in 1956 by President Nasser invited a major Anglo–French invasion of Egypt. The MNCs in Latin America, Africa and Asia exercise a powerful influence on the government's policy-making.

Critics of neo-colonialism point out that investment by multinational corporations enriches few in the developing countries, and causes humanitarian, environmental and ecological devastation to the populations which inhabit the *neo-colonies*. This results in unsustainable development and perpetual underdevelopment; a dependency situation which renders those countries as reservoirs of cheap labour and raw materials, while restricting their access to advanced production techniques to develop their own economies and, thereby, thwarting their pace of development and self-sufficiency.

MNCs also prevent the use of indigenous technology. It is said that the training of manpower in the advanced nations provided at a high degree of sophistication which cannot be sustained by less developed countries leads to brain drain from the poor countries. Thus, increasing their dependence on the developed countries continues.

Treaties and Agreements

The Global North tries to ensure its control over the developing countries of the South through formal treaties and agreements which are mostly designed to serve the interests of the neo-colonial powers. These may be bilateral treaties like the Indo–US Nuke Deal which, to some, have to be looked at with caution or multilateral treaties such as the NPT or CTBT. Both the NPT and CTBT were regarded by the developing countries as discriminatory and they did not end horizontal expansion but tried to stop vertical extension of the nuclear club. Economic agreements and treaties between the developed countries and the poor states are intended to further the neo-colonial exploitation of the poor countries. Therefore, treaties and agreements are also mechanisms to extend control over the developing countries which are mostly former colonies.

Arms Trade

The military–industrial complex is a complicated network of governmental agencies, industrial corporations and research institutes working together to meet a state's military requirement. Both the United States and the Soviet Union have huge military–industrial complex. Other than meeting one's own military requirements, most often the developed states like the United States and the Soviet Union are engaged in arms sale to the developing countries. This serves a dual purpose. One is that they get rid of outdated and also surplus military equipment, and the other is that the money earned is pumped into the military–industrial complex for its survival. Other Western countries such as UK and France also have become major suppliers of arms to the Third World countries. Arms trade diverts the precious foreign exchange from real development of the people and the state to wasteful purposes such as engaging in conflicts and war with other states, or simply engaging in arms escalation resulting in unhealthy arms race with the opponent state, thus obstructing the path of development and continuing their phenomena of dependence.

Transfer of Technology

Transfer of technology is an endeavour on the part of the Third World countries to acquire technology, knowledge, skills, methods, designs and specialized equipments from foreign sources. This, however, only adds up to the burden of the poor developing countries. One UNCTAD (United Nations Conference on Trade and Development) study points out that contracts for transferring technology involves purchases and even imports of raw materials and intermediate inputs resulting in an increase in cost of such transfers and also raises unit costs. This restrains the healthy growth of the economies of the developing countries.

Cultural Device

One variant of neo-colonialism theory suggests the existence of *cultural colonialism*, the alleged desire of wealthy nations to control other nations' values and perceptions through cultural means, such as media, language, education and religion, purportedly ultimately for economic reasons. For this, they use the latest innovations in information and technology, mass media, particularly television with multiple channels, movies, Internet and other devices, to impose a sort of cultural domination on the people of the Third World countries.

The overall international scenario bears testimony to the great divide between the rich and the poor states in the world, with the former extracting the maximum benefits by exploiting the economies and resources, whether natural or human, of the poor countries. The result is that the poor countries remain poor and the rich countries get richer. The World Bank has produced a list of 140 'failed' states which are either developing countries or former socialist countries, but with huge natural resources. In the wake of such a situation, neo-colonialism is assuming its old character of colonialism but in a new garb. This new manifestation of colonialism is referred to as *Post-modern Imperialism* by American and other Western academicians. The aim is to create a "New Imperial Order" to rescue the 'failed' states. The United States is now more interested in establishing a form of international governance that may be described as neo-trusteeship or post-modern Imperialism, and the signs of such post-modern Imperialism is already being seen in Bosnia, Kosovo, East Timor, Sierra Leone, Afghanistan and Iraq. The rationale behind such thinking is that, left to their own devices, collapsed and badly governed states will not be able to improve much with limited administrative capacity and will fail to maintain internal security. Therefore, to reduce international threats, alternative institutional arrangements supported by external actors must be worked out. This might include *de facto* trusteeships and shared sovereignty.[15]

A new dimension has been added to justify physical control of the 'failed' states in terms of inefficiency of their governments to have sustained economic growth. The justification is that inefficient governments breed international terrorism, and to eradicate this menace, control has to be removed from the 'failed' states. As in the Victorian era, the justification of colonialism in terms of "white man's burden" to civilize the "dark continent" now the justification is to save the failed states and spread democracy.[16]

DEMAND FOR NIEO

The dismal picture of the international economic structure had created a discontent among the developing countries. These countries of South had been from the 1970s onwards, pressing for a New International Economic Order where the developing world would have a say. These countries have utilized the Group of G-77, the UNCTAD, the Non- Aligned Conferences, and the General

Assembly of the United Nations to place their demand and realize them through structural adjustment of the existing international economic relations.

By the early 1960s, however, many developing countries were frustrated with their growth prospects and started demanding a better deal. Rallying in such organizations as the Non-Aligned Movement, and establishing the United Nations Conference on Trade and Development (UNCTAD), they argued for fairer terms of trade and more liberal terms for financing development. The North responded with pious declarations of its good intentions—but also with a hard-nosed insistence—that the proper forum for any economic changes continued to be the Bretton Woods institutions where they held the balance of power.

The success of the oil-producing countries of OPEC, in increasing petroleum prices substantially, starting in 1973, served as a catalyst to pull together the developing countries in support of a call for a New International Economic Order in which their interests would be better represented. This call integrated many of the proposals that had been discussed previously at UNCTAD and other world forums.

Specific proposals for changes in the economic system were advanced at the Summit Conference of Non-Aligned Nations held in Algiers in September 1973. Following that, the Sixth Special Session of the UN General Assembly was called hastily in April 1974. This session adopted, without a vote, a manifesto entitled "Declaration and Program of Action of the New International Order". In December 1974, the General Assembly approved the Charter of Economic Rights and Duties of States.

The UN General Assembly, in its Sixth Special Session held in 1974, declared its determination to establish a New International Economic Order (NIEO). It proclaimed that "We, the Members of the United Nations…solemnly proclaim our united determination to work urgently for the establishment of a New International Economic Order based on equity, sovereign equality, interdependence, common interest and cooperation among all states, irrespective of their economic and social systems, which shall correct inequalities and redress existing injustices, make it possible to eliminate the widening gap between the developed and the developing countries and ensure steadily accelerating economic and social development and peace and justice for present and future generations.[17]

In another resolution, the General Assembly adopted at the same Session a programme for establishment of an NIEO. The NIEO is essentially an 18-clause document that seeks certain changes in the international system, which would allow the less developed countries an opportunity to build their way out of the never-ending cycle of poverty. Some of the main clauses were:

1. Fundamental problems of raw materials and primary commodities as related to trade and development

2. International monetary system and financing of the development of developing countries

3. Industrialization

4. Transfer of technology

5. Regulation and control over the activities of transnational corporations

6. Charter of economic rights and duties of states

7. Promotion of cooperation among developing countries

8. Assistance in the exercise of permanent sovereignty of states over natural resources

9. Strengthening of the role of the United Nations system in the field of international economic cooperation

10. Special programme for the most seriously affected developing nations.

The Charter of Economic Rights and Duties, as mentioned in the Programme of Action, was adopted by the UNGA in its Twenty-Ninth Session in 1974. This Charter provided, among others: full sovereignty of states over their natural resources; control over multinationals; nationalization of foreign investment; sharing of common natural resources; equitable terms of trade; duty of the developed countries (DCs) to transfer technology to the less developed countries (LDCs), extension of generalized, non-reciprocal and non-discriminatory tariff preferences by the DCs to the LDCs and others.

Article 8 of the Charter explicitly stated the need for cooperation among states to facilitate more rational and equitable international economic relations and to encourage structural changes in the context of a balanced world economy in harmony with the needs and interests of all countries, especially the developing countries.

In its Twenty-Fifth Session, the UNGA had already declared the period starting from 1 January 1971 to 31 December 1981 as the Second United Nations Development Decade. The UNGA resolution pertaining to the establishment of NIEO, adopted in its Sixth Special Session, specifically recommended the International Development Strategy for the realization of the NIEO. The International Development Strategy aimed at a 6 per cent average annual rate of growth in the GDP of the LDCs during this Second United Nations Development Decade.

The most important provisions in the programme designed to establish the NIEO deal with the management and pricing of at least ten core commodities: cocoa, coffee, tea, sugar, hard fibres, jute, cotton, rubber, copper and tin, and seven other commodities with slightly lower priority: bananas, wheat, rice, meat, wool, iron ore and bauxite. Specifically, the objectives of the commodity programme were: (a) reduction of excessive price and supply fluctuations; and (b) establishment and maintenance of commodity prices which, in real terms, are equitable to consumers and remunerative to producers.

To achieve these goals, the following integrated measures were proposed:

1. Establishment of international buffer stocks

2. Creation of a common fund to finance these stocks

3. Signing of multilateral trade commitments
4. Arrangement of improved compensatory financing to stabilize export earnings.

Realization of these objectives necessarily depended on finding the resources required to achieve the targets visualized in the International Development Strategy. The responsibility of finding the resources lay with the LDCs, which were asked to "continue to adopt vigorous measures for the mobilization of the whole range of their domestic financial resources, both internal and external". A marginal responsibility was also devolved on the developed countries and each developed country was expected to provide by the year 1972, annually to the LDCs financial resource transfer of a minimum amount of 1 per cent of its GNP at market prices in terms of actual disbursements, having regard to the special position of those countries, which were importers of capital. Among other responsibilities, the developed countries were asked to provide, to the greatest extent possible, an increased flow of aid on a long-term and continuing basis, and to make arrangements for the rescheduling and refinancing of debts wherever necessary. The LDCs were asked to "adopt appropriate measures for inviting, stimulating and making effective use of foreign private capital", while the developed countries were asked to "consider adopting further measures to encourage the flow of private capital to developing countries".

The adoption of International Development Strategy, the NIEO, and the Charter of Economic Rights might seem to be grand achievements of the developing states after decades of conference diplomacy by the LDCs but the target remain unfulfilled. Both of these UN documents blame the past exploitation under colonialism and neo-colonialism for the low incomes in the South.

At the UNCTAD IV conference in Nairobi in May 1976, the proposals for the establishment of a New International Economic Order were reworded slightly in some instances, but their essence remained unchanged when they were adopted as resolutions, with only the United States and the Federal Republic of Germany voting against them. Most significantly, the conference laid out a time table for the study and implementation of one of the most controversial proposals involving the integrated programme for commodities, giving them a bureaucratic life of their own and raising exceptions about their ultimate adoption. As things turned out, the NIEO never became much more than a rallying cry for the South.

FATE OF NIEO PROPOSAL

If the resolutions adopted by the UNGA reflect the majority of the LDCs in the UN, their non-implementation as Prof. Jayantanuja Bandyopadhyaya[18] shows the oligarchic and neo-imperialistic control of the developed countries over the total international relations scenario. Even the Charter of the United Nations gave a formal sanction to the neo-imperialistic structure of the international system, which came into existence after the Second World War by according permanent seats to the five members in the Security Council and investing in them the power to veto. The UN sort of revived an international oligarchy, which ruled the world during the phase of European imperialism. Morgenthau asserts that this is a kind of a new Holy Alliance constituting the five permanent members. Therefore, it is too optimistic to consider that the efforts of the LDCs to bring about a revision in the international economic relations would be fruitful.

A UN study led by Wassily Leontief found out that the economic gap between the developed countries and the LDCs would remain unchanged even by the year 2000. If any change occurs that would be marginal. The gloomy picture of the present day remains unchanged and as previously discussed, the continuation of exploitative international economic relations have created more and more failed states. No major developed country has so far been kind enough to transfer even one-third of 1 per cent of the GNP to the LDCs in the form of official development assistance. Neither any sort of international monetary reform, nor the external debt problem of the LDCs have been addressed. Even the activities of the MNCs have expanded and they enjoy their profit from the exploitation of cheap labour and natural resources and transference of technological obsolescence, rather than the supply of sophisticated technology. Even the developed countries, by establishing discriminatory nuclear non-proliferation regimes, have tried to prevent the transfer of nuclear technology. Side by side the developed countries have increased their arms sales compared to the LDCs and definitely the technology transferred is militarily obsolete. This transference of militarily obsolescence only helps to sustain the expensive military–industrial complex of the developed countries. Thus, the North–South dialogues between the developed countries and the LDCs for the establishment of the NIEO, have proved to be "little more than hollow mockery".

The LDCs have alleged that the failure to realize the NIEO is due to the lack of commitment and lack of their 'political will'. The Havana Summit Conference of 1979 of the non-aligned states, comprising an overwhelming number of LDCs noted that even after five years of adoption of the NIEO and the Charter of Economic Rights and Duties of States, there has been no structural change in the international economic scenario and it "continues its pervasive deterioration aggravated and accelerated by the effects of the world economic crisis". It also took into account "the intransigency of most of the developed countries and their refusal to engage in serious negotiations to implement the above-mentioned resolutions which have prevented the fundamental restructuring of economic relations included in the basic objectives of the New International Economic Order".[19]

Scholars also point out the failure of the LDCs to realize NIEO primarily due to the South's lack of power in world politics, and partly because disparities within the South created divergent interests among the member states. Also it became apparent that many of the proposed commodity schemes were not simply a proposal for stable prices, but, high prices. As such, the financial costs of implementing these programmes were way beyond anything the advanced countries were willing to fund. In the 1980s, the terms of trade further deteriorated for the raw material exporters, and the debt problems of many of the nations advocating the NIEO in international forums surpassed all limits.

Under the chairmanship of the former West German Chancellor, Willy Brandt, the Independent Commission on International Development Issues examined the problems being faced by the global economy in the early 1980s. Brandt's panel of former world leaders and other prominent figures found that developing nations were economically dependent on developed nations, which dominated the international rules and institutions for trade, money and finance. This economic division resulted in political instability, not just in poor nations but across the world. According to Brandt "At the beginning of a new decade, only twenty years short of the millennium, we must try to lift ourselves above the day-to-day quarrels (or negotiations) to see the menacing long-term problems. We see a world in which poverty and hunger still prevail in many huge regions; in which resources are squandered without consideration of their renewal; in which more armaments are made and sold than ever before; and where a destructive capacity has been accumulated to blow up our planet several times over" (*North–South*). In *North–South* (1980) and *Common Crisis* (1983), the Brandt Commission made a set of bold recommendations to change the present unequal international economic order. The Brandt Reports called for a full-scale restructuring of the global economy, along with a new approach to the problems of development, including an emergency programme to end poverty in the developing nations.

On the recommendations of Brandt Commission, a Summit Conference was held in Cancun, Mexico on 22–23 October 1981. The Cancun Summit focused on the issue of structuring of global negotiations. The United States however, had its own reservations and it did not want to compromise the supremacy of IMF and the World Bank to United Nations in global negotiations, for in these specialized agencies, the developed countries were the major decision makers than in the UN General Assembly. Though the spirit of Cancun was thought to be providing a boost to NIEO but actually by 1984, the North–South dialogue could not make headway and it stood frozen.

The international community had not responded to NIEO proposals in any meaningful way and though the Brandt Reports though were widely read and discussed, developed nations had focused more on their own interests solely and have not contributed to the realization of NIEO. As documented by the United Nations Development Programme, the World Bank, the International Monetary Fund, and other agencies, the economic disparities outlined in the Brandt Reports had widened significantly since 1980s.

Failure to address the need for NIEO is a lost opportunity for everyone in the world. One should not overlook the benefits of mutual advantage and cooperation. As the Brandt Reports remind us, prosperity in the South can lead to prosperity in the North; but economic trouble in the South can wreak havoc in the North as well. The only alternative in sight is mobilizing the South and working towards a South–South cooperation. The emergence of a new grouping of the developing states, G-15 in 1989 and their subsequent summits are working for forging a strong South–South cooperation. The NAM, CHOGM, G-77 and other international fora outside the UN have also been mobilized to champion the cause for a new world order of developing countries but without much effect. The adoption of the International Development Strategy, the Declaration on the New International Economic Order and the Charter of Economic Rights and Duties of States have been the outcome of decade-long diplomacy and untiring efforts of the developing countries, but in practice, as Prof. Jayantanuja Bandyopadhyaya[20] points out, "the acceptance of this demand by the UN General Assembly has proved to be hardly anything more than a mere nominal recognition of the urge of the LDCs for a greater share in the world distribution of resources. If the resolutions of the General Assembly reflect the majority of the LDCs in the UN, their non-implementation by the developed countries shows the oligarchic and neo-imperialistic control of the developed countries over the concrete structure of contemporary international relations".

EXERCISES

1. What do you understand by neo-colonialism? How is it different from colonialism and imperialism? Trace the growth of neo-colonialism in the post-World War II era.

2. Examine the concept of neo-colonialism with special references to the mechanisms of neo-colonialism.

3. Discuss the demand for a New International Economic Order (NIEO). Has it been achieved by the developing countries? Argue.

4. What were the demands put forward by the developing countries in the form of New International Economic Order (NIEO)? What has been the fate of the New International Economic Order (NIEO) proposal?

REFERENCES

[1] As Quoted in Norman D. Palmer and Howard C. Perkins, *International Relations—The World Community in Transition,* A.I.T.B.S. Publishers, New Delhi, 1997, pp. 159–160.

[2] Melkote, Rama S. and A. Narasimha Rao, *International Relations,* Sterling Publishers, New Delhi, 1983, p. 63.

[3] Palmer and Perkins, *op. cit.*, n. 1, pp. 160–161.

[4] *ibid.*

[5] Padelford, Norman, J. and George A. Lincoln, *International Politics: Foundations of International Relations,* The Macmillan and Co., New York, 1954, pp. 227–239.

[6] Connor, James O', "The Meaning of Economic Imperialism" *in* Richard Little and Michael Smith (Eds.), *Perspectives on World Politics*, Routledge, London, 1991, p. 277.

[7] Lenin, V.I., *Imperialism: The Highest Stage of Capitalism"* Leftword, New Delhi, 2000, pp. 113–123.

[8] Organski, A.F.K., *World Politics*, Alfred A. Knopf, New York, 1960, p. 246.

[9] Melkote and Rao, *op. cit.*, n. 2, p. 138.

[10] http://www.marxists.org/subject/africa/nkrumah/neo-colonialism/index.htm.

[11] Connor, James O', *op. cit.*, n. 6, pp. 283–284.

[12] *ibid.*, p. 288.

[13] Basu, Dipak, "Colonisation in a New Garb", *The Statesman*, Friday 30 September, 2005, Kolkata.

[14] Melkote and Rao, *op. cit.*, n. 2, p. 141.

[15] Easterly, William, *The White Man's Burden: Why the West's Efforts to Aid the Rest Have Done So Much Ill and So Little Good*, Oxford University Press, London, 2006, pp. 238.

[16] Basu, Dipak, *op. cit.*, n. 12.

[17] Bandyopadhyaya, Jayantanuja, *North Over South: A Non-Western Perspective of International Relations,"* South Asian Publishers, New Delhi, 1984, pp. 107–110 (see also http://web.nps.navy.mil/~relooney/routledge_15b.htm).

[18] *ibid.*, p. 10.

[19] *ibid.*, pp. 107–115.

[20] Bandyopadhyaya, Jayantanuja, *op. cit.*, n. 17, p. 110.

10

Regional Arrangements and their Role in International Relations

INTRODUCTION

Since the end of the Second World War, the international scenario has witnessed a certain urge among the states to ensure the well-being, peace and security not only of the states themselves, but also of the individual citizens. But the realization which dawned upon the states was that such endeavour can succeed only if that effort is supplemented by the cooperation of other states belonging to the same region as its. This realization became the basis of regionalism since the late 1940s. The roots of regionalism, therefore, lay in the perception of the national policy-makers that there are certain common interests shared by the states located in a particular region and that these interests could be "most efficiently and effectively promoted by the close and continuing cooperation within a regional framework".[1] Depending on the variety of interests, there arose a number of regional organizations such as the NATO, ASEAN, European Union, OPEC, the Arab League, and a host of others. Regionalism has now become a powerful force in international relations.

REGIONALISM AND INTEGRATION IN INTERNATIONAL RELATIONS

Regionalism definitely pertains to a particular region. There have been untiring efforts on the part of the scholars to define a region. Prof. Palmer and Perkins[2] tried to emphasize that in international relations "a region is invariably an area embracing the territories of three or more states. These states are bound together by ties of common interests as well as geography. They are not necessarily contiguous, or even in the same continent". There are no hard and fast rules to determine what is meant by the term regions. Regions are often constituted by countries sharing common bond of race, institutions and political interests. When these states come together and form an organizational association at the regional level to attain specific objectives, regional arrangements are born. What is important is that, most often, the states joining such regional organizations need not belong to the same geographic region or area. The factor, which reinforces such forging of bond, is perceived as "common interests".

At the San Francisco Conference of 1945, the Egyptian delegation introduced an amendment to the draft text of the United Nations Charter where they limited the term 'regional arrangements' by definition, to "organizations of a permanent nature grouping in a given geographical area several countries which, by reason of their proximity, community of interest or cultural, linguistic, historical, or spiritual affinities, make themselves jointly responsible for the peaceful settlement of any disputes which may arise between them for the maintenance of peace and security in their regions, as well as safeguarding of their national interests and the development of their economic and cultural relations".[3] According to Dr. E.N. Van Kleffens, "...regional arrangement or pact is a voluntary association of sovereign states within a certain area or having common interests in that area for a joint purpose, which should not be of an offensive nature, in relation to that area".[4]

Before discussing about some of the prominent regional arrangements that exist today, it will be worthwhile to take a look at the theory relating to regionalism and regional integration.

Functionalism

As opposed to the sole concerns of the discipline of international relations with security and conflict studies, functionalism arose as an operative philosophy, which visualized a gradual evolution of a peaceful, unified and cooperative world. The earliest and influential exponent of functionalism was David Mitrany. His celebrated work *A Working Peace System* gives a clear exposition of his vision of building peace in the international system. Other proponents were Leonard Woolf, Norman Angell, Robert Cecil and G.D.H Cole. The functionalists do not aim at creating a world federal structure rather, they seek to build "peace by pieces", through transnational organizations, that emphasize the 'sharing of sovereignty', instead of its total surrender. It is a 'bottom up' approach for building cooperative links among states.

Beginning with the assumption that wars are the products of crudely organized international system, which is founded on suspicion, anarchy, sovereignty, and national exclusivism which, in turn, considers war as an accepted means of settling international disputes, functionalists opine that governments will not surrender their national interests and will not dismantle easily. Therefore, they prescribe a realistic means of attaining idealistic ends. They propose a gradual approach towards regional or global unity, which will aim to isolate and, at the end, will render obsolete the stubborn institutional structures of international system, the nation-states.

Functionalists lay emphasis on the socio-economic and welfare needs rather than on the political needs. Functionalism prescribes the development of piecemeal non-political cooperative organizations involving sectors such as economic, technical, scientific, social and cultural. These are regarded as the **functional sectors.** The basic calculation that works behind such assumption is that "it is easier to establish narrow-in-scope functional organizations (in sectors such as energy production and distribution, transportation and communications control, health protection and improvement, labour standards and exchanges and customs unions) than to develop grandiose political institutions that jeopardize the national sovereignty of member states".[5] Such institutions, as Groom[6] observes, would be "international, sub-national and transnational according to their needs". This, Mitrany felt, would to some degree neutralize the antagonisms of the state system by the growth of cross-cutting ties, and the development of a transnational community would emerge with different people working together for different purposes.

The outcome of such functional organizations, which are less opposed by national governments because they revolve around non-political issues and most of the time are mutually beneficial for the participating states, has a 'spillover' effect. This means "if an international cooperative venture works to mutual advantage in the sector of coal and steel production, then it whets the appetite of and creates additional administrative requirements for participating governments to enter into cooperative ventures in related functional areas, such as transportation, pollution control and eventually to political unification".[7]

Such 'spillover' effect will be reinforced by the 'learning process' and ultimately will affect the basic unit of international system—the states, the assumption being that, with the accumulation of a large variety of functional organizations linking people and their interests across national boundaries, a transformation in both national attitudes and institutions will take place. Finally, transnational and supranational attitudes and institutions would render the nation-states useless. People would voluntarily transfer their allegiance and loyalty from individual states to transnational units leading to the emergence of a new 'functional' society with chief focus on 'functional' rather than 'territory'. Therefore, following Mitrany's vision of functionalism, expanding network of international relations and agencies would erase political divisions and integrate the interests and lives of all nation-states. Hence, according to Mitrany[8], there will be "one solid international block of flats" instead of "detached national houses".

Functionalism, however, was not without criticisms. Taylor who wrote on international co-operation, contends that functionalism "is not and never intended to be, a systematic descriptive analysis". Functionalists are regarded as piecemeal social engineers and not the architect or purveyors of blueprints. Claude[9] is critical about the length of time involved in the process of bringing about integration. He says that "Functionalism is not in a hurry, and its claim to offer hope to the world is implicitly based upon the supposition that a long period is both necessary and available for working out solutions to the problems". Many scholars fail to acknowledge the fact that cooperation exists in the social and economic fields; in other words, the non-political sectors. However, such kind of separation between high politics and low politics is hardly tenable. Political issues seem to shape the social or economic activities of the structures of the international system. As Kegley and Wittkopf[10] point out that "the reality is that technical cooperation is often more severely impacted by political considerations than the other way around. The withdrawal from and the subsequent re-entry of the United States into the International Labour Organization (ILO) because of the politicized nature of the organization dramatized the primacy of politics. Indeed, functionalism makes the naive assumption that technical (functional) undertakings and political affairs can be separated. They cannot".

Despite such criticisms, it cannot be denied that functionalism was perhaps the inspiration behind the integrative process in Europe and also the functioning of international organizations like the United Nations along with its specialized agencies.

Neo-Functionalism

Taking cue from functionalism and the experience of Western Europe, theorists of international relations have used the term 'integration' to denote either a 'process' towards or an end product of political unification among separate national units. Neo-functionalism arose as a critique of functionalism, along with the publication of most celebrated works of Ernst B. Hass's *Beyond the Nation-State: Functionalism and International Organization* and *The Uniting of Europe: Political, Social, and Economic Forces, 1950–1957*, and Karl Deutsch and his associates' *Political Community and the North Atlantic Area* and *France, Germany and the Western Alliance: A Study of Elite Attitudes on European Integration and World Politics,* gave impetus to the study of regional integration. This also led to the growth of a body of literature on integration, which tried to explain the process of integration in Europe and other parts of the world, especially the North Atlantic area.

According to Karl Deutsch[*], "Integration… is a relationship among units in which they are mutually interdependent and jointly produce system properties which they would separately lack". He argued that integration between communities would be promoted by the increase in transaction flows, and the multiplication of the channels of communication. Mutually rewarding transactions would lead to better understanding among people (and ultimately to peace). He contended, "Political integration is the integration of political actors or political units such as individuals, groups, municipalities, regions or countries, in regard to the political behaviour". For these integrative efforts, he emphasized certain conditions such as increase in transaction flows, mutual responsiveness, shared values, a relatively high geographic and social mobility of persons.

The transactionalist view does not advocate the case of total surrender of sovereignty or the absolute merger of states into a world federation. The transactionalist simply desire the integration in the form of regional, continental and inter-continental organizations so that the units maintain their interdependence established by a network of mutual transactions. Thus, what Deutsch and other transactionalists do not assume is that the end stage of integration is necessarily a unitary supranational state. Deutsch distinguishes between "amalgamated security community" and "pluralistic security community". In the former, there is a common government that presides over the merger of two or more independent units, into a single larger unit and in the latter there is a peaceful change that is guaranteed and institutionalized in some respects, but in which the individual states retain their legal independence.

But the problems with transactionalists are that they fail to explain whether community formation or integration is the result of increase in transaction flows or precedes it, and also their basic assumption that growth in integration leads to interdependence.[11]

Mitrany argued that international peace may be established through the promotion of cooperation organized around basic functional needs such as health, transportation, educational and cultural activities, trade and other kinds of activities. He opined that there would be as many as international organizations as required, and these would be organized on a universal rather than a regional basis. In contrast to Mitrany, Haas[**] was more interested in the study of regional integration as a process "whereby political actors in several discrete political settings are persuaded to shift their loyalties and political activities towards a new center whose institutions possess or demand

---

[*]Karl W. Deutsch, *The Analysis of International Relations,* Prentice-Hall of India, New Delhi, 1989, p. 212.
[**]E.B. Haas, "The Uniting of Europe: Political, Social and Economic Forces", Stanford University Press, Stanford, 1958.

jurisdiction over pre-existing national states". That is, he wondered whether the establishment of a supranational organization among a group of states (in a region) and the issues around which the process of integration would be set were primarily of economic nature rather than political. For Haas, integration was the tendency towards voluntary creation of larger political units where each avoids the use of force in relations with the participating units and groups. The primary actors in the integration process would be the 'integrationist-technocrats' and various interest groups who would persuade their governments to establish a regional economic integration organization for a variety of 'convergent aims'. Achievement of integration then would result from a cumulative and expansive process through which the functions of the organization would slowly increase, and it would exercise authority over an ever-expanding area of decision-making activities. The necessary assumption that follows, according to Haas, is that progress from a politically inspired common market to economic union, and finally to political union would be automatic.[12]

According to Kegley and Wittkopf[13], neo-functionalism proposes to reach its ultimate goal of a supranational community, not by avoiding controversial issue areas but by stressing cooperation in areas that are politically controversial. It proposes to overcome the political obstacles standing in the way of cooperation by demonstrating the benefits common to all members of a potential union.

Neo-functionalists like Schmitter and Haas, had developed neo-function-alist paradigm for comparative analysis. They had identified nine variables for this. Out of these nine, four were related to background conditions, two pertained to conditions at the time of economic union, and three were conditions of the process itself. Through an automatic and gradual process of politicization of actor's purposes which had initially been technical or non-controversial, they predicted, an organization that scored high in their categories would "be transformed into some species of political union even if some of the members are far from enthusiastic about this prospect when it is argued in purely political terms".[14]

Despite such enthusiasm regarding neo-functionalism, a number of questions have been raised about the usefulness of the neo-functionalist approach for comparative analysis of the degree of integration. But it cannot be said that the total neo-functional framework for analysis is futile because it consists of field work by notable scholars. The original assumptions were later modified by Hass, Nye, and Lindberg in order to explain the process of change in Europe and to free the neo-functionalist theory of its Euro-centric bias. Nye[15] suggested that the following revisions had to be made to accomplish the modification:

1. The dependent variable, automatic politicization, is changed

2. More political actors are added

3. The list of conditions for integration is reformulated in light of the comparative work that has been done on integration processes in less developed areas

4. The idea of a single path from quasi-technical tasks to political union by means of spillover is dropped and other potential process, forces and paths are included.

Haas, in his *The Obsolescence of Regional Integration Theory* (1975), has commented that the study of regional integration was becoming more subsumed under the study of interdependence and system change. He said that themes like interdependence and systems change can profit from the incorporation of diverse aspects of regional integration. "But they are sufficiently different in scope and portent from integration as to suggest that theorizing about it is no longer profitable as a distinct and self-conscious pursuit". This has been a case because the difference between integration and interdependence has faded out.

However, in the face of globalization and with the end of the Cold War, emergence of new forms of competition and cooperation among advanced capitalist economies, increased interdependence of production and trade, rapid growth and shifting patterns of international finance have led to the rise of renewed interest in regionalism and regional integration if not much on a political platform but rather on an economic sphere. Regionalism is now treated as a contingency plan and "as an intermediary between the global and the national and as a market strategy to mitigate the impact of global competition in goods and services".[16] The outcome of this is seen in the nature of adoption of new forms of regional associations involving the development of a complex process of new sets of relationships with other states and macro-regions. Therefore, regions now have come to occupy a preferred place in the life of states in a globalizing world and they are generally regarded as lying at the intersection of the local and the global. Therefore, in the present context, regionalism is viewed by many as "Overwhelmingly the result of a set of strategic calculations by actors located inside states and societies who push for integration as a way of positioning themselves in response to global change".[17]

PROMINENT REGIONAL ORGANIZATIONS

Some of the prominent regional organizations are given hereinafter.

EUROPEAN UNION (EU)

Origin: The European Union (EU) is a geo-political entity covering a large portion of the European continent. It is founded upon numerous treaties and has undergone expansions from the original, six member-states to 27.

After the Second World War which had devastated the European countries, they expressed their desire to move towards the path of integration. The War had left them totally bankrupt and had hit their economies and human resources hard. The European countries enjoying a dominant position in world politics so far, for example, Great Britain, France and Germany, lost their position and the World was soon dominated by the two superpowers—the United States and the

Soviet Union. This period was followed by an extreme superpower rivalry, which came to be known as the **Cold War.** As Europe had always been the centre stage of politics, even after the Second World War and the outbreak of the Cold War, it continued to be the focal point of the superpower politics. Despite the pulls and pressures of the Cold War, there was a desire among the European countries to move towards an integrated Europe, which would work as a bulwark against aggressive nationalism as preached by the Nazi Germany and prevent future holocaust demonstrated in the horrors of war.

The first step towards integration came in the form of a regional arrangement created by the Convention for European Economic Cooperation, signed in Paris on 16 April 1948. The regional arrangement that emerged out of this treaty was called Organization for European Economic Cooperation (OEEC). The chief function of the organization was to act as a coordinating agency of the countries receiving the Marshall Plan aid and it proved to be so useful that it continued to exist even after the Marshall Plan had officially come to an end in December 1951. The Marshall Plan was the primary plan of the United States for re-building and creating a stronger foundation for the countries of Western Europe and repelling communism after World War II. It was within the OEEC that in 1950 the European Payments Union was created to facilitate trade and economic transactions among the member countries. The next boost to European integration came in 1946 with Winston Churchill's call for a "United States of Europe". The ultimate outcome of his speech was the establishment of the Council of Europe in 1949 as the first pan-European organization. Although the Council of Europe was only a limited form of European cooperation, nevertheless, it served as a stimulus for future integration.

On 9 May 1950, the French Foreign Minister, Robert Schuman proposed a community to integrate the coal and steel industries of France and West Germany under a common High Authority. The goal of the proposed community was that France, Italy, West Germany, and the Benelux countries could share the strategic resources in order to "make war not only unthinkable but materially impossible", and to build lasting peace in Europe. The objective of such an integration was made clear in the Schuman Declaration which stated, "the pooling of coal and steel production should immediately provide for the setting up of common foundations for economic development as a first step in the federation of Europe, and will change the destinies of those regions which have long been devoted to the manufacture of munitions of war, of which they have been most constant victims".[18]

The realization of this proposal led to the creation of the European Coal and Steel Community (ECSC) by the Treaty of Paris (1951) and, on 18 April 1951, the leaders of the six member countries signed a European Declaration stating that the signing of this Treaty marked the true foundation of an organized Europe.

The resulting ECSC introduced a common, single steel and coal market, with freely set market prices, and without import/export duties or subsidies. The success of ECSC led to further steps of integration. Leaders met at the Messina Conference and established the Spaak Committee which produced the Spaak report. The report was accepted at the Venice Conference (29 and 30 May 1956). Finally, on the basis of the report, the Intergovernmental Conference on the Common Market and Euratom focussing on economic unity was held. This led to the signing of Treaties of Rome in 1957 which established the European Economic Community (EEC) and the European Atomic Energy Community (Euratom) among the members. From 1 January 1958, they started to function officially.

Another landmark in the process of European integration was the Merger Treaty of 8 April, 1965, which came into force on 1 July 1967. The Treaty established a single executive for the ECSC, the EEC and Euratom, comprising the Council and Commission, based in Brussels. The European Community signalled the coming together of the institutions of the three organizations. There were also other significant developments. For example, 1969 saw the establishment of Customs Union and, in 1978, the European Currency Unit (ECU) was introduced.[19] In 1979 the first direct, democratic elections to the European Parliament were held.

In 1985, the Schengen Agreement created largely open borders without passport controls between most of the member states. In 1986, the European flag began to be used by the European Community. The other milestone towards integration was reached with the signing of the Single European Act (SEA) of 1986 which set 1 January 1993 as the date by which a full internal market was to be established. Through this Act, the process for constructing a truly Single European Market began with the aim of lifting all trade restrictions between the member states.

The European Union was formally established when the Maastricht Treaty came into force on 1 November 1993. The Treaty of Maastricht, which established the European Union, divided EU policies into three main areas called **pillars**.

The Three Pillars

1. The first or "Community" pillar is formed of economic, social and environmental policies.
2. The second or "Common Foreign and Security Policy" (CFSP) pillar is made of foreign policy and military matters.
3. The third or "Police and Judicial Co-operation in Criminal Matters" (PJCC) pillar cooperation in the fight against crime. This pillar was originally named "Justice and Home Affairs".

In 2002, Euro notes and coins replaced national currencies in 12 of the member states.

The process of European integration has also received a boost with the enlargement of the membership of EC. In 1973 the Communities enlarged to include Denmark, the Republic of Ireland, and the United Kingdom. Norway had negotiated to join at the same time but a referendum rejected its membership and so it remained outside. Greece, Spain and Portugal joined in the 1980s. In 1995, Austria, Sweden and Finland joined the newly established EU. Since then, the Eurozone has increased to encompass 16 countries, with Slovakia joining the Eurozone on 1 January, 2009. In 2004, the EU saw its biggest enlargement to date when Malta, Cyprus, Slovenia, Estonia, Latvia, Lithuania, Poland, the Czech Republic, Slovakia and Hungary joined the European Union. On 1 January 2007, Romania and Bulgaria became the EU's newest members and Slovenia adopted the Euro.

The European Constitution was signed on 28 October 2004. Ratification of the treaty was primarily by parliamentary approval but some states held referenda during 2005. The French and the Dutch voters rejected it. Next, in December 2007, the European leaders signed the Lisbon Treaty which was to be ratified before the end of 2008 so that it could come into force on 1 January 2009. This was intended to replace the earlier, failed European Constitution. However, the future of the Lisbon Treaty is also unclear because of its rejection by the Irish voters in June 2008.

Stages of European Integration

1949— The North Atlantic Treaty Organization (NATO) signed.

1950— The Schuman Plan proposed.

1951— The European Coal and Steel Community established with 6 founding members (Belgium, Federal Republic of Germany, France, Italy, Luxembourg and the Netherlands).

1952— The Nordic Council formed to augment cooperation among Denmark, Finland, Iceland, Norway and Sweden.

1954— The Paris Treaty setting up the Western European Union (WEU).

1958— The Treaties of Rome set up the European Economic Community (EEC) and the European Atomic Energy Community (Euratom).

1960— The European Free Trade Association is set up.

1973— The Britain, Denmark and Ireland join the EEC.

1974— The European Council created. The European Regional Development Fund (ERDF) is set up.

1975— The Lomé Convention is signed between the European Communities (EC) and the African–Caribbean–Pacific (ACP) Group.

1978— The European Monetary System (EMS) proposed.

1979— The European Monetary System begins its operations.

1981— Greece becomes member of EC.

1986— Spain and Portugal join the EC.

1989— The fall of Berlin Wall.

1990— East and West Germany reunite. The European Bank for Reconstruction and Development is set up to support economic reforms and transition in the former Communist countries with major contributions from the EC. The Schengen Agreement to remove border controls is signed.

1991— Sweden applies to join EC.

1992— The Treaty of European Union signed in Maastricht on 7 February 1992. Finland and Switzerland apply to join the proposed EU.

1993— The Maastricht Treaty comes into force on 1 November 1993. The European Union came into existence.

1995— Austria, Finland and Sweden join EU. European currency named 'Euro'.[20]

1999— The Treaty of Amsterdam comes into force. A step towards the Common Foreign and Security Policy (CFSP).

2000— The Treaty of Nice.

2004— Constitution of the European Union adopted on 19 June 2004 in Brussels (but never came into force). Malta, Cyprus, Slovenia, Estonia, Latvia, Lithuania, Poland, the Czech Republic, Slovakia and Hungary join EU.

2007— Romania and Bulgaria join EU. Slovenia adopts the Euro.

The Institutions of European Union

1. *Commission of the European Communities:* This constitutes the executive wing of the European Union. It is a body composed of one appointee from each state, and at present there are 27 Commissioners. This body is to initiate proposal for legislation, to act as a "Guardian of the Treaties", and to be the manager and executor of the EU policies and international trade relationships. But in dispensing all its functions, the Commission is designed to be independent of national interests. This body also has the responsibility of dealing with the day-to-day running of the EU.

The Commission is led by a President who is nominated by the Council, in practice the European Council, and approved by the European Parliament. The remaining Commissioners are proposed by the member states, in consultation with the President, and then have to be approved by the European Parliament as a whole before the Commission can take office. The present President José Manuel Barroso and his Commission was elected in 2004 and reelected in 2009 and have a mandate till October 2014.

2. *Council of the European Union:* This **Council of the European Union** is the principal decision-making institution of the European Union (EU). It is often informally called the **Council of Ministers** or just the **Council**. It is the more powerful of the two legislative chambers, the other being the European Parliament.

The Council is composed of 27 national ministers (one per state and one President-in-Office). However, the exact membership depends on the topic being discussed. The European Union's law is limited to specific policy areas; however, it does override the national law. As the EU operates on supranational and intergovernmental platforms, in some areas the Council is superior to the Parliament, having only to consult in order to get assent from the body. In many areas, however, the EU uses the legislative process of co-decision procedure, in which the two bodies are equal in power. Its Presidency rotates between the states every six months, but every three Presidencies now cooperate on a common programme like a "triple-shared presidency".

3. *European Parliament (EP):* It is the only directly elected parliamentary institution of the European Union (EU). It is the bicameral legislative branch of the European Union's institutions and has been described as one of the most powerful legislatures in the world. The Parliament and Council form the highest legislative body within the EU. However, their powers as such are limited to the competencies conferred upon the European Community by the member states. Hence, the institution has little control over the policy areas held by the states and within the other two of the three pillars of the European Union. The EP has supervisory, budgetary and some legislative powers which were increased by the Single European Act, the Treaty of European Union (Maastricht Treaty) and the Treaty of Amsterdam.

The European Parliament has two meeting places: one at the Louise Weiss building in Strasbourg, France, which serves for twelve four-day plenary sessions per year and is the official seat, and the other, the Espace Léopold complex in Brussels, Belgium, the larger of the two, which serves for committee meetings, political groups and complementary plenary sessions. The Secretariat of the European Parliament, is based in Luxembourg.

The Parliament is composed of 785 MEPs (Members of the European Parliament), who serve the second largest democratic electorate in the world and the largest transnational democratic electorate in the world (342 million eligible voters in 2004). It is directly elected every five years by universal suffrage since 1979.

4. *Court of Justice of the European Communities:* The **European Court of Justice** (ECJ) is the highest court of the European Union. It has the ultimate say on matters of the EU law in order to ensure its equal application across all EU member states. It has the function to ensure that the Union's law is uniformly interpreted and effectively applied and has jurisdiction in disputes involving the member states, EU institutions, businesses, and individuals.

The Court was established in 1952 and is based in Luxembourg. It is composed of one judge from each of the member states. The number of judges at present is 27, but only 13 of them can hear a case at any one time in the 'Grand Chamber'. The Court is led by a President. Under the Single European Act, the Court is assisted by a lower court, the Court of First Instance, which has jurisdiction over direct actions brought by natural or legal persons, and by the Civil Service Tribunal which hears cases brought by employees of the EU's institutions.

5. *Court of Auditors:* The European Court of Auditors, despite its name, has no judicial powers. The Court provides an audit report for each financial year to the Council and the Parliament. The Parliament uses this to decide whether to approve the Commission's handling of the budget. The Court also gives opinions and proposals on the financial legislation and anti-fraud actions.

It is composed of one member from each state appointed by the Council, every six years. Every three years one of them is elected to be the President of the Court.

6. *European Economic and Social Committee (EESC):* It was established in 1957. It is a consultative assembly composed of employers, employees and representatives of various industries and work sectors. The committee advises on economic and social policies (principally, relations between workers and employers). It has 344 members, appointed by the Council, for four-year terms. Members of the EESC are divided into three groups of equal number: employers employees and a third group of various other changing interests such as farmers, consumer groups, professional associations, and so on. The members are appointed by the Council following the nominations made by the governments of the respective member states. However, once appointed, the members are completely independent of their governments. The EESC shares the Delors Building in Brussels as its seat, with the Committee of the Regions.

Among the other prominent EU institutions are the Committee of the Regions, European Central Bank, the European Investment Bank and the European Investment Fund.

The present challenges before EU are legitimacy gap, 'widening' and 'deepening', and the future of Common Foreign Security Policy (CFSP). As scholars have pointed out "the main challenge for the EU is the current impossibility of creating a true parliamentary basis of democracy". Although the European Parliament exists, it is regarded as the weakest of the main policy-making institutions. The Maastricht Treaty saw the introduction of the procedure of co-decision with the Council to give a greater say in the European parliament in the legislative process, but this position of co-decision does not extend to all the policy areas. Therefore, there is a so-called democratic deficit in the EU. As a result of widening of the EU, there is a growing demand for reforms of the EU norms to ensure distribution of powers between the member states. Further, deepening of European integration has been achieved through the process of economic integration. However, in the policy fields the principles of subsidiarity and proportionality still operate which are rather abstract and the difference between them is often blurred. The CFSP is another crucial challenge before the EU. It is said, "If one digs deeper into the structure and functioning, it [the CFSP] is neither common, nor foreign, nor dealing with security, nor can be called a policy. Yet, most observers and policy-makers use the acronym CFSP like a magic formula: it is enough to invoke the name and the EU turns into a major actor—if not a superpower—in world affairs. The paradox is that this mantra effect is even stronger outside Europe than inside".[21]

The other kind of threats perceived by the EU range from international terrorism, weapons of mass destruction (WMDs), failed states, regional conflicts due to expansion of the EU to the conflict-prone zone in Central Asia, and organized crimes.

AFRICAN UNION (AU)

The Organization of African Unity (OAU) or Organization de l'Unité Africaine (OUA) was established on 25 May 1963. It was disbanded on 9 July 2002 by its last Chairperson, South African President Thabo Mbeki, and replaced by the African Union by the Sirte Declaration to boost and accelerate the African unity and efforts of integration in the context of the challenges posed by globalization. The AU consists of 53 African States. However, 4 member states, Guinea (2008), Madagascar (2009), Eritrea (2009) and Côte d'Ivoire (2010) have been suspended.

When the OAU was formed, it had two primary aims:

- To promote the unity and solidarity of the African states and act as a collective voice for the African continent. This was important to secure Africa's long-term economic and political future. Years of colonialism had weakened it socially, politically and economically.

- The OAU was also dedicated to the eradication of all forms of colonialism, as, when it was established, there was still a number of states that had not yet won their independence or were minority-ruled. South Africa and Angola were two such countries. The OAU proposed two ways of ridding the continent of colonialism. First, it would defend the interests of the independent countries and help pursue those of still-colonized ones. Second, it would remain neutral in terms of world affairs, preventing its members from being controlled once more by outside powers.

The AU has also been formed with certain purposes and principles in mind. These are reflected in the objectives of the AU.

The objectives of the AU are manifold such as to:

1. Achieve greater unity and solidarity between the African countries and the people of Africa.

2. Defend the sovereignty, territorial integrity and independence of its member states.

3. Accelerate the political and socio-economic integration of the continent.

4. Promote and defend the African common positions on the issues of interest to the continent and its people.

5. Encourage international cooperation, taking due account of the Charter of the United Nations and the Universal Declaration of Human Rights.

6. Promote peace, security and stability of the continent.

7. Promote democratic principles and institutions, popular participation and good governance.

8. Promote and protect human and peoples' rights in accordance with the African Charter on Human and Peoples' Rights and other relevant human rights instruments.

9. Establish the necessary conditions which enable the continent to play its rightful role in the global economy and in international negotiations.

10. Promote sustainable development at the economic, social and cultural levels as well as the integration of African economies.

11. Promote cooperation in all fields of human activity to raise the living standards of African peoples.

12. Coordinate and harmonize the policies between the existing and future Regional Economic Communities for the gradual attainment of the objectives of the Union.

13. Advance the development of the continent by promoting research in all fields, in particular, in science and technology.

14. Work with relevant international partners in the eradication of preventable diseases and the promotion of good health on the continent.

The Organs of the AU

The Assembly: It is composed of Heads of State and Government or their duly accredited representatives. The Assembly of Heads of State and Government is the supreme organ of the African Union. The Assembly meets once a year. The decisions are taken either on the basis of consensus or by a two-thirds majority.

The Executive Council: This is composed of ministers or authorities designated by the governments of member states. The Executive Council is accountable to the Assembly.

The Commission: This body is composed of the Chairperson, the Deputy Chairperson, ten Commissioners and staff members. Each Commissioner shall be responsible for a portfolio.

The Permanent Representatives' Committee: This is composed of Permanent Representatives of the member states accredited to the Union. The Permanent Representatives Committee is charged with the responsibility of preparing the work of the Executive Council.

Peace and Security Council (PSC): By virture of AHG/Dec 160 (xxxvii) of the Summit of Lusaka, July 2001, a decision was made for the creation of a Peace and Security Council (PSC), within the African Union. The protocol establishing the PSC is in the process of ratification. The protocol has devised the PSC as a collective security and early warning arrangement to respond to conflict and crisis situation arising among or within the states of Africa.

Pan-African Parliament (PAP): A Pan-African Parliament is an organ created to ensure the full participation of African peoples in governance, development and economic integration of the continent. The protocol relating to the composition, powers, functions and organization of the Pan-African Parliament has been signed by the member states and is in the process of ratification. The PAP is composed of 265 elected representatives of 53 member states.

ECOSOCC: The Economic, Social and Cultural Council (ECOSOCC) is an advisory organ composed of different social and professional groups of the member states of the Union.

The Court of Justice: A Court of Justice of the Union shall be established and statute defining the powers and functions of the court is under review.

The Specialized Technical Committees of AU: The following specialized technical committees are meant to address the sectoral issues and are at Ministerial level:

- The Committee on Rural Economy and Agricultural Matters
- The Committee on Monetary and Financial Affairs
- The Committee on Trade, Customs and Immigration Matters
- The Committee on Industry, Science and Technology, Energy, Natural Resources and Environment
- The Committee on Transport, Communications and Tourism
- The Committee on Health, Labour and Social Affairs
- The Committee on Education, Culture and Human Resources.

The Financial Institutions: The following are some of the financial institutions of AU:

- The African Central Bank

- The African Monetary Fund
- The African Investment Bank

AU has to go a long way to achieve African solidarity. Its predecessor, OAU had chartered many a rough course and it had its own share of achievements and failures. The OAU played a pivotal role in eradicating colonialism and minority rule in Africa. It gave weapons, training and military bases to colonized nations fighting for independence or majority rule. Groups such as the African National Congress (ANC) and PAC (Pacific Accreditation Cooperation), fighting apartheid, and ZANU (Zimbabwe African National Union) and ZAPU (Zimbabwe African People's Union), fighting for the independence of Southern Rhodesia, were aided in their struggle by the OAU. Various other initiatives undertaken by the OAU were commendable, such as the Lagos Plan of Action (LPA) and the Final Act of Lagos (1980), which incorporated programmes and strategies for self-reliant development and cooperation among the African countries. There was also The African Charter on Human and People's Rights (Nairobi 1981), and the Grand Bay Declaration and Plan of Action on Human Rights are the two instruments adopted by the OAU to promote Human and People's Rights in the continent. The Africa's Priority Programme for Economic Recovery (APPER) adopted in 1985 was an emergency programme designed to address the development crisis of the 1980s, in the wake of protracted drought and famine that had engulfed the continent and the crippling effect of Africa's external indebtedness. The New Partnership for Africa's Development (NEPAD) was adopted as a Programme of the AU at the Lusaka Summit (2001).

Despite such laudable efforts, the OAU often faced and at present the AU faces stiff challenges in fostering African Unity due to differences among the member states, civil strife, ethnic conflicts, continued dependence on the former colonizers, inability to enforce its decision, policy of non-interference, making it virtually ineffective in cases of human rights violation and others. The OAU was often viewed as a bureaucratic 'talking shop' with little power and, thus, the AU has a tough job of making itself a more credible regional organization in the eyes of the international community.

ORGANIZATION OF THE PETROLEUM EXPORTING COUNTRIES

The Organization of the Petroleum Exporting Countries (OPEC) is a permanent intergovernmental organization. This regional body was created at the Baghdad Conference during 10–14 September 1960 by Iran, Iraq, Kuwait, Saudi Arabia and Venezuela. Later, several other countries joined the OPEC: They were Qatar (1961); Indonesia (1962) which was suspended of its membership from January 2009; Socialist Peoples Libyan Arab Jamahiriya (1962); United Arab Emirates (1967); Algeria (1969); Nigeria (1971); Ecuador (1973), which was suspended of its membership from December 1992–October 2007; Angola (2007); and Gabon (1975–1994).

According to OPEC statutes, one of its principal goals is the determination of the best means for safeguarding the Organization's interests, individually and collectively. OPEC also pursues ways and means of ensuring the stabilization of prices in international oil markets with a view to eliminating harmful and unnecessary fluctuations, giving due regard at all times to the interests of the producing nations and to the necessity of securing a steady income to the producing countries; an efficient, economic and regular supply of petroleum to consuming nations, and a fair return on their capital to those investing in the petroleum industry.

Therefore, OPEC has the vital objective to coordinate and unify petroleum policies among the member countries, in order to secure fair and stable prices for petroleum producers; an efficient, economic and regular supply of petroleum to consuming nations; and a fair return on capital to those investing in the industry. This policy is also designed to ensure that oil consumers continue to receive stable supplies of oil.

Article 2 of the OPEC Statute embodies the principles of the Organization. They are:

- The principal aim of the Organization shall be the coordination and unification of the petroleum policies of the member countries and the determination of the best means for safeguarding their interests, individually and collectively.

- The Organization shall devise ways and means of ensuring the stabilization of prices in the international oil markets with a view to eliminating harmful and unnecessary fluctuations.

- Due regard shall be given at all times to the interests of the producing nations and to the necessity of securing a steady income for the producing countries; an efficient, economic and regular supply of petroleum to the consuming nations; and a fair return on their capital to those investing in the petroleum industry.

The OPEC Management

The OPEC Conference is a high-level body and below is the Board of Governors. Below the Board of Governors is the OPEC Secretariat which is a permanent inter-governmental body. The Secretariat, which has been based in Vienna since 1965, provides research and administrative support to the member countries. The Secretariat also disseminates news and information to the World at large. The official language of the Secretariat is English.

The Departments of the Secretariat are:

- Office of the Secretary-General
- Research Division
- Data Services Department

- Petroleum Market Analysis Department
- Energy Studies Department
- Public Relations and Information Department
- Administration and Human Resources Department

The Secretary-General is the legally authorized representative of the Organization and the Chief Executive of the Secretariat. In this capacity, he administers the affairs of the Organization in accordance with the directions of the Board of Governors. The Conference appoints the Secretary-General for a period of three years, whose term may be renewed once for the same period. This appointment takes place upon nomination by the member countries, and after a comparative study of the nominees' qualifications (Article 28 of the OPEC Statute). In the absence of a unanimous decision, the Secretary-General is appointed on a rotation basis for a term of two years, without prejudice to the required qualifications.

The Secretary-General is assisted in the discharge of his duties by the Research Division, the Administration and the Human Resources Department, the Public Relations and Information Department, and by his own Office. The Senior Legal Counsel provides legal advice to the Secretary-General, supervises the Secretariat's legal and contractual affairs, and evaluates the legal issues of concern to the Organization and the member countries, and recommends appropriate action.

The office of the Secretary-General provides him with executive assistance, particularly in establishing and maintaining contacts with governments, organizations and delegations in matters of protocol, in the preparation for and coordination of meetings, and in carrying out any other duties assigned by the Secretary-General.

This regional organization came into prominence during the 1970s, in the backdrop of the Arab–Israeli conflict and marked the beginning of oil diplomacy. The Yom Kippur War of 1973 resulted in a strong Arab opinion against the West. It prompted the OPEC to initiate an embargo against all the states supporting Israel. The rise of Iranian nationalism and the series of clashes with Israel in 1946 and in early 1970s induced the Arab leaders to make use of oil as a weapon to teach the West a lesson. When the United States and the West European states began to supply Israel with huge quantities of arms, which helped them to withstand Egyptian and Syrian forces, the Arab world was infuriated and they imposed the 1973 oil embargo against the United States and the Western Europe. OPEC realized its potential and the significance of oil as a weapon and, thereafter, raised the price of oil per barrel. Finally, long-term price levels were normalized due to the pressure of Saudi Arabia, the richest member of OPEC. The West had learnt a lesson from this crisis.

It is from this time onwards that the OPEC rose to international prominence and it acquired a major say in the pricing of crude oil in the world markets. Under such circumstances, the First Summit of OPEC Sovereigns and Heads of

States was held in Algiers in March 1975. The outbreak of the Iranian Revolution in 1979 also produced another oil crisis, and concerted effort by OPEC had hit the oil market hard.

Following the Iran–Iraq war, the 1980s witnessed another rise in oil prices at the beginning of the decade but soon there was a dramatic decline in prices, which culminated in a collapse in 1986 and set the beginning of the third oil-pricing crisis. Oil prices faced a six-year decline with a 46 per cent price drop in 1986. This also harmed the OPEC unity as the Western nations searched for alternatives to lessen the potential impact of the future price-shock induced by OPEC. This included measures of increasing oil production outside the OPEC like the Central Asian region to tide over the 'oil politics' of the OPEC countries.

In the 1990s, the OPEC came to the relief of the world when a major oil crisis was averted due to the sanctions against Iraq to export oil. A sudden and steep rise in prices on panic-stricken markets was offset by output increases from OPEC members. Collective action by OPEC and some leading non-OPEC producers again brought about a recovery when in 1998 there was a collapse, in the wake of the economic downturn in South-East Asia. The global melt down of 2008, as well as the declining prices of oil, has again called for a concerted effort of the OPEC countries to address the crisis.

ASIA PACIFIC ECONOMIC COOPERATION

Asia Pacific Economic Cooperation (APEC) is a regional organization for fostering Asia-Pacific Community. It was established in 1989 to further enhance economic growth and prosperity of the Asia-Pacific region with the objective of facilitating its economic growth, cooperation, trade and investment.

APEC at present comprises 21 members. They are Australia, Brunei Darussalam, Canada, Chile, People's Republic of China, Hong Kong, Indonesia, Japan, Republic of Korea, Malaysia, Mexico, New Zealand, Papua New Guinea, Peru, the Republic of the Philippines, the Russian Federation, Singapore, Chinese Taipei, Thailand, the United States of America, and Vietnam. APEC countries include the NAFTA, ASEAN and ANZUS countries who are better known as 'Member Economies'.

APEC operates on the basis of non-binding commitments, open dialogue and equal respect for the views of all the participants. Unlike the WTO or other multilateral trade bodies, APEC has no treaty obligations required of its participants. Decisions made within APEC are reached by consensus, and commitments are undertaken on a voluntary basis.

Purposes and Goals

APEC works with a vision to reduce tariffs and other trade barriers across the Asia-Pacific region. Its vision is best reflected in what is referred to as the

"Bogor Goals" *of free and open trade and investment in the Asia-Pacific by 2010 for industrialized economies and 2020 for developing economies.* These goals were adopted by the leaders at their 1994 meeting in Bogor, Indonesia. In 1995, at the Lusaka Summit, an Action Agenda was evolved on the principles of voluntarism and flexibility and consensual approach. APEC also works to create an environment for the safe and efficient movement of goods, services and people across the borders in the region through policy alignment and economic and technical cooperation. By the year 2010, APEC leaders hope to achieve an additional 5 per cent reduction in the trade costs. To this end, a new Trade Facilitation Action Plan has been drafted that places greater emphasis on the transparency initiatives. According to a 2008 research brief published by the World Bank as part of its Trade Costs and Facilitation Project, increasing transparency in the region's trading system is critical if APEC has to meet its Bogor Goal targets.

ORGANIZATION OF AMERICAN STATES

The Organization of American States (OAS) is the world's oldest regional organization, comprising 35 independent states of the Americas—the North, Central and South America—and the Caribbean, with its headquarters in Washington, DC. Government of Cuba, a member state, has been suspended from participation since 1962. Therefore, only 34 countries participate actively. There are also permanent observers. As of 2008, there are 61 permanent observer countries, including the European Union.

The notion of closer hemispheric union in the Americas was first put forward by Simón Bolívar who, at the 1826 Congress of Panama, proposed a creation of a league of American Republics with a common military, mutual defence pact, and a supranational parliamentary assembly. This idea of regional solidarity and cooperation was again raised in 1889–1890, at the First International Conference of American States. Eighteen nations meeting in Washington DC, resolved to establish the International Union of American Republics, served by a permanent secretariat, called the **Commercial Bureau of the American Republics.** These developments were the precursors to the present OAS and its General Secretariat. Since then a number of other initiatives tried to boost the American unity. Finally, in 1948 at the Ninth International Conference of American States held in Bogotá and led by the US Secretary of State, George Marshall, a pledge was taken by the members to fight Communism in America. This perspective of containing Communism ultimately gave birth to the OAS as it stands today. The Charter of the OAS was signed by 21 American countries on 30 April 1948, which came into effect since December 1951. The American Declaration of the Rights and Duties of Man, the world's first general human rights instrument, was also adopted in this meeting.

Article 1 of the Charter embodies the goal of the member nations in creating the OAS. It upholds its primary goal "to achieve an order of peace and justice, to promote their solidarity, to strengthen their collaboration, and to defend their sovereignty, their territorial integrity, and their independence".

Article 2 upholds the eight objectives of the organization. These objectives are to:

1. Strengthen the peace and security of the continent.
2. Promote and consolidate representative democracy, with due respect for the principle of non-intervention.
3. Prevent the possible causes of difficulties and to ensure the pacific settlement of disputes that may arise among the member states.
4. Provide for common action on the part of those states, in the event of aggression.
5. Seek the solution of political, judicial and economic problems that may arise among them.
6. Promote, by cooperative action, their economic, social and cultural development.
7. Eradicate extreme poverty, which constitutes an obstacle to the full democratic development of the peoples of the hemisphere.
8. Achieve an effective limitation of conventional weapons that will make it possible to devote the largest amount of resources to the economic and social development of the member states.

The OAS tries to strengthen cooperation among the member states to enhance democratic values, defend common interests, and debate the major issues facing the region and the world. The OAS is the region's principal multilateral forum for strengthening democracy, promoting human rights, and confronting shared problems such as poverty, terrorism, illegal drugs and corruption. It plays a leading role in carrying out mandates established by the leaders of the hemisphere through the Summits of the Americas.

SOUTH ASIAN ASSOCIATION FOR REGIONAL COOPERATION

The South Asian Association for Regional Cooperation (SAARC) was established when its Charter was formally adopted on 8 December 1985 by the Heads of States or Governments of Bangladesh, Bhutan, India, Maldives, Nepal, Pakistan and Sri Lanka in their First SAARC Summit in Dhaka on 7–8 December 1985. Afghanistan was added to the regional grouping at the behest of India on 13 November, 2005, and became a member on 3 April, 2007. With the addition of Afghanistan, the total number of member states now stands at eight. The observers are Australia, China, the European Union, Iran, Japan Mauritius, Myanmar (Burma), South Korea and the United States.

The South Asian neighbours began to take initiative towards regional cooperation in the 1980s, primarily under the initiative of President Zia-ur Rehman of Bangladesh. Between 1970 and 1980, he paid visits to Nepal, Pakistan, India and Sri Lanka to concretize the idea of cooperation among the South Asian neighbours. Several Foreign Secretary-level meetings followed in Colombo, Kathmandu, Islamabad, and Dhaka. It was followed by the first meeting of the Foreign Ministers at New Delhi in August 1983. It was at this meeting that the Foreign Ministers adopted the Declaration on South Asian Association Regional Cooperation. They also launched the Integrated Programme of Action (IPA) in nine agreed areas, namely, agriculture; rural development; telecommunications; meteorology; health and population activities; transport; postal services; science and technology; and sports, arts and culture.

At the inception of the Association, the IPA consisting of a number of Technical Committees was identified as the core area of cooperation. But given the changed circumstances over the years, the current areas of cooperation, under the reconstituted Regional Integrated Programme of Action which is pursued through the Technical Committees cover:

1. Agriculture and Rural Development
2. Health and Population Activities
3. Women, Youth and Children
4. Environment and Forestry
5. Science and Technology and Meteorology
6. Human Resources Development
7. Transport.

High-level working groups have also been established to strengthen cooperation in the areas of Information and Communications Technology, Biotechnology, Intellectual Property Rights, Tourism and Energy.

Objectives of the Association

The objectives of the Association, as defined in the Charter, are to:

1. Promote the welfare of the peoples of South Asia and to improve their quality of life.
2. Accelerate economic growth, social progress and cultural development in the region and to provide all individuals the opportunity to live in dignity and to realize their full potential.
3. Promote and strengthen collective self-reliance among the countries of South Asia.
4. Contribute to mutual trust, understanding and appreciation of one another's problems.

5. Promote active collaboration and mutual assistance in the economic, social, cultural, technical and scientific fields.
6. Strengthen cooperation with other developing countries.
7. Strengthen cooperation among themselves in international forums on matters of common interest.
8. Cooperate with international and regional organizations with similar aims and purposes.

Principles

The Principles enshrined in the Charter are:

1. Cooperation within the framework of the Association is based on respect for the principles of sovereign equality, territorial integrity, political independence, non-interference in the internal affairs of other states, and mutual benefit.
2. Such cooperation is to complement and not to substitute bilateral or multilateral cooperation.
3. Such cooperation should be consistent with bilateral and multilateral obligations of the member states.

General Provisions

- Decisions at all levels in SAARC are taken unanimously.
- Bilateral and contentious issues are excluded from the deliberations of the Association.

List of SAARC Summits

The list of SAARC Summits are given in details hereinafter.

First Summit: 7–8 December 1985

The First Summit was attended by the Heads of States and/or Governments of Seven South Asian countries: Bangladesh, Bhutan, India, Maldives, Nepal, Pakistan and Sri Lanka. The Declaration of the Dhaka Summit enumerated the objectives and principles of the organization. The Heads of states and/or governments agreed that the guiding principles of the organization will be based on respect for principles of sovereignty, equality, territorial integrity, political independence, non-interference in internal affairs of others, and mutual benefit.

The SAARC Declaration envisaged that the Heads of States and/or Governments shall meet annually and a council of ministers consisting of the foreign ministers of the member states shall be constituted to formulate policies, to review progress of cooperation, to establish additional mechanism, and to decide on matters of general interest. The Declaration also envisioned the setting up of a Technical Committee comprising representatives of the member states for implementation of projects besides the establishment of a SAARC Secretariat.

Second Summit: Bangalore, 16–17 November 1986

The Second Summit was significant as SAARC was institutionalized through the establishment of a permanent Secretariat for implementing, coordinating and monitoring SAARC programmes. The Secretariat started functioning from 16 January 1987. It was also agreed in the Summit to extend cooperation on five additional fields:

(i)   launching of South Asian broadcasting programmes covering radio and television;

(ii) promotion of tourism;

(iii) provisions of facilities to students and academicians;

(iv) harnessing the idealism of the youth; and

(v)   jointly combating terrorism.

Third Summit: Kathmandu, 2–4 November 1987

The Kathmandu Declaration provided a renewed thrust and direction on the future course of regional cooperation. The Heads of States and Governments emphasized that a fundamental goal of SAARC was to promote the welfare of the peoples of South Asia. They expressed their faith in the UN Charter, commitment to the principles and objectives of NAM, resumption of North–South Dialogue, and recognized the need for special measures in favour of the least developed countries in light of recent decisions at UNCTAD VII. A major breakthrough was the signing of the SAARC Regional Convention on Suppression of Terrorism and the Agreement establishing South Asian Food Reserve by the Foreign Ministers of the SAARC member states.

Fourth Summit: Islamabad, 29–31 December 1988

In the Fourth Summit held at Islamabad, the Heads of the States and Governments expressed their concern at the high incidence of drug production, trafficking and abuse. The Year 1989 was, therefore, declared as the "SAARC Year Against Drug Abuse" in order to focus attention on drug-related problems in the region. The Summit welcomed the establishment of a South Asian Food Security Reserve in August 1988 and SAARC Agriculture Information Centre (SAIC). It decided to declare 1990 as the "SAARC Year of the Girl Child". Further, it also agreed to launch "SAARC 2000—A Basic Needs Perspective" which called for a regional plan with specific targets to be met by the end of the century in core areas of interest such as food, clothing and shelter.

Fifth Summit: Male, 21–23 November 1990

The Heads of the States and Governments reaffirmed their faith and their commitment to the principles and objectives of SAARC. They welcomed the signing of the SAARC Convention on Narcotic Drugs and Psychotropic Substances. It was decided to observe 1991 as the Year of Shelter, 1992 as the SAARC Year of Environment, and 1993 as the SAARC year of Disabled Persons. In addition, it was decided to observe the Decade of 1990s as the SAARC Decade of the Girl Child. The Summit also decided to launch the Special SAARC Travel Document, which would exempt its holders from visas for travel within the region.

Sixth Summit: Colombo, 21 December 1991

The Sixth Summit was scheduled for November 1991, but could not be held because of the failure of the member states to arrive at a unanimous decision to hold the Summit in the absence of the King of Bhutan who was unable to attend the Summit due to internal security problems. Ultimately, the seven Heads of States and Governments met for one day at Colombo, on 21 December 1991. The major breakthrough was the approval of the Heads of States and Governments on the establishment of the Inter-Governmental Group (IGG) on the recommendation of the Committee on Economic Cooperation, which had to formulate and seek agreement on an institutional framework under which specific measures for trade liberalization among SAARC member states could be furthered. It was also expected to examine the Sri Lankan proposal to establish a SAARC Preferential Trade Arrangement (SAPTA) by 1997.

Seventh Summit: Dhaka, 10–11 April 1993

The Seventh Summit was postponed twice on account of disturbed situation in Bangladesh in the wake of Babri Masjid demolition in India. Ultimately, it was held in April 1993. The Summit adopted a declaration where the Heads of States and Governments reaffirmed the need to liberalize trade as early as possible. They welcomed the finalization of the framework agreement on SAPTA. The Summit also endorsed an Integrated Programme of Action (IPA) on eradication of poverty in South Asia, trade manufacture and services, environment pollution, population growth, shelter for the homeless child labour, youth unrest and unemployment, disabled persons, women's development, science and technology, terrorism, drug trafficking, security of small states, people-to-people contact, and other.

Eighth Summit: New Delhi, 2–4 May 1995

In the Eighth Summit held in New Delhi, the Heads of States and Governments expressed their satisfaction on the achievements of the First Decade of SAARC and resolved to celebrate the completion of the First Decade by the individual member states and collectively. They endorsed the proposal of the Council of Ministers to convene a Commemorative Session of the Council on the theme "SAARC-Vision for the Second Decade". In addition, they also agreed to operationalize the South Asian Free Trade Area (SAFTA) and its establishment to promote intra-regional trade. Further, they welcomed the establishment of WTO and expressed the hope that it would help to expand international trade particularly that of the developing countries.

Ninth Summit: Male, 12–14 May 1997

In the Ninth Summit hed in Male, the Heads of States and Governments welcomed the entry into force of the Agreement on SAPTA on 7 December 1995. They also recognized the importance of achieving a free trade area by the year 2001. Moreover, they also vowed to fight poverty, combat terrorism and drug trafficking, and create awareness and cooperation in such areas as women's development, child labour, youth unrest and unemployment, disabled persons, shelter for the homeless, increasing literacy, and environment pollution and management.

Tenth Summit: Colombo, 29–31 July 1998

In the tenth Summit held in Colombo, the Heads of States and Governments reaffirmed their faith in the commitment to the objectives and principles of SAARC and called for enhancing political cooperation for promoting peace, stability and amity, and discussed the operation of SAARC in a changed international environment involving economic, technological, and social information. They also called for an acceleration of SAARC economic cooperation, and decided to adopt measures to remove structural impediments to speedily move towards the goal of SAFTA.

Eleventh Summit: Kathmandu, 4–6 January 2002

After a long gap of 42 months, the Eleventh SAARC Summit was held in Kathmandu. The Summit tried to overcome the animosity between India and Pakistan due to increased military build-up of both the neighbours along the LOC (Line of Control) in Kashmir. The Summit resolved to move towards the achievement of the objective of promoting mutual cooperation for the development of the region. Regarding economic cooperation, the Heads of States and Governments recognized the need to move quickly towards SAFTA and they directed the Council of Ministers to finalize the text of the Draft Treaty Framework by the end of 2002. The Kathmandu Declaration called for an intensified coordination among South Asian states on all WTO issues. They stressed the need to intensify coordination among the SAARC missions in Geneva to begin the necessary preparation to advance the common interest of the region in the Fifth WTO Ministerial Conference. In the discussions in the Summit, along with other common concerns such as poverty alleviation, women and children, international political and economic environment, terrorism took the centre stage. The Heads of State and Governments also reiterated their support for the UN Security Council Resolution 1373 of 28 September 2001 and resolved to combat terrorism in all its manifestations. They reaffirmed their commitment to SAARC Regional Convention on Suppression of Terrorism.

Twelfth SAARC Summit: Islamabad, 2–6 January 2004

The Heads of States and Governments resolved to accelerate the economic and trade cooperation among the members and ensure progress towards the realization of SAPTA and the emergence of SAFTA. It was agreed to complete the first level of SAFTA by 2006 and its full operationalization by 31 December 2015. It was also decided to establish an arbitration committee or a Dispute Settlement Body. Overall there was an urge to develop SAARC as a powerful organization like the ASEAN.

Thirteenth Summit: Dhaka, 12–13 November 2005

In the Thirteenth Summit held at Dhaka, three agreements were reached on:

- Limited multilateral agreement on avoidance of double taxation and mutual administrative assistance in tax matters.
- Mutual administrative assistance in customs related matters.
- Establishment of the SAARC Arbitration Council.

The Heads of States and Governments also agreed to declare the years 2006–2015 as the SAARC Decade of Poverty Alleviation and set up a Poverty Alleviation Fund, to grant observer status to China and Japan, to celebrate the year 2007 as the year of Green South Asia, to induct Afghanistan as the eighth member of SAARC by the year 2007, and to ratify the additional protocol to the SAARC Convention on the Suppression of Terrorism. The major breakthrough came in as the Heads of State and Governments agreed to launch the SAFTA with effect from 1 January 2006. Further, it was agreed by the SAARC Foreign Ministers to grant SAARC observer status to the United States, South Korea, and the European Union.

Fourteenth Summit: New Delhi, 3–4 April 2007

The Summit was noteworthy as the bilateral issues did not find a place in the agenda of the Summit proceedings. The Heads of State and Governments reached an agreement to establish a South Asian University and a Food Bank. The South Asian Development Fund was also operationalized with an initial corpus of 300 million dollars. The Summit resolved to work towards trade and economic cooperation and expedite the process and also try to chalk out the future plan for a South Asian Customs Union. It also agreed to combat terrorism among other common concerns. The Indian Prime Minister, Dr. Manmohan Singh outlined four priority areas of cooperation: water, energy, food and environment. The Summit witnessed a high-level of maturity reached by the regional organization.

Fifteenth Summit: Colombo, 1–3 August 2008

The Fifteenth SAARC summit took place during 1–3 August 2008. The Heads of States or Governments reaffirmed their commitment to the principles and objectives enshrined in the SAARC Charter. The offer to host the Sixteenth SAARC Summit by the Maldives was welcomed with appreciation. The Heads of States or Governments stressed on the urgent need to develop the hydro potential, grid connectivity and gas pipelines of the regions concerned.

They also expressed satisfaction at the adoption of a SAARC Declaration on Climate Change for the United Nations Framework Convention on Climate Change (UNFCCC) by the Twenty-ninth Session of the Council of Ministers. The Heads of States and Governments impressed the need for even more expeditious and close regional cooperation in information and communication technology. The Heads of States and Governments emphasized their commitment to implement SAFTA in letter and in spirit, thereby enabling SAARC to contribute to the dynamic process of Asia's emergence as the powerhouse of the world. Recognizing the need to continue to address the major barriers hindering effective trade liberalization in the region, which include sensitive lists of items and Non-Trade Barriers (NTBs), they reiterated their commitment to strengthen the legal regime against terrorism, including their resolve to implement all international conventions relating to combating terrorism to which member states are parties, as well as the SAARC Regional Convention on Suppression of Terrorism and the Additional Protocol to the SAARC Regional Convention on the Suppression of Terrorism.

At the Summit, one of the major points of discussion was the global food crisis, by which they acknowledged the need to forge greater cooperation with the international community to ensure food availability and nutrition security.[22]

Sixteenth Summit: Thimpu, 28–29 April 2010

The Sixteenth SAARC Summit was slated for 2009 and was to be hosted by Maldives, but it backed out from hosting the Summit due to global recession. This opportunity was seized by Bhutan and it hosted the 16th SAARC Summit from 28–29 April, 2010.

The theme of the 16th summit was "Towards a green and happy South Asia". Commemortaing the silver jubilee year, the 16th SAARC Summit adopted the 36-point Thimpu Silver Jubilee Declaration which upholds a pledge to make the regional association effective. The Summit also announced the "Thimpu Statement on Climate Change".

The noteworthy developments in this Summit have been the signing of the SAARC Agreement on Trade in Services and the SAARC Convention on Environment. The leaders also held talks in the area of strengthening regional cooperation by way of forming South Asia Forum for generation of debate, discussion and exchange of ideas on future development. The other issues were: people-centric development and the concept of Gross National happiness, poverty alleviation and realization of SAARC Development Goals (SDGs), education, connectivity, food security, energy security, terrorism, global climate change, women and youth, nomination of a Woman Secretary General as the tenth Secretary General of SAARC, and development of a SAARC Youth Action Plan to guide regional cooperation. The summit further underlined the important role of the SAARC Development Fund (SDF) for financing regional and sub-regional programmes and projects.

However, there was no progress on SAFTA (South Asia Free Trade Agreement) though the leaders reiterated to uphold their commitment to implement the SAFTA in letter and spirit. No effort was also made by the leaders of South Asia to find out any regional solution to the Afghan problem.

Seventeenth Summit: Addu, Maldives, 10–11 November 2011

The Seventeenth Summit was held from 10–11 November 2011 in Addu City, Maldives. The Meeting was opened by the outgoing Chair of SAARC, Prime Minister of the Royal Government of Bhutan, Lyonchhen Jigmi Yoezer Thinley.

The theme of Seventeenth SAARC Summit is *Building Bridges*. The theme is significant as it can be seen as an attempt to bridge the gaps created by uneven economic development and income distribution, the gaps in recognizing and respecting the equality of men and women, the closing of space between intent and implementation. This Summit was seen as a push to boost the building of bridges among SAARC countries to establish an equitable SAARC region.

In this Summit, four agreements were signed which are SAARC Agreement on Rapid Response to Natural Disasters, SAARC Agreement on Multilateral Arrangement on Recognition of Conformity Assessment, SAARC Agreement on Implementation of Regional Standards, and SAARC Seed Bank Agreement. In addition, the **Addu Declaration** on the theme Building Bridges was issued on 11 November 2011, in the Addu Summit. The member states reaffirmed their commitment to peace, confidence building, liberty, human dignity, gender-based violence, democracy, mutual respect, good governance and human rights. They voiced their concerns over terrorism in all its form: trafficking, maritime piracy, environmental degradation and threats of Climate Change. Further, the member states resolved to strengthen the institutional mechanisms of SAARC in order to bolster and enhance regional cooperation.

Eighteenth Summit: Kathmandu, Nepal, 26–27 November 2014

The eighteenth SAARC Summit was hosted by Nepal. It was held in Kathmandu during 26–27 November 2014. The Summit, however, began in the background of grim relation between India and Pakistan over cross-border firing, terrorism and ensuing diplomatic thaw in their relation. The SAARC countries however saw a need to reinvigorate and revitalize SAARC. Despite coldness between India and Pakistan, the SAARC Kathmandu Declaration upholds the theme *Deeper Integration for Peace and Prosperity.* The Declaration underlined deepening of regional integration for peace and prosperity by promoting mutual trust, amity, understanding, cooperation and partnership. The countries pledged to cooperate in the fields of connectivity, energy, poverty alleviation, agriculture, food and security, post-2015 development goals, blue economy, health education, culture, tourism, environment, migration, science technology, telecommunication, youth, women and children, social protection, migration, media, governance, combating terrorism and transnational crimes. They also underlined the importance of progress of SAARC process along with efforts towards building South Asian Economic Union (SAEU) and SAFTA and facilitation of trade.

However, the coldness between India and Pakistan remained throughout the Summit, and it became evident from Indian's newly elected Prime Minister Narendra Modi's statement that India was also proposing several strategies to block China's inroads into SAARC.

Observers were from Australia, The People's Republic of China, the Islamic Republic of Iran, Japan, the Republic of Korea, Mauritius, the Union of Myanmar, the United States of America and the European Union.

The Leaders also agreed to the offer of Pakistan to host the Nineteenth Summit.

Evaluation

The SAARC's balance sheet of success is very limited to adoption of several conventions like the SAARC Regional Convention on Suppression of Terrorism, SAARC Convention on Narcotic Drugs and Psychotropic Substances as well as its concern with issues pertaining to women, children, the youth, and the old and the disabled. There have also been breakthroughs in the form of agreements for establishing SAFTA and SAPTA, but their success at the operational level is yet to be seen. The greatest impediment in the path of achieving success is the political differences between the member states, especially between India and Pakistan, which get reflected during the SAARC sessions. Another inherent weakness of SAARC is that, it totally excludes political issues from its ambit. The operating principle of SAARC is that bilateral and contentious issues must be excluded from the deliberations of the Association. But if there is tension in high politics area, then low politics is sure to suffer. Besides, there is an immense disparity in the developmental pattern within the South Asian region. India, by its sheer size and economic growth, is often considered as a 'Big Brother' of the South Asian region which makes the member states always uncomfortable.

ASSOCIATION OF SOUTH-EAST ASIAN NATIONS

The Association of South East Asian Nations (ASEAN) is a regional organization formed by the governments of Indonesia, Malaysia, the Philippines, Singapore and Thailand through the Bangkok Declaration which was signed by the Foreign Minister of ASEAN countries on 8th August 1967. Since then the membership has expanded and now it stands at 10. Brunei Darussalam joined on 8 January 1984, Vietnam on 28 July 1995, Laos and Myanmar on 23 July 1997, and Cambodia on 30 April 1999.

The dialogue partners are Australia, Canada, the European Union, Japan, New Zealand and the United States. Four more countries have since joined the ASEAN dialogue system: China (1996), India (1996), the Republic of Korea (1991) and Russia (1996). The United Nations Development Programme (1997) is the only dialogue partner that is not a sovereign state.

Objectives

The ASEAN Declaration states that the aims and purposes of the Association are to:

1. Accelerate economic growth, social progress and cultural development in the region.
2. Promote regional peace and stability by abiding respect for justice and the rule of law in the relationship among countries in the region and adherence to the principles of the United Nations Charter.

Fundamental Principles

The ASEAN member countries have adopted the following fundamental principles in their relations with one another, as contained in the Treaty of Amity and Cooperation in South East Asia (TAC) signed in 1976:

• Mutual respect for the independence, sovereignty, equality, territorial integrity and national identity of all nations.

• The right of every state to lead its national existence free from external interference, subversion or coercion.

• Non-interference in the internal affairs of one another.

• Settlement of differences or disputes in a peaceful manner.

- Renunciation of the threat or use of force.
- Effective cooperation among themselves.

Structures and Mechanisms

The highest decision-making organ of ASEAN is the meeting of the ASEAN Heads of States and Governments. The ASEAN Summit is convened every year. The ASEAN Ministerial Meeting (Foreign Ministers) is held annually. The other structures include: the ASEAN Economic Ministers' Meeting, the ASEAN Finance Ministers' Meeting, and the Sectoral Ministers' meeting. There is also the Joint Ministerial Meeting (JMM). ASEAN also has a Secretariat and a Secretary-General.

Ministerial meetings are held regularly in different sectors such as agriculture and forestry, economics (trade), energy, environment, finance, health, information, investment, labour, law, regional haze and youth. Supporting these ministerial bodies are committees of senior officials, technical working groups and task forces.

To support the conduct of ASEAN's external relations, it has established committees composed of heads of diplomatic missions in different cities: Beijing, Brussels, Geneva, Islamabad, London, Moscow, New Delhi, New York, and Washington DC among others.

The Secretary-General of ASEAN is appointed on merit and accorded ministerial status. He has a five-year term; and he is mandated to initiate, advise, coordinate and implement ASEAN activities. The members of the professional staff of the ASEAN Secretariat are appointed on the principle of open recruitment and region-wide competition.

The ASEAN has also several specialized bodies and arrangements, promoting inter-governmental cooperation through various fora such as the:

- ASEAN Agricultural Development Planning Centre
- ASEAN-EC Management Centre
- ASEAN Centre for Energy
- ASEAN Earthquake Information
- ASEAN Specialized Meteorological Centre
- ASEAN Timber Technology Centre
- ASEAN Tourism Information Centre
- ASEAN University Network.

In addition, the ASEAN promotes dialogue and consultations with professional and business organizations with related aims and purposes, such as the ASEAN Chambers of Commerce and Industry, the ASEAN Business Forum, the ASEAN Intellectual Property Association, and the ASEAN Institutes for Strategic and International Studies. Further, there are 58 non-governmental organizations (NGOs), which have formal affiliations with ASEAN.

ASEAN Plus Three Meeting

The ASEAN Plus Three is a meeting held between ASEAN, China, Japan and South Korea, and is primarily conducted during each ASEAN Summit.

Asia-Europe Meeting

The Asia–Europe Meeting (ASEM) is an informal dialogue process initiated in 1996 with the intention of strengthening cooperation between the countries of Europe and Asia, especially members of the European Union and the ASEAN, in particular.

ASEAN–Russia Summit

The ASEAN–Russia Summit is an annual meeting between leaders of the member states and the President of Russia.

East Asia Summit (EAS)

The idea of EAS took root from the discussions regarding the ASEAN plus Three Meetings. It actually became a reality in 2005 and it has become a forum where leaders of 18 countries participate with the objectives of regional peace, security and economic prosperity. The membership comprises ten ASEAN Member states, Australia, China, India, Japan, New Zealand, republic of Korea, Russian Federation and USA.

Achievements

Unlike the SAARC, the ASEAN has been able to make major breakthroughs in economic and political areas, which have resulted either in major political and economic agreements and accords or pledge to reach such agreements and accords, the major objective being to enforce regional peace and stability, and to maintaining its relations with other countries, regions and organizations.

Some prominent political accords are:

1. *Zone of Peace, Freedom and Neutrality (ZOPFAN):*   On 27 November 1971, the foreign ministers of the then five ASEAN members met in Kuala Lumpur and signed the Zone of Peace, Freedom and Neutrality (ZOPFAN) Declaration. It commits all ASEAN members to "exert efforts to secure the recognition of and respect for South East Asia as a Zone of Peace, Freedom and Neutrality, free from any manner of interference by outside powers", and to "make concerted efforts to broaden the areas of cooperation, which would contribute to their strength, solidarity and closer relationship". ZOPFAN recognizes "the right of every state, large or small, to lead its national existence free from outside interference in its internal affairs as this interference will adversely affect its freedom, independence and integrity".

2. *Asean Security Community (ASC)*:   To forge political and security cooperation, the ASEAN leaders have agreed to establish the ASEAN Security Community (ASC) with the aim to ensure that countries in the region live at peace with one another and with the world in a just, democratic and harmonious environment. The members of the Community shall pledge to rely exclusively on peaceful processes in the settlement of intra-regional differences and regard their security as fundamentally linked to one another and bound by geographic location, common vision and objectives. It has the following components: political development; shaping and sharing of norms; conflict prevention; conflict resolution; post-conflict peacebuilding; and implementing mechanisms.

3. *Declaration of ASEAN Concord, Bali, 24 February 1976:*   This Declaration upheld the pledge of the ASEAN countries to work towards the expansion of political co-operation. To this end the Declaration adopted principles for regional stability and a programme of action for political cooperation such as the signing of Treaty of Amity and Cooperation in South East Asia (TAC) and setting of intraregional disputes "by peaceful means as soon as possible".

4. *Treaty of Amity and Cooperation in South East Asia: Bali, 24 February 1976:* The Treaty enshrines the following principles: mutual respect for one another's sovereignty; non-interference in the internal affairs; peaceful settlement of intra-regional disputes; and effective cooperation. The Treaty also provides for a code of conduct for the peaceful settlement of disputes, and it mandates the establishment of a high council made up of ministerial representatives from the parties as a dispute–settlement mechanism.

5. *ASEAN Declaration on the South China Sea, Manila, 22 July 1992:*   This Declaration was adopted to create an atmosphere of peace and stability in the South China Sea. This Declaration urged "all parties concerned to exercise restraint in order to create a positive climate for the eventual resolution of all disputes".

6. *ASEAN Regional Forum (ARF) in 1994:*   In recognition of security interdependence in the Asia-Pacific region, the ASEAN established the ASEAN Regional Forum (ARF) in 1994. The ARF's agenda aims at evolving in three broad stages, namely, the promotion of confidence-building, development of preventive diplomacy and elaboration of approaches to conflicts. The present participants in the ARF include 10 member countries, the dialogue partners and Democratic People's Republic of Korea (North Korea), Republic of Korea (South Korea), and Mongolia. The ARF discusses the major regional security issues in the region, including the relationship among the major powers, non-proliferation, counter-terrorism, transnational crime, South China Sea and the Korean Peninsula, among others.

7. *Treaty on the South East Asia Nuclear Weapon-Free Zone: (SEANWFZ), Bangkok, 15 December 1997:* The leaders of all the ten South East ASEAN countries signed the Treaty on the South East Asia Nuclear Weapon-Free Zone (SEANWFZ). As a key component of ZOPFAN, the SEANWFZ treaty expresses ASEAN's determination to contribute towards general and complete nuclear disarmament and the promotion of international peace and security. It also aims at protecting the region from environmental pollution and the hazards posed by the radioactive waste and other toxic materials. The SEANWFZ treaty came into force on 27 March 1997. The ASEAN is now negotiating with the five nuclear-weapon states on the terms of their accession to the protocol which lay down their commitments under the treaty.

8. *ASEAN Vision 2020, Kuala Lumpur, 15 December 1997:* The ASEAN vision 2020 was adopted by the member states of ASEAN on the 30th anniversary of ASEAN. They agreed on a shared vision of ASEAN as a concert of South East Asian nations, outward looking, living in peace, stability and prosperity, bonded together in partnership in dynamic development and in a community of caring societies.

9. *Declaration of ASEAN Concord II, Bali, 7 October 2003:* This Declaration upheld the resolve of the ASEAN member states to establish an ASEAN Community comprising three pillars: the ASEAN Security Community, the ASEAN Economic Community and the ASEAN Socio-Cultural Community.

In the economic sphere, the ASEAN Free Trade Area (AFTA), launched in 1992, is now in place. It aims at promoting the region's competitive advantage as a single production unit. The elimination of tariff and non-tariff barriers among the member countries is expected to promote greater economic efficiency, productivity, and competitiveness. A series of economic agreements followed, to ultimately reach the ASEAN Vision 2020 of ASEAN Economic Community by 2015. The prominent agreements are:

- Agreement on the Common Effective Preferential Tariff Scheme for the ASEAN Free Trade Area, Singapore, 28 January 1992.
- Framework Agreements on Enhancing ASEAN Economic Cooperation, Singapore, 28 January 1992.
- Protocol to Amend the Agreement on ASEAN Preferential Trading Arrangement, Bangkok, 15 December 1995.
- Protocol for the Accession of the Socialist Republic of Vietnam to the Framework Agreements on Enhancing ASEAN Economic Cooperation, Bangkok, 15 December 1995.
- Protocol to Amend the Agreement on the Common Effective Preferential Tariff Scheme for the ASEAN Free Trade Area, Bangkok, 15 December 1995.

- Protocol for the Accession of Socialist Republic of Vietnam to the Agreement on the Common Effective Preferential Tariff Scheme for the ASEAN Free Trade Area, Bangkok, 15 December 1995.
- Protocol to Amend the Framework Agreements on Enhancing ASEAN Economic Cooperation, Bangkok, 15 December 1995.
- The ASEAN Framework Agreement on the Facilitation of Goods in Transit, Ha Noi, 16 December 1998.
- Protocol on Notification Procedures, Makati, Philippines, 8 October 1998.
- Protocol on the Special Arrangement for Sensitive and Highly Sensitive Products, Singapore, 30 September 1999.
- Protocol regarding the implementation of the CEPT Scheme Temporary Exclusion List, Singapore, 22–25 November 2000.
- Protocol to Amend the Agreement on the Common Effective Preferential Tariff (CEPT) Scheme for the ASEAN Free Trade Area (AFTA) for the Elimination of Import Duties, 31 January 2003.
- Declaration of ASEAN Concord II, Bali, 7 October 2003. The establishment of an ASEAN Economic Community (AEC) was envisaged in this Declaration. This Declaration aimed at the realisation of the ASEAN vision 2020 by the creation of a stable prosperous and competitive ASEAN economic region. It would be based on convergence of interests of the member states with a view to deepen the economic integration. The ultimate aim is the establishment of ASEAN as a single market and production base by using newer mechanisms and utilizing the existing ones like ASEAN Free Trade Areas (AFTA), ASEAN Framework Agreement on Services (AFAS) and ASEAN Investment Area (AIA).
- First Protocol to Amend the Protocol on Special Arrangements on Sensitive and Highly Sensitive Products, 3 September 2004.
- Protocol to Provide Special Consideration for Rice and Sugar, 23 August 2007.
- ASEAN Trade in Goods Agreement, Cha-am, Thailand, 26 February 2009.
- Annexes of the ASEAN Trade in Goods Agreement, Cha-am, Thailand, 26 February 2009.

All these are steps towards the creation of the ASEAN Economic Community which is the end-goal of economic integration measures as outlined in the ASEAN Vision 2020.

A positive step towards establishment of an ASEAN Community was taken at the Twelfth ASEAN Summit at Cebu, the Philippines. The leaders signed the **Cebu Declaration on the Acceleration of the Establishment of an ASEAN Community, by 2015**. The ASEAN Community as envisioned by the leaders is to comprise three pillars. The first one being the ASEAN Political-Security

Community, the second one ASEAN Economic Community and the third ASEAN Socio-Cultural Community. The ASEAN Charter was adopted at the 13th ASEAN Summit in Singapore in November 2007 and it came into force in December 2008. The aim is to establish through the Charter, the legal and institutional framework of ASEAN.

Recent Issues and Concerns

The chief issues affecting peace and security include territorial and jurisdictional disputes in the South China Sea, self-determination for East Timor, nuclear proliferation in North East Asia and South Asia, weapons of mass destruction and the impact of globalization. At the turn of the twenty-first century, issues shifted to involve a more environmental prospective. The ASEAN member states became concerned with environmental issues. This induced them to sign the ASEAN Agreement on Transboundary Haze Pollution in 2002 as an attempt to control the haze pollution in South East Asia which has been disturbing the environment of the region for long. Unfortunately, the attempt proved to be unsuccessful due to the outbreaks of the 2005 Malaysian haze and the 2006 South East Asian haze. The Cebu Declaration on East Asian Energy Security, the ASEAN-Wildlife Enforcement Network in 2005, and the Asia-Pacific Partnership on Clean Development and Climate are other significant environment related Treaties.

However, in the arena of political cooperation, it suffered a setback because of the ambivalent approach of ASEAN to address the human rights and democracy issues in the junta-led Myanmar. Despite global outrage at the military crack down on peaceful protesters in Yangon, the ASEAN has refused to suspend Myanmar as a member and also has rejected proposals for economic sanctions against the regime. This has caused concern, as the European Union, a potential trade partner, has refused to conduct free trade negotiations at a regional level for these political reasons. During the Twelfth ASEAN Summit in Cebu, several activist groups staged an anti-globalization and anti-Arroyo (Head of state and Government, the Philippines) rallies. According to the activists, the agenda of economic integration would negatively affect industries in the Philippines and would cause thousands of Filipinos to lose their jobs.[23] Therefore, the present issues and agenda for integration and furtherance of cooperation have to be worked out with utmost caution.

EXERCISES

1. Discuss the concepts of regionalism and integration in international relations.

2. Describe the origin of European integration by mapping its journey from the formation of European Coal and Steel Community (ECSC) to the European Union (EU).

3. Briefly discuss the institutions of the European Union (EU).

4. Write a note on the African Union (AU).

5. Briefly discuss the role of OPEC in international politics.

6. Comment on the role of Asia Pacific Economic Cooperation (APEC) as a regional organization in world politics.

7. Write a note on Organization of American States (OAS).

8. Comment on the role of South Asian Association for Regional Cooperation (SAARC) as a regional organization.

9. Examine the objectives of SAARC and trace its development over time.

10. Write a note on the composition, objectives, structures and mechanisms of ASEAN.

11. Evaluate the role of ASEAN as a prominent regional organization with special reference to its achievements.

REFERENCES

[1] Bhattacharya, Purusottam, "Globalization and New Regionalism: The EU Experience," *in* Anindyo J. Majumdar and Shibashis Chatterjee (Eds.), *Understanding Global Politics,* Lancer Books, New Delhi, 2004, p. 175.

[2] Palmer, Norman D. and Howard C. Perkins, *International Relations— The World Community in Transition,* A.I.T.B.S. Publishers & Distributors, New Delhi, 1997, p. 559.

[3] *ibid.*

[4] *ibid.*

[5] Couloumbis, Theodore A. and James H. Wolfe, *Introduction to International Relations: Power and Justice*, Prentice-Hall of India, New Delhi, 1981, p. 305.

[6] Groom, A.J.R., *Approaches to Conflict and Cooperation in International Relations: Lessons from Theory for Practice,* The Ford Foundation Lectures in International Relations Studies, M.S. University, Baroda, 1991, p. 66.

[7] Couloumbis and Wolfe, *op. cit.*, n. 5, p. 305.

[8] Mitrany, David, *A Working Peace System*, Quadrangle, Chicago, 1966.

[9] Claude, Inis L., *Sword into Plowshares,* Random House, New York, 1971, p. 289.

[10] Kegley, Charles W., Jr. and Eugene R. Wittkopf, *World Politics—Trends and Transformation,* St. Martin's Press, New York, 1981, p. 454.

[11] Banerji, Arun Kumar (Ed.), *Integration, Disintegration and World Order: Some Perspectives on the Process of Change,* Allied Publishers in collaboration with School of International Relations and Strategic Studies, Jadavpur University, Calcutta, 1995, p. 5.

[12] *ibid.,* pp. 5–6.

[13] Kegley and Wittkopf, *op. cit.,* n. 10, p. 455.

[14] Nye, J.S., *Peace in Parts: Integration and Conflict in Regional Organization,* Little Brown and Company, Boston, 1971, p. 56.

[15] *ibid.,* pp. 56–58.

[16] Bhattacharya, Purusottam, *op. cit.,* n. 1, p. 176.

[17] *ibid.,* p. 179.

[18] http://en.wikipedia.org/wiki/Schuman_declaration

[19] Fink, Marcel and Jain Paterson, "The European Union: Its Past, Present and Future", *West Bengal Political Science Review,* Vol. V, Nos. 1 and 2, January–December, 2002, pp. 36–37.

[20] Butler, Fiona, "Regionalism and Intergration", *in* John Baylis and Steve Smith (Eds.), *The Globalization of World Politics,* Oxford University Press, London, 1997, pp. 426–427.

[21] Fink and Paterson, *op. cit.,* n. 19, p. 63.

[22] http://www.saarc-sec.org/data/summit15/summit15declaration.htm.

[23] http://www.aseansec.org/1814.htm, and http://www.aseansec.org/64.htm.

11

The United Nations and International Relations

INTRODUCTION

The devastating experience of the First World War left the world shocked and petrified. Therefore, attempts were made by the world community to check the horrors of war and search for international peace and security. The League of Nations was the first attempt made by the world community to accomplish world peace through an international organization. However, the political situation and power equations prevalent during the inter-War period paralysed the League from functioning properly and it met a sudden death with the outbreak of the Second World War. However, the idealism of international

251

peace and security did not die down with the League's failure and, with the outbreak of the Second World War, there was a renewed concern for establishment of an international organization as the guardian of international peace and security. This ultimately led to the establishment of the United Nations.

BIRTH OF THE UN

The idealism of the founding fathers of the League of Nations to prevent large-scale war was shattered as the world was caught up again in another massive war—the Second World War. The League failed to prevent the War and its fate became sealed with the outbreak of the War. However, there was a renewed effort on the part of the international community to establish an international organization to save the future generations from the scourge of war. The United States, under President Franklin Roosevelt was in favour of a global peacekeeping agency and Roosevelt himself coined the name "United Nations". In the course of the War, the urge for such an international organization led to the signing of the historic Atlantic Charter on 14 August 1941.

The Inter-Allied Declaration of 12 June 1941 upheld a promise "to work together, with other free people, both in war and in peace". Thereafter, on 14 August 1941 Franklin D Roosevelt, President of the United States and Winston Churchill, Prime Minister of the United Kingdom, signed the Atlantic Charter during their meeting on the ship *HMS Prince of Wales*. This marked the historic beginning of the United Nations.

The next step towards the formation of the United Nations was the Declaration by United Nations on 1 January 1942. Twenty-six allied nations signed the "Declaration by United Nations" in Washington DC. This document contained the first official use of the term 'United Nations'. This initiative was further given a boost in the Moscow Declaration on 30 October 1943, which envisioned "a general international organization based on the principle of sovereign equality of all peace loving states... large and small, for the maintenance of international peace and security".[1] The endeavour picked up momentum and, on 1 December 1943, the Tehran Declaration was adopted, which drew up a plan for an international organization for peacekeeping. The principles of these two declarations were reaffirmed in the Dumbarton Oaks Conference held between 21 September and 7 October 1944, where the blueprint of the international body was prepared. Major decisions relating to the structures and functions of the organs of the United Nations were worked out amidst several objections, adjustments and demands. At the Yalta Conference of 11 February 1945, Roosevelt, Churchill and Stalin declared their resolve to establish "a general international organization to maintain peace and security". Finally, the largest conference for framing of the UN Charter was held in San Francisco from 25 April to 26 June 1945 and it was attended by 280 delegates from 50 invitee nations. After much scrutinization and review of the Dumbarton Oaks proposals and with important changes, finally, the San Francisco Conference ended with the signing of the Charter on 26 June 1945. After the ratification of the Charter by the five permanent members (the P–5) of the Security Council and the majority of the signatories, the Charter came into force with effect from 24 October 1945. October 24 has, therefore, been declared as the United Nations Day. This was the beginning of the world organization and the First General Assembly opened in the Central Hall, Westminster on 10 January 1946, with representatives from 51 nations. The Security Council met for the first time in London on 17 January 1946. Trygve Lie of Norway became the first Secretary-General on 1 February 1946.

Purposes and Principles of the UN

The Charter of the United Nations begins with a Preamble which outlines the purposes or objectives of this international organization. The vision of a world based on the ideals of peace, justice, truth and fraternity is contained in the Preamble. It reads as follows:

"We the peoples of the United Nations determined, to save succeeding generations from the scourge of war, which twice in our lifetime has brought untold sorrow to mankind, and to reaffirm faith in fundamental human rights, in the dignity and worth of the human person, in the equal rights of men and women and of nations large and small, and to establish conditions under which justice and respect for the obligations arising from treaties and other sources of international law can be maintained, and to promote social progress and better standards of life in larger freedom".

The Preamble bears testimony to the devastating and nerve-wracking experiences of the First World War and simultaneous urge on the part of the founding members to save the future generations from the scourge of war. Therefore, it carries a hope of establishing a lasting peace based on respect for the human rights, acknowledgement of sovereign equality of all states and ensuring better living conditions, economic and social, to the peoples of the world. Keeping this in mind, the Preamble to the Charter further carries a set of pledges for realizing the ends whose aims are to:

- Practise tolerance and live together in peace with one another as good neighbours.
- Unite in strength to maintain international peace and security.
- Ensure, by the acceptance of principles and the institution of methods, that armed force shall not be used, save in the common interest.
- Employ international machinery for the promotion of economic and social advancement of all peoples.[2]

Despite such lofty ideals set forth in the Preamble, it is not above criticisms. Scholars find the expression "We the peoples of the United Nations" to be misleading. It neither represents the peoples of the world nor have they created the international organization. The governments representing their respective states concluded the international treaty and these governments, and not the "peoples" were represented in the San Francisco Conference. Nevertheless, it can hardly be doubted that there was a genuine desire on the part of the world community to establish an international organization which would ensure world peace and security.

The purposes of the UN are embodied in the Charter under Article 1 which states that the UN would endeavour to:

- Maintain international peace and security, and to that end: take effective collective measures for the prevention and removal of threats to the peace, and for the suppression of acts of aggression or other breaches of the peace, and to bring about by peaceful means and in conformity with the principles of justice and international law, adjustment or settlement of international disputes or situations which might lead to a breach of peace.

- Develop friendly relations among nations based on respect for the principle of equal rights and self-determination of peoples, and to take other appropriate measures to strengthen universal peace.

- Achieve international cooperation in solving international problems of an economic, social, cultural, or humanitarian character, and in promoting and encouraging respect for human rights and for fundamental freedoms for all without distinction as to race, sex, language, or religion.

- Be a centre for harmonizing the actions of nations in the attainment of these common ends.[3]

Though the purposes of the UN are again quite novel but the very purpose of Article 1(1) gets defeated with Article 2(7) of the Charter debarring the UN from interfering in the cases of strife falling under the domestic jurisdiction of the states. This handicaps the UN from preventing or removing the threats to peace, which may be an internal affair but has a potential to become a threat to peace internationally.

Article 2, in pursuance of the purposes stated in Article 1, prescribes certain principles for their realization. These principles are:

1. The Organization is based on the principle of the sovereign equality of all its members.

2. All members, in order to ensure to all of them the rights and benefits resulting from membership, shall fulfill in good faith the obligations assumed by them in accordance with the present Charter.

3. All members shall settle their international disputes by peaceful means in such a manner that international peace and security and justice are not endangered.

4. All members shall refrain in their international relations from the threat or use of force against the territorial integrity or political independence of any state, or in any other manner inconsistent with the purposes of the United Nations.

5. All members shall give the United Nations every assistance in any action it takes in accordance with the present Charter, and shall refrain from giving assistance to any state against which the United Nations is taking preventive or enforcement action.

6. The Organization shall ensure that states which are not members of the United Nations act in accordance with these principles so far as may be necessary for the maintenance of international peace and security.

7. Nothing contained in the present Charter shall authorize the United Nations to intervene in matters which are essentially within the domestic jurisdiction of any state or shall require the members to submit such matters to settlement under the present Charter; but this principle shall not prejudice the application of enforcement measures under Chapter VII.[4]

The problems with these principles are that, as far as representations of member states are concerned, they have been accorded equal status in the General Assembly, but the composition of the Security Council is very much contrary to the principle of sovereign equality with the preponderance of the permanent five (P-5) members and the system of veto. Nicholas[5] points out that "The Veto in Security Council still protects the Great Powers but at the expense of heightening the disparity between them and the other members, not only of the General Assembly but of the Security Council itself". Further, the procedure for the amendment of the Charter also gives the P-5 a decisive role to play. The limits set by Article 2(7) on the functioning of the international body also have limited its scope. However, it was resolved by the General Assembly that an issue ceases to be of domestic concern if it, having international obligations, endangers international peace and security. The working of the UN, therefore, suffers from structural problems which make the purposes and principles difficult to attain.

Article 55 of the Charter further embodies principles of socio-economic dimension, which are essential in developing friendly relations among the states. It states that with a view to the creation of conditions of stability and well-being which are necessary for peaceful and friendly relations among nations based on respect for the principle of equal rights and self-determination of peoples, the United Nations shall promote:

- Higher standards of living, full employment, and conditions of economic and social progress and development.

- Solutions of international economic, social, health and related problems; and international cultural and educational cooperation.

- Universal respect for, and observance of, human rights and fundamental freedoms for all without distinction as to race, sex, language or religion.

Thus, the UN Charter contains provisions that are noble and lofty but their realization is mostly circumscribed by the oligarchic and hegemonic structure of the UN as reflected in the composition of the Security Council and the preponderance of the P-5.

Membership

Chapter II (Articles 3, 4, 5 and 6) embodies the principle relating to the acquisition and revocation of membership of the UN. Article 3 enunciates that the original members of the UN are those states which, "having participated in the United Nations Conference on International Organization at San Francisco, or having previously signed the Declaration by United Nations on 1 January 1942, sign the present Charter and ratify it" in accordance with their respective constitutional process.

Article 4 states that the membership of the United Nations is open to "all other peace-loving states which accept the obligations contained in the present Charter and, in the judgment of the Organization, are able and willing to carry out these obligations" and the admission of any such state to membership of the United Nations will be effected by a decision of the General Assembly upon the recommendation of the Security Council.

Article 5 contains provisions regarding suspension of exercise of rights and privileges of membership, against whom preventive or enforcement action has been taken by the Security Council, by the General Assembly upon the recommendation of the Security Council. The exercise of these rights and privileges may be restored by the Security Council.

Article 6 goes further to state that any member of the United Nations persistently violating the principles contained in the present Charter may be expelled from the Organization by the General Assembly upon the recommendation of the Security Council.[6]

At present there are 193 member states of the United Nations.

Organs of the United Nations

Article 7(1) outlines the principal organs of the United Nations. They are the:

- General Assembly
- Security Council
- Economic and Social Council
- Trusteeship Council
- International Court of Justice
- Secretariat

Article 7(2) contains such subsidiary organs, as may be found necessary, may be established in accordance with the present Charter.

THE GENERAL ASSEMBLY

Chapter IV of the UN Charter embodies the provisions pertaining to the compositions, powers and functions of the General Assembly. Established in

1945 under the Charter of the United Nations, the General Assembly occupies a central position as the chief deliberative, policy-making and representative organ of the United Nations. Comprising all 193 members of the United Nations, it provides a forum for multilateral discussion of the full spectrum of international issues covered by the Charter. It also plays a significant role in the process of standard-setting and the codification of international law. The Assembly meets in regular sessions intensively from September to December each year, and thereafter as required.

Composition

Regarding the composition of the Assembly, Article 9 states that the General Assembly shall consist of all the members of the United Nations and each member, big or small, shall have not more than five representatives in the General Assembly.

It was at the San Francisco Conference that a limit of five seats was evolved in place of three as in the League Assembly.

Sessions

The General Assembly meets in annual sessions, which usually begins on the third Tuesday in September of each year. The sessions continue almost for three months. At each session the General Assembly elects one President and 21 Vice-Presidents (6 representatives from African States, 5 representatives from Asian States, 1 representative from an Eastern European State, 3 representatives from Latin American States, 2 representatives from Western European or other states, 5 representatives from the P-5 of the Security Council subject to the condition that the election of the President of General Assembly will have the effect of reducing the number of Vice-Presidents by one), and Chairman of Committees. The first session of the General Assembly was held in the Central Hall of Westminster on the twenty-sixth birthday of the League on 10 January 1946.

The agenda for the sessions of the General Assembly revolves around the isssues of International Peace and Security, Economic Growth and Sustainable Development, Development of Africa, Human Rights, Humanitarian and Disaster Relief Assistance, Justice and International Law, Disarmament, Drugs, Crime, International Terrorism, Organizational and Administrative Matters.

Besides the regular sessions, the General Assembly can also meet in special sessions which "shall be convoked by the Secretary-General at the request of the Security Council or of a majority of the Members of the United Nations". [Chapter IV, Article 20]

Any member state can also request the Secretary-General to summon a special session. On receipt of such a request, the Secretary-General immediately informs the other members of the UN of the request and makes sure that there is a general concurrence in the Assembly on the particular matter to be debated. If within thirty days from the date of communication to the Secretary-General, it is found that a majority of the members concur with the request, then a special session of the General Assembly can be summoned.

Several special sessions of the Assembly have been held since its inception. The First Session (1947) and the Second Session (1948) were on Palestine, followed by the Third Session (1961) on Tunisia; many others have followed over the years. Some recent sessions were held like the Session (2005) on the commemoration of the sixtieth anniversary of the liberation of the Nazi concentration camps, Session (2002) on World Summit for Children, Session (2001) on Problem of human immunodeficiency virus/acquired immunodeficiency syndrome (HIV/AIDS) in all its aspects, Session (2001) on Implementation of the outcome of the UN Conference on Human Settlements (Habitat II).

The General Assembly can also meet for emergency special sessions. Under the resolution 377A(V), "Uniting for peace", adopted by the General Assembly on 3 November 1950, an "emergency special session" can be convened within 24 hours.

Several emergency sessions have been held on illegal Israeli actions in Occupied East Jerusalem and the rest of the Occupied Palestinian Territory, the question of Namibia, the situation in Afghanistan, and its implications for international peace and security (1980), the question of Congo, and others.

Subsidiary Organs of the General Assembly

For the proper dispensation of its functions, the Assembly allocates items relevant to its work among its six main committees which discuss them, seeking, wherever possible, to harmonize the various approaches of states, and then present draft resolutions and decisions for consideration to a plenary meeting of the Assembly.

The main commitees are the:

The First Committee (Disarmament and International Security Committee) is concerned with disarmament and related international security questions.

The Second Committee (Economic and Financial Committee) is concerned with economic questions.

The Third Committee (Social, Humanitarian and Cultural Committee) deals with social and humanitarian issues.

The Fourth Committee (Special Political and Decolonization Committee) deals with a variety of political subjects not dealt with by the First Committee, as well as with decolonization.

The Fifth Committee (Administrative and Budgetary Committee) deals with the administration and budget of the United Nations.

The Sixth Committee (Legal Committee) deals with international legal matters.

Other Committees of the General Assembly are the Credentials Committee, the General Committee which is composed of the President and 21 Vice-Presidents of the General Assembly as well as the chairmen of the six main committees. The committee makes recommendations to the Assembly regarding the adoption of the agenda, the allocation of items and the organization of work. Several informal regional groupings have evolved in the General Assembly, which facilitate the procedural work of the Assembly like the groupings of the African states, the Asian States, the Eastern European states, the Latin American and the Caribbean states and the West European and other states.[7]

Article 22 entrusts the General Assembly to establish subsidiary organs as it deems necessary for the performance of its functions.

Commissions

There are several Commissions established by the General Assembly like the Disarmament Commission, the International Civil Service Commission, the International Law Commission, the United Nations Commission on International Trade Law (UNCITRAL), the United Nations Conciliation Commission for Palestine, and the United Nations Peacebuilding Commission [established by GA Resolution 60/180 and UN Securiy Council Resolutions 1645 (2005) and 1646 (2005)].

Advisory Commission

There is also an Advisory Commission on the United Nations Relief and Works Agency for Palestine Refugees in the Near East [established by GA Resolution 302 (IV), 1949].

Working Groups

Working Groups of General Assembly are:

- High-level open-ended Working Group on the Financial Situation of the United Nations [established by GA Resolution 49/143, 1994]

- Working Group on the Future Operations of the International Research and Training Institute for the Advancement of Women [established by GA Resolution 56/125, 2001]

- Working Group on the Finance of the United Nations Relief and Works Agency for Palestine Refugees in the Near East (UNRWA) [established by GA Resolution 2656 (XXV), 1970].

Open-Ended ad hoc Working Groups

There is also an open-ended ad hoc Working Group of the General Assembly on the Integrated and Coordinated Implementation of and follow-up to the major United Nations Conferences and Summits in the Economic and Social Fields [established by GA Resolution 57/270, 2002].

Councils

The Councils established by the General Assembly resolutions are:

- The Human Rights Council [established by GA Resolution 60/251, 1948]
- The Council of the United Nations University [established by GA Resolution 3081 (XXVIII), 1973].

Governing Councils

The Governing Councils of General Assembly are:

- The Governing Council of the United Nations Environment Programme [established by GA Resolution 2997 (XXVII)]
- The Governing Council of the United Nations Human Settlements Programme, UN-Habitat [established by GA Resolution 56/206, 2001].

Panel

There is also a Panel of External Auditors of the United Nations, the Specialized Agencies and the International Atomic Energy Agency [established by GA Resolution 347 (IV) and 1438 (XIV)].

Functions and Powers

Deliberative Functions: It is needless to say that the General Assembly, comprising all the members of the UN, is the central organ of the organization but the primary responsibility of maintaining world peace and security is left to the Security Council. The role of the Assembly in such matters is limited to advisory. The San Francisco Conference set the limits to the functioning of the Assembly on matters pertaining to peace and security. Therefore, under Article 10, the General Assembly may discuss any questions or any matters within the scope of the present Charter or relating to the powers and functions of any organs provided for in the present Charter, and, except as provided in Article 12, may make recommendations to the members of the United Nations or to the Security Council or to both on any such questions or matters. Under Article 12, it should be noted that, while the Security Council is exercising the functions assigned to it in the present Charter in respect of any dispute or situation, the General Assembly shall not make any recommendations with regard to that dispute or situation unless the Security Council so requests. The Secretary-General may, however, with the consent of the Security Council, notify the General Assembly at each session of any matters relating to the maintenance of international peace and security which are being dealt with by the Security Council, and shall similarly notify the General Assembly, or the Members of the United Nations if the General Assembly is not in session, immediately when the Security Council ceases to deal with such matters.

Functions Relating to Maintenance of International Peace and Security: Under Article 11, the General Assembly may consider the general principles of cooperation in the maintenance of international peace and security, including the principles governing disarmament and the regulation of armaments, and may make recommendations with regard to such principles to the members, or to the Security Council, or to both. These functions are also referred to as *teaching functions*. Acting under this authority, the Assembly has adopted various resolutions, for example, the 'Essentials of Peace' in 1949, "Declaration Concerning the Peaceful Coexistence of States", and also established the Atomic Energy Commission in 1946, the Disarmament Commission in 1952, and the Scientific Committee on the Effects of Atomic Radiation in 1955.[8]

Further, the General Assembly may discuss any questions relating to the maintenance of international peace and security brought before it by any member of the United Nations, or by the Security Council, or by a state which is not a member of the United Nations in accordance with Article 35, paragraph 2, and, except as provided in Article 12 and may make recommendations with regard to any such questions to the state or states concerned, or to the Security Council or to both. Any such question on which action is necessary shall be referred to the Security Council by the General Assembly either before or after the discussion. The General Assembly may also call the attention of the Security Council to situations which are likely to endanger international peace and security.

Under Article 14, subject to the provisions of Article 12, the General Assembly may recommend measures for the peaceful adjustment of any situation, regardless of origin, which it deems likely to impair the general welfare or friendly relations among nations, including situations resulting from a violation of the provisions of the present Charter setting forth the purposes and principles of the United Nations.

The 1950s, during the Korean crisis, saw an increase in the importance of the General Assembly. In the backdrop of the Cold War and the continuous tussle between the USA and the USSR resulting in the exercise of veto, and later due to the continuous absence by the Soviet Union, the Security Council reached a deadlock. It was then that the historical "Uniting for Peace Resolution (UPR)", 1950, was adopted by virtue of which "action with respect to threats to the peace, breaches of the peace and acts of aggression", which is solely the responsibility of the Security Council, would be performed by the General Assembly. It was resolved that "if the Security Council, because of lack of unanimity of the permanent members, fails to exercise its primary responsibility for the maintenance of international peace and security in any case where there appears to be a threat to the peace, breach of the peace, or act of aggression, the General Assembly shall consider the matter immediately with a view to making appropriate recommendations to Members for collective measures, including in the case of a breach of the peace or act of aggression the use of armed force when necessary, to maintain or restore international peace and security. If not in session at the time, the General Assembly may meet in emergency special session within twenty-four hours of the request. Such emergency special session shall be called if requested by the Security Council on the vote of any seven members, or by a majority of the Members of the United Nations".[9]

Under the UPR, the General assembly has acted in several international crises, as in Korea, Suez and Hungarian crises, as well as the Jordan and Lebanon crises. It should be remembered that the Assembly reached its zenith acting under the UPR only in the fifties, and from the sixties onwards it was again the Security Council which resumed its responsibilities regarding issues of peace.

While the Assembly is empowered to make only non-binding recommendations to states on international issues within its competence, it has, nonetheless, initiated actions—political, economic, humanitarian, social and legal—which have affected the lives of millions of people throughout the world. The landmark Millennium Declaration, adopted in 2000, and the 2005 World Summit Outcome Document, reflect the commitment of the member states of the UN to reach specific goals in order to attain peace, security and disarmament along with development and poverty eradication; safeguard human rights and promote the rule of law; protect our common environment; meet the special needs of Africa; and strengthen the United Nations.

Functions Relating to Codification of International Law: The functions relating to codification of international law can be regarded as a part of the 'quasi-legislative function' or, as Nicholas[10] refers to, as functions that are "nearest to the law-making activities of a national legislature". According to Article 13 of the Charter, the General Assembly shall initiate studies and make recommendations for the purpose of promoting international cooperation in the (a) political field and encouraging the progressive development of international law and its codification and (b) economic, social, cultural, educational and health fields. The Assembly also assists in the realization of human rights and fundamental freedoms for all without distinction as to race, sex, language or religion.

For performance of its quasi-legislative functions, the Assembly has set up the International Law Commission in 1948 with the primary task of making studies and preparing draft codes and declarations for submission to the

Assembly. On the basis of these recommendations, the Assembly affirmed the principles of international law to exist as embodied in the Charter of the Nuremberg Trial and the judgements of that trial. There are also other instances of such affirmations by the Assembly. Even without the guidance of the Law Commission, the Assembly may prepare and adopt conventions or declarations, which embody a code of behaviour by states.

The General Assembly has also adopted several conventions relating to human rights such as the Universal Declaration of Human Rights, International Covenant on Civil and Political Rights (1966) (ICCPR), International Covenant on Economic, Social and Cultural Rights (ICESR), the Convention on Elimination of All Forms of Racial Discrimination (1965), Convention Against Torture and Other Cruel, Inhuman or Degrading Treatment of Punishment (1984) (CAT) and others.

Supervisory Functions: The Assembly also performs certain supervisory functions under Article 15. It receives and considers annual and special reports from the Security Council. These reports shall include an account of the measures that the Security Council has decided upon or has taken to maintain international peace and security.

The General Assembly also receives and considers reports from the other organs of the United Nations. Under Article 85, the Economic and Social Council and the Trusteeship Council have been placed under the direct supervision of the General Assembly. All specialized agencies should also submit their annual report to the General Assembly.

Under Article 16 the General Assembly is entrusted to perform such functions with respect to the international trusteeship system as are assigned to it under Chapters XII and XIII, including the approval of the trusteeship agreements for areas not designated as strategic.

Budgetary Functions: The budgetary functions form a vital financial activity of the Assembly. Under Article 17, the General Assembly considers and approves the budget of the United Nations. The expenses are to be borne by the members as apportioned by the General Assembly.

The General Assembly also considers and approves any financial and budgetary arrangements with specialized agencies referred to in Article 57, and also examines the administrative budgets of such specialized agencies with a view to making recommendations to the agencies concerned.

Amendment of the Charter: Under Article 108 relating to amendments to the present Charter, the General Assembly, being the forum where all the member states are represented, has been assigned an important position. All amendments can come into force when all the members of the United Nations have adopted it by a two-third majority vote of the members of the General

Assembly and ratified in accordance with their respective constitutional processes by two-thirds of the members of the United Nations, including all the permanent members of the Security Council.

Elective Functions: The General Assembly elects the Secretary-General, judges of the International Court of Justice, and admits new members on the basis of the recommendations of the Security Council. It also exercises exclusive powers to elect the non-permanent members of the Security Council, members of the Economic and Social Council, and several members of the Trusteeship Council.

Voting in General Assembly

Article 18 contains the provisions relating to the voting in the Assembly. These a provisions are:

1. Each member of the General Assembly shall have one vote.

2. Decisions of the General Assembly on important questions shall be made by a two-thirds majority of the members present and voting. These questions shall include: recommendations with respect to the maintenance of international peace and security; the election of the non-permanent members of the Security Council; the election of the members of the Economic and Social Council; the election of the members of the Trusteeship Council in accordance with paragraph 1 (c) of Article 86, the admission of new members to the United Nations; the suspension of the rights and privileges of the membership; the expulsion of members; questions relating to the operation of the trusteeship system; and budgetary questions.

3. Decisions on other questions, including the determination of additional categories of questions to be decided by a two-thirds majority, shall be made by a majority of the members present and voting.

Article 19 contains provisions; which debar a member from exercising the voting rights in the Assembly. It states that "A Member of the United Nations which is in arrears in the payment of its financial contributions to the Organization shall have no vote in the General Assembly if the amount of its arrears equals or exceeds the amount of the contributions due from it for the preceding two full years. The General Assembly may, nevertheless, permit such a Member to vote if it is satisfied that the failure to pay is due to conditions beyond the control of the Member".

In recent years, efforts have been made to achieve consensus on issues, rather than deciding by a formal vote. The President, after having consulted and reached an agreement with the delegations, can propose that a resolution be adopted without a vote.

Evaluation

The General Assembly is by far the most important organ of the United Nations. It is the largest organ comprising all the member states and is known as the **town-meeting of the world**. Given the nature of limited membership of the Security Council, the General Assembly becomes the platform of the developing nations and provides a forum for collective bargaining. The Assembly's power reached its zenith with the passing of the Uniting for Peace Resolution and it met several challenges to peacekeeping using this resolution. But from the sixties onwards, with the resumption of functions relating to matters of peacekeeping and international security, by the Security Council, the role of General Assembly has declined. But this has not made the Assembly an ineffective organ, and it still continues to be the world's Parliament and a forum for deliberation and discussion. The supervisory functions of the Assembly still continue and its effort to work towards a peaceful secure world by promoting peaceful cooperation among nations still remains its main objective. Further, to make the United Nations more effective, the Assembly is the forum which generates ideas and discussions for the proposed reform of the UN and review its work.

THE SECURITY COUNCIL

Composition

CHAPTER V, in particular Article 23 of the Charter, embodies the provisions relating to the membership of the Council. It specifies that the Security Council shall consist of fifteen members of the United Nations. The Republic of China, France, the Union of Soviet Socialist Republics (now Russia), the United Kingdom of Great Britain and Northern Ireland, and the United States of America shall be the permanent members of the Security Council. The admission of People's Republic of China did not take place immediately after the formation of UN due to American veto. At that time, Nationalist China (Taiwan) represented the State of China. However, with the recognition in 1971 of the Beijing Government by the UN, the People's Republic of China was finally admitted to the Council, displacing Taiwan.

The ten non-permanent members are elected by the General Assembly for two-year terms and they are not eligible for immediate re-election. The non-permanent members are selected on the basis of geographical distribution. They are chosen from Asian, African, Latin American and the Caribbean, East European and West European States. The number of non-permanent members was increased from six to ten by an amendment of the Charter, which came into force in 1965. Due regard is specially paid, in the first instance, to the contribution of the members of the United Nations to the maintenance of international peace and security and to the other purposes of the Organization, and also to equitable geographical distribution. Each member of the Security Council shall have one representative.

It has been pointed, however, that the structure of the Council is undemocratic and not based on the principle of sovereign equality. Only the number of non-permanent members was increased and not that of the permanent. Besides, the council has been given sweeping powers relating to the vital matters of international peace and security as compared to the Assembly.

Sessions

Article 28 reflects the desire of the founding members to make it function continuously. It states that the Security Council shall be so organized as to be able to function continuously. Each member of the Security Council shall, for this purpose, be represented at all times at the seat of the Organization.

It also directs that the Security Council shall hold periodic meetings at which each of its members may, if it so desires, be represented by a member of the government or by some other specially designated representative. The Security Council may hold meetings at such places other than the seat of the Organization as in its judgement will best facilitate its work.

Rules 2, 3 and 4 of the provisional rules of procedure of the Security Council adopted by the Council in its first meeting, and amended thereafter several times, specify the procedure of holding sessions of the Council.

The President shall call a meeting of the Security Council at the request of any member of the Security Council and if a dispute or situation is brought to the attention of the Security Council under Article 35 or under Article II (3) of the Charter or, if the General Assembly makes recommendations or refers any question to the Security Council under Article 11 (2) or if the Secretary-General brings to the attention of the Security Council any matter under Article 99. Besides, periodic meetings of the Security Council called for in Article 28 (2) of the Charter shall be held twice a year as the Security Council may decide.

The provisional agenda for each meeting of the Security Council shall be drawn up by the Secretary-General and approved by the President of the Security Council.

The Presidency of the Security Council is held in turn by the members of the Security Council in the English alphabetical order of their names, and each President holds office for one calendar month.

Voting in the Security Council

Article 27 of the present Charter lays down the provisions relating to the voting procedure of the Security Council. The presence of the system of 'veto' is the most conspicuous element in this voting procedure. It calls for an affirmative vote of nine members to arrive at decisions on procedural matters and an affirmative vote of nine members including the concurring votes of the permanent members for all other matters. Each member of the Security Council shall have one vote.

Decisions on procedural matters are made by an affirmative vote of at least nine of the 15 members. Decisions on substantive matters require nine votes, including the concurring votes of all five permanent members. This is the rule of *great Power unanimity*, often referred to as the "veto" power. The exclusive "veto" power of the P-5 reflects the unequal structure of the UN Security Council and also most of ten hinders the UN from taking actions disapproved by the P-5 of the Security Council.

A member state against which preventive or enforcement action has been taken by the Security Council may be suspended from the exercise of the rights and privileges of membership by the General Assembly on the recommendation of the Security Council. A member state, which has persistently violated the principles of the Charter, may be expelled from the United Nations by the Assembly on the Council's recommendation.

Any member of the United Nations, which is not a member of the Security Council, may participate, without vote, in the discussion of any question brought before the Security Council whenever the latter considers that the interests of that Member are specially affected (Article 31).

A State, which is a member of the United Nations but not of the Security Council, may participate, without a vote, in its discussions when the Council considers that the country's interests are affected. Both members of the United Nations and non-members, if they are considered parties to a dispute by the Council, are invited to take part, without a vote, in the Council's discussions, and the Council sets the conditions for participation by a non-member State (Article 32).

Under the Charter, all members of the United Nations agree to accept and carry out the decisions of the Security Council. While other organs of the United Nations may make recommendations to Governments, the Council alone has the power to take decisions and under the Charter member states are obligated to carry out these decisions.

Subsidiary Bodies of the Security Council

The Security Council has established subsidiary organs as it deems necessary for the performance of its functions.

There are at present three **Standing Committees**, and each includes representatives of all Security Council member states. The three standing committees are:

1. Security Council Committee of Experts
2. Security Council Committee on Admission of New Members
3. Security Council Committee on Council Meetings away from the Headquarters

There are also **Ad-Hoc Committees** which are established by the Security Council as and when needed. They comprise all Council members who meet in closed session. Ad-Hoc Committees such as the Governing Council of the United Nations Compensation Commission established by the Security Council resolution 692 (1991), and the Committee set up pursuant to resolution 1373 (2001) concerning Counter-Terrorism—were all established by the Security Council.

The Security Council also formed several **Sanctions Committee**. Some Security Council Sanction Committees established, inter alia pursuant to resolutions adopted, relate to Somalia (1992), Rwanda (1994), Al Qaida and the Taliban and associated individuals and entities (1999), the Democratic Republic of Congo (2004) and Sudan (2006).

There are also several **Working Groups** of the Security Council such as the:

1. Security Council Working Group on Peacekeeping Operations
2. Security Council Ad-Hoc Working Group on Conflict Prevention and Resolution in Africa
3. Security Council Working Group established pursuant to resolution 1566 (2004)
4. Security Council Working Group on Children and Armed Conflict
5. Security Council Informal Working Group on General Issues of Sanctions
6. Security Council Informal Working Group on Documentation and Other Procedural Questions

There is also the Peacebuilding Commission (PBC), the 1540 Committee, and the United Nations Monitoring Verification and Inspection Commission (UNMOVIC). International Tribunals have also been constituted by the resolutions of the Security Council such as the International Criminal Tribunals for the Former Yugoslavia (ICTY), and for the Prosecution of Persons Responsible for Serious Violations of International Humanitarian Law Committed in the Territory of Rwanda and Rwandan Citizens Responsible for Genocide and other such violations committed in the territory of neighbouring states between 1 January and 31 December 1994.

Counter-terrorism bodies have also been constituted such as the:

- Counter-Terrorism Committee
- Al-Qaida and Taliban Sanctions Committee
- 1540 Committee (non-proliferation of weapons of mass destruction)[11]

Functions and Powers

Functions Relating to International Peace and Security: Article 24 entrusts the prime responsibility to maintain international peace and security in accordance with the principles and purposes of the United Nations. Under this Article, the Security Council shall submit annual and, when necessary, special reports to the General Assembly for its consideration.

Under CHAPTER VI relating to Pacific Settlement of Disputes, Article 33 stipulates that the parties to any dispute, the continuance of which is likely to endanger the maintenance of international peace and security, shall, first of all, seek a solution by negotiation, enquiry, mediation, conciliation, arbitration, judicial settlement, and resort to regional agencies or arrangements or other peaceful means of their own choice and the Security Council shall, when it deems necessary, call upon the parties to settle their disputes, by such means.

Article 34 invests upon the Security Council to investigate any dispute, or any situation, which might lead to international friction or give rise to a dispute, in order to determine whether the continuance of the dispute or situation is likely to endanger the maintenance of international peace and security.

According to Article 35, any member of the United Nations may bring any dispute, or any situation of the nature referred to in Article 34, to the attention of the Security Council or of the General Assembly. Even a state which is not a member of the United Nations may bring to the attention of the Security Council or of the General Assembly any dispute to which it is a party if it accepts in advance, for the purposes of the dispute, the obligations of pacific settlement provided in the present Charter. This article also sets restrictions on the proceedings of the General Assembly in respect of matters brought to its attention under this Article. These will be subject to the provisions of Articles 11 and 12 of the Charter.

Article 36 empowers the Security Council to, at any stage of a dispute of the nature referred to in Article 33 or of a situation of like nature, recommend appropriate procedures or methods of adjustment. Further, the Security Council has to take into consideration any procedures for the settlement of the dispute, which have already been adopted by the parties. In making recommendations under this Article, the Security Council should also take into consideration that legal disputes must, as a general rule be referred by the parties to the International Court of Justice in accordance with the provisions of the Statute of the Court.

If the parties to a dispute of the nature referred to in Article 33 fail to settle it by the means indicated in that Article, they shall refer it to the Security Council under Article 37 and, if the Security Council deems that the continuance of the dispute is in fact likely to endanger the maintenance of international peace and security, it shall decide whether to take action under Article 36 or to recommend such terms of settlement as it may consider appropriate.

Article 38 stipulates that without prejudice to the provisions of Articles 33–37, the Security Council may, if all the parties to any dispute so request, make recommendations to the parties with a view to a pacific settlement of the dispute.

Under CHAPTER VII regarding action with respect to threats to peace, breaches of peace, and acts of aggression, the Security Council under Article 39 shall determine the existence of any threat to peace, breach of peace, or act of aggression, and shall make recommendations, or decide what measures shall be taken in accordance with Articles 41 and 42, to maintain or restore international peace and security.

Under Article 40, in order to prevent an aggravation of the situation, the Security Council may, before making the recommendations or deciding upon the measures provided for in Article 39, call upon the parties concerned to comply with such provisional measures as it deems necessary or desirable. Such provisional measures shall be without prejudice to the rights, claims, or position of the parties concerned. The Security Council shall duly take account of failure to comply with such provisional measures.

Articles 41 and 42 include clauses involving enforcement measures, which the Security Council can undertake, as it deems necessary or desirable.

Under Article 41, the Security Council may decide what measures, not involving the use of armed force, are to be employed to give effect to its decisions, and it may call upon the members of the United Nations to apply such measures. These may include complete or partial interruption of economic relations and of rail, sea, air, postal, telegraphic, radio and other means of communication, and the severance of diplomatic relations. If these actions prove to be inadequate, then under Article 42 the Security Council may consider that it may take such action by air, sea, or land forces, as may be necessary to maintain or restore international peace and security. Such action may include demonstrations, blockade and other operations by air, sea or land forces of the members of the United Nations. In compliance with Article 43, all members of the United Nations, in order to contribute to the maintenance of international peace and security, should undertake to make available to the Security Council, on its call and in accordance with a special agreement or agreements, armed forces, assistance and facilities, including rights of passage, necessary for the purpose of maintaining international peace and security. Article 46 provides that plans for the application of armed force shall be made by the Security Council with the assistance of the Military Staff Committee which shall be established under Article 47 to advise and assist the Security Council on all questions relating to the Security Council's military requirements for the maintenance of international peace and security, the employment and command of forces placed at its disposal, the regulation of armaments, and possible disarmament.

The Military Staff Committee under the Security Council shall consist of the Chiefs of Staff of the permanent members of the Security Council or their representatives. Any member of the United Nations not permanently represented on the Committee shall be invited by the Committee to be associated with it when the efficient discharge of the Committee's responsibilities requires the participation of that member in its work. The Military Staff Committee shall be responsible for the strategic direction of any armed forces placed at the disposal of the Security Council. Questions relating to the command of such forces shall be worked out subsequently. The Committee, with the authorization of the

Security Council and after consultation with appropriate regional agencies, may establish regional sub-committees.

Exceptions prevail to these functions of Security Council relating to peace and security. According to Article 51, nothing in the present Charter shall impair the inherent right of individual or collective self-defence if an armed attack occurs against a member of the United Nations, until the Security Council has taken measures necessary to maintain international peace and security. The measures taken by members in the exercise of this right of self-defence shall be immediately reported to the Security Council and shall not in any way affect the authority and responsibility of the Security Council, under the present Charter, to take at any time such action as it deems necessary in order to maintain or restore international peace and security. Another exception is provided under Article 53, which specifies that the Security Council shall, where appropriate, utilize such regional arrangements or agencies for enforcement action under its authority. But no enforcement action shall be taken under regional arrangements or by regional agencies without the authorization of the Security Council, with the exception of measures against any enemy state (as defined in paragraph 2 of this Article).

When a complaint concerning a threat to peace is brought before it, the Council's first action is usually to recommend to the parties to try to reach an agreement by peaceful means. In some cases, the Council itself undertakes investigation and mediation. It may appoint special representatives or request the Secretary-General to do so or to use his good offices. It may set forth principles for a peaceful settlement.

When a dispute leads to full-scale conflict, the Council's first concern is to bring it to an end as soon as possible. On many occasions, the Council has issued ceasefire directives which have been instrumental in preventing wider hostilities. It also sends United Nations peacekeeping forces to help reduce tensions in troubled areas, keep opposing forces apart and create calm conditions in which peaceful settlements may be sought. The Council may decide on enforcement measures, economic sanctions (such as trade embargoes), or collective military action.

Other Functions

Among other functions, the Security Council:

1. Has the power to recommend the name of Secretary-General before he can be appointed by the General Assembly.

2. Shares the power of election of judges of the International Court of Justice with the General Assembly.

3. Is authorized by Article 26 to take necessary measures for arms control and disarmament.

4. Has been vested with powers regarding the amendment of the Charter by Article 108 which states that the amendment proposal must be ratified by the five permanent members.

5. Has the power of granting admission of new members to the UN and approve expulsion of members for violation of the principles of the UN.

Evaluation

Though limited in membership and with sweeping powers to permanent members, the Security Council is the most powerful of all organs of the United Nations. It is the only organ which has the authority to make decisions that are binding and take collective actions to restore international peace and security. However, the *veto* power is the most paralyzing of all the provisions and has led to a number of deadlocks over the years especially during the Cold War years. One such deadlock over the Korean issue arising from the superpower rivalry had prompted the General Assembly to adopt the Uniting for Peace Resolution (UPR) in order to take action whenever the Security Council stands paralyzed. Acting under UPR (1950), the General Assembly usurped the power of Security Council and took action in Korea (1950–1953) and Congo (1960–1964), and virtually bypassed the Security Council.

However, from the late 60s, when the Security Council again resumed its powers and functions, it aptly handled the crises in CONGO (ONUC), the Cuban Missile Crisis (1962), the Cyprus Question (1964), the Rhodesian Embargo Issue (1968), the Arab–Israeli War (1967 and 1973), the Indo–Pak War (1971), the South Africa and Cambodia issues and the later operations. However, post-Cold War and the disintegration of the Soviet Union have left the Security Council as a mere pawn in the hands of the United States which is today the only superpower. For example, the Gulf Crises of 1991 and 2003 show outright assertion of the sole superpower in the world. The action to be undertaken by the Security Council now rests more on the consideration of the Big-Five, especially the US, and much depends on the power relationship of the permanent-5 and their relationship with the non-permanent members. Therefore, the Security Council has failed to deliver its best. Demand is there for an expansion and democratization of the organ and some emerging powers like India, Brazil, Germany and Japan, along with some other claimants desire to become permanent members of the Security Council.[12] Nevertheless, the importance of Security Council in the maintenance of international peace and security cannot be underestimated.

THE UN SECRETARIAT AND THE SECRETARY-GENERAL

Secretary-General

At Dumbarton Oaks, this particular post was given prime importance and the Secretary-General was described as the "Chief Administrative Officer of the UN". He was invested with greater power by the Charter as compared with the league Covenant which restricted the powers of the Secretary-General to the point that "he shall act in such capacity at all meetings of the Assembly and Council". But the Preparatory Commission at San Francisco went further and established the importance of the Secretary-General by highlighting the executive role as a "quite special right, which goes beyond any power previously accorded to the head of an international organization".

Appointment

Chapter XV of the Charter contains provisions relating to the powers and functions of the Secretary-General and his Secretariat. Article 97 states that the Secretariat shall comprise a Secretary-General and such staff as the Organization may require. The Secretary-General shall be appointed by the General Assembly on the recommendation of the Security Council. He shall be the Chief Administrative Officer of the Organization. The term of office has not been specified by the Charter but a General Assembly resolution fixed the term for five years with the provision of reappointment also.

Functions and Powers

Combining in himself the roles of a diplomat, advocate, civil servant and CEO, the Secretary-General is a symbol of the United Nations' ideals and a spokesman for the interests of the world's peoples, in particular the poor and the vulnerable among them. The current Secretary-General, and the eighth occupant of the post, is Mr. Ban Ki-moon of the Republic of Korea (South Korea), who took office on 1 January 2007.

Being the Chief Administrative Officer of the UN, he plays a pivotal role in the overall administration of the UN. From being the chief channel of communication between the UN members and the organs of the UN to being the coordinator of the UN bodies, he has a definite role in determining the direction of the activities of the UN in all its aspects.

Article 98 authorizes the Secretary-General to act in that capacity in all the meetings of the General Assembly, the Security Council, the Economic and Social Council and the Trusteeship Council. It also authorizes him to perform such other functions as are entrusted to him by these organs. This executive function has been entrusted to him to ensure the smooth working of the UN.

The Secretary-General is responsible for the day-to-day functioning of the UN. This includes attendance at sessions of the United Nations bodies, consultations with world leaders, government officials and others, and worldwide travel intended to keep him in touch with the member states and their people, and also keep him informed about the vast array of issues of international concern that top organization's agenda. Further, the Secretary-General has to submit an annual report to the General Assembly on the work of the Organization which is an exhaustive record of all the activities of the Organization. The report also contains some important proposals for better functioning of the UN, such as the Agenda for Peace prepared by Boutros Boutros-Ghali, the proposals for the reform of the UN and revision of the Charter by Kofi Annan. The Secretary-General, therefore, is entrusted to make the widest possible recommendations to the Assembly, but he has also acquired, by the Assembly's Rules of Procedure, the right to put an item on the Assembly's draft agenda and, since 1947, the right "at any time [to] make either oral or written statements to the General Assembly concerning any question under consideration by it".

The Secretary-General is also the Chairman of the Administrative Committee on Coordination (ACC), which brings together the Executive Heads of all UN funds, programmes and specialized agencies twice a year for further coordination and cooperation in the entire range of substantive and management issues facing the United Nations System.

In financial matters, the Secretary-General performs the important task of preparing the annual budget for approval by the General Assembly and determines the direction in which the funds will be allocated for different organs of the UN. He is also responsible for collecting the contribution from the member states and also controls the expenditure of the organs and specialized agencies of the UN.

Under Article 101, the Secretary-General, being the head of the Secretariat, appoints the staff under regulations established by the General Assembly. And it is his prime responsibility to secure the highest standards of efficiency, competence, and integrity. Besides these administrative functions, he has also been assigned a vital political function under Article 99, which states that the Secretary-General may bring to the attention of the Security Council any matter which, in his opinion, may threaten the maintenance of international peace and security. How the Secretary-General would exercise this function is left to the discretion of the incumbent. He should act as a conscience keeper for the whole world as, under Article 35, he has been conferred the status equivalent to a member state or that of the General Assembly. The most important thing to be remembered is that, under Article 100, the Secretary-General has to be politically neutral.

The Secretary-General represents the UN in all its negotiations and interactions with the member and non-member states and other international bodies. The Report of the Preparatory Committee upheld that "The Secretary-General more than anyone else will stand for the UN as a whole. In the eyes of the world, no less than in the eyes of his own staff, he must embody the principles and ideals of the Charter".[13]

One of the most vital roles played by the Secretary-General is the use of his 'good offices'—steps taken publicly and in private, drawing upon his independence, impartiality and integrity—to prevent international disputes from arising, escalating or spreading. Each Secretary-General also defines his role within the context of his particular time in office.

The Secretary-Generals of the UN till date are:

- Trygve Lie (Norway), from February 1946 until his resignation in November 1952

- Dag Hammarskjöld (Sweden), from April 1953 till his death in a plane crash near Nodola, Northern Rhodesia (now Zambia) in September 1961
- U Thant (Burma, now Myanmar), from November 1961, appointed as acting Secretary-General and formally from November 1962 to December 1971
- Kurt Waldheim (Austria), from January 1972 to December 1981
- Javier Pèrez de Cuèllar (Peru), from January 1982 to December 1991
- Boutros Boutros-Ghali (Egypt), from January 1992 to December 1996
- Kofi Annan (Ghana), from 1997 to December 2006
- Ban Ki-moon of the Republic of Korea (South Korea), who took office on 1 January 2007.

Secretariat

In the performance of his duties in the spirit of the Charter, the Secretary-General, is assisted by a staff who are expected to exhibit the highest standards of efficiency, competence, and integrity. He makes the necessary appointments according to the regulations established by the General Assembly under Article 101[1]. Under Article 101[2], appropriate staff shall be permanently assigned to the Economic and Social Council, the Trusteeship Council and, as required, to other organs of the United Nations. All these staff form part of the Secretariat. The prime consideration is placed in the employment of the staff and in the determination of the conditions of service to secure the highest standards of efficiency, competence, and integrity. Due regard shall be paid to the importance of recruiting the staff on as wide a geographical basis as possible.

The staff of the Secretariat comprise linguists, economists, editors, social scientists, legal experts, experts in the various fields of UN activities, librarians, journalists, statisticians, broadcasters, personnel officers, administrators, security officers, besides the clerical and other staff.

Article 100 upholds the international character of the Secretariat. To ward off the national pressures corroding the concept of international loyalty of an international civil service, during the San Francisco Conference (to which mention has already been made), there was a proposal for constituting an independent and internationally responsible Secretariat. Therefore, Charter under Article 100[1] explicitly states that "in the performance of their duties the Secretary-General and the staff shall not seek or receive instructions from any government or from any other authority external to the Organization. They shall refrain from any action which might reflect on their position as international officials responsible only to the Organization". It also contains a plea that each member of the United Nations should undertake to respect the exclusively international character of the responsibilities of the Secretary-General and the staff, and not to seek to influence them in the discharge of their responsibilities.

Duties of the Secretariat

Nicholas[5] points out to the six-fold functions of the Secretariat. The *first* function is similar to the role of a parliamentary clerk and even much wider in scope as the UN requires a wide range of servicing. This function includes interpretation, translation and preparation of drafts, keeping records of proceedings, furnishing documentation and library facilities as well as legal and procedural advice to the General Assembly, the Security Council, the ECOSOC and their sub-committees.

The *second function* is what is generally referred to as the "information function" of the Secretariat. The collection, ordering and providing of information to the centres, which require them, is one of the greatest services rendered by the Secretariat. This enables the delegates, committees and commissions to have access to a whole range of data, technical and others, for the proper discharge of their functions. In other words, it acts as a storehouse of information.

Third, the technical assistance provided by the Secretariat is a part of the executive functions that it performs. It started with the point-4 programme and turned into the Expanded Technical Assistance Programme.

The *fourth function* entails partly the security and partly the administrative function related to transport, maintenance and communication and overall security of the UN Commissions in the field.

The *fifth function*, which involves the overall supervision of the international bureaucracy, is performed by the Secretariat and ranges from recruitment, allocation of functions, to performance assessment of its staff.

Finally the Secretariat performs certain diplomatic and political functions. The UN officials sometimes have to think of alternative courses of action by considering the world public opinion and also pressures of national sentiments and national forces when they persuade and negotiate in crisis situations.[14]

Evaluation

The office of the Secretary-General is quite an important one. The role of the Secretary-General is vital to the functioning of the United Nations system. An analysis of the role played by the different Secretaries-General would reveal that there has sometimes been an increase in prestige of the office while sometimes the office has been sidetracked by major powers.

Trygve Lie (Norway), the first Secretary-General of the United Nations, was a dynamic and energetic person and wanted to ensure a more active role of the Unied Nations in the maintenance of international peace and security. He acted by using his rights under Article 99 on the Spanish and Iranian questions at a time when the big powers were at loggerheads.[15] However, given his background as a former politician, he nurtured strong views on many subjects and made no attempt to conceal them. Therefore, his actions in the case of the Korean War won him both acclaim from some quarters and wrath from the

Soviet Union. His support for the decision of the Security Council to defend South Korea in the wake of an attack by North Korea in June 1950, led to the accusations by the Soviet Union and her allies that the Secretary-General was acting on behalf of the United States and its friends against the Communist states, and they vetoed his nomination for a further term in February 1951. Though the veto was later revoked and he continued his office without a re-election, ultimately he earned the undying criticisms of the USA too for allowing the 'pro-Communist' Americans to work in the Secretariat. Lie finally resigned at the end of 1952 before his extended term expired.[16]

Dag Hammarskjöld (Sweden), the second Secretary-General, was more cautious in his approach. He embarked on what came to be known as "preventive diplomacy" through conciliation and good offices in many situations. He proved his worth in his conciliatory endeavours using his good offices and personal contact with Zhou En-lai (1898–1976), the Chinese Premier, and secured the release of US airmen from China who were imprisoned there in 1955. Thereafter, he played a commending role in the Suez Crisis and the Lebanon Crisis followed by the organization of an observer force in Lebanon in 1958. In 1960, during the Congo Crisis, Dag invoked the powers of the Secretary-General under Article 99 of the Charter and requested a meeting of the Security Council and creation of ONUC and recommended the withdrawal of Belgian troops from Congo. But these were accepted by the Security Council and he was authorized to provide military assistance as he felt necessary. However, the growing role of the Secretary-General was not liked by the Soviet Union and they came up with a proposal known as the **Troika Plan** whereby, instead of one Secretary-General, there would be three Secretaries-General—one from a Western, another from a Communist, and yet another from a neutral country. However, Dag Hammarskjöld died in a plane crash on his way to a personal visit to Tsombe **(President of Katanga)** in his bid to resolve the Congo crisis.

U Thant (Burma, now Myanmar), succeeded Dag as the third Secretary-General. He played a similar kind of role as that of Dag and tried to expand the concept of preventive diplomacy. He played a crucial role during the Cuban Missile Crisis. He also played an effective role in the Congo and Cyprus crises. However, his Vietnam venture could not succeed due to American intransigence and he faced criticisms for removal of UN peacekeeping forces from Sinai just before the Six-day War on the request of Nasser of Egypt.[17] Still, under his leadership, the office of the Secretary-General gained prestige and he tried to act sincerely to further the purposes and principles of the United Nations.

Kurt Waldheim (Austria), the fourth Secretary-General, played great diplomatic role in a number of crisis situations. He presided over the talks between the Greek and Turkish communities in Cyprus, toured Middle East extensively to promote chances of settlement, and helped the United Nations to undertake practical activities like disaster relief, protecting the international environment, running a world university and administering the deep seabed.[18]

Javier Pèrez de Cuèllar (Peru), the fifth Secretary-General, understood the nerves of the office well as he had worked as the Under Secretary-General of the UN. He undertook some significant peacekeeping operations in Namibia, El Salvador and Cambodia. The waning of the Cold War too helped him to dispense his duties in a proper way. He introduced the concept of quiet diplomacy among the P-5 members of the Security Council to prepare the Council to take an agreed course of action on outstanding issues. Thus, Pèrez de Cuèllar was able to strike peace agreements between contending parties in Namibia, Angola, Mozambique, Nicaragua, El Salvador and Cambodia, and deploy UN peacekeeping forces to supervise elections, disarm military units, and check human rights violations. But during the Gulf Crisis of 1991, the position of the Secretary-General got undermined as the US-led forces overstepped their mandate and in many cases the United States did not keep him fully informed.

Boutros Boutros-Ghali (Egypt), the sixth Secretary-General played an important role in several crisis situations around the world in Somalia, Bosnia and Hebron, among the few. But the most significant contribution he made, using his intellectual excellence, was the 52-page "Agenda for Peace" proposing several reforms for making the United Nations more active and functioning.

Kofi Annan (Ghana), the seventh Secretary-General, tried to make the United Nations more active in facing the crises in the post-Cold War era. The American war on terror against Iraq and Afghanistan created a tight situation for the United Nations as a whole and especially the Secretary-General. However, the post-War reconstruction programme earned him praises. But he was accused of corruption relating to the Oil for Food Programme that tarnished the image of his office.

Ban Ki-Moon of the Republic of Korea, took over the office on 1 January 2007 as the eighth Secretary-General. He faced an alarming situation in the tussle between Russia and Georgia over South Ossetia and the increasing violence there. In the face of strong demand for revamping the United Nations and more positive actions of the UN in crisis situations places him in a tough position where every move of his has to take into consideration the post-Cold War international scenario, the presence of the sole superpower, and demands of the developing countries as well as those of the rest of the world community. Ban Ki-Moon has been voted unanimously for a second five year term as the Secretary General of the UN. The second term began from 1 January 2012 and will continue till 31 December 2016. This decision followed a recommendation by members of the Security Council which made Ban the eighth person to be re-appointed and serve a second term.

Therefore, it becomes quite clear that the efficacy of the office of the Secretary-General depends on the personality of the person occupying the office, the current international scenario and, of course, the political equation among the major international players themselves and their relationship with the Secretary-General.[19]

THE ECONOMIC AND SOCIAL COUNCIL

Composition

Chapter X, Article 61 specifies the guidelines for composition of the Economic and Social Council (ECOSOC). It states that the Council shall consist of 54 members of the United Nations elected by the General Assembly. Subject to the provisions of paragraph 3, 18 members of the Council shall be elected each year for a term of three years. A retiring member shall be eligible for immediate re-election. The ECOSOC is composed of 18 members. Later the number increased to 27 and at present it stands at 54. Each member of the Economic and Social Council shall have one representative.

According to Article 68, ECOSOC shall set up commissions in economic and social fields and for the promotion of human rights, and such other commissions as may be required for the performance of its functions. Article 69 also confers upon the ECOSOC the power to invite any member of the United Nations to participate, without vote, in its deliberations on any matter of particular concern to that member. Article 70 states that the Economic and Social Council may make arrangements for representatives of the specialized agencies to participate, without vote, in its deliberations and in those of the commissions established by it, and for its representatives to participate in the deliberations of the specialized agencies.

Voting

Article 67 stipulates that each member of the Economic and Social Council shall have one vote. Decisions of the Council shall be made by a majority of the members present and voting.

Article 72 states that the Economic and Social Council shall adopt its own rules of procedure, including the method of selecting its President. The Council shall meet as required in accordance with its rules, which shall include provision for the convening of meetings on the request of a majority of its members.

Functions and Powers

Article 62 states that the Economic and Social Council may:

1. Make or initiate studies and reports with respect to international economic, social, cultural, educational, health, and related matters and Make recommendations with respect to any such matters to the General Assembly to the members of the United Nations, and to the specialized agencies concerned.

2. Make recommendations for the purpose of promoting respect for, and observance of, human rights and fundamental freedoms for all.

3. Prepare draft conventions for submission to the General Assembly, with respect to matters falling within its competence.

4. Call, in accordance with the rules prescribed by the United Nations, international conferences on matters falling within its competence.

Under Article 63, the Council may enter into agreements with any of the agencies referred to in Article 57, defining the terms on which the agency concerned shall be brought into relationship with the United Nations. Such agreements shall be subject to approval by the General Assembly. It may also coordinate the activities of the specialized agencies through consultation with, and recommendations to, such agencies and through recommendations to the General Assembly and to the members of the United Nations.

According to Article 64 the Council may take appropriate steps to obtain regular reports from the specialized agencies. It may make arrangements with the members of the United Nations and with the specialized agencies to obtain reports on the steps taken to give effect to its own recommendations and to recommendations on matters falling within its competence made by the General Assembly. It may also communicate its observations on these reports to the General Assembly.

Article 65 specifies that the Council may furnish information to the Security Council and shall assist the Security Council upon its request.

Article 66 also specifies that the Council shall perform such functions falling within its competence in connection with the carrying out of the recommendations of the General Assembly. It may also, with the approval of the General Assembly, perform services at the request of the members of the United Nations and at the request of the specialized agencies. It shall also perform such other functions as are specified elsewhere in the present Charter or as may be assigned to it by the General Assembly.

Under Article 71 the Council may make suitable arrangements for consultation with non-governmental organizations, which are concerned with matters within its competence. Such arrangements may be made with international organizations and, where appropriate, with national organizations after consultation with the member of the United Nations concerned.

The Council has been assigned certain new functions as well. At the 2005 World Summit, Heads of States and Governments mandated the Council to hold Annual Ministerial Reviews (AMR) to assess progress in achieving the internationally agreed development goals (IADGs) arising out of the major conferences and summits and a biennial Development Cooperation Forum (DCF) to enhance the coherence and effectiveness of activities of different development partners.

The Council works through several commissions, committees and other subsidiary bodies. The *Functional Commissions* of the Council are the:

1. Statistical Commission
2. Commission on Populations and Development
3. Commission for Social Development
4. Commission on the Status of Women
5. Commission on Narcotic Drugs
6. Commission on Crime Prevention and Criminal Justices
7. Commission on Science and Technology for Development
8. Commission on Sustainable Development

There are five *Regional Commissions* of the Council such as the:

1. Economic Commission for Africa (ECA)
2. Economic and Social Commission for Asia and the Pacific (ESCAP)
3. Economic Commission for Europe (ECE)
4. Economic Commission for Latin America and the Caribbean (ECLAC)
5. Economic and Social Commission for Western Asia (ESCWA)

The *Standing Committees* of the Council are the:

1. Committee for Programme and Coordination
2. Committee on Non-Governmental Organizations
3. Committee on Negotiations with Inter-Governmental Agencies
4. Committee for Natural Resources
5. Committee for Transnational Corporations
6. Committee on Human Settlement.

There are also certain ad-hoc bodies like the Ad hoc Open-ended Inter-Governmental Group of Experts on Energy and Sustainable Development and Ad Hoc Open-ended Working Group on Informatics.

There are certain expert bodies composed of governmental experts such as the Committee of Experts on the Transport of Dangerous Goods and on the Globally Harmonized System of Classification and Labelling of Chemicals and United Nations Group of Experts on Geographical Names.

Besides, there are expert bodies composed of members serving in their personal capacity, like the Committee of Experts on Public Administration, the Committee on Economic, Social and Cultural Rights, and others.

Other related bodies of the Council include the International Narcotics Control Board and the Board of Trustees of the International Research and Training Institute for the Advancement of Women.

Evaluation

Though the Economic and Social Council was created to fulfill the aspirations of the peoples of the United Nations in many cases it has been seen that the

Council has been severely impaired and limited to discussion and recommendation. As in the case of other organs, the Council is also not free from big power politics. Therefore, it has not been able to deliver the goods to the people across the world. Therefore, from time to time, there have been suggestions for reforms. In 1969, a laudable reform effort was made by Sir Robert Jackson and he recommended a creation of a strong central coordinating organization and restructuring of UNDP. In 1974, another effort was made when a resolution was adopted during the Special Session of the General Assembly where the member states asked the Secretary-General to appoint a group of high-level experts to propose structural changes in the United Nations to enable it to deal with matters of international economic cooperation. The group of high-level of experts were soon formed by the Secretary-General and it made many bold recommendations such as clarification of the responsibilities of the Council vis-à-vis the General Assembly and assignment of new responsibilities for the Council in the operational area. The recent proposals came from the former Secretary-General, Kofi Annan in his report entitled *In Larger Freedom*. He made several proposals like the Council arranging for annual ministerial level assessments of progress towards agreed development goals, especially the Millennium Development Goals (MDG).

The Council should also serve as a high-level development cooperation forum. Further, the Council should institutionalize its work in post-conflict management by working with Peacebuilding Commission and various others. Much introspection and reform not in the form of proposals but concrete measures, are needed to increase the efficacy of ECOSOC.

THE TRUSTEESHIP COUNCIL

Chapter XII of the Charter enumerates the provisions relating to the International Trusteeship system and Chapter XIII contains provisions related to the composition and functions of the Trusteeship Council.

Article 76 embodies the basic objectives of the **Trusteeship system** as to:

- Further international peace and security.

- Promote the political, economic, social, and educational advancement of the inhabitants of the trust territories, and their progressive development towards self-government or independence as may be appropriate to the particular circumstances of each territory and its peoples and the freely expressed wishes of the peoples concerned, and as may be provided by the terms of each trusteeship agreement.

- Encourage respect for human rights and for fundamental freedoms for all without distinction as to race, sex, language, or religion, and to encourage recognition of the interdependence of the peoples of the world.

- Ensure equal treatment in social, economic, and commercial matters for all members of the United Nations and their nationals, and also equal treatment for the latter in the administration of justice, without prejudice to the attainment of the foregoing objectives and subject to the provisions of Article 80.

Article 77 specifies the applicability of the Trusteeship system. It says:

1. The trusteeship system shall apply to such territories in the following categories as may be placed there by means of trusteeship agreements:

   (a) Territories now held under mandate

   (b) Territories which may be detached from the enemy states as a result of the Second World War

   (c) Territories voluntarily placed under the system by states responsible for their administration.

Further, it will be a matter for subsequent agreement as to which territories in the foregoing categories will be brought under the trusteeship system and on what terms.

Article 78 enumerates that the trusteeship system shall not apply to territories which have become members of the United Nations, relationship among which shall be based on respect for the principle of sovereign equality.

Article 83 specifies matters relating to the functions of the trusteeship system. It says that all functions of the United Nations relating to strategic areas, including the approval of the terms of the trusteeship agreements and of their alteration or amendment, shall be exercised by the Security Council. Further, the Security Council shall, subject to the provisions of the trusteeship agreements and without prejudice to security considerations, avail itself of the assistance of the Trusteeship Council to perform those functions of the United Nations under the trusteeship system relating to political, economic, social and educational matters in the strategic areas.

Article 85 states that the functions of the United Nations with regard to trusteeship agreements for all areas, not designated as strategic, including the approval of the terms of the trusteeship agreements and of their alteration or amendment, shall be exercised by the General Assembly. Further, the Trusteeship Council, operating under the authority of the General Assembly, shall assist the General Assembly in carrying out these functions.

CHAPTER XIII contains the provisions relating to the constitution of the **Trusteeship Council.**

Composition

Article 86 states that the Trusteeship Council shall consist of the following members of the United Nations:

   (a) Those members administering the trust territories.

   (b) Those members mentioned by name in Article 23 and are not administering the trust territories.

(c) As many other members elected for three-year terms by the General Assembly as may be necessary to ensure that the total number of members of the Trusteeship Council is equally divided between those members of the United Nations who administer trust territories and those who do not.

It also states that each member of the Trusteeship Council shall designate one specially qualified person to represent it in the Council.

Functions and Powers

Under Article 87, the General Assembly and, under its authority, the Trusteeship Council, in carrying out their functions, may:

1. Consider reports submitted by the administering authority.
2. Accept petitions and examine them in consultation with the administering authority.
3. Provide for periodic visits to the respective trust territories at times agreed upon with the administering authority.
4. Take these and other actions in conformity with the terms of the trusteeship agreements.

Voting

Article 89 states that each member of the Trusteeship Council shall have one vote and that the decisions of the Trusteeship Council shall be made by a majority of the members present and voting.

Regarding the procedure of the Trusteeship Council, Article 90 enumerates that the Trusteeship Council shall adopt its own rules of procedure, including the method of selecting its President and that the Trusteeship Council shall meet as required in accordance with its rules, which shall include provision for the convening of meetings on the request of a majority of its members. Article 91 holds that the Trusteeship Council shall, when appropriate, avail itself of the assistance of the Economic and Social Council and of the specialized agencies in regard to matters with which they are respectively concerned.

Evaluation

It should be noted that most of the trust territories have gained independence and the burden of administering the trust territories has been reduced to a great extent. By 1975, 10 out of 11 Trust territories had gained independence and, after 1975, only one Trust territory remained in the pacific islands with the United States as the trustee. Finally, when this trust territory also gained independence in 1994, the Council was left without any work. The composition also changed with the council now consisting of only the five permanent members of the Security Council. There have been proposals from different corners to eliminate the organ, in accordance with Article 108 of the Charter (amendment of the Charter).

THE INTERNATIONAL COURT OF JUSTICE

The International Court of Justice (ICJ) is the principal judicial organ of the United Nations Organization (UNO). It was established in June 1945 by the Charter of the United Nations and began its work in April 1946. The seat of the Court is at The Peace Palace in The Hague (Netherlands).

The Court's role is to settle, in accordance with international law, legal disputes submitted to it by the states and to give advisory opinions on legal questions referred to it by authorized United Nations organs and specialized agencies.

Chapter XIV of the Charter embodies the provisions relating to the composition and functions of the International Court of Justice. Article 92 specifies that the ICJ shall function in accordance with the Annexed Statute, which is based on the Statute of the Permanent Court of International Justice (PCIJ) and forms an integral part of the present Charter.

Membership

Article 93 stipulates that all members of the United Nations are *ipso facto* parties to the Statute of the International Court of Justice. It also states that a state, which is not a member of the United Nations, may become a party to the Statute of the International Court of Justice on conditions to be determined in each case by the General Assembly upon the recommendation of the Security Council.

Under Article 95, nothing in the present Charter shall prevent members of the United Nations from entrusting the solution of their differences to other tribunals by virtue of agreements already in existence or which may be concluded in the future.

Composition

The ICJ is composed of fifteen judges elected for a term of nine years by the concurrent vote of the UNGA and the Security Council. These organs vote simultaneously but separately and in order to get elected, a candidate has to secure maximum votes from both the bodies.

Judges must be elected from among persons of high moral character, who possess the qualifications required in their respective countries for appointment to the highest judicial offices, or are jurisconsults of recognized competence in international law.

Once elected, a member of the Court is a delegate, neither of the government of his own country nor of that of any other state. The members of the Court are independent judges, before taking up their duties, is to make a solemn declaration in open court that they will exercise their powers impartially and conscientiously. In order to guarantee this independence, no member of the Court can be dismissed unless, in the unanimous opinion of the other members, he no longer fulfils the required conditions.

A member of the Court, when engaged in the business of the Court, enjoys privileges and immunities comparable with those of the head of a diplomatic mission. Each member of the Court receives an annual salary with a special supplementary allowance for the President and, on leaving the Court, they receive annual pensions after serving a nine-year term in office.

The Court elects its own President and Vice-President every three years by secret ballot. The President presides at all meetings of the Court and he directs its work and supervises its administration, with the assistance of a Budgetary and Administrative Committee and of various other committees, all composed of members of the Court. During deliberations, the President has a casting vote in the event of votes being equally divided.

The Vice-President replaces the President in his absence, in the event of his inability to exercise his duties, or in the event of a vacancy in the presidency. For this purpose he receives a daily allowance. In the absence of the Vice-President, this role devolves on a senior judge.

Jurisdiction

The Statute confers three types of jurisdiction upon the Court:

- Voluntary
- Compulsory
- Advisory

The Court usually entertains those cases that involve legal disputes between states, which are submitted by them for resolution and also requests for advisory opinions on legal questions referred to the ICJ by the United Nations organs and its specialized agencies.

Voluntary Jurisdiction

The Court on many occasions has assumed jurisdiction on the consent of the parties to any dispute and both the PCIJ and ICJ have accepted the limits of such jurisdiction. The jurisdiction will be extended to that extent which will be acceptable to the state parties to the disputes. States which may use the ICJ fall into three categories:

1. All states which have signed the Charter are automatically parties to the Statute.

2. States which are not members of the UN can avail themselves of the Court's adjudication in terms fixed by the General Assembly on recommendation of the Security Council. For instance, Switzerland in 1948 and Liechtenstein in 1950 had access to the Court this way.

3. States, not parties to the Court's Statute, can also have recourse to the Court on conditions laid down by the Security Council. As in the *Corfu Channel Case* (1948–1949), Albania appeared before the Court, which was a non-member of the UN at that time.[20]

Therefore, the Court's jurisdiction extends only to those cases, which the parties refer to it. Though the UN Charter endeavours for pacific settlement for disputes, it does not make it obligatory for members to seek the assistance of the Court in all cases of disputes. Thus, the jurisdiction of the Court is derived from the consent of the parties to a dispute, which the Court never tries to overreach or overstep.

Compulsory Jurisdiction

In the exercise of this jurisdiction, Article 36 of the Statute (para 1) states that the jurisdiction of the Court comprises all cases which the parties refer to it. Such cases normally come before the Court by notification to the Registry by an agreement, known as a *special agreement* and concluded by the parties especially for this purpose.

The states which are parties to the present Statute may at any time declare that they recognize as compulsory, *ipso facto* and without special agreement, in relation to any other state accepting the same obligation, the jurisdiction of the Court regarding all disputes concerning: (a) the interpretation of a treaty; (b) any question of international law; (c) the existence of any fact which, if established would constitute a breach of an international obligation; (d) the nature or extent of the reparation to be made for the breach of an international obligation.

Article 36 (para 6) of the Statute provides that, in the event of a dispute as to whether the Court has jurisdiction, the matter shall be settled by the decision of the Court. There is also the 'Optional Clause' of this Article under which the terms of compulsory jurisdiction may belong to the Court through voluntary declaration by the member states permitting in certain fields and limiting it in other cases the exercise of such jurisdiction of the Court.[21]

Advisory Jurisdiction

Advisory jurisdiction of the ICJ is exercised when the United Nations General Assembly and the Security Council may request advisory opinions on "any legal question". Other United Nations organs and specialized agencies which have been authorized to seek advisory opinions can only do so with respect to "legal questions arising within the scope of their activities".

On receipt of a request for an advisory opinion, the Court holds the proceedings. The submission by parties may be in either the written or oral form (pleadings). It is rare, however, for the ICJ to allow international organizations, other than the one having requested the opinion, to participate in advisory proceedings. With respect to non-governmental international organizations, the only one ever authorized by the ICJ to furnish information did not in the end, do so (International Status of South West Africa). The Court has rejected all such requests by the private parties.

It is of the essence of such opinions that they are advisory, i.e., unlike the Court's judgements, they have no binding effect. The requesting organ, agency or organization, remains free to give the opinion by any means open to it; or, if it so wishes, it may not give the opinion at all. Certain instruments or regulations can, however, provide beforehand that an advisory opinion by the Court shall have binding force.

Although the advisory opinions of the Court do not have a binding effect yet the advisory opinions of the Court nevertheless carry great legal weight and moral authority. They are often an instrument of preventive diplomacy and have peacekeeping virtues. Advisory opinions also, in their way, contribute to the elucidation and development of international law and thereby to the strengthening of peaceful relations between the states.

According to Article 38 of the Statute, the Court in deciding the disputes submitted to it applies international conventions establishing rules recognized by the contesting states, international custom as evidence of a general practice accepted by the law, the general principles of law recognized by the nations, judicial decisions and the teachings of the most highly qualified publicists of the various nations, as a subsidiary means for determining the rule of law. The Court may decide *ex aequo et bono* (according to what is just and good, i.e., on the basis of practical fairness rather than strict law), but only if the parties concerned so agree.

All important decisions of the ICJ are taken by the majority of judges present. In case the votes are equally divided, the President has the right of his casting vote. Article 94 states that each member of the United Nations undertakes to comply with the decision of the ICJ in any case to which it is a party and, if any party to a case fails to perform the obligations incumbent upon it under a judgement rendered by the Court, the other party may have recourse to the Security Council, which may, if it deems necessary, make recommendations or decide upon measures to be taken to give effect to the judgement.

Article 96 upholds that the General Assembly or the Security Council may request the ICJ to give an advisory opinion on any legal question. Even other organs of the United Nations and specialized agencies, which may at any time be so authorized by the General Assembly, may also request advisory opinions of the Court on legal questions arising within the scope of their activities.[22]

Evaluation

The ICJ has made a great contribution with its legal opinion on contentious issues. It has given its judgements in several cases which have led to a rich discourse on jurisprudence. Its landmark judgements include inter alia, *The Corfu Channel Case* (1949), *Portugal's Right of Passage Case over Enclaves against India* (1960) and the *Case between El Salvador and Honduras*. The Court, in the Nicaragua case against USA (1984–1986), did not allow the case to be removed from its list as desired by USA and issued directions to the United States to refrain from making attacks against Nicaragua. The Court also had given its advisory opinion in several cases. But the problem with the ICJ is its limited operational sphere, coupled with the power politics between the powerful states. This became particularly evident during the Cold War. Even under the present circumstances, the Soviet Union and former Communist states of Europe refuse to submit their case before the ICJ. When a mini-war ensued between Georgia and Russia in 2007, Georgia had brought a case against Russia on the ground of violation of Convention on the Elimination of All Forms of Racial Discrimination (*Georgia* v. *Russia*). Russia was using all means to block the ICJ from dealing with the case.

There is also a belief that legal solutions cannot always be an acceptable one. As such, the activities of the Court are thwarted to a great extent. What can be said is that, despite several weaknesses, the ICJ has played a significant role in resolving disputes brought before it and has contributed to a steady development of international jurisprudence.

REVISION OF THE UN CHARTER

CHAPTER XVIII of the UN Charter contains provisions for the amendments of the Charter. Article 108 of the Charter states that Amendments to the present Charter shall come into force for all members of the United Nations when they have been adopted by a vote of two thirds of the members of the General Assembly and ratified in accordance with their respective constitutional processes by two-thirds of the members of the United Nations, including all the permanent members of the Security Council.

Article 109 states that:

1. A general conference of the members of the United Nations for the purpose of reviewing the present Charter may be held at a date and place to be fixed by a two-thirds vote of the members of the General Assembly and by a vote of any nine members of the Security Council. Each member of the United Nations shall have one vote in the conference.

2. Any alteration of the present Charter recommended by a two-thirds vote of the conference shall take effect when ratified in accordance with their respective constitutional processes by two-thirds of the

members of the United Nations, including all the permanent members of the Security Council.

3. If such a conference has not been held before the tenth annual session of the General Assembly following the coming into force of the UN Charter, the proposal to call such a conference shall be placed on the agenda of that session of the General Assembly, and the conference shall be held if so decided by a majority vote of the members of the General Assembly and by a vote of any seven members of the Security Council.

Besides these formal procedures enunciated in the Charter, several informal and formal changes have been brought to fore, such as in 1965 when the number of non-permanent members was raised, thereby increasing the original membership of the Security Council from 11 to 15. Likewise, the composition of Economic and Social Council was also expanded from 18 to 27 in 1965. Changes can be brought about by non-implementation of the textual provisions as in the case of Articles 43, 45, 47 regarding the constitution of a Military Staff Committee. Further, changes can be effected by institutional adaptation as was the case during the Korean Crisis of 1950 when there was a shift in balance from the Security Council to the General Assembly, *vide* the Uniting for Peace Resolution of 1950. Finally, change can also take place due to the growth of new customs, usages and interpretations. The General Assembly's concerted effort to deal with questions of colonialism and apartheid often led to a non-restrictive interpretation of the domestic jurisdiction clause (Article 2 para 7) on the face of severe reservations of colonial powers like France, Belgium, Netherlands, South Africa and Portugal. Judicial pronouncements in cases like *The Corfu Channel Case of 1948*, *Certain Expenses of the UN Case of 1963*, *South West Africa Case of 1971*, and the *Case of Reparation for Injuries Suffered in the Service of the UN of 1949* also have great impact in ushering change in the UN system. Treaties, agreements and conventions have also made necessary contribution to the UN system.[23]

REFORM OF THE UN

The UN, facing stiff challenges in the present century with its authority being questioned often and its existence being put under great pressure, needs a makeover and needs reinvention. A revitalized UN is the need of the hour. Given the unequal representative structure of the Security Council, the history of inaction of the Security Council during the Cold War, tussle between the P-5 members of the Security Council, the veto factor and, furthermore, hijacking of the Security Council in the post-Cold War era by the United States have undermined the prestige and importance of the UN. The US action in Serbia over the Kosovo issue followed by NATO bombing of Kosovo, US invasion of Iraq and Afghanistan bypassing the UN—all have given deadly blow to the credibility of this world organization. Even the Soviet occupation of Afghanistan in 1979 and bombing in Chechnya and Georgia have also proved the ineffectiveness of the UN system. Further, the allegation of corruption in the Oil-for-Food Programme tarnished the image of this world body. An Independent Inquiry Committee led by Paul Volcker, which unearthed the scandal, suggested measures to strengthen the UN. There were also accusations of sexual exploitation in peacekeeping missions and the Zeid Report entitled "A Comprehensive Strategy to Eliminate Future Sexual Exploitation and Abuse in United Nations Peacekeeping Operations" made recommendations for remedial measures. Reform of the world organization is the need of the hour. Many efforts have been made to revitalize this world body and some measures have also been implemented but the organization has miles to go before some actual structural adjustments can be introduced which would enable it to run effectively.

The Atlantic Council Working Group (1977) on the United Nations proposed a number of reform strategies to revitalize the working of the UN. Some of these strategies were:

- Strengthening of the machinery of pacific settlement of disputes.
- The Secretary-General to be allowed to use his full authority in international diplomacy.
- Development of international bodies and agencies for international management of common problems in the fields of trade, commodity pricing and stocks, monetary management conflict prevention, peacekeeping and the like.
- Effective development of relationship between the United Nations and non-governmental organizations.

Even the former Secretary-General, Boutros Boutros-Ghali submitted an *Agenda for Peace* in which he recognized problems in the UN's capacity to maintain world peace, for instance, resulting from shortages of funds, in particular for reconnaissance, planning and start-up of peace operations. Problems with recruitment and training of personnel proved severe constraints on the UN's ability to deploy its forces quickly, which can be crucial in the effective management of peace processes. Boutros Boutros-Ghali also highlighted the continuing damage to the credibility of the Security Council and the UN in general when the Council made decisions that could not be carried out because sufficient resources were not forthcoming; he urged that in future the availability of necessary troops and equipment be established before authorizing new operations.

Although the *Agenda* was initially received enthusiastically by the UN member states, this enthusiasm waned and many of its recommendations were not implemented. It is observed by many that if support for *Agenda* had been sustained, some of the ensuing disasters, such as those in Somalia, Bosnia and Rwanda, may possibly have been checked. Thus, many problems have not been addressed adequately and remain a hindrance to the UN's capacity to maintain world peace today. Criticisms in Brahimi Report confirm these failures which, for instance, reiterated problems emanating from the Council authorizing mandates without providing sufficient resources.

As a distinguished group, the Panel on United Nations Peace Operations was asked by the Secretary-General, Kofi Annan to outline the processes and changes which shall enable and allow the United Nations to be better prepared to meet the challenges of peacekeeping facing the member states and the United Nations in the twenty-first century. This panel presented its report, which popularly came to be known as the Brahimi Report, and sought pragmatic and practical solutions to matters related to peacekeeping.

The Brahimi Report focuses on:

- Shortcomings in the existing system
- Frank and realistic recommendations for change
- Political and strategic issues
- Operational and organizational issues.

It also called for developing new strategies for peace operations and conflicts, newer strategies of doctrine and mandates, newer system of strategic analysis and intelligence, devising 'rapid and effective deployment capacity', enhancing UNHQ capacity, creation of Integrated Mission Task Forces, and developing a strong responsibility centre for user-level IT strategy and policy in peace operations, and the creation of a Peace Operations Extranet.

An Open-Ended Working Group (OEWG) of the General Assembly was established by the GA Resolution 48/26 in 1994 for an expansion of the Security Council with an aim to democratize it, on the question of equitable representation in the membership of the Security Council and other matters related to the Security Council. It considered many innovative ideas and constructive proposals related to the issues of enlargement and working methods of the UN. In 1997, there was another bout of reform initiative to expand the membership of the Council, but it failed. It included a so-called 'quick-fix' that would have included Germany and Japan as new permanent members did not have much success. The 'Rezali formula'* also proposed an addition of five new permanent members—two from developed, three from the developing (one each from Asia, Africa and Latin America and the Caribbean), and four new non-permanent members. But power politics has prevented introduction of such innovative measures and, therefore, the old non-equitable structure of the Security Council continues.

In January 1997, former Secretary-General, Kofi Annan embarked on a policy of UN reforms. He presented his reform proposals in the following

---

*Another reform initiative was taken during the 51st session of the UNGA. Rezali Ismail, (Malaysia) the elected President of the 51st session of the UNGA (1996–1997) proposed a plan for expansion of UN Security Council.

reports: *Renewing the United Nations: A Programme for Reform* of 14 July 1997; *Strengthening the United Nations: An Agenda for Further Change* of 9 September 2002; *In Larger Freedom: Towards Development, Security and Human Rights for All* in 2005; and *Investing in the United Nations: For A Stronger Organization Worldwide* of 2006.

Kofi Annan proposed in his *In Larger Freedom: Towards Development, Security and Human Rights for All,* that the General Assembly should take bold measures to streamline its agenda and speed up the deliberative process. It should concentrate on the major substantive issues of the day, and establish mechanisms to engage fully and systematically with civil society. The Security Council should be broadly representative of the realities of power in today's world. The Secretary-General supports the principles for reform set out in the report of the high-level panel, and urges the member states to consider the two options, Models A* and B**, presented in that report, or any other viable proposals in terms of size and balance that have emerged on the basis of either of the models. The member states should agree to take a decision on this important issue before the Summit in September 2005 (Millennium + 5 Summit). As far as the Economic and Social Council is concerned, he stated that the Council should be reformed so that it can effectively assess progress in the UN's development agenda, serve as a high-level development cooperation forum and provide direction for the efforts of the various inter-governmental bodies in the economic and social area throughout the UN system. Regarding the Secretariat, the Secretary-General will take steps to realign the Secretariat's structure to match the priorities outlined in the report, and will create a cabinet-style decision-making mechanism. He requests the member states to give him the authority and resources to pursue a one-time staff buy-out to refresh and realign staff to meet the current needs, to cooperate in a comprehensive review of budget and human resources rules, and to commission a comprehensive review of the Office of Internal Oversight Services to strengthen its independence and authority.[24]

Some of the proposals of the former Secretary-General, which were accepted, were:

1. Creation of the position of a Deputy Secretary-General, and the setting up of a senior management group and a strategic planning unit.

2. Strengthening of the United Nations Office at Vienna while downgrading the authority of the Nairobi and Addis Ababa offices.

3. Replacement of the Committee on Administrative Coordination by the Chief Executive Board.

---

*Model A proposes creation of 6 new permanent members, plus 3 new non-permanent members for a total of 24 seats in the Security Council.
**Model B proposes creation of 8 new seats in a new class of members who would serve for 4 years, subject to renewal, plus one non-permanent seat, also for a total of 24.

4. Merger of several departments into one, creation of new departments, and either integration of the United Nations information centres in the resident coordinator's office or their consolidation in regional information hubs.

5. Application of the zero-growth budget, suppression by attrition of personnel posts coupled with the creation of a staff college, reduction of administrative expenditure by 33 per cent, and transfer of such savings to a development account, and reduction of documentation by 30 per cent.

6. Adoption of reforms regarding the UN development activities in the field by establishing a UN House, creating the position of the UN system's resident coordinator, and by enhancing collaboration with civil society components in tackling the various challenges of the world.[25]

For the present Secretary-General, Ban Ki-moon, reform of the UN is a top priority, thereby enhancing its relevance and effectiveness for the world's people in the twenty-first century. With the Organization engaged in a range of pressing global issues in every part of the world, a renewed, revitalized and more responsive United Nations is needed more than ever before.

In January 2008, Secretary-General Ban Ki-moon outlined the broad fronts on which the United Nations needs to advance if it is to meet the challenges facing the member states and their peoples in the twenty-first century. In areas like the environment, public health and human security, the world is facing threats and challenges that respect no boundaries. But by their nature, these challenges also expand the possibilities for collective action by the states and other entities and actors, such as civil society and the private sector, enabling the UN to be the focus for concerted action to advance the common good. The Secretary-General, in consultation with the member states, is also making attempts at ensuring that an efficient, relevant and accountable UN is ready to meet the challenges of today and tomorrow. In other words, he has a vision for a stronger United Nations for a better world.

> In a statement he said: 'Every day we are reminded of the need for a strengthened United Nations, as we face a growing array of new challenges, including humanitarian crises, human rights violations, armed conflicts and important health and environmental concerns. Seldom has the United Nations been called upon to do so much for so many. I am determined to breathe new life and inject renewed confidence into a strengthened United Nations firmly anchored in the twenty-first century, and which is effective, efficient, coherent and accountable'.

UNITED NATIONS AND PEACEKEEPING

United Nations peacekeeping is a unique and dynamic instrument developed by the Organization as a way to help countries torn by conflict and create the conditions for lasting peace. The first UN peacekeeping mission was established in 1948, when the Security Council authorized the deployment of UN military observers to the Middle East to monitor the Armistice Agreement between Israel and its Arab neighbours. Since then, there have been a total of 63 UN peacekeeping operations around the world. At present 15 Peace Keeping Operations are going on along with 17 peace operations under the direction and support of the Department of Peace Keeping Operations.

The term 'peacekeeping' is not found in the United Nations Charter and is difficult to find a simple definition. Dag Hammarskjöld, the second UN Secretary-General, referred to it as belonging to "Chapter Six and a Half" of the Charter, placing it between traditional methods of resolving disputes peacefully, such as negotiation and mediation under Chapter VI, and more forceful action as authorized under Chapter VII.

Peacekeeping is the deployment of a United Nations presence in the field, hitherto with the consent of all the parties concerned, normally involving United Nations military and/or police personnel and frequently civilians as well. It is a technique that expands the possibilities for both the prevention of conflict and the making of peace.

All members of the United Nations share the costs of UNPK operations. The General Assembly apportions the expense for meeting the expenses based on a special scale of assessment applicable to UNPK. The scale often taken into account, is the relative economic wealth of the member state. The permanent members of the Security Council are required to pay a larger share because of their special responsibility for maintenance of international peace and security. As of January, 2008, the top 10 contributors have been the United States, Japan, Germany, the United Kingdom, France, Italy, China, Canada, Spain and the Republic of Korea (South Korea).

With the end of the Cold War, the strategic context for UN peacekeeping dramatically changed, prompting the UN to shift and expand its field operations from 'traditional' missions involving strictly military tasks, to complex 'multidimensional' enterprises designed to ensure the implementation of comprehensive peace agreements and assist in laying the foundations for sustainable peace. Today's peacekeepers undertake a wide variety of complex tasks, from helping to build sustainable institutions of governance, to human rights monitoring, to security sector reform, to the disarmament, demobilization and reintegration of former combatants.

But the nature of peacekeeping has been changing over time, especially after the end of the Cold War. Previously, such UN peacekeeping operations were seen as a means of resolving the conflicts involving states by deploying unarmed or lightly armed military personnel from a number of countries with the consent of the warring parties to keep peace between the armed forces when a ceasefire was in place and to monitor the implementation of the peace agreements. But since the end of the Cold War, peacekeeping has become more complex and now operations involve more non-military elements such as police officers and civilian personnel to perform wide functions beyond assisting ex-combatants in implementing peace agreements, DDRR (Disarmament, Demobilization, Reintegration and Rehabilitation), confidence-building measures, power-sharing arrangements, electoral support, strengthening of the rule of law, and economic and social development.

UN peacekeeping continues to evolve, both conceptually and operationally, to meet new challenges and political realities. Faced with the rising demand for increasingly complex peace operations, the United Nations in the past few years has been overstretched and challenged as never before. The Organization has worked vigorously to strengthen its capacity to manage and sustain field operations and, thus, contributes to the most important function of the United Nations to maintain international peace and security.

UN Department of Peacekeeping Operations

In accordance with the purposes and principles enshrined in the Charter of the United Nations, the Department of Peacekeeping Operations (DPKO) has been established to assist the member states and the Secretary-General in their efforts to maintain international peace and security. The DPKO plans, prepares, manages and directs UN peacekeeping operations so that they can effectively fulfill their mandates under the overall authority of the Security Council and General Assembly, and under the command vested in the Secretary-General.

DPKO provides political and executive directions to UN peacekeeping operations, and maintains contact with the Security Council, troop and financial contributors, and parties to the conflict in the implementation of the Security Council mandates. The Department works to integrate the efforts of UN, and governmental and non-governmental entities in the context of peacekeeping operations. Peacekeeping operations may consist of several components, including a military component, which may or may not be armed, and various civilian components encompassing a broad range of disciplines. The chief concerns are to alleviate human suffering, and create conditions and build institutions for self-sustaining peace. Depending on their mandate, peacekeeping missions may be required to:

- Deploy to prevent the outbreak of conflict or the spill-over of conflict across borders.
- Stabilize conflict situations after a ceasefire, to create an environment for the parties to reach a lasting peace agreement.
- Assist in implementing comprehensive peace agreements.
- Lead states or territories through a transition to stable government, based on democratic principles, good governance and economic development.

List of UN Peacekeeping Operations (1948–2008)

UNTSO	United Nations Truce Supervision Organization (from May 1948 till present)
UNMOGIP	United Nations Military Observer Group in India and Pakistan (from January 1949 till present)
UNEF I	First United Nations Emergency Force (from November 1956 to June 1967)
UNOGIL	United Nations Observation Group in Lebanon (from June 1958 to December 1958)
ONUC	United Nations Operation in the Congo (from July 1960 to June 1964)
UNSF	United Nations Security Force in West New Guinea (from October 1962 to April 1963)
UNYOM	United Nations Yemen Observation Mission (from July 1963 to September 1964)
UNFICYP	United Nations Peacekeeping Force in Cyprus (from March 1964 till present)
DOMREP	Mission of the Representative of the SG in the Dominian Republic (from May 1965 to October 1966)
UNIPOM	United Nations India–Pakistan Observation Mission (from September 1965 to March 1966)
UNAMET	United Nations Mission in East Timor (1999)
UNEF II	Second United Nations Emergency Force (from October 1973 to July 1979)
UNDOF	United Nations Disengagement Force (from June 1974 till present)
UNIFIL	United Nations Interim Force in Lebanon (from March 1978 till present)
UNGOMAP	United Nations Good Offices Mission in Afghanistan and Pakistan (from May 1988 to March 1990)
UNIIMOG	United Nations Iran–Iraq Military Observer Group (from August 1988 to February 1991)
UNAVEM I	United Nations Angola Verification Mission I (from January 1989 to June 1991)
UNTAG	United Nations Transition Assistance Group (from April 1989 to March 1990)
ONUCA	United Nations Observer Group in Central America (from November 1989 to January 1992)
UNIKOM	United Nations Iraq–Kuwait Observation Mission (from April 1991 to October 2003)
MINURSO	United Nations Mission for the Referendum in Western Sahara (from April 1991 till present)
UNAVEM II	United Nations Angola Verification Mission II (from June 1991 to February 1995)

ONUSAL	United Nations Observer Mission in El Salvador (from July 1991 to April 1995)
UNAMIC	United Nations Advance Mission in Cambodia (from October 1991 to March 1992)
UNPROFOR	United Nations Protection Force (from February 1992 to March 1995)
UNTAC	United Nations Transitional Authority in Cambodia (from March 1992 to September 1993)
UNOSOM I	United Nations Operation in Somalia I (from April 1992 to March 1993)
ONUMOZ	United Nations Operation in Mozambique (from December 1992 to December 1994)
UNOSOM II	United Nations Operation in Somalia II (from March 1993 to March 1995)
UNOMUR	United Nations Observer Mission Uganda–Rwanda (from June 1993 to September 1994)
UNOMIG	United Nations Observer Mission in Georgia (from August 1993 till present)
UNOMIL	United Nations Observer Mission in Liberia (from September 1993 to September 1997)
UNMIH	United Nations Mission in Haiti (from September 1993 to June 1996)
UNAMIR	United Nations Assistance Mission for Rwanda (from October 1993 to March 1996)
UNASOG	United Nations Aouzou Strip Observer Group (from May 1994 to June 1994)
UNMOT	United Nations Mission of Observers in Tajikistan (from December 1994 to May 2000)
UNAVEM III	United Nations Angola Verification Mission III (from February 1995 to June 1997)
UNCRO	United Nations Confidence Restoration Operation in Croatia (from May 1995 to January 1996)
UNPREDEP	United Nations Preventive Deployment Force (from March 1995 to February 1999)
UNMIBH	United Nations Mission in Bosnia and Herzegovina (from December 1995 to December 2002)
MICAH	United Nations General Assembly International Civilian Support Mission in Haiti (2000–2001)
UNTAES	United Nations Transitional Administration for Eastern Slavonia, Baranja and Western Sirmium (from January 1996 to January 1998)
UNMOP	United Nations Mission of Observers in Prevlaka (from January 1996 to December 2002)
UNSMIH	United Nations Support Mission in Haiti (from July 1996 to July 1997)
MINUGUA	United Nations Verification Mission in Guatemala (from January 1997 to May 1997)

MONUA	United Nations Observer Mission in Angola (from June 1997 to February 1999)
UNTMIH	United Nations Transition Mission in Haiti (from August 1997 to November 1997)
MIPONUH	United Nations Civilian Police Mission in Haiti (from December 1997 to March 2000)
UNPSG	United Nations Civilian Police Support Group (from January 1998 to October 1998)
MINURCA	United Nations Mission in the Central African Republic (from April 1998 to February 2000)
UNOMSIL	United Nations Observer Mission in Sierra Leone (from July 1998 to October 1999)
UNMIK	UN Interim Administration Mission in Kosovo (from June 1999 till present)
UNAMSIL	United Nations Mission in Sierra Leone (from October 1999 to December 2005)
UNTAET	United Nations Transitional Administration in East Timor (from October 1999 to May 2002)
MONUC	UN Organization Mission in the Democratic Republic of the Congo (from November 1999 till present)
UNMEE	United Nations Mission in Ethiopia and Eritrea (from July 2000 to present)
UNMISET	United Nations Mission of Support in East Timor (from May 2002 to May 2005)
UNMIL	United Nations Mission in Liberia (from September 2003 till present)
UNOCI	United Nations Operation in Côte d'Ivoire (from April 2004 till present)
MINUSTAH	United Nations Stabilization Mission in Haiti (from June 2004 till present)
ONUB	United Nations Operation in Burundi (from June 2004 to December 2006)
UNMIS	United Nations Mission in the Sudan (from March 2005 till present)
UNMIT	United Nations Integrated Mission in Timor–Leste (from August 2006 till present)
UNAMID	African Union/United Nations Hybrid operation in Darfur (from July 2007 till present)
MINURCAT	United Nations Mission in the Central African Republic and Chad (from September 2007 till present)

From the aforesaid list given UNTSO, UNMOGIP, UNFICYP, UNDOF, UNIFIL, MINURSO, UNOMIG, UNMIK, MONUC, UNMEE, UNAMA, UNMIL, UNOCI, MINUSTAH, UNMIS, UNMIT and UNAMID are still being continued.

(**Source:**   http://www.un.org/Depts/dpko/list/list.pdf)

Evaluation

The UN Peacekeeping operations received a much deserved international recognition when, in 1988, the peacekeepers were awarded the Nobel Peace Prize. However, discussed earlier, the nature of peacekeeping has changed over time, especially after the end of the Cold War. Over the years, UN peacekeeping has evolved to meet the demands of different kinds of conflicts and a changing political landscape.

Peacekeeping operations have had their own share of successes and failures. In El Salvador and Mozambique, peacekeeping ensured ways to achieve self-sustaining peace. Sierra Leone, East Timor and Liberia have been successful operations. But UN peacekeeping fared badly and failed in Somalia where peacekeepers were despatched without securing either a ceasefire or the consent of warring parties. Other stories of failures include the genocide in Rwanda in 1994 and the massacre of Srebrenica in Bosnia and Herzegovina in 1995.

Added to this, there is also a mounting expenditure for peacekeeping activities. The costs skyrocketed with the additional requirements for new and expanded missions. Further, there are allegations of sexual abuse by the UN peacekeepers and alleged corruption in procurement by the UN executives in the field and the headquarters. These failures called for introspection and reform of the peacekeeping operations.

The Brahimi Report suggested an adoption of "peacekeeping doctrine that stipulates that once deployed, the United Nations peacekeepers must be able to carry out their mandates, professionally and successfully, and be capable of defending themselves, other mission components and the mission's mandate, with robust rules of engagement, against those who renege on their commitments to a peace accord or otherwise seek to undermine it by violence".[26] In other words, a clear, credible and achievable mandate drawn by the Security Council is to be a vital part of this doctrine.

In 1992, Secretary-General, Boutros Boutros-Ghali, in his *An Agenda for Peace,* held out plans for preventive diplomacy, peacemaking and peacekeeping. He tried to introduce a new dimension to peacekeeping by introducing the concept *preventive diplomacy.* The terms, 'preventive diplomacy', 'peacemaking' and 'peacekeeping', are intimately related and as used in this report, are defined as follows: *Preventive diplomacy* is action to prevent disputes from arising between parties, to prevent existing disputes from escalating into conflicts and to limit the spread of the latter when they occur. *Peacemaking* and *Peacekeeping* are actions to bring hostile parties to agreement, essentially through such peaceful means as those foreseen in Chapter VI of the Charter of the United Nations. The report focused more on these actions to strengthen the post-conflict peacebuilding to prevent recurrence of violence among nations and people.

The former Secretary-General, Kofi Annan also suggested certain reforms relating to the institutions of UN that are engaged in seeking and promoting peace and security. The high-level Panel tasked by him in its report in 2004 recommended the creation of a Peacebuilding Commission (PBC) and a Peacebuilding Support Office (PBSO) to support the Commission. He, in his *In Larger Freedom: Towards Development, Security and Human Rights for All*, suggested that the member states should take steps "to strengthen collective capacity to employ the tools of mediation, sanctions and peacekeeping (including a 'zero tolerance' policy on sexual exploitation of minors and other vulnerable people by members of peacekeeping contingents, to match the policy enacted by the Secretary-General".

Much has been said without any positive actions on any of the recommendations or proposals. The first and foremost thing that has to be done is a full-fledged reform of the United Nations so that it can resurrect with renewed energy and vigour and take up the responsibility of the guardian of international peace and security.

EXERCISES

1. Write a note on the purposes and principles of the United Nations.

2. Discuss the composition, powers and functions of General Assembly.

3. Discuss the composition and functions of Security Council. Do you think a reform of Security Council is much needed?

4. Analyze the role of the Secretary-General of the United Nations.

5. Examine the powers and functions of the Secretary-General of the United Nations. How has his role evolved since the time of the first Secretary-General Trygve Lie?

6. Discuss the composition, powers and functions of ECOSOC.

7. Examine the composition and jurisdiction of the International Court of Justice.

8. Write a note on the procedure for the revision of the UN Charter.

9. Elucidate the various attempts to reform the United Nations.

10. Do you think that a reform of the United Nations is needed? Argue.

11. Discuss the various peacekeeping attempts that have been made by the United Nations, since its birth.

REFERENCES

[1] Chakrabarti, Radharaman, *UNO: A Study in Essential,* K.P. Bagchi & Co, Kolkata, 1998, p. 29.

[2] The Charter of the United Nations.

[3] *ibid.*

[4] *ibid.*

[5] Nicholas, H.G., *The United Nations As A Political Institution,* Oxford University Press, London, 1971, p. 36.

[6] The Charter of the United Nations.

[7] Ping, Jean and Denis Dange Rawka, "Reform of the General Assembly", *in* Ajit M. Banerjee and Murari R. Sharma (Eds.), *Reinventing the United Nations,* Prentice-Hall of India, New Delhi, 2007, p. 77.

[8] Nicholas, *op. cit.,* n. 5, p. 114.

[9] Uniting For Peace Resolution, 1950.

[10] Nicholas, *op. cit.,* n. 5.

[11] *Basic Facts About the United Nations, Sales No.E.98.I.20., Press Release GA/9784 (10 Oct. 2000), and the Office of the Director of Security Council Affairs Division, Department of Political Affairs.*

[12] Chakrabarti, *op. cit.,* n. 1, pp. 50–51.

[13] Nicholas, *op. cit.,* n. 15, p. 170.

[14] *ibid.,* pp. 162–167.

[15] Chakrabarti, *op. cit.,* n. 1, pp. 67–68.

[16] Luard, Evan, *The United Nations: How it Works and What it Does,* Macmillan Press, London, 1979, p. 97.

[17] Chakrabarti, *op. cit.,* n. 1, p. 69.

[18] Luard, *op. cit.,* n. 16, p. 101.

[19] UN News Centre http://www.un.org/aboutun/charter/index.html.

[20] Chakrabarti, *op. cit.,* n. 1, p. 59.

[21] *ibid.*

[22] *ibid.*

[23] Chakrabarti, *op. cit.,* n. 1, pp. 159–160.

[24] http://www.un.org/largerfreedom.

[25] Ping, Jean and Denis Dange Rawaka, *op. cit.,* n. 7, pp. 81–82 (for more check **http://www.un.org/reform/index.shtml**).

[26] Chowdhury, Iftekhar Ahmed, "Keeping and Building Peace: An Evolving UN function," *in* Ajit M. Banerjee and Murari R. Sharma (Eds.), *Reinventing the United Nations,* Prentice-Hall of India, New Delhi, 2007, p. 58.

12

Disarmament and Arms Control

INTRODUCTION

National survival is the prime motive behind every action of each state. Therefore, national security tops the list of 'national interest' of each state. National security is unthinkable without military preparedness and arms production. But military preparedness of one automatically results in active military build-up of the other. This results in an arms race with all the states indulging in massive arms build-up. This, however, not only destabilizes international peace and security but also makes war inevitable. In particular, the possession of nukes, huge stockpile of Weapons of Mass Destruction (WMDs) and chemical and biological weapons makes matters worse and threatens the very existence of humanity and world peace. Therefore, efforts need to be made to reduce the possibilities of war and increase the chances of international peace and security through disarmament and arms control.

MEANING AND CONCEPT

Both the terms 'disarmament' and 'arms control' might seem to be synonymous but there is a subtle line of difference between the two. **Disarmament** means the elimination or reduction of armaments to preserve international peace and security by averting wars. According to Morgenthau[1], "Disarmament is the reduction or elimination of certain or all armaments for the purpose of ending the armament race". According to experts on disarmament and arms control like Charles P. Schleicher disarmament "means of reducing or eliminating the material and human instrumentalities for the exercise of physical violence". According to an authority in international politics, like V.V. Dyke*, "Any regulation or limitation having to do with armed power is treated as a measure of Disarmament".

Couloumbis and Wolfe[2], while showing the difference between disarmament and arms control, opine: "In its absolute sense disarmament requires the global destruction of weapons and the disestablishment of all armed forces". Disarmament for them is quite inclusive and can mean anything from outlawing of all military arsenals and establishments to the banning of particular weapons in the interest of 'humanization' of war and even the implementation of specific agreements designed to prevent the accidental outbreak of war.

While complete disarmament may be difficult to achieve and in some sense is unattainable, the concept of **arms control** has crept in and has gained currency. Couloumbis and Wolfe[3] point out that, as chances of total disarmament become so minimal, its advocates are often regarded as utopians or propagandists and arms control becomes more relevant in the literature of international relations.

Arms control is a generic term and it normally includes two categories: arms reduction and arms limitation. Arms reduction stands for partial disarmament and it implies a mutually agreed-upon set of arms levels for the nation-states involved. The arms reduction formula may apply either to all states worldwide or to a small number of states on a regional basis. Arms limitation, on the other hand, stands for the wide variety of international accords designed to limit the impact of war and to prevent the accidental outbreak of war. Under arms limitations there can be infinite measures such as the installation of fail–safe devices designed to detonate nuclear missiles in midair, should they be fired accidentally, hot lines to keep the key decision-makers in constant contact during crises, moratoriums on specific types of nuclear testing and agreements between two or more countries restricting the sale of arms and the transfer of nuclear technology.[4]

According to Schleicher, arms control is used to "include any kind of cooperation with respect to armament which could curtail the arms race, reduce the probability of war, or limit its scope and violence".[5]

---

*Vernon Van Dyke, *International Politics,* Appleton-Century-Crofts, New York, 1957.

In the views of Kegley and Wittkopf[6], arms control means "cooperative agreements between states designed to regulate arms levels either by limiting their growth or by placing restrictions on how they might be used. Arms control is less ambitious than disarmament, since it seeks not to eliminate weapons but to regulate their use or moderate the pace at which they are developed".

Since the First World War, efforts towards disarmament and arms control have been made by the world leaders to save humanity. US President Woodrow Wilson in his **Fourteen Points** upheld the need for abolition of arms and ammunitions. He also stated that armament should be reduced to "the lowest point consistent with domestic safety". Even the **Treaty of Versailles** (1919), concluded at the end of the First World War specified that: "the maintenance of peace requires the reduction of national armaments to the lowest point consistent with national safety and the enforcement by common action of international obligations". Under the League of Nations too, efforts were made to curb arms build-up. A Temporary Mixed Commission was set up in 1921 followed by a Preparatory Commission in 1925 on the issue of disarmament but these commissions failed to deliver the goods.

However, a landmark development towards disarmament was seen in 1925, namely, the Geneva Protocol for the Prohibition of the Use in War of Asphyxiating, Poisonous or Other Gases, and of Bacteriological Methods of Warfare. The parties to the Protocol condemned the use of asphyxiating, poisonous or other gases, and of all analogous liquids, materials or devices in war, and agreed that this prohibition should be universally accepted as a part of International Law, binding both the conscience and the practice of nations.

Serious thoughts about disarmament and arms control began after the devastation experienced by humanity in the Second World War. The UN Charter emphasized the need for a regulation of armaments, and thereafter several steps have been taken to effect disarmament and arms control.

Some of the major developments that have taken place in the field of disarmament and arms control since the Second World War are now discussed.

1. *The Four Power Declaration, 1945:* The United States of America, Great Britain, the erstwhile Soviet Union and China signed a declaration on 3 October 1945 on general security by which these four powers declared to bring about a practical agreement on regulation of armaments in the post-War period.

2. *Atomic Energy Commission:* The United Nations Atomic Energy Commission (UNAEC) was founded on 24 January 1946 by the first resolution of the United Nations General Assembly "to deal with the problems raised by the discovery of atomic energy".

The Commission comprised one representative from each of those states represented in the Security Council. The Commission was expected to enquire into all phases of the problems of disarmament and make recommendations from time to time and make specific proposals for:

(a)   Extending between all nations the exchange of basic scientific informations for peaceful ends.

(b)   Control of atomic energy to the extent necessary to ensure its use only for peaceful purposes.

(c)   The elimination from national armaments for atomic weapons and of all other weapons adaptable to mass destruction.

(d)   Effective safegurads by way of inspection and other means to protect the complying states against the hazards of violations and evasions.

The Commission was supposed to submit its reports and recommendations to the Security Council. It started to work from 14 June 1946 by holding its first meeting but subsequently failed to perform its function due to opening up of the hostilities between the USA and the USSR. The Soviet refusal to sign the 'Baruch Plan' placed by the US (prepared by Bernard Baruch) to the UNAEC in its first meeting in June 1946, was responded by the US with massive nuclear weapons testing and development programmes. Therefore, disarmament efforts got a deadly blow and the Atomic Energy Commission was finally dissolved by the General Assembly Resolution No 502 (VI).[7]

3.   *Commission on Conventional Armaments:*   The United Nations Commission on Conventional Armaments was formally established by the Security Council on 15 February 1947 in pursuance of the General Assembly Resolution of December 1946. The Commission was established with the goal of finding ways to reduce the size of non-nuclear armaments around the world. It was expected to prepare and submit within three months proposals for general regulation and reduction of armaments and armed forces to the Security Council. Ultimately, the Commission adopted a resolution on 12 August 1948 where it recommended the following measures:

(a)   Setting up a system for the regulation and reduction of armaments of all states, initially those having substantial military resources.

(b)   Taking measures for the reduction and regulation of armaments to encourage further regulation and reduction.

(c)   Establishment of an adequate system of international control of atomic energy and conclusion of peace settlement with Japan and Germany.

(d)   Regulation and reduction of armaments to make possible the least diversion for armaments of the world human and economic resources and maintenance of armaments and armed forces which are indispensable for the maintenance of international peace and security.

(e)   Adequate method of safeguards and provision for effective action in case of violation.

The five permanent members of the United Nation Security Council could not, however, agree on how to achieve this aim and, therefore, the first report of the Commission made no substantial recommendations. When the resolution finally came up for discussion, it was opposed by the Soviet Union and it presented its own proposal for disarmament. The Soviet proposal looked forward for disarmament to the extent of one-third of the military power by the permanent members of the Security Council which was not accepted by the members of the Security Council. Thus, not much success was achieved by this disarmament effort also. Further, in 1950, the Soviet Union refused to sit with the representatives of the 'Kuomintang group', (the non-Communist Chinese representatives) on the Commission. This brought an effective end to the Commission's discussion. It was formally dissolved in 1952. The Commission on Conventional Armaments was finally dissolved by the Security Council on 30 January 1952 following a recommendation contained in the General Assembly Resolution 502 (VI).

4. *Disarmament Commission:* The General Assembly, by its resolution 502 (VI) of January 1952, created the United Nations Disarmament Commission under the Security Council with a general mandate on disarmament questions.

5. *Atoms for Peace:* The speech of President Eisenhower on 8 December 1953 did not by itself spell out a disarmament plan, but was like an initiative to open up the benefits of atomic energy to the world community. The speech, however, contained proposals of arms control and security considerations. Ultimately, this gave impetus to organization of the Conference on the Statute of International Atomic Energy Agency (IAEA) at the UN headquarters in New York in 1956. Following this conference on the IAEA Statute, the Agency was formally inaugurated on 29 July 1957. The hidden agenda of Eisenhower's speech was a cut-off in the production of fissile nuclear materials with an aim to curb the Soviet capacity of procuring fissile materials and producing nuclear weapons to match that of the United States. Therefore, the key idea of the speech was transferring of significant amount of fissile materials to the IAEA by the USSR and the USA to be used for peaceful purposes.[8]

MAJOR ARMS CONTROL AGREEMENT SINCE 1960

1. *Partial Test Ban Treaty (PTBT):* The PTBT was signed on 8 August 1963 in Moscow and it came into force on 10 October 1963. The basic features of the treaty are:

(a) Under Article I, each of the Parties to the Treaty undertook the responsibility to prohibit, to prevent, and not to carry out any nuclear weapon test explosion, or any other nuclear explosion, at any place under its jurisdiction or control: (i) in the atmosphere; beyond its limits, including outer space; or under water, including territorial waters or high seas; or (ii) in any other environment if such explosion causes radioactive debris to be present outside the territorial limits of the state under whose jurisdiction or control such explosion is conducted.

(b) Each of the Parties to the Treaty undertook further responsibility to refrain from causing, encouraging, or in any way participating in, the carrying out of any nuclear weapon test explosion, or any other nuclear explosion, anywhere which would take place in any of the environments described, or have the effect referred to, in paragraph 1 of this Article.

The Treaty though was a significant step towards disarmament as it aimed to reduce the dangers of radioactive fallout from the nuclear tests in the atmosphere; it was partial because it did not prohibit the nuclear test underground. Both the Soviet Union and the United States conducted a large number of tests underground. France and China declined to sign the Treaty and continued with their nuclear tests in the atmosphere.

2. *Outer Space Treaty, 1967:* The Outer Space Treaty opened for signature on 27 January 1967 and came into force from 10 October 1967.

Article IV of the Treaty stipulates that Parties (states) to the Treaty should undertake not to place in orbit around the Earth any objects carrying nuclear weapons or any other kinds of weapons of mass destruction, install such weapons on celestial bodies, or station such weapons in outer space in any other manner. The Moon and other celestial bodies shall be used by all Parties to the Treaty exclusively for peaceful purposes. The establishment of military bases, installations and fortifications, the testing of any type of weapons, and the conduct of military manoeuvres on celestial bodies shall be forbidden. The use of military personnel for scientific research or for any other peaceful purposes shall not be prohibited. The use of any equipment or facility necessary for peaceful exploration of the Moon and other celestial bodies shall also not be prohibited. Under Article XII, all stations, installations, equipment and space vehicles on the Moon and other celestial bodies shall be open to representatives of other Parties to the Treaty on a reciprocal basis.

3. *Nuclear Non-Proliferation Treaty (NPT), 1968:* The NPT was signed simultaneously in London, Moscow and Washington on 1 July 1968 and came into force on 5 March 1970. The Treaty aims at limiting the spread of nuclear weapons globally. About 189 countries are till date party to the treaty. Five members among these have nuclear weapons. They are the United States, the United Kingdom, France, Russia, and the People's Republic of China. India, Israel, Pakistan and North Korea are not signatories to this Treaty. India and Pakistan both possess and have openly tested nuclear bombs. Israel has adopted a policy of deliberate ambiguity regarding its own nuclear policy. North Korea acceded to the Treaty, violated it, and later withdrew itself.

The Treaty consists of a Preamble and eleven articles and is considered as having three pillars: non-proliferation, disarmament, and the right to peacefully use nuclear technology.

(a) *Non-proliferation:* Under Article I, the five Nuclear Weapon States (NWS) agree not to transfer "nuclear weapons or other nuclear explosive devices" and "not in any way to assist, encourage, or induce" a Non-Nuclear Weapon State (NNWS) to acquire nuclear weapons. Article II contains that NNWS parties to the NPT agree not to "receive," "manufacture" or "acquire" nuclear weapons or to "seek or receive any assistance in the manufacture of nuclear weapons". Article III states that NNWS parties also agree to accept safeguards by the IAEA to verify that they are not diverting nuclear energy from peaceful uses to nuclear weapons or other nuclear explosive devices.

(b) *Disarmament:* Article VI urges all state Parties to the NPT, both nuclear-weapon states and non-nuclear-weapon states, "to pursue negotiations in good faith on effective measures relating to cessation of the nuclear arms race at an early date and to nuclear disarmament, and on a treaty on general and complete disarmament under strict and effective international control".

(c) *Peaceful use of nuclear energy:* The NPT allows for and agrees upon the transfer of nuclear technology and materials to NPT signatory countries for the development of civilian nuclear energy programmes in those countries, as long as they can demonstrate that their nuclear programmes are not being used for the development of nuclear weapons. The Treaty recognizes the inalienable right of sovereign states to use nuclear energy for peaceful purposes, but restricts this right for NPT parties to be exercised "in conformity with Articles I and II".

There have been severe criticisms regarding the language of the Treaty, especially from the countries interested in developing their nuclear capabilities. India, Pakistan, Brazil, Argentina are among the many countries who refused to sign the Treaty because they thought that the Treaty was discriminatory. The Treaty, while on the one hand was aiming to limit the vertical expansion was, on the other hand, silent on horizontal expansion. In other words, it was silent about the control of possessions of the nuclear capabilities of the states belonging to the Nuclear Club. The Treaty was viewed as being aimed at perpetuating nuclear dependence of non-nuclear states on the nuclear states and, therefore, increased the gap between them. The NPT failed to bring about any positive disarmament and arms control.

4. *Sea-Bed Treaty, 1971:* On 11 February 1971, the UK, the United States and the USSR signed the treaty and it came into force on 18 May 1972.

The provisions under this Treaty embody that the state Parties to this Treaty undertake not to implant or emplace on the sea-bed and the ocean floor and in the subsoil thereof, beyond the outer limit of a sea-bed zone, any nuclear weapons or any other types of weapons of mass destruction as well as structures, launching installations or any other facilities specifically designed for storing, testing or using such weapons. There are also various measures for verification and it states that in order to promote the objectives of and ensure compliance with the provisions of this Treaty, each state Parties to the Treaty shall have the right to verify, through observations, the activities of other state Parties to the Treaty on the sea-bed and the ocean-floor and in the subsoil thereof beyond the zone referred to in Article I of the Treaty provided that the observation does not interfere with such activities.

5. *Biological Weapons Convention, 1972:*   The Convention on the Prohibition of the Development, Production and Stockpiling of Bacteriological (Biological) and Toxin Weapons and on their Destruction opened for signature on 10 April 1972 and came into force on 26 March 1975. Its objective was to achieve effective progress towards general and complete disarmament, including the prohibition and elimination of all types of weapons of mass destruction.

Under Article I, the state Parties to this Convention undertook to develop, produce, stockpile or otherwise acquire or retain under any circumstances: (a) Microbial or other biological agents, or toxins, whatever their origin or method of production, of types and in quantities that have no justification for prophylactic, protective or other peaceful purposes; (b) Weapons, equipment or means of delivery designed to use such agents or toxins for hostile purposes or in armed conflict.

Article II underlines that state parties to this Convention, must undertake to destroy, or to divert to peaceful purposes, as soon as possible but not later than nine months after the entry into force of the Convention, all agents, toxins, weapons, equipment and means of delivery specified in Article I of the Convention, which are in its possession or under its jurisdiction or control. In implementing the provisions of this article, all necessary safety precautions shall be observed to protect populations and the environment.

Ariticle III enumerates that each state Parties to this Convention undertakes not to transfer to any recipient state whatsoever, directly or indirectly, and not in any way to assist, encourage, or induce any state, group of states or international organizations to manufacture or otherwise acquire any of the agents, toxins, weapons, equipment or means of delivery specified in Article I of the Convention.

6. *Strategic Arms Limitation Talks (SALT I):*   These refer to efforts made by the two superpowers to ease off the Cold War tensions and enhance the spirit of détente by developing means of arms limitations. SALT I froze the number of strategic ballistic missile launchers at existing levels, and provided for the addition of new Submarine Launched Ballistic Missile (SLBM) launchers only after the same number of older intercontinental ballistic missile (ICBM) and SLBM launchers had been dismantled.

After a long deadlock, the first results of SALT I came in May 1971 when an agreement was reached over ABM systems. The Agreement included: (a) the Anti-Ballistic Missile Treaty and (b) the Interim Agreement between the United States of America and the Union of Soviet Socialist Republics (now Russia) on Certain Measures With Respect to the Limitation of Strategic Offensive Arms.

The Treaty required both the countries to limit the number of sites protected by an anti-ballistic missile (ABM) system to two each. The Soviet Union had deployed such a system around Moscow in 1966 and the United States announced an ABM program to protect 12 ICBM sites in 1967. The Interim Agreement covered both land-based ICBMs and SLBMs. The USSR was permitted to have 1618 ICBMs while the number for USA was fixed at 1054 on the basis of their actual strength as on 1 July 1971.

7. Threshold Test Ban Treaty, 1974: The Treaty on the Limitation of Underground Nuclear Weapon Tests, also known as the **Threshold Test Ban Treaty** (or **TTBT**), was signed in July 1974 by the USA and the USSR. It established a nuclear 'threshold', by prohibiting nuclear tests of devices having an yield exceeding 150 kilotons (equivalent to 150,000 tons of TNT).

The TTBT was militarily important since it prohibited the possibility of testing new or existing nuclear weapons going beyond 150 kilotons. The Treaty imposed a mutual restraint and thereby sought to reduce the degree of explosive force of new nuclear warheads and bombs which could otherwise be tested for weapon systems.

8. Convention on Prohibition of Military or Other Hostile Use of Environment Modification Techniques, 1977: This Convention opened for signature in Geneva on 18 May 1977 and came into force on 5 October 1978.

Article I contains provisions under which each state Parties to the Convention undertook not to engage in military or any other hostile use of environmental modification techniques having widespread, long-lasting or severe effects as the means of destruction, damage or injury to any other state Party. The Treaty also required that each state Party should refrain from assisting, encouraging or inducing any state, group of states or international organization to engage in activities contrary to the provisions of this article.

Under Article III, the state Parties to this Convention further undertook responsibility to facilitate, and have the right to participate in, the fullest possible exchange of scientific and technological information on the use of environmental modification techniques for peaceful purposes. The provisions of the Treaty also upheld co-operation among states parties and other states or international organizations, to international economic and scientific cooperation for the preservation, improvement and peaceful utilization of the environment, with due consideration for the needs of the developing areas of the world.

9. Strategic Arms Limitation Talks (SALT II): This was the second round of talks from 1972 to 1979 between the United States and the Soviet Union and signified the continuation of the progress made during the SALT I talks which aimed at curtailing the manufacture of strategic nuclear weapons. This Treaty was to remain in force for five years. It talked about real reductions in strategic forces to 2,250 of all categories of delivery vehicles on both sides, such as the ICBM launchers, Long Range Bombers and SLBMs. A ceiling was also imposed on Multiple Independently Targetable Reentry Vehicles (MIRVs), and provisions were included for slowing down the pace of new strategic weapons.

Six months after the signing of the Treaty, the Soviet deployment of troops in Afghanistan and refusal of the American Senate to formally ratify the Treaty, it met a fateful end. The outbreak of the new Cold War embittered the relations between the two states and disarmament missions received heavy blows.

10. *The INF Treaty, 1987:* This is the **Intermediate-Range Nuclear Forces Treaty** which was an agreement between the United States and the Soviet Union signed in Washington, DC by the US President Ronald Reagan and the General Secretary of the Communist Party of the Soviet Union, Mikhail Gorbachev on 8 December 1987. It was ratified by the United States Senate on 27 May 1988 and came into force on 1 June of that year. The Treaty is formally titled as *The Treaty Between the United States of America and the Union of Soviet Socialist Republics on the Elimination of Their Intermediate-Range and Shorter-Range Missiles*.

Before the Treaty opened for signature, a series of negotiations and tussle between the two superpowers took place. Finally, in January 1985, George Shultz, Secretary of State of the United States and Andrei Gromyko, the Soviet Foreign Minister agreed to have separate but parallel negotiations on INF, Strategic Arms Reduction Treaty (START), and defence and space issues as part of a new bilateral forum called the Nuclear and Space Talks (NST). Thereafter, formal talks started in March 1985 covering all the three areas.

Following the talks between President Reagan and General Secretary Gorbachev in Geneva in 1985, where they issued a joint statement calling for an "interim accord on intermediate-range nuclear forces" and Reykjavik, Iceland, in 1986, both sides finally cleared the obstacles to the INF Treaty. On 23 July 1987, Gorbachev announced the Soviet acceptance of "double global zero", i.e., total elimination of INFs under NATO and the USSR, worldwide. Finally, the Treaty was signed on 8 December 1987 in Washington, DC.

The provisions of the INF Treaty were aimed at elimination of the ground-launched ballistic and cruise missiles with ranges between 500 and 5500 kilometres. This Treaty called for the elimination of Pershing II and GLCMs on the US side and SS-4, SS-5, SS-12, SS-20, SS-23 and SSC-X-4 on the part of USSR.

Scholars point out the novelty of the treaty, namely, its verification procedures. Verification of the Treaty was assured through on-site inspections and National Technical Means and was supposed to continue for 13 years. The on-site inspections include baseline data inspections, closed-out facility inspections, and missile systems elimination inspections. The Treaty established continuous portal and perimeter monitoring activities at former missile production facilities in the territory of each Party. Moscow was given the right to carry out 240 inspections in the USA and West Europe. The USA obtained the right to carry out about 400 inspections in the former USSR, the former GDR and Czechoslovakia. The United States was given greater inspection quota because the USSR had a greater number of missiles. Thirty-two facilities in the USA and 117 facilities in the USSR were opened to each other's inspection.[9]

11. *Conventional Arms Cut Treaty, 1990:* This Treaty was signed by the European countries, the United States and the erstwhile USSR on 19 November 1990 in Paris and it entered into force on 9 November 1992.

Under this Treaty, each state Party is under the obligation set forth in this Treaty, including those obligations relating to the following five categories of conventional armed forces: battle tanks, armoured combat vehicles, artillery, combat aircraft and helicopters. This should be done within the area of application, as has been defined in Article II of the Treaty. Article II defines the term "area of application" as the entire land territory of the states Parties in Europe from the Atlantic Ocean to the Ural Mountains, and for the Union of Soviet Socialist Republics, the area of application includes all territories lying West of the Ural River and the Caspian Sea.

Each state Party was required to limit and, as necessary, reduce its battle tanks, armoured combat vehicles, artillery, combat aircraft and attack helicopters so that, 40 months after entry into force of this Treaty and thereafter, the aggregate numbers do not exceed: (a) 20,000 battle tanks, of which no more than 16,500 shall be in active units; (b) 30,000 armoured combat vehicles, of which no more than 27,300 shall be in active units. Of the 30,000 armoured combat vehicles, no more than 18,000 shall be armoured infantry fighting vehicles and heavy armament combat vehicles; of armoured infantry fighting vehicles and heavy armament combat vehicles, no more than 1,500 shall be heavy armament combat vehicles; (c) 20,000 pieces of artillery, of which no more than 17,000 shall be in active units; (d) 6,800 combat aircraft; and (e) 2,000 attack helicopters.

12. *START I 1991:* The Strategic Arms Reduction Treaty is a treaty between the United States of America and the Union of Soviet Socialist Republic (USSR) on the Reduction and Limitation of Strategic Offensive Arms. The Treaty barred both the signatories from deploying more than 6,000 nuclear warheads atop, a total of 1,600 ICBMs, submarine launched ballistic missiles and bombers. START I was the most negotiated and the largest and complex arms control treaty in history. It was proposed by President Reagan of the United States. It was renamed START I after negotiations began on the second START Treaty, which became START II.

However, START negotiation was delayed several times because of differences between the United States and the Soviet Union regarding the terms of the Treaty. President Reagan's introduction of the Strategic Defense Initiative Program in 1983 or his Star War was regarded as a threat by the Soviet Union, and the Soviets withdrew from further negotiations. Failure in these talks resulted in heavy nuclear arms race during the 1980s and finally ended in 1991. The Treaty was ultimately signed on 31 July 1991, five months before the collapse of the Soviet Union.. Its coming into force was delayed due to the collapse of the USSR and awaiting an Annex that enforced the terms of the Treaty upon the newly independent states of Russia, Belarus, Kazakhstan and the Ukraine. The latter three agreed to transport their nuclear arms to Russia for disposal. It remains in effect between the United States and Russia, Belarus, Kazakhstan and Ukraine.

13. START II, 1993: The Strategic Arms Reduction Treaty (START) was signed by the President of United States, George Bush and the Russian President, Boris Yeltsin on 3 January 1993 which banned the use of MIRVs on ICBMs.

However, the signing of the Treaty was postponed a number of times following the non-ratification by the Russian Duma and also the invasion of Iraq by USA. The Treaty was ultimately officially bypassed by the **Strategic Offensive Reductions Treaty (SORT),** agreed to by Presidents George W. Bush and Vladimir Putin at their summit meeting in November 2001. It was signed at the Moscow Summit on 24 May 2002. Both sides agreed to reduce by 2012, the operationally deployed strategic nuclear warheads from the existing number to 1,700–2,200.

14. Chemical Weapons Agreement, 1993: The Agreement was signed in Paris on 13 January 1993 and came into force on 29 April 1997.

Article I provides the general obligations of this Treaty. It states that each state Parties to this Convention undertakes never, under any circumstances to:

(a) Develop, produce, otherwise acquire, stockpile or retain chemical weapons, or transfer, directly or indirectly, chemical weapons to anyone.

(b) Use chemical weapons.

(c) Engage in any military preparations to use chemical weapons.

(d) Assist, encourage or induce, in any way, anyone to engage in any activity prohibited to a state Party under this Convention.

Article I also provides that each state Parties should undertake to destroy chemical weapons it owns or possesses, or that are located in any place under its jurisdiction or control, in accordance with the provisions of this Convention. Simultaneously, it also contains provisions that each state Party must undertake to destroy all chemical weapons it has abandoned on the territory of another state Parties, in accordance with the provisions of this Convention, any chemical weapons production facilities it owns or those possesses, or those that are located in any place under its jurisdiction or control, in accordance with the provisions of this Convention and refrains itself from using riot control agents as a method of warfare.

15. Indefinite Extension of NPT, 1995: On 11 May 1995, at a Global Conference held to review the NPT, the state Parties to the Treaty agreed by consensus and without formal dissent that the Treaty would continue in force permanently and unconditionally. The extension of NPT, however, legitimized the possession of nuclear weapons by the five nuclear powers. India, Pakistan and Israel still rejected the Treaty as discriminatory.

16. *Comprehensive Test Ban Treaty (CTBT), 1996:* The Treaty was opened for signature at New York on 24 September 1996 and it is yet to come into force. It bans all nuclear explosions in all environments, for military or civilian purposes. The general obligations under this treaty are contained in Article I which states that each state Party to the Treaty must ensure that it does not carry out any nuclear weapon test explosion or any other nuclear explosion, and must take steps to prohibit and prevent any such nuclear explosion at any place under its jurisdiction or control. The state Parties must also refrain from causing, encouraging, or in any way participating in the carrying out of any nuclear weapon tests explosion or any other nuclear explosion.

Seventy-one states, including five of the eight the then nuclear-capable states signed the Treaty. At present, the CTBT has been signed by 180 states and ratified by 145 states. India, Pakistan and the Democratic People's Republic of Korea (North Korea) did not sign. In fact, India and Pakistan conducted back-to-back nuclear tests in 1998, while North Korea withdrew from the NPT in 2003 and tested a nuclear device in 2006.

17. *Landmines Ban Treaty, 1997:* The Treaty was formally signed in Ottawa in December 1997 and entered into force on 1 March 1999.

The general obligations under this Treaty embody that each state Party undertakes never, under any circumstances to:

(a) Use anti-personnel mines.

(b) Develop, produce, otherwise acquire, stockpile, retain or transfer to anyone, directly or indirectly, anti-personnel mines.

(c) Assist, encourage or induce, in any way, anyone to engage in any activity prohibited to a state Party under this Convention. Each state Party must also undertake to destroy or ensure the destruction of all anti-personnel mines in accordance with the provisions of this Convention.

Unfortunately, the major landmine-producing and user countries of the world such as China, India and Russia are non-signatories to the Treaty. The United States rejected the draft Treaty and Japan desired 'more flexibility'.

DISARMAMENT AND THE UNITED NATIONS: STRENGTHENING PEACE AND SECURITY THROUGH DISARMAMENT

The United Nations was founded on the belief that peace and security for all peoples would only be possible through disarmament. Article 26 of the United Nations Charter calls for "the establishment and maintenance of international peace and security with the least diversion for armaments of the world's human and economic resources". The UN Charter also provides for necessary commitments towards disarmament and arms control. Article 11 of the UN Charter declares "The General Assembly can consider the general principles of cooperation for the maintenance of international peace and security. These can include the principles governing disarmament, and the regulation of armaments". Article 26 outlines the functions of the Security Council on matters relating to disarmament. It states that in order to promote the establishment of international peace and security, "the Security Council shall be responsible for formulating plans to be submitted to the members of the United Nations for the establishment of a system for the regulation of armaments". Article 47 embodies provisions for the creation of a Military Staff Committee for advising and assisting the Security Council "on all questions relating to the Security Council's requirements for the maintenance of international peace and security, the employment and command of forces placed at its disposal, the regulation of armaments, and possible disarmaments".

The United Nations has worked for nuclear disarmament ever since its first resolution in 1946 entitled "The Establishment of a Commission to Deal with the Problems Raised by the Discovery of Atomic Energy". The UN works for three types of nuclear disarmament:

- *General disarmament:* allows nations to keep minimum necessary police force.
- *Quantitative and qualitative disarmament:* involves overall reduction and abolition of only certain types of armaments.
- *Total disarmament:* the complete elimination of armaments.

The UNGA has adopted a number of resolutions and established a number of international regimes to work towards effective disarmament and arms control. The institutions comprise the:

1. General Assembly First Committee
2. The 1540 Committee (set up by Security Council Resolution in 2004)
3. UN Disarmament Commission
4. Conference on Disarmament
5. Secretary-General's Advisory Board
6. UNIDIR (United Nations Institute for Disarmament Research)

The United Nations also tries to reach the goal of disarmament through its Office for Disarmament Affairs (UNODA). The Office promotes the goal of nuclear disarmament and non-proliferation and the strengthening of the disarmament regimes in respect of other weapons of mass destruction, chemical and biological weapons. It also promotes disarmament efforts in the area of conventional weapons, especially land mines and small arms. UNODA provides substantive and organizational support for the norm-setting in the area of disarmament through the work of the General Assembly and its First

Committee, the Disarmament Commission, the Conference on Disarmament and other bodies.

PROBLEMS OF DISARMAMENT

The United Nations was founded on the belief that peace and security for all peoples would only be possible through disarmament. However, the track record of disarmament efforts is not praiseworthy. Morgenthau[10] points out that success or failure of any particular disarmament effort depends on:

- The ratio among the armaments of different nations.
- The standard according to which, within the ratio, different types and quantities of armaments are to be allocated.
- What is the actual effect in view of intended reduction of the armaments.
- Bearing of disarmament on the issues of international order and peace.

The primary obstacles to disarmament arise from these problems, especially the ones related to the ratios of strength. As there are no fixed ratios among weapons, the questions of standards of allocation of different types and quantities of armaments to be allotted to various nations remain unresolved. Further, the existence of mutual distrust among states frustrates disarmament efforts. National interest and security also make the states cautious on the issues of disarmament and arms control. Political rivalry and disputes also fuel arms race and disarmament commitments break down. Advancement in military R&D and technological innovations induce the states to go on procuring arms and nukes which give rise to proliferation of nuclear weapons and an ensuing nuclear arms race, as was evident during the Cold War between the US and the USSR or as seen between the two South Asian neighbours, India and Pakistan. Besides, the Military Industrial Complex (MIC) also prevents any sort of policy barring the reduction of arms production. The MIC is a lucrative industry in the United States, France, Britain and Russia. The manufacture and sale of weapons is the most profitable business, and unless the MIC is restrained, disarmament measures will not reach its fruition.

Though states suffer from the fears of dangers of nuclear war or destruction from the WMDs or international or regional instability from unregulated arms race, they may gear their efforts towards disarmament and arms control, yet a major breakthrough is still a dream. Till then disarmament and arms control measures will continue to be small and quite slow.

EXERCISES

1. What do you understand by disarmament? Comment on the major developments in the field of disarmament and arms control since the Second World War.

2. Write briefly on any three: PTBT, NPT, INF, CTBT.

3. Discuss the disarmament attempts made by the United States and Russia to reduce their armament stockpiles. (SALTI, SALTII, INF, STARTI, STARTII, SORT).

4. Write on any four: Outer Space Treaty (1967), Sea-bed Treaty (1971), Biological Weapons Conventions (1972), Convention on Prohibition of Military or other Hostile Use of Environment Modification Techniques (1977), Chemical Weapons Agreement (1993).

5. Discuss the role of the United Nations in the field disarmament.

REFERENCES

[1] Morgenthau, Hans J., *Politics Among Nations: The Struggle for Power and Peace*, Kalyani Publishers, New Delhi, 1985, p. 419.

[2] Couloumbis, Theodre A. and James H. Wolfe, *Introduction to International Relations—Power and Justice*, Prentice-Hall of India, New Delhi, 1986, p. 233.

[3] *ibid.*, p. 234.

[4] *ibid.*

[5] Quoted in Vinay Kumar Malhotra, *International Relations*, Anmol Publications, New Delhi, 2006, p. 354.

[6] Kegley, Charles W., Jr. and Eugene R. Wittkopf, *World Politics—Trends and Transformation*, St. Martin's Press, New York, 1990, p. 404.

[7] http://www.undemocracy.com/A-RES-1(I).pdf.

[8] Howlett, Darryl, Nuclear Proliferation, *in* John Baylis and Steve Smith (Eds.), *The Globalization of World Politics,* Oxford University Press, London, 1997, p. 351.

[9] Banerjee, Jyotirmoy, *Strategic Studies*, Allied Publishers, New Delhi, 1998, pp. 143–144.

[10] Morgenthau, *op. cit.*, n. 1, p. 424.

13

Globalization

INTRODUCTION

As a central concept in the present day international scenario, globalization is hard to define. Still, scholars have made attempts to provide a basic understanding of the concept. The concept has got inextricably linked with the process of transformation touching upon every aspect of social, political and economic development around the globe. It can be seen as a process by which the population of the world is increasingly bonded into a single society. In the social front, globalization signifies closer interaction of people and homogenization of culture and values and the world being transformed into a 'global village'. Politically, it refers to the complex networks of global governance and shared political values resulting in the development of a tendency towards homogenization of global political culture. Economically, it is manifested in the form of liberalization tendencies, privatization, deregulation leading to a free market regime. On a greater plane, globalization has posed challenges to the raison d'être of the states—the dominant actors in international relations.

CONCEPT OF GLOBALIZATION

Scholars like Anthony Gidden (1990) a British sociologist conceive globalization as "the intensification of worldwide social relations which link distant localities in such a way that local happenings are shaped by events occurring many miles away and vice versa". Robert Cox an American political Scientist (1994) visualizes globalization from a different perspective. For him, "The characteristics of globalization trend include the internationalizing of production, the new international division of labor, new migratory movements from South to North, the new competitive environment that accelerates these processes, and the internationalizing of state...making states into agencies of the globalizing world". For some others, "The world is becoming a global shopping mall in which ideas and products are available at the same time". According to Scholte, globalization refers to processes by which social relations acquire relatively distanceless and borderless qualities so that human lives increasingly play out in the world as a single place.[1]

According to Deepak Nayyar*, eminent academic and administrator, globalization can be more precisely defined as "a process associated with increasing economic openness, growing economic independence and deepening economic integration between countries of the world economy".

According to David Held a British political scientist and a notable figure in the field of international relations and others, the understanding of the world as reflected in the idea of globalization is one that is "rapidly being moulded into a shared social space by economic and technological forces and that developments in one region of the world can have profound consequences for the life chances of individuals and communities on the other side of the globe". Held and his fellow scholars look at globalization as "widening, deepening and speeding up of worldwide interconnectedness in all aspects of contemporary social life...".[2]

The central point is that under the forces of globalization, the greater part of social life is determined by global processes in which it seems as if national cultures, national economies and national borders are fast integrating under one universal umbrella. The term 'globalization' encompasses various aspects including expanded international trade, telecommunications, monetary coordination, multinational corporations, cultural exchanges of new types and scales, migration and refugee flows, and relations between the world's rich and poor countries.[3]

FEATURES OF GLOBALIZATION

Globalization is marked by liberalization, privatization, free trade, deregulation of tariff barriers, internationalization of national economies, global movement

---

*Deepak Nayyar (ed.), *Governing Globalization: Issues and Institutions*, Oxford University Press, Oxford, 2002.

of capital, information and technology, increased activities of economic and political organizations, and rapid growth in globalized social movements. Most importantly, globalization has come to signify 'deterritorialization', and geography is becoming less relevant to how people live and interact. Globalization is characterized by increasing in flow of trade, capital and information, as well as mobility of individuals across borders.

Therefore, globalization signifies:

1. Opening up of national economies to foreign capital, foreign direct investment and foreign technologies.

2. Efforts of integrating national economies with the global economy.

3. Free trade, meaning free flow of trade and removal of tariff and trade barriers, protective regimes including granting of Most Favoured Nation (MFN) status.

4. Privatization is the key to liberalization which means less and less control of state over ownership of means of production and distribution.

5. Increased proliferation of agents of globalization in the form of multinational corporations and international institutions such as the World Trade Organization (WTO), International Monetary Fund (IMF), the World Bank and others.

6. Information and technological revolution, bringing about a sea-change in modes of communication, has resulted in fast movement of capital, goods, information and people around the globe.

7. Deterritorialization is making geography irrelevant. Global stock and bond trading and fixation of international financial and exchange rate transactions have really made geography a thing of the past.

8. Globalized social movements have resulted in global civic activism and range from movements for human rights, women's issues, greenpeace and other environment movements to HIV/AIDS.

9. Global governance is through suprastate agencies such as international and regional organizations, the United Nations, the IMF, the World Bank, WTO, and a host of regional arrangements like the ASEAN, European Union and others.

EFFECTS OF GLOBALIZATION

The effects of globalization are difficult to discuss as some view globalization as the fruition of liberal economic principles, while some others are sceptical about it. The former perspective regards that a global marketplace has brought prosperity and growth, not to all, but positively to those integrated with the global market. They talk about dilution of state authority and highlight the importance of supranational institutions like the IMF, the World Bank and EU, and also the pre-eminence of transnational actors like the MNCs. The sceptics, on the other hand, regard the deepening of gap between the rich and the poor countries and their contention that the geographical distinction such as the North–South divide is disappearing in favour of a single global market is hardly tenable.[4] The world has witnessed series of protests and movements against globalization with its apparatus, especially those like the IMF and the World Bank, and the mantra of liberalization and privatization. The movement against globalization took a concrete expression in Seattle where thousands of people gathered to show their discontent against globalization during the annual WTO meeting in 1999. That was a significant beginning as, after Seattle meeting, there were series of movements across the globe at different times. Another significant protest was held in a big way in Genoa in 2001. From Seattle to Genoa is a long history of struggle against globalization, which has not yet died down and is still continuing. The world once again witnessed violent anti-G 20 protest in Toronto in Canada during the G-20 summit in June 2010. Police vehicles were set ablaze and windows of stores and banks were thrashed with stones and damaged by protestors.

Professor Bhagwati[5], in his *In Defense of Globalization*, points out that there are two groups of critics of globalization. He identifies as one of these two groups as hard-core protestors who have deep-seated antipathy towards globalization. Though they come from different intellectual and ideological backgrounds and do not share the same kind of sentiments, yet they have some commonness in their discontent, towards globalization. This discontent according to Prof. Jagdish Bhagwati, is a trilogy. The trilogy of discontents against globalization is:

- Anti-capitalism
- Anti-globalization
- Anti-corporation mindset

The second group of critics, whose discontents are within the parameters of mainstream dissent and discourse, engage in translating their discontents into arguments that economic globalization is the cause of several social evils today, such as poverty in developing countries and deterioration of the environment worldwide. He refuted the claim that globalization is the root cause of many of the social evils and in several chapters in his book he demonstrates that, in fact, the various social causes that we all espouse, such as advancement of gender equality and reduction of poverty, are advanced and not set back by globalization.[6] Therefore, he rejected the arguments put forward by a prominent women's group who expressed their fears concerning the impact of globalization on their agendas and interests involving global care chains, unpaid housework, intra-family decision-making, and WTO rulings without analyzing the gender effects of such rulings, the IMF and World Bank conditionalities which are part of structural adjustment programmes and their impact upon women, tourism induced prostitution and trafficking of women. Professor

Bhagwati concluded that the broader criticisms that many women's groups have voiced about the negative effects of globalization on women are not convincing.[7] He even rejects the claims that globalization and democracy are at odds. For him, "It is precisely the growing awareness that globalization creates a web of relationships that introduce such complexity, and hence prudence and pause in the policy choices of nation-states, has led to the charges that globalization and democracy are at odds. But the question whether democracy is enhanced or diminished by globalization is not so easily answered".[8] For him, it should be the endeavour of the world community to consider the ways in which they can reinforce the social effects of globalization.

Stiglitz,[9] in his *Globalization And Its Discontent,* however, is of the opinion that opening up to international trade has helped many countries to develop at a rapid pace though it may have hit the local enterprises hard. Similarly, foreign aid, despite its pitfalls, has succeeded to bring benefits to many. Globalization has also opened up to millions in developing countries access to knowledge well beyond their reach. Therefore, globalization is not all that bad. However, Stiglitz opines that the proponents of globalization have forwarded an unbalanced form of it. To them globalization, typically associated with the American style, is progress, and developing countries must accept it if they want to grow and fight poverty effectively. But the fact remains that, despite embracing the forces of globalization, the conditions of the poor and developing countries of the world have not developed much and the world remains divided between the haves and the have nots.

Stiglitz while analyzing annual publications of *World Development Report, World Economic Indicators* and *Global Economic Prospects and the Developing Countries 2000* is quite critical and shows that the Developed West has succeeded in forcing the poor countries to remove trade barriers while retaining their own restrictive regimes and deprived the poor countries from export income. Even the developed countries retained their quotas on a multitude of goods from textiles to sugar and continued subsidizing agriculture while pressurizing the poor countries to eliminate their subsidies. Western banks benefited from the loosening of capital market controls in Asia and Africa, whereas these regions suffered when inflows of speculative hot money got reversed.[10] Undoubtedly, these economies suffered as can be seen during the Global Economic Crisis of 2008. Therefore, globalization has neither succeeded in reducing poverty nor has it brought in stability in the financial market. The economic crises in Asia and Latin America in 1997 and 1998 and the current global crisis of 2008 have proved that collapse of one emerging market currency will pull the others down. The benefits of globalization appear to be too meagre compared to the price paid in terms of the social, political, economic, cultural and environmental problems it has created.

Economic globalization results in integration of national economies into global economy such that the global forces that act upon the domestic economies are out of control of national governments. Nevertheless, globalization has been able to bring in certain positive benefits too. A *World Bank Report: Globalization, Growth and Poverty: Building an Inclusive World Economy* states that 24 developing countries of the world have managed to integrate their economy into the world economy over two decades by the end of 1990s and have now achieved higher growth in incomes, longer life expectancy, and better schooling as in the case of China, India, Hungary and Mexico. Globalization has also enabled easy flow of capital into domestic economy, commercial borrowings, collaborations, transfer of technology, service-based knowledge, and so on. But the global movement of capital and services, the MNCs and global stock and bonding have given rise to such a system where the sovereignty of the state becomes limited. Besides, world organizations controlled by the developed countries of the West, such as the WTO or the World Bank and their programme of *structural adjustments* in the domestic economies of languishing economies seeking aid clearly reduces the sovereignty of the state.[11]

"Globalization often has been a very powerful force for poverty reduction, but too many countries and people have been left out. Important reasons for this exclusion are weak governance and policies in the non-integrating countries, tariffs and other barriers that poor countries and poor people face in accessing rich country markets, and declining development assistance.

Some anxieties about globalization are well-founded, but reversing globalization would come at an intolerably high price, destroying the prospects of prosperity for many millions of poor people. We do not agree with those who would retreat into a world of nationalism and protectionism. That way leads to deeper poverty and it is fundamentally hostile to the well-being of people in the developing countries. Instead, we must make globalization work for the poor people of the world."

—**Nicholas Stern, Former Senior Vice President and Chief Economist, The World Bank**[12]

Cultural dimension of globalization has entailed a grave problem of what is sometimes identified as *cultural imperialism*. The predominant culture of globalization is the American culture, which now seems to proliferate deep into indigenous societies and threaten the very existence of such local indigenous cultures. McDonald's, Microsoft and Madona (to name a few) or Michael Jackson seem to be reaching the remotest corner of the globe. Hollywood seems to have its sway all around the globe. It is true when cultures come into contact there is going to be some mixing, but the fact is that American culture is the dominant culture that prevails. So it is not the folk songs which attract the youth now but it is the American pop and Indi-pop, and the Indian version of American pop that seem to be popular in a country like India. Therefore, it is actually global culture in the form of 'Americanization' that underlies fear and apprehensions about vanishing indigenous culture.

The political dimension of globalization has resulted in the formation of a *universal political culture*. This culture advocates the cause of democracy and democratic institutions. The enthusiasts of globalization with great vigour had championed the cause of democracy and viewed globalization and democratization to be the two sides of the same coin. With the collapse of communism and the conceived victory of capitalism, the liberalists thought that this wind of change would help in ushering democracy throughout the world and in some instances also suggested exporting democracies to countries which are under authoritarian rule. But in reality it has been seen that in most cases even democratic states are unable to control the global flows. They, in most cases, cannot secure public opinion in matters related to global capital, information flow or environment related issues. Actually, the whole idea of democratization is related to market democracy. The market provides larger scope for the popular participation. Money and materialism are the most sought after. Traditional democratic concerns for human dignity and equal opportunity have been replaced by obsessions for managerial efficiency and product quality.

Globalization has also resulted in increased activities of transnational agents such as the terrorists, transborder criminals, drug-traffickers, and even arms transfer across the border. The pathbreaking advancements in technology and information revolution have made their work easier. The Mumbai terrorist attack of 26/11 revealed the use of hi-tech equipment, including satellite phones by the terrorists. Globalization, therefore, has brought human insecurity into the forefront. It has gone into the psyche, specially of the city dwellers and is keeping the security agencies on their toes all the time.

Professor Bhagwati recommends that globalization must be wisely regulated to ensure its benign effects. Stiglitz[13] insists that globalization must have a human face. He, while outlining certain reforms, like the need for reforms in international public institutions, system of governance of international monetary institutions like the WTO, the IMF, and the World Bank, and development assistance and other reforms, opines that these would make globalization fairer and more effective in raising living standards, especially of the poor. The need of the hour is not just institutional changes but changing the mindset about globalization. He concludes by saying: "If we are to address the legitimate concerns of those who have expressed a discontent with globalization, if we are to make globalization work for billions of people for whom it has not, if we are to make globalization with a human face succeed, then our voices must be raised. We cannot, we should not, stand idly by".

GLOBALIZATION AND THE SOVEREIGNTY OF THE STATE

The Westphalian model of state system has come under the threats of globalization. Though the states, still surviving, exercise their power and authority in certain respects, but the core of the Westphalian model, that is, the concept of sovereignty, has been deeply undermined in a fast globalizing world.

The concept of sovereignty pertains to a specific reference, to a specific territory where governments exercise absolute authority. But the forces of globalization have rendered the territorial limits useless. In other words, there has been a deterritorialization of the world.

The state in a globalizing world has to work along with the forces which are not under its control even such as surveillance by global governance agencies, nationalism, global ecological problems, satellite communications, electronic money transfers, multinational companies, migration, information flows, technology transfers and, most importantly, nuclear weapons and weapons of mass destruction. Scholars point out that the concept of absolute sovereignty was developed under conditions of relatively low level of interdependence among the states. However, the complex level of interdependence with large flow of capital, labour, technology and information across border has now emerged within the changing patterns of sovereignty and its meaning and conditionality are continuously changing in a fast globalizing world.

The suprastate global governance system has also limited the state sovereignty. In several fields, ranging from macroeconomic policy, conflict management, to human rights and environmental movements more than the state it is now the suprastate agencies such as the United Nations, the IMF, the WTO, the World Bank, and various regional arrangements have significant roles to play.

Global social movements have also now come to undermine the sovereignty of states. These movements on various social, political, economic issues or even ecological issues exploit the benefits of globalization, that is, fast travel and communication, the Internet, developments in telecommunication, awareness about global laws help to conduct transborder social movements which pervade the sovereign authority of the states. These social movements to some extent succeed in bringing about changes in the policies of the states.

The operation of MNCs and their interference with the domestic policies of their host countries have really undermined the sovereignty of the states. Some of the industrial MNCs have annual sales of tens of billions of dollars each. No wonder, MNCs like IBM, GE, Microsoft, Wall-Mart, and others have become more powerful than many sovereign states.

Nuclear weapons have changed the whole perception of security of the state. The states are no longer invincible. They have become vulnerable preys to the latest technological discoveries of long-range cruise missiles, intercontinental ballistic missiles (ICBMs), short-range ballistic missiles (SRBMs), multiple independently targetable reentry vehicles(MIRVs), and a host of other improved newer weapons of mass destruction, which have completely made the concept of territoriality passé.

It might seem that under such circumstances, globalization has really brought an end to state sovereignty. But this argument is hardly tenable. Experiences show that states do continue to be the most powerful actors and, in times of turbulence, such as the present global economic crisis states have again reaffirmed their authority as ultimately it is the governments who are providing bailout packages for the financial institutions in their respective countries. It becomes clear that under the pressures of globalization today states have to perform roles different from the earlier times, but in no way have states become less significant.

EXERCISES

1. Discuss the concept of globalization with special mention about its features and effects on world politics.

2. Critically analyze the effects of globalization on state sovereignty. Has globalization meant an end of state territoriality?

REFERENCES

[1] Scholte, John Aart, "The Globalization of World Politics," *in* John Baylis and Steve Smith (Eds.), *The Globalization of World Politics,* Oxford University Press, London, 1997, pp. 14–15.

[2] Lawson, Stephanie, *International Relations,* Polity Press, UK, Cambridge, 2003, First Indian Reprint, 2004, p. 118.

[3] Goldstein, Joshua S., *International Relations*, Pearson Education, New Delhi, 2006, p. 330.

[4] *ibid.*, p. 331.

[5] Bhagwati, Jagdish, *In Defense of Globalization* ,Oxford University Press, Oxford India Paperbacks, OUP, New Delhi, 2007, p. 4.

[6] *ibid.*

[7] *ibid.*, p. 91.

[8] *ibid.*, p. 92.

[9] Stiglitz, Joseph, *Globalization and Its Discontent*, Penguin Books India, New Delhi, 2003, pp. 1–22.

[10] *ibid.*

[11] World Bank Report *Globalization, Growth and Poverty: Building an Inclusive World Economy,* World Bank Washington, DC published in May, 2001.

http://econ.worldbank.org/external/defaultmain?menuPK=477838&pagePK=64168092&piPK=64168088&theSitePK=477826.

[12] *ibid.*

[13] Stiglitz, Joseph, *op. cit.* n. 9, pp. 215–252.

14

Development and International Relations

INTRODUCTION

Development has been a central theme of discussion in social science discourses for a long time but what is noteworthy is the expansion of the meaning of the term development. The economic disparity between the rich and the poor countries, the obstacles faced by the poor developing countries in the path of their development and the causes behind their underdevelopment have created immense enthusiasm among the scholars belonging to the different genres to probe into the questions of development. Whether development should be, strictly speaking, seen to be something related to economic growth or it is something beyond that has created myriad perspectives on development. There are the liberal and alternative views on development accompanied by the Marxian concept on what constitutes underdevelopment. There is also now the current definition of development provided by the United Nations, Development Programme (UNDP) along with the Human Development Index (HDI), 1990. The United Nations Conference on Environment and Development (UNCED) and also referred to as the Rio Summit or the Earth Summit), 1992 gave a new direction to the concept of development which upheld 27 principles intended to guide the future sustainable development around the world.

CONCEPT OF DEVELOPMENT

Since the end of the Second World War, the dominant understanding of development was akin to the concept of economic growth within the context of a free market international economy. It was believed that only economic growth was a panacea for poverty. Therefore, measurement of economic growth in terms of Gross Domestic Product per capita, industrialization and agriculture came to be acknowledged as criteria for categorizing countries on the scale of development. Likewise, World Bank reports reflected categorization of countries as low-income, lower middle-income, upper middle-income, or high-income countries.

This perception of development, as synonymous with economic growth, took firm root in the aftermath of the Second World War. In post-War years, the reconstruction of the war-torn economies of the developed world, especially of Europe, became a priority. The course of the reconstruction process was, however, guided by the Cold War calculations and it saw huge transfer of money from the United States to Europe in the form of bilateral aid through the Marshall Plan of 1947. Harry S. Truman, the 33rd President of the United States, gave meaning to the concept of development and also adopted it as a goal of state policy. It is generally accepted that Truman's Point Four Program, launched on 10 January 1949, endowed the term 'development' with a special meaning in the sense that development was linked with economic growth (in the war torn Europe) which in turn was linked with the growth of liberal international economic order and containment of communism. Therefore, post-War international order exhibits an attempt by the West to create a stable international order through the United Nations and its affiliates, such as the International Monetary Fund (IMF) the World Bank and GATT. These affiliates were supposed to provide the institutional bases of a liberal international economic order. Simultaneously, around this time, there was a wave of decolonization and numerous countries emerged on the political scenario. They were ascribed as 'Third World' countries and now the focus shifted towards them. The international organizations and agencies as well as the United States and the West now tried to focus on the needs of the developing countries. With the international atmosphere already charged with the Cold War temperament, there started a tussle between the Western bloc and the Eastern bloc to win over the 'Third World'. Each presented its model of development as the best. The United States believed that there always is a possibility of unlimited economic growth in a free-market system. Economies would reach a 'take-off' point and thereafter wealth would trickle down to those at the bottom. The underlying assumption was the superiority of the 'Western' model and knowledge. The process would involve reliance on 'expert knowledge', generally Western and external, large capital investments in large projects, advanced technology, and expansion of the private sphere. On the other hand, the USSR projected its pattern of development as the model means of progress in which they upheld the central planning in the socialist sphere by the state as the preferred method of ushering in economic growth as opposed to market-driven economic growth in the capitalist system. But both these models heavily relied on industrialization and GDP per capita economic growth. But the assessment of the post-War international economic order portrayed a dark picture of the Third World economies. On the one hand, the developing countries were caught up in a vicious circle of debt trap and could not disentangle themselves from it and, on the other, they were suffering so severely from the structural adjustment programmes of the IMF and the World Bank that they neither could register a positive rate of development nor could they ensure the well-being of their people. An estimate shows that from 1970 to 1982, the developing countries were encouraged to borrow more since the real interest rates were extremely low. Further, the export revenue with which they were reimbursing their debt increased due to the increase in the price of raw materials. However, by the end of 1979, the sudden increase in the interest rates imposed on the world unilaterally by the United States resulted in an increase in the sums to be repaid. Matters were made worse with the fall in commodity prices followed by drop in the price of crude oil. This made it difficult for the oil-producing countries such as Mexico to repay the loan. Many Latin American, Asian and the sub-Saharan countries faced an extreme debt crisis.[1]

Therefore, it was thought that there was a necessity for reassessment of the post-War international economic order. What emerged was obviously a critical alternative assessment of the post-War international economic order and a critical alternative view of development. The first and the foremost thing that was focused was the statistical measurements of economic growth, and the GDP per capita did not reveal the true story of development process in the developing countries, especially the quality of life in a particular Third World country. The critics of development orthodoxy emphasized more on the *pattern of distribution* of gains within the global society and within the individual state. The economic liberalism has fostered a great divide between the rich and the poor countries and increased dependency of the developing states on the developed ones.

The great divide led to a revival of Marxist and neo-Marxist tradition, identified as the dependency school which highlighted that the under-development of the Third World countries placed in the periphery was the result of the development and growth of wealth of the Western countries placed in the core. The dependency scholars like Andre Gunder Frank (1967) and others highlighted that:

- Underdevelopment is a historical process. It is not a condition necessarily intrinsic to the Third World.
- The dominant and the dependent countries together form a capitalist system.

- Underdevelopment is an inherent consequence of the functioning of the world system. The periphery is plundered of its surplus; this leads to development of the core and underdevelopment of the periphery.

They also highlighted how multinationals add up to the underdevelopment of the periphery. Further, these scholars emphasized that MNCs:

- Impose a universal consumption pattern, without taking local needs into account.
- Use capital-intensive techniques in areas with large labour resources.
- Out-compete national capital, or undertake joint ventures with local capital.
- Use a variety of methods to transfer the capital.
- Involve themselves in national, political and economic affairs via (among others) their relationships with the local bourgeoisie.

Frank's ideas were further reinforced by the World Systems theorists like Immanuel Wallerstein. Like Frank, Wallerstein also saw that a capitalist world economy had existed since the sixteenth century, that is, from the beginning of the Colonial era. Increasingly, countries which were previously isolated and self-supporting were drawn into the world economy. This ultimately resulted in the creation of an industrialized core, the underdeveloped periphery, and the Newly Industrialized Countries (NICs) semi-periphery. The relation between the core and the periphery is one of dependency and that between core and periphery is a go-between. Semi-peripheral countries import sophisticated and advanced technologies from the core and in return export semi-manufactured goods to the core. There is also import of raw materials from the periphery and export of industrial end products.[2] Therefore, a consciousness grew regarding such exploitative international economic order.

On the practical front, this was reflected in the demand of New International Economic Order (NIEO). Specific proposals for changes in the economic system were advanced at the Summit Conference of Non-Aligned Nations held in Algiers in September 1973. Following that, the Sixth Special Session of the UN General Assembly was called hastily in April 1974 where it declared its determination to establish a New International Economic Order. But this was highly unsuccessful. The Session adopted, without a vote, a manifesto entitled "Declaration and Program of Action of the New International Order". In December 1974, the General Assembly approved the Charter of Economic Rights and Duties of States. However, even with all the Declaration and the approval of the Charter, the exploitative and unequal international economic order continues.

Despite such failure, what was realized was that the traditional or the orthodox conception of the 'trickle down' failed to bring about substantial development, and inequalities continued in the international economic order. Some of the developing countries did see an increasing rate of growth in terms of GDP per capita, but this was not reflected in their societies at large, that is, in terms of the well-being of the majority of the population. The South Commission observed, "Inequalities tended to widen as the economy grew and became more industrialized... Increasingly, the rich and powerful countries of the South were able to enjoy the lifestyle and consumption patterns of developed countries of the North. But large segments of the population experienced no significant improvement in their standard of living, while being able to see the growing affluence of the few". [3]

Further, the plight of the sub-Saharan Africa in the 1980s identified as the 'lost decade', with declining GDP per capita in most of the developing countries, coupled with the stringent structural adjustment policies, increasing debt burden, declining terms of trade, uncertain markets for goods, protectionist policies pursued by developed countries, and insufficient technological and financial transfers to the developing world from the developed countries provided impetus to think in different terms while looking at development.

Thus, there was the 1987 UNICEF report entitled *Adjustment with A Human Face*, which highlighted the social cost of structural adjustment policies. This report also argued for a redesigning of the structural adjustments taking into account the social costs.

A breakthrough came in 1990 with the attempt of the United Nations Development Programme (UNDP) to define development. The First Report on Human Development tries to define it "as a process of enlarging the range of people's choices increasing their opportunities for education, health care, income and employment and covering the full range of human choices from a sound physical environment to economic and political freedom". The Report further stated, "This report is about people and about how development enlarges their choices. It is about more than GNP growth, more than income and wealth and more than producing commodities and accumulating capital. A person's access to income may be one of the choice, but it is not the sum total of human behaviour". It viewed human development as "a process of enlarging people's choices. The most critical of these wide-ranging choices are to live a long and healthy life, to be educated and to have access to resources needed for a decent standard of living. Additional choices include political freedom, guaranteed human rights and personal self-respect". The 1990 report introduced the Human Development Index (HDI) and identified three essential elements as essential to human life: *life expectancy*, *knowledge*, and *decent standard of living*. Subsequent Human Development Reports have led to the broadening of the concept of development.

The Human Development Report 1995 talked about gender equality and it stated, "human development if not engendered is endangered". Further, the 1997 Human Development Report considered poverty eradication to be the prime objective of human development. It not only looked at poverty from the perspectives of income, basic needs and capacity but also outlined the criteria of ill-being which is inevitable for assessing capacity-building and measurement of well-being. This included criteria like being disabled, lacking land, livestock, etc., being unable to bury their dead ones, being "poor in people" lacking social support, having to accept demeaning low status work and others. Another aspect of this report was the preparation of Human Poverty Index (HPI-1) and (HPI-2) for the developed and the developing countries, respectively. Considering the three elements of human life as prescribed by the Human Development Index, the HPI highlighted deprivation of these three elements in the form of deprivation related to:

1. Survival—vulnerability to death at a relatively early age.
2. Knowledge—being excluded from the world of reading and communication.
3. Decent living.

The Human Development Report of 2003 was a reflection of a pledge by the international community to combat poverty and hunger. It set the "Millennium Development Goals: a compact among nations to end human poverty". The declaration made by the Heads of States made it binding on them to "attack inadequate income, widespread hunger, gender inequality, environmental deterioration and lack of education, health care and clean water". These also included actions on the part of the developed countries to reduce debt and increase aid, trade and technology transfer to poorer countries. Some of the targets outlined by the Millennium Development Goals were:

• Eradication of extreme poverty and hunger
• Achieving universal primary education
• Promotion of gender equality and empowerment of women
• Reduction of child mortality
• Improvement of maternal health
• Combating HIV/AIDS, malaria and other diseases
• Ensuring environmental sustainability
• Development of a global partnership

Therefore, there was a sea-change in the concept of development, so much so that the critical assessment of the post-War international economic order led to the formation of a critical alternative view of development. This view stated that the process of development should be

• need-oriented (material and non-material);
• endogenous (coming from within a society);
• self-reliant (in terms of human, natural and cultural resources);
• ecologically sound; and
• based on structural transformations (of economy, society and power relations).

This vision of development championed by the NGOs and the two-year preparatory process before the UN Conference on Environment and

Development (UNCED) in Rio in June 1992, gave a chance to the voiceless groups like the indigenous people, women and children to express their views. This further got a boost with the organization of an alternative NGO forum in Copenhagen, parallel to the UN World Summit for Social Development there in 1995. The *Alternative Declaration* produced by the NGO Forum at the Copenhagen Summit highlighted the principles of community participation and empowerment. Equity, participation, self-reliance, role of women and youths and sustainability were also given importance. The Summit Declaration condemned economic liberalism and identified trade liberalization and privatization as the causes of concentration of wealth. It also demanded immediate cancellation of debt, improved terms of trade, transparency and accountability of IMF and the World Bank, and the regulation of the activities of the multinationals.[4]

Therefore, the mainstream debate is now centred around sustainable development. The concept of development now not only stands broadened but also related to environment and sustainability. This brings us to the discussion of sustainable development at length.

SUSTAINABLE DEVELOPMENT

The idea of sustainable development found roots in the thinking of some scholars, popularly known as 'Club of Rome' in the year 1972. They argued that if the pattern of limitless growth continued, then there would arise problems of sustainability.

The same year, the United Nations Conference on the Human Environment (also known as the **Stockholm Conference**) was held under the auspices of the United Nations in Stockholm Sweden, during 5–16 June 1972. There were serious concerns about the patterns of ongoing limitless development as the world was becoming incapable of supporting and sustaining present rates of economic and population growth vis-à-vis resource depletion and ecological crisis. It was the UN's first major conference on international environmental issues, and marked a turning point in the development of international environmental politics. The Conference was opened and addressed by the Swedish Prime Minister Olof Palme and the UN Secretary-General, Kurt Waldheim to discuss the state of the global environment. It is recognized as the beginning of modern political and public awareness of global environmental problems. It was attended by the representatives of 113 countries, 19 inter-governmental agencies, and more than 400 inter-governmental and non-governmental organizations.

The landmarks, however, in the sustainable development thinking are obviously the *World Conservation Strategy* (1980), *Our Common Future* (1987), and *Caring for the Earth* (1991).[5]

The World Conservation Strategy (WCS) was prepared in the 1970s by the International Union for the Conservation of Nature and Natural Resources (IUCN), the World Wildlife Fund (WWF), and the United Nations Environment Programme (UNEP), and published in 1980. It represented a shift in thinking about conservation as it highlighted cure for the loss of wildlife species and habitats rather than prevention. It upheld that both conservation and development were the key to a sustainable society. The WCS identified three objectives for conservation. The first two were *maintenance of essential ecological processes* and *preservation of genetic diversity*. The third principle followed from the above two. It was the *sustainable utilization of resources*.

A more concrete development towards the concept of sustainable development came with the publication of the Report of the Brundtland Commission. The Report of the Brundtland Commission (officially known as the *World Commission on Environment and Development*) was prepared under the aegis of the United Nations World Commission in 1983 on Environment and Development elucidating the concept of sustainable development. The Commission was created to address the growing concern "about the accelerating deterioration of the human environment and natural resources and the consequences of that deterioration for economic and social development" and it was felt that it was in the common interest of all nations to establish policies for sustainable development. The Report entitled *Our Common Future* was published in 1987. The report tried to recapture the spirit of the United Nations Conference on the Human Environment—the **Stockholm Conference**—which had introduced environmental concerns to the formal political development sphere.

According to the report of the Commission, sustainable development is "Development that meets the needs of the present without compromising the ability of future generations to meet their own needs, improved living standard for all, better protected and managed ecosystem and a safer; more prosperous future".

The critical objectives for environment and development policies proposed in the Brundtland Report are:

- Reviving growth
- Changing the quality of growth
- Meeting essential needs for jobs, food energy, water and sanitation
- Ensuring a sustainable level of population
- Conserving and enhancing the resource base
- Reorienting technology and managing risk
- Merging environment and economics in decision-making.[6]

Caring for the Earth was prepared in 1991 by the International Union for the Conservation of Nature and Natural Resources (IUCN) and it identified nine principles of sustainable development. The priority requirements of Caring for the Earth are as follows:

- Respect and care for the community of life
- Improve the quality of human life

- Conserve the Earth's vitality and diversity
- Minimize the depletion of non-renewable resources
- Keep within the Earth's carrying capacity
- Change personal attitudes and practices
- Enable communities to care for their own environments
- Forge a global alliance.[7]

The publication of *Our Common Future** and the work of the *World Commission on Environment and Development* laid the groundwork for the convening of the 1992 Earth Summit and the adoption of Agenda 21, the Rio Declaration, and also the establishment of the Commission on Sustainable Development.

The United Nations Conference on Environment and Development (UNCED also referred to as the *Rio Summit* or the *Earth Summit*) was held from 3 June to 14 June 1992. The chief achievement of this Summit was the **Agenda 21: Green Paths to the Future** or the **Rio Declaration of 1992**. The Rio Declaration consisted of 27 principles intended to guide future sustainable development around the world. Some of the principles contained in the Rio Declaration may be regarded as the third generation rights.

PRINCIPLES OF RIO DECLARATION

PRINCIPLE 1
> Human beings are at the centre of concerns for sustainable development. They are entitled to a healthy and productive life in harmony with nature.

PRINCIPLE 2
> States have, in accordance with the Charter of the United Nations and the principles of international law, the sovereign right to exploit their own resources pursuant to their own environmental and developmental policies, and the responsibility to ensure that activities within their jurisdiction or control do not cause damage to the environment of other States or of areas beyond the limits of national jurisdiction.

PRINCIPLE 3
> The right to development must be fulfilled so as to equitably meet developmental and environmental needs of present and future generations.

PRINCIPLE 4
> In order to achieve sustainable development, environmental protection shall constitute an integral part of the development process and cannot be considered in isolation from it.

PRINCIPLE 5
> All States and all people shall cooperate in the essential task of eradicating poverty as an indispensable requirement for sustainable development, in order to

---

*"Our Common Future", United Nations World Commission on Environment and Development; 1987.

decrease the disparities in standards of living and better meet the needs of the majority of the people of the world.

PRINCIPLE 6

The special situation and needs of developing countries, particularly the least developed and those most environmentally vulnerable, shall be given special priority. International actions in the field of environment and development should also address the interests and needs of all countries.

PRINCIPLE 7

States shall cooperate in a spirit of global partnership to conserve, protect and restore the health and integrity of the Earth's ecosystem. In view of the different contributions to global environmental degradation, States have common but differentiated responsibilities. The developed countries acknowledge the responsibility that they bear in the international pursuit of sustainable development in view of the pressures their societies place on the global environment and of the technologies and financial resources they command.

PRINCIPLE 8

To achieve sustainable development and a higher quality of life for all people, States should reduce and eliminate unsustainable patterns of production and consumption and promote appropriate demographic policies.

PRINCIPLE 9

States should cooperate to strengthen endogenous capacity-building for sustainable development by improving scientific understanding through exchanges of scientific and technological knowledge, and by enhancing the development, adaptation, diffusion and transfer of technologies, including new and innovative technologies.

PRINCIPLE 10

Environmental issues are best handled with the participation of all concerned citizens, at the relevant level. At the national level, each individual shall have appropriate access to information concerning the environment that is held by public authorities, including information on hazardous materials and activities in their communities, and the opportunity to participate in decision-making processes. States shall facilitate and encourage public awareness and participation by making information widely available. Effective access to judicial and administrative proceedings, including redress and remedy, shall be provided.

PRINCIPLE 11

States shall enact effective environmental legislation. Environmental standards, management objectives and priorities should reflect the environmental and developmental context to which they apply. Standards applied by some countries may be inappropriate and of unwarranted economic and social cost to other countries, in particular developing countries.

PRINCIPLE 12

States should cooperate to promote a supportive and open international economic system that would lead to economic growth and sustainable development in all countries, to better address the problems of environmental degradation. Trade policy measures for environmental purposes should not constitute a means of arbitrary or unjustifiable discrimination or a disguised restriction on international trade. Unilateral actions to deal with environmental challenges outside the jurisdiction of the importing country should be avoided. Environmental measures addressing transboundary or global environmental problems should, as far as possible, be based on an international consensus.

PRINCIPLE 13

States shall develop national law regarding liability and compensation for the victims of pollution and other environmental damage. States shall also cooperate in an expeditious and more determined manner to develop further international law regarding liability and compensation for adverse effects of environmental damage caused by activities within their jurisdiction or control to areas beyond their jurisdiction.

PRINCIPLE 14

States should effectively cooperate to discourage or prevent the relocation and transfer to other States of any activities and substances that cause severe environmental degradation or are found to be harmful to human health.

PRINCIPLE 15

In order to protect the environment, the precautionary approach shall be widely applied by States according to their capabilities. Where there are threats of serious or irreversible damage, lack of full scientific certainty shall not be used as a reason for postponing cost-effective measures to prevent environmental degradation.

PRINCIPLE 16

National authorities should endeavour to promote the internalization of environmental costs and the use of economic instruments, taking into account the approach that the polluter should, in principle, bear the cost of pollution, with due regard to the public interest and without distorting international trade and investment.

PRINCIPLE 17

Environmental impact assessment, as a national instrument, shall be undertaken for proposed activities that are likely to have a significant adverse impact on the environment and are subject to a decision of a competent national authority.

PRINCIPLE 18

States shall immediately notify other States of any natural disasters or other emergencies that are likely to produce sudden harmful effects on the environment of those States. Every effort shall be made by the international community to help States so afflicted.

PRINCIPLE 19

States shall provide prior and timely notification and relevant information to potentially affected States on activities that may have a significant adverse transboundary environmental effect and shall consult with those States at an early stage and in good faith.

PRINCIPLE 20

Women have a vital role in environmental management and development. Their full participation is, therefore, essential to achieve sustainable development.

PRINCIPLE 21

The creativity, ideals and courage of the youth of the world should be mobilized to forge a global partnership in order to achieve sustainable development and ensure a better future for all.

PRINCIPLE 22

Indigenous people and their communities and other local communities have a vital role in environmental management and development because of their knowledge and traditional practices. States should recognize and duly support their identity, culture and interests and enable their effective participation in the achievement of sustainable development.

PRINCIPLE 23

The environment and natural resources of people under oppression, domination and occupation shall be protected.

PRINCIPLE 24

Warfare is inherently destructive of sustainable development. States shall, therefore, respect international law providing protection for the environment in times of armed conflict and cooperate in its further development, as necessary.

PRINCIPLE 25

Peace, development and environmental protection are interdependent and indivisible.

PRINCIPLE 26

The states shall resolve all their environmental disputes peacefully and by appropriate means, in accordance with the Charter of the United Nations.

PRINCIPLE 27

The states and the people shall cooperate in good faith and in a spirit of partnership in the fulfilment of the principles embodied in this Declaration and in the further development of international law in the field of sustainable development.[8]

The momentum continued and another Summit, the United Nations World Summit for Social Development, was held at Copenhagen in 1995 to discuss the issues of poverty reduction, social disintegration and employment. But due to the differences of opinion between the countries of the North and South no successful breakthrough was achieved. There was disagreement on issues such as debt, structural arrangements, regulation of multinationals and reform of the Bretton Woods Institutions. Therefore, the intergovernmental *Summit Declaration and Programme of Action* contained only passing references to these issues.

Thus, it is clear that there has been a substantial change in the mainstream thinking about development. There has also been an encouraging shift from economic growth to sustainable development. However, this has not altered the dominant position enjoyed by the orthodox development paradigm. A long and continuous struggle has to be embarked upon to make the core values of the alternative model of development more credible and acceptable. Therefore, some scholars are of the opinion that to ensure the long-term credibility of sustainable development, the proponents have to focus on certain issues. They have to:

- Reject the temptation to focus on economic growth.
- Recognize the 'internal inconsistencies and inadequacies of neo-classical economics' and redirect economic analyses.
- Accept the structural, technological and cultural causes of poverty and environmental degradation.
- Understand that sustainable development has multiple dimensions.
- "Explore what patterns and levels of resource demand would be compatible with different forms or levels of ecological or social sustainability, and different notions of equity and justice".[9]

Nevertheless, the alternative view of development has led to serious changes and modifications in the orthodox view of development and, in future, might be able to represent a clearer concept and come to occupy a sound position within the development discourse.

RIO + 20-UNITED NATIONS CONFERENCE ON SUSTAINABLE DEVELOPMENT, 13–22 JUNE 2012

The United Nations Conference on Environment and Development (UNCED and also referred to as the Rio Summit or the Earth Summit) was held during 3–14 June 1992. The chief achievement of this Summit was the *Agenda 21: Green Paths to the Future* or the *Rio Declaration of 1992*. The Rio Declaration consisted of 27 principles intended to guide future sustainable development around the world. Some of the principles contained in the Rio Declaration may be regarded as third generation rights. [See Chapter 14, pages 328–332]

Rio + 20 was a 20-year follow-up to the 1992 Rio Earth Summit/United Nations Conference on Environment and Development (UNCED) and the 10th anniversary of the 2002 World Summit on Sustainable Development (WSSD) in Johannesburg. It was hosted by Brazil in Rio de Janeiro from 13–22 June 2012.

Rio + 20 Summit was focussed on two themes: A green economy in the context of sustainable development and poverty eradication and the institutional framework for sustainable development. The Conference focused on critical issues like jobs, energy, cities, food, water, oceans and disasters and preparedness to tackle them.

The outcome document of Rio + 20 is *The Future We Want By, For and With All Stakeholders Redefining the Multi-Stakeholder Partnership Contract*. The Future We Want emphasizes the process to establish sustainable development goals; detailing how the green economy can be used as a tool to achieve sustainable development; strengthening the UN Environment Programme (UNEP); promoting corporate sustainability reporting measures; taking steps to go beyond gross domestic product to assess the well-being of a country; developing a strategy for sustainable development financing; and, adopting a framework for tackling sustainable consumption and production. Alongside, the document underscores the importance of establishing gender equity; recognized the importance of voluntary commitments on sustainable development; and stressed the need to engage civil society and incorporate science into policy; among other points.

Rio + 20 harped on the concept of inclusion of stakeholders at all levels, which will benefit in decisions which will be participatory rather being ad hoc. Partnership between government and stakeholders will ensure viability, equitability and sustainability of environment and life on the Earth. Rio + 20 was an exercise by countries attending the Conference to rethink and redefine the way in which all stakeholders can engage, participate and shape decisions at all levels of government processes.

Gender and Development: GDI, GII and GEM

The **Millennium Development Goals (MDGs)** very much uphold gender equality and women's empowerment and identified goals for achieving the same. The Millennium Project Task Force on Gender Education has developed a framework outlining why gender equality is so important to each of the MDGs. The Framework in the line of the Task Force is provided in Table 14.1.

Table 14.1   MDGs and Vision of Gender Equality

MDGs	Importance of Gender Equality
Goal 1: Eradicate extreme poverty and hunger	Addressing Women's health and nutritional issues and giving them access to basic infrastructure facilities will increase economic activity, productivity and well being.
Goal 2: Achieve universal primary education	Addressing women's primary education will help them in greater decision-making in issues related to fertility, public domain, child's education, health and nutritional values.
Goal 3: Promote gender equality and empower women	Addressing the goal of gender equality and empowerment will automatically help in solving gender related problems and bridge gender gap.
Goal 4: Reduce child mortality	Addressing goals of women's education and empowerment will help in lowering child mortality.
Goal 5: Improve maternal health	Addressing goals of women's education, health, nutrition along with empowerment will reduce maternal mortality.

(Contd.)

Table 14.1   MDGs and Vision of Gender Equality

Goal 6: Combat HIV/AIDS, Malaria and other diseases	Economic independence, increased ability to negotiate for safe sex, raising consciousness and awareness about sexual relations will help in preventing HIV/AIDS. Similar consciousness about epidemic diseases can stop their outbreak at a massive scale.
Goal 7: Ensure environmental sustainability	Gender-equitable property and resource ownership policies would enable women to manage them in a sustainable manner.
Goal 8: Develop global partnership for development	Developing global partnership for gender-sensitive development with greater gender equality in the political sphere will lead to higher investments in development cooperation.

[**Source:** Adapted from Grown et el., 2005][10]

Human Development Index (HDI) gave a new dimension to development by considering factors or indicators, other than the economic ones. HDI components include the basic dimensions of human development-health, knowledge and living standards. HDI, however, does not reveal the disparity of development between males and females. Therefore, keeping the same components of HDI, the UNDP formulated a **Gender Development Index** (GDI) in its Report in 1995. The GDI is the ratio of the HDIs calculated separately for females and males using the same methodology of HDI. It is a direct measure of gender gap showing the female HDI as a percentage of male HDI. Gender gap reveals the percentage of under-development of females in the three indicator areas, i.e., health, knowledge and living standards as compared to their male counterparts. A diagrammatic exposition of GDI is given in **Figure 14.1.**

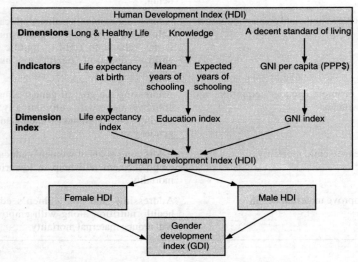

Figure 14.1   Gender Development Index (GDI).

Source: Adapted from UNDP

The GDI is calculated at present for 166 countries which are grouped into five categories based on the absolute deviation from gender parity in HDI values: [1] Very High Human Development, [2] High Human Development, [3] Medium Human Development, [4] Low Human Development and [5] Other Countries or Territories.

Along with GDI, another measure which is used to calculate gender inequality is **Gender Inequality Index** (GII). GII was introduced in 2010 Human Development Report in the 20th Anniversary Edition by the UNDP. It measures Gender inequality in three important aspects of human development – [1] Reproductive health, measured by maternal mortality ratio and adolescent birth rates, [2] Empowerment, measured by proportion of parliamentary seats occupied by females and proportion of adult females and males aged 25 years and older with at least some secondary education and [3] Economic status expressed as labour market participation and measured by labour force participation rate of female and male population aged 15 years and older. The higher the GII value the more disparities between females and males amounting to low human development gender-wise. A diagrammatic exposition of GII is given in **Figure 14.2.**

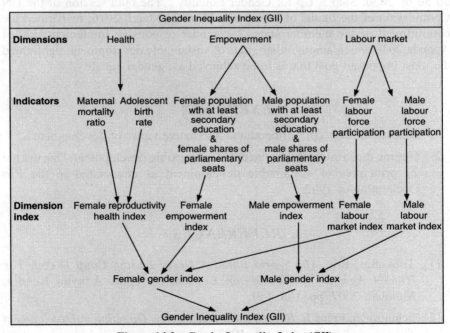

Figure 14.2 Gender Inequality Index (GII).

Source: Adapted from UNDP

Gender Empowerment Measure (GEM) was also introduced by UNDP Human Development Report of 1995. This uses estimated earned income based on non-agricultural wages, percentage of Parliamentary seats by gender, percentage of technical positions held by women and percentage of legislators, senior officials and managers who are women as indicators. The three dimensions considered in GEM are [1] political participation and decision making, [2] economic participation and decision-making and power over economic resources. The index runs from 0 to 1 with 1 being the maximum, a higher score is always desirable.

If we consider the case of India and its ranking or values in each of the categories we can assess the gender gap in India. According to Human Development Report 2015 India ranks 130 as far as HDI is concerned. The value of Gender Development Index (GDI) is 0.795 and falls under Group 5 of the GDI groups. The Gender Inequality Index (GII) value is 0.563 which shows great disparity between male and female in the indicators and indices shown in Figure 14.2. Percentage of female participation in Parliament is 12.2%.

A striking development took place in the year 2016. 8 March, which is celebrated every year as International Women's Day, saw the adoption of a pledge by the UN on 8 March, 2016, for working towards and achieving 'gender equality'. The 2016 theme for International Women's Day was "Planet 50-50 by 2030: Step It Up for Gender Equality". The 60th session of the UN Commission of the Status of Women, held on 24 March 2016, reaffirmed the commitment of the member states for gender-responsive implementation of Agenda 2030 which among other goals of sustainable development highlighted the most important goal that is to be achieved as 'gender equality.'

EXERCISES

1. Discuss the concept of liberal and alternative views of development.

2. Outline the growth of the concept of sustainable development. Discuss the 27 principles of sustainable development as enunciated in the Rio Declaration of 1992.

REFERENCES

[1] Toussaint, Eric, *The World Bank: A Never Ending Coup D'état, The Hidden Agenda of Washington Consensus*, Vikas Adhyan Kendra, Mumbai, 2007, pp. 158–159.

[2] Schuurman, Frans J., *Beyond the Impasse: New Direction in Development Theory*, Zed Books, London, 1993, pp. 1–9.

[3] Thomas, Caroline, "Poverty, Development, and Hunger" *in* John Baylis and Steve Smith (Eds.), *The Globalization of World Politics,* Oxford University Press, London, 1997, pp. 456–457.

[4] *ibid.,* p. 460.

[5] Schuurman, *op. cit.*, n. 2, p. 208.

[6] Schuurman, *op. cit.*, n. 2, p. 212.

[7] Schuurman, *op. cit.*, n. 2, p. 218.

[8] Annex 1 of Report of the United Nations Conference on Environment and Development (Rio de Janeiro, 3–14 June 1992).

[9] Schuurman, *op. cit.*, n. 2, p. 218.

[10] Grown, C., Rao Gupta, G. and Kes, A (2005) *Taking Action: Achieving Gender Equality and Empowering Women*, UN Millennium Project Task Force on Education and Gender Equality, London and Sterling, VA, Earthscan *http://www.unmillenniumproject.org/documents/Gender-complete.pdf*

15

Human Rights

CONTENTS

Evolution
The UN and Human Rights

INTRODUCTION

"Of all animals with which this globe is peopled, there is none towards whom nature seems, at first sight, to have exercised more cruelty than towards man, in the numberless wants and necessities with which she has loaded him, and in the slender means which she affords to the relieving of these necessities".[1] This was the view of David Hume. Therefore, from this observation it is clear that that there is a need for protection of man not only from society but also from his fellow human beings in fulfilling his wants which invariably make it necessary to have certain 'rights' for man. From this urge, therefore, there arose a whole new way of looking at rights of man, which came to be identified as the human rights. These are currently embodied in several international treaties, declarations and charters as well as contained in several constitutional provisions of the states of the world.

EVOLUTION

The concept of rights is nothing new and its genesis can be traced to the philosophical foundations of the liberal democratic tradition in Europe, especially in Great Britain, France and also the United States. Human rights got philosophical treatment in the works of Thoreau* in his treatise, *Civil Disobedience,* of the English Philosopher John Stuart Mill, in his essay *On Liberty* (1859), and of the American Political theorist Thomas Paine in his essay, *The Rights of Man* (1791). But before that the Reformation and the Age of Reason (Renaissance), the Puritan Revolution and the Glorious Revolution of the seventeenth century also saw contributions of philosophers to the issue of rights of man in the works of Hobbes in his *Leviathan* (1651), Locke in his *Two Treatises on Government* (1689), and Rousseau in his *Contract Sociale* (1762) through his notion of *vox populi* or *General Will*. The ideas expounded by these philosophers to a great extent influenced the formulation of human rights documents, declarations, conventions and treaties at international, national and regional levels.

One of the earliest documents on human rights was the *Magna Carta*, which was forced on King John in 1215 by the English Barons. The *Magna Carta* embodied such principles as trial by jury of peers, an end to feudal forced labour, no confiscation of property without compensation, equality of all before the law, and the right to free migration. It established the right of widows who owned property to choose not to remarry and the principles of due process. It also contained provisions forbidding bribery and official misconduct.[2]

Almost a century later, in 1776, most of the British colonies in North America, which proclaimed their independence from the British Empire in the document, "The American Declaration of Independence", said, with reference to natural rights, that "We hold these truths to be self-evident, that all men are created equal, that they are endowed by their Creator with certain unalienable rights, that among these are life, liberty and the pursuit of happiness". It further enumerated, "that to secure these rights Governments are instituted among men deriving their just powers from the consent of the governed; that whenever any form of government becomes destructive of these ends, it is the right of the people to alter or abolish it".[3] This was the reflection of Locke's idea of resistance, which conveys the idea that Government is not their master; it is created by the people voluntarily and maintained by them to secure their own good. Individuals give up to the society those rights which are essential to perform certain functions but retain all other natural rights to himself including the right to resistance if the government endeavours to invade the arbitrary rights, liberties or fortunes of the people.[3a]

However, the American Declaration contained relatively very few explicit guarantees of individual rights. Under strong demands, the first ten amendments to the US constitutions, generally referred to as the Bill of Rights, were made to address the shortcomings. Additional amendments, adopted in succeeding years, guaranteed equal rights for racial minorities and for women. The French Declaration of the Rights of Man and the Citizen adopted in 1789 was

---

*Henry David Thoreau, *Civil Disobedience*, an essay published in 1849.

analogous to the British and American traditions. The second Article of this Declaration proclaimed, "The aim of all political association is the conservation of the natural and inalienable rights of man". The rights being liberty, property, security and resistance to oppression. This Declaration proclaimed major rights of man, which came to be identified as civil and political rights. The basic principle that all men are born free and remain so and are equal in their rights; in case of particular rights, such as equality before law, freedom not to be arrested except in conformity with law, freedom of opinion, freedom of expression which were upheld in the Declaration.[4] This liberal, democratic tradition of human rights were later incorporated in the Constitution and legal systems of the other countries of the world in varying degrees. But conspicuous developments have taken place after the Second World War when efforts were made to institutionalize and guarantee human rights, either through the United Nations or through other regional instruments.

The formation of the United Nations was a landmark in the institutionalization of human rights. The UN Charter and the Universal Declaration of Human Rights are the most explicit expression of human rights and dignity. Human rights, as enshrined in the major international instruments, are embodiments of basic rights of individuals, which they are entitled to enjoy as human beings. These are certain standards set to induce the states to respect the fundamental freedoms of their citizens. Apart from the UN Charter and the Universal Declaration of Human Rights (UDHR) of 1948, a host of other international instruments on human rights such as the International Covenant on Economic, Social and Cultural Rights (ICESR) 1966, International Covenant on Civil and Political Rights (ICCPR) 1966, the Convention on the Prevention and Punishment of Crime and Genocide (1948), the Convention relating to the Status of Stateless Persons (1954), the Convention on the Elimination of Racial Discrimination (1965), the Convention on the Elimination of Discrimination Against Women (1979), the Convention Against Torture and Other Cruel, Inhuman or Degrading Treatment of Punishment (1984), the Convention on the Rights of Child (1989) and others have been adopted. Certain regional instruments have also been adopted pertaining to human rights and fundamental freedoms, such as the European Convention of Protection of Human Rights and Fundamental Freedoms (1950) and the American Convention on Human Rights (1981). These are nothing but exuberant and exotic expressions of the basic rights of individuals, which supposedly should be guaranteed by the states to their citizens. These constitute the **first and second generations** of human rights, which mainly aim at seeking economic, political and social rights for men by asking for or forbidding some kind of actions on the part of the state Parties to the treaties and conventions. Universal human rights are often expressed and guaranteed by law, in the form of treaties, customary international law, general principles, and other sources of international law. International human rights law lays down obligations of governments to act in certain ways or to refrain from certain acts, in order to promote and protect human rights and fundamental freedoms of individuals or groups.

A **third generation** of rights has come up for discussion pertaining to environment and sustainable development. This got expression in a number of efforts by world leaders and NGOs relating to environment, climate change, ozone depletion, carbon emission, and a host of other problems, making the future of the Earth bleak. Among these, the most significant was the Rio Declaration of 1992 underlying the 27 principles of sustainable development.

Through ratification of international human rights treaties, governments undertake to put into place the domestic measures and legislation compatible with their treaty obligations and duties. Where domestic legal proceedings fail to address human rights abuses, mechanisms and procedures for individual complaints or communications are available at the regional and international levels to help ensure that international human rights standards are indeed respected, implemented and enforced at the local level. The principle of universality of human rights is the cornerstone of international human rights law. This principle, as first emphasized in the Universal Declaration of Human Rights in 1948, has been reiterated in numerous international human rights conventions, declarations and resolutions. The 1993 Vienna World Conference on Human Rights, for example, noted that it is the duty of the states to promote and protect all human rights and fundamental freedoms, irrespective of their political, economic and cultural systems.

THE UN AND HUMAN RIGHTS

The Preamble to the UN Charter of 1945 contains a number of provisions pertaining to the promotion of human rights. It proclaims, "We the peoples of the United Nations, determined…to reaffirm faith in fundamental human rights, in the dignity and worth of the human person, in the equal rights of men and women and of nations large and small…have resolved to combine our efforts to accomplish these aims". The purpose set forth in the Preamble among others is "to cooperate…in promoting respect for human rights and fundamental freedoms for all". Article 1(3) stating the purposes and principles of the UN, envisages, "To achieve international co-operation in solving international problems of an economic, social, cultural, or humanitarian character, and in promoting and encouraging respect for human rights and for fundamental freedoms for all without distinction as to race, sex, language, or religion". Article 55 calls for promotion of, inter alia, "universal respect for, and observance of human rights and fundamental freedoms for all without distinction as to race, sex, language or religion".[5] Apart from the UN Charter, a major breakthrough in the development of an international human rights regime was achieved when the UN General Assembly adopted the Universal Declaration of Human Rights on 10 December, 1948. Since then, 10 December is observed as the World Human Rights Day.

The Preamble to the Declaration embodies that "recognition of the inherent dignity and of the equal and inalienable rights of all members of the human family is the foundation of freedom, justice and peace in the world, whereas disregard and contempt for human rights have resulted in barbarous acts which have outraged the conscience of mankind, and the advent of a world in which human beings shall enjoy freedom of speech and belief and freedom from fear and want has been proclaimed as the highest aspiration of common people". The General Assembly proclaimed that "this UNIVERSAL DECLARATION OF HUMAN RIGHTS as a common standard of achievement for all peoples and all nations, to the end that every individual and every organ of society, keeping this Declaration constantly in mind, shall strive by teaching and education to promote respect for these rights and freedoms and by progressive measures, national and international, to secure their universal and effective recognition and observance, both among the peoples of Member States themselves and among the peoples of territories under their jurisdiction".[6]

Initially, the United Nations Human Rights Programme organizationally started as a small division at the United Nations Headquarters in the 1940s. The Division later moved to Geneva and was upgraded as the Centre for Human Rights in the 1980s. At the World Conference on Human Rights in 1993, the international community decided to establish a more robust human rights mandate with stronger institutional support. Accordingly, the member states of the United Nations created the Office of the High Commissioner for Human Rights (OHCHR) by a General Assembly Resolution in 1993.

All the principal organs of the United Nations are involved in the protection of human rights. Article 13 enshrines the responsibility of the General Assembly to: "The General Assembly shall initiate studies and make recommendations for the purpose of: **a.** promoting international co-operation in the political field and encouraging the progressive development of international law and its codification; **b.** promoting international co-operation in the economic, social, cultural, educational, and health fields, and assisting in the realization of human rights and fundamental freedoms for all without distinction as to race, sex, language, or religion".

The Economic and Social Council has been charged with the responsibilities, which are directly linked to the protection and upliftment of the human rights. Under Articles 62/1 and 62/2 the Council may make or initiate studies and reports with respect to international economic, social, cultural, educational, health and related matters and may make recommendations with respect to any such matters to the General Assembly to the members of the United Nations, and to the specialized agencies concerned. It may also make recommendations for the purpose of promoting respect for, and observance of, human rights and fundamental freedoms for all. Under Article 68, the Council shall set up commissions in economic and social fields and for the promotion of human rights, and such other commissions as may be required for the performance of its functions.

Even specialized bodies such as the ILO, UNICEF, UNESCO and the United Nations High Commissioner for Refugees (UNHCR) are engaged in human rights protection in one form or the other.

The growth in United Nations human rights activities has seen an increase with the growth of the strength of the international human rights movement since the United Nations General Assembly adopted the Universal Declaration of Human Rights on 10 December 1948. The Universal Declaration of Human Rights, together with the International Covenant on Civil and Political Rights and its two Optional Protocols, and the International Covenant on Economic, Social and Cultural Rights, form the "International Bill of Human Rights".

Alongside the development of international human rights law, a number of United Nations human rights bodies have been established to respond to changing human rights challenges. There are certain Charter-based bodies and eight treaty-based bodies which work towards the monitoring of human rights situations worldwide. These constitute the Human Rights Monitoring mechanisms under the UN. There is also the Office of the High Commissioner for Human Rights (OHCHR) to support and assist these human rights monitoring mechanisms of the UN.

The **Charter-based bodies** include the former Commission on Human Rights, the Human Rights Council, Universal Periodic Review and Special Procedures. Between 1946–2006, the Human Rights Commission, which was established by the UN Economic and Social Council, was responsible for monitoring human rights protection. The Universal Declaration, the ICCPR, the ICESR all were formulated with active help from this body. However, in 2006 this Commission was replaced by the Human Rights Council.

Human Rights Council was created by the UNGA on 15 March 2006 by adopting the resolution A/RES/60/251 which replaced the Commission on Human Rights. It held its first meeting on 19 June 2006. This intergovernmental body, which meets in Geneva 10 weeks a year, is composed of 47 elected United Nations member states who serve for an initial period of three years, and cannot be elected for more than two consecutive terms. The Human Rights Council is empowered to prevent abuses, inequity and discrimination, protect the most vulnerable, and expose the perpetrators.

The Human Rights Council is different from OHCHR as both have separate mandates given by the General Assembly. Nevertheless, the OHCHR provides, substantive support for the meetings of the Human Rights Council, and follow-up to the Council's deliberations.

The **Universal Periodic Review** (UPR) is a process by which a review of the human rights records of all the member states of the UN is done once in every four years.

Special Procedures constitute the mechanisms established by the Commission on Human Rights and assumed by the Human Rights Council after its creation in 2006 to address either specific country situations or thematic issues in all parts of the world. Special Procedures are either an individual—a special rapporteur or representative of the Secretary General, or an independent expert—or a working group.

Special Procedures' mandates usually call on mandate-holders to examine, monitor, advise and publicly report on human rights situations in specific countries or territories, known as **country mandates**, or on major phenomena of human rights violations worldwide, known as **thematic mandates**. There are 30 thematic mandates and 8 country mandates. All report to the Human Rights Council on their findings and recommendations. They are sometimes the only mechanism that will alert the international community on certain human rights issues.

There are nine core international human rights treaties, two of which—on persons with disabilities and enforced disappearance—have not yet come into force. Since the adoption of the Universal Declaration of Human Rights in 1948, all UN member states have ratified at least one or more of core international human rights treaty.

There are eight human rights **treaty-based bodies** which are committees of independent experts that monitor implementation of the core international human rights treaties. They are created in accordance with the provisions of the treaty that they monitor. OHCHR assists the treaty bodies in harmonizing their working methods and reporting requirements through their secretariats.

The eight human rights treaty-based bodies that monitor implementation of the core international human rights treaties are:

1. International Covenant on Civil and Political Rights (ICCPR)
2. Committee on Economic, Social and Cultural Rights (CESCR)
3. Committee on the Elimination of Racial Discrimination (CERD)
4. Committee on the Elimination of Discrimination against Women (CEDAW)
5. Committee Against Torture (CAT) and Optional Protocol to the Convention against Torture (OPCAT)—Subcommittee on Prevention of Torture
6. Committee on the Rights of the Child (CRC)
7. Committee on Migrant Workers (CMW)
8. Committee on the Rights of Persons with Disabilities (CRPD)

The Office of the High Commissioner for Human Rights (OHCHR)

The High Commissioner for Human Rights is the principal human rights official of the United Nations. The High Commissioner heads the OHCHR and works towards the realization of the United Nations human rights efforts. This body offers leadership, works objectively, educates and takes action to empower individuals, and assists states in upholding human rights. The OHCHR, with its headquarters in Geneva, is a part of the United Nations Secretariat.

It supports the work of the United Nations human rights mechanisms, such as the Human Rights Council, and the core treaty-based bodies set up for monitoring the state Parties' in compliance with the international human rights treaties, promotes the right to development, coordinates United Nations human rights education and public information activities, and strengthens human rights across the United Nations system. This body works to ensure the enforcement of universally recognized human rights norms, including promoting both the universal ratification and implementation of the major human rights treaties and respect for the rule of law.

Mandate

The Office of the High Commissioner for Human Rights (OHCHR) is mandated to promote and protect the enjoyment and full realization, by all people, of all rights established in the Charter of the United Nations and in international human rights laws and treaties. OHCHR is guided in its work by the mandate provided by the General Assembly in resolution 48/141, the Charter of the United Nations, the Universal Declaration of Human Rights and subsequent human rights instruments, the Vienna Declaration and Programme of Action, the 1993 World Conference on Human Rights, and the 2005 World Summit Outcome Document.

The OHCHR mandate upholds the broad principles of preventing human rights violations, securing respect for all human rights, promoting international cooperation in protecting human rights, coordinating related activities throughout the United Nations, and strengthening the United Nations activities in the field of human rights. The OHCHR also makes efforts to integrate a human rights approach within all work carried out by the United Nations agencies.

Mission Statement

The mission of the OHCHR is to work for the protection of all human rights for all people; to help empower people to realize their rights; and to assist those responsible for upholding such rights in ensuring that they are implemented.

In carrying out its mission, OHCHR:

- Gives priority to addressing the most pressing human rights violations, both acute and chronic, particularly those that put life in imminent peril.
- Focuses attention on those who are at risk and vulnerable on multiple fronts.
- Pays equal attention to the realization of civil, cultural, economic, political and social rights, including the right to development.
- Measures the impact of its work through the substantive benefit that is accrued through it to individuals around the world.

Operationally, OHCHR works with governments, legislatures, courts, national institutions, the civil society, regional and international organizations, and the United Nations system. This, it does to develop and strengthen capacity, particularly at the national level, for the protection of human rights in accordance with international norms. It serves a forum for identifying, highlighting and developing responses to as human rights challenges, and encourages in human rights research, education, public information, and advocacy.

OHCHR's method of work focuses on three major dimensions: standard-setting, monitoring and implementation of programmes. It offers the expertise, and substantive and secretariat support to the different United Nations human rights bodies. It also tries to ensure that the international human rights standards are implemented in reality.

EXERCISES

1. Examine the evolution of the concept of human rights in international relations.

2. How is the United Nations involved in the noble mission of protecting and safeguarding the human rights of the 'peoples' of the world?

REFERENCES

[1] Laqueur, Walter and Rubin, Barry, *The Human Rights Reader,* A Meridian Book, New American Library, Times Mirror, New York, 1979, p. 3.

[2] *ibid.*, pp. 101–102. (See also http://www.hrweb.org/history.html.)

[3] Pandey, Veena Pani, *International Perspectives on Human Rights,* Mohit Publications, New Delhi, 1999, pp. 4–7.

[3a] Ghosh, Birendranath, *Glimpses of Political Thought: Western and Indian,* Mahila Mangal Prakashani, Kolkata, 2004, p. 63.

[4] Pandey, *op. cit.*, n. 3, pp. 4–7.

[5] United Nations Charter of 1945, http://www.un.org/en/documents/Charter.

[6] Universal Declaration of Human Rights, 1948 http://www.un.org/en/documents/udhr/.

[7] http://www.ohchr.org/EN/AboutUs/Pages/WhoWeAre.aspx and http://www.un.org/rights/.

16

Terrorism

CONTENTS

Terrorism: A Threat to International Peace and Security
International Terrorism: An Overview
Combating Terrorism

INTRODUCTION

The September 11, 2001 attacks on the twin towers of the World Trade Center, New York, the symbol of prowess and of prestige of the most powerful state in the world, came as a rude shock not only to the Americans but also to the people in other parts of the world. The attacks signalled to the fact that states are no longer impermeable and even a superpower like the United States of America can easily become a victim of attacks launched, not by states but by invisible actors, the most dangerous being the forces of terrorism, which are at work globally.

TERRORISM: A THREAT TO INTERNATIONAL PEACE AND SECURITY

The terms, *terrorism* and *terrorist* are used very frequently in the present day world but their origin can be traced to the French Revolution when they were used to mean different persons/events of that time. The 1798 supplement of the

Dictionnaire of the Académie Française gave the meaning of terrorism as *système, régime de la terreur*. These terms referred to that period of French Revolution between 1793–1794, identified as the *Reign of Terror*. Later, it came to acquire a much broader connotation and one of the few attempts made to define and explain 'terrorism' has been that of Hardman's entry in the *Encyclopedia of Social Sciences* published in 1930s. Here he tried to define terrorism as the method (or the theory behind the method), which an organized group or party sought to achieve its avowed aims chiefly through the systematic use of violence.[1] The central point is that terrorism is an act which uses violence to achieve its ends and is characterized by certain forms of actions such as assassinations, bombings, taking people as hostages, and hijacking of planes. The striking feature is the globalization of terrorism. Most of the countries in the world like Afghanistan, Brazil, Myanmar, Canada, Egypt, France, Germany, United Kingdom, USA, India, Indonesia, Italy and others suffer from terrorist onslaughts. The Ejercito Revolutionary del pueblo (People's Revolutionary Group) of Argentina, the Front de Liberation due Quebec (Quebec Liberation Front) of Canada, the Baader Meinhoff Group (Baader Solidarity Group) of Germany, the Jammu Kashmir Liberation Front, the United Liberation Front of Assam (among others) in India, the Provisional Irish Republican Army (IRA) of Ireland, the Red Brigades of Italy, the Japanese Red Army of Japan, the Palestinian Liberation Movement and other Arab terrorist Groups such as Black September Organisation of Palestine, the Huklalahaps of the Philippines, the Tupamaros of Uruguay, etc. are some of the terrorist organizations in the world which are disrupting peace and security. But the new epicentre of terror since the 9/11 tragedy is the Al-Qaeda and the name associated with it is that of Osama bin Laden. Worldwide improvement in telecommunications, transportation and technology have helped to heighten the links between terrorist outfits that are, in some way, connected with each other either through finances, training or common enemy, commiting terrorist acts assuming transnational character. International terrorism of the 20th Century made its debut in the 1970s, with the Lod airport assault in Israel on 30 May, 1972 when three terrorists killed 27 persons and injured 77 others in an operation carried out by the Popular Front for the Liberation of Palestine (PFLP). What is remarkable is that, from the 1970s onwards, terrorism assumed a global nature, i.e. it became international.

International terrorism has often been described as *warfare without territory, waged without armies...It is warfare that is not limited territorially, sporadic battles may take place worldwide. It is warfare without neutrals, and with few or no civilian bystanders*. International terrorism covers the categories of terrorist outfits outside the country of their origin or where they are active. It is also said to comprise "those incidents of terrorism that have clear international consequences: incidents in which terrorists go abroad to strike targets, select victims or targets, because of their connections to a foreign state (diplomats, executives of foreign corporation), attack airliners on international flights, or force airlines to fly to another country".[2]

Certain key criteria have been identified with terrorism such as target, objective, motive, perpetrator, and legitimacy or legality of the act. Acts of terrorism can be identified from some of the features usually associated with it. They are:

1. *Use of Violence:* Acts of terror are usually associated with violence, the chief aim being to create shock in the minds of the people at large as well as the ruling elite. The aim is to send their message clearly to the target audience by using violence, organized crimes and destruction of property. To give a jolt to the national morale and blow to the national security becomes the ulterior motive of the terrorist. The Mumbai siege of 26/11 and the destruction of the heritage building of Hotel 'Taj', Oberoi Trident Hotel and Nariman House, alongside butchery of the foreign nationals as well as Indians inside the sieged buildings were nothing but use of violent methods to send tremors of terror to India and Indians.

2. *Psychological Impact and Fear:* Along with the use of violence, the terrorists aim at breaking the morale of the people by raising insecurity in their minds. With the severity of the attacks the terrorists try to create massive psychological impact and fear in the minds of the people. The objective is to shock and awe large audiences with acts of terror. Terrorists also attack national symbols to show their power and to shake the foundation of the country or society they are opposed to. This may sometimes negatively affect a government's legitimacy, while increasing the legitimacy of the given terrorist organization and or ideology behind a terrorist act. The Mumbai siege and attack on the Taj are pointers in this direction. The attack on the World Trade Center was a direct assault to American national pride.

3. *Perpetration for a Political Goal:* Most often terrorist attacks have, as their goal, the achievement of a political purpose. Terrorism then becomes a political tactic. The perpetration of terrorist acts is often directed in giving shocks to the government so that the government succumbs under its pressure.

4. *Deliberate Targeting of Non-Combatants:* The choice of targets also becomes important. Generally, terrorists aim soft targets like civilians. Most of the time, the victims of terrorism are targeted not because they are threats, but because their suffering accomplishes the terrorists' goals of instilling fear, sending a message out to the world, to the specific government, specific community or just trying to accomplish their political ends indirectly.

5. *Use of Disguise:* Terrorists almost invariably pretend to be non-combatants, hide among non-combatants, fight from in the midst of non-combatants. This was seen during the Mumbai siege of 26/11/2008.

6. *Unlawfulness or Illegitimacy:* Though some official definitions try to characterize terrorist activities on the basis of illegitimacy or unlawfulness, there is an inherent difficulty in this. The use of the criteria on terrorism becomes problematic when one considers the cases of state-sponsored terrorism.

INTERNATIONAL TERRORISM: AN OVERVIEW

The history of terrorism, however, can be traced to the 1st century C.E. when two Jewish groups, the Zealots and the Sicarii were formed to launch terrorist campaigns against the Roman occupation of Judea. In 666 C.E., a radical Muslim group, the Kharjites carried out routined assassinations of Muslim leaders who were found to be at fault by them. The 'Assassins' were another Muslim terrorist group, which was active during the twelfth and thirteenth centuries. The 'Hashashin' was another such group of medieval Islam.[3]

The Nardonaya Volya (the Peoples Will) of the nineteenth century was one of the first modern kind of terrorist groups and it targeted the Czarist officials for assassinations to arouse social revolt. The assassinations of Czar Alexander II in 1881 and that of Archduke Franz Ferdinand in 1914 are some of the noteworthy events of the nineteenth century where violence was used by some political groups especially by the anarchists and the nationalists to achieve their goals.[4] The 1920s witnessed an active right-wing terrorism among the German Nazis and the Italian Fascists to intimidate political enemies and attract public attention. However, the functioning of some groups in Eastern Europe, unlike the present terrorists, were almost like that of criminal gangs. Similarly, the contras of Nicaragua associated with the anti-communist dictatorship in Haiti, Argentina and Mozambique relied heavily on the right-wing 'death-squads'. They were active throughout the 1980s but their functioning was more or less like the criminal gangs. But the irony is that the West working with their Cold War calculations seemed to tolerate terrorism by such gangs regarding it as a lesser menace than the threat of communism. Therefore, President Ronald Reagan and George W. Bush (Sr.) regarded the contras and the Mujahideen guerillas of Afghanistan as 'freedom fighters' and at present the paradox is that against the backdrop of 9/11, the USA is fighting the War on Terror in Afghanistan and Iraq. Personal interpretation plays a critical role in assessing modern terrorism. Terrorist to one is often a 'freedom fighter' to another. Sometimes, other terms are also euphemistically used such as separatists, liberator, revolutionary, militants, guerilla, rebel, jihadi or fedayeen or any other terms in other languages by either the terrorists themselves or, by their supporters, or protectors or by the victim states.

It is on the basis of such personal interpretation that guerilla warfare or movements against the colonial rule became the dominant form of terrorism after the Second World War in the developing world which were dubbed as legitimized movements by the political leaders of this part of the world. A plethora of examples are available to support such argument. Irgun and Stern Gang used terrorism against the British rule in Palestine. Algerian revolutionaries systematically assassinated the French police officers during the 1950s and the anti-British 'Mau Mau' activities in Kenya during the same period are a few to add to the list. The African National Congress (ANC) of South Africa too was engaged in bombings and other acts of terrorism against the system of apartheid and racial segregation policy of the Whites.

Apart from that, the 1980s witnessed the rise of Islamic fundamentalism in several Muslim countries, which became the harbinger of Islamic terrorism on a global scale affecting the safety, security and sovereignty of the nation states. In 1992, Algeria witnessed Islamic revolt when a military takeover of the independent government in Algeria had denied the Islamicists, engaged in aircraft hijackings, a parliamentary victory in Algeria. Acts of violence and counter-violence on the part of Islamicists started against the local governments in Israeli occupied territories and Egypt clearly revealed that the terrorists' target was the Western-style secular governments in this part of the world.[5] This reflected their unacceptability and intolerance towards the Western model of democracy. Facing the challenges of globalization and spread of liberal democratic ideals, this intolerance grew more virulent and got its ultimate expression on 11 September 2001 when two planes crashed into the WTC Twin Towers—the symbol of US pride and prudence—another crashed into the Pentagon and the other missed the White House by sheer luck. This was followed by an all out 'War on Terror' on the part of the United States and its allies in Afghanistan and Iraq. But this has backlashed in the form of a series of terrorist attacks since then on the United States and its allies, globally. Thus, terrorism has transcended from the local character and has assumed perilous proportions and transnational character at an alarming pace.

State-Sponsored Terrorism

Another form of terrorism, which has emerged, is the state-supported terrorism. Between 1970s and 1980s it became quite clear that an increasing number of states supported the idea of providing support to the insurgents and terrorists in another state as an instrument of statecraft. Shultz[*], an expert on Low-Intensity Conflict, observes that "it is an indirect and potentially low-cost means of attacking an adversary without having to resort to open, interstate armed conflict". The USSR and its East European allies, the Western bloc as well as several Middle Eastern countries such as Iran, Iraq, Syria and Libya have allegedly been aiding and abating terrorism. Cuba, North Korea and Yemen reportedly also support terrorism. In the South Asian context, Pakistan is alleged of extending support and training to the separatist elements in India and the Mumbai terror siege of 26/11/2008 revealed the Pakistani connections. Bangladesh too serves as a safe haven for terrorist elements who also have links with the Pakistani intelligence and international terrorist organizations. They too pose a security threat to the Indian state. Therefore, state-sponsored terrorism is a real challenge to the security and existence of a state with a number of adversaries, each wanting to score a victory over it through subversive means.

---

[*]Richard H. Shultz, "The Low-Intensity Conflict Environment of the 1990's" *Annals*, AAPSS, September, 1991.

Cyber-Terrorism

Improvement in technologies and telecommunication system is gradually changing the face of terrorism. Attacks by terrorists are not confined to the real world only, for they have made inroads into the virtual world too. Security risks emanating from disruption of working of computer systems, networks, Internet with an objective to cause harm, threaten or shock the target audience/group, individual or a particular government tantamount to cyber-terrorism.

There may be ordinary to professional hackers who might also commit cyber crime, but that may be a bit different from the cyber-terror attack. These people or group might perform such functions purely for economic gains and not for the sake of committing terror attacks. However, scholars and intelligence officials find it difficult to draw a line of distinction between cyber crimes and suspected terrorist cyber attacks. What can be said is that, the latter aims to generate fear in the similar fashion as a traditional terrorist attack would do or may even try to cause severe economic, political or security damage.

E-mail bombings, defacing websites, hacking governmental confidential database, disrupting computer systems either by jamming or by sending computer viruses, and credit card frauds are the most common kinds of cyber terrorism. Besides, internet, e-mails and improvised telecommunication systems help the terrorists to stay connected, pass on information and commands, plan and conduct operations, proselytize, recruit, train and obtain logistical and financial support. The serious part is that more and more terrorist outfits are collaborating and hiring professional hackers and cyber criminals to facilitate them to perform these functions and also conduct narco-terrorism.

Therefore, use of the cyber space by the terrorist either for complimenting large conventional attacks or using it to communicate or conduct planning and operation, equals to loss of confidentiality, security and integrity.

Despite significant investment in technology and infrastructure, cyber terrorism represents one of the greatest challenges when it comes to combating terrorism. Every day, the Internet and countless other computer systems are under attack. A global strategy and policy for combating this type of terrorism is the need of the hour.

Narco-Terrorism

Terrorist activities are not limited to only causing physical or psychological damage to a state or even tarnishing its image. The effects of terrorism go much deeper into the society when it destroys the very basis of the state—the population, especially the younger generation, by creating addiction among its population to drugs, heroin, cocaine, and the like. This is solely done by the terrorist organizations to pump in money to support their planning and conduct their operations. Illegal drug trafficking carried out through the nexus between terrorist outfits and the transnational criminal gangs or mafia is a threat to national as well as international peace and security.

Earlier, narco-terrorism was identified as activities or methods used by drug mafia to carry out assault on anti-narcotics agencies/forces which roughly used the tactics of terrorist organizations like the use of car bombs, assassinations and kidnappings, against anti-narcotics police forces. Narco-terrorists in this context refer to individuals such as the drug lord Pablo Escobar from the Medellý´n cartel in Colombia and other members of drug cartels, mafia or other criminal organizations. But the present world scenario reveals that more and more terrorist organizations are using narcotics trafficking for the purpose of gaining revenue and for this they are developing partnerships with transnational drug cartels, mafia or other criminal organizations. The U.S. Department of State's International Narcotics Control Strategy Report documents report that there is a direct connection between traditional Colombian drug trafficking and money laundering organizations and Middle Eastern money launderers tied to Hezbollah. The Talibans even collected money from drug trafficking to facilitate their resurgence in Afghanistan.

Alongside narco-terrorism, terrorist organizations are linked with transnational criminal organizations of all kinds in carrying out illegal arms trafficking, extortion, kidnapping, prostitution and human trafficking, credit card fraud, social security and immigration fraud and identity theft, tax fraud; counterfeiting currencies, pharmaceuticals, cigarettes, alcohol, pirating videos, compact discs, tapes, and software and illegal oil trade. The unity and integrity of a state, therefore, is challenged from many corners, which is making the task of maintaining law and order a problem. When state leaders like Hugo Chavez, President of Venezuela are on the side of the drug cartels, then the problem becomes more acute. He stopped cooperating with the U.S. drug eradication efforts in 2005 and provided safe haven to the anti-American narco-terrorist groups, which facilitates transfer of money, arms and operatives to and from Syria, Southern Lebanon and Iran.[6] The international community must gear up to tackle these transnational criminal activities to save the future generations.

COMBATING TERRORISM

There have been several International Conventions which someway or the other aimed at combating terrorist kinds of activities prior to 9/11/2001, when terrorism reached its climax. Some prominent among them are the Tokyo Convention on Offences and Certain Acts Committed on Board Aircraft, 1963, the Hague Convention on Unlawful Seizure of Aircraft, 1970, the International Convention against the Recruitment, Use, Financing and Training Mercenaries adopted by the General Assembly in 1989 and others.

Some other Conventions adopted by the UN are:

- Convention on the Prevention and Punishment of Crimes against Internationally Protected Persons, including Diplomatic Agents, adopted by the General Assembly of the United Nations on 14 December 1973.
- International Convention against the Taking of Hostages, adopted by the General Assembly of the United Nations on 17 December 1979.
- International Convention for the Suppression of Terrorist Bombings, adopted by the General Assembly of the United Nations on 15 December 1997.
- International Convention for the Suppression of the Financing of Terrorism, adopted by the General Assembly of the United Nations on 9 December 1999.
- International Convention for the Suppression of Acts of Nuclear Terrorism New York, 13 April 2005.

The UN has been quite active in dealing with the problem of Terrorism worldwide. In 1994, the UNGA condemned "all acts, methods and practices of terrorism, as criminal and unjustifiable, wherever and by whomever committed, including those which jeopardize the friendly relations among States and peoples and threaten the territorial integrity and security of States", and for this purpose it noted that the states should "refrain from organizing instigating, facilitating, financing, encouraging or tolerating terrorist activities...". The UN Millennium Summit Declaration also upheld the immediacy of preventing and eliminating international terrorism. After the 9/11 attacks on the WTC and Pentagon the UN members found it necessary to develop international legal framework to tackle terrorism. The September 11 attacks called for more serious measures in combating terrorism. The United Nations Security Council (UNSC) in the immediate aftermath of 9/11 attacks passed the Resolution 1373 under Chapter VII of the United Nations on 28 September 2001. This resolution imposed several obligations on the member states including efforts to prevent and suppress financing of terrorist acts, to criminalize the willful provision or collection, by any means, of funds, by their nationals or in their territories, to freeze without delay the funds, financial assets and economic resources of persons committing or participating in the commission or facilitating commission of terrorist acts.[7]

Some of the regional instruments to combat terrorism are:

- Arab Convention on the Suppression of Terrorism, signed at a meeting held at the General Secretariat of the League of Arab States in Cairo on 22 April 1998.
- Convention of the Organization of the Islamic Conference on Combating International Terrorism, adopted at Ouagadougou on 1 July 1999.

- European Convention on the Suppression of Terrorism, concluded at Strasbourg on 27 January 1977.

- OAS Convention to Prevent and Punish Acts of Terrorism Taking the Form of Crimes against Persons and Related Extortion that are of International Significance, concluded at Washington, DC on 2 February 1971.

- OAU Convention on the Prevention and Combating of Terrorism, adopted at Algiers on 14 July 1999.

- SAARC Regional Convention on Suppression of Terrorism, signed at Kathmandu on 4 November 1987.

- Treaty on Cooperation among States Members of the Commonwealth of Independent States in Combating Terrorism, signed at Minsk on 4 June 1999.

Despite several attempts to tackle the menace of terrorism, it is on the rise. A word of caution rings all over the globe that states now have to counter invisible forces with might equivalent to a state, operating transnationally, involved in smuggling, narco-terrorism, running a risk of chemical and biological weapons and nuclear terrorism. As President Bush has opined, "This is a different kind of a war. Our enemies are not organized into battalions, or commanded by governments. They hide in shadowy networks and retreat after they strike".[8] The peoples of the world, not guided by their narrow interests, acting in accordance to the principles as envisaged in the Charter of the United Nations have to come together and fight against these invisible forces and protect the future generations from the scourge of not only visible wars but also invisible wars.

EXERCISES

1. Critically discuss how terrorism has become a menace to the international community.

2. Write an overview of international terrorism and also discuss the various mechanisms to combat international terrorism.

3. How do you think that terrorism has become a threat to international peace and security? Elucidate.

REFERENCES

[1] Laqueur, Walter, *A History of Terrorism*, Transaction Publishers, New Brunswick, USA, 2002, pp. 6–7 and 135.

[2] Panna Kaji Amatya, *International Terrorism: Threat to Global Security, in* Verinder Grover (Ed.), *Encyclopedia of International Terrorism:*

History and Development, Vol-1, Deep & Deep Publications, New Delhi, 2002, pp. 316–317.

[3] Magill, Frank N. (Ed.), *International Encyclopedia of Government and Politics*, Vol-2, Fitzroy Dearborn Publishers, Chicago, 1996, pp. 1350–1352.

[4] Krieger, Joel (Ed.), *The Oxford Companion to Politics of the World*, Oxford University Press, London, 2000, pp. 829–831.

[5] Rachel Ehrenfeld, "Defeating Narco-Terrorism", *Huffington Post*, 17.3.2009.
http://www.acdemocracy.org/article/invent_index.php?id=683

[6] Magill, Frank N. (Ed.), *op. cit.*, n. 3, pp. 1350–1352.

[7] Sreenivasa Rao Pemmaraju, "An Indian Response to International Terrorism: A Comprehensive Convention on International Terrorism", *in* Omprakash Mishra and Sucheta Ghosh (Eds.), *Terrorism and Low Intensity Conflict in South Asian Region*, Manak Publications, New Delhi, 2003, pp. 190–193.

[8] "A different war against terror: Bush" *The Statesman*, 24 August, 2005.

17

International Law, International Morality and World Public Opinion

INTRODUCTION

Securing national interest is the prime motive of states in international relations and to that end they strive to amass national power vis-à-vis the other states, in order to gain control over them. But international relations is not left to the whims of the states as actors, and there are certain limitations to the actions of the states. These limitations act as constraints on the exercise of national power. International law, international morality and world public opinion act as definite constraints on national power. Even the sole surviving superpower, the United States, is not above international law, international morality, and world public opinion. It may manipulate, manoeuvre all the three to justify its actions, but it cannot ignore the three principal restraining factors in international relations.

INTERNATIONAL LAW

Even before the emergence of the sovereign states as major political units in the Westphalian sense, sovereign political units had always felt the need to regulate their relations with other states by adopting rules and institutions, thus, enabling them to conduct their relations, in a peaceful manner, abhorring the path of war and violence.

The modern system of international law is mainly a product of the customs, usages and practices of modern European states and have been greatly influenced by the writings of the jurists of the sixteenth, seventeenth and eighteenth centuries. These customs and practices in the course of time have developed and some were even codified and have gradually come to constitute the body of International Law. However, we may note that treaties, usages of war, immunities for diplomatic personnel, and other customary laws were prevalent in ancient India, China and Egypt for many centuries before the advent of Christianity.

Hugo Grotius (1583–1645) is regarded as the "Father of International Law". His *De jure belli ac pacis* (*On the Law of War and Peace*), published in 1625, codified international law as it had developed up to that time. Later, various attempts were made by the jurists to codify international law. In 1863, Francis Lieber (1800–1872) prepared *A Code for the Government of Armies* used during the Franco–Prussian War. In 1868 Bluntschli (1808–1872) made a more comprehensive attempt towards codification. In 1872, David Dudley Field (1805–1894) issued a *Draft Outline of an International Code*. An Italian jurist, Pasquale Fiore (1837–1914) published in 1899 a code covering various fields of international law.[1]

Besides, individual attempts by jurists, several institutes also contributed sufficiently towards the codification of international law. The prominent among them is the *Institut de Droit International* (founded in 1873) and the Association for the Reform and Codification of the Law of Nations, which in 1895 changed its name to International Law Association. The American Institute of International Law also made notable contributions. Codification attempts were also made under the auspices of the League of Nations. In 1924, the League Assembly and the Council set up a Committee of Experts to codify certain international laws. A Codification Conference met at the Hague to consider the subjects related to nationality, territoriality and responsibility of states for damage caused within their territory to the person and properties of foreigners. The United Nations created the International Law Commission in 1927 which prepared a Declaration on Rights and Duties of States, and formulated some principles underlying the Nuremberg War Crimes Tribunal (1946) and others. The Human Rights Commission drafted the Universal Declaration of Human Rights (1948) and the International Covenant on Civil and Political Rights (1966), the International Covenant on Economic Social and Cultural Rights (1966), and the Convention on Genocide (1948).

International law is generally acknowledged as a body of rules accepted by civilized nations, which define their rights and obligations and the procedures enforcing them.

Definitions of International Law

According to Oppenheim[2] international law is "the name for the body of customary and conventional rules which are considered legally binding by civilized states in their intercourse of states with each other". And it is "a law between, and not above, the single states".

Stowell[3] defined international law as embodying "certain rules relating to human relations throughout the world, which are generally observed by mankind and enforced primarily through the agency of the governments of the independent communities into which humanity is divided".

According to Jessup[4], in the study of international law, "The recent trend in the West, particularly in the United States, is toward a less technical view of the law. The increasingly influential School of International Law created by Myres S. McDougal of Yale University regards law as a process of decision into which all relevant factors, and not merely technical norms, enter. It virtually identifies law with policy and calls the study of law a policy science".

Fenwick[5] regards international law as primarily "the body of rules accepted by the general community of nations as defining their rights and the means of procedure by which those rights may be protected or violations of them redressed".

According to Starke[6] "International law may be defined as that body of law which is composed for its greater part of the principles and rules of conduct which states feel themselves bound to observe, and therefore, do commonly observe in their relations with each other...".

Sources of International Law

The material sources of international law fall into five principal categories: These are now briefly dealt with.

1. _Custom:_ Customs and usages over a long period of time have come to acquire legal validity with their recognition by the international community. In the _Paqueta Habana_ (175 US 677 1900), the US Supreme Court upheld the validity of customary international law. Though the preponderance of traditional customary laws has declined due to the conclusion of a large number of law-making treaties, for example, the Vienna Conventions of 18 April 1961, of 24 April 1963 and 22 May 1969 on Diplomatic Relations, Consular Relations, and the Law of Treaties, respectively, scholars still acknowledge the significant role played by international customs.

2. _Treaties:_ Even before Grotius codified international law, treaties existed as a source of international law since the written records of man. Treaties are binding on states who are parties to them and are under the obligation to respect the terms contained therein. A treaty can be

(a) law making, laying down the rules of universal or general applications such as the Covenant of the League of Nations and the Charter of the United Nations; or

(b) contracts between two or only a few states concerning a specific matter involving these states exclusively.

3. *Decisions of Judicial or Arbitral Tribunals:* International judicial decisions of International Court of Justice and its predecessor, the Permanent Court of International Justice, are important sources of international law. The advisory opinions of both these Courts contributed to the development of international jurisprudence. The judgement delivered by an international judicial body like the Military Tribunal at Nuremberg in 1946 laid down important principles pertaining to crimes against peace and humanity. The newest body in this regard is the International Criminal Court (ICC). The ICC became a reality on 1 July 2002 when the Rome Statute came into force. Initially, the Court has jurisdiction over genocide, war crimes, and crimes against humanity. The crime of aggression will be added once a definition has been agreed upon and added to the Rome Statute by an amendment. The ICC is meant to complement national legal structures, and will act only when the national systems are either unwilling or genuinely unable to proceed. Besides the regional courts, international courts also play an important role in the development of international law. The decisions of the state courts also lead to the formation of rules of international law.

4. *Juristic Works:* The works of reputed jurists also contribute to the development of international law. Article 38 of the International Court of Justice directs the Court to apply judicial decisions and the teachings of the most highly qualified publicists of the various countries as subsidiary means for the determination of rules of law.

5. *Decisions or Determinations of the Organs of International Institutions:* These may lead to the formation of rules of international law when they have been adhered to in practice, or are in the form of binding determinations and sometimes may be general decisions or directives of quasi-legislative effect.

Under Article 38, paragraph 1 of its present Statute, which is similar to the corresponding provision in Article 38 of the Statute of Permanent Court of International Justice, the International Court of Justice is directed to apply the following:

(a) International treaties

(b) International customs, as evidence of a general practice accepted as law

(c) The general principles of law recognized by the civilized nations. "General principles" refer to those principles accepted by all nations in the municipal sphere, such as certain principles of procedure, the principle of good faith, and the principle of *res judicata*.

(d) Judicial decisions and the teachings of the most highly qualified publicists of the various countries as subsidiary means for the determination of rules of law.

Scope of International Law

The scope of international law is ever expanding and is generally considered to include the following laws.

1. Laws of Peace: These include laws relating to states as subjects of international law pertaining to the birth, recognition and death of a state, succession, territorial sovereignty, rights and duties of states, jurisdiction, laws of the sea and maritime highways, state responsibility, nationality, international economic and monetary law, disarmament, development and environment.

2. Laws of War: International Humanitarian Law (IHL), often called the *law of armed conflict* and earlier referred to as *the law of war*, is a special branch of law governing situations of armed conflict, i.e., war. IHL seeks to mitigate the effects of war by limiting the choices and methods of conducting military operations and also obliges the belligerents to spare persons who do not or no longer participate in hostile actions. *IHL has been formulated through various codes and conventions such as the Convention for the Amelioration of the Condition of the Wounded in Armies in the Field* (22 August 1864) *which was first revised in 1906, Four Geneva Conventions adopted in 1949, the Geneva Convention for the Amelioration of the Condition of the Wounded and Sick in Armed Forces in the Field* (12 August 1949), *the Geneva Convention for the Amelioration of the condition of the Wounded and Sick and Shipwrecked Members of Armed Forces at Sea* (12 August 1949), *the Geneva Convention Relative to the Treatment of Prisoners of War* (12 August 1949), *the Geneva Convention Relative to the Protection of Civilian Persons in Time of War* (12 August 1949), *and Protocols Additional to the Geneva Conventions of* 12 August 1949.

In the First Peace Conference in Hague, in 1899, four Conventions were established and in the Second Peace Conference, in 1907, 13 Conventions were established. The 1907 *Conventions on the Laws and Customs of War on Land* and the annexed *Hague Regulations* contained provisions on the treatment of prisoners.

3. Laws of Neutrality: The status of neutrality relates to the rights and duties of neutral states on the one hand and of belligerent states on the other. The duties under such circumstances of both the neutrals and the belligerents include:

(a) duties of abstentions from giving any sort of assistance direct or indirect to either belligerent sides by the neutrals and the prohibition of commitment of warlike acts on the neutrals by the belligerents.

(b) duties of prevention by the neutrals within their territory and warlike measures, enlistment of troops and the like, and also the belligerent's duty to prevent the ill-treatment of neutral envoys or neutral subjects and any injury to neutral property on enemy territory occupied by it.

(c) duties of acquiescence in the acts of the belligerent states by the neutral states with respect to the commerce of its nationals if they are duly warranted by laws of war-like seizure of vessels under its flag for carriage of contraband, adjudications by Prize Courts and the like. Similarly, belligerent states must also acquiesce in by neutral states of such members of its armed forces as taking refuge in neutral territory or in granting of temporary asylum by the neutral ports to hostile warships so that necessary repairs may be effected.

Is International Law a Proper Law?

Many consider international law as the vanishing point of jurisprudence. The characteristic feature of international system is the sovereignty and unaccountability of states, which makes the applicability of international law less effective. Hoffman[7] argues, "International law like its Siamese twin and enemy, war, remains a crystallization of all that keeps world politics *sui generic*". In times of political harmony, international law is applicable and, in times of dissonance, war takes over.

One theory has upheld that international law is not a true law but a code of moral force only. The forerunner of this school of thought was the English Jurist, John Austin (1790–1859). He in his *Lectures on Jurisprudence* (published posthumously by Sarah Taylor Austin in 1863) enunciated the Austinian theory of law. According to Austin, law is the command of the sovereign and international laws are issued not from a sovereign authority which is politically superior. Therefore, in the absence of a visible sovereign authority the rules cannot be legal rules, but rules of moral of ethical validity only. Austin, contends that, in case of international law, as there is no visible authority with the legislative power and even with any determinate power over the society of states, rules on international law is not true law but positive international morality or opinions or sentiments current among nations generally.

However, there are some scholars who consider international law as a law. Starke gives certain arguments refuting the Austinian view on international law. He contends:

1. Austin's general theory of law has been refuted by modern jurists. They have shown that earlier times many communities without a formal legislative authority had a system of law, which was observed and had also the binding effect like the law of any state with true legislative authority.

2. At present a huge body of 'international legislation' has come into existence as a result of law-making treaties and conventions and, therefore, the proportion of customary international law has diminished in proportion. Though there is an absence of sovereign legislative authority at the international level, the procedure for formulating these rules of international legislation by means of international conferences or through international organizations is settled, if not quite similar or as efficient as any legislative procedures of a state.

3. The authoritative agencies responsible for conducting international business like those occupying positions in various foreign offices, do not consider international law as merely a moral code.

Therefore, Starke opines that international law is law proper and not the vanishing point of jurisprudence. It has a binding force which limits the exercise of national power, though its nature is different from the nature of municipal law as it is law among states and regulates the conduct of the states.

There exists another debate regarding the relationship between international law and municipal law. Which one has a primacy over the other? If municipal law is taken in the first instance, one would find that it is generated by well-developed legislative institutions such as the Parliament (UK, India, for instance) or the Congress (e.g. USA) or the like. International law, as compared to the municipal law, has no institutionalized legislative sources. The United Nations General Assembly (UNGA) may resemble a legislature of a state and can be regarded as a global legislature, but the decisions taken in the UNGA reflect the aspirations and wishes of the majority of governments represented in the United Nations. These resolutions have neither legal nor substantive binding power.

Further, municipal laws have proper agents for their execution such as the executive branch of a government of a state. Such institutions do not exist at the global level. Even the United Nations cannot be regarded as an executor of International law. In case of municipal law there is also a system which enables such laws to be interpreted and applied to specific cases by the municipal courts that have compulsory jurisdiction regardless of consent over their subjects. On the other hand, the International Court of Justice can hear only those cases referred to it by the consenting governments or international organizations. The greatest weakness of this whole system is that there is no executive authority to enforce the Court's decision. It is entirely up to the states to adhere to the verdict of the Court.

The adoption or adherence to international law in most cases depend on how far the specific municipal measure of statutory or judicial incorporation has been undertaken by a state so that the international law becomes binding within the municipal sphere too. Therefore, regarding the question of primacy, it is often considered that municipal laws enjoy a primacy over international laws. In India, e.g., the Directive Principles of the State Policy under Part IV of the

Indian Constitution, Article 51 contains provisions that the state shall endeavour to:

1. Promote international peace and security.
2. Maintain just and honourable relations between nations.
3. Foster respect for international law and treaty obligations in the dealings of organized peoples with one another.
4. Encourage settlement of international disputes by arbitration.

In Britain, the customary rules of international law are deemed to be part of the law of the land and are applied by the British municipal courts with certain qualifications. The rules must not be inconsistent with the British statute and that once the scope of such customary rules has been decided by the British courts of final authority, all British courts are thereafter bound by that decision even though a divergent customary rule of international law later develops. As far as treaties are concerned, the negotiation, signature and ratification of treaties are matters belonging to the prerogative powers of the Crown and the legislative domain of the Parliament.

The American practice relating to customary rules of international law is very similar to the British practice. Such rules are administered as part of the law of the land. Regarding treaties, the American practice rests upon the provisions of the US Constitution stipulating that "all Treaties made, or which shall be made under the Authority of the United States", shall be "the supreme Law of the Land" (Article VI, para 2).

However, it has also been pointed out by experts on international law that if international law draws its validity from a state constitution, it will cease to be in force once the constitution on which its authority rests, disappears. The operation of international law has proven that it is independent of change or abolition of constitutions. The London Conference of 1831 upheld that "treaties do not lose their force despite internal constitutional changes". Even the entry of new states into the international society binds the new states with international law without its consent and such consent, even if it is expressed is merely declaratory of the true legal position. The dismemberment of the erstwhile Soviet Union and the emergence of new states did not end the Soviet Union's Treaty obligations with other states, and the newly independent states could not make themselves insulated from international law. Above all, it is the duty of every state to bring not only its laws but also its constitution into harmony with international law so that international peace and security can be preserved.

In reality, states conduct their relations with other members of the international community on the basis of international law and in most cases they do adhere to or uphold international law. During peace and also during war, the states try to justify their actions as valid in the eyes of international law. Despite the weaknesses of international law, when compared to the municipal laws, it cannot be said that international law is a weak law. It upholds the sovereignty of states and preserves that sovereignty by defining the rights and obligations of the states.

INTERNATIONAL MORALITY

International morality is not only difficult to define but it also involves a cumbersome exercise to understand its effectiveness on the actions of states in pursuit of their national power. In such a discussion, there is always a chance of either overestimating the impact of ethics or underestimating its influence on the actions of statesmen and diplomats. If international politics is perceived as a Hobbesian state of nature, then the statesmen and diplomats would exceed all limits to pursue their power objectives. In reality, however, they do much less than they actually could have done and this is because their actions violate or are limited by certain moral rules. The restraining function of the moral rules is "most obvious and most effective in affirming the sacredness of human life in times of peace".[8] This is international morality which consists of moral principles agreed upon by the comity of nations. They comprise rules of customary international law, general principles, conventions and treaties.

The sanctions behind international morality are domestic public opinion and world public opinion. While domestic public opinion is an internal constraint on the foreign policy decision-makers, world public opinion is the external restraint on the actions of statesmen and diplomats. It is for their own interests that the states subject themselves to such restraints. States are always concerned with their image and in no way can risk jeopardizing their 'decent' image by dishonouring domestic or world public opinion. Even, a superpower like the United States, due to its heavy involvement in the Vietnam War in the 1960s, had to succumb ultimately to the growing adverse domestic as well as world public opinion.

Role of International Morality

Morgenthau highlights the importance of international morality. According to him, it has three dimensions.

1. *Protection of Human Life in Peace:* The Covenant of the League of Nations contained and the Charter of the United Nations contains provisions regarding the use of force by states. Force can only be used either for self-defence or in pursuance of a decision made collectively by the members of UNO. In other words, the UN Charter is the embodiment (earlier the Covenant was) of protection and safeguard of international peace and security.

Various Conventions and Declarations also try to safeguard human life and dignity such as the Universal Declaration of Human Rights (1948), the International Covenant on Civil and Political Rights (1966), the International Covenant on Economic Social and Cultural Rights (1966), the Convention on Genocide (1948).

2. *Protection of Human Life in War:*   Moral limitations are also imposed during times of war by various Conventions and Declarations. In Chapter IV, Book III of *On the Law of War and Peace*, under the heading "On the Right of Killing Enemies in a Public War and on Other Violence against the Person", Grotius presented a catalogue of acts of violence committed in ancient history against enemy persons without discrimination. He himself justified some on the ground that the war was waged for a just cause. Since then the whole concept of war has undergone change and it is now accepted that war is not a contest between whole populations, but only between the armies of the belligerent states. Therefore, a distinction between combatants and non-combatants became fundamental legal and moral principles governing war. These found expressions in the Hague Conventions, with respect to the *Laws and Customs of War on Land* of 1899 and 1907 and the Geneva Conventions of 1864 superseded by those of 1906, 1929 and 1949, and their additional Protocols. The International Red Cross Society (ICRC) is entrusted with the mandate to uphold the International Humanitarian Law.

3. *Moral Condemnation of War:*   There is increasing realization on the part of the states that use of war as an instrument of foreign policy is restricted by certain moral limitations. The two Hague Conferences of 1899 and 1907, the League of Nations (1919), the Kellog–Briand Pact of 1928—all outlaw aggressive war, and the United Nations (1946) upholds the avoidance of war as its ultimate objective. War in the present has assumed perilous proportions due to the advent of newer technologies and nuclear materials resulting in the production of weapons of mass destruction like the nuclear bomb. Therefore, efforts towards disarmament and arms control are also being made to prevent arms race and outbreak of war among states.

WORLD PUBLIC OPINION

It is widely acknowledged that world public opinion acts as an external restraint on the foreign policy decision-makers of any state. However, the effectiveness of the world public opinion of restraining a particular state from performing an action, which might violate international law and morality, is questionable. It is equally difficult to define and even harder to prove the existence of world public opinion.

Morgenthau has offered a definition which partially covers the element and extent of world public opinion. He states, "World public opinion is obviously a public opinion that transcends national boundaries and that unites members of different nations in a consensus with regard to at least certain fundamental international issues". The question which arises is: Does such consensus exist and if so, can it be regarded as world public opinion? It is true that human beings have a desire for freedom, self-expression, self-development, and therefore, develop a certain perspective, opinions or expectations regarding certain fundamental aspects of foreign policy behaviour of states. It is hardly tenable that there is a tremendous psychological unity of the world and upon this psychological conviction, similar ethical postulates and political aspirations may be shared by all men under certain conditions. Most often this is not the case. This world is an unequal world with unequal distribution of power and great economic disparity dividing the globe into the haves and the have nots, the North and the South, the Developed World and the Third World, and so on. Even the same moral precepts may assume different meanings in different environments. As imperialism, racialism, colonialism, neo-colonialism and dependency might have different interpretations for the once colonial powers and the Third World, perceptions regarding some particular issues like the given ones may give rise to consensus among some groups of states which in most cases are driven by their common historical experiences and their struggle against particular actions of other groups of states, which for them might be exploitative and discriminatory. Earlier, such common perceptions had united a certain part of the world and given rise to powerful movement like the NAM. However, it can hardly be agreed upon that this movement was able to forge world public opinion as it was critically viewed by the Western states.

Massive technological revolution and invasion of information technology have undoubtedly removed the barriers between the individuals and have increased the chances of their contacts, and thus greater opportunity for building up of world public opinion; but very rarely we can perceive the existence of world public opinion on fundamental issues in international relations. Morgenthau points out that the information and ideas that are transmitted are reflections of the experiences that have moulded philosophies, ethics and conceptions of different people belonging to different states. If these experiences and their intellectual derivatives are identical throughout humanity, then the free flow of information and ideas would indeed create by itself a world public opinion; but this is hardly the case. Thus, an American perception would differ from a Russian and an Indian perception from a Pakistani. Therefore, it is hard to get an aggregate of their opinion, that will give rise to world public opinion.

In the past there have been attempts to mobilize public opinion against the foreign policy of certain governments like the Japanese aggressions against China in the 1930s, the German foreign policies since 1935, the Italian attack against Ethiopia in 1935, and the Russian suppression of the Hungarian revolution of 1956. However, even if these attempts were successful in generating world public opinion, these did not have restraining effects on the policies of those opposed. A more recent example is the US action in Iraq and Afghanistan in the name of "War on Terror" disregarding the world public opinion alongside projecting its action as justified and trying to build up a consensus globally to support its action in the name of 'War on Terror'.

Nationalism also prevents the crystallization of world public opinion. Morgenthau stated that between the elemental aspirations for life, freedom and power which unite mankind and which could provide the roots for a world society and universal morality and the political philosophies, ethics and objectives held by individuals, there intervenes the nation. Therefore, the intellectual derivatives from this nation and nationalism conception disunite the human beings of the world. Hence, for an American, the image of the Soviet Government during the Cold War days was that of a deceitful, untrustworthy, aggressive, unreliable nation which represented an evil empire and must be "contained".

However, it would be too pessimistic to totally negate the importance of world public opinion. World public opinion was supposed to be the foundation of the League of Nations (1919) which was to be the enforcement agency for the Kellog–Briand Pact of 1928, the decisions of the Permanent Court of International Justice and international law in general. Under the present situation, because of globalization and immense revolution in technological front and information technology (IT), common problems relating to peace, war, environment, development, sustainable development, disarmament, equity and justice, democracy and other issues have induced individuals to transcend national barriers and establish a psychological unity among peoples of different states and thus pave the way for the development of world public opinion. It must also be acknowledged that world public opinion does have a restraining effect on the actions of the states. Even the sole surviving superpower, viz. USA, cannot disregard the world public opinion and hence it is often engaged in the task of justifying its action as one upholding international law, international morality and world public opinion. Most governments are very much concerned with their prestige and cannot afford the world to be critical of its policy abroad. It is only under certain crisis situations that the states are bent on defending their objectives even at the risk of breaking commitments, violating norms while strictly following national imperatives. But under normal conditions, the statesmen and diplomats choose policy alternatives which are likely to meet less hostile reaction and evoke world public opinion.

EXERCISES

1. Define the concept of international law. Is it a proper law?

2. What are the sources of international law?

3. Discuss the nature and scope of international law.

4. What do you understand by international morality? Examine the role of international morality in international relations.

5. Comment on the role of world public opinion in restraining the actions of states in international relations.

REFERENCES

[1] Sharma, Urmila and S.K. Sharma, *International Relations*, Atlantic Publishers, New Delhi, 2000, p. 31.

[2] Oppenheim, L., *International Law,* Longmans, Green & Co., New York, 1905, p. 2.

[3] Stowell, Ellery C., *International Law*, Holt, New York, 1931, p. 10.

[4] Jessup, Phillip C., *Transnational Law,* Yale University Press, New Haven, 1956.

[5] Fenwick, Charles G., *International Law*, Century, New York, 1924, p. 34.

[6] Starke, J.G., *Introduction to International Law*, Aditya Books, New Delhi, 1994, p. 3.

[7] Hoffman, Stanley, "International Systems and International Law," *in* Richard Falk and Saul H. Mendlovitz (Eds.), *The Strategy of World Order, International Law,* Vol. 2, World Law Fund, 1966, p. 134, cited in Theodore A. Couloumbis and James H. Wolfe, *Introduction to International Relations: Power and Justice*, Prentice-Hall of India, New Delhi, 1981, p. 257.

[8] Morgenthau, Hans. J., *Politics Among Nations: The Struggle for Power and Peace*, Kalyani Publishers, New Delhi, 1985, p. 249.

18

Indian Foreign Policy

INTRODUCTION

India has travelled a long way since her Independence in 1947 and is gradually assuming the status of an 'emerging power'. Despite several challenges from within her polity arising from her unique character as a sub-continental, multilingual entity, severely constraining her ability, India has managed to exhibit her prowess in terms of nuclear as well as military capabilities while exercising restraint whenever required.

India's foreign policy has evolved over the years under the influence of the country's geo-strategic location, economic conditions, political tradition, societal fabric, national character, national morale and personality traits of the leaders. If these constitute the internal factors shaping the Indian Foreign Policy, then international political environment, foreign policies of major powers and those of the neighbouring countries comprise the external determinants of Indian foreign policy. It must be noted here that Indian foreign policy has never been a static one and it has undergone changes due to the changing domestic as well as international scenario.

BASIC OBJECTIVES

It can be said with certainty that certain basic objectives, which enshrine the main principles of Indian foreign policy, have remained unchanged overtime and constitute the pillars of Indian foreign policy. These basic principles are now outlined.

1. *Non-Alignment:* The chief architect of non-aligned policy was Pandit Jawaharlal Nehru, the first Prime Minister of India. His main concern was consolidating the Independence earned after years of struggle and ensuring peace and economic development of India. Nehru's ardent desire, therefore, became an effort to keep India out of 'entangling alliances'. However, the immediate impetus to the formulation of non-alignment was provided by the Cold War between the two superpowers, the United States and the Soviet Union, which divided the world into two hostile camps. Further, the US attempt to rope in a number of Asian countries into various military alliances like the Baghdad Pact (1955–1958), SEATO (1954) and CENTO (1958–1979) as part of their 'containment' policy, and to which India's neighbour Pakistan was also being drawn into, made non-alignment a better option to Nehru.

Nehru professed distancing India from the two power blocs, with the aim of ensuring development and fighting social evils such as poverty, hunger and death. India also preferred to keep away from the power politics of groups aligned against one another which had led in the past to two World Wars, and which might again lead to disasters on an even vaster scale in the future. Nehru felt that "to enter into an alliance was to lose one's independence because at times of emergency the recipient country will have to take orders from the country supplying the arms. Worse still, Asian countries entering into alliance with the West, would give the West an opportunity to solve Asian problems minus Asia".[1]

2. *Anti-Colonialism and Anti-Imperialism:* The roots of India's anti-colonial and anti-imperialistic politics lie in her own experience of British imperialism. The anti-imperialist feeling, which gathered during the Indian freedom movement, through mass struggles such as the Swadeshi Movement, Non-Cooperation Movement, Civil Disobedience Movement, and Quit India Movement, got expression in the foreign policy posture adopted by India after Independence.

Therefore, post-Independence, India expressed solidarity with the national liberation movements in Asia, Africa and Latin America. India used the NAM forum and also the UN platform to fight for the cause of the people still under the colonial rule. India extended help to the people fighting for independence of Indonesia, Libya, Tunisia, Algeria, Morocco, and most importantly, the decolonization of Namibia and South Africa. She even played a vital role in the evolution of independent Bangladesh with her support to the people of East Pakistan to liberate themselves from the yoke of West Pakistan. India never ceased its struggle against colonialism as increasingly traditional colonialism was being replaced by neo-colonialism. India also continued to play a vital role in the Third World's struggle to establish a New International Economic Order (NIEO), with a vision of international equity and justice.

3. *Anti-Racialism:* Like imperialism, racialism also can be traced to India's historical experiences. The British racialist policy in India "permeated all the services and constituted the distinguishing characteristic of British rule in the East in the nineteenth century".[2] Therefore, post-Independence anti-racialism became one of the major principles of Indian foreign policy. By 1947, anti-imperialism and anti-racialism became categorical imperatives of the Indian national mind and Nehru only expressed a deep Indian sentiment when in 1946 as the Prime Minister of the Interim Government of India, he stated that anti-imperialism and anti-racialism were the "kernel of our foreign policy".

Soon after Independence, India began to play a pioneering role in condemning the policy of apartheid and racial discrimination pursued by the Government of South Africa. India sought to rally the international community to force the Pretoria Government to abandon its policy of apartheid. In 1952, India, along with 12 other Afro-Asian states, raised the issue of apartheid in the UN and expressed her grave concerns regarding the practice as it was tantamount to open violation of the UN Charter and the Universal Declaration of Human Rights and constituted a threat to international peace. India also took up the cause of the 'black' population in USA and also the African population of Rhodesia (Zimbabwe). She had also used the NAM platform to support the struggle of the people against racialism and apartheid. India still believes in the relevance of its anti-racial policy, and therefore, continues to fight against such practice against humanity.

4. *Panchsheel or Peaceful Coexistence:* The cardinal principle of Indian foreign policy is *Panchsheel* or peaceful coexistence. It was in 1954 that Beijing and New Delhi jointly proposed *Five Principles of Peaceful Coexistence* (known as **Panchsheel** in India) primarily to guide the bilateral relations between them. The Five Principles of peaceful coexistence, collectively known as *Panchsheel,* were enunciated by the Chinese Premier Zhou Enlai and the Indian Prime Minister Jawaharlal Nehru during the negotiations on the India–China Agreement on Tibet concluded on 29 April 1954. But the Five Principles were nothing new to India and can be found in the ancient scriptures. Moral, spiritual, religious and cultural teachings have been inculcating the spirit of mutual respect, tolerance, peaceful coexistence and respect for each other's integrity and independence among its people for centuries.[3]

These five principles of Panchsheel are:

1. Mutual respect for each other's territorial integrity and sovereignty
2. Mutual non-aggression

3. Mutual non-interference in each other's internal affairs
4. Equality and mutual benefit
5. Peaceful coexistence.

The *Panchsheel* became the moving force behind Asian and African movements for equality and freedom against domination of the world by colonial and imperialist powers and was also endorsed by the UN. Although the Five Principles of Panchsheel are quintessentially reflected in the UN Charter, drafted a decade earlier than the *Panchsheel,* the then UN Secretary-General Dag Hammarskjold aptly described them as "reaffirmation of the aims and obligations of the United Nations". *Panchsheel* got wider acceptability when the resolution moved by Yugoslavia, Sweden and India on 11 December 1957 in the UN was adopted unanimously in the UN General Assembly.

Although the 1962 Sino–Indian crisis came as a Chinese betrayal, India continues to have faith in these principles in her relations with her neighbours as well as with other members of the international community. In his bid to improve India's relations with her neighbours, Prime Minister I.K. Gujral reaffirmed those principles and gave them a new dimension. This was known as the **Gujral Doctrine.** Under this doctrine, unilateral concessions were made to the neighbouring countries with regard to trade and travel without expecting reciprocity.

5. *Disarmament:* Another important foreign policy posture of India is that of disarmament and arms control. India herself is not a signatory to Non Proliferation Treaty (NPT, 1968) and Comprehensive Test Ban Treaty (CTBT, 1996) as these international regimes are considered discriminatory and create nuclear 'haves' and 'have nots'. It was under India's initiative that broad proposals were forwarded at the Six-Nation Summit in 1985 held in New Delhi. But the irony is that India and Pakistan have entangled themselves in an arms race and both conducted nuclear tests in 1998. Experts opine that this arms race might destabilize the peace and security of the South Asian region. The danger increases manifold as Pakistan, India's menacing neighbour, is involved in clandestine transfer of nuclear R&D from North Korea, Libya and Iran, which poses a threat not only to India but to the entire South Asian region. Besides, Pakistan being a country facing political turmoil, economic instability and gradually becoming a safe haven for the terrorists with increasing intrusion of Talibans into Pakistan and their increased activities, there is every possibility that the nukes might fall into the wrong hands, which will be the worst nightmare coming true. On the other hand, Indian democracy faces stiff challenges from within, but the polity is still strong enough to adopt a nuclear doctrine characterized by restraint and notable non-proliferation credentials. India earned criticisms after the 1998 nuclear tests but she has shown restraint and has adopted the posture of No-First-Use (NFU), unlike Pakistan which proposes First-Use (FU) of nukes. Besides, India has always championed the cause of peaceful use of nuclear energy. Even the Indo–US Nuclear Deal of 2008 contained provisions for use of nuclear energy for civilian purposes.

6. *Faith in the United Nations:* India has always reposed great faith in the United Nations and always upheld its basic principles and objectives. It has also taken part in a number of peacekeeping activities under the auspices of the United Nations. India contributed an infantry battalion to UN operations in the Gaza strip from 1956 onwards. Another large contingent of the Indian Army and Air Force was sent for the Congo peacekeeping mission in 1961. Smaller groups comprising Indian military personnel have been involved in UN monitoring and peacekeeping exercises in Korea (1953), Indo–China (1954), Lebanon (1958), Angola (1988) and along the Iran–Iraq border. Troops were also sent to Rwanda in 1994, Somalia in 1993–1994, and to a host of other UN peacekeeping missions.

Simultaneously, India has made a strong plea for an overall reform of the United Nations in order to make it more representative and democratic. India is also striving for a permanent seat in the United Nations Security Council. Just before the G–8 Summit in July 2009, Prime Minister Dr. Manmohan Singh has called for reform in the UN and also pleaded for inclusion of India as a permanent member of the UN Security Council.

7. *Ties with Commonwealth:* India continues to nurture her relation with the Commonwealth. Though, initially there were apprehensions about India's membership to the Commonwealth as a compromise on its sovereignty, yet India with its Republican constitution continues to have good ties with the Commonwealth which in reality helps India to develop economic and other relations with the members of the Commonwealth.

8. *Fight against Terror:* International terrorism is an increasing menace to international peace and security. India herself bore the brunt of terrorist onslaughts over the past several years. India has always voiced her concern over the issue of terrorism. After the 9/11 attacks on the US, terrorism became a global concern and there have been several attempts to combat terrorism. India has used the UN, the NAM and the SAARC platforms to mobilize the international community to fight terrorism. India and the other South Asian states signed the SAARC Regional Convention on Suppression of Terrorism, at Kathmandu on 4 November 1987. India continues her fight against terrorism along with the world community.

EVOLUTION OF INDIA'S FOREIGN POLICY: 1947–PRESENT

Foreign Policy under Jawaharlal Nehru: The Formative Years

Pandit Jawaharlal Nehru (1947–1964) was not only the first Prime Minister of India but also the chief architect of the Indian foreign policy; for nearly twenty years, he guided the country's participation in the world affairs. Even after his death, his legacy continued till the end of the Cold War and cessation of bipolar politics. This was more because of the fact that the environment of Indian foreign policy did not change much—bipolarity continued till 1990, incessant bitter relations with Pakistan and the China factor remained as constant determinants of the course of Indian foreign policy.

Further, Nehru's views persisted because he was succeeded by individuals who were either unskilled in foreign policy [Lal Bahadur Shastri (1964–1966)] or those who were committed to Nehruvian principles [Indira Gandhi (1966–1977) and (1980–1989) and Rajiv Gandhi (1984–1989)] who were also his daughter and grandson, respectively. Though both had introduced changes in Indian foreign policy, yet they expressed their commitments to the Nehruvian principles. Besides, the long single party domination of Indian politics by the National Congress created generations of Indian politicians and bureaucrats committed to Nehruvianism.[4]

Under Nehru's guidance, Indian foreign policy was the inevitable consequence of the geo-strategic realities of India. Nehru's worldview was conditioned by his belief that the world is not necessarily friendly to a weak and vulnerable state such as India, and that national interests must shape the foreign policy of any state. This way, Nehruvian internationalism was realistic but it was also liberal in the sense that he thought states can rise above "the rigors of anarchy and fashion at least seasons and locales of peace and cooperation. They must do so because power politics is flawed and will end in catastrophe". Therefore, in many instances, Nehru himself wavered continually between idealism and national egoism or realism and, under such reductionist realism, Nehru pursued policies that advanced national interest as well as included a good measure of idealism or liberal internationalism.

India under Nehru, therefore, embarked on the policy of non-alignment as she was keen to preserve her national interest by keeping away from either the Western capitalist bloc led by the United States or the Socialist bloc led by the Soviet Union. Nehru told the Constituent Assembly on 4 December 1947: "Whatever policy we may lay down, the art of conducting foreign affairs of a country lies in finding out what is most advantageous to the country. We may talk about international goodwill and mean what we say. But in the ultimate analysis government functions for the good of the country and no government dare do anything, which in the short or long run is manifestly to the disadvantage of the country".[5]

Another major challenge faced by India was economic development. After independence, India faced the serious problem of poverty alleviation and for that she realized that dependence on both the blocs was necessary to spearhead India's economic and industrial development. Nehru was quite realistic to recognize the economic strength that was central to the stability and social coherence of the country. Economic development would help to build up a strong India. Therefore, in March 1947, he stated in the Constituent Assembly, "if we had been some odd little nation in Asia or Europe it would not have mattered much, but because we counted and because we're going to count more and more in the future, everything we do becomes a matter of comment and many people do not like our counting so much. It is not a question of our viewpoint or of attaching ourselves to this or that bloc, it is merely a fact that we are potentially a great nation and a big power and possibly it is not liked by some people that anything should happen to strengthen us".

Simultaneously, Nehru rejected isolationism and he clearly stated that " we maintain our old ties with those countries because no nation can live in isolation....That some people obsessed by passion and prejudice disapproved of our relations with the Anglo-American bloc is not sufficient reason for us to break any bond which is of advantage to us". Thus, Nehru, despite vehement criticisms, forged the membership of the Commonwealth. He viewed that it did not compromise the country's freedom in international affairs, but it acted as a shield against the reigning powers of the day.

Nehru was against the creation of military blocs in Asia and Africa and he saw their creation as a manifestation of neo-colonialism. He also abhorred racialism and delivering the Presidential address of the Indian National Congress session on 24 January 1954, Nehru said the issues confronting the Third World countries were colonialism and racialism. India under Nehru also showed a strong commitment to the struggle against imperialism and colonialism as well as a commitment to the unity of the struggling nation of the world. India gave a call for the freedom of all countries under the colonial rule and solidarity with the worldwide anti-imperialist struggle and was vocal in various international fora like the General Assembly, Conferences of Non-aligned Movement, and spoke in unison with the Third World countries for a New International Economic Order.

Regarding Nehru's policy towards India's neighbour, it can be said that India's bilateral relations with Nepal, Bhutan and Sri Lanka remained, by and large, cordial. There were some irritants in Indo–Nepal relations, which stemmed from Nehru's reaction to the Royal Coup in Nepal in 1960 and also in India–Sri Lankan relations because of granting citizenship to the Tamil plantation workers in northern Sri Lanka.[6]

LAL BAHADUR SHASTRI TO INDIRA GANDHI— THE CONSOLIDATION PHASE

Lal Bahadur Shastri (1965–1966)

After the death of Jawaharlal Nehru, Lal Bahadur Shastri became the Prime Minister of India for a very brief period. He gave currency to the slogan *Jai Jawan, Jai Kisan* on the wake of the first real Indo–Pak War, which took place in September 1965. Under his leadership India gave a befitting reply to Pakistan between Indian and Pakistan and the Indian army reached almost the outskirts of Lahore. Ultimately, ceasefire was declared under the auspices of the United Nations Security Council. The Soviet Union took the initiative to bring about peace negotiations between India and Pakistan and Shastri met Field Marshal

Ayub Khan, President of Pakistan, in Tashkent (now the capital of Uzbekistan) and the Tashkent Declaration was signed on 10 January 1966. This provided for the following:

1. Restoration of normal and peaceful relations between India and Pakistan.
2. Reaffirmation of their obligations under UN charter to settle their disputes through peaceful means.
3. Agreement to base their relations on the principle of non-interference in the internal affairs of each other.
4. Meetings at the highest level as also at other levels to discuss matters of direct concern to both.

Lal Bahadur Shastri also took initiative to improve India's relationship with her other neighbours such as Nepal, Myanmar and Sri Lanka. With Sri Lanka, Shastri signed an Agreement with Sirimavo Bandaranaike in October 1964. Under this agreement, out of the 775,000 Indian Tamil settlers in Sri Lanka, 300,000 were to be granted Sri Lankan citizenship and 325,000 were to be repatriated to India within a period of 15 years. The status of the future of the remaining 150,000 Tamils was to be settled later.

He also tried to build good relations with both the superpowers and succeeded in procuring military and economic assistance from them. Only the 1965 War between India and Pakistan provided the occasion for Washington and London to suspend the military aid and sales programmes to both India and Pakistan.

Shastri's greatest achievement was the Indo–Pak War of 1965, which, partly helped boost the morale of the army that had been shattered by the border war with China in 1962. Unfortunately, Shastri passed away with a massive heart attack soon after signing the Tashkent Agreement. In January 1966, Indira Gandhi became the first woman Prime Minister of independent India.

Indira Gandhi (1966–1977) and (1980–1984)

When Indira Gandhi came to power, India was grappling with hard times during 1966–1969. The troubles had arisen in the aftermath of border war with China and these increased with two years of severe drought accompanied by flooding in other parts of the country which had grave impact on the economy of the country and also constrained India's assertiveness and capacity to take initiatives in international relations and on her policy of non-alignment.

Soon after Indira Gandhi assumed the office, she expressed her solidarity and moral support to the principles of non-alignment. Tito and Nasser arranged a meeting with her and she visited UAR and Yugoslavia in July 1966. The Third Tripartite Conference of the leaders of UAR, Yugoslavia and India was held in New Delhi in October 1966. The proceedings of these meetings and the joint communiqué reflected the concern of Mrs. Gandhi and others over the imposition of various forms of imperialism and neo-colonialism and the threat to world peace posed by gross interference in the internal affairs of independent countries followed by economic and financial assistance as an instrument of pressure. The three, Gandhi, Tito and Nasser, also expressed their deep concern for the sufferings of the Vietnamese people and demanded a cessation of the bombing of North Vietnam. This was rather a courageous stand taken by Mrs. Gandhi as the economic crisis had made India heavily dependent on the United States.

Mrs. Gandhi visited the United States from 28 March to 1 April 1966 and agreements on US aid followed one after another in the coming years in the fields of supply of fertilizers, mineral exploration and a food agreement in which Washington undertook to supply 3.5 million tons of food grains, 856,000 bales of cotton and other commodities. This was a supplement to the PL–480 Agreement of 30 September 1964. Another food agreement under PL–480 was implemented on 20 February 1967. This was followed by further food agreements and also funds to finance development projects mutually agreed upon.[7] The point to be noted here is that, the US administration, while publicly giving the impression that it was going all out to help but actually it was trying to twist India's arm with regard to her foreign policy, particularly in relation to her friendly ties with Moscow. Further, the Indo–US relations suffered several setbacks because of India's role in the Bangladesh crisis, Nixon's tilt towards Pakistan and the Pokhran explosion of 1974. Still Mrs.Gandhi continued her efforts to improve India's relation with the United States. She met President Ronald Reagan for the first time during a World Summit at Cancun (Greece) in October 1981. This was followed by her visit to the United States in September 1982 with the objective of reducing the differences and enhancing mutual understanding. However, basic differences persisted over West Asia, the Indian Ocean, and South-East Asia.

The revival of economic and political momentum between 1969 and 1971 once again helped India to regain her assertiveness in her foreign policy decisions as well as voicing the concerns of the developing world. Mrs. Gandhi projected India's image abroad as not an image of a country which follows any group or country, but as an image of a country standing or trying to stand on her own feet.

The most critical and dangerous challenge to India which she faced in the 1970s was the Bangladesh crisis. She gave top priority to this crisis as India's security and stability were jeopardized. Refugee influx became a grave concern for India. But India, under Mrs. Gandhi took calculated move at every stage of the crisis. Besides the Prime Minister and the Foreign Minister, a nucleus for high-level planning was made by the Principal Private Secretary to the Prime Minister, Mr. P.N. Haksar and the Foreign Secretary, Mr. T.N. Kaul.

At about the same time, simultaneous developments could be seen in other parts of the world where the Nixon–Kissinger duo was eager to mend fences with China, and China too under Mao–Zhou partnership was determined to end her isolation. Therefore, there developed a rapprochement between the two to balance off Russia. It was under these circumstances that India concluded with the Soviet Union, The Indo–Soviet Treaty of Peace Friendship and Cooperation in August 1971. This treaty provided that the two countries would keep in touch with each other on major international problems affecting the interests of both the parties. They agreed not to enter into or participate in military alliance, which is directed against any one of them. The treaty stipulated that if there was aggression against any of the two parties, they would immediately consult each other on how to meet the aggression. They would abstain from providing assistance to any third party that emerged in armed conflict with one of them. The Treaty was like a shield against both Washington and Chinese designs of any military action against India in the unfolding Bangladesh Crisis.

India played a prominent role in the emergence of Bangladesh, which became an independent state on 16 December 1971 after the surrender of the Pakistani troops in the erstwhile East Bengal to the Indian army. India gave immediate recognition to the state of Bangladesh. Ultimately, the Indo–Pak relations were normalized with the Simla Summit held on 1 July 1972 which sought to resolve several thorny issues in their bilateral relations. The Simla Agreement provided that:

1. Both the parties would resolve their differences by peaceful means through bilateral negotiations, and committed themselves to peaceful coexistence, respect for each other's territorial integrity, sovereignty and non-interference in each other's internal affairs.
2. Hostile propaganda against each other would be stopped.
3. Meeting between the Heads of the two countries would be convened to discuss the future ways and means for the establishment of durable peace and normalization of relations.

Mrs. Gandhi too was keen on improving India's relations with other neighbours such as Nepal and Sri Lanka. She adopted a soft policy towards Nepal and even visited Nepal in October 1966 and held out largest aid package for India's small neighbour. She always tried to win the goodwill of India's other neighbour, Sri Lanka.

During both her terms, Mrs. Gandhi had tried to improve India's relation with China. She met Hua Guofeng, the then Chinese Prime Minister in Belgrade in 1980 and later Premier Zhau Ziyang at Cancun in 1981. Beijing also made efforts for the betterment of relations to that end and sent, one of its senior Vice Premiers, Huang Hua to New Delhi in June 1981.

India again faced another dilemma when the Soviet Union invaded a non-aligned country like Afghanistan. It was a tightrope walk for India. India's response to the Afghanistan issue disappointed the Americans as they thought New Delhi would come down heavily on the presence of the Soviet troops in Afghanistan. India again was vocal against the US supply of the most advanced and lethal armaments to Pakistan as a part of its containment policy. It was only during the Cancun Summit that President Ronald Reagan and Mrs. Gandhi evolved a good personal equation that served to limit the damage caused.

India also hosted the Seventh NAM Summit in 1983 and Mrs. Gandhi was elected as the Chairperson for the next three years. The 1982 Asian Games was another achievement of Mrs. Gandhi's government. In 1983 Commonwealth Heads of Government Meeting (CHOGM) was held in New Delhi. These events showed that India was gaining a prominent position in the international arena.

The Janata Party (1977–1979): Good Neighbourly Policy

The Janata Party came to power for a very brief period from 1977 to 1979. This was the first non-Congress government formed under Morarji Desai since the time of Nehru. It was expected that there would be drastic changes in the foreign policy posture of India under the Janata Government. This was specially so because they vehemently criticized India's intimacy with the Soviet Union as a violation of the principle of non-alignment. On the Janata Party's assumption of office, the leaders talked about genuine non-alignment and maintaining distance from both the superpowers. But soon they were disillusioned as Jimmy Carter's Government refused shipment of enriched uranium to Tarapore plant on the ground that India was non-commital to the signing of the NPT and was "insensitive to human rights violations in Kashmir". Therefore, Indo–US relations did not improve but the Janata government realized the utility of special relationship that was initiated in 1971 with the Soviet Union. It got itself reconciled with the tilt in non-alignment and continued good relations with the Soviet Union.

As far as India's relations with her neighbours were concerned, there were tremendous improvements. The Janata government made possible the Salal Agreement with Pakistan. The Indo–Bangladesh Agreement on Ganga Water Sharing was also concluded. Two separate agreements on Trade and Transit were signed with Nepal. Atal Bihari Vajpayee, the then External Affairs Minister, made every effort to improve India's relation with her South Asian neighbours which he propounded as 'beneficial bilateralism'. Critics often point out that the shifts in the policy that were visible in the foreign policy under Janata government were neither new nor a marked departure from the earlier policies. They were just continuing adjustments according to the needs of the time in domestic and external contexts.

Rajiv Gandhi (1984–1989): The Globalization Spree

After the assassination of Mrs. Gandhi in October 1984, Rajiv Gandhi became the youngest Prime Minister of India. He was inexperienced but "A young man with a modern outlook, Rajiv Gandhi was a technophile with great faith in modern management ways".

His foreign policy did not mark a departure from his predecessors'. His worldview reflected the perspectives of Nehru and Mrs. Gandhi. Rajiv Gandhi was in favour of nuclear disarmament, consolidation of non-aligned movement, reaffirming faith in the United Nations, supporting the struggle against racialism, and was inclined to work for narrowing the international economic disparities.

On 28th January 1985, a Six-Nation Meeting was held in New Delhi attended by Sweden, Mexico, Greece, Tanzania, Argentina and India which was presided over by Rajiv Gandhi. He made an appeal to the five nuclear powers (USA, Russia, France, Britain and China) to stop further production and testing of nuclear devices as the "first credible and reassuring step" towards nuclear disarmament and reduce their stockpiles. This appeal was reiterated in the joint statement issued by the leaders of the six countries at the end of the meeting.

He also had a vision of improving relations with the Soviet Union, the United States and China. Simultaneously, he gave priority to the betterment of relations with the neighbours, especially Pakistan and Sri Lanka. With the neighbours he was bent on pursuing a bilateral foreign policy based on the spirit of peace, friendship and cooperation, non-interference and also intended to work towards the concept of common regional development in South Asia.

Rajiv Gandhi realized the complexities in the relation between the United States and India. Thus, he took an early opportunity to visit the United States in June 1985 and struck a rapport with President Ronald Reagan. He, however, took the opportunity and pointed out the lurking dangers of a rapidly nuclearizing Pakistan. The initial bonhomie was, however, over by the time he visited the United States in October 1985, coinciding with the 40th Anniversary of the United Nations, as the American desire of dilution of Indo–Soviet relationship was never materialized. Despite such irritants, Indo–US relationship did not reach a nadir and there was considerable interchange in various fields like political, economic, cultural and social.

Rajiv Gandhi adopted caution while cultivating yet protecting, India's ties with the Soviet Union. This bilateral tie served the interests of both the sides. It not only enabled India to fend off a number of hostile challenges that came from China, Pakistan and from the West in the form of support to Pakistan but also helped Soviet Union to expand its ties with non-aligned countries in the face of continuous attempts of the West to Isolate it form world politics. Rajiv Gandhi went on his first visit to Moscow from 21 to 26 May 1985 which resulted in fruitful interactions in strategic as well as economic fields. The return visit by the Soviet President Mikhail Gorbachev to India in November 1986 was a landmark in India's relation with the Soviet Union. New agreements were signed between India and the Soviet Union in the field of economic and technical cooperation.

Rajiv Gandhi was successful in melting the ice in Indo–China relations. His visit to China in December 1989 was symbolic in the sense that India accepted the Chinese viewpoint of broadening exchange in other areas without making these developments contingent on the resolution of the border issue. A much more relaxed relationship evolved after Rajiv Gandhi's visit to China, which was briefly disturbed due to the Pokhran explosion of May 1998. Nevertheless, after a short interregnum of strained relations between the two, normalcy returned and relations continued on the course set by Rajiv Gandhi.

Rajiv Gandhi tried to mend fences and took several confidence-building measures to boost India's relations with Pakistan. After the death of General Zia-ul-Haq (17 August 1988) in a plane crash, democracy was restored in Pakistan for a very brief period under Benazir Bhutto, which was welcomed by India. Rajiv Gandhi even went to Islamabad to attend the SAARC Summit (1988) and held "constructive and cordial talks" with his Pakistani counterpart. But his hopes were soon belied and he became apprehensive of Pakistan's endeavour to develop its nuclear capacity, particularly Benazir Bhutto's visit to Pyongyang to negotiate a deal for the exchange of missiles and missile technology from North Korea. Thus, Rajiv Gandhi made efforts to secure India's security by advocating nuclear and general disarmament.

The tensions emanating in Sri Lanka due to ethnic conflict also affected India's domestic politics and also her security when a large number of Tamilians fled from Sri Lanka and crossed over to India. This created a serious refugee problem for India. Tensions cropped up between India and Sri Lanka, especially due to air-dropping of supplies for the suffering Tamilians. Improvement of bilateral relationship began with the signing of the accord between Rajiv Gandhi and President Jayewardane on 29 July 1987. The Indian Peacekeeping Force's (IPKF) action thereafter, drew criticisms from different quarters and is seen as India's greatest foreign policy blunder, yet it had helped in restoring peace in Sri Lanka.

Alongside the traditional concerns of Indian Foreign Policy, Rajiv Gandhi realized the changed global economic scenario. Therefore, on the economic front due to the globalization and liberalization spree, Rajiv Gandhi wanted to introduce changes to the old economic conservatism and dogmas. Thus, he introduced newer dimensions to India's development strategy so that India could respond favourably to the global market forces. This was followed by the policy of liberalization, deregulation and privatization, which was furthered by Prime Minister Narasimha Rao with the active effort of the then Finance Minister Dr. Manmohan Singh.

V.P. Singh (December 1989–1990)

When the National Front came to power in 1989 under Prime Minister V.P. Singh, the world scenario was rapidly changing and the Indian foreign policy posture needed to be adjusted accordingly. While Iraq's invasion of Kuwait under Saddam Hussein resulting in the First Gulf War of 1990 marked the beginning of American armed superiority, the break-up of the Soviet Union altered the balance of power in the world. The collapse of the communist regimes in Eastern Europe and the dismemberment of the Soviet Union substantially changed the world order and a new post-Cold War order emerged. India's foreign policy had to be formulated keeping these changes in mind.

Under such circumstances, V.P. Singh made a visit to the Soviet Union in July 1990. During this visit, he and the Russian President Gorbachev reaffirmed the continuation of their traditional ties of friendship and cooperation and also readjusted their economic and trade ties according to the needs of the time. Simultaneously, under him India's relationship with the other superpower, viz. the United States, began to show improvement and financial assistance from world agencies such as the World Bank and the IMF increased. which helped India to tide over the economic crisis caused by the First Gulf War. With China, the National Front Government did not deviate from the course set by Rajiv Gandhi and made efforts to maintain cordial relationship.

V.P. Singh's National Front Government also tried to improve India's relations with her neighbours, especially with Nepal, Sri Lanka and Bangladesh. With Nepal several irritants had developed soon after the expiry of the Trade and Transit Treaty in 1989 including Nepal's attempts for overland import of weapons from China. However, the then Foreign Minister I.K.Gujral's visit to Kathmandu in August 1990 eased the tensions and improved the relation. Regarding the pull out of the IPKF, which had created tensions between Sri Lanka and India, India under V.P. Singh withdrew the forces even before the set deadline of 31 March 1990. Gujral's visit to Bangladesh and talks about river water sharing also turned out to be fruitful.

V.P. Singh held office from 2 December 1989 to 10 November 1990. After the BJP withdrew support to the V.P. Singh government, he resigned after losing the trust vote. Chandra Shekhar broke away from the Janata Dal with 64 MPs and formed the Samajwadi Janata Party. He got outside support from the Congress and became the 11th Prime Minister of India. He finally resigned on 6 March 1991, after the Congress withdrew support from his government. For the brief term when Chandra Shekhar became the Prime Minister, he did not introduce any radical change in the course of Indian foreign policy.

Narasimha Rao (1991–1996): The Phase of Liberalization

The Indian National Congress with a nominal majority came to power with Narasimha Rao as the Prime Minister after the general election of 1991. When Rao assumed office, India faced a crumbling economy with a balance of payment crisis which had left India's foreign exchange reserves for only two weeks. Therefore, Dr. Manmohan Singh, the then Finance Minister began a more substantial economic reform to help the dwindling economy and boost production. Therefore, greater emphasis was placed on economic diplomacy a departure from the traditional foreign policy stance of India.

Now that the Soviet Union or the USSR had disintegrated and a new Commonwealth of Independent States (CIS) comprising Russia, Belarus and Ukraine had emerged, the Rao Government was forced to renegotiate various ties which were in place with the erstwhile Soviet Union. India also slipped from the privileged position, which it used to enjoy under the USSR. To India's greatest dissatisfaction, Russia voted in favour of a Pakistani-sponsored resolution declaring South Asia as a nuclear-free zone. Further, the supply of cryogenic engines by Moscow to aid India's space programme for peaceful explorations was disrupted under immense US pressure which also created apprehensions in Indian minds. However, the initial misunderstandings soon gave way to newer bonds between the two. Relations improved greatly with Russian President Boris Yeltsin's visit to India in January 1993. During this visit not only was the Rupee–Rouble exchange rate was resolved but also the 1971 Indo–Russian Treaty of Peace, Friendship and Cooperation was substituted by a new 14-clause Treaty of Friendship and Cooperation valid for 20 years. This Treaty stipulated that the two countries would refrain from taking any action that might affect the security interests of the other, pledging support to each other's territorial integrity and non-interference in internal affairs.

Alongside, the Rao government began pursuing a policy of improving relation with the United States. There persisted several hiccups in the Indo–US relation centring around Kashmir, India's nuclear and missile programmes, the US tilt towards Pakistan, attempts to modify Pressler amendment and supply of military equipment to Pakistan, differences on Non Proliferation Treaty (NPT), and nuclear free zone in South Asia. Despite such irritants there was a remarkable improvement in the Indo–US relations and the two countries held Joint Naval Exercise in May 1992. In 1995, following the visits by the US Defence and Commerce Secretaries the signing of several agreements took place. Prime Minister Narasimha Rao paid an official week-long visit to the United States in May 1994 which helped to strengthen ties and was followed by signing of several Memorandum of Understandings (MOUs).

India established full diplomatic ties with Israel during this period. India, on 29 January 1992 announced its decision to establish full diplomatic ties with Israel and opening of embassies at Tel Aviv and New Delhi "as soon as it is physically possible". India also supported the US-sponsored resolution, which sought to repudiate the 1975 UN Resolution equating Zionism with racism.

With China, India under Narasimha Rao continued her efforts to nurture good relations. This was followed by several high-level visits from both the countries. The Prime Minister of China visited India from 11 to 16 December 1991. The first Indian President to visit China was President R. Venkataraman. He made a six-day trip to China from 19 to 25 May 1992. Prime Minister Narasimha Rao also visited China in 1993. On all these occasions the border problem was kept aside and negotiations were held in other fields of interests of both the countries.

Rao also tried to improve India's relation, with her neighbours, especially with Nepal, though with Sri Lanka there remained a little irritant over forcing a SAARC Summit in the absence of the Bhutanese King. Indo–Pak relations continued to be strained following the accelerated pace of development of Pak's nuclear capability with assistance from China and North Korea. Further, the demolition of Babri Masjid on 7 December 1992 deteriorated the relation between the two.

I.K. Gujral (1997–1998): The Gujral Doctrine

The 11th Lok Sabha elections resulted in a hung Parliament and two years of political instability during which the country had three Prime Ministers. First A.B.Vajpayee took over as the Prime Minister on May 16 and tried to get support from the regional parties in Parliament. He failed and resigned 13 days later. Then Janata Dal leader Deve Gowda formed a United Front coalition government on 1 June 1996. His government lasted 18 months. I.K. Gujral, who was the Foreign Minister in Gowda's cabinet, took over as the Prime Minister in April 1997 after the Congress agreed to support a new United Front Government from outside. But Gujral was an interim arrangement. The country witnessed another round of elections again in 1998.

· The United Front Government, first under Deve Gowda and then under I.K. Gujral did not introduce any significant change in India's foreign policy posture. Both inherited a stable economy registering a good rate of growth. The foreign exchange position also showed improvement. The most noteworthy contribution was made by Prime Minister I.K. Gujral who gave to the world an innovative doctrine. This came to be identified as the *Gujral Doctrine* and it was chalked with a vision to improve India's relations with her neighbours without expecting reciprocity. India held out unilateral concessions to the neighbouring countries in matters relating to trade and travel without expecting reciprocity. The basis of his thought was that India being the largest country in the region could afford to be more generous while protecting her fundamental interests.

Thus, there was considerable improvement of relations with Bangladesh and the greatest breakthrough came in the form of signing a 30-year Treaty between the then West Bengal Chief Minister, Jyoti Basu and the Bangladesh Foreign Minister, Abdus Samad Azad on the sharing of the Ganga waters. Relations with Sri Lanka also showed a general improvement after the temporary thaw following the assassination of Rajiv Gandhi. The rise of democratic and friendly governments in Nepal, Bangladesh and Sri Lanka in the 1990s helped to instill the spirit of good relations between India and her neighbours. With Pakistan, no significant development was planned out because of its efforts to develop nuclear capability and provide sanctuary to terrorists.

With regard to India's emerging ties with the major global powers such as the United States, Germany, France, United Kingdom, Canada and Japan, the United Front Government continued with the existing policy of mutually beneficial cooperation on issues such as trade, Foreign Direct Investment (FDI) and technical assistance. With Russia, defence ties were strengthened with the signing of a number of agreements. Regarding India's relation with the United States, it also improved significantly despite the differences over the CTBT and India's refusal to sign the Treaty. But there was also a failure to be taken into account during the United Front Government's tenure. There was an all round criticism for India's dismal performance and failure of her diplomacy for which she lost a race with Japan for a non-permanent Asian seat at the UN Security Council.

With China, the United Front Government followed the course chartered by Rajiv Gandhi and made significant developments and a high-level visit was made by the Chinese President and General Secretary of the Communist Party, Jiang Zeminin, in November 1996.

Before the Gujral government could make its impact felt, it fell when the Congress withdrew its support leading to fresh elections, which was again followed by a period of political instability.

A.B. Vajpayee (1998–2004): The Pokhran Explosion

The 12th Lok Sabha was constituted on 10 March 1998, and a coalition led by the Bharatiya Janata Party (BJP) leader Atal Bihari Vajpayee was sworn in nine days later. It had a lifespan of 413 days, the shortest till date. The dissolution came in the absence of a viable alternative after the 13-month-old Bharatiya Janata Party-led government was ousted by one vote on 17 April, 1999. This was the fifth time the Lok Sabha was dissolved before completing its full tenure. On April 26, the then President of India, late K.R. Narayanan, dissolved the Lok Sabha and called for early elections. Vajpayee continued as the caretaker Prime Minister. As General Elections had previously been held in 1996 and 1998, those of 1999 were the third in 40 months. In the election of 1999 the National Democratic Alliance (NDA), a conglomeration of 32 right-wing centrist and regional parties, won majority of seats and A.B.Vajpayee was sworn in as the Prime Minister on 13 October 1999.

The highlight of the Vajpayee government's foreign policy was the Pokhran explosion on 11 May 1998 and the Kargil War. With the nuclear tests of 1998, codenamed *Shakti 1*–V, India proved to the world that she had developed nuclear capability to miniaturize nuclear weapons and mount warheads on Agni and Prithvi missiles. These nuclear explosions, however, earned criticisms from the world community, especially the United States, which imposed sanctions on India. The United States also pressurized the World Bank and the IMF and other international financial institutions to withhold new assistance. The nuclear powers organized themselves into Nuclear Suppliers Group (NSG) that decided how much and to whom nuclear materials, even for peaceful purposes, would be supplied. Hence, the United States denied any such hi-tech and scientific exchanges to India. However, due to increased activities of terrorists in Pakistan, the US stance towards India began to change and President Clinton visited India in March 2000. When President Bush assumed office in 2001, despite several irritants, he did not stop searching for avenues for new relationship with India. However, it was only after 9/11 attacks on the United States and the 13 December attack on the Indian Parliament in 2001 did Indo–US relationship take a new turn as both pledged to fight against international terrorism.

India's relation with Russia also improved and was followed by continuation of their defence ties. A ten-year defence cooperation programme was finalized in 1998 between India and Russia. India and Russia also signed a $2.5 billion deal to set up a nuclear power station in Koodankulam in Tamil Nadu. Further, Indo–Russian ties were strengthened by Putin's visit to India in October 2000. India and Russia also signed the technology transfer deal for production of 150 Sukhoi Su–30 MKI multirole jets in India under Russian licence in December 2000.

China sent a high-powered delegation, led by her Chief of General Staff of the People's Liberation Army (PLA), General Fu Quanyou to India in April 1998 to discuss several bilateral issues. But the Indo–China relations got a jolt due to the Pokhran explosion and also because of identifying China as a potential threat to India's security. This earned the Chinese wrath and the Chinese condemnation of the nuclear tests along with the other major powers. However, gradually, Indo–China relationship began to get normalized following visits by the then External Affairs Minister, Jaswant Singh in 1999 and President K.R. Narayanan in 2000 to China.

India in her bid to normalize relationship sent feelers to Pakistan too. Vajpayee as a part of confidence-building measure with Pakistan inaugurated a bus service from Lahore–Amritsar in February 1999 and he himself took the inaugural bus service to visit the then Prime Minister of Pakistan, Nawaz Sharif in February at Lahore. This was followed by signing of the Memorandum of Understanding (MOU) reaffirming their unilateral moratorium on further nuclear testing and spelling out their confidence-building measures. But the Kargil adventurism of Pakistan during May–June 1999 under General Pervez Musharraf disrupted the peace process. Gradually, relations showed improvement and this was followed by General Musharraf's visit to India for talks held in Agra in July 2001. But the talks failed to make any notable breakthrough and even later the strain in Indo–Pak relation continued because of Pakistan's insistence of linking *Kashmir* as the core issue which has always been rejected by India, and India's stand on cross-border terrorism which Pakistan always rejects out of hand. The Kandahar episode revealed the Pakistani connection with the militants, either helped or given shelter by Pakistan. Therefore, like the efforts of the previous governments, the Vajpayee government failed to melt the ice in the Indo–Pak relations.

The Vajpayee government also sought to improve relations with India's neighbours Nepal, Bangladesh and Sri Lanka. With Nepal, India signed a new Transit Treaty in January 1999 and worked out matters relating to hydro-power, flood control, terrorism and extradition. Bangladesh and India expressed their commitments to further bilateral relations and a bus service was started between Dhaka and Kolkata in June 1999. With Sri Lanka, India signed a Free Trade Agreement in 1998.

Dr. Manmohan Singh (2004–2009) and (2009–2014): The Nuclear Deal

The BJP-led NDA government, headed by Prime Minister Atal Bihari Vajpayee completed five years of its rule in 2004 and elections to the 14th Lok Sabha was held in 2004. Congress was able to manage a majority of more than 335 members out of 543 (including external support from parties like the BSP, SP, MDMK, and the Left front) with the help of its allies and formed the post-poll alliance, which came to be known as the **United Progressive Alliance (UPA).** Dr. Manmohan Singh, who had previously served as the Finance Minister in the Narasimha Rao Cabinet in the early 1990s, became the Prime Minister.

Manmohan Singh's foreign policy posture marked a continuity rather than a change, except that he sped up the process of improving relations with the United States, China and Pakistan and India's neighbours. In case of Nepal there were a few problems because Nepal was suffering from Maoist insurgency and political instability.

The most remarkable breakthrough that Manmohan Singh's Government was able to make was the Nuclear Deal with the United States. The process started with Dr. Singh's assumption of office and met its culmination in October 2008 when the final nuclear deal was signed between the two countries. Earlier on 18 July 2005, India and the United States signed the landmark Civilian Nuclear Agreement in Washington DC. Next on 2 March 2006, a Separation Plan was initiated by India and the United States which listed out which reactors would New Delhi put under safeguards. On 18 December 2006, the Hyde Act was passed by the US Congress which led to the amendment of the US Atomic Energy Act. The next breakthrough came in 27 July 2007 when the 123 Agreement was signed by India and the United States outlining the terms of nuclear trade between the two countries. On 1 August 2008, International Atomic Energy Agency (IAEA) cleared India-specific Safeguards Agreement that defined the level of supervision of civilian plants. The Nuclear Suppliers Group (NSG) waiver came ultimately after intense negotiation among its 45 members to allow nuclear trade with India on 6 September 2008. Ultimately, India and the United States struck the Nuclear Deal on 8 October 2008. As the nuke deal is in place now, India can formally begin trade in civilian nuclear technology while continuing its nuclear weapons programme but expecting severe consequences if it conducts a test in future.[8] The real factor behind the US decision to sign the Nuclear Deal was to balance off China in Asia that would help to maintain its primacy in the region without isolating China. India, therefore, was key to the US game plan. Besides the strategic factor, Washington's decision to upgrade its relation with India was also a result of the growing worldwide acknowledgement of the image of India as a rising power, particularly in economic terms.

With Russia also Dr. Singh's Government tried to work out the glitches involved in the relationship. Some of the irritants in the relationship between Russia and India were related to the pricing and supply of the spare parts and the

Intellectual Property Rights (IPRs) issue over the supply of latest armaments by Russia to India. These became the subject matter of a marathon Summit between Russian President Putin and Dr.Singh in New Delhi on 3 December 2004. No positive outcome was visible then until the Putin–Manmohan Singh Summit in December 2005, where some of the glitches were sorted out.

Regarding India's relation with China, she was making a laudable progress and the highlight of the relationship during this period was the Chinese Prime Minister Wen Jiabao's visit in April 2005 and President Hu Jintao's visit in November 2006. Yet irritants still remained centring around issues of unresolved border problems and Chinese policies towards Pakistan.

In respect of relations with Pakistan, despite several confidence-building measures, bus diplomacy and summit meetings; no improvement was noticed and stalemate continued. President Musharraf, during his second visit to New Delhi on 17 April 2005, declared that the peace process had become irreversible and, despite fresh confidence-building measures, such as pledge to solve the Kashmir issue, the possible resumption of Lahore–Amritsar bus service and reestablishment of consulates at Karachi and Mumbai, nothing concrete was actualized in reality. Efforts of peace dialogue made, thereafter, were severely paralyzed due to the increasing number of terrorist acts in India and alleged involvement of Pakistan or of terrorists based in Pakistan. India under Dr. Singh expressed a grave concern over the safety of Pakistan's nuclear arsenal, as there always looms a possibility of the nuclear arsenals falling into the hands of the terrorists, especially the Taliban and the Al-Qaeda. Therefore, stalemate continued as far as the Indo–Pak relation is concerned.

India's vote against Iran in International Atomic Energy Agency (IAEA) general body was in favour of a resolution warning Iran that its case could be referred to the UN Security Council for possible sanctions if it did not fully cooperate with the IAEA on its investigation about any secret efforts at enrichment of uranium to a degree that would make it possible for Iran to develop an atomic device. This had opened floodgates of criticisms against the Manmohan Government as India had to pursue the Oil Pipeline Programme from Iran through Afghanistan and Pakistan. India under Dr. Singh also strove to improve ties with the Association of South East Asian Nations (ASEAN) and the European Union (EU).

The second term of Dr. Manmohan Singh began with the victory of the Congress and its allies in the 15th Lok Sabha election. The highlights till now have been the Indo–Pak relations, Indo–US Nuclear deal and climate-change related emission issue.

On the sidelines of the 15th NAM Summit (Sharm el-Sheikh, 2009) Dr. Manmohan Singh met the Pakistani PM Yousuf Raza Gilani and both strove to make serious efforts towards positive improvement in Indo–Pak relations despite several glitches. India dropped her insistence of holding talks with Pakistan only after those involved in Mumbai terror attacks have been punished.

India delinked 'composite dialogue' from terrorism. The joint statement issued after the second top level meeting since the 26/11 Mumbai terror attacks declared "Both the Prime Ministers recognized that dialogue is the only way forward. Action on terrorism should not be linked to the composite dialogue process and these should not be bracketed."[8] Kashmir did not figure in the joint statement which is always under the composite dialogue process. Prime Minister Manmohan Singh expressed India's readiness to "discuss all issues with Pakistan including all outstanding issues". Responding to Dr. Singh's statement in the Lok Sabha on the India–Pakistan joint statement in Egypt, Pakistani PM Gilani reciprocated the 'sentiments of peace' and expressed the meeting as one where both leaders had agreed that terrorism was a common threat and dialogue is the only way to take relations in a positive direction. But the opposition slammed New Delhi's stance for delinking of the "composite dialogue"[9] with Pakistan. Dr. Singh, however, reaffirmed that delinking of dialogue process with Pakistan from its action against terrorism was not a dilution of India's stand but strengthening of it.

As far as the Indo–US relation is concerned, there are serious apprehensions among the oppositions following the visit of the US Secretary of State, Mrs. Hillary R. Clinton in July 2009. The message of the Obama administration is to link the implementation of the nuclear deal to an end-use monitoring agreement for military supplies from America which would result in the signing of a defence pact with the US. India's stand on entering into an understanding on End-Use-Monitoring Agreement (EUMA) has raised severe criticisms from the opposition. PM Dr. Singh has tried to defend his government's posture on the face of allegations about dilution of India's stand on the EUMA. He said that the text of EUMA contains no provisions that compromises India's sovereignty and calls for unilateral verification by the USA on imported defence equipment.

A recent development of Dr. Singh's government has been the signing of a partial free-trade agreement with ASEAN on 13 August, 2009 at the beginning of the 41st ASEAN Economic Ministers meeting in Thailand. With this agreement in place the annual bilateral trade would get a boost.

The year 2010 began with several developments in Indo-Pak relations, though not very fruitful in every respect. Despite Pakistan's accusation that India has broken off the Composite dialogue process and tried to isolate it diplomatically, the major events have been – (i) Foreign Secretary Level Talk (FSLT)—February 25, 2010; (ii) Sidelines Meeting at the 16th SAARC Summit, Thimpu, April 2010; (iii) Foreign Secretary Level Talk, June 24, 2010; and (iv) SAARC Home Ministers Meeting, Islamabad, June 25, 2010.

The February FSLT between Indian Foreign Secretary Nirupama Rao and Pakistani Foreign Secretary Salman Bashir took place in the backdrop of a bomb blast in a popular Café in Pune, after a 14 month lull that followed 26/11, which was seen as an attempt to derail the dialogue process. Still, the talks took place and can be regarded as the first official dialogue and an ice-breaker since the 2008 Mumbai terror attack as India insisted that there would be no resumption of dialogue with Pakistan until it took action against the perpetrators of 26/11 terror attacks. The issues included terrorism, Kashmir, Afghanistan and water sharing. Although both the sides claimed the talks to be encouraging, Pakistan reiterated the resumption of composite dialogue while India insisted that it has to wait till greater trust and confidence is built.

On the sidelines of the 16th SAARC Summit at Thimpu on April 29, 2010, Prime Minister Manmohan Singh and Pakistan's Prime Minister Yousuf Raza Gilani met and agreed that foreign secretaries of both countries should meet again and Indo-Pak dialogue should resume as without dialogue there was no other means of addressing the bilateral issues. On the sidelines of Nuclear Security meeting in April 2010, there were no meetings between the two countries, but India made it clear that it will only resume talks if Pakistan takes action against Lashkar-e-Taiba (LeT) and perpetrators of 26/11 terror attacks.

On the completion of one year of the second term of the UPA government on May 25, 2010, while producing the 'report card' of the government's performance in a press meet, Manmohan Singh stated that Indo-Pak relation was suffering from 'trust deficit' and reducing this 'trust deficit' was essential to improve their relations.

Another FSLT was planned on 24th June, 2010 which was thought to be aiming at reducing this 'trust deficit' and, as advocated by India, to find "creative solutions" on Jammu and Kashmir and other issues to build on the progress made earlier through the Composite Dialogue and back channel diplomacy.

But before the June 2010 Indo-Pak talks, both countries got engaged in another major dispute. Both got set to fight a legal battle over Kishenganga power project under construction in J&K in an international court of arbitration. Pakistan is objecting to construction of 330 MW hydropower plant on Kishenganga, a tributary of the Jhelum under the 1960 Indus Water Treaty.

Uneasiness arose just before June 24, 2010 when Pakistani troops fired on Indian positions on the Line of Control in J&K, killing 2 civilians and injuring 2 jawans. However, India made it clear that it will focus on cross-border terrorism and would adopt "an exploratory approach" to work out steps to reduce post-Mumbai attack trust deficit between the two countries.

June 24, 2010 FSLT took place in Islamabad. Though there was no breakthrough, a positive step towards bridging the trust deficit between the two countries was made. During the talks, India raised the "core concern of terrorism" including the activities of the Laskar-e-Taiyyaba (LeT) and Jamaat-ud-Dawah (JuD) and Hafiz Muhammad Saeed. The other issue discussed was Pak's concern about Indian presence in Afghanistan, and the Indian stand was clarified by making it related to the developmental works in Afghanistan. India, however, made it clear that attacks on Indian assets could not be allowed to continue as it affected relations between New Delhi and Islamabad. The FSLT, though not very substantial consequencewise, was not merely "exploratory" as both sides tried to "understand each others' position".

SAARC Home Ministers' Meet, Islamabad, June 25, 2010 witnessed a meeting between Indian Home Minister Mr. P. Chidambaram and his Pakistani counterpart Mr. Rahman Malik during the conference. He was the first Indian Minister to visit Pakistan in three decades where he was accorded a red carpet welcome and a ceremonial Guard of Honour. He pressed for action against JuD Chief Hafiz Saeed and the handlers of the 26/11 terrorists including those who are believed to be in the Pak army. Chidambaram is believed to have sought voice samples of the Pak handlers and raised issues such as infiltration in J&K also.

However, the mood that was set by these two meetings was suddenly dampened by a diplomatic show down during the Foreign Ministers' Meet in Islamabad on 16 July, 2010. Indian Foreign Minister S.M. Krishna and his Pak counterpart Shah Mahmood Qureshi soon got caught in a diplomatic imbroglio when Pak refused to engage in any substantial manner with the critical areas of 26/11, cross-border terrorism and infiltration by arguing that it could not speed up the judicial process. Further, a diplomatic spat broke off during the joint press conference on Balochistan and infiltration in J&K. Another undiplomatic posture adopted by Pak Foreign Minister Qureshi spoiled the whole atmosphere when he spoke to the Pak journalists while Mr. Krishna was still in Islamabad that Indian delegation was not "fully prepared" for the talks and that his counterpart had repeatedly sought directions from Delhi when the deliberations were on. Thus, the diplomatic parleys ended amidst sharp differences and undiplomatic gestures ruining the spirit of bilateral negotiations. Further, the Wagah land export deal between Pakistan and Afghanistan shuts out India completely, where no Indian export to Afghanistan would be allowed through Wagah, but Afghanistan would have the opportunity to export to India. This was signed in the presence of the US Secretary of States, Hillary Clinton. India, faced with a dilemma, cannot obstruct the entry of Afghan goods because that will antagonize Kabul and add to its ever-increasing poverty. But this treaty can give strategic one-upmanship to Pakistan. US, however, wanted continuation of Indo-Pak talks. Soon after the diplomatic showdown between India and Pakistan, the US Secretary of States, Hillary Clinton, during her visit to Islamabad for the US-Pakistan strategic Dialogue in 19 July 2010, made it clear that USA is interested that the process between Pakistan and India is sustained and both amicably resolve their outstanding issues.

Indo-US relations saw new developments with Manmohan Singh's four-day visit to the US in November 2009. The visit was followed by high level talks on strengthening cooperation in counter-terrorism, counter-intelligence to prevent Mumbai-type attacks, implementation of the Indo-US civil nuclear deal, US-India financial and economic partnerships and strengthening and reforming global economic and financial architecture in the G-20 and the World Bank. India and the US also agreed to expand trade and investment in sectors such as infrastructure, informatics and communication technologies. Manmohan Singh expressed India's willingness for a strong and sustained engagement between India and the US. US President Barack Obama acclaimed India as an "indispensable partner" as both nations, the two global leaders, would strive to build a future of security and prosperity for all nations. Further, he assured India that the US-China Joint Statement on the Indo-Pak dialogue does not mean involvement of a 'third power' in the bilateral engagement.

During the Nuclear Security Summit in Washington on April 11, 2010, Manmohan Singh met President Obama once again and discussed the key concerns of both the countries, including US policies towards Pakistan and Afghanistan' as well as other bilateral matters. Singh conveyed India's concern about the enduse of military aid given to Pakistan by America and expressed apprehensions of their usage against India's national interest. Among other issues discussed were Afghanistan, Civil Nuclear Liability Bill (then caught in a political battle between the government and the opposition), and David Coleman Headley, the chief plotter of Mumbai terror attack and activities of LeT.

The Indo-US Strategic Dialogue took place on June 3, 2010 when Foreign Minister S.M. Krishna visited the United States. The issues discussed included the situation in Afghanistan-Pak region and expansion of cooperation in a wide range of areas such as defence, security, nuclear energy, climate change, education and agriculture. The two sides exchanged views regarding necessary reforms of the international economic and security architecture including the UNSC. Recognizing India as a "rising global power", the US Secretary of State, Hillary Clinton declared that the USA today was definitely committed "to consider India's bid for a permanent seat in the UNSC." The two countries also pledged to deepen people-to-people contact, business-to-business and government-to-government linkages for the mutual benefit of both the countries and also for the promotion of global peace and stability, economic growth and prosperity. President Obama also expressed his intention to visit India in November as he considered India to be a rising and responsible global power "indispensable" to a future American strategy.

The US President Obama's visit to India from 6–9 November, 2010 has been a visit of a President who has just lost ground in the elections to the Senate and the House of Representatives and who wanted to show that his four-nation visit to India, Indonesia, South Korea and Japan were aimed at opening up new markets for US companies and create jobs at home. His visit ultimately proved to be full of promises of US supporting India's membership to multilateral export control regimes like NSG, MTCR, the Australian Group (AG) and the Wassenaar Arrangement (WA) in a phased manner and removal of India's defence and space related entities from the US 'Entity List'. But the former cannot be done soon, for the membership criteria for these have to be amended to make India eligible and the latter, as US Fact Sheet reveals that such changes have been initiated by Obama administration from 2009 and will bring about fundamental changes in the export relationship with India. This is yet to be seen how it influences Indo-US export relationship. Another promise made by

President Obama is the US support for India's bid for a permanent seat in the UN Security Council. In his address to the Indian Parliament, Obama, however, clearly said that to earn this seat, India has to follow Washington's line on key global issues like Iran and Myanmar with whom India has good relations. Regarding terrorism and Pakistani safe havens for terrorists, India was upset because in October 2010 the US announced $2-billion annual defence aid package to Pakistan. Again, Obama in his address stated that India and the US both have an interest in an Afghanistan and a Pakistan that is stable, prosperous and democratic. In other words, he tried to justify the aid that had been given to Pakistan just before his arrival in India. On the Kashmir issue, he said that the US was not in favour of imposing any solution but can always lend a helping hand if needed. Behind the scene, of course, another motive of trying to win over India comes from the US compulsion to have India as a strategic ally, which would help to contain a rising China.

The US President, as discussed earlier, came with lots of promises in order to secure financial benefits, which would help in recovering the dwindling American economy. India hosted a US business delegation of 200 CEOs of US Corporations and the deals struck are expected to bring benefit export wise and jobwise to the US. Twenty deals were struck which were worth $10 billion and can create 53,000 jobs in America. Therefore, Obama has tried to push American strategic and business interests during his visit, with holding out promises for lots of things for India. Time can only say that whether Obama's visit has been gain for India or the US. Obama was also silent about the corporate accountability in the 1984 Bhopal Gas Disaster while he has insisted on corporate accountability in the Gulf of Mexico oil spill.

Indo-Russian relations saw an upsurge with several pacts signed between both the countries in the course of the visits by Russian Prime Minister Vladimir Putin to New Delhi and Indian Prime Minister Manmohan Singh to Moscow.

India and Russia reinforced their ties with an expanded civil nuclear deal and three military pacts. They also raised voices of concern over growing menace of terrorism. This was done in the course of a three-day visit to Moscow by Indian Prime Minister Manmohan Singh during December 2009. Dr. Singh also upheld that India's relations with third countries will never be at the cost of "time-tested ties" with Russia.

Again, during Russian Prime Minister Putin's visit to New Delhi during March 2010, 19 pacts were signed. Some prominent among them are Agreement on Cooperation in the use of Atomic Energy for Peaceful Purposes, Agreement on Road Map for the Serial Construction of Russian Designed Nuclear Power Plants (Russia to build 6 atomic plants in Kudankulan and 6 in Haripur, West Bengal), Agreement on Protocol of Cooperation signed between ONGC and Russia's Gazprom, revised agreement on Gorshkov aircraft carrier deal, agreement for sale of MiG-29K aircraft carrier-based fighters by Russia to India under a USD 15 billion contract, two pacts in the field of fertilizers and five pacts in the diamond sector.

Besides, on bilateral issues, both the Prime Ministers had comprehensive talks regarding regional situation as in Afghanistan and some Central Asian Republics. On the whole, both sides expressed their desire to deepen their relationship.

In December 2010, Russian President Dmitry Medvedev visited India. The outcome of the visit was reflected in the signing of 30 agreements during his visit on 21–22 December 2010. The agreements were signed in key areas like defence, energy, nuclear, space, science & technology, pharma, IT, bio-technology etc. Russian President also showed strong and unambiguous support to India's bid for the UNSC permanent membership. He also expressed a strong desire to stabilize the situation in Afghanistan through joint efforts. Therefore, Indo-Russian relationship received another boost with Medvedev's visit to India.

India and Britain also looked afresh at their relations with the new leadership in Britain under the youngest Prime Minister of Britain, David Cameron. Cameron came on a two-day visit to India at the end of July 2010. There was delegation level talk between the two Prime Ministers and both addressed a joint press conference. Terror was seen as a biggest threat and Cameron emphasized that existence of terror groups like Laskar-e-Taiyyaba (LeT) on Pakistani soil was unacceptable and must be eliminated. MoUs were signed for cooperation in the areas of culture. Both sides agreed to establish a new India-UK CEOs Forum to help boost bilateral trade and India-UK Infrastructure Group to identify barriers to investment and potential solutions. There was also talks regarding cooperation in the education sectors and British Minister for State for universities David Willets evinced interest in the proposed Innovation Universities during meeting with Indian HRD Minister Kapil Sibal. The British Prime Minister also met the Indian President Pratibha Devisingh Patil and discussed a number of bilateral issues, including trade, counter-terrorism and cultural ties, but ruled out the return of Kohinoor diamond to India.

Indo-French relations also took a new turn with President Nicolas Sarkozy visiting the country in December 2010. In a joint press conference with Prime Minister Manmohan Singh, Sarkozy backed India in its efforts to tackle terror and offered unlimited French cooperation on counter-terrorism. India and France also signed five atomic pacts for building two 1,650 MW nuclear reactors at Jaitapur in Maharashtra including an early works agreement and a general framework agreement between French nuclear giant Areva and the Nuclear Power Corporation of India Limited (NPCIL) for implementation of two European Pressurized Reactors (EPRs) at Jaitapur.

With Germany, India for the first time discussed the possibilities of entering into a bilateral cooperation in civil nuclear energy. This has given a boost to India-Germany partnership. Germany also expressed its willingness to back India's bid to secure membership of the NSG. There were also discussions about relaxation of German export control laws which was thought to increase the volume of bilateral trade.

On the regional front, India also tried to improve her relations with neighbours like Sri Lanka, Bangladesh and Bhutan.

As far as Indo-Sri Lankan relation is concerned, there have also been significant developments. After the 26th January, 2010 Presidential elections in Sri Lanka, the newly elected President Mahindra Rajapakse met the Indian Foreign Secretary Nirupama Rao in Colombo on March 7, 2010. An official statement released from the Presidential Secretariat upheld India's willingness to assist Sri Lanka in the resettlement of the Tamil IDPs (Internally Displaced Persons) from the war-ravaged areas in North Sri Lanka. India also expressed her intention to assist Sri Lanka in the restoration of the railway line in the North. Other issues discussed were problems being faced by fishermen of both countries, proposed coal power powered project in Trincomalee, environment related issues and other issues of mutual concern.

The Sri Lankan President Rajapakse visited India on June 9, 2010 and there was a wide-ranging delegation level talk between the President and Indian Prime Minister Manmohan Singh. The main focus was the settlement of the longstanding Tamil issue. Other matters included bilateral and global issues, economic ties, energy security and increased cooperation in the areas of development and counter terrorism. An MoU on interconnecting electricity grids of the two countries, two MoUs on the transfer of sentenced persons and mutual legal assistance in criminal matters that aim at enhancing counter-terror cooperation, a pact on laying Talaimannar-Madhu rail link, and an MoU on special projects and community learning centre by SEWA were signed.

With Bangladesh, India maintained cordial relations. Bangladesh Prime Minister Sheikh Hasina visited India in early January 2010. India extended a line of credit worth one billion dollars on the terms of Asian Development Bank for infrastructural upgradation of Bangladesh. India also agreed to construct the Akhaura-Agartala rail link, provide 250 megawatts per day from the Indian power grid and deferred plans to construct the 1500 MW Tipaimukh hydroelectric dam on the Barak in Manipur to which Bangladesh has reservations. It was also agreed that border markets would be set up along the Bangladesh-Meghalaya border and land customs posts on the Mizoram border. Forty-seven commodities were removed from the negative list, despite serious concern about the fallout. Bangladesh promised India access to the Ashuganj inland port and India, Nepal and Bhutan access to deep-water ports at Mongla and Chittagong. Bangladesh also expressed willingness to revive old land-border rail transit points and also prevent its soil from being used against India. Bangladesh also agreed to negotiate an extradition treaty, formation of a joint boundary group to address the land border and a team from Bangladesh to discuss maritime boundary. Sheikh Hasina expressed her satisfaction over the visit.

With Bhutan, India continues to nurture the good relation it had maintained for years. Earlier, in December 2009, the Bhutanese King Jigme Khesar Namgyel Wangchuck visited India and held wide-ranging talks with the Indian Prime Minister Manmohan Singh and both sides signed several pacts in different sectors. Again in 2010, the Indian Prime Minister Manmohan Singh held a bilateral meeting with Bhutanese King on the sidelines of 16th SAARC Summit in Kathmandu in April. Dr. Singh also laid the foundation stones of the India-funded state-of-the-art medical institute, two hydroelectricity plants and an IT project before returning to India after the three-day trip to the Himalayan kingdom to attend the SAARC summit. The Bhutanese King again graced the 2010 Convocation ceremony of the Calcutta University and delivered the Convocation address on 5 October, 2010.

Indo-China relations also witnessed certain ups and downs. The Indian President Pratibha Devisingh Patil arrived in Beijing on 27 May 2010 for a six-day visit to China and was welcomed by Chinese Premier Wen Jiabao at the Purple Light Pavilion. She received red carpet welcome as the first Indian Head of the State to visit China in a decade. Both sides discussed bilateral issues pertaining to trade and commerce. Particularly, sources said that Mrs Patil sought China's support for India's bid for the permanent seat in the UNSC. Further, an agreement streamlining the visa formalities of airline staff of two countries by Indian Foreign Secretary Nirupama Rao and Chinese Assistant Foreign Minister Hu Zhengyue during Mrs. Patils's visit to China was signed. A MoU for cooperation in the field of civil services and public administration was also signed between the two.

Prime Minister Manmohan Singh met his Chinese counterpart Wen Jiabao at Hanoi on the sidelines of ASEAN Summit. The controversial issue of stapled Chinese visa to Kashmiris and Sino-India economic ties were the core issues of the talks. This was the first top-level contact since the Sino-India defence exchanges were suspended in July 2010 following Beijing's decision to issue such stapled visa to India's Northern Area Commander Lt-Gen B.S. Jaiswal. The two sides agreed to work out solutions to the "difficult" problems, and Wen Jiabao's visit to India in December 2010 would be an effort to find ways to cooperate and collaborate, as there was enough space in the world for both the countries.

Premier Wen Jiabao's arrived in India on a three-day visit on 15 December, 2010. Before his arrival, the Chinese envoy to India stated that relations between the two countries are "fragile and can be damaged easily." Thus, Wen's visit can be seen as an effort to shore up "fragile" Indo-China relations. But the focus of the Chinese delegation was more on economic issues of trade and commerce rather that China's support for India's candidature for the permanent seat in the UN Security Council or Pakistani support of terrorists. The issue of stapled visa was, however, brought up by Wen and it was agreed that Indian and Chinese officials should meet and resolve the issue. The positive thing that happened was launching of a hotline between the two Prime

Ministers of China and India as a step towards building up trust. India and China signed six agreements in areas like media and cultural exchanges, green technologies, sharing of hydrological data on the Sutlej river and collaboration between their banks.

With several other countries, in the year 2010, India tried to draw new roadmaps for strategic partnerships. The External Affairs, Minister S.M. Krishna, went on a three-day official visit, to Republic of Korea (RoK) in June 2010 and he co-chaired the 6th meeting of India-Republic of Korea (RoK) Joint Commission along with his Korean counterpart Yu Myung- Hwan. During this visit India and Korea inked 3 accords to enhance economic and cultural ties in Seoul and also agreed to launch negotiations for the conclusion of an Inter-Governmental Agreement on Peaceful Uses of Nuclear Energy nuke energy pact. The two countries also signed three MoUs, including one on Cooperation in the field of Small and Medium Enterprises, Cooperation between ICCR and Korea Foundation and Cooperation between Indian Council for World Affairs (ICWA) and the Institute for Foreign Affairs and National Security (IFANS) of the RoK.

With South Korea, India reached an agreement on civil nuclear operation, making it the ninth country with which India signed nuclear agreement after it got the NSG waiver in 2008. This announcement was made after Prime Minister Manmohan Singh met South Korean President Lee Myungbak at Hanoi on the sidelines of the ASEAN Summit. The $12 billion dollar Posco project of South Korea, the largest foreign investment project in India, has got delayed because of clearances. Korea has been concerned about the delay. Thus, on the eve of the meeting Indian Commerce Minister promised to address the issue of clearance in a "very constructive manner."

With Saudi Arabia, Indian Prime Minister Manmohan Singh was able to forge a major advance in the two countries' bilateral relation. Dr. Singh had the opportunity to address the Shura Council and was conferred an honorary degree. The two countries agreed the India-Saudi ties to a strategic relationship. The Riyadh Declaration underpins the partnership to which the two countries aspire.

India, in its spree to develop her look-east policy, has also nurtured the existing relations with her eastern neighbours. As far as Indo-Myanmar relation is concerned, it received a boost when Myanmar's Military ruler General Than Shwe visited India in July 2010. The Indian Prime Minister Manmohan Singh and General Than Shwe signed five agreements to increase cooperation in counter-terror activities, legal assistance in criminal matters and others. Talks were also held on a wide range of issues including counter-terrorism, enhanced energy ties, collaboration in several developmental projects.

India also set a positive tone in her relation with Malaysia. Indian Prime Minister Manmohan Singh visited Malaysia on 27 October 2010 ahead of his ASEAN-India and East Asia Summits at Hanoi. Both countries formally announced boosting up of Comprehensive Economic Cooperation Agreement

(CECA) for improving trade relations and cooperation in various sectors including freer movement of goods, services and investments which would come into effect from 1 July, 2011. Five other pacts were signed after wide-ranging talks between Indian Prime Minister Manmohan Singh and his Malaysian counterpart Mohd Najib Tun Abdul Razak.

India's relation with Japan also saw improvement. Prime Minister Manmohan Singh went for a two-day visit to Japan in October 2010. He met his Japanese counterpart Mr. Naoto Kan and held discussions on several issues including civil nuclear energy cooperation, free trade agreement, situation in Afghanistan, ways to combat climate change and reform of UN. After the extended delegation level talks, the two leaders officially endorsed the Comprehensive Economic Partnership Agreement (CEPA). This was seen as a historic achievement, which would hopefully open up new economic opportunities.

In the international sphere, India too had quite a number of progresses made. In the Nuclear Security Summit held in Washington on 11 April, 2010, India had raised the twin dangers of clandestine nuclear proliferation and international terrorism and the resonance of the same could be found from the views expressed by the 47 nations gathering of heads of states and governments.

After attending the N-Security Summit, Dr. Singh left for Brazil to participate in the IV BRIC (Brazil-Russia-India-China) Summit. On the sidelines, Dr. Singh held talks with Chinese President Hu Jintao on several bilateral issues, particularly trade and investment. The Chinese President looked forward to Indian President Pratibha Patil's visit to China. The Indian President Pratibha Devisingh Patil visited China in May 2010.

Following his BRIC Summit, Dr. Singh also went to attend the IBSA (India-Brazil-South Africa) Summit where Iran's controversial nuclear programme and the impending UN sanctions were the 'focused agenda'.

On Prime Minister Manmohan Singh's visit to Hanoi during the ASEAN Summit, he expressed high hopes regarding the completion of all formalities of India-ASEAN Trade in Goods Agreement signed in Bangkok in August 2009 after six years of negotiations and coming into force from 1 January 2010. He also announced extension of visa-on-arrival facility to travellers from Cambodia, Vietnam and Philippines as part of the overall package for the initiative for ASEAN integration. He pushed for ASEAN unity and emphasized that the ASEAN is the "core around which the process of economic integration of the Asia-Pacific region should be built."

On the whole, the year 2010 has been quite an eventful year for India, with a number of visits by important dignitaries from important countries and consequential diplomatic parleys. What is most remarkable is that in one year there were visits from P-5 members countries in 2010. India has also been elected as a non-permanent member of the United Nations Security Council with an overwhelming number of countries endorsing its sole candidature from the Asian group. In polling for 10 seats that took place at the UN headquarters in New York on 10 October, 2010, India received the highest number of votes—187 out of 192—among all countries in the fray. However, given the background of power equations, one cannot be jubilant over the Security Council membership until and unless a permanent seat is not secured by India.

There has been certain setbacks in Indo-Pakistan relations, but attempts have already been made by India to decrease the trust deficit. Indo-US relations also saw improvements.

2011 was also an eventful year as far as Indian foreign policy is concerned. The year began with the visit of the President of Indonesia, Susilo Bambang Yudhoyono, who was the Chief Guest at the Republic Day celebrations on 26 January 2011. This can be seen as a further boost to India's Look-East Policy. This visit was followed by signing of a number of Memoranda of Understanding (MoU) and agreements for cooperation in combating terror, extradition, curbing money laundering and others.

India's Minister of External Affairs, S.M. Krishna, and the US Secretary of State, Hillary Rodham Clinton, met in New Delhi on 19 July 2011, for the second Annual Meeting of the India-US Strategic Dialogue. The leaders recognized the achievements made since the inaugural Strategic Dialogue in June 2010, and President Obama's visit to India in November 2010 in advancing two countries' shared interests—pluralism, tolerance, openness, and respect for fundamental freedoms and human rights. They committed to continue to broaden and deepen the India-US global strategic partnership for the benefit of their countries; and for peace, stability, and prosperity in Asia and the world.

Three focal areas of interaction were highlighted by Ms. Clinton. They are like lower tariff barriers along with further opening of markets, involving India in maritime security and selling equipment especially to the Navy and civil nuclear cooperation. India-US Strategic Dialogue Joint Statement issued on 19 July 2011 also made reference to a number of other issues like the UN and peacekeeping operations, bilateral defence cooperation in maritime security and strengthening further defence cooperation through technology transfer, joint research, development and production of defence items. Ms. Clinton also visited Tamil Nadu, and shared her concern over Sri Lankan Tamils living in camps, with Chief Minister Jayalalithaa. Chief Minister Jayalalithaa also requested Ms. Clinton to restore the quota of HIB visas to original level of 1,95,000.

Dr. Manmohan Singh paid a five-day visit to China and Kazakhstan from 12–16 April 2011. He visited China to attend the BRICS Summit. Thereafter, he arrived at Astana in Kazakhstan to finalize the long-pending oil exploration contract which will give India an opportunity to get access to the Caspian oil.

In the sidelines of the BRICS Summit, Dr. Singh met Chinese President Hu Jintao. Both sides agreed to work towards removing the major irritants in the Sino-Indian relation and initiate coordination and consultation on border related matters, along with resumption of senior-level defence exchange, initiation of economic dialogue for redressal of investment and market-related grievances.

In April 2011, Dr. Manmohan Singh visited Asatana, Kazakhstan, to consolidate strategic partnership with Kazakhstan. Both sides signed seven pacts, including a framework agreement in civil nuclear field and a stake-sharing accord in oil sector. The Kazakh President also announced that Kazakhstan would supply India with 2,100 tons of uranium. A great breakthrough was a package of three agreements signed by India and Kazakhstan in the hydrocarbon sector. Under these, ONGC Videsh Limited would acquire 25 per cent stake in Satpayev oil block in Caspian Sea. The two sides also signed a mutual legal assistance treaty and agreed to intensify dialogue in counter-terrorism and drug trafficking. This can be seen as a major boost to India's Central Asian policy and her quest for an alternative source of oil and natural gas supply besides West Asia and the Gulf countries.

As far as Indo-Sri Lankan relations is concerned there was a visit by the Foreign Minister of Sri Lanka in May 2011. Delegation-level talks, between the two External Affairs Ministers, were held on 16 May 2011. Issues relating to regional and international issues of common concern were mainly focussed. The Sri Lankan Foreign Minister also upheld his country's commitment to ensuring expeditious and concrete progress in the ongoing dialogue between the Government of Sri Lanka and representatives of Tamil parties. On 17 August 2011, IRCON and Sri Lankan Railways signed a pact for supply and installation of signaling and telecommunication system for railway network in Northern province of Sri Lanka.

Uzbek President's visit on 17 May 2011 was followed by signing of 34 agreements relating to important strategic issues as well as several business contracts in Telecom & IT, Pharmaceuticals, Textiles & leather, Chemicals and fertilizers and hydrocarbons. Joint Statement on Strategic partnership between the Republic of India and the Republic of Uzbekistan declared a strategic partnership between India and Uzbekistan detailing the outcomes of the visit along with a vision for future cooperation.

In May 2011, Prime Minister Manmohan Singh visited two African countries—Ethiopia and Tanzania. He arrived in Ethiopia to attend the Africa-India Forum Summit on 23 May 2011. He offered, at the plenary on 24 May 2011, lines of credit to Africa to achieve development goals.

Japan and India on 6 June 2011, signed seven agreements under which loans would be provided as Official Development Assistance (ODA) for various infrastructure development projects in different states including Bangalore Metro. In December 2011, the Prime Minister of Japan paid a three day visit to India. Japan expressed its desire to expand cooperation in the nuclear sector while taking into consideration of safety aspects.

On the India-Pakistan relations front, the Minister of External Affairs of India, S.M. Krishna and the Minister of Foreign Affairs of Pakistan, Ms. Hina Rabbani Khar met in New Delhi on 27 July 2011. The meeting reviewed the status of bilateral relations on the issues of Counter-Terrorism (including progress on Mumbai trial) and Narcotics Control; Humanitarian issues;

Commercial and Economic cooperation; Wullar Barrage/Tulbul Navigation Project; Sir Creek; Siachen; Peace and Security including CBMs; Jammu and Kashmir; and promotion of friendly exchanges. The Ministers attached importance to promoting peace and security, including confidence-building measures, between India and Pakistan and agreed to convene separate meetings of the Expert Groups on Nuclear and Conventional CBMs, in Islamabad in September 2011. The Ministerial level talks were preceded by a meeting between the Foreign Secretaries of India and Pakistan on 26 July 2011.

President Pratibha Devisingh Patil visited Seoul in July 2011, and also to Mongolia thereafter. India and Republic of Korea signed an agreement for cooperation in the peaceful use of nuclear energy.

Indo-Bangladesh relations also got a boost with the Prime Minister's visit to Bangladesh in September 2011. The two countries discussed matters like mutual legal assistance in criminal matters, transfer of sentenced persons and fight against international terrorism, organized crime and illicit drug trafficking. The highlight of this meeting has been the signing of a new land border agreement to resolve long-standing border dispute. A vision statement laying out a long-term relationship between India and Bangladesh was signed. However, on sharing of waters of Teesta River, no deal could be struck due to the objection raised by the Chief Minister of West Bengal, Smt. Mamata Banerjee.

There was a visit by the President of Afghanistan, Hamid Karzai in October 2011. Two MoUs signed during visit of President of Afghanistan, were Memorandum of Understanding on Cooperation in the field of Development of Hydrocarbons, and Memorandum of Understanding on Cooperation in the field of Mineral Resources Development. The first ever Strategic Partnership Agreement (SPA) was signed during this visit on 4 October 2011. The agreement was aimed to provide training to the Afghan National Security Forces. Prior to this visit there was a visit by the First Vice President of Afghanistan to India on 16 June 2011. Soon after this, there was again another visit by Professor Burhanudin Rabbani, Chairman of the High Peace Council and former President of Afghanistan, who visited India from 14–15 July 2011. During this visit, there was a detailed discussion on the peace process in Afghanistan. On 3 June 2011, India under its Duty-Free Tariff Preference (DFTP) scheme agreed to provide duty-free market access to Afghanistan.

President of Vietnam visited India on 12 October 2011. An agreement was signed between India and Vietnam during this visit to promote oil exploration in South China Sea along with other pacts regarding extradition, trade, security and strategic ties between the two countries. Six agreements were signed after comprehensive talks on issues of mutual interest along with a desire to launch a biennial security dialogue between Home Ministries of India and Vietnam.

Prime Minister Manmohan Singh met the President Thein Sein during his visit to Myanmar in October 2011. Both agreed to examine the feasibility of railway links, accelerate work of two hydel projects in Myanmar, review working out a rout into north-east, and also the Mae Sot road linking India and Thailand via Myanmar which would be a direct link between ASEAN and India.

Prime Minister was on a visit on November 17 to attend the Ninth ASEAN-India Summit and the Sixth East Asia Summit in Bali, Indonesia. The visit to Bali was followed by an official visit to the Republic of Singapore from 19–20 November 2011. Prime Minister Manmohan Singh met President Obama at Bali on 18 November 2011, and both explored how both countries can work together not only on bilateral issues, but also in multilateral fora, like the East Asia Summit and on a wide range of issues, such as maritime security or non-proliferation, strengthening cooperation on disaster relief and humanitarian aid.

Prime Minister Manmohan Singh visited Addu to attend the Seventeenth SAARC Summit from 10–11 November 2011. In the sidelines of SAARC he met the Prime Ministers of Pakistan, Bhutan, Bangladesh and Presidents of the Maldives and Sri Lanka.

India and Nepal signed a revised Double Taxation Avoidance Agreement (DTAA) on 27 November 2011, to improve Indian investment in Nepal and ease procedures for stakeholders with commercial interest in both countries. Earlier during the visit of Nepalese Prime Minister Baburam Bhattarai to India in October 2011, both sides formalized the long pending Bilateral Investment Promotion and Protection Agreement (BIPPA). The visit was aimed at building trust between the two countries and two people.

Indo-Russian relation took a positive turn with the visit of Prime Minister Manmohan Singh to Russia on 15–17 December 2011. The India-Strategic Summit focused on economic ties as well as cooperation in the fields of nuclear, defence, science and space. Talks were held regarding Comprehensive Economic Partnership for East Asia (CEPEA), Kudankulam nuclear plant in Tamil Nadu among other issues. As far as international issues are concerned both sides expressed concerns over Syria, Iran, Afghanistan, terrorism and security in the Asia-Pacific region. Russian also supported India's bid for permanent membership in UNSC and also her membership in the Shanghai Cooperation Organization.

On 23 December 2011 there was a visit by Foreign Minister of Thailand. There was a wide range of discussions covering bilateral, regional and international issues. Both leaders affirmed the strong bilateral ties between India and Thailand, and discussed ways to further strengthen cooperation in diverse areas such as trade, investment, security and defence cooperation, tourism, education, culture, science and technology, energy, infrastructure and civil aviation, etc.

There were also visits of German Chancellor Dr. Angela Merkel, 30 May 2011, followed by signing of several MoUs and agreements. There were also visits by Dr. Ram Baran Yadav, President of Nepal from 27 January–5 February 2011, Foreign Minister of Bahrain to India, 30 March 2011, visit of Secretary General of the National Security Council of Saudi Arabia, 29 March 2011,

Foreign Minister of Nigeria for Joint Commission Meeting, 15–17 March 2011, visit of Foreign Minister of Philippines for the Meeting of India-Philippines Joint Commission on Bilateral Cooperation, 15 March 2011 and Foreign Ministers of Brazil and South Africa on 7–8 March 2011. There were also visits of Malaysian Deputy Prime Minister on 10 March 2011, visit of Prime Minister of Thailand, 5 April 2011, and visit of Foreign Minister of Cyprus on 19 April 2011. Month of May 2011 was followed by visits by Foreign Minister of Egypt and Iceland. Prime Minister of Slovenia, John Key visited India on 14 June 2011. Prime Minister of New Zealand paid a State visit to India in June 2011. July 2011 also saw a series of visits by Foreign Minister of Netherland, Libya and Poland and on 01August 2011 Foreign Minister of Syria.

The **year 2012** began with the visit of Minister of State (External Affairs) to Vietnam for attending the commemorative event for the 40th anniversary of establishment of full diplomatic relations between India and Vietnam (5 January). This was followed by another visit by Minister of State (External Affairs) to Palestine and Israel (10 January). External Affairs Minister, S.M. Krishna visited Sri Lanka from 16–19 January 2012. Both sides reviewed progress in various areas, including trade, services and investment, development cooperation, science and technology, culture and education. MoUs were signed for Housing Project, on cooperation in the field of Agriculture, and also a MoU between Telecom Regulatory Authority of India and Telecommunication Regulatory Commission.

The External Affairs Minister visited China on 8 February 2012. They reviewed the outstanding issues in Indo-China relations and agreed to work towards resolving them. To take the relations beyond bilateral cooperation they agreed that these irritants do not adversely affect the growing cooperation in other areas. Both sides pledged to carry that forward into 2012 and agreed to mark as the **"Year of India-China Friendship and Cooperation."**

The External Affairs Minister also visited Egypt and Singapore in early March 2012. The Prime Minister of India, Dr. Manmohan Singh paid an official visit to the Republic of Korea (ROK), at the invitation of President Lee Myung-bak, on 25 March 2012. The *India-Republic of Korea Joint Statement: Deepening the Strategic Partnership* upheld the multi-faceted bilateral relationship, which has rapidly acquired greater depth and vitality since its elevation to a Strategic Partnership during the landmark State visit to India of President of ROK in 2010 and State visit of President Pratibha Devisingh Patil to the Republic of Korea in July 2011. They expressed satisfaction at the increasing high-level exchanges, growing economic, trade, security and cultural ties, as well as people-to-people exchanges. The two leaders also held wide-ranging discussions on regional, international and multilateral issues. This visit was followed by signing of an agreement and MoU, (i) Agreement on Simplification of Visa Procedures, (ii) MoU on Cooperation between KNDA (Korea National Diplomatic Academy) and FSI (Foreign Service Institute).

Prime Minister Dr. Manmohan Singh visited Seoul on 27 March 2012, to attend the Nuclear Security Summit. He presented the national progress report. He upheld that India supports implementation of the Washington Summit Communiqué and Work Plan. India contributed to the NSS process, including hosting of a meeting of the Sherpas in New Delhi 16–17 January 2012.

The External Affairs Minister visited Russia on 13 April 2012 to attend the Eleventh Trilateral Meeting of the Foreign Ministers of India, Russia and China. The Joint Communiqué of the Eleventh Meeting of the Foreign Ministers of the Russian Federation, the Republic of India and the People's Republic of China upheld the importance attached by Russia, India and China to their constructive cooperation in the trilateral format. They stressed that this cooperation was not directed against any other country, was conducive to the promotion of regional peace, security and stability and served to benefit their peoples. The External Affairs Minister also talked about the multi-dimensional relationship that has evolved in different ways on the occasion of the 65th anniversary of establishment of India-Russia Diplomatic Relations.

The Prime Minister visited Myanmar on 28 May 2012. The Indian Prime Minister and U. Thein Sein, President of the Republic of the Union of Myanmar held a restricted meeting, followed by delegation level talks on bilateral, regional and international issues of mutual interest. They agreed to cooperate in the areas such as border area development, transportation, connectivity, agriculture, trade and investment, promotion of friendly exchanges and human resource development. They recognized that peace and stability in the region is necessary for development and well-being of the people. Several MoUs were signed during this visit between India and Myanmar. President of India visited Seychelles and South Africa from 29 April–7 May 2012.

In the months of June and July 2012, the External Affairs Minister visited a number of countries which included Cuba, USA, Tajikistan, Japan and Cambodia.

The External Affairs Minister participated in the 10th ASEAN-India Ministerial Meeting, the 2nd East Asia Summit Foreign Ministers Meeting and the 19th ASEAN Regional Forum Ministerial Meeting in Phnom Penh, Cambodia from 11–12 July 2012. In his statement at the 10th ASEAN-India Ministerial Meeting he upheld India's commitment to its partnership with ASEAN. He reiterated India's conviction that this partnership's would help in the achievement of the goal of the ASEAN Community by 2015, the Initiative for ASEAN Integration (IAI), the Master Plan on ASEAN Plus Connectivity (MPAC), the Declaration for a Drug Free ASEAN by 2015 and to the collective capacity building in this region.

S.M. Krishna, Minister of External Affairs, co-chaired with US Secretary of State Hillary Clinton the third India-US Strategic Dialogue on 13 June 2012 in Washington DC. The Joint Statement contained a satisfaction of both the sides on the remarkable expansion and growth of the bilateral relationship since the inaugural Strategic Dialogue in 2010. Both USA and India committed to further broaden and deepen the US-India global strategic partnership and charted a vision for the future, centered on promoting shared prosperity, peace and stability. On the sidelines of this Strategic Dialogue, number of sub-dialogues took place on various issues like the Global Issues Forum, S&T Joint Commission Meeting, the Counter terrorism Joint Working Group, the Higher Education Dialogue, Cyber Consultations, the Information and Communications Technology Working Group, the Women's Empowerment Dialogue, Homeland Security Consultations and other events. Prior to this meeting, the US Defence Secretary, Leon Panetta visited India from 5–6 June 2012.

In 15 June 2012, Prime Minister Manmohan Singh visited Los Cabos, Mexico, to attend the G-20 leaders Summit. He also visited Rio de Janeiro, Brazil to attend the Rio + 20-United Nations Conference on Sustainable Development, from 13–22 June 2012.

Prime Minister had bilateral meetings on 21 June 2012 in the sidelines of Rio+20 with Prime Minister of Nepal Mr. Baburam Bhattarai and with President of Sri Lanka Mahinda Rajapaksa. With President Mahinda Rajapaksa of Sri Lanka, PM had first a one-on-one discussion and then a delegation-level meeting. The issues discussed were economic relations, updating on Sampur Power Project, a joint venture between the Ceylon Power Board and the NTPC and also the rehabilitation of Internally Displaced People. As far the Prime Minister's Meeting with the Prime Minster of Nepal was concerned, Manmohan Singh felt that as the constitution-making process is underway, soon investment climate would improve. There was a hope that investment would be favourable as India and Nepal have entered into both a Bilateral Investment Promotion Agreement and a Double Taxation Avoidance Agreement in 2011 which have also been ratified.

Prime Minister Manmohan Singh also had a meeting with the Chinese Prime Minister Wen Jiabao in Rio de Janeiro on sidelines of Rio + 20 Summit in June 2012. Both agreed to carry on close political dialogue as well as dialogue among sectoral level officials. They also made reference to the boundary question and agreed the working of joint mechanism as a positive step. They also discussed issues pertaining to continuance of Defence and Strategic Dialogue, boosting bilateral trade, addressing the Indian trade deficit, investment flows, trans-border rivers and increasing people to people contacts with creating more scope for academics, media and other sections of civil society to engage with each other between India and China.

Prime Ministers visited Iran to attend XVI NAM Summit on 26 August 2012. While highlighting the radical changes in West Asian and North African region, Dr. Singh underscored India's support for popular aspirations for a democratic and pluralistic order. He urged all parties to recommit themselves to resolving the crisis peacefully through a Syrian-led inclusive political process that can meet the legitimate aspirations of all Syrian citizens. Dr. Singh also harped on an early resolution of the Palestinian question. Regarding India's policy towards the NAM movement, the Indian think-tanks have envisaged a policy which they have identified as **NAM 2.0: A Foreign and Strategic Policy for India in the Twenty First Century** (January 2012). This is an attempt to a re-work for present times of the fundamental principle that has defined India's international engagements since Independence. Nam 2.0 prescribes that Indian foreign policy must be defined keeping in mind the broad perspective and approach which India should adopt as it works to enhance its strategic autonomy in global circumstances that, for some time to come, are likely to remain volatile and uncertain.

In the sidelines of NAM Summit, a trilateral meeting between the Deputy Foreign Ministers of the Islamic Republic of Iran, the Islamic Republic of Afghanistan and Foreign Secretary of the Republic of India was held in Tehran on 26 August 2012. The objective of the meeting was to explore ways to expand trade and transit cooperation, including investment among the three countries. Setting up of a Joint Working Group (JWG) comprising representatives of the three countries would meet within next three months at Chahbahar to take the discussions forward.

The Minister of Foreign Affairs of Pakistan Hina Rabbani Khar, and the Minister of External Affairs of India S.M. Krishna met in Islamabad on 8 September 2012, for a meeting to review progress in the dialogue process. The ministerial level talks were preceded by a meeting between the Foreign Secretaries of Pakistan and India on 7 September 2012. They held substantive discussions on a wide range of issues within the framework of the dialogue process, and expressed satisfaction over the progress achieved since their last review meeting in July 2011. They upheld the importance of carrying forward the dialogue process with a view to resolving peacefully all outstanding issues through constructive and result-oriented engagement, and to establish friendly, cooperative and good neighbourly relations between Pakistan and India.

During 5–6 November 2012, the External Affairs Minister, Salman Khurshid visited Lao PDR to attend the 9th ASEM Summit. Prime Minister Dr. Manmohan Singh visited Cambodia to attend the 10th India-ASEAN Summit on 19 November 2012. He attended the 7th East Asia Summit in Phnom Penh, Cambodia on 20 November 2012. He welcomed the launch of the Regional Comprehensive Economic Partnership negotiations and also extended support for the Phnom Penh Declaration on East Asia Summit Development Initiative. Prime Minister Dr. Manmohan Singh met Prime Minister of Japan Mr. Yoshihiko Noda on the sidelines of 7th East Asia Summit. Dr. Singh also met Chinese Prime Minister Wen Jiabao in Phnom Penh on 19 November 2012, and talked about a variety of cooperative initiatives in global as well as bilateral arenas as well as growing dialogue in international for a like BRICS, G 20, East Asia Summit (EAS) and also on issues of climate change.

During 14–15 December 2013, the External Affairs Minister, Salman Khurshid visited Myanmar. This visit aimed at strengthening the multifaceted ties with Myanmar.

There was also a number of **incoming visits** from foreign dignitaries to India in the year 2012. On 13 January 2012, the EU High Representative

Baroness Catherine Ashton, the High Representative of the European Union for Foreign Affairs and Security Policy, visited India. During this visit there were discussions over issues covering the entire spectrum of EU-India relations ranging from bilateral, regional to international issues of mutual interest.

On 09 February 2012, President of the European Council, Herman Van Rompuy and José Manuel Durão Barroso, President of the European Commission visited India to attend the 12th India-EU Summit held in New Delhi on 10 February 2012. Both sides discussed bilateral, regional and multilateral issues of mutual concern with a view to, inter alia, strengthen their multifaceted bilateral cooperation, coordinate responses to regional issues, and tackle international challenges including the current financial crisis. This was followed by signing of a MoU and an agreement between EU and India.

President of the General Assembly of the United Nations visited India on 14 February 2012. There were discussions on several global challenges that the United Nations is currently seized with. At the same time India reiterated its commitment to principle of multilateralism and to the UN's leadership in confronting the current global challenges.

On 27 February 2012, there was a visit by the Minister of Foreign Affairs of Italy to India. This was the first high level visit from Italy since the new government was formed in Italy in November 2011.

India hosted the Fourth BRICS Summit 2012 from 26 to 29 March 2012. Discussions were held on the broad theme, *"BRICS Partnership for Global Stability, Security and Prosperity"*. The Summit was held under the leadership of Prime Minister Dr. Manmohan Singh. Ms. Dilma Rousseff, President of Brazil, Mr. Dmitry Medvedev, President of Russia, Mr. Hu Jintao, President of China and Mr. Jacob Zuma, President of South Africa attended the Summit. An ambitious action plan was drawn which was adopted on the 29 March along with the BRICS Delhi Declaration. India stated that BRICS countries must collaborate and cooperate with each other to shape global developments and bring tangible benefits to their people.

The President of Pakistan, Asif Ali Zardari paid a visit to India on 08 April 2012. President Zardari was on a private visit to Ajmer Dargah. However, Prime Minister Dr. Singh and President Zardari met for forty minutes and discussed various bilateral issues. Both sides felt that the dialogue process should steadily progress, addressing the bilateral problematic issues step by step and moving forward in trade-related issues. The leaders discussed the problem of terrorism, and Dr. Singh told President Zardari that it was imperative to bring the perpetrators of the Mumbai attack to justice, and prevent activities aimed against India from Pakistani soil especially the activities of Hafiz Saeed. President Zardari said the matter needed to be discussed further between the two Governments.

Minister for Foreign Affairs of Afghanistan to India visited New Delhi from 30 April–2 May 2012 at the invitation of S.M. Krishna, External Affairs Minister. The Ministers co-chaired the inaugural session of the India-

Afghanistan Partnership Council, which has been mandated to implement the Strategic Partnership Agreement signed by the Prime Minister and the President of Afghanistan in October 2011. Both sides acknowledged the successful conduct of the first meeting of the Joint Working Group on Political and Security Consultations. Further, they decided that the three Joint Working Groups on Trade and Economic Cooperation, Capacity Development and Education, and Social, Cultural, Civil Society and people to people contacts will be worked out expeditiously.

At the invitation of the External Affairs Minister, the Foreign Minister of Bangladesh Dr. Dipu Moni paid an official visit to India during 7–8 May 2012. The first meeting of the India-Bangladesh Joint Consultative Commission (JCC), as envisaged in the Framework Agreement on Cooperation for Development signed during the visit of the Prime Minister of India to Bangladesh, was held in New Delhi on 7 May 2012. Discussions were held around issues like political and security cooperation, trade and connectivity, development cooperation, bilateral cooperation in water resources and power, sub-regional cooperation and people-to-people contacts.

US Secretary of State Ms. Hillary Clinton paid a visit to India on 08 May 2012. External Affairs Minister S.M. Krishna projected an optimistic vision of Indo-US relation in the future. However, India expressed her concerns about the continuing difficulties on mobility of professionals, especially for our IT companies, and protectionist sentiments in the US with regard to global supply chain in services industry. Further both sides had an in-depth discussion about fostering commercial cooperation in civil nuclear energy. As far as Afghanistan is concerned, India stressed the need for sustained international commitment to build Afghan capacity for governance, security and economic development, and to support Afghanistan with assistance, investment and regional linkages. India also underscored the importance of peaceful settlement of the Iranian nuclear issue through dialogue and negotiations. There was also discussion on the Asia Pacific and Indian Ocean region, including relations with China, and developments in countries in India's immediate neighbourhood. Both sides exchanged views on their recent interaction with their Bangladeshi counterpart also.

Dr. Ali Akbar Salehi, Minister of Foreign Affairs of the Islamic Republic of Iran visited India from 31 May–1 June 2012 as Special Envoy of the President of Iran to hand over an invitation to Prime Minister to attend the 16th NAM Summit to be held in Tehran in August 2012. Sharing the same neighbourhood, India and Iran both are interested in the stability of Central Asia and the Gulf and also share the same concern about terrorism. Iran is not only an important neighbour but also a crucial trade partner for India, and also a major source of our energy supplies. Therefore, this visit was crucial and the timing is also noticeable as it followed immediately after the visit of US Secretary of State.

The Prime Minister of Singapore Lee Hsien Loong paid a State Visit to India from 10–12 July 2012 at the invitation of Prime Minister Dr. Manmohan

Singh. Several important MoU related to facilitation of cooperation in field of vocational education and skills development, facilitation of the setting up of a Greenfield World Class Skills Development Centre in Delhi to provide state-of-the-art facility for skills development and continuation of armed forces joint training and exercises.

On 27 July 2012, Dr. Marty Natalegawa, Foreign Minister of Indonesia visited India to co-chair the fourth meeting of the India-Indonesia Joint Commission with S.M. Krishna. Two agreements were signed during the visit. They are: avoidance of Double Taxation and the prevention of fiscal evasion with respect to taxes on income, and Agreed Minutes of the 4th Joint Commission Meeting between Republic of India and Republic of Indonesia.

Community of Latin American and Caribbean States (CELAC) is a newly formed regional group comprising 33 Sovereign States of Latin America and the Caribbean region (LAC) region. The First India-CELAC Troika Foreign Ministerial meeting was held on 7 August 2012 in New Delhi. Thus, there were visits of Foreign Ministers of Chile and Venezuela and Vice Foreign Minister of Cuba for the First CELAC Ministerial TROIKA Meeting to India on this occasion. Discussions revolved around regional and multilateral issues of mutual interest like strengthening the multifaceted bilateral cooperation between India and CELAC, coordinating responses to regional issues and addressing international challenges including UN reforms, the international financial crisis, climate change and international terrorism. The Foreign Ministers agreed to enhance exchange of visits at all levels including at the Summit level leading towards realization of a strategic partnership between India and CELAC.

On 7 August 2012, there were visits by the Deputy Prime Minister and Foreign Minister of Belgium. Emomali Rahmon, President of Tajikistan was on his fifth State Visit to India on 31 August 2012. Tajikistan is a key partner of India in the Central Asian region. This visit is significant from the perspective of India's gaining access to Central Asian hydrocarbon reserves. India and Tajikistan both have a common interest in the security transition in Afghanistan as well as counter-terrorism cooperation.

There were quite a number of significant visits in the month of September 2012. There were visits by the President of Palestine, 9 September 2012, Minister of Foreign Affairs of Canada, 11 September 2012, President of Burundi, 17 September 2012 and President of Sri Lanka, 19–22 September 2012.

Deputy Chairman of Russian Federation, Dmitry Rogozin, visited India on 13 October 2012. India and Russia reviewed bilateral collaboration in the field of Science and Technology and welcomed the operationalization of the offices of the India-Russia Joint Technology centres in the two countries. Both countries emphasized on strengthening contacts in the IT and hydrocarbons sector, particularly the energy sector as an important area for expansion of cooperation between our two countries.

The Australian Prime Minister Julia Gillard visited India on 15–17 October 2012. Three Memorandum of Understandings (MoUs) were signed pertaining to:

1. Civil Space Science, Technology and Education;
2. Field of Wool and Woolen products;
3. Student Mobility and Welfare;
4. Mining and National Skill Development Cooperation.

The second India-Japan 2 + 2 Dialogue was held in Tokyo on 22 October 2012. The Indian delegation was led by Foreign Secretary Ranjan Mathai and Defence Secretary Shashi Kant Sharma. The Japanese delegation was led by Deputy Foreign Minister Akitaka Saiki and Administrative Vice Defence Minister Hironori Kanazawa. These 2 + 2 consultations at Senior Official level are mandated by the Action Plan to Advance Security Cooperation concluded between the two countries in December 2009. These consultations were built on the last round of the 2 + 2 Dialogue held at New Delhi in June 2010. Apart from briefing each other on their respective defence and security policies in the background of each country's security environment, there was a review of bilateral security and defence cooperation and discussed ways of further expanding such ties. The two delegations also exchanged views on maritime, cyber and outer space security. They agreed to an early meeting of the new India-Japan Cyber Security Dialogue.

There was a State Visit of King of Spain to India on 26 October 2012. Five agreements/MoUs were signed during the visits pertaining to:

1. The avoidance of double taxation and the prevention of fiscal evasion with respect to taxes on income and on capital;
2. Roads and Road Transport Sector;
3. Defence Cooperation;
4. Audiovisual Co-production;
5. Technical cooperation in the field of railway sector

Increased Chinese activities in the South China Sea provide the background for India, USA and Japan to work out cooperation in maritime security and shaping the Asia-Pacific architecture. India hosted the 3rd round of India-Japan-US Trilateral Dialogue on 29 October 2012. The trilateral dialogue seeks to address the three major themes—the evolving Asian security architecture, non-traditional security issues, and prospects and challenges for this process.

Begum Khaleda Zia paid a visit to India from 28 October to 3 November 2012. She met new External Affairs Minister of India, Salman Khurshid. She focused on the future vision of Indo-Bangladesh relations without harping on the past.

The External Affairs Minister of India, Salman Khurshid met Jean Paul Adam, Minister of Foreign Affairs of Seychelles, Samson Ongeri, Minister of

Foreign Affairs of Kenya, Pierrot Jocelyn Rajaonarivelo and Minister of Foreign Affairs of Madagascar on 1 November 2012.

India hosted the 12th Meeting of the Council of Ministers of IOR-ARC on 02 November 2012. The *Gurgaon Communiqué - IORARC at 15 – The Next Decade* was adopted which pledged for stronger cooperation within the maritime domain of the IOR-ARC member states. In the sidelines of the IOR-ARC meeting the External Affairs Minister of India, Salman Khurshid met the Foreign Minister of Oman Yousuf Alawi, Foreign Minister of Yemen Abu-Bakr Al-Qirbi, Foreign Minister of Sri Lanka Prof. G.L. Peiris, and Foreign Minister of Comoros Mohamed Bakri Ben Abdoul Fatah.

Prime Minister of Canada Mr. Stephen Harper paid a visit to India from 4–9 November 2012. Both the Prime Ministers in their joint statement pledged to work out a forward-looking relationship by deepening bilateral engagement at strategic level as well as identifying areas of mutual interests like energy security, agriculture, food security, education, science and technology, mineral resources, infrastructure, defence and the like. The visit was significant as it marked the 65th Anniversary of the opening of the High Commission of Canada in India.

William Hague, the Secretary of State for Foreign and Commonwealth Affairs, of United Kingdom visited India from 7–9 November, 2012. During this visit India and the United Kingdom issued a Joint Statement on Cyber Security. They also agreed to hold 'Cyber Dialogue' on a bi-annual basis.

The 2nd India-China Strategic Economic Dialogue took place in New Delhi on 26 November 2012, which emphasized the increasing economic engagement between India and China.

Aung San Suu Kyi, Chairperson of the National League of Democracy of Myanmar visited India from 13–18 November 2012. She delivered the Nehru Memorial lecture to mark the birth anniversary of Pt. Jawaharlal Nehru on 14 November 2012. From 9–13 November, President of Islamic Republic of Afghanistan, Hamid Karzai was on a State Visit to India. Both countries looked forward to consolidate their strategic partnership and also took up bilateral, regional and global issues for discussions.

India hosted the ASEAN-India Commemorative Summit in New Delhi on 20–21 December 2012. This marked the 20th anniversary of the ASEAN-India dialogue partnership and the 10th anniversary of ASEAN-India Summit-level partnership. The theme of the Summit was *ASEAN-India Partnership for Peace and Shared Prosperity*. The summit witnessed the adoption of the ASEAN-India Vision Statement 2020. This can be seen as a major achievement for India in marking a tremendous progress of ASEAN-India relations.

The Russian President Vladimir Putin was on an official visit to New Delhi on 24 December 2012 to attend the 13th India-Russia Annual Summit. A joint statement was issued during this Summit under the theme *Partnership for Mutual benefit and a Better World*. The year 2012 ended with the official visit of the President of Nepal, Dr. Ram Baran Yadav from 24–29 December 2012.

India's foreign policy is showing signs of maturity. It is reflecting India's intent on the improvement of its Look-East policy, boosting its Central Asian policy, engaging with Latin American and Caribbean States and improving economic engagements with the newer economic arrangements as well as negotiating bilateral CECAs and CEPAs with countries like Australia, Malaysia, Singapore, Indonesia, Japan, South Korea and Bangladesh to mention a few. As part of the foreign investment policy of the Government of India negotiations have been undertaken with a number of countries to enter into Bilateral Investment Promotion and Protection Agreement (BIPAs/BIPPAs) in order to promote and protect on reciprocal basis investment of the investors. Government of India have, so far, (as on July 2012) signed BIPAs with 82 countries, out of which 72 BIPAs have already come into force and the remaining agreements are in the process of being enforced. Alongside, India is also engaging in various security dialogues with various countries like Japan and the US. However, India has to aim at stabilizing relations with her neighbours especially with Pakistan. With China, India has to be cautious, as in 2013 there would be a change in Chinese leadership which means re-orientation of India's policy towards China. Indo-US relations now has to be adjudged from the view-point of President Obama's disposition towards India in his second term, in addition to how he balances China and India. Another important factor will be the direction of his Af-Pak policy.

INDIA AND THE MAJOR POWERS

India and United States of America

In the present international scenario, with the overwhelming presence of United States of America as the sole surviving Super Power, it is important for any student of Indian foreign policy to analyze the ever-evolving Indo-US relations in the post-cold war international relations.

Immediately after independence, till the end of Cold War, and a decade after that, Indo-US relations did not mark any significant developments. Bilateral relations between the two could not develop properly, because of Cold War calculations that conditioned Indo-US relations. Initially, India's posture of non-alignment did not find favour in the US. John Foster Dulles condemned non-alignment as "immoral". Later, certain other issues cropped up which obstructed the natural growth of bilateral relations between the two. Kashmir has been one such issue and the US favouring a plebiscite in Kashmir as per the UN resolution of 1948 and 1949, made India cautious about the US. Moreover, India's recognition of Communist China in 1949, roping in of Pakistan into military alliances like Baghdad Pact (1955–1958), SEATO (1954) and CENTO (1958–1979) and subsequent US arms supply to Pakistan to "contain" Communism became major irritants in the Indo-US relations. The Korean crisis and India's refusal to endorse the US sponsored "Uniting for Peace Resolution" distanced the two. The Indo-Russian Treaty of Friendship of 1971 further embittered the Indo-US relations. Again during the 1971 Bangladesh liberation war, relations reached a low point. The US supported Pakistan and even tried to negotiate a cease-fire through the UNSC. However, the Soviets vetoed it. The US even moved their 7th Fleet to the Bay of Bengal to create pressure on India. The Soviet Union had come to India's rescue and they sent their Fleets to Bay of Bengal to counter the US pressure. The 1974 Pokhran Nuclear explosion by India also distanced the two countries. But one point of consideration is that, despite such irritants, in the spheres of economic, culture and education, cooperation continued. The US also provided technical assistance and also supplied food grains (PL-480) to meet the scarcity of food (see Indian Foreign Policy under Indira Gandhi page 373). A Joint Commission was also established to explore possibilities of fostering cooperation in economic, commercial, scientific and technological, educational and cultural sectors. Bilateral relations suffered a setback in 1979 due to Soviet invasion of Afghanistan. India refused to rally behind the US and ascribe Soviet Union as an aggressor (see page 374). India also was critical about US supply of arms sell to Pakistan. During the tenure of Ronald Reagan, bitterness increased due to differences over Diego Garcia and India wanted dismantling of the US base in Diego Garcia. India demanded establishment of Indian Ocean as a 'Zone of Peace'. The US refused to supply nuclear fuel to Tarapur Atomic Power Station. Refusal of India to sign NPT and US intent on enforcement of Super 301* and Missile Technology Regime against India further added to bitterness.

It was only during Rajiv Gandhi's tenure that little improvement could be perceived. He visited the United States in June 1985, and struck a rapport with President Ronald Reagan. He, however, took the opportunity and pointed out the lurking dangers of a rapidly nuclearising Pakistan. During the National Front Government, there was further improvement in the Indo-US relations and financial assistance from world agencies like the World Bank and the IMF increased which helped India to tide over the economic crisis caused by the First Gulf War. For the first time also the US agreed to drop its insistence for a plebiscite in Kashmir and resolution of the crisis on the lines of the Simla Accord, 1972. In 1990-1991, the collapse of Soviet Union, the end of Cold War and the economic liberalization of India, the two countries looked afresh at their bilateral relations. During Narasimha Rao's tenure, therefore, despite several irritants both sides tried to move forward with their bilateral relations. Two countries held Joint Naval exercise in May 1992. Prime Minister Narasimha Rao paid an official week-long visit to the US in May 1994, which helped to strengthen ties and was followed by signing of several Memorandum of Understandings (MoUs).

In 1995, following the visits by the US Defence and Commerce Secretaries several agreements were signed. However, US trade law Super 301 still affected

---

*Super 301 Section 301 of the US Trade Act, 1974

India's export which again was a disturbing factor in Indo-US relations which was only removed in 1994. Relations saw set back by the passing of Pressler Amendment in 1995 regarding sale of 28 F-16 aircrafts to Pakistan. Again supply of nuclear fuel to Tarapur reactor suffered, cryogenic sales was hit and the issue of Super 301 resurfaced, which created discomfort between the two.

In 1998, relations totally took a reverse turn with the Pokhran II explosion and India's refusal to sign the CTBT during the tenure of Vajpayee Government. However, due to increased functioning of terrorists in Pakistan, the US stance towards India began to change and President Clinton visited India in March 2000. When President Bush assumed the office in 2001, despite several irritants did not stop searching for avenues for new relationship with India. Only after 9/11 attacks on the United States and the 13 December attack on the Indian Parliament that Indo-US relationship took a new turn as both pledged to fight against international terrorism.

India and the US both agreed to foster military cooperation according to the Kickleighter proposals. However, differences over reforms of US, supply of F-16s to Pakistan, GATT negotiations, Cryogenic engine sales, refusal to supply nuclear fuels for Tarapur reactor, imposition of tariff restrictions of India's textile exports and other issues persisted. Relations took off significantly in the 1999–2000. In 1999, both India and USA entered into Bilateral Extradition Treaty, Treaty on Mutual Legal Assistance in Criminal Matters and several defence cooperation deals. President Clinton visited India in March 2000, and Prime Minister Vajpayee visited the US in September. In 2001, the US lifted the nuclear sanctions. In 2002, a major milestone was achieved when Vajpayee and Bush met in New York. They identified sectors of cooperation like high technology, space research, civilian nuclear technology, economic, defence and also addressing various global issues. In 2002, National Security Strategy was agreed upon and in January 2004 President Bush announced 'Next Steps in Strategic Partnership' (NSSP) with India. With these India acquired the status of 'strategic partner' of the US.

The year 2008 is important in the sense that with the assistance of US and other countries India managed to get a Nuclear Suppliers Group (NSG) waiver. The 123 Agreement was rectified. The ultimate result was that India and USA struck the historic nuke deal.

In July 2009, Hillary Clinton, the US Secretary of State paid a visit to India to further boost the Indo-US relations. Indo-US relations saw new developments with Manmohan Singh's four-day visit to the US in November 2009. The visit was followed by high level talks on strengthening cooperation on various global and regional issues like counter-terrorism, counter-intelligence to prevent Mumbai-type attacks, implementation of the Indo-US civil nuclear deal to mention a few. The US President, Barack Obama acclaimed India as an "indispensable partner" as both nations would strive to build a future of security and prosperity for all nations. Thus, a new phase of 'strategic partnership' between India and USA took off. In November 2009 only, India and US signed the India-US Counter Terrorism Initiative which aims at strengthening cooperation to counter terrorism.

The Indo-US Strategic Dialogue took place on 3 June 2010 when Foreign Minister S.M. Krishna visited the United States. Recognizing India as a "rising global power", the US Secretary of State, Hillary Clinton declared that the USA today was definitely committed "to consider India's bid for a permanent seat in the UNSC." The US President Obama's visit to India from 6–9 November 2010, further brought the two countries closer. President Obama expressed US support for India's membership to multilateral export control regimes like NSG, MTCR, the Australian Group (AG) and the Wassenaar Arrangement (WA) in a phased manner and removal of India's defence and space related entities from the US 'Entity List'. (see pages 387–388)

India's Minister of External Affairs, S.M. Krishna and the US Secretary of State Hillary Rodham Clinton met in New Delhi on 19 July 2011, for the second Annual Meeting of the India-US Strategic Dialogue. Three focal areas of interaction were highlighted by Ms. Clinton. They are—lower tariff barriers along with further opening of markets, involving India in maritime security and selling equipment especially to the Navy and civil nuclear cooperation.

US Secretary of State Ms. Hillary Clinton paid a visit to India 08 May 2012. External Affairs Minister S.M. Krishna projected an optimistic vision of Indo-US relation in the future. However, India expressed her concerns about the continuing difficulties on mobility of professionals, especially for our IT companies, and protectionist sentiments in the US with regard to global supply chain in services industry. S.M. Krishna, Minister of External Affairs, co-chaired with the US Secretary of State Hillary Clinton the third India-US Strategic Dialogue on 13 June 2012 in Washington DC. The Joint Statement contained a satisfaction of both the sides on the remarkable expansion and growth of the bilateral relationship since the inaugural Strategic Dialogue in 2010.

As far as Indo-US **economic relations** are concerned, it started improving after 2000. The year 2000 witnessed the initiation of trade partnership between the two countries. On 21 March 2000, Prime Minister of India and President of United States released a document in the theme *India-US Relations: A Vision for the 21st Century* at New Delhi. Obviously, despite such remarkable steps, scholars point at the slow rate of progress as compared to progress of US-China trade. In 1991, the figure stood at US $ 5.91 billion, in 2000 US $14.35 billion, in 2004 US $ 37.1 billion, in 2008 US $43.4 billion and in 2010 the figure stood at US $ 48.75 billion. US-China trade in the year 2010 has been to the tune of US $ 456.82 billion. Despite such sluggish pace of progress of Indo-US trade India seems to be lucrative destination for FDI and huge market for US exports and MNCs. IT sector is the major sector of cooperation between the two countries. However, outsourcing has been a serious problem and the domestic public opinion in USA is quite averse to outsourcing of jobs to India, China and elsewhere. In 2010 both countries to boost the bilateral trade in macroeconomic policy, financial sector and infrastructure financing launched a new Economic and Financial Partnership between India's Ministry of Finance and the Department of the Treasury in April 2010. Earlier in 2005, to promote real and meaningful cooperation in trade and investment a US-India Trade Policy Forum set up followed by the establishment of a Private Sector Advisory Group (PSAG) in 2007.

The Indo-US Nuke deal is well-known and quite a path-breaking success for India. The most remarkable breakthrough that Manmohan Singh's government was able to make was to enter into the nuclear deal with the United States. The process started with Dr. Singh's assumption of office and met its culmination in October, 2008 when the final nuclear deal was signed between the two countries. Earlier on 18 July 2005, India and the US signed the landmark Civilian Nuclear Agreement in Washington DC. Next on 2 March 2006, a Separation Plan is initialed by India and the US which listed out which reactors New Delhi would put under safeguards. On 18 December 2006, the Hyde Act was passed by the US Congress which led to the amendment of the US Atomic Energy Act. The next breakthrough came in 27 July 2007 when the 123 Agreement was signed by India and the US outlining the terms of nuclear trade between the two countries. On 1 August 2008, IAEA cleared India-specific safeguards agreement that defined the level of supervision of civilian plants. The Nuclear Suppliers Group (NSG) waiver came ultimately after intense negotiation among its 45 members to allow nuclear trade with India on 6 September 2008. Ultimately India and the US struck the nuclear deal on 8 October 2008. As the nuke deal is in place now India can now formally begin trade in civilian nuclear technology while continuing its nuclear weapons programme but expecting severe consequences if it conducts a test in future.

As far as cooperation in other sectors is concerned, both countries pledge to work towards achieving energy security, use of clean energy and working out climate change negotiations. Both sides look forward for fruitful cooperation in the health, science and technology. USA and India also cooperate in high technology area pertaining to aerospace, IT and communication, pharmaceuticals and bio-technology. Education is also another significant area of cooperation. During Prime Minister Manmohan Singh's visit to Washington in 2009 both countries launched *Obama-Singh 21st Century Knowledge Initiative* aimed at increasing linkages and faculty development programme between US and Indian Universities. USA is also a vocal supporter of India's bid for a permanent seat in the UNSC.

However, certain grey areas still persist. India's stand on entering into an understanding on End-Use-Monitoring Agreement (EUMA) with the US, which has raised severe criticisms from several quarters. Some see the provisions of EUMA as a compromise of India's sovereignty. CITBT can again prove a stumbling block. Doha rounds of negotiations under WTO and the continuing stalemate brings to the fore the differences of perspectives of the US and India on matters hurting the developing world especially subsidies on agriculture by USA and other developed countries. Differences exist over climate change and global warming issues, especially regarding matters on carbon emission level and necessary cut to be imposed by India and China. Above all, US Af-Pak policy immensely affects India. USA is soft on Pakistan, and in the war against terrorism, Pakistan has emerged as the major ally of the US. India's hue and cry over Pakistan's policy of sheltering terrorists and evidences given by India after the 26/11 Mumbai attacks did not result in change in the US policy towards Pakistan. Pakistan goes on receiving generous amount of military and economic aid from the US. Just before President Obama visited India in November 2010, the US announced $2-billion annual defence aid package to Pakistan in October 2010. US Drone attacks (starting from 2004) in the Federally Administered Tribal Areas (FATA) along Afghan border on northwest of Pakistan and killing of Osama bin Laden by the US Navy SEAL in May 2011 prove beyond doubt the gravity of the terrorist activities in Pakistan. Again, regarding the Haqqani group, US has warned Pakistan of military action in North Waziristan. However, the US administration refused to endorse the ISI and Haqqani linkage. The haziness over US stand on David Coleman Headley also is a distressing factor between India and the US. The Chicago Court sentenced Headley to 35 years of imprisonment in January 2013. India has pleaded for his extradition in the past and also would like to have Headley now but this has not been responded favourably by the US.

Therefore, what emerges in the present scenario is that India should not become a tool in the hands of the US in her strategic design in the Asia-Pacific. India must not try to alienate herself from the Chinese and be blind on containing China. Again India must also engage with the US to balance the overwhelming presence of China. Thus, engagement and accommodation of the three powers can ensure peace and stability in the region.

India and Russia

Indo-Russian friendship is a time-tested relationship. No one has been such a trusted friend as has been Russia for India. Undoubtedly, there have been some hiccups immediately after the disintegration of Soviet Union and certain matters related to defence deal, yet both have nurtured strong bond over the years. Immediately after the independence of India, there were some differences on international issues related to India's membership to Commonwealth, opposition to Communist revolution in Malaya, adoption of non-alignment policy, and also support to Greece among others. Soviet Union was suspicious about India's foreign policy posture as pro-West. However, the initial misgivings soon disappeared with the death of Stalin and Khrushchev's assumption of office of the President. In the 1950s when military pacts were being formed by USA to counter Communist threat, India's refusal to join such pact/alliances as opposed to Pakistan, and sticking to non-alignment, brought the two countries together. Thereafter, both had agreed on matters like Suez crisis and disagreed on Hungary, yet both moved on amicably in their bilateral relations. In 1962, during the Sino-Indian war, Soviet Union supported India whole heartedly, sided with India and also extended proposals for defence cooperation like manufacture of M.I.G Fighter Planes. During the 1965 Indo-Pak war, Soviet Union mediated peace between India and Pakistan and thus the Tashkent Declaration (1966) was signed.

The year 1971 was eventful, and Soviet Union and India entered into the Treaty of Friendship and Cooperation. The Preamble to the Treaty reaffirms both countries' faith in "the principles of peaceful co-existence and co-operation between states with different political and social systems." The noticeable point of this treaty was that there would be reciprocal consultations in case either of parties was subjected to an attack. Both also pledged to refrain from concluding military alliances against each other. Both also committed to enhance economic, scientific and technological cooperation. Thus, we find that Soviet Union helped India to set up Iron factory at Bhilai and Iron and steel factory at Bokaro. Arya Bhatta, the first artificial satellite was sent from Soviet Union. During the Janata government's tenure, it was expected that there would be drastic changes in the foreign policy posture of India. This was specially because they vehemently criticized India's intimacy with the Soviet Union as a violation of the principle of non-alignment. However, it got itself reconciled with the tilt in non-alignment and continued good relations with the Soviet Union.

With the coming back of Indira Gandhi, relations became more cordial which were further strengthened by Rajiv Gandhi. Rajiv Gandhi went on his first visit to Moscow from 21–26 May 1985, which resulted in fruitful interactions in strategic as well as economic fields. The return visit by the Soviet President Mikhail Gorbachev to India in November 1986, was a landmark in India's relation with the Soviet Union. New agreements were signed between India and the Soviet Union in the field of economic and technical cooperation. During all these years one thing that was happening was that there was voluminous rise of bilateral trade between both the countries. The National Front Government under V.P. Singh and then Chandra Sekhar did not dramatically change Indo-Russian policy and continued the same traditional policy of amity and cooperation.

With the disintegration of the Soviet Union in December 1991 problems surfaced. There was no clear idea about what the Russian policy towards India would be. Yeltsin and his close associates like Gaider and Kosyrev were pro-West. Therefore, Indo-Russian relations suffered a setback. In the meantime, the historic Indo-Soviet Treaty of Peace and Friendship and Cooperation was extended for another two decades. Several irritants cropped up regarding the cryogenic deals, arms transfer, rupee-rouble exchange, and Kashmir issue among others. Narasimha Rao Government had to renegotiate various ties in place with the erstwhile Soviet Union. India also slipped from the privileged position, which it used to enjoy under the erstwhile USSR. To India's greatest dissatisfaction, Russia voted in favour of a Pakistani-sponsored resolution declaring South Asia a nuclear-free zone. The supply of cryogenic engines by Moscow to aid India's space programme for peaceful explorations, ultimately disrupted under immense US pressure, also created apprehensions in Indian minds. However, the initial misunderstandings soon gave way to newer bonds between the two. Relations improved greatly with Russian President Boris Yeltsin's visit to India in January 1993. During this visit not only was the rupee-rouble exchange rate resolved but also the 1971 Indo-Russian Treaty of Peace, Friendship and Cooperation was substituted by a new 14-clause Treaty of Friendship and Cooperation valid for 20 years. This Treaty stipulated that the two countries would refrain from taking any action that might affect the security interests of the other, pledging support to each other's territorial integrity and non-interference in internal affairs.

The visit of Prime Minister Narasimha Rao to Moscow in June 1994 saw further improvement of relations. Russia also refrained from supply of arms to Pakistan. Primakov, first as Russian Foreign Minister, 1996 and then as Prime Minister in 1998 made all effort to boost the bilateral relations. During the visit of Indian Prime Minister H.D. Deve Gowda to Moscow in March 1997, Russia agreed to help India set up a nuclear power plant at Kudankulam. The United Front Government first under Deve Gowda and then under I.K. Gujaral did not introduce any significant change in India's foreign policy posture.

During Vajpayee's Prime Ministership, a breakthrough came in the year 2000. In the same year relations took a new turn with Putin assuming the office of the President of Russia. Putin visited New Delhi in 2000. The Declaration on strategic partnership was signed in 2000. This was not directed against any State/groups of states, and did not aim at creating military-political alliances. This declaration also set up the framework for convening Annual Summit Level Meetings, closer cooperation at international and regional forums, deepening and diversifying cooperation in sectors such as metallurgy, fuel and energy, information technology, communications and transport, consolidating defence and military cooperation, cooperation in the peaceful use of nuclear energy and outer space, cooperating in combating international terrorism and organized crimes among others. The idea of North-South Corridor was also floated in September 2000.*

Again during the Vajpayee Government's tenure, the relations got a boost with another visit form Putin to New Delhi in 2002. The *Delhi Declaration* was signed on 'Further Consolidation of Strategic Partnership'. Both countries agreed to set up a joint group on fighting terrorism, and emphasized on promotion of scientific and cultural cooperation.

During UPA-I and UPA-II Indo-Russian relations saw an upsurge with several pacts being signed between both the countries in the course of the visits by Russian Prime Minister Vladimir Putin to New Delhi, and Indian Prime Minister Manmohan Singh to Moscow. India and Russia reinforced their ties with an expanded civil nuclear deal and three military pacts. They also raised

---

*North-South Corridor-stretches from the ports of India across the Arabian Sea to the Southern Iranian port of Bandar Abbas and then goods transit Iran and the Caspian sea to the ports in the Russian sector of the Caspian Sea. From there, the corridor stretches along the Volga River to the port of Astra Khan before reaching Moscow and finally Europe.

voices of concern over growing menace of terrorism. This was done during the course of a three-day visit to Moscow by Indian Prime Minister Manmohan Singh during December 2009. Dr. Singh also upheld that India's relations with third world countries will never be at the cost of "time-tested ties" with Russia. Again during Russian Prime Minister Putin's visit to New Delhi during March 2010, 19 pacts were signed. Some prominent among them are Agreement on Cooperation in the use of Atomic Energy for Peaceful Purposes, Agreement on Road Map for the Serial Construction of Russian Designed Nuclear Power Plants (Russia to build 6 atomic plants in Kudankulan and 6 in Haripur, West Bengal), Agreement on Protocol of Cooperation signed between ONGC and Russia's Gazprom, revised agreement on Gorshkov aircraft carrier deal, agreement for sale of MiG-29K aircraft carrier-based fighters by Russia to India under a USD 15 billion contract, two pacts in field of fertilizers and five pacts in the diamond sector. In December 2010, Russian President Dmitry Medvedev visited India. The outcome of the visit was reflected in the signing of 30 agreements during his visit on 21–22 December 2010. The agreements were signed in key areas like defence, energy, nuclear, space, science & technology, pharma, IT, bio-technology, and so on. Russian President also showed strong and unambiguous support to India's bid for the UNSC permanent membership. He also expressed a strong desire to stabilize the situation in Afghanistan through joint efforts. Therefore, Indo-Russian relationship received another boost with Medvedev's visit to India.

Indo-Russian relation took a positive turn with the visit of Prime Minister Manmohan Singh to Russia on 15–17 December 2011. The External Affairs Minister visited Russia on 13 April 2012 to attend the Eleventh Trilateral Meeting of the Foreign Ministers of India, Russia and China. Deputy Chairman of Russian Federation, Dmitry Rogozin, visited India on 13 October 2012. (see Indian Foreign Policy developments in the Year 2011-2012 for details).

India and Russia have been successful in forging strong ties at the international levels too. The India-Russia-China Trilateral is showing signs of positive development. The 10th IRC Ministerial Meeting was held in Wuhan in November 2010. Russia's solid support gave India access to Shanghai Cooperation Organization (SCO) despite initial Chinese stubbornness. Russia backs India's full-fledged membership of SCO. This is essential to give India's Central Asian policy a major boost. Both are involved in the East Asia Summit (EAS) which gives both access to conduct strategic dialogue and enhance security cooperation in Asia-Pacific Region. Russia also backs India's entry into APEC. India supports Russia's entry into the Asia-Europe Meeting (ASEM) for better enhancement of cooperation in Eurasia. BRICS* has given both India and Russia another dialogue forum for enhancing cooperation. Both interact and share similar views in various international organizations like the UN, G20, ASEAN Regional Forum on Security (ARF) and the Asia Cooperation Dialogue (ACD). In case of voting in UNSC for passing Resolution 1973 for

*BRICS—an economic grouping comprising Brazil, Russia, India, China and South Africa. (see Chapter 20)

establishing no-fly zone over Libya, Russia and India abstained among 10 other abstaining members. Russia has outrightly supported India's bid for a permanent seat in the Security Council.

Defence cooperation between India and Russia is quite old, and has been growing over the years. Both sides have, on their agenda, issues related to ongoing projects like Fifth generation Fighter Aircraft, Multi-role Transport Aircraft, T-90 tanks, AWACS, SU-30 MKI upgrade, aircraft carrier Admiral Gorshkov and Medium Lift Helicopters. Both sides are keen on expediting the projects. The 10th Indo-Russia Inter-Governmental Commission on Military Technical Cooperation (IRIGC-MTC) was held in New Delhi in 2010, which pointed to the positive dynamics of the defence cooperation. The tenure of the Indo-Russian Inter-Governmental Commission on Military Technical Cooperation (IRIGC-MTC) was extended by another ten years on the expiry of its term in 2010. However, the delay in delivery of aircraft carrier Admiral Gorshkov is causing discomfort in the bilateral relations. The delivery was pushed back to 2013, and in 2012 reports came out of further delay. This is costing India more than the amount signed in the original contract in 2004. India defence supply diversification has also caused displeasure at the diplomatic level. India has developed closer ties with Israel, France, UK and Germany to name a few of the prominent countries with which India is negotiating defence deals. In a latest historic purchase by the Indian Air Force in January 2012, the Dassault Rafale won the bid from among the chief contenders like the Russian MIG-35, Lockheed Martin's F-16 Falcon, Boeing's F-18 Hornet, the Swedish Saab Gripen and Eurofighter Typhoon. This deal shows how India has diversified her defence procurement and also plans to issue global tenders for future purchases too.

In the Indo-Russian trade front however, things are not showing positive signs. There has been a trade slump. It is slowly picking up from $1,339 million in 1997 to $1,406 million in 2000–2001 and further to $1,954 million in 2004–2005 and $2878 in 2006–2007. Sino-India trade witnessed an upsurge of $33.4 billion in 2006 whereas Indo-Russian trade showed a bare $3.3 billion figure.

However, both sides still continue to forge ties in the fields of Science and technology, energy and nuclear sectors. Both sides have ongoing cooperation in the Russian Global Navigation Satellite System (GLONASS), joint lunar exploration (Chandrayan-2), joint development and launch of youth satellite for educational purposes, joint collaborative ventures in technology and bio-technology among others. In the field of nuclear cooperation, Tarapur and Kudankulam are worth mentioning. As far as energy cooperation is concerned Indian and Russian oil companies have acquired 20% stake in Sakhalin-1 project from Rosneft-S. Both have huge prospect of cooperation in these sectors.

The Russian President Vladimir Putin was on an official visit to New Delhi on 24 December, 2012 to attend the 13th India-Russia Annual Summit. The mechanism of Annual Summit began with the signing of the *Declaration of*

Strategic Partnership between India and the Russian Federation in October 2000. The Summits are held annually on a rotational basis. A joint statement was issued during this Summit under the theme *Partnership for Mutual benefit and a Better World.* Both sides emphasized the deepening of the strategic partnership between the two countries. Both sides stressed to improve ties in the fields of trade and investment, energy, science and technology, culture and humanitarian exchanges, education, military-technical cooperation, space, terrorism, regional and international issues, disarmament and non-proliferation efforts as well as matters concerning Syria, Afghanistan, Iran's nuclear programme, recovery of global economy, and environment and sustainable development. A number of agreements/MoUs were also signed between India and Russia.

From the above analysis of indo-Russian relation, one can come to the conclusion that the irritants have not been able to dampen the cooperative spirit of both the countries at the bilateral level. Currently, in the various international fora like the SCO, G 20 and the BRICS, they are getting along well. So both India and Russia must make earnest effort to nurture the cooperative spirit that they have cultivated over the years.

India and China

India and China, two big neighbours vying for leadership in Asia, have over the years cultivated bilateral relations involving rivalry and engagements. A number of irritants have severed the relation between the two. Long pending border dispute, territorial claims, Chinese incursions, Tibet and Dalai Lama, burgeoning trade deficit, assistance to Pakistan, developing closer ties with India's neighbours, China's strategy of 'Strings of Pearls' and Indo-US Nuclear deal are some major drawbacks in the Sino-Indian relations among others.

As far as the border dispute is concerned which is a pricky and disturbing factor there have been claims and counter claims over certain territories by both. China has forwarded claims over Arunachal Pradesh and the dispute centres around the acceptance of McMohan Line [Line of Actual Control (LAC)] by China. China refuses to accept the LAC while India regards McMohan Line as a permanent border. There is also bitterness over Aksai Chin and again the dispute is regarding the acceptance of John Ardagh-Johnson Line and the Macartney-MacDonald Line by one and rejection by the other. The former puts Aksai Chin within Indian territory and the latter puts it outside the Indian territory. Such divergent perspectives had been uncompromising and complicating relations. In 1963, against Indian objections, Pakistan handed over the Trans-Karakoram Tract to China as this area is claimed as a part of Jammu and Kashmir. There are also eight pockets of disputes between the two. In the Western sector—(1) Trig Heights and (2) Demchok; in the Middle sector—(3) Barahoti; in the Eastern Sector- (4) Namka Chu, (5) Sumdorong, (6) Chantze,

(7) Asaphila, and (8) Lonju. Chinese incursions into the Western Sector (Ladakh), Middle (Uttarakhand and Himachal) and Eastern (Sikkim and Arunachal) have also disturbed the relations. China also has made a claim over the Finger Area* in Sikkim.

Tibet has been a vexing issue since the Chinese started their mission to liberate Tibet in the late 1940s and completed its occupation by 1951. Dalai Lama following the uprising in Tibet in 1959 fled to India and established a government in exile in India in *Dharamshala*. From then onwards, the issue of Dalai Lama has been a vexing topic in Sino-India relation. China alleges the hands of Dalai Lama for formenting troubles in Tibet. China uses all means to integrate Tibet into mainland China. It has built roads and rail links like the Beijing-Lhasa road, and had plans for constructing a road up to Mount Everest. With the Chinese occupation of Tibet India lost a buffer state between China and herself, and now every single Chinese defence designs involving Tibet gives her a nerve shock, because these connectivity between Tibet and China can well be mobilized to move troops upto Indian border.

The widening trade gap is a matter of worry for India. In 2006, the Joint Economic Group (JEG) which met in New Delhi made commitments to diversify India's exports and improve market access for Indian companies to China. However, the trade deficit has grown from US $4 billion to US $14 billion in 2009.

Bilateral trade fell by 20% in 2009 due to global meltdown and hit Indian exports. However, one big allegation against China is 'dumping' of Chinese goods in India and thus spoiling the domestic market of India. India since September 2008 has extended a ban on milk and milk products from China due to high amount of melamine content. Further, China has also tried to block the US $2.9 billion development fund for India out of which $60 million development project was meant for Arunachal Pradesh from the Asian Development Bank (ADB) in March 2009. China insisted that Arunachal Pradesh must be removed from the development project plan. Earlier China also had attempted to block a waiver by the Nuclear Suppliers Group (NSG) which cleared global nuclear trade for India.

China's closeness to Pakistan is a matter of concern for India. China has given assistance both in the military and the nuclear sector which are disturbing factors in the Sino-Indian relations. Sino-Paksitani collaboration in the building up of the nuclear reactor (Khusab Nuclear Reactor) has made Indian allegations of clandestine dealings between China and Pakistan proved beyond doubt. Further, Chinese design of 'Strings of Pearls' which is a strategy to encircle India by building or developing relations with States around India and isolate India in South Asia and limit her extension of activities beyond this region and

---

*Finger Area is a territory which is located in the north of Gyangyong in Sikkim and strategically overlooks the important valley-Sora Funnel. This is the northernmost tip of Sikkim which appears like a protruding finger on the map.

also check India's activities in the South China Sea, Indian Ocean and Arabian Sea. China also is aware that it has to limit growing India's influence in Southeast Asia, Central Asia and Persian Gulf to ensure China's energy security supplies. China wants to achieve this by establishing economic and military nodes in various countries by using diplomacy and economic packages. China has targeted countries like Myanmar, Bangladesh, Nepal, Sri Lanka, Maldives, Mauritius and Seychelles, Thailand and Cambodia and above all Pakistan. In 2005, Chinese Premier Prime Minister Wen Jiabao inaugurated the deep-seaport at Gwadar on the coast of Arabian Sea which obviously was constructed with Chinese assistance. In Sri Lanka, China is assisting in construction of Hambantota port in southern Sri Lanka. Strategic investments are being made by China in Hainan Island in the South China Sea, the Straits of Malacca, port developments in Chittagong in Bangladesh, Sittwe, Coco, Hianggyi, Khaukphyu, Mergui and Zadetkyi Kyun in Myanmar, Laem and Chabang in Thailand and Sihanoukville in Cambodia.

The issue of stapled visas is another recent irritant in the Sino-Indian relation. Chinese and Indian Naval warships had been paying goodwill visits to each other's ports since 2004. The armies of both countries also had conducted joint military exercises in 2008 in China and in India in 2009. These naval exchanges were suspended on July 2010 after issuance of stapled visa* to Lt. Gen BS Jaswal who was commanding Indian troops in Jammu and Kashmir. However, before the BRICS summit in China, Beijing issued normal visas to four Kashmiri. Yet during the meeting between Manmohan Singh and Hu Jintao during the BRICS Summit in Sanya in April 2011 they could not resolve the issue of stapled visa. Earlier China began issuing visa on a separate piece of paper to the citizens of the Indian state of Jammu and Kashmir, which challenges the territorial integrity of India.

The Sino-Indian relations in the present international scenario has to be perceived by taking into consideration the presence of USA. India's nuclear deal with USA can be seen as a strategy to balance off China. Therefore, a balance of power situation in South Asia has emerged where US economic and strategic partnership with India can help India to gain a stronger foothold in South Asia.

India was quick in extending official recognition to the emergence of Peoples Republic of China in 1949. Diplomatic relations between the two were established on 1 April 1950. In 1954, a pathbreaking agreement between China and India which recognized the five principles of *Panchsheel* of mutual existence. India also formally recognized Chinese sovereignty over Tibet. From the year 1954–56, the spirit of friendship *hindi-chini bhai bhai* flourished. There were visits by Chinese Premiere Zhou Enlai to India and also Nehru to China. However, this spirit soon witnessed a downturn with publications of

---

***Stapled Visas** When the visas for a visiting country are issued on a separate paper rather than on the passport it is called stapled visa. After the immigration, officers would not stamp one's passport if one is carrying a stapled visa's.

Chinese maps showing large portion of Indian territory as Chinese possessions. In late 1950s, the Chinese started building Sinkiang-Tibet road followed by several Chinese incursions in Barahoti and Aksai Chin areas. In 1958, Chinese troops intruded Lohit division of NEFA/Arunachal. In 1959, Chinese suppression of Tibetan revolt and fleeing of Dalai Lama to India where he was given political asylum hurt terribly the bilateral relations. The year 1962 was an eventful year as the two neighbours clashed. The Sino-Indian border war embittered relations further. Taking advantage of Sino-Indian animosity, Pakistan seized the opportunity to develop friendly relations with China. However, relations eased in early 1970s. Mao emphasized the re-establishment of friendship in 1970 which came to be known as 'Mao Smile'. In 1971, an Indian Table Tennis team participated in the Afro-Asian Friendship Table tennis Championship. During the Bangladesh war and India's role in it, China though was not on Indian side yet reaction was not hostile. Again a jolt in the relationship came with the Pokhran-I explosion and Sikkim's accession to India. In 1975, there was restoration of normalcy, and K.R. Narayan was designated as India's ambassador to China. Later in the 1970s economic relations witnessed a positive turn. In 1979, after 30 years of any visist by high level dignitary to China, Vajpayee visited China but midway terminated the visit and returned due to Chinese aggression of Vietnam. The year 1980 again saw differences over Chinese policies towards Afghanistan, Pakistan, Vietnam, Cambodia and boundary issues. Regarding border negotiations differences arose over whether there would be separate discussions on each sector as per Indian demand or a package deal as per Chinese intentions. In 1986, despite boundary negotiations, China intruded into Indian territory in Arunachal Pradesh.

However, a positive change in the bilateral relations with Rajiv Gandhi's visit to China. His visit to China in December 1989, was symbolic in the sense that India accepted the Chinese view-point of broadening exchange in other areas without making these developments contingent on the resolution of border issue. A much more relaxed relationship evolved after Rajiv Gandhi's visit to China, which was briefly disturbed due to the Pokhran explosion of May 1998. Nevertheless, after a short interregnum of adverse reaction between the two, normalcy resumed and relations continued on the course set by Rajiv Gandhi. Two sides arrived at a decision to constitute a Joint Working Group (JWG) to deal with boundary dispute. In December 1991, the Chinese Premier Li Peng visited India, the first visit by a Chinese PM after a lapse of 31 years. Both sides agreed to maintain tranquility in the area along LAC pending final settlement. The first Indian President to visit China was President R. Venkataraman. He made a six-day trip to China from 19–25 May 1992. Prime Minister Narasimha Rao also visited China in 1993. On all these occasions, the border problem was kept aside and negotiations were held in other fields of interest of both the countries.

In 1993, another major breakthrough came when P.V. Narasimha Rao visited China, and two signed an *Agreement on Maintenance of Peace and*

Tranquility Along the Line of Actual Control in the China-India Border Areas. The implication of this agreement was that the two sides would respect the LAC along the Himalayan frontier and not to conduct military manoeuvre in the designated zones. It was also agreed to set up India-China Expert Group of Diplomatic and Military officers to assist the work of JWG. During the United Front Government tenure, with China, the UF Government followed the course chartered by Rajiv Gandhi and made significant development and a high level visit was made by the Chinese President and General Secretary of the Communist Party, Jiang Zeminin November, 1996.

In 1995, both India and China agreed to dismantle four closed military posts, setting up of four border pots, establishment of four meeting points between their military personnel and pull back their troops in close proximity to the Sumdorong Chu Valley in the eastern sector. The year 1996 also saw the visit by the First President of China till then. Jian Zemin visited India and both sides agreed to take several confidence building measures.

In the year 1998, with Vajpayee as the Prime Minister there were some ups and downs in Sino-Indian relations. China sent a high-powered delegation led by China's Chief of General Staff of the People's Liberation Army (PLA) General Fu Quanyou to India in April 1998 to discuss several bilateral issues. But the Indo-China relations got a jolt due to the Pokhran explosion and also because of pointing out to China as an impending danger to India's security. This earned the Chinese ire and its condemnation of the nuclear tests along with the other major powers. However, gradually, Indo-Chinese relationship began to get normalized following visits by the then External Affairs Minister, Jaswant Singh in 1999, and President K.R. Narayan in 2000. In 1999, border negotiations were held. In 2000, both countries celebrated 50th anniversary of their diplomatic relations between the two countries. In 2001, Li Peng visited India. In 2002, Chinese Premier Zhu Ronji visited India. Several agreements and MoUs were signed pertaining to tourism, sharing of hydrological information regarding the Brahmaputra river, peaceful use of outer space, cooperation in science technology and exchange of personnel. In March 2002, Air links were established with China Eastern Airlines starting direct services and Air India commencing services from December 2003. In 2003, Indian Prime Minister Vajpayee paid a visit to China. The signing of a memorandum on opening border trade through Sikkim is thought to have its obvious implications in starting the process of China recognizing—de facto first, but eventually de jure—that Sikkim is a part of India after its accession in 1975 to India. Sikkim was also dropped from the Chinese website after Vajpayee's path-breaking visit to China. In 2004, India and China signed an agreement on border trade which aimed at opening a border trading point through Nathu La followed by China's acceptance of status of India as part of India. Border Trade with India through Nathu La was opened in 2006. The other two passes were opened earlier in 2003. They are Namgaya Shipkila in Himachal Pradesh and Lipulekh (Gunji) in Uttaranchal.

During the first term of UPA-I in April 2005, Chinese Premier Wen Jiabao visited India, and in November 2006 President Hu Jintao visited India. Yet irritants remained regarding unresolved border problems and Chinese and Pakistani bonhomie. In 2007, Chinese President visited India and 13 Agreements and MoUs were signed. In 2008, Prime Minister Manmohan Singh visited China and both sides expressed eagerness to strengthen India-China Strategic and Cooperative Partnership for Peace and Prosperity and upheld the success of first joint military training exercise. In 2009, the 13th round of border talks took place despite China reassertion of Arunachal Pradesh as part of its territory. The 14th round of boundary talks focussing on finding a framework for a final settlement of disputed areas was held in Beijing in November 2010. There was no headway in this round of talks like earlier ones and deadlock still continues, because of mutual accusation of retaining or intruding and occupying areas along boundary.

The year 2010 marked the 60th anniversary of establishment of diplomatic relations between the two countries. The Indian President Pratibha Devisingh Patil arrived in Beijing on 27 May 2010 for a six-day visit to China and was welcomed by Chinese Premier Wen Jiabao at the Purple Light Pavilion. She received red carpet welcome as the first Indian Head of the State to visit China in a decade. Both sides discussed bilateral issues pertaining to trade and commerce. Particularly, sources said that Mrs. Patil sought China's support for India's bid for the permanent seat in the UNSC. Further, an agreement streamlining the visa formalities of airline staff of two countries by Indian Foreign Secretary Nirupama Rao and Chinese Assistant Foreign Minister Hu Zhengyue during Mrs. Patils's visit to China was worked out. A MoU for cooperation in the field of civil services and public administration was also signed between the two. Prime Minister Manmohan Singh met his Chinese counterpart Wen Jiabao at Hanoi in the sidelines of ASEAN Summit in July 2010. Premier Wen Jiabao's arrived in India on a three-day visit on 15 December 2010. (See details on pages 391–392).

In 2011, Prime Minister Manmohan Singh visited China to attend the BRICS Summit at Sanya, China. In the sidelines of the BRICS Summit, Dr. Singh met Chinese President Hu Jintao in April 2011. The External Affairs Minister visited China on 8 February 2012. India-China relations were aimed at transcending differences in their bilateral matters. They reviewed the outstanding issues in Indo-China relations and agreed to work to resolve them. To take the relations beyond bilateral cooperation they agreed that these do not adversely affect the growing cooperation in other areas. Both sides pledged to carry that forward into 2012 and agreed to mark it as the "**Year of India-China Friendship and Cooperation.**" Prime Minister Manmohan Singh also had a meeting with the Chinese Prime Minister Wen Jiabao in Rio de Janeiro on sidelines of Rio + 20 Summit in June 2012. He met his Chinese counterpart on the sidelines of the ASEAN summit in Cambodia, where the two leaders discussed ways to move forward on the vexed boundary issue in November.

However, soon after this a fresh row erupted again over China's depiction of Arunachal Pradesh and Aksai Chin as part of its territory in maps of China in its new e-passports. Despite such uneasiness, the 2nd India-China Strategic Economic Dialogue took place in New Delhi on 26 November 2012, which emphasized the increasing economic engagement between India and China.

China has bypassed USA, as India's largest trading partner in 2008. However, the trade imbalance is a worrying factor. India's trade deficit stands at over $20 billion, which is higher that the trade deficit in 2009 that stood at $15.87 billion. Both again are competing in African and Latin American countries to get access to oil reserves. China's intention to divert the Brahmaputra River is also a major fear for India. With much reluctance and initial negation, China accommodated India into Shanghai Cooperation Organization (SCO) as an observer. This was again done to protect its Central Asian interest and curb growing American presence in the Central Asian and Caspian Sea region for the hydrocarbon reserves. China openly does not support India's bid to permanent member of UNSC. However, both India and China have started interacting at the BRICS multilateral. They also participate in the Trilateral Summit involving Russia, China and India. The Tenth Trilateral Foreign Ministers Meet was held in Wuhan in 2010. The Eleventh Trilateral was held in April 2012. However, India is worried about the border problems and China's military design over Indian territories like Aksai Chin, Sikkim, Arunachal Pradesh and road buildups in Tibet and largest land port in Nepal, which will connect Xigaze with Nepal by rail. To ward-off the Chinese threat, India has plans to upgrade six air-strips (Advanced landing Ground) along the 40 km of the border, revamp border posts modernization of Airfield infrastructure and other measures.

Nuclear deal signed between India and United States of America can be seen as a strategy by India to balance China's growing influence over India's neighbours. The India-Japan-South Korea trilateral seeks to reinforce the India-Japan-US trilateral dialogue that also focuses on expanding strategic and maritime cooperation. Beijing has not come out in the open about the India-Japan-South Korea trilateral, but it has been uneasy about the three powers in the region getting together which can be dubbed as an exercise in encirclement of a rising China.

INDIA AND HER NEIGHBOURS

India and Pakistan

Two Countries, India and Pakistan were born out of the partition of British India, in 1947. The two, since their births, have been archrivals. Their relationship has seen many ups and downs. The major irritants in their relation have been disputes pertaining to borders, distribution/sharing of river waters, territorial disputes, Afghanistan, cross-border terrorism and above all Kashmir.

Liberation of Bangladesh in 1971 and India's role in it still disturbs the Pakistani minds.

The two countries have problem over the Siachen Glacier. India's position is that Pakistan should accept the **actual ground position line** (AGPL) on Siachen where its troops have been in position since 1984. Pakistan demands that India should pull back to the position occupied in 1972. The Siachen figures as one of the eight issues of the composite dialogue process. Regarding Sir Creek* both sides are forwarding their claims and undefined boundary is complicating the issue. Fishermen are often caught and jailed. The Wullar Barrage-Tulbul Project dating back to 1985 also invited the Pakistani ire. Pakistan saw it as a violation of the Indus Water Treaty (IWT), 1960. After rounds of failed negotiations in the recent years both sides have agreed to work out an early and amicable solution on the basis of technical consultations and the provisions of the IWT, 1960. The Baglihar Hydropower project was started by India in 1999. This has also been objected to by Pakistan on similar grounds. Pakistan alleges India of violating the IWT, 1960. In January 2005, Secretary-level talks were held, but without much result. Ultimately the matter was referred to the World Bank which appointed Prof. Raymond Lafitte as the Neutral Expert (NE) to study the project and consider Pakistan's objections to the project. The Kishenganga Hydropower project being built by India on the Jhelum River has been objected to by Pakistan. Similar arguments and allegations of violation of IWT, 1960 have been raised. There is also apprehension on the part of Pakistan regarding manipulation of water flow of river by India. Pakistan has also objected to the construction of the Nimoo Bazgo project in Leh on the grounds of pondage level and slit flushing.

However, the two major irritants that have embittered the Indo-Pak relations have been the issues of Kashmir and terrorism. Kashmir, from the very inception has been a contentious issue. Failing to wrest Kashmir from India immediately after independence by sending the Pushtun raiders in September 1947, and in 1965, Pakistan opted for subversive means of disturbing peace and security of India. Proxy war in Kashmir and Punjab was damaging for India. In 1971, following the Bangladesh liberation war, another Indo-Pak war was fought. In the context of the 1965 and 1971 war two milestone agreements were reached between India and Pakistan. The first one was the Tashkent Declaration of 10 January 1966 and the other one was the Simla Agreement of 1972. However, Kashmir still is a thorny issue between the both, and relations suffer much due to Pak support of militants who receive training and sanctuary in Pakistan.

Significantly attached to the Kashmir issue is the case of terrorism and Pakistani involvement not only in Kashmir but also aiming to destabilize entire Indian peace and security. The 26/11 Terrorist attack in Mumbai, Pune blasts and a series of blasts in different parts of India, and their Pakistani connection

---

*Sir Creek**   A 60 miles of long strip of watery marsh with patches of land situated in the Rann of Kutch. Sir Creek divides the Kutch region of Gujarat and the Sind province of Pakistan.

have pushed the Indo-Pak relations to a nadir. The David Headley episode and the ISI connections and operations of militant groups in Pakistan like the Lashkar-e-Taiba point to the gravity of India's security concerns.

Added to this was the military buildup and ensuing arms race between both the countries, which threatens the stability of South Asian region. Alarming is that Pakistan from very early stage received arms and financial assistance from USA who aimed at containment of Communist expansion. Apprehensions of diversions of these assistances against fuelling proxy war against India have always troubled India. Another worrying factor for India was roping in of Pakistan into US sponsored Military alliances like the Baghdad Pact (1955-58), SEATO (1954) and CENTO (1958-79). This had conditioned Indian posture of adopting the non-aligned stance.(see Chapter 8 on Non-Alignment-Page 164) The Indo-China war of 1962 derailed the relations and taking advantage of the animosity between India and China, Pakistan began cultivating ties with China.

Despite such differences, both sides have struggled to move ahead in their bilateral relations. In 1983 Joint Commission was set up to increase cooperation in various sectors like industry, culture, education, tourism, information and scientific exchanges. Both reiterated to develop peaceful relations on the basis of mutual cooperation. This positive development got a jolt due to acquisition of Harpoone missiles by Pakistan and supply of arms and training to Sikh militants. In 1984, after the assassination of Indira Gandhi when her son Rajiv Gandhi became the PM he took up measures to improve relations with Pakistan. Another Joint Commission was set up to look into various aspects of bilateral cooperation.

In 1985, both countries pledged not to attack each other's nuclear installations. However, again relations got a blow and Rajiv Gandhi postponed his visit to Islamabad. In 1987, virtually the relations got ruptured due to heavy troop movements on both sides and clashes in the undemarcated region of the Siachen Glacier as well as acquisition of sophisticated weapons by Pakistan from USA. In 1988, with the restoration of democracy in Pakistan and assumption of the office of PM by Benazir Bhutto, relations again eased. Rajiv Gandhi visited Islamabad an signed three accords pertaining not to attack each others nuke installations, promotion and development of relations in the sectors like art, culture, archeology, education, mass media and sports and avoidance of double taxation on income derived from international air transport to facilitate airlines operation to both countries. India also facilitated Pak's entry into Commonwealth from which Pak had withdrawn in 1972. Again relations got strained as Pakistan tried to develop nuke capacity. Bhutto visited Pyongyang to negotiate a deal for exchange of missiles and missile technology from North Korea. In 1989, there was slight improvement of relations with several cooperative measures in economic, medical, agricultural and cultural fields and easing of travel facilities as well as decision for coordinated patrolling by both sides. The years 1990 and 1991 also saw some more improvements and high-level meetings between the two countries. However, there were clashes between

Pak troops and Indian army in September in the Kemi area of Poonch sector, and in October 1991 there was a Pak attack on an Indian outpost in Kargil. In 1992, tension arose due to Ayodhya crisis, failure of Siachen talks and even attempt by Azad Kashmir force to cross border. In 1994, Indian Consulate in Karachi was closed.

During the Prime Ministership of P.V. Narasimha Rao (1991–1996) Indo-Pak relations continued to be strained following the accelerated pace of development of Pak's nuclear capability with the assistance from China and North Korea. Further, the demolition of Babri Masjid on 7 December 1992 deteriorated the relation between the two.

In 1996, when the United Front Government under I.K. Gujral came to power, Prime Minister Gujral introduced a new dimension of India's foreign policy. He introduced a concept which came to be identified as *Gujral Doctrine*, and it was chalked with a vision to improve India's relations with her neighbour without expecting reciprocity. India tried to melt the ice by initiating the process of bilateral talks, but Pakistan under Bhutto backed out. With the assumption of office of PM by Nawaz Sharif there were certain improvements in the Indo-Pak relations. Though there was no substantial breakthrough and Kashmir remained the most contentious issue, yet both sides agreed to carry out the dialogue process.

With the assumption of Prime Ministership of A.B. Vajpayee, relations suffered due to the Pokhran explosion on 11 May 1998. Pakistan responded by nuke explosions at Chaghai on 13 May 1998. India however, again made efforts to improve the bilateral relations. Vajpayee as a part of confidence-building measure with Pakistan inaugurated a bus service in February 1999, and he himself took the inaugural bus service to visit the then Prime Minister of Pakistan, Nawaz Sharif in February at Lahore. This was followed by signing of Memorandum of Understanding (MoU) reaffirming their unilateral moratorium on further nuclear testing and spelling out their confidence-building measures. But the Kargil adventurism of Pakistan in May-June 1999 under General Musharraf disrupted the peace process. Gradually, relations showed improvement and this was followed by General Musharaff's visit to India for talks in Agra in July 2001. But the talks failed to make any notable breakthrough and even later the thaw in Indo-Pak relation continued because of Pakistan's insistence of linking Kashmir as the core issue always rejected by India and cross border terrorism being highlighted by India and rejected by Pakistan. The Kandahar episode (hijacking of an Indian Airlines Plane IC 814 after it left Kathmandu to Kandahar) revealed the Pakistani connection of the militants either helped or given shelter by Pakistan. Therefore, like the efforts of the previous governments, the Vajpayee government failed to melt the ice in the Indo-Pak relations and stalemate continued.

President Musharaff during his second visit to New Delhi on 17 April 2005 declared that the peace process had become irreversible and there was again another round of fresh confidence-building measures, pledge to solve the

Kashmir issue, the possible resumption of Lahore-Amritsar bus service and re-establishment of consulates at Karachi and Mumbai. However, nothing concrete was actualized in reality. Efforts of peace dialogue made thereafter were severely paralyzed due to increasing number of terrorist acts in India and alleged involvement of Pakistan or of terrorists based in Pakistan. India, under the Prime Ministership of Dr. Manmohan Singh expressed grave concern over the safety of Pakistan's nuclear arsenal, as there always looms a possibility of the nuclear arsenals falling into the hands of terrorists. Further relations got derailed with the 26/11 Mumbai terror attacks and revelations of Pakistani connections.

However, again on the sidelines of the 15th NAM Summit (Sharm el-Sheikh, 2009) Dr. Manmohan Singh met the Pakistani PM Yousuf Raza Gilani and both strove to make serious efforts towards positive improvement in Indo-Pak relations despite several glitches. India dropped her insistence of holding talks with Pakistan only after those involved in Mumbai terror attacks have been punished. India delinked 'composite dialogue' from terrorism. The joint statement issued after the second top level meeting since the 26/11 Mumbai terror attacks declared, "Both the Prime Ministers recognized that dialogue is the only way forward. Action on terrorism should not be linked to the composite dialogue process and these should not be bracketed." Kashmir did not figure in the joint statement which is always under the composite dialogue process. Prime Minister Manmohan Singh expressed India's readiness to "discuss all issues with Pakistan including all outstanding issues". Responding to Dr. Singh's statement in the Lok Sabha on the India–Pakistan joint statement in Egypt, Pakistani PM Gilani reciprocated the 'sentiments of peace' and expressed the meeting as one where both leaders had agreed that terrorism was a common threat and dialogue is the only way to take relations in a positive direction. But the opposition slammed New Delhi's stance for delinking of the 'composite dialogue' with Pakistan. Dr. Singh, however, reaffirmed that delinking of dialogue process with Pakistan from its action against terrorism was not a dilution of India's stand, but strengthening of it.

The year 2010 began with several developments in Indo-Pak relations though not very fruitful in every respect. Despite Pakistan's accusation that India has broken off the composite dialogue process and efforts to isolate it diplomatically, there were Foreign Secretary Level Talk (FSLT) on 25 February 2010; Sidelines Meeting at the 16th SAARC Summit, Thimpu, on April 2010; Foreign Secretary Level Talk on 24 June 2010; and SAARC Home Ministers Meeting, Islamabad, 25 June 2010. However the Indo-Pak relations suffered a setback during the Foreign Ministers Meet in Islamabad on 16 July 2010. Indian Foreign Minister Krishnan and his Pak counterpart Shah Mahmood Qureshi soon got caught in a diplomatic imbroglio when Pak refused to engage in any substantial manner with the critical areas of 26/11, cross-border terrorism and infiltration by arguing that it could not speed up the judicial process (see page 385–387 for details).

On 28–29 March 2011, a meeting was held between the Home Secretary of India, G.K. Pillai and Interior Secretary of Pakistan, Q.Z. Chaudhury. This was a step towards further easing of the tensed bilateral relations and resumption of talks. These talks were followed by a meeting of the India Pakistan Judicial Committee on Prisoners to discuss the issue of inadvertent boundary crossers and other related issues like verification of nationality and humane treatment of prisoners especially women and children. Both sides had released a number of fishermen and civilians who were languishing in the jails of the two countries.

The Minister of External Affairs of India, S.M. Krishna and the Minister of Foreign Affairs of Pakistan, Ms. Hina Rabbani Khar met in New Delhi on 27 July 2011. The Ministerial level talks were preceded by a meeting between the Foreign Secretaries of India and Pakistan on 26 July 2011. The meeting reviewed the status of bilateral relations on the issues of Counter-Terrorism (including progress on Mumbai trial) and Narcotics Control; Humanitarian issues; Commercial and Economic cooperation; Wullar Barrage/Tulbul Navigation Project; Sir Creek; Siachen; Peace and Security including CBMs; Jammu and Kashmir; and promotion of friendly exchanges.

The Minister of Foreign Affairs of Pakistan Hina Rabbani Khar and the Minister of External Affairs of India S.M. Krishna met in Islamabad on 8 September 2012, for a meeting to review progress in the Dialogue process. The Ministerial level talks were preceded by a meeting between the Foreign Secretaries of Pakistan and India on 7 September 2012. They held substantive discussions on a wide range of issues within the framework of the dialogue process, and expressed satisfaction over the progress achieved since their last review meeting in July 2011. They upheld the importance of carrying forward the dialogue process with a view to resolving peacefully all outstanding issues through constructive and result-oriented engagement, and to establish friendly, cooperative and good neighbourly relations between Pakistan and India. Keeping with the spirit of the Agreement reached between the two countries on 8 September 2012, the Seventh Round of Expert Level Talks on Nuclear CBMs was held on 28 December 2012. India and Pakistan reviewed the implementation and strengthening of Nuclear CBMs like the existing Agreements on pre-Notification on Flight Tests of Ballistic Missiles and Reducing the Risk from Accidents relating to Nuclear Weapons. However, in early January 2013, the alleged killing of two Indian soldiers along the LOC by Pakistani troops and insistence of Pakistan to involve UN Military Observer Group for India and Pakistan (UNMOGIP) to probe the incident have again derailed the bilateral relation between India and Pakistan.

India's relation with Pakistan is always not at ease. The Kashmir issue and cross-border terrorism haunt the relations especially with India insisting action being taken against those involve in a spate of terror acts/attacks in India. India has handed over a list of "most wanted" including the names of Hafiz Saeed (founder of Lashkar) and also Dawood Ibrahim and others involved in 26/11 attack, 1993 Mumbai serial blasts, IC-814 hijacking, 2001 attack on Parliament and other terror activities in Punjab, J&K and in other parts of India. **Operation Neptune Spear** conducted by US Navy SEAL that carried out the killing of Osama bin Laden in Abbottabad surely affirms India's hue and cry over the issue of cross-border terrorism and security threat is not unreal. The closeness of Pakistan to China and the latter's interest to fully utilize Pakistan's strategic position as a gateway to the Persian Gulf, West Asia and Africa is surely of a great concern to India. With this intention China has helped Pakistan develop it Gwadar Port. Pakistan's nuclear design is a sure threat to India's security. The emergence of the Beijing-Pyongyang-Islamabad-Naypyidaw-Tehran axis must condition India's foreign policy concern. Internal condition of Pakistan which is quite unstable is a concern for India. How much political power is under the control of civilian government is questionable. Military plays a decisive role. The ISI is alleged to be operating from the soil of India's other neighbours like Nepal and Bangladesh, and also trying to establish links with India's insurgent forces, which is hindering security of India. Further, Pakistan is a prominent member of Coffee Club.* Yet, the silver lining is that both are keen to increase their economic cooperation. Pakistan gave India the assurance to grant MFN status. India has to make efforts to reduce the 'trust deficit' if she wants to ensure the actualization of the Turkey-Afghanistan-Pakistan-India (TAPI) and Iran-Pakistan-India (IPI) pipelines. Both should think beyond the contentious issues and try to improve relations and establish peace and security in the South Asian region by combating terrorism and other subversive activities hindering peace and security.

India and Bangladesh

India had played a pivotal role in the emergence of the current state of Bangladesh on 26 March 1971. India had given full-fledged support to the Bangladesh's 'Mukti bahini' in its fight for the liberation of Bangladesh from Pakistan. India and Bangladesh share a common border of approximately 4096 km bordering 4 Indian states of West Bengal, Assam, Meghalaya, Tripura and Mizoram. Both countries share cultural affinities, especially the state of West Bengal and also ethnic linkages with the North Eastern states.

However, tensions in the Indo-Bangladesh relation crop from various issues like the Farrakha Barrage, Moore island, border-dispute (including Teen Bigha Corridor), border fencing, illegal migration, Chakma refugees, border crimes, human trafficking, smuggling, trade and transit issues and Land Boundary Agreement.

Coffee Club* Countries that strongly oppose the G4 countries—Brazil, Germany, India, and Japan's bids for permanent seats in the United Nations Security Council have formed the *Uniting for Consensus movement*, or the *Coffee Club*. The most vocal countries of this group are Italy, South Korea, Mexico, Argentina and Pakistan. In East Asia, both China and South Korea heavily oppose Japan's bid. In Europe, Italy, Spain and the Netherlands all oppose a seat for Germany. In Latin America, Argentina, Colombia and Mexico are opposing a seat for Brazil. In Asia, Pakistan is opposing India's bid.

Right after its birth, Bangladesh entered into a 25 year Treaty of Cooperation, Friendship and Peace. This was patterned almost on the lines of Indo-Soviet Treaty of Peace, Friendship and Cooperation signed in 1971. Both countries pledged to fight against colonialism, racialism, imperialism and work towards strengthening peace and security. Both countries also agreed to cooperate in various sectors like economic, scientific, technical, trade, transport and communication. The Land Boundary Agreement (LBA) was signed between both the countries in 1974. However, the LBA has not been implemented in totality. Three issues still create trouble in Indo-Bangladesh relation. They are like the demarcation of 6.5 km of the border in three sectors of Lathililla-Dumabari (Assam Sector), South Berubari (West Bengal Sector) and Muhuri river/Belonia sector (Tripura Sector), exchange of adverse possessions and exchange of enclaves. In 2001, the two countries established the Joint Boundary Working Group (JNWG) to make recommendations for the contentious border issues.

The Nuclear test by India in 1974 was not looked at adversely by Bangladesh. However, later differences over Farakka barrage, Mujib's policies, New Moore island dispute and Chinese and Pakistani propaganda against India as having an imperialist agenda over Bangladesh embittered the relation. However, beginning of 1980s saw a change. In 1977, a short-term agreement was signed. This agreement specified the quantum of water that the two countries were to withdraw. In 1982, the two countries reached an interim accord on Ganga water. Under this agreement the Farakka Agreement of 1977 was terminated. Subsequently in 1983, 1985 accords were signed for sharing of Ganga water. However, tensions continued over inclusion of Nepal and plan of action for dry season flow of Ganga and augmentation of water supply at Farakka and sharing of waters. In 1996, Indo-Bangla Ganga Accord was signed. This was a 30 year water sharing Treaty, which was signed in New Delhi. This Treaty is reviewed after every five year. It was agreed that if water level drops sharply then both sides will share the available quantum of water on a 50:50 basis.

The Chakma problem have disturbed for long the Indo-Bangladesh relations. For long, there have been allegations against India of supporting the *Shantibahini* (the armed wing of the Parbatya Chattagram Jana Sanghati Samiti (PCJSS). However, with the signing of the Peace Accord between the Chakmas and the Awami League, and finally assassination of Manabendra Narayan Larma, the movement faded. In 1997, Bangladesh agreed to repatriate 80,000 tribal Chakma refugees from India. In 1999, both countries started Calcutta-Dhaka bus service followed by signing of an agreement to resume goods train link after 26 years in 2000. In 2003, India gave some trade benefits to Bangladesh. India agreed to grant duty-free access to some Bangladesh products. The year 2003 marked the beginning of comprehensive talks about Free Trade Agreement (FTA). The External Affairs Minister of India Natwar Singh visited Bangladesh in August 2005. Further, Prime Minister of India visited Dhaka in November 2005 on the occasion of attending SAARC Summit and met Bangladesh Prime Minister Begum Khaleda Zia. Begum Khaleda Zia also visited India in March 2006. This visit was followed by two agreements which were regarding Revised trade Agreement and the Agreement for Mutual Cooperation between India and Bangladesh for Preventing Illicit Trafficking in Narcotic Drugs and Psychotropic Substances. In 2007 the then External Affairs Minister Pranab Mukherjee visited Bangladesh and extended invitation to the Bangladeshi Prime Minister to participate in the 14th SAARC Summit which was to be held in New Delhi from 3–4 April 2007. The Foreign Office Consultations (FOC) were held in Dhaka in June 2007. Eighth Home Secretary level talks were held in New Delhi in August 2007 regarding border management. The biannual border coordination conference was held in New Delhi in October 2007. According to the decision of the third Joint Boundary Working Group meeting which was held in Dhaka July 2006, delegations from both sides for the first time made joint visits to a few enclaves and adverse possessions in May 2007.

In 2008, Sheikh Hasina won the election and became the new Prime Minister of Bangladesh. India extended its feelers to Bangladesh. Former External Affairs Minister Pranab Mukherjee visited Bangladesh and held comprehensive discussions regarding security matters, issues of common concern like cross-border terrorism, peaceful management of the indo-Bangladesh borders, demarcation of land boundaries and Indian maritime boundaries. Two agreements were signed on bilateral trade and bilateral investment promotion and protection. This was followed by visit by Foreign Minister of Bangladesh Dipu Moni to India from 7–10 September 2009. This visit was followed by discussions on bilateral issues and also the contentious issue over a proposed hydel dam in India's North-east. Both India and Bangladesh agreed to conclude three agreements pertaining to—mutual legal assistance on criminal matters; transfer of sentenced persons; and combat of international terrorism, organized crime and illegal drug trafficking.

During 10–13 January 2010, the Prime Minister of Bangladesh, Sheikh Hasina visited India. India extended a line of credit worth one billion dollars on the terms of Asian Development Bank for infrastructural upgradation of Bangladesh. India also agreed to construct the Akhaura-Agartala rail link, provide 250 megawatts of electricity per day from the Indian power grid and deferred plans to construct the 1500 MW Tipaimukh hydroelectric dam on the Barak in Manipur to which Bangladesh has reservations. It was also agreed that border markets would be set up along the Bangladesh-Meghalaya border and land customs posts on the Mizoram border. Forty-seven commodities were removed from the negative list, despite serious concern about the fall out. Bangladesh promised India's access to the Ashuganj inland port and also India, Nepal and Bhutan's access to deep-water ports at Mongla and Chittagong. Bangladesh also expressed willingness to revive old land-border rail transit points and also prevent its soil from being used against India. Bangladesh also agreed to negotiate an extradition treaty, formation of a joint boundary group to address the land border and a team from Bangladesh to discuss maritime boundary. Sheikh Hasina expressed her satisfaction from the visit.

In August 2010, the Finance Minister Pranab Mukherjee visited Dhaka to witness the signing of US $1 billion Line of Credit Agreement to Bangladesh. In November 2010, Bangladeshi Foreign Minister, Dipu Moni visited Tripura and 'Bharat-Bangladesh Maitree Udyaan' was also inaugurated at Chottakhola in Tripura. Her visit was followed by visit by Advisors to Prime Minister to India in December 2010. They held discussions on bilateral issues and follow up of the spirit of Joint Communiqué issued during the visit of Prime Minister Sheikh Hasina. In May 2011, a high powered Indian delegation visited Bangladesh under the Vice President of India, Hamid Ansari to commemorate the 150th birth anniversary of Rabindranath Tagore.

In July 2011, the External Affairs Minister of India, S.M. Krishna paid a visit to Bangladesh and held discussions with Bangladeshi Foreign Minister Dipu Moni. Both sides reviewed the progress made in the bilateral relations since the signing of the Joint Communiqué during the visit of Sheikh Hasina.

Prime Minister Dr. Manmohan Singh visited Bangladesh in September 2011. The two countries discussed matters like mutual legal assistance in criminal matters, transfer of sentenced persons and fight against international terrorism, organized crime and illicit drug trafficking. The highlight of this meeting has been the signing of a new land border agreement to resolve long-standing border dispute. A vision statement laying out a long-term relationship between India and Bangladesh was signed. However, on sharing of waters of Teesta River, no deal could be struck due to the objection raised by the Chief Minister of West Bengal, Smt. Mamata Banerjee.

At the invitation of the External Affairs Minister, the Foreign Minister of Bangladesh Dr. Dipu Moni paid an official visit to India during 7–8 May 2012. The first meeting of the India-Bangladesh Joint Consultative Commission (JCC), as envisaged in the Framework Agreement on Cooperation for Development signed during the visit of the Prime Minister of India to Bangladesh, was held in New Delhi on 7 May 2012. Discussions were held around issues like political and security cooperation, trade and connectivity, development cooperation, bilateral cooperation in water resources and power, sub-regional cooperation and people-to-people contacts.

Begum Khaleda Zia, leader of the opposition party in Bangladesh, the Bangladesh Nationalist Party (BNP), was on a week-long visit to India from 28 October to 3 November 2012. She met new External Affairs Minister of India, Salman Khurshid. She focused on the future vision of Indo-Bangladesh relations without harping on the past. Her party Bangladesh Nationalist Party (BNP) has traditionally taken anti-India stance. She met Prime Minister Manmohan Singh and External Affairs Minister Salman Khurshid. She reassured that Bangladeshi soil will not be used for anti-Indian activities. She also pressed India for signing the Teesta Pact. Her visit however, was not received with much ease by Sheikh Hasina's Government. A number of outstanding pacts between India and Bangladesh involving Teesta water sharing, land demarcation and land boundary agreements may well be used by Begum Zia during election in 2013. India is quietly performing a balancing act. India's traditional pro-Awami League policy is being balanced by India's efforts to reach out to the BNP as in the 2013 elections, there may be change in government in Bangladesh. So India by inviting Begum Zia kept the doors of negotiations open.

Problems persist in the Indo-Bangladesh relations relating to boundary, water sharing, terrorism and other issues. Yet both countries have taken steps to do the damage control. A Joint Boundary Working Group (JBWG) has been established which aims at resolution of outstanding land boundary related issues. India also had offered support to the Cyclone Sidr hit Bangladesh, in 2007. The Bilateral Investment Promotion and Protection Agreement (BIPPA) signed on 9 February 2009, and enforced on 7 July 2011, is hoped to improve investment flows between the two. Substantial duty concession has also been extended by India to Bangladesh under SAFTA, SAPTA and APTA. India already has declared at the 14th SAARC Summit held in New Delhi in April 2007, that it will give zero duty market access, w.e.f. 1 January 2008, for products originating from SAARC LDCs including Bangladesh except for some items on the sensitive list. India also has extended a huge line of credit to Bangladesh. Various MoUs related to trade, enhanced power sector cooperation and waiving of ban on rice and wheat export to Bangladesh among others show a positive progress in the bilateral relations. Bangladesh also supports India's bid to the permanent membership in the UNSC.

However, there are certain issues which continue to estrange relations. The illegal cross-border migration from Bangladesh which is creating tensions in India's North-east. Most importantly, the increase of fundamentalist forces in Bangladesh and their connection with international terrorist organization is a matter of serious concern for India. Added to this is the ISI links with the anti-Indian terror outfits operating from Bangladesh or aiding those operating in India. In 2007, only several hundred alleged members of two banned organizations, Harkat-ul-Jihad-al-Islami, Bangladesh (Huji-B) and Jamaatul Mujahideen Bangladesh (JMB) were arrested. There are reports of other groups operating in Bangladesh and some having links with international terrorist organizations. Above all, Chinese connection with Bangladesh again is a worry for India. Sheikh Hasina visited China in March 2010, and the two countries have agreed to help each other. Bangladesh has agreed to provide transit facility to China, requested China to assist in construction of a highway passing through Myanmar to Yunnan province of China and construction of a rail network following the same path. Bangladesh has also sought assistance in development of the Chittagong port and deep sea port at Sonadia Island along with defence cooperation. In 2008, Bangladesh with the assistance of China constructed a missile launch pad near Chittagong port. Chinese Vice President Xi Jinping paid a return visit to Bangladesh. Even Begum Khaleda Zia, prior to her visit to India, paid a visit to China on 14 October 2012. Thus, this growing influence of China over Bangladesh must be taken into consideration by India. India must try to bolster bilateral relations with Bangladesh as it is trying to do so by concretizining economic relation. Territorial dispute, illegal migration, terrorism and even problem of water sharing are problems quite difficult to be resolved so India must enhance strategic cooperation with Bangladesh.

India and Sri Lanka

India has very old ties with Sri Lanka dating back to the times of Ashoka. Ashoka had sent his son Mahendra and daughter Sanghamitra for propagation of Buddhism in the island country. The year 2011 marked the celebration of 2600th anniversary of the enlightenment of Buddha in both India and Sri Lanka.

The major irritants however, in Indo-Sri Lankan relations have been the issue of stateless persons of Indian origin, issue of Liberation Tigers of Tamil Eelam (LTTE), demand of establishing Indian Ocean as a zone of peace, differences on the issue of NPT and CTBT, declaration of South Asia as a nuclear free zone, issue of trade imbalance between both the countries among others. The major disturbing factor over the years has been the issue of civil war in Sri Lanka and the case of the Sri Lankan Tamils.

Since independence of the island country in 1948, Sri Lanka has got embroiled in ethnic problems between the Sinhalese and the Tamils of Indian origin. Since the very inception, the Tamils have been deprived of basic rights, and successive governments in Colombo have adopted discriminatory policies pertaining to land settlement, citizenship rights, official languages, employment opportunities, inclusive education, political freedom and host of other fundamental rights against the Tamils. Matters came to a head with the enactment of the Official Languages Act of 1956. This Act introduced the 'Sinhala only' language policy. Further, there was a massive disenfranchisement of the Tamil workers following the abolition of the colonial system of contractual labour, followed by simultaneous denial of citizenship to these people. They became the 'stateless' people. The Tamils had often been victims of ethnic clashes taking place in the 1950s, 1970s and 1980s. The rise of Tamil insurgency especially after the armed attack and killing of Tamil prisoners and attacks on Tamils in general during 1983 more or less started civil war in Sri Lanka. The demand for a separate 'Eelam' crystallized. Several Tamil militant organizations like Eelam Revolutionary Organization of Students (EROS), the Tamil Eelam Liberation Organization (TELO) and the Liberation Tigers of Tamil Eelam (LTTE) formed a united front. They also received support from the People Liberation Organization of Tamil Eelam (PLOTE).

It is in this context that India-Lanka relation has to be assessed. India's commitment to the unity and integrity of Sri Lanka was upheld in the Nehru-

Kotelewala Pact, 1954 (addressing the problem of citizenship) and the Sirimavo-Shastri Pact, 1964 (regarding repatriation of 5,25,000 stateless people to India and granting of Sri Lankan citizenship to 3,00,000 Tamils.) However, with the escalation of Tamil insurgency and subsequent suppression by the Sri Lankan Government, India had to take notice of the situation in 1983. A large number of Tamils left Sri Lanka and crossed over to India, and created refugee problem in 1984–85. Under such circumstances, there was a strong demand from the Tamil Nadu state government on the intervention of the Indian Government. India however, resisted from such intervention and pressed the Sri Lankan Government for finding out a political situation.

Around May-June 1987, India responded in the wake of large scale massacre of Tamils in Jaffna by security forces of Sri Lanka Government. India air-dropped humanitarian assistance to the suffering Tamils. This created tension in the Indo-Sri Lanka relation as Sri Lanka viewed it as an interference/intervention by India. However, things started showing improvement with the signing of an accord between the then Indian Prime Minister Rajiv Gandhi and Sri Lankan President Jayewardane on 29 July 1987. Relations eased after the accord. India sent the Indian Peace-keeping Force (IPKF) for fulfillment of the obligations under the accord. India assumed the responsibility of disarming the Tamil militants, but very soon troubles began to emerge. The LTTE refused to surrender arms and engaged in violence against other Tamils preferring to contest provincial elections. The IPKF also got embroiled in many controversies like human rights violations and its presence on the Sri Lankan soil started to be protested by Sri Lankans. Even Sri Lankan President Premadasa wanted India to recall the IPKF and as a protest Sri Lankan Foreign Minister did not participate in the meeting of Foreign Ministers of SAARC held in 1989. Ultimately, the IPKF was withdrawn in 1990. In 1992, following the SAARC Summit President Premadasa taking advantage of India's absence left no room for pouring out his bitter feeling against India. He even held informal talks with Pakistan, Bangladesh and Maldives where he displayed open hostility against India.

However, relations again became normal in 1992. By July 1992, more than 23,000 of Tamil refugees in India were repatriated. President Premadasa visited India in October 1992. India expressed her willingness to extend support for effective devolution of power within the framework of an early solution to the ethnic problem. President Chandrika Kumartunga visited India again in 1995. Her visit greatly helped in re-establishing friendly tie between the two countries. In 1997, India's External Affairs Minsiter I.K. Gujral visited Colombo and announced certain concessions in various matters including trade without expecting any reciprocity. In December 1998, the India-Sri Lanka Free Trade Agreement (ISFTA) was signed which became operational from March 2000. Under this agreement both sides are committed to eliminate tariff barriers in a phased manner. India has kept its commitment of reducing its duty to zero except for 429 items in the negative list. In 2003 breakthrough in the economic relation of both the countries took place with the signing of Comprehensive Economic Cooperation Agreement (CECA). A defence agreement also followed the CECA.

With the assumption of Office by Mahinda Rajapakse, Indo-Sri Lankan relations took a new turn. He visited India in 2004. India agreed to help in the rehabilitation and reconstruction of North-eastern province of Sri Lanka. India time and again reassured Sri Lanka that the only way the ethnic problem can be solved is by pursuing a dialogue process and not a 'military solution'. India even backed Sri Lanka in the Human Rights Council in 2009. In 2009, things again took a different turn as the LTTE leader Prabhakaran was killed. With his death the process of devolution started, and India assured Sri Lanka of her assistance for rehabilitation of the displaced people.

After the 26th January 2010 Presidential elections in Sri Lanka, the newly re-elected President Mahinda Rajapakse met the Indian Foreign Secretary Nirupama Rao in Colombo on 7 March 2010. An official statement released from the Presidential Secretarial upheld India's willingness to assist Sri Lanka in the resettlement of the Tamil IDPs (Internally Displaced Persons) from the war-ravaged areas in North Sri Lanka. India also expressed her intention to assist Sri Lanka in the restoration of the railway line in the North. Other issues discussed were problems being faced by fishermen of both countries, proposed coal powered project in Trincomalee, environment related issues and other issues of mutual concern.

Again in June 2010 President of Sri Lanka, Mahinda Rajapakse visited India. This visit was followed by a number of agreements like the contract for the reconstruction of the Madu-Talaimannar railway line by IRCON, Treaty on Mutual Legal Assistance on criminal matters and Agreement on Transfer of Sentences Prisoners.

In October 2010 President Rajapakse along with his External Affairs Minister, G.L. Peiris, visited India to attend the closing ceremony of the Commonwealth Game in New Delhi. On 26 November 2010 on the Seventh session of the Sri Lanka-India Joint Commission was held in Colombo which was co-chaired by Indian External affairs Minister S.M. Krishna and Minister of External Affairs of Sri Lanka G.L. Peiris.

In January 2011, Foreign Secretary of India visited Sri Lanka and expressed his concern for the violent clashes in the waters between India and Sri Lanka resulting in the deaths of two fishermen. In May 2011, G.L. Peiris visited India. Both sides upheld their commitment for the resolution of the crisis and resettlement in a progressive manner. India focused on the meaningful devolution of power on the basis of the 13th Amendment to the Sri Lankan Constitution and also assurance for every possible assistance in the task of rehabilitation, resettlement and reconstruction. Both sides in keeping with the spirit of the Joint Declaration of June 2010, agreed to expedite the process of signing agreements related to Joint Venture Thermal Power Projects at Sampur, and Trincomalee, finalization of the agreements including reconstruction of Palai-KKS railway line, cooperation in the energy sector, continuance of the ongoing dialogue for the finalization of Comprehensive Economic Partnership

Agreement (CEPA) and others. Some important projects which have been launched in Sri Lanka in collaboration with Indian companies are a 500 MW coal-based thermal power plant at Trincomalee by NTPC, exploration of oil and gas blocks in Mannar by ONGC and upgradation of Colombo-Matara railway by RITES-IRCON.

The External Affairs Minister, S.M. Krishna visited Sri Lanka from 16-19 January 2012. Both sides reviewed progress in various areas, including trade, services and investment, development cooperation, science and technology, culture and education. MoUs were signed for Housing Project, on cooperation in the field of Agriculture, and also a MoU between Telecom Regulatory Authority of India and Telecommunication Regulatory Commission. President of Sri Lanka visited India during 19-22 September 2012. However, on 19 October 2012, the Cabinet took a tough decision to silently send a message to Sri Lanka that India would not keep mum and watch China expand its influence in Sri Lanka, especially after the Sri Lankan Government awarded the Colombo Port expansion project to China, whereas a major source of income of Colombo Port come from trans-shipment cargo coming from Indian ports. The cabinet took a decision to relax India's policy on granting the right to operate in its waters ("cabotage policy") as per the Merchant Shipping Act of 1958 for trans-shipment of export-import (EXIM) containers to and from the International Trans-shipment Terminal (ICTT) at Vallarpadam, Cochin. The outcome of this relaxation is to attract trans-shipment of Indian cargo from ICTT, Vallarpadam and reduce dependence on nearby foreign ports (read Sri Lanka).

Sri Lanka, like the other neighbours of India, suffers from the fear of 'big brother' India. This threat perception, not only is difficult to overcome but also both cannot avoid the pangs of proximity which affects their bilateral relation. Sri Lanka has tried to assert its independent stance many a times. It has been vocal for establishing a nuclear free zone in South Asia and played ambivalent role during the Indo-China war of 1962, Indo-Pak war of 1971 and even Indian Peaceful Nuclear explosion of 1974. Yet currently, Sri Lanka supports India's bid for permanent membership in the Security Council. Certain issues still persist and stir tensions at times or have the potential of causing bitterness between the two in future. The first of it is the Kachhativu island, where Sri Lanka wanted to establish a military base which was ceded by India as per the 1974 agreement. The rights of Sri Lanka were established by the 1974, and 1976 Treaty. However, some disturbing incidents do occur between the Sri Lankan naval patrols and the India fishermen. Further, the 18th Amendment to the 1978 Constitution has lifted the two term limit on the post of the President. India has to be cautious because a longer reign of a pro-Chinese President would be quite alarming for India. Already China has extended its feelers to Sri Lanka. China is developing Sri Lanka's Hambantota harbour. Sri Lanka has also announced purchase of equipments for its Northern province from China. Sri Lanka is also increasing its collaboration with Pakistan. This became evident with the visit of President Asif Ali Zardari to Sri Lanka in

November 2010. India has every point to become concerned about such developments. India needs to look afresh at its relation with Sri Lanka and concentrate on gaining more economic clout, and thereby more meaningful partnership which will ultimately help in betterment of political relation and help in neutralizing Chinese and Pakistani influence in Sri Lanka.

India and Nepal

Indo-Nepal relations has to be viewed from the perspective of Nepal's political regime with long period of monarchy and interjections by brief periods of experiments with democracy, Maoist insurrection and capture of power and ultimately abolition of Monarchy and emergence of Nepal as a republic. Relations between these two countries must be analyzed from the geo-strategic location of Nepal sandwiched between two major powers and from the lens of Chinese threat and India's counter measures. The main guideline of Indo-Nepal relation has been the Indo-Nepal Peace and Friendship Treaty of 1950. The Treaty provides that, "neither government shall tolerate any threat to the security of the other by a foreign aggressor. To deal with any such threat the two governments shall consult with each other and devise effective counter measures." This was primarily aimed at blocking Nepal's bid to develop relations with China. Therefore, India gave huge economic, technological and other kinds of support to Nepal to help in emergence of a strong Nepal. Nepal is dependent on India for its trade and transit which was also given by India. India's sole aim was to secure her northern frontier. Therefore, when India became independent she tried to create a ring of buffer states to secure her northern frontier. She thus, concluded a Treaty with Bhutan in 1949 and 'Standstill agreements' with Nepal and Sikkim in 1950. Further, with the Chinese occupation of Tibet the outer line of defence of India was abolished. Thus, India became desperate to develop closer ties with Nepal and also ensuring internal stability in Nepal.

In her bid to have a strong Nepal, India had played a central role in abolishing Rana oligarchy in Nepal and restoration of Monarchy and gradual working towards Parliamentary democracy. Under the auspices of India, a tripartite negotiation was held among King Tribhuban, Nepali Prime Minister Mohan Shamsher Janga Bahadur Rana and the then Indian Prime Minister Jawaharlal Nehru in February, 1951. All through, the anti-Rana movement, India made it clear that the primary objective of India is to make Nepal, independent, progressive and strong. Further, from the 1960–1990 political parties were banned in Nepal, but parties like Nepali Congress, Communist Party of Nepal and other parties operated from India. India always wanted a strong and democratic Nepal to act as a bulwark against Chinese designs. Under the Primeministership of B.P. Koirala, the Nepali Congress formed the government after the elections in 1958. However, this government was short-lived and was brought to an abrupt end by the 'Royal Coup' in December 1960. King Mahendra assumed direct and absolute control of the state.

With the assumption of Mahendra of complete state power, Nepal gradually tried to assert itself independent of Indian directions. He tried to cultivate relations with China quite against the provisions of the 1950 Treaty. Sino-Indian conflict of 1962 made Nepal and China come closer. The Chinese even proclaimed to provide help to Nepal if it were attacked. They also signed with Nepal an agreement to construct a road to link Kathmandu with the Chinese border. Thereafter, King Birendra who succeeded King Mahendra, even raised a plea to declare Nepal as a 'Zone of Peace'. India looked at this as a violation/dilution of the 1950 Treaty. Nepal tried to develop relations with Pakistan too which was reciprocated by Pakistan. Even a trade agreement was signed between both in 1962, whereby Pakistan extended port facilities to Nepal through Chittagong. Another transit agreement was also signed with Pakistan. However, during the India-Pakistan war of 1965, Nepal maintained a neutral stance and emphasized on the re-establishment of friendly relations between India and Pakistan. India also tried to mend fence with Nepal around this time. Nepal had to do a tight rope walking while maintaining good relations with both China and India. The era of 1970s could be seen as a period when the Indo-Nepal relations saw a positive turn. King Birendra emphasized peace and amity between countries with contiguous borders. During this time, minor irritants were kept aside and both tried to settle problems mutually and peacefully.

In 1983, India extended the treaty of trade for another five years which underscored cooperation of both as well as many trading facilities being provided by India. India also committed to purchase power generated from the proposed MW Karnali hydro-electric project. However, in 1987, India's action of air dropping food supplies and aid to Tamils in Jaffna in Sri Lanka created tension between India and Nepal. The signing of the peace Accord between India and Sri Lanka in July 1987 was welcomed by Nepal. With the introduction of work permit to foreigners seeking employment, which also included India, created tension. Again this was seen as a violation of the terms of 1950 Treaty. Yet relations between both the countries went on well. Both signed an agreement for setting up of a Joint Commission to increase cooperation. Tensions again surfaced in 1989 with the differences between the two over signing of a new trade and transit Treaty. With the lapse of the Treaty, Nepal was badly hit and there was acute shortage of diesel, petrol and essential commodities. With the coming of the National Front government, things again started taking a positive turn. While Nepal insisted on two separate trade and transit Treaties, India insisted on a single consolidated Treaty. Both sides however, struck at a cordial note and restored *status quo ante* on 1 April 1987 in trade and transit agreement. This was followed by India reopening its land customs stations and reactivating transit points. Nepal also agreed to restore tariff preference for Indian goods. The Treaty of 1950 contained formal provisions of trade which was modified in 1961 and 1971 and provisions for transit facilities were incorporated. In 1978, in place of a single Treaty, three different agreements were signed. These treaties were modified significantly in 1991. In December 1991, a Summit meeting at New Delhi was held between Prime Ministers of both the countries which was followed by signing of several agreements. India also signed two treaties on trade and transit with Nepal in 1991. The Treaty of Trade was again revised and renewed through an exchange of letter on 3 December 1996. The Treaty of Transit, 1991 came up for renewal in December 1998, and following bilateral talks, a renewed Transit Treaty was signed on 5 January 1999. The Protocol to the India-Nepal Treaty of Trade was renewed with some modifications in February 2002.

In 1992, an understanding was reached between increasing bilateral cooperation and providing duty free and quota free access to Nepalese exports to Indian market. They also reached an agreement to prepare project reports for Karnali, Pancheshwar, Sapta Koshi, Buri Gandaki, Kamala and Bagmati Projects and to install flood fore casting and warning system.

In 1994 however, doubts loomed in the minds of Indian foreign policy makers over the assumption of political power by the first Communist Government in Nepal as they had long opposed the terms of the 1950 Treaty. However, relations by far remained amicable and a number of agreements were signed pertaining to construction of bridges on the Kolhapur Mahakali Sector, Raxaul Sirsya broad gauge rail link, joint survey of East-West Electric Railway and others. India additionally agreed to provide transit facilities for Nepalese goods at Kandla and Mumbai. In February 1996, Nepalese Prime Minister Sher Bahadur Deuba visited India, and this resulted in the signing of Treaty on Integrated Development of Mahakali River. This Treaty was on integrated development of Mahakali basin along with construction of Pancheshwar power project. With the coming of United Front government and introduction of **Gujral Doctrine** relations further improved. India unilaterally gave Nepal greater access for Nepal's civil aviation sector, free movement and access to jobs for Nepalese citizens and provision of corridor through the **Chicken Neck** to Bangladesh on an experimental basis. The years 1997 and 1998 also witnessed good relations between the two neighbours followed by signing of MoU in civil aviation sector, providing alternate 61 km transit route to Bangladesh, opening of Kakkarbitta-Phulwari-Bangband route on an experimental basis holding of secretary level meeting for review and implementation of Sarada Barrage, Tanakpur Barrage and the Dodhara-Chandani and Tanakpur Mahendragarh road under the Mahakali Treaty. In 1999, another Treaty was signed which simplified transit of Nepal's Cargo through Kolkata port. However, in December 1999 relations received a jolt with the hijacking of IC 814 Indian Airlines aircraft from Kathmandu. Before this even India had been complaining about the use of Nepalese soil by ISI to sponsor insurgency in India especially in the North-east. Relations became strained further when a Pakistani embassy employee was found to possess fake Indian currency. However in 2000, the Nepalese Foreign Minister visited India and convinced India to resume the flights of Indian Airlines and lift the travel restrictions.

The Royal killings in June 2001, and accession of Gyanendra as the King followed by resignation of G.P. Koirala and intensification of the Maoist activities the situation within Nepal became turbulent and unstable. Sher Bahadur Deuba assumed Prime Ministership and tried to seek peace with the Maoists but failed. State of emergency was imposed. In 2002, Gyanendra dismissed Deuba, dissolved the Parliament and indefinitely put off elections. He appointed Lokendra Bahadur Chand as the PM who resigned in 2003. Thereafter, Surya Bahadur Thapa was appointed as PM who resigned in 2004. Sher Bahdur Deuba was again appointed as the PM. However, under the pretext of continuance of Maoist insurgency, Gyanendra declared a state of emergency, dismissed the Deuba government, and took complete control over the administration in February 2005. Indian condemned the 'Royal Coup' as a setback for democracy. Indian PM Manmohan Singh cancelled his visit to Dhaka for the SAARC Summit. India, USA and Britain stopped supply of arms to Nepal which put the Nepalese government in trouble and it faced difficulty in tackling Maoist insurgents. In April 2005, after a meeting between King Gyanendra and Manmohan Singh in the sidelines of the Afro-Asian Summit, India agreed to provide non-lethal military supplies to Nepal if the King facilitated the restoration of democracy. Seizing this strong stand of India, China jumped into the scene and Gyanendra responded quickly and started playing the China card. China promised to help Nepal to fight the Maoists. Chief of Army Staff of Nepal visited Beijing in June 2004. Gyanendra also met Chinese President Hu Jintao in the sidelines of the Afro-Asian Summit who reciprocated quite positively and impinged upon improving Sino-Nepal relations as China sees Nepal as an entry point into South-Asia.

In 2006, anti-monarchy sentiment became strong. G.P. Koirala became the PM and the Parliament curtailed the power of the King and his legal immunity was removed and he was brought under the ambit of taxation. At the same time, a Comprehensive Peace Agreement was struck that ended the 10 year Maoist conflict in Nepal. However, the future of the Maoists remained uncertain. In 2007, there were some visits from both sides. Nepalese Foreign Minister Pradhan visited India from 6–9 December and participated in the SAARC Council of Ministers Meeting. Indian Foreign Secretary, Shivshankar Mennon visited Nepal in September 2007. In October 2007, Shyam Saran, Special Envoy of PM visited Nepal. However, around this time anti-Indian sentiments were high in Nepal. There were massive anti-Indian demonstrations near the Indo-Nepal border gate, and they agitated against the suppressive and land expansionist policies of India.

In 2008, there was change in the political scenario in Nepal. King was removed and Nepal became a Republic. Prachanda became the PM and Ram Baran Yadav, a Madhesi, became the first President of Nepal. Prachanda soon started developing closeness with China. He visited China and both sides arrived at a large number of agreements on various sectors like hydro-power, agriculture, tourism and infrastructure in Nepal. Prachanda visited India soon thereafter, but without much effect followed by a visit by Pranab Mukherjee former Minister of External Affairs to Nepal in November 2008. However, Prachanda had to resign on 4 May 2009 after his attempt to sack the army chief, General Rookmangud Katawal, was opposed by President Ram Baran Yadav. Thereafter, Madhav Kumar Nepal became the PM of Nepal. There have been efforts on both the sides to improve relations. Indian Foreign Secretary visited Nepal in February 2009. In August 2009, Nepalese Foreign Minister Sujata Koirala was on an official visit to India in order to bridge the widening gap between the two neighbours. She had tried to downplay the growing Chinese influence and underscored the necessity of increasing cooperation with India for collaborating on more projects and also cooperation on development of water resources, bilateral trade and transit, control of cross-border crimes, border issues and inundation problems among many other things. In the sidelines of the SAARC Summit at Thimpu in April 2010, PM Manmohan Singh and Nepalese PM Madhav Kumar Nepal met and had talks. Jairam Ramesh, Minister of State for Environment and Forests visited Nepal in October 2010 to attend an international symposium on Climate Change. In January 2011, India Foreign Secretary visited Nepal and held talks to expand the bilateral cooperation. President of Nepal Ram Baran Yadav visited India from 27 January to 5 February 2011. His visit was aimed at consolidating the bilateral relations. In 2011, there were further visits by the External Affairs Minister to Nepal in April and before that in March a group of 6 Young MPs from India visited Nepal. Therefore, both the countries are trying to put the relations back into proper track. India and Nepal signed a revised Double Taxation Avoidance Agreement (DTAA) on 27 November 2011, to improve Indian investment in Nepal and ease procedures for stakeholders with commercial interest in both countries. Earlier during the visit of Nepalese Prime Minister Baburam Bhattarai to India in October 2011, both sides formalized the long pending Bilateral Investment Promotion and Protection Agreement (BIPPA). The visit was aimed at 'building trust between the two countries and two peoples.'

Yet tensions persists on issues of water sharing, border dispute including the Kalapani issue where Nepal has sought Chinese help in its resolution, insurgents and connections with Nepalese Maoists, pending extradition treaty, fake currency, persecution of India traders, and above all the fear of growing Chinese influence into Nepal jeopardizing India's security interests. However, India and Nepal must embark on more confidence building measures and work out bilateral problems amicably.

India and Bhutan

Bhutan seems to be sandwiched between its two gigantic neigbours—India and China. Therefore, this geo-strategic location of Bhutan has raised geo-political concerns for her two 'big' neighbours as well as for itself. Bhutan being a buffer state between India and China has significantly figured in foreign policy postures of both its giant neighbours on its north and south. Besides, both India and China embark cautious policy towards Bhutan in order to preserve their national interests vis-à-vis each other, respectively. Therefore, China is a constant factor in Indo-Bhutan relation.

India's big and powerful neighbour China is a constant worry for New Delhi. Bhutan along with Nepal and Sikkim had acted as buffers between India and China since the British period. For long however, China had laid claim to all three Himalayan Kingdoms and parts of Indian territory in north and north-east. China claimed that the Himalayan region was "within her natural sphere". China even drew an analogy in its relation with Bhutan when it compared the Union of China, Tibet, Nepal, Sikkim and Bhutan to the blending of the five principal colours, yellow, red, blue, black and green. China further compared the position of Tibet, Nepal, Sikkim and Bhutan to that of the molar teeth side-by-side in a man's mouth. Therefore, when India became independent, she tried to create a ring of buffer states to secure her northern frontier. She thus, concluded a Treaty with Bhutan in 1949 and 'Standstill agreements' with Nepal and Sikkim in 1950. Bhutan too needed to protect itself from Chinese menace. So the need was both ways.

China's attempts to win over Thimpu have made India reluctant to do anything significant and risky, losing an important diplomatic and economically. Bhutan had 15 rounds of boundary talks with People's Republic of China since 1984. Though the talks have not yielded positive results for Bhutan yet both countries have signed an agreement on "Maintenance of Peace and Tranquility in Bhutan-China Border Areas" during the 12th round of talks in Beijing in 1998. This is a matter of concern for India.

Further, India is worried about the presence of anti-Indian insurgents especially from North-east who are alleged to be using the Bhutanese soil for their activities. The North-east insurgency problem has made India sensitive towards Bhutan for without its active cooperation India would not be able to combat the insurgency problem. After years of hesitation, the Bhutan National Assembly in the year 2000 finally authorized the use of force to tackle terrorism by the Government against the ULFA and Bodo militants operating from Bhutan. This was a welcome step by India. This has exactly been proved when on 15 December 2003 the Royal Bhutan Army launched an offensive against the Indian Insurgent groups operating from its territory. The move was closely coordinated with the centre, and the goal was to wipe out the 30 camps of the militant outfits in southern Bhutan. The Royal Bhutanese army has just 6,000 soldiers fighting against 2,500 insurgents, which might seem too insufficient for the "Operation All Clear".

The Gorkhaland problem has also made India very cautious towards her relations with Bhutan. The resurgence of the Gorkhaland problem in 2007-2008 under Bimal Gurung and the Gorkha Janamukhti Morcha (GJM), with their demand for a "Gorkhaland" which plans to incorporate areas within the plains in Siliguri and Duars as well, the India Government continues to be cautious while addressing the Lhotshmapa* refugee crisis. It continues to exhibit the posture of neutrality regarding the crisis and treats the matter as a bilateral issue between Nepal and Bhutan.

However, China has always been a constant factor in Indo-Bhutan relation. The British India Government was also cautious about Chinese intentions and so is the Government of Independent India. The 1949 Treaty concluded between Bhutan and Independent India is nothing but a continuation of the British legacy and it continued to be the guiding principle of Indo-Bhutan relation till 2007 when the Treaty was renegotiated and a new Treaty came up in its place.

Article 2 of the 1949 Treaty upheld that:

"The Government of India undertakes to exercise no interference in the internal administration of Bhutan. On its part the Government of Bhutan agrees to be guided by the advice of the Government of India in regard to its external relations."

Article 2 of the new Indo-Bhutan Friendship Treaty of 2007 now read as follows:

"In keeping with the abiding ties of close friendship and cooperation between Bhutan and India, the Government of the Kingdom of Bhutan and the Government of the Republic of India shall cooperate closely with each other on issues relating to their national interests. Neither Government shall allow the use of its territory for activities harmful to the national security and interest of the other."

Recognizing Bhutan's maturity as a nation and its transition to a democracy, the language in the Treaty pertaining to foreign policy now talks in terms of "co-operation". The new Treaty in essence emphasize Bhutan's sovereignty and it's right to pursue an independent foreign policy as long as it does not compromise Indian interests.

Although relations remained close and friendly, the Bhutanese government expressed a need to renegotiate parts of the Treaty of 1949 in order to enhance Bhutan's sovereignty. Following the India-China border war of 1962, Bhutan was facing a tough choice. On the one hand, the Royal Government harboured doubts about India's capability to assist, and on the other hand, Bhutan was apprehensive of Chinese designs in the Himalayan region. Bhutan also realized its vulnerability to possible Chinese threat emanating from its alignment with India. Therefore, for the time-being, the Royal Government of Bhutan tried to follow the 'Nepali model' of equal friendship with India and China. But in the long run, Bhutan relinquished the 'Nepali model' as the fear of Chinese policies in Tibet influenced the Royal Government to extend closer ties with India. Formal bilateral relations between Bhutan and India were established in

---

*Lhotshampas   The southern Bhutanese of Nepalese origin who have been evicted from Bhutan in the early 1990s. They have been staying in the UNHCR administered refugee camps in Nepal for over 20 years. Following Bhutan's stringent attitude of continuous refusal to take back the Lhotshampas, UNHCR have started the process of Third Country Resettlement of Bhutanese refugees in Nepal.

January 1968 with the appointment of a special officer of the Government of India to Bhutan. The India House (Embassy of India in Bhutan) was inaugurated on 14 May 1968 and Resident Representatives were exchanged in 1971.

Bhutan began to slowly assert an independent attitude in foreign affairs by joining the United Nations in 1971, recognizing Bangladesh and signing a new trade agreement in 1972 that provided an exemption from export duties for goods from Bhutan to third countries. Bhutan exerted its independent stance at the Non-Aligned Movement (NAM) summit conference in Havana, Cuba also in 1979, by voting with China and some South-east Asian countries rather than with India on the issue of allowing Cambodia's Khmer Rouge to be seated at the conference. Bhutan also signed the Nuclear Non-proliferation Treaty in 1985 to which India is a non-signatory. Bhutan also took steps to rechristen the Bhutanese Embassy in New Delhi as the Royal Bhutanese Embassy (1978), opening of diplomatic relations with Bangladesh (1979) and the inauguration of Druk Air Service (1983) in order to expand Bhutan's external contacts. All these steps account for attempts made by Bhutan to come out of India's influence and assert itself internationally. However, unlike in Nepal, where the 1950 Treaty with India is subject of great political controversy and nationalist resentment for decades, the nature of Bhutan's relationship with India has not been affected by concerns over the Treaty provisions and differences between India and Bhutan in certain cases.

Thereafter, relation between Bhutan and India which started-off due to their mutual need of preservation of their respective national interests has come a long way and has become stronger. India has maintained a position of neutrality regarding more than 20 years long Lhotshampa refugee crisis, whereby Bhutanese Royal Government drove out a large section of its population who are of Nepalese origin from southern Bhutan. The reason is obviously geo-strategic, political and security considerations which have been discussed above. Most importantly, India refrains herself from antagonizing Bhutan, which had launched operations against anti-Indian insurgents operating from its soil from 2003 to 2004. Furthermore, as long as China remains a potential threat to India, Bhutan will figure prominently in Indian foreign policy posture.

On the whole, relations between India and Bhutan has been one of peace and amity. There has been a number of Treaties between the two countries pertaining to matters of trade and commerce and also extradition. The Treaties in place are the Indo-Bhutan Trade Treaty of 1972, the Chukha Hydropower Project Agreement of 1974, Indo-Bhutan Trade Treaty of 1995, the Extradition Treaty with India of 1997. Bhutan began its planned economic development growth in 1961. The First Five Year Plan was launched in 1961. Since then India has provided generous financial assistance for Bhutan's Five year Plans. Tala Hydro Electric Project, Kurichu Hydro Electric Project and Dungsum Cement Plant are three major projects which were taken up during the VII Five Year Plan. Other important projects were Sankosh Multipurpose and Bunakha Projects, Hospitals, Paro Airport Development Project, Renovation of Punakha

Dzong and Pasakha-Monitar Road, Indo-Bhutan Microwave link, Exploration of Mineral Resources and Survey and Mapping. In August 2003, during the visit to India by the Crown Prince and the present King the India-Bhutan Foundation was established. In 2005, the India-Bhutan Trade and Commerce Agreement was renewed for another ten years. MoUs were also signed for Air Service Management and also cooperation between UPSC and Royal Civil Service Commission of Bhutan also in 2005.

During the visit of the King of Bhutan in July 2006, an Agreement laying down the framework for cooperation in the field of hydropower, Protocol to the Inter-Governmental Agreement on the Tala Hydroelectric Project which worked out the commercial arrangements for purchase of power from the project and the Agreement on Trade, Commerce and Transit were signed. In 2007, the 57 year long Treaty of 1949 was renegotiated and a new Indo-Bhutan Friendship Treaty was signed. Other MoUs between the two countries are the twelve MOUs/Agreements in areas of hydropower, IT, health/medicine, narcotics, civil aviation, agriculture and environment which were signed during the visit of His Majesty Jigme Khesar Namgyel Wangchuck in December 2009. Another MoU is on Nehru-Wangchuk Scholarship, which was signed during External Affairs Minister's visit to Bhutan in June 2009. Prime Minister Manmohan Singh during his visit to Bhutan in May 2008 announced the proposed construction of the 17.5 km railway line starting from Hasimara in West Bengal going through Satali, Bharna Bari and Dalsingpara to Toribari in Bhutan. This was named as the *Golden Jubilee Rail Line* to mark the golden jubilee of the visit of India's first Prime Minister Jawaharlal Nehru to the Himalayan kingdom in 1958. The rail link, was envisaged to counter China's design of building railway network to enter into South Asia. However, this project is now facing uncertainties due to problems of land acquisition in Bengal. During Prime Minister Dr. Manmohan Singh's visit to Bhutan in April 2010 for the 16th SAARC Summit, Implementation Agreements for the Punatsangchhu'II and Mangdechhu Hydro Electric Projects (HEPs) were signed by the Minister of Economic Affairs of Bhutan Lyonpo Khandu Wangchuk and the External Affairs Minister of India S.M. Krishna, in the presence of the Prime Ministers of India and Bhutan. Bhutanese King Jigme Khesar Namgyel Wangchuk was the Chief Guest for the 64th Republic Day celebrations on 26 January 2013.

The new Treaty of 2007 is most unlikely to bring in qualitative changes in Indo-Bhutan relation. Given the need, both ways, India and Bhutan most likely would follow the same amicable relations. The updated Treaty of 2007 like the 1949 Treaty, reiterates that there shall be perpetual peace and friendship between India and Bhutan.

India's Look-East Policy

It was only in 1992 that India's Look East Policy (LEP) was launched. This was a foreign policy posture of India to reach out to their South-eastern neighbours and also connect with East Asia. The chief objectives of LEP are to renew political contacts with the countries of South-east Asia and East Asia, increase economic cooperation and most importantly secure strategic defence cooperation to balance expanding Chinese influence in South-east Asia and South China Sea and areas beyond that.

Earlier, during the Cold War years, India's insistence on non-alignment had retracted India to limit her activities to South Asia. Again, with the defeat of India in the hands of China compelled India to restrain herself to expanding beyond South Asia. Further, India refrained from entering into a broad alliance being envisaged by the South-east Asian countries to counter China. This also distanced India from them. Later, also India's obsession with South Asia greatly hindered her vision of expanding beyond this region. With the end of Cold War, followed by economic liberalization of India, launching LEP became a need of the hour for India. Seeking economic cooperation of immediate neighbours was a viable option rather than negotiating economic ties with the bigger countries, especially the developed ones. With this objective an initiative to develop policy towards South-east Asia and East Asian countries started making rounds in the MEA in the early 1990s. Ultimately, the LEP was launched in 1992.

Immediately, it started reaping dividends for India. India's contact with ASEAN was rewarding. India was made the Sectoral Dialogue Partner in 1992, and become the Full Dialogue Partner in the Fifth ASEAN Regional Forum (ARF) on 23 July 1996. India became Summit Level Partner (A+1) in 2002. At the Second India-ASEAN Summit in Bali, Indonesia in October 2003, India and ASEAN signed a **Framework Agreement on Comprehensive Economic Cooperation** aiming at creation of Free Trade Area (FTA) by 2011 in goods, services and investments. India also acceded to the Treaty of Amity and Cooperation in South-east Asia. Both also signed an agreement on forging cooperation to combat international terrorism. Another event took place in the Third India-ASEAN Summit is historic Partnership Pact for Peace, Progress and Shared Prosperity in Vientiane, Laos in 2004. In 2007, India and ASEAN agreed on different modalities for FTA with the acceptance of a list of products that would not be subject to any tariff cuts till 2022. In the case of these products, the total value should not exceed 5 per cent of the total. On the rest of 95 per cent goods there would be elimination or reduction of duties by 2022. In 2009, the Free Trade Agreement (FTA) in Goods was signed between India and ASEAN as part of the Comprehensive Cooperation Agreement (CECA) in Bangkok. This aimed at integration of two economic blocks as well as regions.

Areas of economic cooperation are quite wide including food, energy, security, infrastructure, human resource development, oil and natural gas, agro-chemicals, fertilizers, healthcare, tourism, pharmaceuticals and automobiles. Both can exploit each other's market for capital investment in various sectors. ASEAN-India partnership can gain fullest expression with gradual emergence of ASEAN Community of nations. This would be 'arc of advantages' for India.

At the sub-regional level India has bolstered (MGC) strong ties with South-east Asian countries in economic arrangements like Mekong-Ganga Cooperation (MGC), BIMSTEC and IOR-ARC (see Chapter 20 for details).

At the bilateral level, India is cultivating her relations at economic and also defence spheres with Cambodia, Indonesia, Laos PDR, the Philippines, Malaysia, Thailand, Vietnam and Singapore. Some important achievements in strengthening economic cooperation with individual ASEAN countries are either completion or ongoing negotiation for signing Comprehensive Economic Cooperation Agreements (CECAs) with Malaysia, Singapore, South Korea and Indonesia.

China is the largest trading partner of the ASEAN countries. As of 2007 Chinese trade with ASEAN is around US $202 billion. China replaced USA as the largest trading partner in 2006. Therefore, by forging strong economic ties with South-east Asian countries, India must try to cut a niche for herself in the economic sector. Growing Chinese influence in the South China Sea is of increasing strategic concern for India. The geo-strategic importance of South China Sea as far as the world shipping activities are concerned cannot be denied. In addition to this it has huge oil and gas reserves. Yet, it is at the centre of controversy as China, the Philippines, Vietnam, Taiwan, Brunei and Malaysia all have conflicting claims to parts of the South China Sea. China claims almost the entire body of South China Sea. China is also trying to restrict India's activities in the South China Sea. In November 2011, China send out a warning to India when it said that it would not allow "outside forces" and "foreign companies" to either get involved in the South China Sea dispute or engage in oil exploration with littoral states. USA too has geared up its presence in South China Sea to counter China. Under such circumstances India has to stay guard and forge more strong bonds with the ASEAN Countries in order to fulfill her economic as well as strategic interests while balancing-off Chinese threat in a rational way.

To further boost the LEP, India is making all out effort to reach out to Japan, Korea and Australia. India and Japan have entered into a global partnership after the conclusion of joint statement titled **Japan-India Partnership in the New Asian Era: Strategic Orientation of Japan-India Global Partnership** in 2006. Both concluded a Comprehensive Economic Partnership Agreement (CEPA) in October 2010 and further strengthened their global and strategic partnership. India-Japan 2+2 Dialogue is another platform for defence cooperation which is a very recent initiative. Further, both have multi-layered cooperation in several regional forums like ASEEAN Regional Forum (ARF), Regional Cooperation Agreement on Combating Piracy and Armed Robbery against Ships in Asia (ReCAPP) processes and most importantly East Asia Summit (EAS). Both have also agreed to cooperate in areas of energy, security, youth exchange and evolving Comprehensive Economic Partnership in East Asia (CEPEA). With Republic of Korea (RoK) India has started cultivating her relations. The **Long Term Cooperative Partnership** is the bedrock of India-RoK relationship concluded in 2004. With Australia, India is developing closer economic and strategic cooperation. India is negotiating a CECA with Australia. Both interact with ARF, EAS, and Asia-Europe Meeting. India envisions to extend her LEP beyond South-east Asia to East Asia and gradually India is consolidating her relations with these countries.

India also has another interest in successful fruition of LEP. India wants to foster economic development of its North-eastern states by cultivating economic ties with South-east Asian neighbours who are in closer proximity to India's North-eastern frontier. North-east which touches upon the border with Mynamar can be considered as the gateway to ASEAN. India envisions increasing connectivity with her South-eastern neighbours through North-east. To realize this vision, India embarked on projects like the Kaladan Multi-Modal Transit Transport facility connecting Indian ports on the eastern sea board to the Sittwe Port in Myanmar and upgradation of the Tamu-Kalewa-Kalemyo Road in Myanmar. Negotiations are going on to establish connectivity between Moreh in Manipur to Mae Sot in Thailand via Bagan in Myanmar. Projects have been undertaken for upgradation of road links too. An ambitious project, if turned into reality, will be a great achievement of LEP is a road link from Jiribham in Assam to Hanoi in Vietnam via Myanmar. ASEAN countries also want to cultivate the huge potential of India's North-east. Laos sees huge potential in North-east's tourism and agricultural sectors. There were visits to North-eastern states in 2007 and 2008 by Thai Minister of Commerce and Thai Deputy Ministry of Industry, to give a further boost to investment and explore potentials of trade. India has issued Visas on Arrival (VoA) to foreign tourists of 10 countries including Indonesia, Singapore, the Philippines, Vietnam, Myanmar, Cambodia, Japan among others.

ASEAN and India share some common interests like combating trans-national terrorism in all its forms like drug trafficking, smuggling; securing Indian Ocean and maritime resources; exploring oil and gas reserves; counterbalancing China; protection of sea lanes; combating piracy to mention a few. India must continue cultivating her ties with ASEAN countries and East-asian countries which will necessarily bring her rich dividends and give her a strong foothold in Asian politics vis-à-vis China.

INDIAN FOREIGN POLICY UNDER PM NARENDRA MODI (2014–)

The 16th Lok Sabha elections conducted during April–May, 2014 in phases witnessed a landslide victory for NDA led by Bharatiya Janata Party. Sri Narendra Modi became the new Prime Minister of India, and with his assumption of office there were much activities on the foreign policy front as the Prime Minister made many outgoing visits to neighbouring countries as well as important countries of the world.

The first State Visit made by PM Modi was to Bhutan, India's most significant neighbour from 15–16 June 2014, on the invitation of the King of Bhutan Jigme Khesar Namgyel Wangchuk. They held talks on bilateral relations and economic cooperation along with cooperation in regional and multilateral forums. India promised to double the Nehru-Wangchuk Scholarship to Rs/Nu. 20 million per year as well as assistance in setting up digital section/E.library in the National Library of Bhutan in all 20 districts too. Both sides expressed satisfaction at the completion of the Supreme Court Building and commencement of the Kholongchhu Hydroelectric Project. The President of India also visited Bhutan from 7–8 November 2104. The President held wide-ranging discussions with His Majesty the King of Bhutan including bilateral and regional issues. Among other issues, GOI reiterated its commitment to support Bhutan's socio-economic development and also support for successful implementation of 11th Five Year Plan of the Royal Government of Bhutan (2013–2018).

During 26–30 June 2014, the Vice-President of India, Mr. Hamid Ansari went on an official visit to China. Memorandum of Understandings were signed regarding cooperation on Industrial Parks in India, communication and cooperation of training in area of Capacity Building of Public Officials and Implementation Plan for Provision of Hydrological Information of the Yarlung Zangbu/Brahmaputra River in Flood Season by China to India. The Vice-President of India also conveyed his good wishes on the occasion to commemorate the 60th Anniversary of Panchsheel during his visit.

PM Modi also visited Brazil for attending 6th BRICS Summit from 14–16 July 2014. This was his first visit to the BRICS Summit. He hinted at restoration of climate of peace and stability which is an urgent global need. For this, he called for newer avenues of cooperation and collaboration. He said that BRICS brings together a group of nations on the parameter of 'future potential' rather than existing prosperity or shared identities. BRICS, therefore, should play an active role in global discourse on Growth and Development including shaping the post-2015 Development Agenda to alleviate poverty, reforming international financial institutions and UN Security Council.

With Brazil, India signed Implementing Arrangement for Establishing Cooperation in Augmentation of a Brazilian Earth Station for receiving and processing data IRS satellites and Memorandum of Understanding on establishment of a consultation mechanism on consular and mobility issues on 16 July 2014.

Prime Minister, Mr. Modi also visited Nepal during 3–4 August 2014. The Indian PM addressed the Constituent Assembly and legislature Parliament of Nepal and prior to this address PM had a meeting with the Chairman of the Constituent Assembly, Rt. Hon'ble Subhas Chandra Nembang. The Indian PM had a meeting with the PM of Nepal Mr. Sushil Koirala followed by delegation level talks. The two PMs were the witnesses to the signing of the Exchange Letters regarding Terms of Reference of the Pancheshwar Development Authority. The two sides also signed MoUs on Cooperation in the Goitre Control and on Cooperation between Doordarshan and the Nepali television. Nepal urged India to adopt measures to help Nepal to tide over the trade deficit it is facing vis-a-vis trade with India.

From 30 August–3 September, PM Modi visited Japan to strengthen the global strategic partnership between the two countries. On 1 September 2014, PM Modi held the Japan–India Summit with Japanese PM Shinzo Abe. A number of important agreements were signed, and both sides talked about deepening of comprehensive security and defence cooperation as well as strengthening of Japan–India 2 plus 2 dialogue along with establishment of the Trilateral foreign Ministers Meeting of Japan, US and India to bolster regional security. Economic cooperation was discussed along with cooperation in infrastructural development in India and improving of business environment in India. India was able to get $35 billion worth of Japanese investment including Official Development Assistance (ODA) during a 5-year period will be under the aegis of India–Japan Investment Promotion Partnership for development of projects including infrastructure and building of smart cities. Partnership city arrangement between India's Varanasi and Japan's Kyoto was also worked out and also agreement for public-private partnership for setting up of Industrial Electronic Parks in India and Japan. India's maiden bullet train project with Japanese funding was also promised by Japan. Japan also agreed to remove six of India's space and defence related entities from its Foreign End User List and for the first time since World War II Japan agreed to sell military equipment to India and expedite the talks for sale of US-2 amphibian aircraft for maritime security. Though the Japan–India Summit was a mega success yet the two countries despite their efforts to forge a special strategic global partnership did not conclude a civil nuclear deal with Japan agreeing to speed up the talks for nuke deal.

The Secretary of State of USA paid a visit to India from 30 July–1 August, 2014. External Affairs Minister, Smt. Sushma Swaraj and US Secretary of State, John Kerry co-chaired the 5th India-US Strategic Dialogue which was launched in 2009. Both sides reiterated their commitment to fight terrorism, proliferation of WMDs, nuclear terrorism, cross-border terrorism, cross-border crime and address the misuse of the internet for terrorist purposes in compliance with respective laws. They reaffirmed their commitment to the full implementation of the India–US civil nuclear agreement. They welcomed the Authorization to Proceed provided to Westinghouse to implement the pre-Early Works Agreement with NPCIL as of September 2013 and also commitment to work towards a successful outcome in Paris in 2015 of the work of the AD-hoc Working Group on the Durban Platform under the UN Framework Convention on Climate Change.

The Indian PM visited USA from 26–30 September 2014. He address the 69th Session of UNGA on 27 September 2014. He addressed the public at the Global Citizens Festival, Central Park, New York City on 28 September 2014. The Indo–US talks saw the unfurling of a vision of a transformative relationship as trusted partners in the 21st century which would be a model for the rest of the world. Both leaders announced on 29 September 2014, the *Vision Statement for the US–India Strategic Partnership—Chalein Saath Saath: Forward Together We Go*.

Another significant event was the State visit of President of China Xi Jinping to India from 17–19 September 2014. The two sides decided to strengthen political communication, deepen strategic trust and political dialogue and consultations at all levels. The two sides decided to designate 2015 as the *Visit India Year* in China and 2016 as the *Visit China Year* in India. Among others, the agreements on establishing a provincial partnership between Gujarat and Guandong Province and Sister-City relationship between Mumbai–Shanghai and Ahmedabad–Guangzhou were signed. Both sides recognized that there are several mutual interest areas, like climate change, Doha Development Round of WTO, energy, food security, reform of international institutions and global governance. This is reflected in their cooperation and coordination in BRICS, G-20 and other fora. The leaders assigned Strategic Economic Dialogue (SED) to explore new areas for economic cooperation in different fields, like industrial investment, infrastructure development, energy conservation and environment protection, high-tech industry, clean energy and sustainable urbanization. Both sides evaluating the progress in their relations focused on considering the relation form an overall perspective.

Australia was also on the agenda of PM Modi. He visited Australia from 14–18 November 2014. His visit followed a visit by PM of Australia Tony Abbot from 4–5 September 2014. Both countries in New Delhi signed agreements regarding Cooperation in the Peaceful Uses of Nuclear Energy, MoUs on Cooperation in Technical Vocational Education and Training (TVET) and Cooperation in Sport as well as Renewal of MoU on Cooperation in the Field of Water Resources Management.

PM Modi while in Australia attended the BRICS Leader's Meeting in Brisbane on 15 November 2014. In the bilateral talks held between two countries during 16–18 November, both sides recognized that the partnership has a great room for growth and agreed to unlock the vast potential of the economic relationship in priority areas such as resources, education, skills, agriculture, infrastructure, investments, financial services and health. Both countries have decided to establish a Framework for Security Cooperation to intensify bilateral cooperation and consultation on areas of mutual interests which will be implemented by an Action Plan which was also worked out. Agreements were signed concerning Social Security, Transfer of Sentenced Persons and MoUs concerning cooperation in the field of Arts and Culture and field of Tourism as well as combating narcotics trafficking and developing police cooperation.

PM Modi again visited Nepal in November to attend the 18th SAARC Summit. Against the backdrop of cynicism and scepticism, he said that SAARC countries are gradually coming together and are trying to forge bonds through rail, road, power and transit. He said that India is aware of its own share of responsibility and announced India's gift of satellite for SAARC region by the SAARC Day, 2016. However, India has maintained its stance of keeping China out of SAARC. PM Modi announced India's pledge to provide regional investments in infrastructure, health facilities, and lucrative export facilities for smaller countries. All these evidently were steps to counter China's growing inroads into India's backyard. China has been already lobbying Pakistan, Sri Lanka and Bangladesh for SAARC membership. It was Pakistan which mooted the idea, in the 18th SAARC Summit, of pushing for China's full-fledged membership from observer status. India-Pakistan coldness in their bilateral relations overshadowed the atmosphere of SAARC. In the sidelines of SAARC, PM had bilateral talks with all other members of SAARC except PM Nawaz Sharif of Pakistan. Pakistan also blocked three projects—an electricity grid and trade in electricity and road and rail connectivity on the ground that it has still to conclude its "internal processes."

Another landmark event has been the *India Global* broadcast on AIR FM Gold on 28 November 2014 which is a mark of India's relationship with Germany.

The last month of year 2014 saw the visit by President of Russian Federation Vladimir V. Putin from 10–11 December 2014. Both leaders acknowledged "Our partnership and the strong sensitivity that we have always had for each other's interests will be a source of strength to both countries." Putin came to attend the 15th Annual India–Russia Summit. A *Druzhna-Dosti: A Vision for Strengthening the Indian Russian Partnership over the next decade* was announced in a joint statement on 11 December 2014. The leaders expressed their confidence that a strong bilateral strategic partnership advances the national interests of the two countries and contributes to a more stable and secure world order. Both countries pledged to further their cooperation in fields of energy, technology and innovation, expanded economic engagement, global order, world peace and people-to-people ties. India always considers the importance of Russian relationship and its unique position in Indian foreign policy. Both sides felt confident to propel their bilateral relationship to a new level where aspirations of the people will be met. Both sides acknowledged that Indo-Russian relationship has been a time-tested one based on trust and will grow in future. A number of bilateral agreements and commercial contracts were signed during this visit. The most notable among them were Strategic Vision for Strengthening Cooperation in Peaceful Uses of Atomic Energy, Supplement to the General Framework Agreement (GFA) for Units 3 & 4 of Kudankulam Nuclear Power Project between Nuclear Power Cooperation of India Limited (NPCIL) and ATOMSTROYEXPORT (ASE) and Contract between NPCIL and ASE for Units 3 & 4 Kudankulam Nuclear Power Plant.

However, India–Pakistan relation reached a nadir in 2014. There were cross-border firing and violations of LOC and mutual accusations of violations along with stagnation over terrorist issue and extradition of Mumbai blast terrorists. India called off the talks with Pakistan slated for August 2014 on the grounds that New Delhi-based High Commissioner of Pakistan invited Kashmiri separatist leaders or consultation ahead of the Summit. The coldness in their relation was reflected in 18th SAARC Summit also. Even after suicide bombers massacred a Peshawar Army School killing over hundred school kids and Tehreek-e-Taliban claiming the responsibility for the attack on 16 December 2014, on 18 December 2014, the anti-terrorism court in Pakistan gave bail to Lt. commander Zakiur Rehman Lakhvi, the key planner of Mumbai 2008 attacks. After India's reaction and international pressure, he was detained under the Maintenance of Public Order (MPO) rules for three more months at Rawalpindi's Adiala Jail. It is to be seen how both sides take initiatives to improve relations. India-Pakistan relationship is an integral ingredient of sustainable peace in Afghanistan also.

The President of Bangladesh, Mr. Md. Abdul Hamid, paid an official visit to India from 18–23 December 2014 on an invitation of the Indian President Sri Pranab Mukherjee. Earlier the First India–Bangladesh High Commissioner's Summit was held on 14 November 2014. This visit is supposed to strengthen and expand the bilateral relations between the two countries.

On the regional front, pursuing "Look East Policy", India hosted the round table Meetings on innovations among Asia-Europe Meeting (ASEM) countries and Inauguration Virtual Knowledge Portal (VKP) and meetings of the 24 × 7 Points of Contact (PoC) of the East Asia Summit (EAS) countries on 4–5 December 2014 at New Delhi. It focused on innovative technologies for disaster risk reduction and disaster rescue efforts amongst participating countries with a plan for broad structure and functioning of VKP.

On 17 December 2014, the Minister of State for External Affairs General (Dr.) V.K. Singh (Retd.) held interactions with African Heads of Missions in New Delhi. India assured that safety and security of all foreign nationals including those of African countries as India has a long history of inclusive and cosmopolitan culture and has zero tolerance for racism in any form.

The First Meeting of the India–US Contact Group on Civil Nuclear Cooperation was held from 16–17 December 2014. This Group was formed in pursuant of the Joint statement of 30 September 2014 during PM Modi's visit to the US. The discussions were held between the Nuclear Power Corporation of India (NPCIL) from Indian side and Westinghouse and GE-Hitachi from the US side regarding implementation issues, administrative issues, liability, technical issues and licensing to facilitate US designed power plants in India.

Besides the PM's visit to important countries, the External Affairs Minister also visited Dhaka in June 2014, Nepal in July 2014 prior to PM's visit to Nepal, Nay Pyi Taw, Myanmar, Vietnam and Singapore in August 2014, Bahrain, Tajikistan and Afghanistan in September 2014, United Kingdom, USA (prior to the visit of the PM) in October, 2014, Mauritius, Maldives, UAE and Nepal in November 2014.

The year 2015 started with the high profile visit of the US President Barack Obama to India. He was the Chief Guest for the Republic Day celebration on 26 January, 2015. There were high level talks and indications of intensifying Indo-US ties in field of climate change, PACE (Partnership to Advance Clean Energy), incentivizing trade investments among others.

The year 2015 has witnessed frequent visits of PM Modi to a number of countries in his bid to engage India in constructive relationship as well as project the prowess of India in international fora. There were about 28 foreign trips made by the PM in 2015 to countries like USA, UK, Russia, France, China, Germany, some other European countries, Canada, Japan as well as neighbouring countries in South-east Asia and South Asia, island countries deep down into the Indian Ocean like Mauritius and Seychelles, Central Asian countries, Iran, Turkey to mention a few. His multilateral engagements have been followed up by his visits to BRICS Summit at Ufa, G-20 at Antalya, EAS Summit at Kuala Lumpur, Shanghai Cooperation Organization (SCO) Summit at UFA and India-Africa Summit at New Delhi. The most surprising moment came when suddenly PM Modi made a visit to his counterpart Nawaz Sharif in Pakistan on 25 December, 2015. However, this not reciprocated equally by Pakistan, as soon after this visit, there were terror attacks on India's Pathankot Airbase (2–5 January, 2016). Still it can be said that India under his leadership is following an active foreign policy. It is said to be based on five pillars:

1. Economic development and technological progress,
2. Greater orientation of domestic and foreign policies towards the fulfillment of these objectives,
3. Recognition of importance of national power both economic and military,
4. Focus on 'soft power' which can be said to be utilizing cultural diplomacy and interacting with India Diaspora, and
5. Eliminations of constraints while engaging with other countries.

It can be said that the focus is now on South Asia, South-East Asia (from Look-East to Act-East), Far-East, Central Asia, rediscovery of the importance of Indian Ocean, strengthening of cultural linkages, winning the Diaspora and renewed focus on climate change, nuclear power and terrorism.

It is to be seen how these pro-active engagements are beneficial for India and what dividends it can bring for India.

EXERCISES

1. Discuss the basic objectives of Indian Foreign Policy.
2. Trace the evolution of India's foreign policy from Nehru to Indira Gandhi.
3. Examine the changes and shifts in Indian foreign policy in post-Indira Gandhi era.
4. Examine India's foreign policy in the post-Cold War era.
5. Analyze the development of the Indo-US relations during the tenure of UPA-I and UPA-II and the nuke deal.

6. Comment on the evolution of Indo-US relations.

7. Do you think an Indo-Russian relation is a 'time-tested' tie? Argue.

8. Discuss the evolution of Indo-Russian relations in the post-Soviet era.

9. Highlighting the major irritants discuss the Indo-China relations.

10. Discuss the major disturbing factor leading to the 'trust deficit' between India and Pakistan.

11. Comment on the development of Indo-Pak relations over the years.

12. Point out the major irritants in the Indo-Bangladesh relations. Analyze the trend of development of Indo-Bangladesh relations.

13. How has the Indo-Sri Lankan relations have grown over the years?

14. Discuss the evolution of Indo-Nepal relations.

15. Why do you think Bhutan figures significantly in the India-Bhutan relations? In this context discuss how both have cultivated their relations over the years?

16. Comment on India's Look-East Policy (LEP).

REFERENCES

[1] Doctor, Adi H., *Essays on India's Foreign Policy*, National Publishing House, New Delhi, 1977, p. 36.

[2] Bandyopadhyaya, Jayantanuja, *The Making of India's Foreign Policy,* Allied Publishers, New Delhi, 1991, p. 74.

[3] Asopa, Sheel K., "Fifty Years of Panchsheel and India–China Relations," in Mahavir Singh (Ed.) *Panchsheel: Retrospect and Prospect*, Maulana Azad Institute of Asian Studies, Kolkata, Shipra Publications, New Delhi, 2005, pp. 89–90.

[4] Cohen, Stephen P., *Emerging Power India,* Oxford India Paperbacks, New Delhi, 2006, p. 38.

[5] Dutt, V.P., *India's Foreign Policy Since Independence,* National Book Trust, New Delhi, 2007, p. 5.

[6] Mishra, Pramod Kumar, "Responding to the Changing Global Milieu From Nehru to Vajpayee," in Nalini Kant Jha (Ed.), *India's Foreign Policy in a Changing World*, South Asian Publishers, New Delhi, 2000, p. 51.

[7] Dutt, V.P., *India's Foreign Policy,* Vikas Publishing House, New Delhi, 1987, p. 83.

[8] Chengappa, Raj, "The New Nuclear Future", India Today, 20 October, 2008, pp. 44–47.

[9] "PM, Gilani agreed: Talks must resume", *The Statesman,* 17 July, 2009.

SUGGESTED READING

Chakrabarti, Radharaman and Lahiri, Iman Kalyan (Eds.), *India's Constructive Engagement in Asia and Around,* Academic Excellence, Delhi, 2012.

Dubey, Muchkund, *India's Foreign Policy: Coping with the Changing World*, Pearson Education, Delhi, 2012

Kothari, Rajkumar (Ed.), *Indian Foreign Policy in the New Millennium,* Academic Excellence, Delhi, 2010.

Kothari, Raj Kumar (Ed.), *Emerging India as a Global Partner: Growing Ties and Challenges,* Atlantic Publishers and Distributors, New Delhi, 2012.

19

Environment and International Relations

The Earth Day (April 22) and the World Environment Day (June 5) are celebrated every year, all around the globe, to raise awareness about environmental problems and to work for a more concerted action towards tackling them. But the question is, how far is the world community aware of the challenges to the environment? As discussed in Chapter 4 under the section on sustainable development, the environment has been a prime concern of international community for a long time. With the onset of globalization, growth of market economy and technological revolution, the global environment, especially that of the developing countries, stands threatened. Therefore, time has come to rethink about international relations and its connection with the environment. The noteworthy initiative that was taken by the international community to voice their environmental concerns was the Stockholm Conference (1972) on Environment under the auspices of the United Nations. Since then, a number of summits and conferences have been held and a number of conventions have been passed to sensitize the states and the world population about the environmental problems such as global warming, climate change, pollution (air, water and sound) and sustainable development.

GLOBAL INITIATIVES, CONFERENCES AND SUMMITS RELATING TO ENVIRONMENT SINCE 1972

As we have seen in Chapter 14, the whole initiative regarding the world environment took root with the formation of 'Club of Rome' in the year 1972. They argued that if the present increasing trend in population, food and pollution continue, given finite resource supplies, the limits to growth on the planet will be reached within the next 100 years and there would arise problems of sustainability.

The same year, the United Nations Conference on the Human Environment (also known as the **Stockholm Conference**) was held in Stockholm, Sweden, during 5–16 June 1972. It was the UN's first major conference on international environmental issues, and it marked a turning point in the development of international environmental politics. The **Declaration of the United Nations Conference on the Human Environment**, or **Stockholm Declaration**, was adopted on June 16, 1972 by the United Nations at the 21st plenary meeting as the first document in the international environmental law to recognize the right to a healthy environment.

The other landmarks in the environmental awareness thinking were obviously the *World Conservation Strategy* (1980), *Our Common Future* (1987), and *Caring for the Earth (*1991) (see Chapter 14).

Besides these landmark events in arousing environmental awareness, the other remarkable summits and conferences were as follows:

1. *UNEP, 1972:* United Nations Environment Programme (UNEP) was formed as a result of the United Nations Conference on the Human Environment in June 1972. Its main function is to coordinate the UN environment programmes at the global and regional levels.

2. *Bucharest Population Conference, 1974:* The year 1974 had been designated as the World Population Year and with this theme in the backdrop, the first World Conference on Population was held in Bucharest, Romania under the auspices of the UN. 135 countries participated in the Conference. The Conference focused on the relationship between population issues and development, and proposed the World Population Plan of Action. It was followed up by the International Conference on Population, which was held in Mexico City in 1984.

3. *Cocoyoc Declaration, 1974:* A symposium in Cocoyoc, Mexico was held in 1974. It was chaired by the late Barbara Ward. This symposium was organized by the UNEP and the United Nations Commission on Trade and Development (UNCTAD). The remarkable feature of this symposium was the adoption of the **Cocoyoc Declaration,** which was viewed as a proclamation of sustainable development.

The **Cocoyoc Declaration** ends with the following observation:

> *The road forward does not lie through the despair of doom watching or through the easy optimism of successive technological fixes. It lies through a careful and dispassionate assessment of the 'outer limits', through cooperative search for ways to achieve the 'inner limits' of fundamental human rights, through the building of social structures to express those rights, and through all the patient work of devising techniques and styles of development which enhance and preserve our planetary inheritance.*[1]

4. *Rome Food Conference, 1974:* This was the first **World Food Conference** held in Rome in 1974 under the auspices of the UN Food and Agriculture Organization (FAO). The outcome was the formation of the World Food Council and World Food Programme. It also also led to the follow-up World Food Conferences.

5. *Habitat Conference, 1976:* The United Nations convened the Habitat: United Nations Conference on Human Settlements in Vancouver, Canada, from 31 May till 11 June 1976. This Conference focused on the plight of cities as a result of increased urbanization, especially in the developing countries, and it resulted in the establishment of a new Habitat programme in the UN system.

6. *Green Belt Movement, 1977:* Professor Wangari Maathai established the organization in 1977, under the auspices of the National Council of Women of Kenya in order to take a holistic approach to development by focusing on environmental conservation, community development and capacity building.

7. *Desertification Conference, 1977:* This Conference on Desertification was held under the auspices of the UN in Nairobi, Kenya from 29 August to 9 September, 1977. This was the first international conference where the issue of desertification on a global scale was addressed. The outcome of this conference was the Plan of Action to Combat Desertification.

8. *Water Conference 1977:* This United Nations Water Conference was held in Mar del Plata, Argentina from 14 to 25 March, 1977. This Conference recognized the central role of water in public health and environmental planning. Freshwater issues were thus discussed and that too in the context of sustainable development. It also recognized that:

- global climate change could affect freshwater resources and the hydrological cycle through higher temperatures and decreased precipitation leading to decreased water supplies and increased demand for water;

- increases in climate extremes, such as floods or droughts, could further stress water resources;
- a sea level rise would put low-lying countries at risk; and
- atmospheric pollutants could affect freshwater resources.

The Conference recommended a number of measures/techniques that the international community can develop and apply in assessing the potential adverse effects of the above.

9. *World Climate Conference, Geneva, 1979:* The World Climate Conferences actually are a series of international meetings organized by the World Meteorological Organization (WMO) on global climate issues. The **First World Climate Conference** was held on 12–23 February 1979 in Geneva and it focused on the increasing emission of carbon dioxide resulting in "greenhouse" effect. The outcome of this Conference was the establishment of the World Climate Programme (WCP), the World Climate Research Programme and the Intergovernmental Panel on Climate Change (IPCC) by WMO and UNEP in 1988. The **Second World Climate Conference** was held from 29 October to 7 November 1990, Geneva. The notable feature of this Conference was the establishment of the United Nations Framework Convention on Climate Change (UNFCC) amidst differences over climate change issues. The **Third World Climate Conference** was held from 31 August to 4 September, 2009 Geneva. The focus was on climate predictions and information for decision-making that help to cope with the changing conditions.

10. *Brandt Commission Report, 1980:* The Brandt Commission was the Independent Commission on International Development Issues and it was chaired by the former West German Chancellor, Willy Brandt. In the report entitled *North-South: A Programme for Survival,* he recommended an increase in aid to developing countries and also called for environmental impact assessments of development proposals.

11. *Charter for Nature, 1982:* The UN General Assembly adopted a **World Charter for Nature** prepared by IUCN on 28 October, 1982. It proclaimed five "principles of conservation by which all human conduct affecting nature is to be guided and judged."

The general principles of the **World Charter for Nature** are:

(i) Nature shall be respected and its essential processes shall not be impaired.

(ii) The genetic viability on the earth shall not be compromised; the population levels of all life forms, wild and domesticated, must be at least sufficient for their survival, and to this end necessary habitat shall be safeguarded.

(iii) All areas of the earth, both land and sea, shall be subject to these principles of conservation; special protection shall be given to unique areas, to representative samples of all the different types of ecosystems and to the habitat of rare or endangered species.

(iv) Ecosystems and organisms, as well as the land, marine and atmospheric resources that are utilized by man, shall be managed to achieve and maintain optimum sustainable productivity, but not in such a way as to endanger the integrity of those other ecosystems or species with which they coexist.

(v) Nature shall be secured against degradation caused by warfare or other hostile activities.[2]

12. *Montreal Protocol, 1987:* This **Montreal Protocol on Substances that Deplete the Ozone Layer** was a protocol to the Vienna Convention for the Protection of the Ozone Layer. This protocol aimed at reducing depletion of the ozone layer and it was negotiated in Montreal under the auspices of UNEP. The treaty was opened for signature on 16 September, 1987, and was brought into force on 1 January, 1989. Since then, it has undergone seven revisions, in 1990 (London), 1991 (Nairobi), 1992 (Copenhagen), 1993 (Bangkok), 1995 (Vienna), 1997 (Montreal), and 1999 (Beijing).

13. *Global Environment Facility (GEF):* The World Bank, UNDP, and UNEP created this intergovernmental financial organization. GEF provides grants to developing countries for projects related to biodiversity, climate change, international waters, land degradation, the ozone layer, and persistent organic pollutants.

14. *Rio Conference, 1992:* The United Nations Conference on Environment and Development (UNCED), also referred to as the *Rio Summit* or the *Earth Summit*, was held from 3 June to 14 June 1992. The major breakthrough achieved in this Summit was the **Agenda 21: Green Paths to the Future** or the **Rio Declaration of 1992**. The Rio Declaration consisted of 27 principles intended to guide future sustainable development around the world [see Chapter 14 for details]. The UNGA created the **Commission on Sustainable Development** (CSD) to coordinate the implementation of *Agenda 21* into the programmes and processes of the UN system.

15. *Cairo Conference, 1994:* The United Nations coordinated an **International Conference on Population and Development (ICPD)** in Cairo, Egypt from 5 to 13 September 1994. The recommendations that came up from this Conference were in the issues of improving reproductive health services and the position of women in society. The outcome of the Conference was the Programme of Action, which became the guiding document for the United Nations Population Fund (UNFPA).

According to the official ICPD release, the conference delegates arrived at a consensus on four qualitative and quantitative goals for universal education, reduction of infant and child mortality, reduction of maternal mortality and access to reproductive and sexual health services including family planning.

16. *Habitat II, 1996:* The Second United Nations Conference on Human Settlements, called Habitat II, was held in Istanbul, Turkey from 3 to 14 June, 1996. The primary focus of Habitat II was adequate shelter for all and sustainable cities.

17. *Kyoto Protocol, 1997:* The third meeting of the Conference of Parties to the UN Climate Change Convention in Kyoto, Japan adopted the Kyoto Protocol (features discussed later) to reduce global emissions of greenhouse gases.

18. *Millennium Development Goals (MDGs), 2000:* At the United Nations Millennium Summit, the UN General Assembly approved eight Millennium Development Goals, all of which are interrelated, aimed at ensuring "environmental sustainability" (Goal-7).

Goal-7, aimed to ensure environmental sustainability, upholds:

- Target 7A: Integrate the principles of sustainable development into country policies and programmes; reverse loss of environmental resources.

- Target 7B: Reduce biodiversity loss, achieving, by 2010, a significant reduction in the rate of loss.

- Target 7C: Halve, by 2015, the proportion of the population without sustainable access to safe drinking water and basic sanitation.

- Target 7D: By 2020, to have achieved a significant improvement in the lives of at least 100 million slum-dwellers.

19. *Johannesburg Summit, 2002:* World Summit on Sustainable Development (WSSD) (also known as Rio+10) under the auspices of the UN was held in Johannesburg, South Africa, to assess the global situation and progress in implementing international agreements adopted at Rio in 1992 and at the 1972 UN Conference on the Human Environment in Stockholm.

The Political Declaration that was adopted stated that the members would undertake "a collective responsibility to advance and strengthen the interdependent and mutually reinforcing pillars of sustainable development, economic development, social development and environmental protection at the local, national, regional and global levels" and a Plan of Implementation for achieving this.

20. *Vienna Climate Change Talks, 2007:* A round of climate change talks under the auspices of the United Nations Framework Convention on Climate Change (UNFCCC) was held in Vienna, Austria. At Vienna, the "Ad Hoc Working Group" (AWG) on Further Commitments of Annex I Parties (industrialized countries) under the Kyoto Protocol officially recognized the Intergovernmental Panel on Climate Change's indication that global emissions of greenhouse gases need to peak in the next 10–15 years and then be reduced to very low levels, well below half of levels in 2000 by mid-century, if concentrations are to be stabilized at safe levels. The group also officially recognized that avoiding the most catastrophic forecasts made by the IPCC, including very frequent and severe droughts and water-shortages in large parts of the world, would entail emission reductions.

21. *High-level conference on World Food Security, 2008*:   The High-level Conference on World Food Security: The Challenges of Climate Change and Bioenergy was held from 3 to 5 June 2008 in FAO Headquarters in Rome. 181 member countries participated in this Conference. The highlight of the Conference was the adoption of a declaration calling on the international community to increase assistance for developing countries, in particular the least developed countries, which are affected by high food prices.

22. *United Nations Framework Convention on Climate Change*:   Alongside the noteworthy developments mentioned before in the environmental sphere, another progress took place after the Rio Summit, better known as the United Nations Conference on Environment and Development (UNCED) held in Rio de Janeiro from 3 to 14 June 1992. This was the creation of the **United Nations Framework Convention on Climate Change** (UNFCCC).

The treaty itself sets no mandatory limits on greenhouse gas emissions for individual countries and contains no enforcement mechanisms, but it provides for updates (called protocols) that would set mandatory emission limits. The principal update is the Kyoto Protocol of 1997. The UNFCCC was opened for signature on 9 May 1992. It came into force on 21 March 1994. As of December 2009, UNFCCC had 192 parties. The significance of the UNFCCC since it has come into force, can be found in the annual **Conferences of the Parties (COP)** to assess progress made in dealing with climate change. Since 1995 till the present, COP meets annually to discuss issues of climate change. The Kyoto Protocol is the result of such meetings.

Since 1995, sixteen such annual COPs have been held in Berlin (1995), Switzerland (1996), Kyoto (1997), Buenos Aires (1998 and 2004), Bonn (1999 and 2001), The Hague (2000), Marrakech (2001), New Delhi (2002), Milan (2003), Montreal (2005), Nairobi (2006), Bali (2007), Poznañ (2008), Copenhagen (2009) and Cancún (2010).

Some of the important Conferences and their outcomes are discussed below.

UN Climate Change Conference 2005 was held in Montreal. This was significant as this was the first **Meeting of the Parties** (MOP-1) to the Kyoto Protocol since their initial meeting in Kyoto in 1997. The **Montreal Action Plan** is an agreement reached out at the end of the conference to extend the life of the Kyoto Protocol beyond its 2012 expiration date and negotiate deeper cuts in greenhouse gas emissions.

UN Climate Change Conference 2007 was held at Bali, Indonesia where the notable event was the adoption of the **Bali Action Plan** for structured negotiation on the post-2012 framework (the end of the first commitment period of the Kyoto Protocol).

UN Climate Change Conference 2009 was held at Copenhagen, Denmark. It was the 15th Session of the Conference of the Parties to the UNFCCC and the fifth Meeting of the Parties (MOP). The goal of this meeting was to establish a successor to the Kyoto Protocol so that a global climate agreement could come into effect from 2013 after the expiry of the first commitment period under the Kyoto Protocol.

The **United Nations Climate Change Conference 2010** that took place in **Cancun**, Mexico, was the sixteenth Conference of the Parties (COP) and the sixth Meeting of the Parties (MOP) to the Kyoto Protocol.

The UN Climate Change Conferences have never been able to register historical breakthroughs ever since their initiation chiefly because of the North-South divide on climate change and other environment issues. Consensus among the participating countries is always difficult. The Kyoto Protocol has been only a major achievement, but negotiations for the post-Kyoto successor are proving to be a stumbling block. The Copenhagen Conference 2009 could not hammer out a new treaty.

Again, the differences between the developing countries and developed countries came to the fore. The developing countries, least developed countries and small island countries refused to budge from their position and reiterated the historical responsibility of the developed countries for maximum greenhouse emission. They demanded that climate change action should be guided by principles of historical responsibility and common and differentiated responsibility. They also wanted the extension of the Kyoto Protocol which gives some relief to developing countries. However, the US and the developed countries wanted to replace the Kyoto Protocol whereby cuts in emission of greenhouse gases become applicable to poor countries too and also wanted large emitters like India and China to be more transparent about domestic emission curbing actions. India did not shift her position during the Copenhagen negotiations, but clauses in the Accord suggest that emission cut by her even those not supported by foreign finance may be open to international consultations. Further, there was no agreement on designing a legally binding instrument that will govern climate change beyond 2012. Thus, the Copenhagen Accord has failed to deliver the goods to the countries of the South, and many feel that there is a tilt towards the developed countries.

The Cancun Conference, 2010 also could not be said to be successful in delivering the goods to the world. The Cancun documents recognize emission targets set by industrialized and developing countries and require that inventories of the national emissions are shared annually by industrialized countries and once every two years by the developing countries. The agreements are expected to be transformed into a legal treaty at next December 2011 conference in Durban, South Africa. There is also a pledge of $30 billion fast-start finance from industrialized countries to support climate action in developing countries. However, the environment groups point out that the Cancun Agreement has failed to establish any mechanism to ensure that the industrialized countries did not break the pledges made. They also fear that the Cancun Agreement might finally provide a platform to abandon the Kyoto Protocol. Further, India's action has been criticized. India has shifted from her earlier position and has given a hint that she would eventually consider legally binding curbs on emissions, which has been viewed as a betrayal. The poor countries have seen this as a keen India to become a part of the global alliance of polluters at the cost of poor countries. Thus, the politics of environment will continue in the future also as long as there is the North-South divide and the world is divided into haves and have-nots.

SOME INTERNATIONAL CONVENTIONS ON ENVIRONMENT AND ENVIRONMENT RELATED MATTERS

Several Global Conventions relating to environmental protection have been ratified by a large number of states. Some of them are:

- Convention on the International Trade in Endangered Species of Wild Flora and Fauna (CITES), 1973
- The Convention on Wetlands of international Importance Especially as Waterflow Habitat, 1971
- The Convention Concerning the Protection of the World Cultural and Natural Heritage, 1972
- The Convention on the Prevention of Marine Pollution by Dumping Wastes and Other Matter, 1972
- International Convention for the Prevention of Marine Pollution by Dumping from Ships and Aircraft, 1973
- International Convention Relating to Intervention on the High Seas in Cases of Oil Pollution Casualties, 1969
- International Convention on Civil Liability for Oil Pollution Damage, 1969
- United Nations Convention on the Law of the Sea, 1982

CONVENTIONS REGARDING REGULATION OF HAZARDOUS WASTES AND HAZARDOUS CHEMICALS

- European Agreement concerning the International Carriage of Dangerous Goods by Road, Geneva, 1957
- FAO International Code of Conduct on the distribution and use of Pesticides, Rome, 1985
- Basel Convention on the Control of Transboundary Movements of Hazardous Wastes and their Disposal, Basel, 1989

- Convention on Civil Liability for Damage Caused during Carriage of Dangerous Goods by Road, Rail, and Inland Navigation Vessels (CRTD), Geneva, 1989
- Convention on the ban of the Import into Africa and the Control of Transboundary Movements and Management of Hazardous Wastes within Africa, Bamako, 1991
- Convention on the Transboundary Effects of Industrial Accidents, Helsinki, 1992
- Convention to ban the Importation into Forum Island Countries of Hazardous and Radioactive Wastes and to Control the Transboundary Movement and Management of Hazardous Wastes within the South Pacific Region, Waigani, 1995
- Rotterdam Convention on the Prior Informed Consent Procedure for Certain Hazardous Chemicals and Pesticides in International Trade, Rotterdam, 1998.
- European Agreement Concerning the International Carriage of Dangerous Goods by Inland Waterways, Geneva, 2000
- Stockholm Convention on Persistent Organic Pollutants, Stockholm, 2001

CONVENTIONS RELATING TO NUCLEAR SAFETY

- Vienna Convention on Civil Liability for Nuclear Damage, Vienna, 1963
- Treaty Banning Nuclear Weapon Tests in the Atmosphere, in Outer Space, and Under Water, (PTBT) 1963
- Convention on Assistance in the Case of a Nuclear Accident or Radiological Emergency (Assistance Convention), Vienna, 1986
- Convention on Early Notification of a Nuclear Accident (Notification Convention), Vienna, 1986
- Convention on Nuclear Safety, Vienna, 1994
- Comprehensive Test Ban Treaty, 1996

FEATURES OF KYOTO PROTOCOL, 1997

The final shape to the Kyoto Protocol could be given after much bargaining and adjustments. It was adopted on 11 December, 1997. The main features of the Kyoto Protocol are as follows:

1. Under the Protocol, 37 countries ("Annex I countries") commit themselves to a reduction of four greenhouse gases (GHG) (carbon dioxide, methane, nitrous oxide, sulphur hexafluoride) and two groups

of gases (hydrofluorocarbons and perfluorocarbons) produced by them, and all member countries give general commitments. Annex I countries agreed to reduce their collective greenhouse gas emissions by 5.2% relative to levels prevailing in 1990.

2. Most non-Annex I Parties belonged to the low-income group, with a very few classified as middle-income. They are not obligated by the limits of emissions in the Kyoto Protocol. Fast growing economy countries like China, South Africa, India and Brazil are still in this non-obligated group.

3. The agreement aims to lower overall emissions from a group of six greenhouse gases by 2008–12. Cuts in the three most important gases – carbon dioxide (CO_2), methane (CH_4), and nitrous oxide (N_2O) and cuts in three long-lived industrial gases – hydrofluorocarbons (HFCs), perfluorocarbons (PFCs), and sulphur hexafluoride (SF_6) were agreed upon.

4. The commitment period was to be from 2008–12.

5. Inclusion among cuts of sources and removal of defined 'sinks' or carbon absorbent material was limited to aforestation, reforestation and deforestation since 1990.

6. Clean Development Mechanism (CDM), emissions trading and joint projects implementation were agreed upon towards fulfilling emission cuts which came to be identified as 'voluntary' commitments of non-Annex 1 or developing countries.

7. Absence of any mechanism to ensure compliance or punitive measures for non-compliance.

The Kyoto Protocol was about to expire at the end of 2012 but it was extended at the UN Climate Change Conference which was held at Doha, 26 November–8 December 2012. It was extended till 2020. In this Climate Change Conference it was also agreed that a successor to the Kyoto Protocol would be formulated by 2015 and implemented by 2020.

The environment is the prime concern of the international community at present. But a lot of politics is involved in it as we have seen in the UN Climate Change Conferences or any of the environment related negotiations. Despite such lack of consensus among the members of the international community, certain landmark agreements and conventions have come into force. Several of these legal instruments are based on the realization that environmental protection alone is not sufficient and that it must be seen within the overall context of the many socio-economic and developmental issues that challenge the nations of the world. Sustainable development is the key to progress as well as to a safe earth that we can give to our future generations. A common concern of mankind should prevent the world community from committing the 'tragedy of the commons'*. The motto should be "Give Earth a Chance" and thereby secure our future.

United Nations Climate Change Conference, Paris, 30 November–11 December, 2015

The UN Climate Change Conference held in Paris, 30 November–11 December, 2015 has to be analysed in the backdrop of UN Climate Change Conference of 2011, 2012, 2013 and 2014.

The UN Climate Change Conference held in Durban from November 28–December 9, 2011 (COP17/CMP7) showed a pledge on the part of International Community to implement the Kyoto Protocol, 1997, Bali Action Plan, 2007 and the Cancun Agreement, 2010. A decision was also taken by the Parties to adopt a universal legal agreement on climate change which was to take effect in 2020.

The UN Climate Change Conference held in Doha, 26 November–8. December, 2012 was quite remarkable as it agreed to extend the validity of the Kyoto Protocol till 2020. It also for the first time incorporated the 'Loss and Damage' mechanism by which the rich nations agreed finance to help developing countries to work towards clean energy and adapt to climate change. It also agreed to formulate a successor to Kyoto Protocol.

The UN Climate Change Conference held in Warsaw, from 11 November–23 November, 2013 (COP19/CMP9) ended with the adoption of key decisions regarding (1) further advancing the Durban Platform, (2) the Green Climate Fund and Long-Term Finance, (3) the Warsaw Framework for REDD Plus, (4) the Warsaw International Mechanism for Loss and Damage among others.

The UN Climate Change Conference, held in Lima, 1 December–12 December, 2014 (COP20/CMP10) was intended to increase the pace of adoption of a Universal Climate Agreement in Paris in 2015 and to galvanize transformative action in all countries to reduce emissions.

The UN Climate Change Conference held in Paris, 30 November–11 December, 2015 (COP21/CMP11) was a breakthrough in a sense that 195 nations agreed on a plan, which they have been deliberating for years, to reduce the greenhouse gases and address the problem of global warming. The goal of the Paris Plan is to bring down pollution levels so that the rise in global temperature can be limited to 2 degrees celsius. It includes commitments by majority countries of the 195 signatories to cut or limit the rise of their greenhouse gas emissions. The signatories also agreed to the convening of meetings every 5 years to take stock, and realfirm their pledges so that the 2 degrees goal is not lost midway. The Paris Agreement also includes regular

---

*The notion that 'rational' individual actions can lead to 'irrational' collective practices resulting in catastrophic over-exploitation of common resources.

transparent reporting of every country's carbon reductions. The stupendous job involved in the signing of the Paris Agreement by countries between 22 April, 2016 (Earth Day) and 21 April, 2017 has to be followed by adoption/ratification according to national procedures of signatories.

However, observers pointed out that much success of the Paris Agreement depend on the goodwill of individual signatories especially the two largest carbon emitters of the world—the USA and China. However, it must be noted that in November 2014, both the USA and China had agreed to limit greenhouse gases emissions (US–China Joint Announcement on Climate Change and Clean Energy Co-operation, 2014). Only future can speak whether Paris Agreement will live upto its expectations or not. Never-the-less the UN Secretary-General Ban Ki-Moon called it a "monumental success for the planet and its people". A safe and green planet needs to be ensured for our future generations and for this climate change issue needs to be addressed on an emergency basis.

EXERCISES

1. Discuss the gradual evolution of the consciousness about the environment through various conferences and adoption of various conventions.

2. Discuss the UNFCCC and the efforts of the subsequent UN Climate Change Conferences to tackle global climate change. Briefly state the features of the Kyoto Protocol.

REFERENCES

[1]   http://www.unep.org/geo/geo3/english/045.htm.

[2]   http://eelink.net/~asilwildlife/wcn.html.

20

![decorative band]

Prominent Economic Institutions/ Arrangements

INTRODUCTION

We have seen in Chapter 10 that how States located in a particular region identifying their common mutual interests have created regional arrangements. Thus, what we observe in the present international scenario is that Regional Trading Agreements (RTAs) have gained increased prominence. Repeated failures of multilateral negotiations, especially at various ministerial meets of the World Trade Organization (WTO), have lead to an increase in the number of

RTAs. Another trend which is noticeable is that emerging economies are fostering economic bonds among themselves. There has been steady rise of many a new economic groupings and initiatives alongside the existing international institutions like IMF, World Bank and WTO and regional arrangements like, European Union, SAARC, ASEAN, AU, OPEC and several others. In the context of Indian foreign policy these have important bearings. Therefore, this Chapter attempts to take up a few of such groupings/initiatives for analysis. This will enable the students to grasp the current trend of international political economy.

INTERNATIONAL MONETARY FUND (IMF)

The **International Monetary Fund (IMF)** was conceived by 45 States in the United Nations Monetary and Fiscal Conference held immediately after the Second World War in Bretton Woods, New Hampshire, 1944. As a part of the "Bretton Woods Agreement" the International Monetary Fund (IMF) and the International Bank for Reconstruction and Development (IBRD) were evolved to stabilize the international monetary system in the aftermath of the 'Great Depression'. IMF came into existence on 27 December 1945 when 29 countries signed the agreement, with a goal to stabilize exchange rates and assist the reconstruction of the world's international payment system.

IMF therefore, functions as an organization to foster global monetary cooperation, secure financial stability, facilitate international trade, promote high employment and sustainable economic growth, and reduce poverty around the world. As of 2011, IMF had 187 members. In April 2012, Republic of South Sudan joined the IMF, becoming the institution's 188th member.

The purposes and functions of the IMF were stated to be:

1. to promote international economic cooperation,
2. to facilitate the expansion and balanced growth of international trade,
3. to create more employment opportunities,
4. to promote exchange rate stability,
5. to assist in the establishment of a multilateral system of payments,
6. to solve the problems of international liquidity by suggesting various measures including efforts by which resources are made available to member countries to meet balance of payments needs.

Its headquarter is in Washington, D.C. Each member country of the IMF is assigned a quota, based broadly on its relative size in the world economy. It is on the basis of this quota that a member's organizational relation with IMF determines its voting power, Special Drawing Rights (SDR) and also access to financing. On 28 June 2011, Christine Lagarde was named Managing Director of the IMF, replacing Dominique Strauss-Kahn (1 November 2007–18 May 2011).

India joined the IMF on 27 December 1945 and IMF credit during turbulent period of India's economy in 1981–1982 and 1991–1993 had helped to tide over the balance of payment deficit. Yet, India and other emerging economies like the BRICS countries have been demanding reforms of the quota system and voting rights. The G-20 countries also want a dynamic system of calculating the economic weightage of a country.

THE WORLD BANK

The World Bank is also the outcome of the Bretton Woods Conference in 1944 like the International Monetary Fund. The World Bank is headquartered in Washington D.C.

The World Bank is a vital source of financial and technical assistance to developing countries around the world. Its mission is to "fight poverty with passion and professionalism for lasting results, and to help people help themselves and their environment by providing resources, sharing knowledge, building capacity and forging partnerships in the public and private sectors."

World Bank is not a usual bank we are used to. As it targets to alleviate poverty and augment development among poorer nations of the world, it functions through collaborative institutions which are two in number. These, in turn, embark on development projects for the targeted countries. These development institutions are owned by 188 member countries, collectively. The two development institutions are the International Bank for Reconstruction and Development (IBRD) and the International Development Association (IDA). IBRD target middle-income, but credit worthy poorer countries and IDA target poorest countries. These development institutions are supported by International Finance Corporation (IFC), Multilateral Investment Guarantee Agency (MIGA) and the International Centre for the Settlement of Investment Disputes (ICSID).

World Bank Group Branches

- International Bank for Reconstruction and Development (IBRD)
- International Development Association (IDA)
- International Finance Corporation (IFC)
- Multilateral Investment Guarantee Agency (MIGA)
- International Centre for the Settlement of Investment Disputes (ICSID)

Together, these branches provide low-interest loans, interest-free credits and grants to developing countries for a wide array of purposes that include investments in education, health, public administration, infrastructure, financial and private sector development, agriculture and environmental and natural resource management.

To become a member of the Bank, under the IBRD Articles of Agreement, a country must first join the International Monetary Fund (IMF). Membership in IDA, IFC and MIGA are conditional on membership in IBRD. Member countries govern the World Bank Group through the Boards of Governors and the Boards of Executive Directors. These bodies make all major decisions for the organizations.

Total member countries in each institution

The International Bank for Reconstruction and Development (IBRD)	**188**
The International Development Association (IDA)	**172**
The International Finance Corporation (IFC)	**184**
The Multilateral Investment Guarantee Agency (MIGA)	**177**
The International Centre for Settlement of Investment Disputes (ICSID)	**147**

India joined the World Bank in 1944, and therefore, is one of the oldest members. It is the World Bank's largest single borrower, in market-based loans from the International Bank for Reconstruction and Development (IBRD) and development credits from the International Development Association. Andhra Pradesh was the first state to benefit from of state-focused lending and Uttar Pradesh the Second in 2000.

However, the World Bank activities like the IMF have invited criticisms from the developing world. There is a hegemony of developed world, and the transactions lack transparency and democracy. The Structural Adjustment Programmes have created hurdles for the poor developing countries, and have added to their dismal economic performance. The 1980s witnessed the sub-Saharan countries facing tremendous crisis due to the Structural Adjustment Programmes. There is strong demand for democratization of the institutions dominating the international political economy.

WORLD TRADE ORGANIZATION (WTO)

The General Agreement on Tariffs and Trade (GATT) was established in 1 January 1948 after the end of the Second World War. It was a multilateral instrument with the aim to liberalize world trade with a view to promote economic growth and development and welfare of the people all around the globe. The significant rounds of GATT were the First Round at Geneva in 1947, the Kennedy Round of 1964–1967, the Tokyo Round of 1973–1979 and the Uruguay Round of 1986–1994. The Final Act of the Uruguay Round establishing the WTO regime was signed in 15 April 1994 during the Ministerial Meeting at Marrakesh, Morocco. With the signing of the Marrakesh Agreement the WTO came into existence on 1 January 1995.

Members can join the system of WTO through negotiation and consequently acquire memebership. For this, they have to make commitments to open their markets and to abide by the rules. These commitments arise out of membership or accession to negotiations. Countries at present negotiating membership are WTO "observers", and they are 27 in number including the Holy See. With the exception of the Holy See, observers must start accession negotiations within five years of becoming observers. The total number of members is 157 as on 24 August 2012. Laos has negotiated its membership accession package to WTO in October 2012. After ratification, Laos will become 158th member of WTO after thirty days of ratification.

The WTO agreements provide legal basis of rules. These are negotiated in bulk and also signed by the world's trading nations in bulk, as mentioned above, in several rounds of GATT negotiations. Currently, negotiations are on through the Doha rounds. The objective of the WTO is to ensure free trade flow by removing obstacles on the basis of rules which will be transparent and predictable.

WTO has a unique dispute settlement procedure through rulings by a panel which are then either endorsed or rejected by the all the members of WTO. Disputes may continue for a long period of time and sometimes even there can be 'out of court' settlement. As of January 2008, out of 369, 136 cases have been settled by the Panel and rest of the cases have been mostly 'out of court' settlement.

The functioning components of the WTO are:

1. Multi-Fibre Agreement (MFA)
2. Agreements on Agriculture (AoA)
3. Trade Related Investment Measures (TRIMs)
4. Trade Related Intellectual Property Rights (TRIPS)
5. General Agreement on Trade and Services (GATS)

The WTO is currently the host to new negotiations, under the 'Doha Development Agenda' launched in 2001. The Doha Round began with a ministerial-level meeting in Doha, Qatar in 2001. Subsequent ministerial meetings took place in Cancún, Mexico in 2003, and Hong Kong in 2005. Related negotiations took place in Paris, France (2005); in Potsdam, Germany (2007); and Geneva, Switzerland (2004, 2006, 2008) and as of May 2012 the future of the Doha Round remains uncertain.

The WTO regime has been fraught with controversy. The developing countries allege that WTO policies are discriminatory. The Intellectual Property Rights (IPR) and Patent regime, labour policies, environment, dumping, agricultural, subsidies among many have raised waves of controversies. India's position for a long time is to have a kind of fair use of the IPR regimes, and allowing the best use of the existing modalities of the IPR regimes under the WTO in the TRIPS.

THE GROUP OF TWENTY (G-20)

Group of Twenty (G-20) is a group of Finance Ministers and Central Bank Governors from 20 economies. The G-20 comprises 19 countries plus the European Union, which is represented by the President of the European Council and by the European Central Bank.

The backdrop for the formation of G-20 was provided by the economic crisis of the late 1990s. This crisis brought the emerging market countries closer, and their regular interactions at fora like the G-7, G-22 and G-33 showed the benefit of regular dialogue with a constant set of participating countries to address global financial issues and reduce the risk of global economic crisis. This gradually led to the institutionalization in the form of G-20 in 1999. From 2008 the G-20 Heads of State Summits initiated.

The objectives of the G-20 Summit are:

1. Policy coordination between its members in order to achieve global economic stability, sustainable growth;

2. To promote financial regulations that reduce risks and prevent future financial crises; and

3. To create a new international financial architecture.

The member countries are Argentina, Australia, Brazil, Canada, China, France, Germany, India, Indonesia, Italy, Japan, Mexico, Russia, Saudi Arabia, South Africa, Republic of Korea, Turkey, United Kingdom, United States of America. Several countries that are not permanent members of the G-20 are extended invitations to participate in the summits. The invitees are chosen by the host country. As in the 2010 Summits, both Canada and South Korea invited Ethiopia (Chair of NEPAD), Malawi (Chair of the African Union), Vietnam (Chair of ASEAN), and Spain. Canada also invited the Netherlands, while South Korea invited Singapore. Both Canada and South Korea invited seven international organizations— the United Nations, the International Labour Organization, the World Bank, the International Monetary Fund, the Organization for Economic Cooperation and Development, the World Trade Organization, and the Financial Stability Board.

The G-20 has made quite a progress on a wide range of issues since 1999, including agreement about policies for growth, reducing abuse of the financial system, dealing with financial crises and combating terrorist financing. It also tries to establish international financial standards based on transparency and exchange of information on fiscal matters to tackle problems like money laundering and financing terrorism.

The global melt down of 2008 made it essential for the G-20 to address the global recession. G-20 member countries pledged to strengthen their cooperation to tackle the economic crisis. It was from 2008 that the G-20 Leaders Summits started to be organized. Accordingly, the G-20 Summits have been held in Washington in 2008, in London and Pittsburgh in 2009, and in Toronto and Seoul in 2010. The Seoul Summit was the first G-20 Summit to be hosted by an emerging country. At this Summit, the Leaders endorsed the *Seoul Action Plan*, a comprehensive package of country-specific policy actions to support strong, sustainable and balanced economic growth.

The G-20 2011 Summit in Cannes pledged to strengthen the progress of G-20, and ensure an active follow-up on processes already underway. It also addressed the critical issues such as the reform of the international monetary system, volatility of commodity prices, adoption of coherent measures to guide the management of capital flows, common principles for cooperation between the IMF and Regional Financial Arrangements and to an Action Plan for local currency bond markets and also the Eurozone crisis.

The G-20 Summit 2012 was held in Los Cabos from18-19 June 2012. The *Los Cabos Declaration* addressed issues like supporting economic stabilization and the global recovery, employment and social protection, trade, strengthening the international financial architecture, reforming the financial sector and fostering financial inclusion, enhancing food security and addressing commodity price volatility, meeting the challenges of development, promoting longer-term prosperity through inclusive green growth and intensifying the fight against corruption. Table 20.1 shows the list of G-20 Summits.

Table 20.1   List of G-20 Summits

Year	Host Country and City
2008 G-20	USA, Washington
2009 G-20	UK, London
2009 G-20	USA, Pittsburgh
2010 G-20	Canada, Toronto
2010 G-20	South Korea, Seoul
2011 G-20	France, Cannes
2012 G-20	Los Cabos, Mexico
2013 G-20	Streina, Saint Petersburg, Russia
2014 G-20	Brisbane, Australia
2015 G-20	Belek, Antalya, Turkey

India has been successful in G-20 in pursuing her objective of inclusion of things like the Mutual Assessment Process (MAP) for measuring imbalances between surplus and deficit economies. India has been cautious over competitive devaluation and advocated that any resurgence of protectionism be resisted and is also against putting a cap on current account balance, proposed by the US at 4 per cent of the Gross Domestic Product (GDP) in the 2010 Summit for it was difficult for individual countries to reach the proposed sustainable current account balances given the structural differences across the countries. In April 2012, prior to the Los Cabos Summit, former Finance Minister Pranab Mukherjee made clear India's intentions. India has called upon G-20 nations, to work out a "credible and ambitious" action plan to put the global economy firmly on the path of recovery as also promote strong, sustainable and balanced growth. In future, India is expected to play greater role in the G-20 along with her BRICS partners.

Eighth G-20 Heads of the States Summit, 5–6 September, 2013, Streina, Saint Petersburg, Russia

G-20 Summit took place in Streina, Saint Petersburg, Russia during 5–6 September 2013. It was the **Eighth G-20 Head of the States Summit**. There was a bit of a rift between Russia and USA regarding providing asylum to Snowden charged of leaking classified information from the National Security Agency (NSA). President Obama called off meeting with President Putin just before the G-20 Summit slated for September 2014. However, the summit took place and the G-20 **5ᵗʰ Anniversary Vision Statement** reaffirmed the commitment of the G-20 countries to act together to

- Raise growth, create jobs and boost confidence;
- Maintain fiscal sustainability;
- Continue to reduce internal and external imbalances;
- Keep markets open for trade and investment;
- Promote a rule-based international economy;
- Ensure a stable, well-functioning and transparent global financial system;
- Support strong and more representative global institutions;
- Promote open and transparent governments; and
- Build an inclusive and sustainable global economy for all.

For these, the G-20 countries proposed strong collective action. The *St. Petersburg Action Plan* upheld strengthening of growth and creation of jobs as top priority and the commitment of G-20 countries to take decisive actions to return to a job-rich, strong, sustainable and balanced growth path.

Ninth G-20 Heads of the States Summit 15–16 November, 2014, Brisbane, Australia

The **Ninth Summit of G-20 Heads of the States** was held in Brisbane, Australia, which was hosted by the Australian President, Tony Abbott, from 15–16 November 2014. There was a tremendous reaction whether Russia should be allowed to participate in the G-20 meeting or not. This was because of Russia's policy towards Ukraine, Russia's response over crash of Malaysian Airlines Flight 17 and also sending of fleet of warships into international waters near Australia to accompany Putin's visit. Stephen Harper, the Canadian President, created an uncomfortable atmosphere for President Putin by asking him to 'get out of Ukraine'. The joint communiqué released after the Summit highlighted the efforts to act together to lift growth and create jobs, to build a stronger, more resilient global economy, to strengthen global institutions, and also addressed issues like energy supply, climate change as well as Ebola virus in west Africa.

Turkey assumed the Presidency of G-20 from 1 December 2014. The priority for Turkish Presidency Summit has been upheld as 'Collective Action for Inclusive and Robust Economic Growth'.This can be done by three 'I's-Inclusiveness, Implementation and Investment for growth. Three pillars for fulfilling this objective will be:

[1] Strengthening the global recovery and lifting the potential

[2] Enhancing resilience

[3] Buttressing sustainability

Tenth G-20 Heads of the States Summit, 15–16 November, 2015, Belek, Antalya, Turkey

The backdrop of Tenth G-20 Summit was much tensed because it took place immediately after the terrorist attacks on Paris. It took the centre stage of the G-20 leaders' discussion. Terrorism, mass migration and global refugee issues were of great concern to the G-20 leaders, and they deliberated on them at full length. Syria, which has a border very close to Antalya, also topped the agenda. Fullest implementation of Bali package addressing the climate change was also discussed and they looked forward for a commitment to a successful Paris Climate Conference. As the global economic growth is uneven and falling far short of expectation, the G-20 leaders discussed concrete steps to boost growth and job creation. The aim is achieving strong, sustainable and balanced global economic growth as well as an all inclusive global economic growth. G-20 leaders also talked about ways of strengthening global financial system. These were reflected in the Antalya-Action Plan which provides for G-20's plan for decisive action for global economic recovery.

BRICS (BRAZIL, RUSSIA, INDIA, CHINA, SOUTH AFRICA)

BRIC was a grouping acronym that referred to the countries of Brazil, Russia, India and China. South Africa was officially admitted as a BRIC nation on 24 December 2010 after being invited by China and the other BRIC countries to join the group. The capital "S" in BRICS now stands for South Africa. In April 2011, South African President Jacob Zuma attended the 2011 BRICS summit in Sanya, China, as a full member. There can be further expansion of BRICS and there is proposed inclusions of Mexico and South Korea.

Goldman Sachs Bank predicted that the economic potential of Brazil, Russia, India and China is such that they could become among the four most dominant economies by the year 2050. Vladimir Putin, President of Russia, was the driving force behind this original cooperative coalition of developing BRIC countries. BRICS countries hold regular Summit level meetings. Table 20.2 gives the list of BRIC/BRICS Summits.

Table 20.2   List of BRICS Summits

Summit	Date	Host Country, City	Host Head of State
1st BRIC	16 June 2009	Russia, Yekaterinburg	Dmitry Medvedev
2nd BRIC	16 April 2010	Brazil, Brasília	Luiz Inácio Lula da Silva
3rd BRICS	14 April 2011	China, Sanya	Hu Jintao
4th BRICS	29 March 2012	India, New Delhi	Manmohan Singh
5th BRICS	26 March 2013	South Africa, Durban	Jacob Zuma
6th BRICS	14 July 2014	Fortaleza & Brasilia, Brazil	Dilma Rousseff
7th BRICS	8 July 2015	Ufa in Bashkortostan, Russia	Vladimir Putin

2011 BRICS Summit took place in Sanya on the island of Hainan, China, on 14 April 2011, and the Theme was *Broad Vision, Shared Prosperity*. The main agenda of the Summit was current international scenario, international economic, financial and trade issues, challenges of sustainable development and cooperation among BRICS countries. The Summit focused on the following:

1. Early conclusion to deadlocked talks on anti-terror law under UN auspices that would curtail funding for illegal groups that partake in violence against states and deny their supporters access to funds, arms, and safe havens
2. United Nations Security Council reform
3. Withdrawal from loans in American dollars
4. Libyan conflict among others

The leaders of BRICS states expressed misgivings about NATO air strikes and urged an end to the two-month conflict in Libya. It is to be noted that in 2011 all five members were present in the UNSC, two as permanent members and other three as non-permanent members and all of them abstained from voting on a resolution 1973 authorizing establishment of 'no-fly zone' over Libya.

The *Sanya Declaration* upheld that by cooperating in economic, financial and trade matters, the BRICS countries will ensure that they enjoy strong and sustained economic growth, unaffected by uncertainties of global economic ups and downs. The Sanya Summit emphasized reforms and improvement of the international monetary and financial system and also proposed for introduction of Special Drawing Rights (SDR) which can be swapped with dollars at a pre-fixed rate. This will give BRICS countries an alternative if not replacement of dollar as the global currency. BRICS countries also envision mutual payments of loans in national currencies rather than in dollars. They propose strict international financial regulation to curb price volatility and strengthening of policy coordination and financial regulation and cooperation to check functioning of international financial and banking systems.

India hosted the Fourth BRICS Summit in New Delhi on 29 March 2012 under the leadership of Prime Minister Dr. Manmohan Singh. Ms. Dilma Rousseff, President of Brazil; Mr. Dmitry Medvedev, President of Russia,

Mr. Hu Jintao, President of China; and Mr. Jacob Zuma, President of South Africa attended the Summit. The theme of the Summit was *BRICS Partnership for Global Stability, Security and Prosperity*.

The *Delhi Declaration*, put forth common position of BRICS countries on various economic and political issues of global and regional importance was issued at the end of the Summit. The Declaration included Delhi Action Plan which highlights the activities to be undertaken under India's chairmanship of BRICS for further cooperation. Leaders focused their discussions on issues of global governance—both political (UN) and economic (IMF and World Bank). They also covered global economic and financial situation, with special focus on the Eurozone sovereign debt crisis, as well as the political issues like developments in Afghanistan, Iran, Syria, etc. The Delhi Declaration also focused on BRICS efforts towards sustainable development and prepared the ground for Rio+20 in Brazil and Conference of the Parties to the Convention of Biological Diversity (CBD-COP11) to be held in Hyderabad in October 2012.

BRICS Leaders held an informal meeting on 18 June 2012 ahead of the formal opening of the G-20 Summit in Los Cabos. Among other issues the Leaders discussed swap arrangements among national currencies as well as reserve pooling. They agreed that G-20 must take serious measures to combat the Eurozone crisis. Therefore, the importance of BRICS as a dialogue forum cannot be denied. If the members are able to sustain this coordination and cooperation to tackle international issues, then BRICS will be a success.

Fifth BRICS Summit 26–27 March, 2013, Durban, South Africa

The **Fifth BRICS Summit** was hosted by South Africa and held at Durban during 26–27 March 2013. With the Durban Summit, BRICS completed the first cycle of all the member countries hosting the summits. The BRICS Summit being held in South Africa coincided with 50th Anniversary celebrations of Organization of African Unity, now renamed as African Union. Landmark decisions taken were regarding establishment of new Development Bank, Contingent Reserve Arrangement (CRA), establishment of BRICS Think Tank and BRICS Business Council. Two Agreements were concluded under auspices of the BRICS Interbank Cooperation Mechanism.

1. The BRICS Multilateral Infrastructure Co-Financing Agreement for Africa paves the way for the establishment of co-financing arrangements for infrastructure projects across the African continent.

2. The BRICS Multilateral Cooperation and Co-Financing Agreement for Sustainable Development sets out to explore the establishment of bilateral agreements aimed at establishing cooperation and co-financing arrangements, specifically around sustainable development and green economy elements.

The BRICS Countries reiterated their position of demanding reform of International Monetary Fund and election to the post of Director-General of World Trade Organization to be held in 2014.

Sixth BRICS Summit, 14–16 July, 2014, Fortaleza and Brasilia, Brazil

The **Sixth BRICS Summit** was hosted by Brazil and held at Fortaleza and Brasilia during 14–16 July 2014. This summit witnessed the official inauguration of New Development Bank. BRICS leader also met eleven leaders from Union of South American Nations (UNASUR)* on 16–17 July 2014. The Summit outcome documents known as the *eThekwini Declaration and Fortaleza Action Plan* were adopted at the conclusion of the Summit.

Seventh BRICS Summit, 8–9 July, 2015, Ufa in Bashkortostan, Russia

The Seventh BRICS Summit was hosted by Russia in Ufa. Here the leaders deliberated on issues like rising terrorism, inclusion of India, Brazil and South Africa as permanent members of UN Security Council, the Ukraine issue and imposition of sanctions by the West of Russia, climate change, greater South-South cooperation, cooperation in Scientific research and innovation initiatives, reaffirming faith in the UN as it celebrated 70th Anniversary of its foundation in the year 2015 and also commemorated the victims of WWII at the 70th Anniversary of the end of the War among other issues. It must be noted that the BRICS Summit took place ahead of the G-20 Heads of the States Summit. BRICS leader reviewed the progress made in setting up of the New Development Banks as well as a $100 billion liquidity reserve fund for boosting up the emerging economies. India, as PM Narendra Modi, emphasized will guide the BRICS nations' $50 billion New Development Bank in BRICS's effort to build a rival to the World Bank. The prime objective will be to finance "inclusive and responsive" needs of particularly emerging economies of the world. BRICS leaders are looking forward for the 8th BRICS summit to be hosted by India in 2016.

INDIA-BRAZIL-SOUTH AFRICA (IBSA) TRILATERAL

IBSA is a trilateral, developmental initiative between India, Brazil and South Africa to promote South-South cooperation and exchange. During the G-8 meeting that took place in Evian in 2003, the Heads of State and Government of the IBSA countries floated the idea of this trilateral initiative. This was followed up by trilateral consultations, and finally, the trilateral took concrete shape when the Foreign Ministers of the respective countries met in Brasilia on 6 June 2003. At this meeting between Ministers Nkosazana Dlamini Zuma from South Africa, Celso Amorim from Brazil and Yashwant Sinha from India, the launching of the IBSA Dialogue Forum was formalized through the adoption of the Brasilia Declaration.

The main objectives of the IBSA Dialogue Forum are as follows:

1. To promote South-South dialogue, cooperation and common positions on issues of international importance

2. To promote trade and investment opportunities between the three regions of which they form a part

3. To promote international poverty alleviation and social development

4. To promote the trilateral exchange of information, international best practices, technologies and skills, as well as to compliment each other's competitive strengths into collective synergie.

5. To promote cooperation in a broad range of areas, namely agriculture, climate change, culture, defence, education, energy, health, information society, science and technology, social development, trade and investment, tourism and transport.

The IBSA Dialogue Forum has regular consultations at Senior Official (Focal Point), Ministerial (Trilateral Joint Commission) and Heads of State and/or Government (Summit) levels, but also facilitates interaction amongst academics, business and other members of civil society. Table 20.3 shows the list of IBSA Summit.

Table 20.3   List of IBSA Summits

Summit	Date	Host Country, City	Host Head of State
1st IBSA	13 September 2006	Brazil, Brasília	Luiz Inácio Lula da Silva
2nd IBSA	October 2007	South Africa, Pretoria	Thabo Mbeki
3rd IBSA	October 2008	India, New Delhi	Manmohan Singh
4th IBSA	15 April 2010	Brazil, Brasília	Luiz Inácio Lula da Silva
5th IBSA	October 2011	South Africa, Pretoria	Jacob Zuma
6th IBSA	6 June 2013	India, New Delhi	Manmohan Singh

The next Summit is to be hosted by New Delhi in 2013.

The areas of cooperation of IBSA countries are primarily agriculture, climate change, culture, defence, education, energy, health, information society, science and technology, social development, trade and investment, tourism and transport. In the backdrop of the global melt down, the Third IBSA Summit was held at New Delhi in 2008. The major thrust of this Summit was therefore the financial crisis as well as energy and food security, WTO, Climate Change and terrorism. A trilateral trade target of US $25 billion was set to be achieved by 2015. The fourth IBSA Summit held at Brazil adopted two documents along with the Brasilia Declaration. One was the Social Development Strategies and the other was the Future of Agricultural Cooperation in India, Brazil and South Africa. Two MoUs were also signed pertaining to Science, Technology and Innovation and Solar Energy.

IBSA is a fast-emerging trilateral initiative and has a great prospect. IBSA envisions partnership among equals, and if it can successfully prove its credentials, then the members countries would be playing important role in international arena too. These three IBSA countries are the ones which are also forwarding their bid for permanent membership in the UNSC. Therefore, forging a strong tie at this trilateral level would definitely give them an advantage of pushing forward their views at the international level on matters of common concerns of these three countries.

India hosted the Sixth IBSA Summit in New Delhi, on 6 June 2013, which was preceded by a number of meetings of Joint Working Groups and People-to-People Forums. This Summit was very significant as it marked the completion of 10 years of the establishment of the dialogue forum, and the **10th** **anniversary** of the *Brasilia Declaration*. The IBSA members reiterated their pledge to bolster South-South cooperation and not to slip away the agenda. They talked about three concern areas where cooperation can be developed like reaching out to other democracies, sharing of IBSA's democratic experiences and developing new format for ocean governance. Its time they thought for IBSA to mature and deliver.

INDIAN OCEAN RIM ASSOCIATION FOR REGIONAL COOPERATION (IOR-ARC)/INDIAN OCEAN RIM ASSOCIATION (IORA)

Mauritius Government sought to enhance economic co-operation among countries of the Indian Ocean Rim. Therefore, it convened a meeting in March 1995 which was attended by representatives from the government, business sectors and academia, from Australia, India, Kenya, Mauritius, Sultanate of Oman, Singapore and South Africa, known as the "Core Group States" or M-7. What emerged out of this meeting was a joint statement with a vision to practice *Principles of Open Regionalism and Inclusivity of Membership, with the objectives of Trade Liberalization and Promoting Trade Co-operation. Activities would focus on Trade Facilitation, Investment Promotion and Economic Co-operation*. The IOR-ARC was formally launched at the first Ministerial Meeting in Mauritius on 6–7 March 1997. This meeting adopted the IOR-ARC Charter, and determined a number of administrative and procedural matters.

All Sovereign States of the Indian Ocean Rim are eligible for membership. To become members, States must adhere to the principles and objectives enshrined in the Charter. Member states can decide on the expansion of membership of the association. The member countries of IOR-ARC are Australia, Bangladesh, India, Indonesia, Iran, Kenya, Madagascar, Malaysia, Mauritius, Mozambique, Oman, Singapore, South Africa, Sri Lanka, Tanzania, Thailand, the United Arab Emirates, and Yemen. The Seychelles announced its withdrawal from the Association in July 2003, but rejoined in November 2011 taking the membership to 19. The Dialogue Partners are China, Egypt, France, Japan, United Kingdom. The IOR-ARC Observers are currently limited to the Indian Ocean Tourism Organization (IOTO) and the Indian Ocean Research Group (IORG).

IOR-ARC activities include several on-going projects and work programmes conducted by member countries with shared interests, all of which are under the umbrella of three separate working groups. These are the Working Group on Trade and Investment (WGTI), the Indian Ocean Rim Business Forum (IORBF), and the Indian Ocean Rim Academic Group (IORAG). The Association holds a Council of Ministers meeting once every two years. The working groups have business and academic representatives to ensure that different points of view and interests are fully reflected in IOR-ARC's work programme.

The IOR-ARC *Action Plan* is a vision enumerated in Article 3.2 of IOR-ARC Charter. IOR-ARC aims to formulate and implement projects for economic co-operation relating to trade facilitation, promotion and liberalisation; promotion of foreign investment, scientific and technological exchanges, and tourism, movement of natural persons and service providers on a non-discriminatory basis; and development of infrastructure and human resources, as laid down in the Work Programme of the Association. (Art. 3.2 of IOR-ARC Charter)

India is interested in reaching out to the Indian Ocean Rim countries not only for economic engagements but also to counter the menace of piracy. India also calls for people-to-people contact and more joint projects between India and the Rim countries. The Government of India is offering scholarships to meritorious students from Malaysia, for Postgraduate courses only, for the academic year 2011–2012 under the Indian Ocean Rim Association for Regional Cooperation (IOR-ARC) Scholarship scheme. The Indian Council for Cultural Relations (ICCR) administers the scholarship programme. The first Indian Ocean Rim Association for Regional Cooperation (IOR-ARC) Film Festival was hosted by New Delhi on 22 February 2008. India had offered to host this Festival at the 7th Council of Ministers Meeting of IOR-ARC held in March 2007.

The IOR-ARC must engage more in maritime cooperation which have got a very little attention and only been limited to developing, upgrading and management of ports. The Indian Ocean forms an important channel for drugs and arms. Afghanistan, Iran and Pakistan, form the 'Golden Crescent' and two member countries, viz, Iran and Pakistan are part of it. Again Myanmar and Thailand are part of the 'Golden Triangle' encompassing Myanmar, Vietnam, Laos and Thailand. Both 'Golden Crescent' and Golden Triangle' are infamous for illegal drug production. Therefore, there arises a prime need to address the issues of transnational threats encompassing narco-terrorism, arms running and sea piracy. The IOR-ARC must also beef-up cooperation for providing assistance during natural disasters such as cyclones, famines, Tsunamis which can be dubbed as "out of area operations." The Tenth Council of Ministers

Meeting held on 5 August 2010 at Yemen, emphasized cooperation among IOR-ARC members in the areas like promotion of trade and investment, tourism, culture, education, combating communicable diseases and natural disasters and challenges of Climate Change. They also agreed to take up initiatives for combating piracy in the Gulf of Aden and other parts of Indian Ocean. India has assumed the Chair of IOR-ARC from 2011.

The12th Meeting of the Council of Ministers of IOR-ARC was hosted by India. *The Gurgaon Communiqué-IORARC at 15—The Next Decade* underlined the geo-strategic importance of the Indian Ocean and garner the capabilities at hand of the Rim countries to meet common challenges. They reaffirmed the maintenance of freedom of navigation and safety and security of Sea Lanes of Communication the Indian Ocean as piracy is a growing threat and also pledged to fight natural disasters in the IOR-ARC maritime domain. Union of Comoros was inducted into the IOR-ARC as the twentieth member of the Association. The members of IOR-ARC also have agreed to admit the United States of America as the 6th Dialogue Partner of IOR-ARC.

Currently the name of this regional bloc has been changed to **Indian Ocean Rim Association (IORA).**

The Government of Mauritius in collaboration with the Indian Ocean Rim Association hosted the First IORA Ministerial Blue Economy Conference on the theme "Enhancing Blue Economy Cooperation for Sustainable Development in the IORA Region", at Le Meridien, Pointe aux Piments, Republic of Mauritius from 2-3 September 2015.

The Council of Ministers' Meeting of IORA on 6-9 October 2014 in Perth, Australia adopted the Blue Economy as the top priority for generating employment and ensuring sustainability in business and economic models. An IORA Secretariat draft paper identified **eight priority** areas for cooperation in the Blue Economy:

1. Fisheries and Aquaculture
2. Renewable Ocean Energy
3. Seaports and Shipping
4. Seabed Exploration and Minerals
5. Marine Biotechnology, Research and Development
6. Tourism
7. Ocean Knowledge Clusters
8. SIDS and LDCs

The First IORA Ministerial Blue Economy Conference addressed the first four priority areas. The remaining priority areas will be addressed in subsequent meetings, events and deliberations. How best the IOR countries can use such windows of opportunities and gear up their economic cooperation and undertake plans of actions, will determine the direction of IOR region in world politics.

BAY OF BENGAL INITIATIVE FOR MULTI-SECTORAL TECHNICAL AND ECONOMIC COOPERATION (BIMSTEC)

Another regional initiative which is to emerge as an important economic bloc connecting South Asia and South-east Asia is the BIMSTEC. Earlier it was BIST-EC, an economic cooperation initiative comprising Bangladesh, India, Sri Lanka and Thailand. It came to existence on 6 June 1997 in Bangkok with the adoption of the Bangkok Declaration. Later, with Myanmar joining the grouping in a Special Ministerial Meeting in Bangkok in December 1997, the name was changed to BIMSTEC. Nepal became an observer country in the Second Ministerial Meeting in Dhaka in 1998, and acquired full membership in 2003. Bhutan also became a full-fledged member in 2003.

The Bangkok Declaration on the Establishment of BIST-EC embodies the aims and objectives of BIMSTEC. They are:

1. to create an enabling environment for rapid economic development and to accelerate social progress in the sub-region,

2. promote active collaboration and mutual assistance on matters of common interest,

3. provide assistance to each other in the form of training and research facilities,

4. cooperate more effectively in joint efforts that are supportive of, and complementary to national development plans of member states,

5. maintain close and beneficial cooperation with existing international and regional organizations, and

6. cooperate in projects that can be dealt with most productively on a sub-regional basis, and which make best use of available synergies.

BIMSTEC was initiated with the goal to combine the 'Look West' policy of Thailand, and ASEAN with the 'Look East' policy of India and South Asia. Thus BIMSTEC may be seen as a link between ASEAN and SARRC, i.e., South Asia and South-east Asia.

In the first Summit on 31 July 2004, leaders of the group agreed that the name of the grouping should be known as BIMSTEC or the **Bay of Bengal Initiative for Multi-Sectoral Technical and Economic Cooperation**. The Chairmanship of BIMSTEC is done on a rotation basis. Table 20.4 gives the list of Chairmanship and years of assumption of the Chair by member countries.

The BIS-TEC or Bangkok Declaration, 1997, lays down the organizational arrangement of BIMSTEC. It comprises the Annual Ministerial Meeting to be hosted by member states on rotational basis according to the alphabetical order, Senior Officials Committee, A Working Group for preparatory works before each Annual Ministerial Meetings and Specialized Task Forces, which may be deemed necessary.

Table 20.4   List of Chairing BIMSTEC countries with year

Sl. No	Countries	Year
1.	Bangladesh	1997–1999
2.	India	2000–2001
3.	Myanmar	2001–2002
4.	Sri Lanka	2002–2003
5.	Thailand	2003–2005
6.	Bangladesh	2005–2006
7.	India*	2006–2009
8.	Myanmar	2009–2014
9.	Nepal	2014–till date

*Bhutan skipped so Chairmanship turned to India.

BIMSTEC has identified six priority sectors at the 2nd Ministerial Meeting in Dhaka on 19 November 1998, and for each there is a 'lead country'. Trade and investment is under Bangladesh, technology under Sri Lanka, transport and communication under India, energy under Myanmar, tourism under India and fisheries under Thailand. After the 8th Ministerial Meeting in Dhaka on 18-19 December 2005, a number of new areas of cooperation emerged which include agriculture, public health, poverty alleviation, counter-terrorism and transnational crime, protection of Biodiversity/Environment and natural disaster management, culture and people to people contact.

One achievement of BIMSTEC is the setting up of BIMSTEC Free Trade Area Framework Agreement on 8 February 2004. The Framework Agreement includes trade in goods, trade in services, investment and economic cooperation and the products, except those included in the Negative List, shall be subject to tariff reduction or elimination on the basis of fast track or normal track. BIMSTEC grouping also signed a convention in December 2009, to combat terrorism and agreed to conclude a Free Trade Agreement (FTA) soon. Apart from the convention on terrorism, the grouping adopted a Memoranda of Association (MoA) on the establishment of a BIMSTEC Energy centre, a centre for Weather and Climate and a Cultural Industries Observatory.

India views the seven-nation organization as 'a bridge' linking South and South-east Asia with India's north-eastern states, and underline the need for greater regional economic integration. This is also part of India's Look-East Policy. If India succeeds in cementing her ties with BIMSTEC, then economic engagements with the member countries would help India to tackle Chinese policy of isolating India.

Second Summit of BIMSTEC was hosted by India, New Delhi on 13 November 2008. Member states agreed to intensify efforts to strengthen cooperation and also establish institutional structures to implement and coordinate Summit decisions, Ministerial meetings and other official meeting follow ups and establish a permanent secretariat.

The Third BIMSTEC Summit Meeting took place on 1–4 March 2014 at Nay Pyi Taw, Myanmar and was attended by Prime Ministers of Bangladesh, Bhutan, India, Myanmar, Nepal, Sri Lanka and Thailand. It was decided that the fourth BIMSTEC Energy Ministerial Meeting was to be held in Bhutan in 2015 after the Third in Nepal. Among other important activities of the BIMSTEC, the member countries applauded the creation of BIMSTEC Network of Policy Think Tanks, agreed to promote BIMSTEC Network of National Centres of Coordination, recognized the role of BIMSTEC Energy Centre in Bengaluru, expressed desire to improve people-people exchanges and linkages including facilitating BIMSTEC Business Visa Scheme and BIMSTEC Visa Exemption Scheme and implementation of BIMSTEC Poverty Plan of Action.

Three BIMSTEC Instruments were signed as follows:

[1] Memorandum of Association on the Establishment of the BIMSTEC Permanent Secretariat

[2] Memorandum of Understanding on the Establishment of the BIMSTEC Cultural Industries Commission (BCIC) and BIMSTEC Cultural Industries Observatory (BCIO)

[3] Memorandum of Association Among BIMSTEC Member Countries Concerning Establishment of a BIMSTEC Centre for Weather and Climate

Since March 2014, the Chairmanship is with Nepal.

Bangladesh Prime Minister Sheikh Hasina inaugurated the permanent secretariat of the Bay of Bengal Initiative for Multi-Sectoral Technical and Economic Cooperation (BIMSTEC) in Dhaka in September 2014. During the 13th BIMSTEC ministerial meeting held in Nay Pyi Taw in Myanmar in 2011, it was unanimously decided that the secretariat would be set up in Bangladesh and the first Secretary General would be appointed from Sri Lanka. The secretariat has been set up in Dhaka's diplomatic enclave of Gulshan. The first Secretary General, Sumith Nakandala, of Sri Lanka joined the secretariat in July and assumed office in Dhaka from August 2014.

The year 2015 was marked by series of meeting of BIMSTEC countries over a number of issues. The Sixth Meeting of the BIMSTEC Sub-Group on Legal and Law Enforcement Issues discussed counter-terrorism and transnational crime during 17-18 December, 2015 at New Delhi. Negotiations were held to outline the Draft Text of the BIMSTEC Convention on Transfer of Sentenced Persons.

The Second meeting of the BIMSTEC Network of Policy Think Tanks was held in Bangkok, Thailand from 08-09 October 2015. They focused ways and means of revitalizing cooperation among the Member States to further enhance people-to-people contact in the Bay of Bengal region, and also to increase visibility of BIMSTEC.

The Twentieth Meeting of BIMSTEC Trade Negotiating Committee was held during 7-9 September 2015, Pullman Khon Kaen Raja Orchid, Thailand.

The Third Meeting of the BIMSTEC Expert Group on the Establishment of the Technology Transfer Facility was held from 25-26 August 2015 at Colombo, Sri Lanka.

The Seventh Meeting of the BIMSTEC Joint Working Group on Counter-Terrorism and Transnational Crime was held in Bangkok, Thailand from 04-05 August 2015. They discussed issues pertaining to Counter Terrorism and Transnational Crime in the Bay of Bengal Region. The Meeting also finalized the BIMSTEC Convention on Mutual Legal Assistance in Criminal Matters.

MEKONG-GANGA COOPERATION (MGC)

The MGC was formally launched on 10th November 2000 in the Laotian capital of Vientiane. MGC focuses on building cooperation in sectors of tourism, culture, educational contacts and transport and communications between India and these five Greater Mekong Sub-region (GMS) countries which are Cambodia, Lao PDR, Myanmar, Thailand and Vietnam. These five GMS countries had begun, much before the formation of MGC, a cooperation initiative named 'Mekong-Ganga Swarnabhoomi Programme'. MGC only institutionalized their cooperation by providing a much stronger platform.

First MGC Ministerial Meeting was held at Vientiane (Lao, PDR) on 10th November 2000. This led the foundation of the MGC. The outcome of the Meet was the adoption of the *Vientiane Declaration*. This Declaration underscored the identification of the member countries' common heritage and desire to enhance friendship. The Declaration outlined MGC objectives in four specific sectors of—Tourism, Culture, Education and Transport and Communications. It also committed the member states to strengthen their cooperation in the development of Information Technology (IT) infrastructure. The Second MGC Ministerial Meeting was held in Hanoi, 28 July, 2001. The Meet concluded with the adoption of the Hanoi Programme of Action affirming their commitment to cooperate in four areas of cooperation. The Hanoi Programme of Action targeted 6 years timeframe from 2001 to 2007 with the progress of its implementation being reviewed after every two years. The Third MGC Ministerial Meeting was held in Phnom Penh on 20 June 2003. The Phnom Penh Road Map was adopted as a plan to accelerate the implementation of all MGC projects and activities. In the absence of Fourth Ministerial Meeting taking place in 2004 or 2005, the Annual MGC Senior Officials Meeting was held in New Delhi on 25th May 2005. The long-awaited Fourth MGCI Ministerial Meeting was held in New Delhi on 12 October 2006. The then Indian foreign minister, Pranab Mukherjee reiterated India's commitment to strengthen India's cultural and commercial ties with GMS countries. The Fifth MGC Ministerial Meeting, Cebu, 12 January 2007. In this meeting, Thailand has handed over the chairmanship of MGC to India.

The Sixth Mekong–Ganga Cooperation meeting was held in New Delhi on 3-4 September 2012 ahead of the ASEAN-India commemorative summit. This Summit is slated for 20–21 December 2012 to be held in New Delhi. This ASEAN-India commemorative Summit will mark the 20th anniversary of the ASEAN-India dialogue partnership and the 10th anniversary of ASEAN-India Summit-level partnership. Therefore, the MGC meeting was significant as it provided another platform for the member countries to strengthen cooperation, especially among the overlapping members of MGC and ASEAN. The Sixth MGC Meeting recognized the need for short gestation projects that could directly benefit local communities, with results that are immediate and visible. The Ministers felt that these would give fresh impetus to cooperation under MGC. In this context, the Ministers welcomed the announcement by India on the establishment of the India-Cambodia-Laos-Myanmar-Vietnam (CLMV) Quick Impact Projects (QIP) Revolving Fund with an annual contribution of $ 1 million. The members of the meet appreciated the completion of construction of the MGC Traditional Asian Textiles Museum building at Siem Reap, Cambodia in December 2011. India's association with MGC cannot be seen in isolation but must be viewed as a part of India's Look-East policy. Therefore, India is making all out efforts to solidify the cooperation with her MGC partners.

A boost to Mekong-Ganga cooperation was given during the visit of India's Vice-President Hamid Ansari to Cambodia during September 2015 where he signed two MoUs on tourism and Mekong-Ganga Cooperation with Cambodian PM. The Mekong-Ganga MoU was related to five "quick impact projects" related to [1] $50,000 grant to Cambodia for the upgradation of an Entrepreneurship Development Centre, [2] two projects in health care, [3] one project in agriculture [4] one project in women's empowerment.

As per the Press release of the Ministry of External Affairs dated 23 December, 2015, it has declared that through the ASEAN-India Cooperation Fund, India has granted six scholarships to students from Cambodia, Laos, Myanmar and Vietnam to pursue Masters degree at Nalanda University. Selected students are eligible for waiver of full fees, including tuition fees, boarding, lodging and travel fare, for the period of study. A total of 4 students (2 from Laos, 2 from Myanmar and none from Cambodia) are currently studying at Nalanda University under this scholarship.

NAFTA

The North America Free Trade Agreement (NAFTA) was implemented on 1 January 1994 among United States, Canada and Mexico. This agreement was arrived at with the aim to remove trade and investment barriers among these three countries. Remaining duties and quantitative restrictions were eliminated in 1 January 2008. USA and Canada signed the Canada-USA Free Trade Agreement (CUFTA) in the year 1989. Some provisions of CUFTA like those related to agriculture were incorporated into NAFTA. Under NAFTA all non-tariff barriers to agricultural trade between USA and Mexico were eliminated. Further, some major tariff barriers were removed immediately after emergence of NAFTA while others were being passed out over periods of 5 to 15 years. Mexico and Canada arrived at a separate NAFTA agreement on market access for agricultural products. This agreement eliminated almost all the tariffs, some immediately and others over a period of 5 to 15 years. However, tariffs affecting trade in dairy, poultry, eggs and sugar remained. NAFTA created the world's largest free trade area, which now links 450 million people producing $17 trillion worth of goods and services.

Trade between the United States and its NAFTA partners has soared since the agreement entered into force. US goods and services trade with NAFTA amounted to $1.6 trillion in 2009. Exports amounted to $397 billion. Imports were to the tune of $438 billion. The US goods and services trade deficit with NAFTA was $41 billion in 2009. Not only this, NAFTA had a great impact on US job market. Some allege NAFTA responsible for huge job loss. Some uphold creation of huge employment. Others contend that high-paying manufacturing jobs are being lost and replaced by lower paying jobs and is causing wage deflation in certain sectors. For Canada the picture is also not so pleasing. Canada also did not benefit much from NAFTA. Mexico has been worst affected. Subsidized corn supplies (read 'dumping') from USA are destroying the income opportunities of poor Mexican corn farmers. Mexico witnessed Zapatista Uprising in response to NAFTA in Chiapas. Indian trade with NAFTA countries are mostly dominated by Indo-US trade exchanges. The India-United States Commercial Dialogue was signed on 23 March, 2000. The India-US Trade Policy Forum (TPF) was announced during Manmohan Singh's visit to the US in July 2005. India has emerged as a thriving market for US exports and FDI destination. With Canada India has modest trade partnership while with Mexico it is much below the actual potential.

MERCOSUR

If NAFTA is a trading arrangement among the North African countries, then MERCOSUR, is a trading bloc among the Latin American Countries. It came into existence with the conclusion of the Treaty of Asunción, 1991. This 1991 Treaty was amended and updated in 1994 by the Treaty of Ouro Preto. The member countries are Argentine, Brazil, Paraguay, Uruguay and Venezuela. The associate members are Bolivia, Chile, Colombia, Ecuador and Peru. This trading bloc also envisages free movement of goods, services, capital and people among the member countries. MERCOSUR is growing from strength to strength when compared to already existing regional arrangements like European Union, NAFTA and ASEAN.

India also aims at developing her economic relations with MERCOSUR. A Framework Agreement was signed between India and MERCOSUR in June 2003 at Asunción. There were twin objectives to the Agreement. Firstly, both countries would grant reciprocal tariff preferences and this will pave way for both to negotiate for establishment of a Free Trade Area (FTA) between India and MERCOSUR. To further strengthen their efforts to establish the FTA, both concluded a follow up of the Framework Agreement in the form of a Preferential Trade Agreement in New Delhi, in January 2004.

Further, the five Annexes of the PTA have been signed in New Delhi, in March 2005. However, as far as India is concerned the PTA is not much lucrative as the Regional Trade Agreements (RTAs) that have been concluded between MERCOSUR and Andean Community*. Yet India should move ahead with the economic cooperation with MERCOSUR as developing ties with Latin American countries will enhance South-South cooperation and definitely will increase market opportunities for emerging India.

EXERCISES

1. State the modus operandi of IMF in the international political economy.

2. Comment of the activities of World Bank.

3. What does the WTO stand for? How does it function? Comment on the Doha Rounds.

4. Discuss the role of G-20 in the current international scenario.

5. Discuss importance of BRICS as an emerging economic arrangement.

6. Comment on the role of IBSA as a new economic initiative.

7. Discuss the importance of the functioning of IOR-ARC.

8. Comment on BIMSTEC as an economic grouping.

9. Analyze the importance of Mekong Ganga Cooperation.

10. Comment on NAFTA as an important economic arrangement.

11. Analyze the importance of MERCOSUR as a regional economic arrangement.

---

*Andean Community   The Andean Community is a customs union comprising the South American countries of Bolivia, Colombia, Ecuador and Peru. With the new cooperation agreement with MERCOSUR, the Andean Community gained four new associate members: Argentina, Brazil, Paraguay and Uruguay in July 2005.

21

Current Concerns in International Relations: India and the World

PATHANKOT TERROR ATTACK (INDIA)

The year 2016 for India started with a terror attack on her Pathankot's Air Force Station on 2 January. It was a few days after PM Narendra Modi's surprise visit to his counterpart Nawaz Sharif in Pakistan on 25 December 2015. There were six attackers who put up a long and tough fight, in which seven security personnel were martyred. The fight continued for almost 38 hours and rest of the time was spent on combing operations. Some reports suggested that the attack took place at this time to derail the high level talks between the two neighbours. Again allegations are that the Pakistan based militants are behind this terror attack. This disastrous incident proves beyond doubt how terror attacks can aim not only 'soft' civilian targets, but also defence targets. If the security and intelligence are not beefed up and coordination among countries are not designed strategically, the countries all across the globe will fall easy prey to terrorists whether state-sponsored or Al-Qaeda or any other terror outfit.

ISIS

The November 2015 Paris terror attacks followed by the devastating terror explosions in the Brussels airport (March 2016) show the emergence of a new pivot of terror alongside the existing ones – the ISIS. It would be too far-stretched to say that the Al-Qaeda has become non-functional, but currently the focus is on increased activities of the ISIS.

The ISIS is the acronym for the Jihadi militant outfit who calls themselves as Islamic State of Syria and Iraq. By mid-2014, the ISIS took control of Mosul, Fallujah and Tirkit. They have extended their activities into Libya too and has established a strong foothold in Sitre.

An international coalition of almost 60 countries has been fighting against the ISIS since 2014. The USA is taking a leading role in these actions against ISIS. It is leading two coalitions carrying out air strikes targeting ISIS in Iraq and Syria and Libya. Britain, France and Russia are among other major coalition partners. Germany's lower House of Parliament also gave a green signal for Germany to join the international coalition against ISIS at the end of 2015.

In early 2016, the US-backed forces were successful in pushing back the ISIS from the Syrian town of Shadadi. Iraq has also launched military offensive to reclaim its largest city of Mosul. No solution is in sight and terrorism and counter-terrorism activities will go on, but sufferers will be innocent people who are fleeing their countries and taking refuge in other countries especially European countries. Europe is experiencing the tragedy of 'boat people' from Syria and Iraq.

GLOBAL FALL IN CRUDE PRICES

15 September 2008 is an important date as **Global Financial Crisis** started with global share market crash, liquidity crisis, and currency crisis and is still continuing. Typicality of the crisis is that it was not a usual economic crisis of cyclical burst. Essentially it is burst of a Financial Bubble on which the current phase of capitalism was surviving. The world is grappling to tide over the crisis including the advanced economies of the US and Europe as well as the developing countries. To make matters worse there is a continuous fall of crude prices. Since June 2014, when it was $115 per barrel. It is down to $39.39 as on 29.3.2016. The 1 year forecast is $45 per barrel.

The ups and downs in oil prices in world market is partially determined by actual supply and demand and partly by expected demand for energy which is closely related to the economic conditions. However, in reality over the years a lot of international politics and bargaining have been determining the oil prices. After the first global oil shock following the 1973 Middle-East War, Saudi Arabia, the ultra-low-cost producer of oil, has influenced geopolitics at will by turning the taps on and off. It is again playing politics with oil to force down the price with three major objectives. One being hurting Iran and Russia's oil incomes and rendering the U.S. shale production unviable. This emanated from the threat from the shale project to the oil producers in the sense that the U.S. is projected to become a net petroleum exporter before 2020. Saudi Arabia also wants to counter the attempts of the Rouhani regime in Iran at dominating the Middle-east region.

The impact of Western sanctions caused Iranian production to drop by about one million barrels a day in recent years and blocked Iran from importing the latest Western oil field technology and equipment. With sanctions now being lifted, the Iranian oil industry is expected to open the taps on production soon.

However, the current fall in crude price will affect not only the US but also Russia, Venezuela, Nigeria, Ecuador, Brazil and Iran. Russia loses about $2 bn in revenuès for every dollar fall in the oil price, and the World Bank has warned that Russia's economy would shrink by at least 0.7% in 2015 if oil prices do not recover.

On 16 February 2016, OPEC members Saudi Arabia, Venezuela and Qatar, along with Russia, announced a plan to freeze output at current levels. This is a reversal of stand by Saudi Arabia which refused to even listen to cuts in productions and continued to increase its production despite landslide fall in oil prices.

However, if prices remain low for another year or longer, King Salman, who is in power since January 2015, may find it difficult to persuade other OPEC members to keep steady against the financial strains. The International Monetary Fund estimates that the revenues of Saudi Arabia and its Persian Gulf allies will slip by $300 billion this year. The price of crude has to be closely watched because the direction of internal political economy will be determined by the fluctuations in crude prices.

EUROPE'S BOAT PEOPLE: A REFUGEE CRISIS IN EUROPE UNFOLDING

Since the World War II, the world has not experienced such a massive emergency refugee crisis where thousands of "boat people" from Iraq, Afghanistan, Syria and war-torn Libya and Somalia are seeking asylum or have set up migrant camps or are heading towards many European Countries like Greece, Germany, Italy and others. This reminds the world of the "boat people" crisis after the Vietnam War in the 1970s. Around 1975 and even over next two decades more than 3 million people fled from Vietnam, Cambodia and Laos after Communist victories in these countries. Unwilling to live under Communist regimes, people started fleeing these countries. Almost 80,000 Vietnamese according to UNHCR Reports fled by boats. It was a massive exodus during peacetime. A large number of people died even before reaching shores from pirate attacks, drowning or starvation.

But current crisis is unprecedented and of a larger volume. At least 60 million people have been displaced because of war, conflict, persecution and unrest in Afghanistan, Iraq, Somalia, Syria, Yemen and elsewhere. More than 4 million refugees have escaped Syria where Civil War has out-broken and has killed people in large numbers. Since the beginning of the conflict in Syria in 2011, two million Syrians have been registered as refugees with the United Nations High Commissioner for Refugees (UNHCR). Most have crossed over to other countries and live in shanties, camps or poor local communities in Turkey, Jordan, Lebanon, Iraq and Egypt to mention a few. Others have tried to reach some other countries via sea-route. The exodus trends show the direction towards Europe. Greece is becoming a first destination for Syrian escaping the civil war back at home. Many are taking a direct but a longer sea route to Italy. In 2014 Italy was mainly the destination of refugees from Eritrea and Syria. However, a sizeable number have been given refugee status by mid-2014.

The UN reports that since the war began, more than 500,000 Syrians (of the 4.2 million Syrian refugees overall) have applied for asylum in Europe. Sweden accepted around 10,000 Syrian asylum-seekers in 2013 alone. The EU as a whole permanently resettled some 30,000 Syrian refugees from 2011 through 2014 and several thousand Iraqi refugees during the Iraq War.

The world is facing a humanitarian crisis. It is not only a migration issue or a refugee issue but also the 'vulnerability' of a section of people fleeing persecution by boats. The women and young girls and children are the worst sufferers. The most important question for the 'boat people' is the question of 'survival' in the sea and when touching a territory their safety and security in that territory. The international community might feel that cessation of war in these war-torn countries might stop such exodus. However, the reality shows that stability and peace in these countries are far too long to achieve very fast. Concerted effort on parts of international community and the United Nations and the European Union is the only visible conflict resolution method in site.

EUROZONE CRISIS

The Global recession of 2007-2008 followed by world-wide recession from 2008-2012 and bubble burst had already send nerve shocks around the world. The Eurozone was not immune from it too. Coupled with this were the fiscal policies of some of the peripheral Eurozone countries. The net result was that the Eurozone was caught in sovereign-debt crisis. To make matters worse in 2009 Greece's new Government unveiled the fact that the previous government had grossly under–reported its budget deficit which was a sheer violation of EU policy and raised fears of a Euro collapse via political and financial contagion (financial pollution or corruption). Soon it came to be known that the financial positions of several Eurozone countries have made them unsustainable.

The problem spiraled in 2010 with rising spreads on sovereign bond yields among the peripheral Eurozone countries like Greece, Ireland, Portugal and Spain and also Germany. Greece was alone burdened with debt amounting to

113% of GDP-nearly double the Eurozone limit of 60%. The Greece yield diverged in 2010 and Greece needed eurozone assistance. It received two bailout packages from the EU over the following five years during which the country adopted EU-mandated austerity measures to cut costs while Greece experienced a further economic recession but faced massive social unrest and protest. By mid-2015 the sovereign debt crisis became acute. In July 2015, the Greek people however, voted against further austerity measures. There was also a possibility of Greece moving towards an exit from European Monetary Union or 'Grexit'. Greece in total received three bailout packages but it is still grappling with an acute crisis, and Eurozone leaders are searching for solutions. Greece's matters have become worse as there is a heavy influx of refugees from Iraq, Syria and other war-torn countries. The Greece debt crisis has put the future of European political and economic union at stake. Britain went on a referendum on the issue of 'Brexit' from the EU in June 2016. Approximately 51.9% vote for Brexit and approximately 48.1% voted against Brexit. This definitely has created uneasiness in EU, and developments have to be watched seriously in the Eurozone regarding the future of EU.

EXERCISES

1. Comment of the terror attacks at the Pathankot's Air Force Base on 2 January, 2016.
2. How do you think that the ISIS is a threat to world peace?
3. Analyze the fall in crude prices in international market and its necessary fall outs.
4. Write a note on the 'boat people' moving towards Europe.
5. Examine the Eurozone crisis as a growing threat to the sustainability of the EU.

Index